MARTIN BUBER

A CENTENARY VOLUME

Edited by

HAIM GORDON and JOCHANAN BLOCH

KTAV PUBLISHING HOUSE, INC.
FOR THE FACULTY OF HUMANITIES
AND SOCIAL SCIENCES
BEN-GURION UNIVERSITY OF THE NEGEV

Library of Congress Cataloging in Publication Data

Martin Buber, Me'ah shanah le-huladeto. English.
  Martin Buber, a centenary volume.

  Translation of: Martin Buber, me'ah shanah le-huladeto.
  Includes bibliographical references and index.
  1. Buber, Martin, 1878-1965—Congresses.
I. Buber, Martin, 1878-1965. II. Gordon, Hayim.
III. Bloch, Jochanan, 1919-   . IV. Title.
B3213.B84M4313   1984   296.3'092'4   84-4410
ISBN 0-88125-026-0

Contents

Preface

The participants who came to the Buber Centenary Conference which was held at Ben Gurion University of the Negev in January 1978 were a living testimony to the deep influence of the person whom they honored. From Europe and North America, from Japan and from Israel came many who endeared his memory. In addition to the differences in spiritual and religious background, the participants represented four generations. Among the elderly were septuagenarians and octogenarians, from Germany and central Europe, upon whose lives Buber had had a deep personal impact. Participants in their fifties or sixties had often been acquainted with Buber after the Second World War, and his influence upon them was mainly a result of his contribution to contemporary spiritual life. Another group consisted of younger scholars for whom Buber was already a heritage, an important part of the spiritual history of the twentieth century. And lastly there were groups of younger people, in their twenties and thirties, for whom Buber's writings had opened a new perspective to comprehend their lives, and perhaps a new relationship to the world. Thus, four generations convened in Beer Sheva to commemorate Martin Buber, to survey and to discuss his works.

In editing this book we attempted, not only to present what was essential at the conference, but also to give a broader picture of Buber the person, and his thought. Therefore, we added a chapter on Buber's life, we asked the participants to add here and there to their papers; two papers were somewhat extended to add some aspects of Buber's political thought; in contrast, the discussions were shortened in order to avoid repetitions.

Most of the articles in the book deal with two central themes: Buber's I-Thou philosophy and his theological thought. When the conference was planned it was clear that Buber's main contribution to contemporary thought is in these two areas, which somewhat overlap. Such an overlapping in certain articles, such as that of Jochanan Bloch and Steven Katz, is important, since the point of departure and the background of the thinkers are quite different. For reasons beyond the control of the editors an article which deals with Buber's contribution to Hasidism is not included in this volume.

The book is dedicated to Jochanan Bloch, who was killed in an accident in Thailand in February 1979. His talent, his spirit, and his untiring endeavors to realize the Buber Centenary Conference contributed to its success and to its being a major historical and scholarly event.

The conference was advised by an international advisory committee under the chairmanship of Jochanan Bloch; other members were Zwi Werblowsky from Israel, Michael Theunissen from West Germany, Marvin Fox and Walter Kaufmann from the United States. The organizing committee included Jochanan Bloch, Haim Gordon, Walter Ackerman, Rivka Horwitz, Ilan Troen, Yair Magen, and Pinhas Peli, all from Ben Gurion University of the Negev. We were also assisted by Joseph Tekoah, the president of the university and Moshe Rosen, the rector. Nathan Rotenstreich helped with much needed advice.

The main endowment for the conference came from the Fritz Thyssen Foundation in West Germany. Israel Discount Bank contributed at the beginning, and again towards the end. We were also helped by the estate of Isidor and Dora Shavin and by the Lakritz Foundation.

In editing the English volume I was helped by Pinchas Peli, Yair Magen and Yoram Neuman. I want to extend special thanks to David Wolff and Yair Magen for their continuing support of my efforts.

The English translation was done by Esther Kameron and in the preparation of the volume I was greatly assisted by Alexandra Meiri.

We also want to thank Rafael Buber for allowing us to quote freely from his father's works and Margot Cohen from the Buber archives in Jerusalem for her continuing help in problems which arose.

H.G.

Introduction

HAIM GORDON

Martin Buber—if he could have—certainly would have enjoyed reading this book, which criticizes his teaching and questions central points in his thought. He knew that important and original ideas demand critical appraisal; moreover, ideas that do not demand such an appraisal are quickly forgotten. During his life he learned that a teacher who arouses his pupils usually also arouses them to criticize him. And also that only thoughts which touch on areas central to our life encourage us to return to examine them again and again.

What unites all the essays which appear in this book, from Steve Katz's analytic article to the development of Rosenzweig's critique of Buber by Bernhard Casper, is the ambivalent approach of the authors. On the one hand the authors express a deep personal relationship to Buber, a relationship which is difficult to define and which stems from the fact that they saw in Buber more than a thinker whose thoughts are worthy of being understood; on the other hand, the authors struggle in order to clarify to themselves Buber's continuing influence and contribution both to the development of their thought and also to the forming of their own life. Such a clarification requires an objective and at times critical examination of his writings. Walter Kaufmann clearly expresses this ambivalent relationship when, on the one hand, he denies the dichotomy between I-Thou and I-It, and, on the other hand he relates to Buber an epigram from Hamlet:

> He was a man, take him for all in all.
> I shall not look upon his like again.

The participants in the volume at times examine Buber's thoughts in order to clarify to themselves the problems which perturb them. Jochanan Bloch's paper is such an examination and the same is true of Helmut Gollwitzer, who often disagrees with Bloch. They were assisted by Buber's writings in their struggle to develop their own unique thinking and found in the Buber conference an opportunity to examine their own originality.

Few thinkers attract us to reread their writings again and again. I believe that Buber's writings encourage us to return to them frequently because they allow us to bury the dreams of our youth (to borrow a phrase from Nietzsche). Some of the authors in this volume criticize Buber in a manner which allows them to understand their own personal development beyond former dreams. Robert Perkins, who criticizes Buber while comparing him to Kierkegaard, expresses some disappointment with Buber, especially since, as he personally confided: "Buber's writings sing in my ears whenever I open his books . . ." A similar disappointment is found in Menachem Dorman's essay.

The volume opens a new direction in relating to Buber's thoughts. The period of the 50s and 60s, when Buber was overly lauded and applauded, has passed. The time has come for his teaching to assist us in opening new realms of thought and in deepening our research in those areas to which he brilliantly contributed. His writings assist in such a research because they are not a closed system and they do not ignore the paradoxes of human existence. They point to the difficulties of formulating experiences central to our life, such as religious or interpersonal relationships. In other words, Buber's writings encourage us to open a dialogue with them, and after the dialogue to reach conclusions which allow us to transcend that conversation. Such a possibility is found in the essay by Binyamin Uffenheimer who discusses Buber's ability to listen to a Biblical text and his intuition in discovering its secrets. Another possibility is found in the essays of Robert Wood and Yoshimori Hiraishi, who revealed a closeness between Buber's writings and Eastern thought. They also point to an area of research to which Buber's thought can serve as a basis: constructing a bridge between Eastern and Western thought.

Some authors examine here Buber's contribution to contemporary thought by comparing that thought to the contributions of other thinkers such as A. D. Gordon, Gabriel Marcel, Karl Barth. These comparisons reveal Buber's broad influence: on the founders of Zionism and its thinkers, on Catholic and Protestant theology, on Japanese philosophy, on German Jewish youth that decided to immigrate to Israel, on psychotherapy, etc. His thought inspired persons, encouraged them and charged them with a mission; many attempted to realize his writings, each in his own manner and place. Yet while contemplating all this the reader discovers an interesting phenomenon: Buber the person is hidden from our view. His photographs will continue to decorate his books, but the person who wrote the books is only partially revealed. Thus this volume points to a need of a comprehensive biography of Martin Buber.

I opened by noting that this book criticizes Martin Buber, but it is important to add that the critique reveals the intellectual struggle of scholars with the teachings of their teacher. During the conference there reigned a sort of tranquility in daily life, while participants attempted to evaluate what Buber contributed to us and to our generation. An atmosphere of mutual education prevailed, somewhat like beautiful moments described in Plato's dialogues. The participants in this volume discuss Buber, but they are also speaking to each other, and while struggling with the depth of the writings of their teacher, each one discovers his own uniqueness. Buber would have willingly accepted a critical volume dedicated to his writings, but he would have especially enjoyed the dialogue that arose between the participants of the conference—due to him and his writings.

August, 1983

Jochanan Bloch speaking at the opening of the conference

Speech of the President of Israel

PROFESSOR EFRAIM KATZIR

Distinguished Guests:

I am happy to welcome you to the Martin Buber Centenary Conference.

I became acquainted with Buber when I was a student of the Hebrew University on Mount Scopus. Since I studied Natural Sciences, I was not among his students, but I could not but perceive how highly esteemed he was among my fellow-students. Although I did not always agree with his political views I kept returning to his writings over the years. Later, when he became President of the Israeli Academy of Science, I met with him quite often.

Any reader of Buber cannot but be impressed by his wisdom, his fruitfulness and his breadth of mind. Buber was a wonderful Biblical scholar and an excellent linguist who translated the Bible into German with Franz Rosenzweig. I can still remember my father reading this translation and delighting in it each day anew. His tales of the Hasidim are still an aesthetic and spiritual source of pleasure. His sociological research influenced the kibbutz movement, and his Zionist doctrine was and is still interesting and inspiring. Buber of course became well-known through his book *I and Thou* and through his philosophical Weltanschauung.

Martin Buber was born in Vienna in 1878; until the age of fourteen he lived with his grandfather who was an outstanding Midrashim scholar; later he studied at the Universities of Vienna, Zurich and Berlin. In 1899 he was a delegate to the third Zionist Congress at which he spoke of the importance of culture, education, and spiritual values—issues which should also be of great concern today. Later in his life he was part of the Democratic Zionist Fraction which opposed Herzl, and there too he emphasized the importance of cultural and educational activity. In 1902 together with Weizman and Bertold Feivel he wrote the famous pamphlet on the Jewish School of Higher Learning which laid the foundation of the Hebrew University. His many other activities are written in the annals of our time.

It is good to know that at this conference Buber's philosophical writings will be discussed and analyzed, as well as his phenomenological-religious view, his contribution to the Jewish thought and his unique approach to the similarities and dissimilarities between Judaism and Christianity. For me his book *I and Thou* has special appeal. I agree with him that men of science are indeed involved in an "I-It" world and are mostly preoccupied with the relation between the "I" and the "It" and not with the relationship between "I" and "Thou". However, having been the President of the State of Israel for the last four and a half years, I can understand the great importance of the relationship between "I and Thou". We need dialogue. And those who understand the importance of and seek to intensify their relationship with the "Thou" will understand better the concept of the Jewish God, the one Being with whom dialogue is always possible and to whom one may always turn.

A quotation from Buber's collection *Tales of the Hasidim*, in which he compiled the wonderful tales of the Hasidim and presented them with subtlety and sensitivity, comes to my mind:

> Rabbi Elazar said:
> When the Lord perceived the unjust deeds of the generation of the Flood and the generation of the Tower of Babel He hid the Light of the first day of Creation from them.
> —For whom did He hide it?
> —For the righteous to come.
> —Where did He hide it?
> —In the Torah.
> —If so, will the righteous not find some of the hidden Light while studying the Torah?
> —They will.
> —If so, what will the righteous who will find some of the hidden Light in the Torah do?
> —They will show it in their way of life.

I would like to wish you all that you may find some of that hidden Light of the Torah to illuminate your lives and our lives in the discussions of this conference.

Opening Remarks

JOCHANAN BLOCH

The man whom we are discussing and in whose memory we have convened was blessed—and in many ways. Among the many gracious qualities with which he was endowed was the tremendous gift of pleasing and impressing people without getting into a heated confrontation with them. This also accounts for his fame—and in this too he was exceptional. He did not know the pains of struggle for recognition at the beginning of his career. Already in his youth his talent was honored. In his old age he was not abandoned nor forgotten. On the contrary, in his declining years his reputation attained its height. Indeed, his is a rare case. But he also had a special charm which was beyond praise—that element of his magic which became a source of legend. It was not a legend of struggle and sorrow, like the legend of A. D. Gordon or the legend of Jabotinsky, for example. Buber was an aesthetic legend.

All this tends to conceal one fact, which is worth emphasizing: the man was courageous. He had a native courage that was truly extraordinary. He never followed the beaten track. With an astounding self-confidence he found his own way, a rebellious, unconventional way. An astonishing anecdote is known to us. When he was a student in his early twenties, he was already editing the central organ of the Zionist movement, *Ha-Olam*. After a few months he told Herzl that he no longer wished to continue in this work—to appreciate this one must know what Herzl was then to those who surrounded him and followed him. "Why?" Herzl asked. "Because I want to go over to the opposition," he replied.

This rebelliousness characterized his whole way. He sought a Judaism which would correspond to his religious and spiritual desire and which would provide an answer for his generation. He was convinced that the traditional forms would not suffice for this, and that the forces of creativity and renewal in Judaism must be liberated. Therefore he did not hesitate to demand the breaking of the accepted forms. There was in him a revolutionary and anarchist element; to be sure, this revolutionary element was well stylized and captured many hearts with the magic of style, which sometimes concealed the extremism and the breaking of vessels.

Gershom Scholem called him a religious anarchist. There is some truth in this. But it seems to me that this characterization requires a more precise definition. Buber had a lifelong tendency for lack of specificity. A kind of conceptual abstraction prevailed in him, which shied away from a specific commandment, specific contents, and if you like—from the crudeness of life, with its burdens, its materialistic and rigidified element, its cruelty. In his eyes this was not a deficiency, but an asset. God, he thought, is not caught in the specificity of "this and just this"—and therefore there are no fixed commands to guide us through life.

Buber paid a high price for this lack of specificity. You cannot teach men a way nor lead a people if you do not point to *this* specific way and to *this* goal and *these* means. To be sure, every specific truth of life is for a limited time, and that time passes. But on the other hand great persons are remembered for their commitment to *one* clear truth, even if in the passage of time this truth is revealed as fragile and partial, like everything human.

That breaking of vessels, without any new vessel alongside or within it, is certainly also the root of a strange phenomenon, which many have already observed: in the eyes of the Gentiles Buber was a spokesman of Judaism, a kind of uncrowned representative of Judaism, but among us his voice was heard sparsingly. Concerning this there are two observations to be made; first, it is rightly said that Buber was a religious anarchist. But after all, Gershom Scholem is also a religious anarchist, and certainly no less than Buber. And Ahad ha-Am, who seems so orderly and so traditional, was an agnostic and even a religious nihilist. And Bialik? What did Bialik believe? One may also ask what was the Judaism of Herzl, Ben Gurion and Jabotinsky? But these men felt a command from which Buber was very distant. Therefore it is better not to continue with this comparison. Nevertheless we may conclude that as regards the religious, spiritual tradition of Judaism, that disclarity was the property of the entire generation. And second—it is true that Buber has not achieved popularity among us, but his hidden influence has been very considerable. Gershom Scholem once said, "We are all disciples of Buber". If the reference is to those philosophers and scholars of Judaism who passed through the melting-pot of assimilation—and who among us is not an "assimilated Jew?"—this saying is largely true, although not in all areas.

One may also understand the measure of his influence. Buber was not a spokesman of Judaism, but his being was impressed by the fate of Judaism in our time, and the decisions of that fate. He partook in them. He is united with us in that extreme renewal which begins almost from nothing, and whose goal is nevertheless to preserve the existence of Judaism and to renew its days as of old. The paradox lies in the fact that the renewal of Judaism, and the striving to break through its contents and forms, were the product of a generation which was cut off from Judaism and could not continue the tradition of the fathers. The generation wanted two mutually contradictory things, and sometimes it accuses itself. We must be grateful that Buber found an attractive and impressive way out of this maze, which is the maze of the generation and ours too.

But all this did not make him popular. Almost everyone attacks him severely. The younger generation asks: Is this enough? That dialogue between I and Thou, that mystical experience—is it sufficient? Buber was a socialist. But the socialists claim that he cut himself off from the socio-economic foundation. He was a Zionist, but the Zionists claim that he was blind to the demands of political power. He was a religious Jew, but the Orthodox will never forgive him for not keeping the 613 commandments.

Nevertheless, Buber does not require defence. He was a man at peace with himself as few are, a man who found his way. We shall not adequately fathom his character unless we remember that he himself knew his own limitations. He did not speak of it much, and the words which he said on this matter are not clear, as if they were spoken clandestinely. But if we listen closely, we shall hear them. Perhaps it is said most beautifully in the afterword to his novel *Gog und Magog* (For the Sake of Heaven), which for some reason appeared only in the German, and not in the English or Hebrew edition. There he writes: "My heart belongs to those in Israel in whom the struggle which precedes the renewal of the form of faith and the form of life is taking place. In that struggle Hasidism finds its continuation—this, however, in an hour of the world when darkness has replaced the gradual shining-forth of the light. . . . It seems to me that in this hour of the world it is not at all important to possess a fixed doctrine, but rather to know eternal reality and to hold out, by its power, against the reality of the present. There is no way in this desert night. We can only wait in readiness of soul until light dawns and the way is revealed—in a place which no man today can anticipate."

Indeed, in this hope we too participate, and in this hope he is close to us, whatever our arguments against him may be. If we can each make some personal contribution of hope to this expectation, we shall all be his partners and disciples—faithful or rebellious, but still: Martin Buber's disciples.

THE MAN AND HIS WORK

Buber's Failures and Triumph

WALTER KAUFMANN

1

Martin Buber's manysidedness distinguished him even in his own time. On the hundredth anniversary of his birth, such manysidedness has become an outright anomaly. Specialization has grown rapidly during the twentieth century, especially since the second World War. No religious writer today invites comparison with Martin Buber—no Jew, Christian, Hindu, Buddhist, or Muslim. We may feel that religion and perhaps also philosophy are the poorer for that; or we may wonder whether there are not good reasons for the increase in specialization; or both. In any case, to gain an understanding of Buber, we should recall not only particular themes in his work but also the whole man.

When Buber was in his eighties, he published his works in three volumes, devoting each volume to one of his central concerns. In the first volume he collected his writings on philosophy, in the second his writings on the Bible, and in the third his writings on Hasidism. Simultaneously, another publisher brought out, also in German, his essays and lectures on *Der Jude und sein Judentum, The Jew and His Judaism*. Even these four tomes do not represent the whole of his work. We must add to them the four volumes that contain his German translation of the Hebrew Bible.

His major writings, then, by which he wished to be remembered can be found in eight volumes which span five major concerns. Yet, we must add a sixth dimension, for Buber was not only a writer but also a teacher, and what was best in his teaching was not necessarily the content of his lectures that survives in print. He was, at least part of the time, a charismatic teacher who impressed his listeners profoundly during informal sessions and during the discussions that sometimes followed his lectures. On such occasions the point was less to communicate knowledge than it was to change the participants in the dialogue.

At the very least, then, we must distinguish six major endeavors: translating the Bible, writing about the Bible, about Hasidism, about Jewishness and Zionism, philosophy, and dialogical teaching. But it

3

would be better to add a seventh project. Even as we must distinguish Buber's translation of the Bible from his more or less scholarly writings about the Bible, we should also distinguish Buber's more or less scholarly writings about the Hassidim from his one-volume collection of their tales and his novel *Gog and Magog*.

His manysidedness should be plain by now. Buber confronts us with an imposing and multi-dimensional achievement that has won him countless admirers. If one is satisfied with what Kierkegaard called the aesthetic orientation—that is, content to pay homage to what is profound and beautiful, but *ganz unverbindlich*, without incurring any obligation, merely as a spectator who enjoys a diversion, applauds, and goes home—then one has an easy time of it. There is much in Buber that is profound and beautiful, and it is a pleasure to express one's gratitude for that. But Buber presumably did not write or teach in order to win gratitude or appreciation. A serious author and teacher is no mere entertainer. His aim transcends applause. He wants to make an enduring difference. To be appreciated is child's play compared to that.

We must ask to what extent Buber succeeded in what he tried to do. This is an uncomfortable question and therefore mostly avoided. It brings us face to face with Buber's failures.

We should face up to them to learn something not only about Buber but also about success and failure and what it means to be human. The failures that concern us here are not mistakes. It is not as if Buber had taken examinations and failed them. The most devastating failures in life are different. We set our own goals, and those who aim low enough often succeed. Those who aim at applause often get it. Those who aim to win riches often do. Buber's goals were exceptionally ambitious. Even taken singly, his aims were extraordinarily high, making success unlikely from the beginning. But Buber did not confine himself to one or two of these aims. We have distinguished seven major endeavors and shall consider them one by one, not in a censorious spirit but recalling the splendid line (7488) in Goethe's Faust:

> *Den lieb ich, der unmögliches begehrt.*
> I love him who desires the impossible.

2

In all of his seven major endeavors Buber accomplished a great deal and came nowhere near total failure. Consider his Bible translation. The first volume appeared in 1926; by 1933 there were twelve volumes, and when Buber left Germany in 1938, fifteen. For almost two decades this was probably his most quixotic undertaking. It tells us a great deal about the state of German Jewry in the thirties that Buber's continued work on his German translation was not considered grotesque. The strange style that Buber and Rosenzweig developed for this project was criticized, and many people preferred Torczyner's version, which also appeared in Germany in the thirties. But the need for a new German Bible was felt intensely at that time. Thousands of Jews in Germany went back to reading the Bible and did not know Hebrew enough to study it in the original. And many turned to Buber's version.

When the war ended, scarcely any Jews were left in Germany, and Buber might have written off this undertaking as a noble failure. Yet a German publisher asked him to finish the project, and Buber began by revising what he had done years ago, before he completed the remaining books, and the whole translation was finally finished in 1962, almost forty years after it was begun. During his last years Buber kept revising his German Bible, enabling his son to publish in 1976 the ninth edition, again revised and improved, of the new edition of 1954 of Buber's German Torah, and the fourth revised edition of the new edition of 1962 of the *Schriftwerke (Ktuvim)*. Obviously there is a market though it does not consist of the readers whom Buber and Rosenzweig had had in mind when they started *"In the beginning" (Breshit)*. The culture that this translation was meant to change has perished. In an important sense this undertaking was a tragic failure.

The German Jews who survived the war are widely scattered. Few of those living in Israel read the Bible in German, and of those who went elsewhere some no longer read the Bible at all while others no longer have enough German to wrestle with Buber's version which was never meant to be read without effort. It was meant to be studied by people who wished to "learn Bible"; and I still recall Buber talking about *"Bibel lernen"* in 1934. I do not know *who* reads Buber's version in Germany in the seventies, or *how* it is read. That it keeps being read is surely a triumph.

Buber's way of translating, which owes a great deal to Rosenzweig, has many roots in Germany and invites comparison with Rudolf Borchardt, whose translations have had even less influence, and Martin Heidegger, whose versions of the Greek materials he quotes, have found many imitators among German academics. But all such comparisons only redound to Buber's credit. While Heidegger insisted that an interpretor must use "violence" and made a practice of ripping short texts from their context, Buber paid more attention to the context than previous translators and tried to teach us respect for the distinctive voice of the original. Far from concentrating merely on fragmentary quotations, like Heidegger, Buber always felt a responsibility to the Hebrew Bible as a whole. He insisted that we must ask where else a word occurs. If there should be few who have learned from this approach to translation, I am one of them and am glad to acknowledge my debt to Buber and Rosenzweig.

Buber's way has not prevailed. Publishers still press translators to give them easily readable versions that are idiomatic, and any profound concern for the original voice is equally rare in prose and in poetry. While I often prefer other versions to Buber's, it was Buber who taught me to listen for the original voice; and if he failed to impress this lesson on many others, I cannot help feeling that it was better to stand for noble principles than to adopt a more popular position and have more influence.

Buber's writings *about* the Bible present a similar picture. His books on the kingship of God, Moses, and the faith of the prophets have not become standard works and have not succeeded in redirecting Biblical scholarship. Scholars have largely ignored his Biblical studies, which are considered excessively impressionistic and personal. Yet much that was more highly regarded when Buber's studies appeared has by now been forgotten. Buber remains.

3

Buber's writings on "The Jew and his Judaism" can be seen as another failure. He was one of the leading Zionists of his time but stayed in Germany until 1938, and when he finally went to Palestine he never gained anything like the influence that he had had on the German Jews in the thirties. In Palestine he was, and in Israel he remained, a marginal figure. Yet the writings in which he developed concepts of Zionism and of Judaism different from the more widely accepted ones still confront us. Some of the Hebrew prophets were failures, too; but their writings still haunt humanity.

Success is no proof of virtue, nor is failure. But we come nowhere near an understanding of Buber if we ignore the brute fact of his repeated failures. The Judaism and the Zionism that he espoused have not gained wide acceptance. The culture that has developed and the policies that are espoused in Israel today are not what Buber had hoped for.

One might have thought that as a teacher Buber must have had a great impact. It is surprising how little he changed most of his listeners who sat at his feet in Germany, Israel, and the United States. Of course, he did make a profound difference in the lives of a few, but it is sad how few eminent men and women were changed by being his students. Was Buber's insistence on personal contact misguided? Can even a charismatic teacher accomplish little in person?

Counterexamples abound. Some charismatic teachers have had many followers who became teachers in their own right and wrote books. Wittgenstein did, for example, but as one talks to people who knew him one gains the impression that he may have considered his disciples proof of his failure. Nor did Buber envy Heidegger *his* followers.

It may be objected that one can teach a method, which is true. Freud certainly did; yet he said to Ludwig Binswanger, who came from Switzerland to visit him and attended one of the evening sessions of the Vienna Psychoanalytical Society: *So, haben Sie jetzt diese Bande gesehen!* Well, have you seen these gangsters now?[1]

Craftsmen can teach many students their craft. Teachers whose stature is inseparable from their individuality will often have a wide appeal but cannot hope to turn out many students who have much in common with them. Followers of widely different teachers usually have more in common with each other than they do with their masters.[2] And if the disciples emulate their master and he retains his integrity, he will probably feel as Freud did.

Buber's failure as a teacher is poignant but not accidental; it is a corollary of the kind of man he was. And it may remind us that no major modern philosopher could point to students he had taught as some measure of his success. The greatest philosophers from Descartes to Hume did not teach philosophy. Kant was the first great philosopher of modern times who was also a professor, and he taught only one student who became a major figure: Herder. But when Herder published a major philosophical work, Kant reviewed it very disparagingly[3], and later on Herder published a two-volume attack on Kant.[4] Hegel had some remarkable students, but those who became philosophers in their own right, like Ludwig Feuerbach, did not remain Hegelians. Some of Schelling's lectures were attended by Engels, Bakunin, and Kierkegaard, but he would surely have felt dismayed by all of them.

In sum, no great philosopher of modern times was a successful teacher in the sense that he turned out disciples who carried on and developed his work. But whether Buber was a great philosopher is, of course, another question.

4

Buber confronts posterity as, above all, a philosopher. The most important book about him bears the title *The Philosophy of Martin Buber.*[5] He himself contributed to it. And most people would say, if asked to identify him, that he was a Jewish philosopher. Finally, he himself considered *I and Thou* his most important book, and he saw it as his contribution to philosophy.

In some ways *I and Thou* has been a great success. Tens of thousands of students still read it year after year in the United States alone, and philosophers keep writing articles and books about it. The books differ widely but have one thing in common: all are many times as long as *I and Thou*.

Of course, interest in Buber's *I and Thou* is not confined to philosophers and philosophy students. The first English version of the book was the work of a Christian clergyman, and it has long enjoyed a marked popularity among Protestant theologians.

We have finally reached a drastic reversal. In the areas where Buber failed to have as wide an impact as he might have wished we could say that this may actually be to his credit. Conversely, the relative popularity of *I and Thou* is not necessarily to its credit. It is a flawed work and owes its success not least to its timely failings.

The most obvious of these is the style, which is affected rather than ruthlessly honest. To compare it with *The Prophet* by Khalil Gibran, which was published the very same year and has enjoyed an enormous success, might be too unkind, but both books are influenced by the pose of Nietzsche's *Zarathustra* without remotely approaching its riches or its irony. Authenticity is not everything, and the very category of authenticity is simplistic. Nietzsche, for example, used masks and knew and said that he did. But the inauthenticity of Buber's *I and Thou* is a serious flaw in a book that *is* simplistic. We are confronted by a pose without redeeming wit or irony. It approximates the oracular tone of false prophets.

It is not fashionable to pay attention to style in philosophy, but as long as we do not we cannot fully understand a philosopher. Kant or Hegel, Nietzsche or Heidegger in another style would no longer be the same men. For better or worse, their philosophy and their language belong together. Those who think of philosophy as a science may wish to deny this, but Buber himself never considered language as merely accidental and external but attached immense importance to it.[6] Hence the note of falseness in *I and Thou* cannot be discounted. It is a warning sign.

Discussing *I and Thou* in his "Replies to My Critics" at the end of *The Philosophy of Martin Buber*, he claimed to have written the book "under the spell of an irresistible enthusiasm. And the inspiration of such enthusiasm one may not change any more, not even for the sake of exactness. For one can only estimate what one would gain, but not what would be lost".[7]

Although Nietzsche had not paused to revise his *Zarathustra*, he did revise his other books before publication. On December 8, 1888, less than a month before his final breakdown, Nietzsche wrote Peter Gast that he had returned the manuscript of *Ecce Homo* to the publisher "day before yesterday after laying it once more on the gold scales from the first to the last word to set my conscience finally at rest".[8]

Such scrupulous weighing of every word was not in fashion in 1923 when *I and Thou* first appeared. Nor was the point Nietzsche made in section 319 of *The Gay Science* popular:[9]

> One sort of honesty has been alien to all founders of religions and their kind: They have never made their experiences a matter of conscience for knowledge. "What did I really experience? What happened in me and around me at that time? Was my reason bright enough . . ." But we, we others who thirst after reason, are determined to scrutinize our experiences as severely as a scientific experiment—hour after hour, day after day. We ourselves wish to be our experiments and guinea pigs.

It was also in 1923 that Rilke published both his *Duino Elegies* and his *Sonnets to Orpheus*. In a letter from Muzot (February 11, 1922) he claimed that both had been written "in a few days, it was a nameless gale, a hurricane in the mind."[10] There was much in these volumes that belongs with the best verse ever written in German. And yet, as any reader of Rilke's letters knows even if he should not notice it in Rilke's poetry, he was addicted to poses, and one often encounters a disturbing note of falseness in his letters.

In Heidegger, who wrote *Being and Time* in the twenties, this falseness is more pronounced and took a different, much more scholastic but no less oracular form. Walter Benjamin's affections and obscurantism were different again but equally palpable.

We should reject the claim that "the inspiration of such enthusiasm

one may not change any more, not even for the sake of exactness".
Even in poetry that is not true, and in philosophy it is quite
unacceptable. Goethe kept revising the products of his inspiration,
including the original versions of his *Iphigenie* and *Faust*, and did not
even take pains to preserve the text of the *Urfaust*, which was
discovered only in 1887 in a copy made by someone else. It is
arguable that in places the *Urfaust* is preferable to the final version,
but a truly inspired writer will not shrink from the experiment of
rewriting and will try to see what can be improved, unless the first
draft seems more or less perfect. Those who keep having intuitions,
hunches, and inspiration can afford to be ruthless with themselves,
while the writer who has been under the spell of an irresistible
enthusiasm only once will naturally guard its fruit more anxiously.

Was *I and Thou* more or less perfect? Is it credible that the reason
for not changing anything was that it could have been changed only
for the worse? Surely, the central dichotomy of the book did not bear
close examination. Buber refused to go over his text critically, feeling
perhaps, if only dimly, that genuine self-criticism might have required him to abandon the central idea.

It is not true—and this is the crux of my criticism—that a genuine
relationship to another human being can be achieved only in brief
encounters from which we must always relapse into states in which
the other human being becomes for us merely an object of experience
and use. If one takes this dichotomy seriously and identifies with the
person who championed it instead of treating it scholastically, one
realizes that it reveals a deep existential malaise both in the writer
and in the young people who clasp his book to their bosoms. In
Buber's case one can scarcely resist the surmise that he was permanently damaged by his mother's abandonment of him when he was a
small child.

My relationship to students who come to ask me something and to
other partners in a conversation, whether a man or woman in a store
or Ernst Simon or Gershom Scholem, is not punctuated by brief
moments of genuine encounter; neither—and this is crucial—do I
confront them as mere objects of experience or use. Precisely if they
matter much to me, I also find myself thinking *about* them, sometimes in an effort to understand better how they feel and think. Such
thoughts are not a fall from grace, a relapse into inauthenticity, or a
betrayal to be atoned for in another ecstasy.

Some of my published photographs may help to show what I
mean.[11] When I photograph a person—and most of my photographs of

people are of poor men, women and children whose names I do not know—they become objects of experience for me, but most certainly not merely objects. The ethos of the photographs is to reveal the "You".

This crucial point can be illustrated best with Rembrandt's portraits. Think of some of the most eloquent portraits, like that of his mother in Vienna (Br. 71) or that of his father in Boston (Br. 73), the two of Margaretha Trip in London (Br. 394f.), or the Woman Holding a Carnation in New York (Br. 401), and ask yourself whether the following passage from *I and Thou* stands up.[12] These crucial paragraphs are found in the center of the first part (pp. 68f. of my English version) and summarize what is said repeatedly elsewhere:

> This, however is the sublime melancholy of our lot that every You must become an It in our world. However exclusively present it may have been in the direct relationship—as soon as the relationship has run its course or is permeated by *means*, the You becomes an object among objects, possibly the noblest one and yet one of them, assigned its measure and boundary. The actualization of the work involves a loss of actuality. Genuine contemplation never lasts long; the natural being that only now revealed itself to me in the mystery of reciprocity has again become describable, analyzable, classifiable—the point at which manifold systems of laws intersect. And even love cannot persist in direct relation; it endures, but only in the alternation of actuality and latency. The human being who but now was unique and devoid of qualities, not at hand but only present, not experienceable, only touchable, has again become a He or She, an aggregate of qualities, a quantum with a shape. Now I can again abstract from him the color of his hair, of his speech, of his graciousness; but as long as I can do that he is my You no longer and not yet again.
>
> Every You in the world is doomed by its nature to become a thing or at least to enter into thinghood again and again. In the language of objects: everything in the world can—either before or after it becomes a thing—appear to some I as its You. But the language of objects catches only one corner of actual life.
>
> The It is the chrysalis, the You the butterfly. Only it is not always as if these states took turns so neatly; often it is an intricately entangled series of events that is tortuously dual.

To be painted or photographed, "You must become an It in our world", and the portrait is of course "an object among objects". But does seeing the portrait involve a fall into the realm of the "describable, analyzable, classifiable" and a loss of the "You"? Is a "He" or

"She" necessarily an "It", that is "an aggregate of qualities, a quantum with a shape"? On the contrary, I can look at a portrait of an old man or woman, mindful that this human being is old, and feel addressed by him or her, knowing that this is a "He" or a "She" while not at all admitting that "Every You in the world is doomed by its nature to become a thing".

To be sure, Buber himself says that "everything in the world can . . . appear to some I as its You", and this obviously includes portraits as well as van Gogh's paintings of flowers and trees. But the painter does not lapse from the genuine I-You relationship into a deplorable attitude in which he notes the color of the hair or other qualities, reducing the You to a mere It. On the contrary, he must pay some attention to qualities and details to reveal the You on the canvas. It is not "the sublime melancholy of our lot" that we cannot help thinking about the You that confronts us. Those who refuse to do this live in illusions and cultivate a relationship to an idol instead of truly confronting a You.

There is a Manichaean strain in *I and Thou* that is unworthy of Buber and that he himself might have eliminated if he had been more severe with the child of his inspiration. His faults here are of one piece. In line with his Manichaean denigration of the I-It and his unduly romantic and ecstatic notion of the I-Thou, he refused to treat his brainchild as a good painter treats one of his paintings or as Goethe treated his poems, even *Faust*, subjecting it to rigorous criticism until it becomes the better for that. Buber mistook intense emotion for revelation and did not realize how much rational reflection is needed if we really want to encounter the You rather than an illusion.

If ever a great artist worked under the spell of ecstasy and inspiration, it was Vincent van Gogh. He created literally hundreds of the finest paintings in the world in a mere four years. Of his high emotional tension and total, self-sacrificing devotion there can be no doubt, yet his copious letters show how far he was from regarding the fruits of his inspiration as sacrosanct. Even when committed to an asylum, he never lost or disparaged his critical powers. He discussed his works as well as his situation with a rarely equaled lucidity that furnishes a really startling contrast to Buber. Freud's and Kafka's letters are equally free of falseness, pretense, and murkiness but not so intense. All three men—van Gogh, Kafka and Freud—were distinguished by an amazing capacity for detachment from themselves and could see themselves from above.

It is really not surprising that Rilke liked Buber's books while Freud and Kafka did not, but the vehemence of Kafka's dislike *is* astonishing. In January 1918 he wrote Max Brod what he thought of "Buber's last books. Revolting, repulsive *(Abscheuliche, widerwärtige)* books, all three of them."[13] Yet only three days after Kafka had written his friend, Felice, on January 16, 1913, that he had heard Buber lecture and "he makes a dreary impression on me; everything he says lacks something", Kafka wrote her: "Yesterday I also spoke with Buber, who is in person fresh and simple and remarkable *(bedeutend)* and seems to have nothing to do with the lukewarm things he has written."[14] But this did not change his view of Buber's books and only a day or two later he wrote Felice that he found Buber's reworking of the tales of Rabbi Nachman (1906) and the Baalshem (1908) "insufferable".

Many others, including Gershom Scholem, who described much the same ambivalence in his autobiographical book, *Von Berlin nach Jerusalem* (Frankfurt, 1977), felt that in person, though not necessarily when he was lecturing, Buber was truly impressive, but that the tone of some of his writings was affected and not genuine. His later treatment of Hasidic materials was very different from his first two efforts and will be discussed later on, but in *Ich und Du* his affectation was, I think, especially disturbing.

My fundamental criticism, however, does not concern Buber's style but his claim that "Every You in the world is doomed by its nature to become a thing or at least to enter into thinghood again and again." This unacceptable claim was meant to prepare the ground for the eternal You or God of whom Buber said in the last part of the book (p.147 of my English version): "Only one You never ceases, in accordance with its nature to be You for us."

I hesitate to compare Buber with other philosophers because he so clearly differed from them. But something needs to be said in his defense. In the 1920's when "authenticity" became a watchword in philosophy, authenticity actually declined. One might suppose that it declined first and that the philosophers then called attention to this *malaise*. But the melancholy fact is that precisely those who made the most of the contrast of authenticity and inauthenticity exhibited nothing short of a cultivated inauthenticity. Compared to some of the others—Adorno and Benjamin, Heidegger and Sartre (in his philosophic themes)—Buber remained relatively clear, and certainly unambiguous in his stand against totalitarianism from both the right and the left. "The Jargon of Authenticity"[15] may well be one of the best things Adorno ever wrote. It was a splendid attack on Heidegger, but Adorno evidently failed to notice how much of this critique was applicable to himself.

The whole complex of problems relating to authenticity is too vast to be unraveled here. I hope to deal with it at greater length in a forthcoming work. What should be said here is that Buber ought to be compared with his contemporaries and that he fares better as a philosopher when we do that than he does when we measure him against major philosophers of the past, like Kant, Hegel, or Nietzsche, whose thought was marked by an abundance, a range, and a sweep not even remotely approximated by Buber.

5

This critique of *I and Thou* is corroborated by Buber's correspondence with Rosenzweig, published in 1973.[16] In September 1922 Rosenzweig wrote Buber after reading the first installment of the printer's proofs of *I and Thou* that he found the central dichotomy of the book unacceptable. He put the point differently from the way I put it here or, for that matter, in the Prologue to my translation in 1970: "With the I-It you give the I-You a cripple as an opponent". Rosenzweig then introduced God as *Er*, "He", and reproached Buber for his undue "narrowing down to the I-You (which incidentally you share with Ebner)."[17]

In his reply of September 14, Buber told Rosenzweig of his plans for volumes II through V,[18] and five days later he wrote Rosenzweig that *I and Thou* "is after all not a whole but a scanty and rough beginning and yet must go out into the world like that. The second volume, on which I am working hard and which . . . is to be called, non-religiously (*religionslos*), *Holy Action*, will become simpler and more transparent, it seems to me." But the second volume never appeared any more than the third, fourth and fifth, for Buber could not build on the foundation he had laid.

Against Rosenzweig's criticism one could cite passages in which the I-It does not seem to be a cripple, but in his letter of September 22 Rosenzweig himself replied: "Yes, the It receives its full rights in a few places, but that is not to your credit but to its own, for these passages fall out of the line of your thought". My concern in any case is not to eulogize the I-It but rather to insist that it is false that every You except for God must again and again become a mere thing for us.

To be sure, we are not eternal, and in death we become dust and ashes, but as long as I live the dead whom I love are not mere things for me, and thanks to Rembrandt's art his father and mother are not mere things for me either. Nor are Buber and Rosenzweig. They still address me, and I am not trying to score points but rather to respond to them.

I am much closer to Buber's more humanistic orientation than to Rosenzweig's philosophical theology. But Rosenzweig was not only Buber's close friend and a man whose indomitable wit in the direst of circumstances remains a challenge though he is long dead, but he was also an extraordinarily perceptive reader. And it is fascinating to discover how he questioned Buber's central contrast of the I-You and I-It before *I and Thou* was published, though *too late* for Buber to make major changes; how Buber kept insisting that after all this was only the first volume; how a few weeks later, as Buber reported on February 10, 2000 copies had been sold; and how Buber, though he kept considering *I and Thou* his major contribution to philosophy, abandoned the project of which it had been meant to be no more than a scanty beginning. In a significant sense, *I and Thou* was a failure.

6

Two dimensions of Buber's work remain to be discussed briefly: his writings on Hasidism and his collection of Hasidic lore. To begin with the former, it is now widely acknowledged that Buber's portrait of Hasidism does not stand up under scholarly scrutiny and that it was rather partisan and impressionistic. Far from being in a position to dispute this verdict, I can only say that this was surely obvious from the beginning. Buber's Hasidim bore little resemblance to any Hasidim to be found anywhere nowadays, and the inherent likelihood that people like that should have lived in the places where Hasidim flourished around 1800 was surely nil. When the scholars' verdict came in, I did not feel that I had been betrayed and that Buber's essays had been a waste of my time. Buber's writings on the Hasidim served three crucial functions.

First, they served as introductions and commentaries to his collections. If the collections were worth having, then these writings filled an important place.

Secondly, these essays explore a possible meaning of religiousness and expanded our conception of the religious life. If we compare

them with William James' *Varieties of Religious Experience*, Rudolf
Otto's *Das Heilige*, and the vast literature on mysticism that appeared
during the first half of this century, Buber's essays easily hold their
own value as an important and illuminating contribution.

Finally, it was Buber who opened up the subject. In this respect,
one could compare him with Moses and Scholem with Joshua.

Die Erzählungen der Chassidim and *Gog und Magog* are Buber's
most enduring creations. They are masterpieces of religious literature. In an essay written in 1957 for *The Philosophy of Martin Buber*
(the original English version appeared in 1967, while the German
version of the book was published in 1963), I argued at some length
that Buber's *Erzählungen* were "one of the great religious books of all
time."[19] That estimate and the arguments produced in its support still
strike me as sound. It depends on the assumption that great religious
books rarely stand or fall with their historical accuracy. The question
of what really happened is always interesting and worth discussing,
and when a religious book departs from the facts that is worth
pointing out. But religious works have other dimensions as well, and
Buber's two books have a literary quality that leads me to cite the
original German titles. To do him justice, one must read the originals.
I still feel that Hermann Hesse was right when he said in a published
letter in January 1950 that Buber, "like no other living author, has
enriched world literature with a genuine treasure."[20]

7

Buber's motivation has been overlooked not only by his critics but
also by most of his admirers. Wilhelm Dilthey was his teacher, and
Dilthey struggled his life long to spell out the difference between the
natural sciences and the mental sciences, or rather what he called *die
Geisteswissenschaften*. But Dilthey also wrote a remarkable book on
the young Hegel,[21] reporting on unpublished Hegel manuscripts that
one of Dilthey's students, Herman Nohl, published a year later, in
1907.[22] The earliest manuscripts in this volume have not been included in the English version of Hegel's *Early Theological Writings*,[23]
but I have included some striking quotations from this material in an
essay on "The Young Hegel and Religion".[24] In the 1790s the young
Hegel, then in his twenties, was interested in the possibility of a "folk
religion" that would be free of all irrational elements. It was Dilthey
who made this known in 1905, in a lecture a few months before his
book appeared, and it was then that Buber began his efforts to

construct a Jewish folk religion that would contain nothing contrary to reason. His work on the Hasidim and his Biblical studies are misunderstood when they are viewed as historical studies, as *I and Thou* is misunderstood when it is considered as a contribution to epistemology.

The young Hegel wrote "life of Jesus" in which Jesus teaches Kant's moral philosophy, but this was grotesque and Hegel did not publish it. This had been *his* attempt to furnish a scripture for his "folk religion". Buber's Hasidic tales are not grotesque, and he did publish them, but they have to be understood along with his Biblical Studies and *I and Thou* as parts of an epic effort to create a viable humanistic religion—a non-theological, non-halachic, Judaism. That was Buber's most ambitious and fascinating undertaking, and it was, of course, a failure.

One aspect of *I and Thou* that was much more important to Buber than to most of his readers was that the book ruled out all discourses about God, including all of theology. He did not like to be called a theologian or a mystic. He associated mysticism with the drowning of the I in the divine Thou, and theology with the reduction of the divine Thou to an It. He wanted a religion in which the individual could address God and be addressed by God, but a religion that left no room for talk about God, nor did Buber attend religious services. The only rabbis, not to speak of ministers and priests, for whom Buber had any use were dead rabbis—whose stories he cut to create stunning gems. Of course, he respected men who happened to be rabbis, like Leo Baeck, for example; but as a religious person he had no need of rabbis.

As long as we fail to see Buber's central attempt to create a humanistic religion, we do not understand him.

8

It is easy to chalk up Buber's failures as a scholar and a teacher, as a translator and a philosopher, and as a Zionist. But we should recall what Gilbert Murray once said: "There is not one play of Euripides in which a critic cannot find serious flaws." The same could be said of Buber's books; but one should add, as Murray did: "the worse the critic, the more he will find."[25] Why? Because the faults are really not hard to discover, and the critic who gloats over them is likely to be so immersed in details that he fails to see what transcends such faults.

One flaw remains crucial. This is not, as one might suppose, that

Buber did too many things and did not specialize enough. It is rather the false dichotomy that Buber presented to us in *I and Thou* and henceforth assumed to be fundamental instead of questioning it: that of the I-You and I-It. By associating the former with a kind of ecstasy while relegating all objectification, reflection, examination, and careful thought to the I-It, he provided a philosophical justification for excessive subjectivity, illusions, and murkiness.

That Buber ranged as widely as he did was precisely what still makes him interesting and important. That he was not more rigorous, self-critical, as scholarly is a fault—but not a price one must necessarily pay for breadth.

If we compare Buber with our contemporaries and above all with the teachers and scholars at our universities today, his stature seems secure. As specialization has increased, something important has been lost. Buber created a cosmos from the chaos of the modern world, and when you encountered him you encountered his world as well. It was not a small and merely academic world, but a world that embraced past and present. It was not oppressive because it was not a finished system to be handed over to students or younger colleagues with the demand that they should become interior decorators. The soul of this world was Buber's ceaseless striving through the whole length of his rich life. He was not free from vanity, but he was never self-satisfied or complacent and kept trying to improve his translation of the Bible, for example, until he died.

In conclusion, I feel like saying of him what Hamlet says of his father:

> He was a man, take him for all in all.
> I shall not look upon his like again (I.ii.187f.).

Discussion Following Walter Kaufmann's Lecture

S. KATZ

You placed so much importance on authenticity and inauthenticity and on style in some broad sense in your criticism of *Ich und Du* and generally of Buber's work. And yet we lacked a criteria of your sense of what makes something authentic or inauthentic. I find certain aspects of Hegel equally difficult to cope with. I was therefore wondering if you might say a bit more about your canons of authenticity and of stylistic credentials.

W. KAUFMANN

I find the category of authenticity interesting but of limited usefulness. I did say more than once that there is a certain falseness to the style, the tone of *Ich und Du* in many places. I did not say that this is anything singular or unusual about Buber, I wouldn't dream of holding up Hegel as an example of authenticity, or as someone whose style is not full of faults; in fact, the badness of Hegel's style is such that one has to start at the other end and see how in some ways this style is functional and not merely bad.

Buber at his best was a really great writer, but in *Ich und Du* there is in places a false, oracular tone that is affected and brings to mind role-playing. Buber certainly was not beyond doing that; but at his best he transcended that, and there was an electrifying directness that spoke directly to the listener.

D. MOORE

I would like to defend Buber's dichotomy of the I-Thou and the I-It. One point which you omitted in that passage you gave us from *I and Thou* deals with need of presence, of wholehearted presence, when we are confronting the Thou of our life, or any Thou of our life. The fact that the Thou becomes an It doesn't mean quite what you seem to infer in your talk, that this is therefore an object to be used, an experience, because it does say right there in that citation it might be the noblest of objects; nevertheless it is an object, but that's not

19

something obviously evil or wrong; it is something which for Buber is necessary. The idea of presence is rather key here in differentiating the I-Thou and the I-It. Because I cannot be wholeheartedly and continuously present to someone I love, it seems to me, that that is why Buber relegates even the beloved to the realm of the It. Wholeheartedness implies precisely that this object is the only one before me. When I confront the Thou, I know the Thou and nothing but the Thou at the moment. Do you see the problem?

W. KAUFMANN

I see the problem. There must be many people in the room who agree much more with you than they do with me. All I can say is that I think I understand the usual position and I think it is wrong. What we have in Buber is rooted in an existential, human reality; an account of two attitudes, even vis-à-vis people to whom one is very close. On the one hand there is the satisfactory, the authentic Ich-Du relationship, which Buber associated with rare moments. On the other hand he associated the It with an object of experience and use. Now, this seems to me to be a sickness of the soul, a deep malaise, if in my relationship to other people I can only in rare moments transcend the attitude in which they are for me objects of experience and use.

If I truly encounter another person, this involves also paying attention to details; this is not an alternative to the I-You but one of the building blocks. I must observe others, I must think about how I might have misunderstood them; I must ask myself, perhaps in a sleepless night in bed, how they may have felt. Empathy is not a matter of pure ecstasy and pure feeling, but it is something that involves thinking about. Just so, a painter has to pay attention to details in order to bring to life the You for others. In some of his better moments Buber realized this, but in *Ich und Du* he occasionally says the opposite. I find some of his other books more satisfactory, but because he was never really willing to criticize *Ich und Du* because it was sacred to him, he again and again repeats in other works what I take to be a fundamental error of *Ich und Du*.

J. BLOCH

I strongly object to the main point in your lecture. I think that if we would take out the so-called dichotomy of Buber's teaching, nothing really would remain of him. His *Tales of the Hasidim,* his Bible translation—this is all very impressive. But what did make him an outstanding feature, what was considered after all to be a Copernican revolution at the time within theology vis-à-vis the natural sciences, vis-à-vis the scientific approach, the realistic approach, was the I-Thou, this dualism, this dichotomy. It is not a question of ecstatic moments; it is a question of a fundamental relation of being which was not made a subject matter of philosophical thinking before Dialogism. Buber accentuated it perhaps in a way which made it strained, which made it sound strained, but he touched upon a fundamental reality which is revealed, for instance, in religious existence. And it is not only a question of religious existence. The difficult thing is that, quite as Prof. Kaufmann has pointed out, there is a very realistic approach to things, taking a certain position, taking a certain line, taking certain figures. And that is the thing we have to ponder about, that in these I-It figurations, something exists which is not addressed by I-It. It is not a question of ecstatic moments, it is a question of a constant unity as real distinctive dimensions.

W. KAUFMANN

Obviously I am not trying to reduce everything to the I-It. There is more than one way of denying the dichotomy, and I am suggesting that this is a loaded alternative. Further I would say, Buber had the great merit of calling attention to a crucial problem even if he offered what I consider an untenable solution.

Z. KURZWEIL

I feel rather strongly that there is no fundamental fault in Buber's distinction between I-Thou and I-It. The I-Thou is certainly not an ecstatic state; I object to this adjective which Prof. Kaufmann used. I was once in Jerusalem, in the house of the late poet Agnon, when this point was raised and discussed. I remember the very words he used to characterize the I-Thou. He used two Hebrew words—"ricuz atzum", enormous concentration or powers of concentration—that is to say that at that moment, which is of course passing, there is nothing else in the world for me but this I-Thou situation.

A. W. DAVIS

In relation to what Prof. Kaufmann said about *Ich und Du*—it was not about the translation, I realize, it was about the work . . . But he said that such scrupulous weighing of every word was not in fashion in 1923, when *I and Thou* first appeared. Well, it was certainly in fashion in 1947-1948, when I was translating Torat Hanevi'im, because not only every word, but every comma, every full stop, had to be agreed by Martin Buber.

W. KAUFMANN

In his Bible translation Buber weighed every word and was endlessly dissatisifed with himself. *Ich und Du* stands out as an exception. This was the one work that Buber treated differently because somehow he considered it inspired.

I certainly didn't expect that I would convert everybody to my view of *Ich und Du*. Many of you have given a great deal of thought to these problems and will continue to disagree with me. Nevertheless it might be worthwhile to open up a problem here and lead people to think a little more about it. Buber said some very interesting things about the I-You relationship. From that it doesn't follow that there are only two basic relationships, and that the other one is the one that he describes as the I-It relationship. When I translated *Ich und Du* I wrote a prologue in which I suggested a pluralistic perspective: there are quite a number of possible relationships, of which these are merely two, and a number of others are also very interesting. My criticism concerns at least as much the I-It as the I-You, but mostly the dichotomy, the claiming that there are just these two. That claim has Manichaean overtones. Asked whether he considered the I-It something bad, evil or despicable, Buber would have said no. Yet there are in this distinction some overtones of authentic and inauthentic, of a good and a bad relationship to another person. And this does not do justice to the realities.

It is possible to maintain human relationships in which one does not constantly glide off into what Buber describes as the I-It relationship. Buber opened up this subject in an interesting and important way. In some ways he made a bad start, some things aren't quite right with it; but it is typical of philosophy, science and scholarship that somebody makes a start and leads you to rethink things. There is a great deal in Buber that remains. In fact, every one of his books remains. A body of work remains to comfort and to haunt us, something to return to and think about. And those of us who knew Buber personally will always be grateful for having had the chance to meet such a wonderful person. Bloch has his differences with Buber,

I have my differences with Buber, and most of us have some differences with Buber; in spite of that his books are worth going back to, and are something to be immensely grateful for.

Notes

WALTER KAUFMANN

1. L. Binswanger, *Erinnerungen an Sigmund Freud* (Bern, 1956), p. 13.
2. See 21, "Followers", in W. Kaufmann, *Critique of Religion and Philosophy* (New York, 1958).
3. *Ideen zur Philosophie der Geschichte der Menschheit*, 4 vols. (Riga & Leipzig, 1784-91). Kant reviewed volume 1 in *Jenaische Allgemeine Literaturzeitung*, January 4, 1785.
4. *Eine Metakritik zur Kritik der reinen Vernunft* (Leipzig, 1799).
5. Ed. P. A. Schilpp and M. Friedman (LaSalle, Ill., 1967).
6. See, e.g., *Die Schrift und ihre Verdeutschung* (Berlin, 1936), p. 137: "As if a genuine message . . . contained a What that could be detached without any damage from its How; as if the spirit of a speech could be discovered anywhere else than in its linguistic body . . ."
7. p. 706; p. 604 of the German ed.; my translation.
8. See W. Kaufmann, *Nietzsche*, 4th ed. (Princeton, 1974), p. 435.
9. Translated with Commentary, by W. Kaufmann (New York, 1974).
10. Rilke, *Briefe aus Muzot* (Leipzig, 1937).
11. W. Kaufmann, *Religions in Four Dimensions* (New York, 1976); also the trilogy *Man's Lot* (New York, 1978), especially the third part, *What is Man?*
12. Buber, *I and Thou: A New Translation with a Prologue "I and You" and Notes*, by W. Kaufmann (New York, 1970) p. 68f.
13. Franz Kafka, *Briefe 1902-1924* (New York, 1958), p. 224.
14. Franz Kafka, *Briefe an Felice* (New York, 1967), pp. 252ff. *Briefwechsel aus sieben Jahrzehnten*, ed. Grete Schaeder, vol. I, Heidelberg, 1972.
15. *Der Jargon der Eigentlichkeit* (Frankfurt, 1964).
16. Grete Schaeder, *op. cit.*, vol. II.
17. Friedrich Ebner, *Das Wort und die geistigen Realitäten* (Innsbruck, 1921).
18. Buber's outline of the five-volume project was first published in facsimile and English translation in my version of *I and Thou* (1970), pp. 49f. Cf. Schaeder, vol. I (1972), p. 73. Yet Buber's admirers have for the most part ignored the fact that *I and Thou* was the first volume of a work Buber abandoned.
19. The essay has been reprinted in W. Kaufmann, *Existentialism, Religion, and Death* (New York, 1976).
20. H. Hesse, *Briefe* (Berlin & Frankfurt, 1951).
21. *Die Jugendgeschichte Hegels* (Berlin, 1906).
22. *Hegels theologische Jugendschriften*, ed. Herman Nohl (Tübingen, 1907).
23. Translated by T. M. Knox and Richard Kroner (Chicago, 1948).
24. W. Kaufmann, *From Shakespeare to Existentialism* (Boston, 1959 and Garden City, N.Y., 1960); *Hegel: A Collection of Critical Essays*, ed. A. MacIntyre (Garden City, N.Y., 1972). An earlier and shorter version of this essay appeared in *The Philosophical Review*, 1954.
25. *The Literature of Ancient Greece* (1897), 3rd ed. (Chicago, 1956), p. 273.

The Sheltered Aesthete: A New Appraisal of Martin Buber's Life

HAIM GORDON

Man is a riddle, writes Nikolai Berdyaev, it is because he possesses personality that he is a riddle. Often great persons harbor disturbing riddles, Martin Buber being a case in point. For many of his students and readers he was an enigma around whom myths thrived, often with his silent approval. These myths concealed his personality and its riddle. The time has come to cut through the myths and describe his personality and personal history realistically.

Martin Buber was born in Vienna in 1878, in a period which Stefan Zweig called the golden age of security. He soon encountered the profound personal loneliness that underlay this facade of security, a loneliness intimated by Freud's psychoanalytic studies and Schnitzler's stories and plays, and clearly expressed in Rilke's haunting poems and Egon Schiele's portraits. His mother eloped with a lover when he was three years old and he was packed off to Lemberg to be raised by his affluent and scholarly grandparents, Solomon and Adele Buber. It must have been a traumatically lonely period, especially since nobody spoke to him about the rift between his parents. When he was four years old an older girl confided to him that his mother would never return, and he intuitively knew that her pronouncement was true. More than three decades later his mother visited him and his wife and children. But then he could no longer relate to her as a mother, but rather as an elderly woman with beautiful eyes who had in one period of her life begotten him.

Buber's feeling of abandonment was intensified by his not being exposed to outward expressions of affection and intimacy. His grandparents immersed themselves in their business pursuits and in the world of learning and were disinclined to talk over affairs of their own existence. He emulated them and seems to have skipped much of the romping and playing of childhood in which one learns to relate spontaneously to others. His children do not recall him ever mentioning playmates or childhood games, and no such experiences appear in his writings. He seems to have been a delicate and reserved child who did not know how to spontaneously reach out to another person and initiate a warm, affectionate, and intimate relationship.

Buber was endowed with an exceptional talent for languages. As a child he easily mastered the five languages spoken and read in and about his grandparents' home: Hebrew, Yiddish, Polish, German, and French. At school he acquired Latin and Greek. In later years he gained command of English and Italian. This broad scope of linguistic proficiency was prompted by his enchantment, nay, often obsession, with what he termed the mystery of language, an enchantment which continued throughout his life. Half a century later while climbing the Dolomite mountains with his wife, Paula, and his granddaughters, Buber would draw out of his pocket the proofs of his Bible translation at every respite, and with Paula, examine the exact meaning of key words. Even Alpine beauty could not lessen his preoccupation with language.

As a child and youth Buber fled from his loneliness into the world of books; they mirrored reality in a manner that was ordered and could be conquered by thought; their voice appealed to him, he met himself in their pages. When at the age of fourteen the order of his daily reality was threatened by his inability to resolve the problem whether time was finite or infinite, he contemplated suicide; he found salvation in a book—Kant's *Prolegomena*. And since books seemed to be the *raison d' être* of his admired grandparents, one need only unravel and master the mystery of the printed word to prove that he, Martin Buber, also had the right to exist in this world, despite the fact that his beautiful mother had forgotten that he existed.

In addition to being a famous Midrashim scholar, Solomon Buber was a director of two banks and a member of the chamber of commerce. Adele Buber managed the household and the business of their large estate. Martin led a sheltered life in their spacious home surrounded by servants who catered to his every whim. He accepted it as natural, and I doubt that he ever learned to fry an egg or to sweep the floor. Later, during his student years, he was always accompanied by a servant, and until his sixtieth birthday, when he emigrated to Palestine, he never experienced life without servants. What is more, he almost never descended from his intellectual perch to relate personally to those who served him. His household employees in Heppenheim, where he resided for twenty two years, distinctly remember his aloofness and detachment. His relation to them was I-It, never I-Thou.

As a child recluse Buber learned to employ his seclusion creatively. He confided to a friend that in his sixth or seventh year his best playmates were dramas that he composed in his mind, and in which he would play-act the different parts. What is more he learned not to fear being alone. Throughout his life his stance on moral and political issues was never hampered by a hesitancy to struggle alone for the realization of his views.

Sigmund Freud, Robert Musil, and Stefan Zweig, each in his own manner, described and discussed the repression of sex in the Hapsburgian upper and middle classes. Buber seems to have internalized such an attitude at an early age. In elementary school he once nearly wept himself unconscious when questioned by the director of the school about the sexual diversions of two of his classmates. Many persons remembered his repression of his physical self. He rarely embraced a person, even those closest to him such as his granddaughters; he refrained from creating spontaneous physical contact, such as the sudden grasping of another person's hand; sports hardly interested him, and although he was an accomplished dancer and horseback rider in his youth he soon gave up these activities.

The emphasis on the theatrical, on the need to strike a pose, flourished in the last years of the Hapsburgian monarchy and influenced persons as remote from each other as Theodor Herzl and Crown Prince Rudolf. Elements of this attitude were absorbed by the young Buber; throughout his life he delighted in being photographed and enjoyed being lauded and applauded. He always dressed impeccably and with style. The aesthetic presentation of himself was a way of life, and when it aroused admiration, all the better. His relative Ahron Eliasberg recalled that, from early childhood, Martin's many talents were held in esteem by his extended family and he seemed to enjoy playing the role of the family *Wunderkind*.

From early in his life Buber took himself very seriously and felt comfortable when others complied with such an approach. When at the age of fourteen he moved to his father's and stepmother's house in Lemberg he spent much spare time at his grandparents helping his grandfather with his scholarly pursuits. In the memoirs of his youth and student years he never described pranks or frivolous behavior. The few jocular episodes that Ahron Eliasberg described from the year they studied together at the University of Leipzig are rather mild, such as writing a drunkard's poem to a female cousin. Judaism for Solomon and Adele Buber seems to have been much more of an intellectual engagement than a way of life. They did not oppose their grandson choosing a text from Schiller's poetry rather than a passage from the weekly Biblical portion for the theme of his Bar Mitzvah sermon. Moreover, the Hebrew date of the Torah-reading does not appear on the Bar Mitzvah invitations. Nor does there seem to have been family opposition to Martin's giving up morning prayers and the donning of the phylacteries at the age of fourteen. As a teenager he immersed himself in German culture and rejected many aspects of Judaism. Ahron Eliasberg recalled that when Buber came to Leipzig in 1898 he was somewhat of a Jewish anti-Semite—"genuinely Jewish," in his vernacular, was a derogatory term. That summer he read Mathias Archer's work on Modern Judaism and became a zealous Zionist. But he viewed his Zionist activity primarily as an intellectual engagement.

During the four years that Martin lived with his remarried father, Carl Buber, a warm relationship seems to have developed between them. But the relationship was not built on a deep understanding of each other. Martin admired his father's ability to relate to nature and to his employees, but he made almost no attempts to emulate him. And Carl found it difficult to accept his son's dedication to scholarly pursuits. Years later, when writing to congratulate him on his thirtieth birthday, he vigorously urged him to abandon such "unfruitful themes" as the study of Hasidism. Martin's relationship with his stepmother was cool and his relationship with his stepsister developed much later. He makes no mention of the give-and-take of family life in Carl Buber's household and seems to have pursued his scholarly reclusion in that environment. We may safely assume that in his childhood and youth Martin Buber internalized no familial model.

Buber's student life commenced at the University of Vienna in 1896, and after spending some time at the universities of Leipzig, Berlin, and Zürich, he returned to Vienna to write his PhD dissertation which he completed in 1904. His wandering from university to university was prompted by his wish to encounter the broad spectrum of German academic achievement; it was also his manner of meeting the world and asserting his independence. In his first year at Vienna he was deeply moved by the contemporary art scene, fascinated by the poetry of Beer Hoffman and Hofmansthal, and enchanted by the theater. These interests did not hinder his being a brilliant student, indefatigable in his reading and with a unique ability to express his profound insights without arousing the animosity of his peers. These qualities probably impressed Paula Winkler, a young Christian girl with beautiful eyes whom he met while studying in Zürich and who after a brief romance, which included a memorable Alpine dancing party till the early morning hours, agreed to become his life partner. They set up house together and Raphael, their son, was born in 1900.

Taller, huskier, and in worldly affairs more strong-willed than her spouse, Paula shouldered the many tasks of their family life and encouraged Martin to dedicate himself fully to the expression of his creative powers. She sheltered him, served him, challenged him, and tenderly loved him; he was her lover and very much the child of her creative will. In one revealing love letter he admitted that he had found in her his long lost mother. Paula's many intellectual talents prompted him; she read every line he wrote before he sent it to the publisher, often commenting on the ideas he expressed or on the unclarity of his over-picturesque style. Later she became an accomplished novelist, adopting the pseudonym of Georg Munk. But throughout the half century of their life together Martin's talents always took precedence over her own.

Although Paula's attachment and conversion to Judaism were new, she immediately grasped the significance of her spouse's attempts at the turn of the century, together with Weizmann and Feivel, to imbue the Zionist movement with cultural and educational goals, which, in the spirit of Achad Haam, would revive the entire Jewish nation in the Diaspora. She supported Buber's agitation against Herzl's charismatic manner of directing the Zionist movement primarily towards economic and political goals. During this period Paula became pregnant and gave birth to their daughter, Eve; Buber continued his studies at the University of Berlin and travelled in Europe to spread his views. They settled down to a more stable life with their two children in 1903, when Buber decided to return to Vienna in order to write his PhD dissertation and subsequently, he became less involved in the Zionist movement.

Buber was not an active father. Bringing up the children was undertaken by Paula, assisted by the *Kindermadchen*, the nanny. Needless to say he probably never changed a diaper; nor do his children remember his romping with them when they grew older. This approach pretty much accorded with the norms of his milieu, but in Buber's case it was strengthened by he himself not having experienced childhood with his parents, and by Paula doing her utmost to not let the children "disturb" their father.

Undoubtedly, Buber's limited contact with his children—they remember only his reading them stories—strengthened the image he wished to project. Whether we like it or not our children see through us; we cannot pose as a hero or a sage or a prophet in front of them; or rather, we can pose, but they will soon discern that we are posing. But a person whose contact with his children is minimal can persist in perfecting his image—in Buber's earlier years it was the image of a budding genius and later it was the image of a sage, or perhaps even a prophet.

The preceding paragraph should not be misunderstood. Buber *was* a budding genius and later in his life he *was* very much of a sage. But in addition to being such a person he enjoyed playing the role of himself in society. His "Autobiographical Fragments" (published in The Philosophy of Martin Buber) bear witness to such an approach. Each fragment describes an episode in his life which supposedly led to a subsequent triumph, i.e. the bringing of Hasidism to the West, the writing of *I and Thou*, the translation of and commentaries on the Bible. He describes no dead ends in his development and conceals his personal and family life. He thus encouraged his readers to read his personal history backward, from his successes to what he presented as their humble beginnings. Such an historical approach is, of course, hortatory and uncritical; but more important for our understanding of Buber is the fact that only a person who decided what role he played in history and has greatly enjoyed playing that role can write thus.

Buber was not a person who savored participating in conflicts, particularly political conflicts. Hence he disengaged himself from Zionist activity and its conflicts and sought a new personal approach to Judaism. He renewed his reading of Hebrew and quite accidentally encountered a book on the heritage of the Baal Shem Tov. His genius was aroused; he sensed that underlying these seemingly simple texts and tales lay a profound religious message. He also sensed, albeit vaguely, that the study of Hasidism could serve as an anvil upon which he could forge his talents, prominent among them his ability to listen to the voice of a text and to transmit it. Fortunately, at that period his grandmother mended the rift that had arisen between Martin and his family—they seemed to have been unhappy that their Wunderkind should marry a convert to Judaism. In 1905 Adele Buber treated her beloved grandson and his young family to a year vacation in Italy. Buber utilized this year to immerse himself in Hasidism.

Hasidism for Buber was a scholarly, philosophical, and aesthetic engagement. As Gershom Scholem has noted, Buber was initially the reporter and transmitter of Hasidism, later he became its interpreter and herald. He sought the living and creative elements of Hasidism not in order to personally realize these elements, but rather so as to present what he believed to be the mystical or existential message of Hasidism to the world. The only manner in which Hasidism seems to have been expressed in his personal life was through his reading of his Hasidic tales to his children and grandchildren.

Buber's presentation of Hasidism is based on description, explanation and judgement connected by empathy and to the exclusion of piecemeal analysis. Such a presentation accords with what the social historian Ralf Dahrendorf calls the German idea of truth; it is poetic, profound, thought provoking, and authoritarian, but it is lacking in definiteness and in necessity, because it contains no falsifiable statements, it cannot be proven mistaken. In this context one can understand Buber's rejection of Scholem's attempt in 1943 to prove that he had misrepresented Hasidism. Instead of examining Scholem's arguments, Buber indicated that his own intuition and authority carried much more weight than Scholem's piecemeal analysis of the evidence.

Buber was also authoritarian in his family life; there were not many discussions with the children on educational problems. Thus Eve Buber remembers that she had no say in her parents' decision never to send her to school but to tutor her themselves with the help of hired teachers. His authoritarianism was probably nurtured by his early successes, such as his being hired in 1905 by Verlag Rutten and Loening in Frankfurt to edit "Die Gesellschaft", a series of monographs by eminent psychologists and sociologists, each in his area of specialization. In 1912 when the series was completed forty monographs had been published. As editor Buber was not tied down to an office or to a specific geographical location and he enjoyed the freedom to travel with his young family whenever he wished and the leisure to pursue his own research.

During this period Buber became closer to Gustav Landauer, who was eight years his senior, and whom he had met in Berlin when they both participated in the discussions of the "Neue Gemeinschaft" circle on the possibility of establishing a new communal life. Although Landauer was an accomplished writer and translator he had often worked at odd jobs in order to support his family; he was an active agitator for socialism who had twice been convicted and jailed

for expressing his views in public—once for eleven months and once
for six months. He had a difficult first marriage and only in his second
wife did he find a compatible companion. Perhaps Landauer's courageous history was what enabled him to disregard the distance Buber
kept from all his acquaintances and to relate both seriously and
jocularly to Buber's qualities and failings. He also seems to have been
one of the few persons whose relationship with Buber spilled over to
engulf the entire family. Eve remembers going to play with Landauer's daughter and Raphael remembers looking forward to the
visits of Uncle Landauer who was real fun. But Buber did not learn
from this meaningful relationship how to establish additional friendships.

At the invitation of the Bar Cochba Jewish High School in Prague
in 1909 Buber presented his "Drei Reden uber Das Judentum",
(Three Speeches on Judaism). The speeches deeply impressed the
students; when they were subsequently published in 1911 they
enthused hundreds of German speaking Jewish youth. But this initial
enthusiasm slowly dwindled and in many cases estrangement towards
Buber followed. This phenomenon of initial enthusiasm followed by
estrangement was to repeat itself with at least four generations of
pupils during Buber's lifetime. (See, for instance the essay by
Menachem Dorman in this volume.) Gershom Scholem has suggested that Buber's concept of Judaism, which was "heretical" played
a crucial role in bringing about this estrangement. He also pointed
out, in accord with Dorman, that many pupils felt that when the
chips were down Buber did not personally realize what he himself
had indicated needed to be realized. All this is true, but there is an
additional educational point that Scholem and Dorman have not
sufficiently articulated.
  Buber had a unique talent for sensing and eloquently expressing a
need, a mood, a craving that lay dormant in the hearts of youth; he
also presented a vague challenge which they could pursue in response to that need, that mood, that craving. But he gave no specific
guidelines. And since, as Buber himself wrote, it is the responsibility
of the educator to lay down specific guidelines we can only conclude
that he evaded the role of an educator. Even at home he did not
concern himself much with his children's non-academic problems,
their interests, their affairs. Only much later did he and Paula realize
how difficult it must have been for a high spirited boy like Raphael to
grow up with a secluded yet famous father.
  For many years Buber was "an oracle" (he termed himself thus)

whom young people sought out to consult, but who uttered vague, non-committing answers. He cites as the reason he abandoned this approach an encounter with a young man who died soon after he came to Buber in quest of a human response and in its stead received general advice. But it seems that other factors were equally prominent, such as Gustav Landauer's influence; in a scathing letter during the war he criticized Buber's oracular tendencies. Also, one can safely assume that when in 1917 Raphael joined the Austrian Army, the horrors and fears of war struck home and the uniqueness and significance of every living person became meaningful for Buber.

In 1916 the Buber family rented a nine room house in Heppenheim, not far from Frankfurt, they purchased the house two years later. Even today the house and its surrounding garden conveys the impression of composed affluence. Next door to the house one discovers that the bookstore which Buber frequented weekly to order books and journals is still in business, and as one's eyes wander along the surrounding Odenwald hills, the towering medieval church on the hill above the town commands one's attention. Although he had few acquaintances among the town's people, Buber loved the calm and seclusion of Heppenheim, and he probably would have never left it if the Nazis had not come to power.

During the decade of the First World War Buber was extremely self centered, as a writer and as a person. He enjoyed his popularity as an initiator of a renaissance in German Jewry, but he does not seem to have worried if people acted in accordance with his writings or merely read them because they plucked their heartstrings. At home he often sided with Paula against his own better judgement, so that his equanimity would be preserved. Eve sadly remembers that after she reached the age of eighteen her parents refused to allow her to leave home in order to study gardening at Stuttgart. Buber argued that she was needed in Heppenheim to help Paula, and that every person should be where he is needed in life. His exaggerated paternalism was, of course, unwarrented. And his lack of sensitivity to his daughter's need to strike out on her own bears witness to an attitude which I would be bold enough to term egotistical.

The following letter which Franz Rosenzweig wrote to a friend following a visit to Buber in December 1921 describes the beginning of the fruitful relationship between these two original thinkers:

> We reached Heppenheim in the afternoon . . . In the course of conversation, while we were having coffee, I suddenly realized that

Buber was no longer the mystical subjectivist that people worship, but that even intellectually he was becoming a solid and reasonable man. I was rather astonished and impressed by the extreme honesty with which he spoke. In referring to his books on Hasidism, he remarked that he was surprised only one person had asked for his sources in all these years. He was planning to add a list of sources to his new book. What he said struck home with me. I had been searching all along for the East European Jewish sources of his tales with some success. I told him I thought there were quite a few people including myself, who simply hadn't written to him. He said he would like, sometime, to present the sources to a few persons, whereupon I said I could gather those few persons, not during the winter but during the summer, and I at once outlined a plan how in the mornings we could take hikes and then stop over at his place in Heppenheim in the afternoons. But I had to know how he would go about it so I could tell people. When he said he couldn't tell exactly, I suggested that since he and two of his students were there he might give us a trial lesson. We moved into the other room. He disappeared among his bookshelves, returned with two or three texts, and we started reading. He proved a rather awkward teacher; . . . Only during the trip home did it occur to me that it was cheaper to transport the prophet than twenty of his disciples. I wrote to him to this effect. I had already told him about the Lehrhaus (The Frankfurt Jewish Lehrhaus which Rosenzweig had established) per- haps also shown him one of the programs. He replied that, to his own surprise, though refusing had been second nature to him for many years, he had immediately felt disposed to accept my proposal. After some further exchange the rest of the arrangements were made.

Buber's willingness to teach at the Lehrhaus was one of a series of attempts he made during that period to reach out to the world. A few months earlier he had represented the socialist working party in Palestine, Hapoel Hatsair, in the first postwar Zionist congress which met in Karlsbad. It was a bitter experience for Buber to have his resolution concerning a basis for mutual understanding with the Arabs watered down and finally accepted for reasons of political expediency. He once again withdrew from active political involve- ment, but seems to have sought other avenues of participation in German Jewish life.

Some of these avenues were made accessible by Franz Ro- senzweig. He invited Buber to take part in the management of the Lehrhaus; and when he succumbed to paralysis he nominated Buber to replace him in the chair of Jewish Philosophy and Ethics at the University of Frankfurt, which became Buber's first academic post.

In addition to being a profound thinker Rosenzweig was blessed with a delicate sense of humor and keen organizational abilities. He challenged and criticized Buber in a warm, penetrating and enlightening manner and prompted him to be less romantic and more down to earth. In retrospect Buber admitted that he had learned much from Rosenzweig, the creative thinker, but that his encounter with the courage and vivacity of his paralysed dying colleague instructed his very existence.

In April 1925 Lambert Schneider, a young Christian who had recently established a publishing house, asked Buber to help him bring out a revised translation of the Old Testament. Later Buber wrote an essay describing how, at that time, he and Rosenzweig had reached the stage of maturity in their personal relation to the Bible which allowed them to undertake such an endeavor; but it seems that he is once again reading his life history backward in a self centered manner. Without Lambert Schneider's courage and perseverance Buber and Rosenzweig—despite their maturity—would probably never have dreamed of such an undertaking.

Translating the Bible together with Rosenzweig was a boon for Buber because his work was constantly subject to competent criticism which he learned to accept and to appreciate. Furthermore, he and Rosenzweig had to come to terms with various established traditions of Biblical research and by piecemeal investigation demonstrate the validity of their own approach. In short, the translation of the Bible and later his books on the Bible taught Buber the value of give and take, of conflict and compromise in the scholarly world. During this period all his writings became less imbued with pathos and more research oriented.

After Rosenzweig's death in 1929 Buber continued the Bible translation by himself. His work was interrupted in 1938, he resumed it after the Second World War, and completed it in 1961. For years he spent many hours each day seeking the appropriate rendering of the Hebrew into German, his lifelong love of linguistic proficiency found here its greatest challenge. Many commentators have noted that the merit of his translation stemmed from his ability to listen to the voice of a text. But this ability was directed only to those texts to which Buber seems to have felt a personal relationship, such as the Hasidic lore or the Bible. He does not seem to have attempted to listen to the voice of those of his contemporaries whose writings disturbed him, such as Sartre, or Kafka, or Freud. Much of his life Buber sat alone listening to voices from a distant past.

Although Buber and Paula went to court to obtain the custody to raise their granddaughters following Raphael's divorce from his first wife—according to the German law at that time, following a divorce daughters go with the mother, sons with the father—this did not change much the way of Buber's life. One of the first things the granddaughters, Barbara and Judith, learned was not to interfere with the work of their grandfather, Vater Martin. Paula enjoyed her second opportunity at child raising and vehemently opposed Raphael's wish to have his daughters live with him after his second marriage. But Buber continued his secluded existence and never became intimate with the young girls.

A person who immerses himself in the past is often able to ignore persecution. Such an immersion partially accounts for the Jews' ability throughout the centuries to disregard their degradation and humiliation. Buber's immersion in the past might explain his rather mild reaction to the terror and oppression which characterized the Nazi regime. Before 1933 he did not publicly denounce the Nazi party and after Hitler's rise to power he did not advocate any decisive action. Instead, he suggested to his fellow Jews that they learn to live with the hatred and mendacity which pervaded Germany by initiating a renewal of their spiritual life, by immersing themselves in their heritage.

Now we know that Buber's suggestions were frightfully wrong. We also know that he had the courage of his convictions. From 1933 until 1938 Buber spent much of his time and energy strengthening his fellow Jews' alliance to their heritage. He lectured, he taught, and he wrote about seemingly neutral subjects, such as the Bible, which would not arouse the suspicion of the Gestapo infiltrators to his lectures or his Nazi readers. But he always chose topics which in-between the lines would reject the regime; thus "The Question to the Single One", a polemic against Kierkegaard published in 1936, also attacks in a round about way, those "conscientious Germans" who placidly accepted Nazism.

During the five years that Buber spent in Nazi Germany he at times frequented a synagogue. But his reason for doing so seems to have been to express solidarity toward his Jewish brethren rather than to pray to God in a communal service. His dislike of organized Jewry did not earn him many friends among Orthodox Jews or Jews of the establishment. The events surrounding his move to Jerusalem to a chair at the Hebrew University exemplify the estrangement of the Jewish establishment towards Buber. In 1934 the senate of the

Hebrew University offered Buber the chair of religious sciences, which he willingly accepted. But at a stormy Board of Trustees meeting in 1935 this offer was withdrawn after the English trustees under the leadership of Harry Sacher threatened to cut off funds if Buber was hired for that position. The official reason for withdrawing the offer was that the senate of the university had not proven that a chair of religious sciences was needed. But one can sense, even from the dry minutes of the meetings, that the English trustees were unhappy with Buber, the person, and with what he represented. After two additional years of bickering about who would pay the first three years of his salary, (finally a special fund outside the regular budget was set up under the sponsorship of Zalman Schocken,) Buber was called to Jerusalem to accept the chair of social philosophy.

Buber's move to Jerusalem in 1938 together with Paula and their granddaughters united them with his immediate family: Eve with her husband, Ludwig Strauss, and their two sons, and Raphael with his second wife, Ruth had all moved to Palestine earlier. But, he was abruptly cut off from the milieu which had nurtured him and to which he had substantially contributed. The Jewish settlement in Palestine at that time was new and pioneering in spirit, informal in manners, and often disinclined to respect scholars from the Diaspora. Hence, throughout the rest of his life Buber was somewhat of a stranger in his own land, admired in academic circles and among his fellow German expatriates, but often ignored or repudiated by the populace.

The move to Jerusalem was very difficult for Paula. She made some attempts to study Hebrew but with little success; consequently she confined herself to the house and was no longer a major link between Buber and the everyday world. Fortunately, she was able to dedicate her free time to her own writing. The Bubers also faced financial difficulties. After 1939 money no longer came from the estate in Poland or from Buber's publications in Germany and he had to live on a professor's salary, which was quite a drop in his standard of living.

Buber does not seem to have been perturbed by any of these problems; he immersed himself in his academic activity and the years from 1938 until 1947 were very fruitful. Some of his classical essays, such as "The Education of Character," "What is Man?" and "Two Types of Faith" belong to this period. He also began to write in Hebrew and to edit the translation of some of his German writings. But the mystery of Hebrew evaded him and his style lacks the appeal of his German. Even today, one of the reasons Buber is not popular among Israeli students is that his style "turns them off!"

World wide fame slowly converged on Buber in the 1950s. He accepted it placidly; since his student years he was used to moving in and out of the public spotlight. After becoming professor emeritus at Hebrew University in 1951 he traveled much in the world, giving seminars, speeches and talks. He was awarded prizes and honors which he accepted with aristocratic flair and eloquent modesty; he was often approached for personal advice and was happy to give it. Jochanan Bloch, who early in his career was referred to Buber for academic assistance and encouragement and received it, recalled that although Buber did not court admiration, neither did he discourage it. He subterraneously invited the admiration that flowed from a person's being toward him and accepted it as his natural desert. Such a relationship probably suited both participants. The person who turned to Buber probably was elated that he had found an opportunity to express his admiration towards and receive advice from a renowned philosopher, and Buber himself probably felt that he was coming in contact with the world outside the academic ivory tower and responding to a person's needs. And since by accepting admiration a person hides his true self behind the image of him in his admirer's mind, Buber could render advice with very little disclosure of his own person. He could remain a riddle, and a pleasant one at that.

It is not difficult to list the striking inconsistencies and riddles which characterize Buber's personal history and personality. He became famous as advocate of the life of dialogue, in which one says *du*—Thou—to the other, but in the eighty seven years of his life he himself said *du* to less than a handful of persons. He was a man who professed straightforwardness, but whose decorative style of writing (especially in Hebrew) was far from straightforward. He was a theologian who made new inroads into the essence of religious experience, but he shunned religious services. He was a vindicator of utopian socialism who for periods of his adult life had his income supplemented from the toil of Polish peasants. He educated three or four or perhaps even five generations of pupils, most of whom abandoned his teachings later in life. He was a fervent Zionist who constantly encouraged his pupils to emigrate to Palestine; but he himself might never have reached Israel if Hitler had not come to power.

But such a list is misleading because each inconsistency or riddle views Buber from one specific aspect, and consequently the whole person remains veiled. Yet one can obtain glimpses of Buber, the entire person, from his writings, from some of his letters, and from some of the events described above. He was a secluded aesthete who sought truth and beauty and a meaningful way of relating to man and to God. He had the courage to reject half truths as answers to the questions which perturbed him and the perseverence to fulfill great challenges, such as the translation of the Bible. He was satisfied with himself (and at times vain) because many of his creative potentials had been fulfilled. And he was unsatisfied because he was a visionary who was willing to dream about a more meaningful and just way of life and to demand of his fellow man that he attempt to realize that life. He was lucky and lonely, admired and often misunderstood and he knew it. These glimpses suggest that perhaps Martin Buber, the entire person, may be described with a bit of irony by the first three verses of the book of Psalms:

Happy is the man that hath not walked in the counsel of the wicked,
Nor stood in the way of sinners,
Nor sat in the seat of the scornful.

But his delight is in the law of the Lord;
And in His law doth he meditate day and night.

And he shall be like a tree planted by streams of water,
That bringeth forth its fruit in its season,
And whole leaf does not wither;
And in whatsoever he doeth he shall prosper.

DIALOGICAL THINKING

The Justification and the Futility of Dialogical Thinking

JOCHANAN BLOCH

Such is the problem of dialogical thinking, that it reflects upon and discourses about a human reality about which it is essentially impossible to think or to speak. But we have not yet said enough. Because no one denies that there are many human states which urgently press for expression and in their pressing give rise to a similar dilemma, and yet these states are not the subject of dialogism, nor its basic problem. Feelings, for example: they accompany and develop the contents of daily life, which are stamped with the patterns of our intellect. These feelings are not insignificant. They determine our days for good or for bad, for significance or for emptiness. They endow their color to the lived moment, the quality of our existence. They appear in our consciousness as unstable fluctuations, at times obscure, at times with burning intensity, but always with an indubitable qualitative uniqueness. It is possible to distinguish *types* of feelings: fear, love, pain, anger, longing, depression, etc. But feelings still remain the problem children of consciousness, since we cannot delimit them clearly, nor can we conceptually analyze them and incorporate them in a rational context. Our understanding is forced to acknowledge a certain helplessness towards feelings; it is at a loss with them and fears them. Thus it seems as though feelings flood our consciousness or penetrate it as outsiders. Of a different sort are basic moods of our existence, such as the tide of satisfaction that accompanies creative work, or the sadness and fears of a life that has failed, or that nameless sensation which signals the crises and turning-points of fate. Such is also the drive to act, emerging from desires, passions from our primal history which is a "repetition" of what was and occurred already. Each of these has its own psychic *Gestalt*, and yet they elude clear perception, so that our consciousness, with fear or an anxious tremor, merely grazes their surface. But dialogism refers to something else. It refers to something primordial, which Buber calls the fundamental reality of man. Presumably this reality occurs throughout all our lives, at every moment, though with varying intensity; certainly it occurs in unique moments with such decisive

43

predominance that its influence can be recognized throughout our existence, although the occurrence does not continue. Although the occurrence is elemental to our existence, we know nothing about it. Or rather, strictly speaking, we do not know "something" about it. For we do not relate to it as to an object, of whatever kind, whether a certain process or an existing thing. After all we do relate to a feeling or a mood as "an existing thing". This does not mean that we are dealing here with something unconscious. The occurrence is of the nature of consciousness, even if we cannot say without reservation that it is known, since it is not "known as something". In this sense it is likewise not an occurrence which we can talk or think "about". Thus arises our uncertainty as to whether this reality occurs throughout our lives or only at isolated moments.

Indeed, this true element of human existence is by its very nature concealed in a sort of secret. Our consciousness is always a knowledge of something. To be sure, Franz Rosenzweig is correct in saying that "I see the tree" and "I am conscious of the tree" are sentences only a philosopher would say.[1] But it is enough if I simply say "tree", if I think "tree" or see a tree; for in all these cases I am speaking and thinking and knowing "something", and there indeed exists here a subject-object relation which corresponds to the philosophical formulations. But now if there is a consciousness which contains no object, or which departs from the subject-object relation, or denies it, then this consciousness cannot even exist side by side with our consciousness as knowledge-of-something. At most it can exist in its shadow. Whatever this consciousness is: now when I speak "about" it, when I reflect on it, the reflection necessarily covers this "fundamental reality", and drives it, if it exists, into an existence concealed from my consciousness.

Against this concealment, dialogical thinking wants to show us that reality, to bring us to it—despite and because of the fact that it is hidden. A certain "nevertheless" accompanies all the attempts of dialogism, like a constant reservation. For even while pointing to the reality it intends, dialogism claims (and without this explicit claim the pointing could not be carried out) that that reality cannot be known as something, as a content, and thus it cannot be expressed nor spoken "about". Therefore dialogism knows that its thinking is an ascetic thinking, which knows that it cannot truly grasp and fix, by its concepts, that toward which they are directed. Its speaking is not informative, not a direct depiction. Nonetheless it wants to speak and must speak: how can it depict by speaking a thing of which one cannot truly speak?

It makes use of metaphors. That is, it employs word-combinations in which words are separated from the informative significance which generally belongs to them. As parts of a metaphor, words do not mean exactly what they mean "according to the dictionary". They change their function, somewhat as rebellious students change the function of a public lecture, whose basic purpose is to inform, into a "happening". Thus words, when joined in metaphor, can present a reality which is no longer the reality that accords with the clear objective knowledge of he who is present. They do this by means of an associative aura which is the heritage of words, which seems to draw power from a hidden analogy among all existent things. To put it another way, in metaphor the thing is no longer the object confronting us in its exact measurements. It is as it were split open; it becomes, in this language-event, so really present that it can no longer be grasped in rational concepts, much as we cannot grasp all true presence. To use Alan Watts' analogy: True presence is like flowing water: we grasp it with our concepts the way we catch a stream of water in buckets. In this way we obtain "water", but not the flowing water of reality.[2] Here in metaphor is reflected the stream of reality itself, in which live the forms in all that is present to us.

But even metaphor is not enough for dialogism, which aspires to more than the living presence of this thing or that. It aspires to more than the Gestalt or the specific existent thing to which every metaphor is still bound, however living, however "real" that thing may become in the language-event of metaphor. Dialogism directs itself to a reality which by its very nature cannot be in any way specific. Whatever this reality may be: metaphor itself cannot represent it, and if metaphor still wants to lead us to the fundamental event of dialogism, it has to transcend itself, that is, to become a "leap word".[3] The speech of dialogism is a kind of pointing-to which does not show the indicated thing itself, but only points to its direction, in which we, as it were, leap from the pointing words to reach the presence of the reality which has no description.

All this has a very banal consequence, whose significance should not be downplayed, namely: we do not know exactly what Buber means when he points to reality. We all know the names of this reality: I-Thou, relationship, dialogue, the interhuman. Buber's literary achievement can be measured by the fact that these names have become part of the general vocabulary and have divested themselves of their authorship and source. But each of us who has to explain to his students what those terms originally meant finds himself confronted with a problem which—we had better admit it—confronts us all: we are not certain what is the essence of the reality which we are discussing.

Let us first of all make clear that by the nature of things we cannot truly "know" what is meant. For, strictly speaking, dialogic philosophers do not "mean something". If we attempt to clarify "what Buber means", we may be pulled in the wrong direction from the beginning of our attempt. But even if we are aware that objective statements are not appropriate here, and that we have to leap from the informative meaning of the words that point, we are still caught in much uncertainty. After all our point of departure is a state of uncertainty. In general, dialogical words are addressed to those who are in a state of insecurity because of the "hiddenness" of dialogical reality. This hiddenness is increased, apparently, by the historical situation in which we are living. Buber says that in our time that fundamental reality is neglected, disparaged, or covered over, and that this is part of the qualitative peculiarity of the time. In any case, this reality is hidden at the point of departure, and hence Buber's call for attention, the demanding character of his teaching: Consider, he says, your own experience, "and what you cannot recollect, dare to attain it as experience . . . I take him who listens to me by the hand and lead him to the window. I open the window and point to what is outside".[4]

But this again leads us into a state of uncertainty, or, we may say, into the second and more serious state of uncertainty. It is more serious because this time it is apparently final; it cannot be overcome. We can follow, more or less, the indications of dialogism, we can give them a meaning appropriate to our life-experience, and thus we can know the meaning. But in truth we are not certain that this experience is identical with the fundamental reality to which dialogism points.

The source of uncertainty is above all an obstacle which we may call our "noetic prejudice". It is in the nature of our consciousness— to the extent that it is objective recognition and attainment, that is, to the extent that it is "noesis"—that we find security in any state that satisfies the criterion of objective recognition. Security, is therefore found in constancy, in self-identity, and in the possibility of identification, by which we orient ourselves in actuality. From this perspective, dialogism points to a reality that is "not secure". According to Buber's descriptions it is entirely bound up with the "person", it is bound up with the uniqueness of the person, which has no definition. Moreover, it is the reality of a situation which is always unique, and therefore it is unverifiable. It belongs to the moment, that "atom of

eternity" (Kierkegaard's phrase) which is always being swallowed up
in the contexts and processes of things. (These descriptions do not
give us much hope of security; they confirm our insecurity with
regard to the reality of dialogism.)

This uncertainty seems to contradict our statement that there is
here a fundamental reality; for how can there be a *fundamental*
reality which has no constancy, no identified existence of any kind?
But there is, in truth, no contradiction. To understand this we must
leave generalities and finally demonstrate the reality in question in its
basic characteristics, even while keeping in mind that the words used
in this demonstration cannot directly describe what we are aiming at,
and obviously do not have an informative function. The reality of
which we are speaking, then, occurs when we encounter some
presence and are affected by it; that is, in that unity of being without
which there can be no encounter—no encounter "between" us and
the one who encounters us, between man and the "Thou" which he
addresses. This reality incarnates itself in the act of speaking, is
essentially speech. But that is the difficulty: *this* speech does not say
anything specific, it is not "something". This speech is what the
presence of the situation in my life says to me, each time, here and
now, in a uniqueness which, cannot be explained—because it is
unique. It is the "speech" of the concreteness of the moment which
has no fixed meaning, such as one might look up in a dictionary, and
sometimes the speech does not occur through the pronunciation of
words.[5] Thus at a certain moment a landscape may speak, or the gaze
of a person. This reality is fundamental existence, primordial existence, if we concentrate on the "how"—on the act of speech, on the
address as such, on the reciprocity of beings. But it is characterized
by complete insecurity, it is even nonexistent, if we try to comprehend it as a fixed "something" or as a fixed "content". We must
renounce this attempt. Once we have renounced it, we shall also be
freed from the "noetic prejudice" of our consciousness, which is
forever seeking to know something and to determine the "what". And
then the lack of "content" in the aforesaid reality will not threaten us
as offending a norm of security or hinder with its uncertainty the
understanding of the descriptions of dialogism.

But this is not yet all. Even if we overcome this obstacle, we shall
not be fundamentally free from insecurity. We are dealing, in my
opinion, with an insecurity which cannot really be overcome.
Strangely enough, it is bound up precisely with the connection
between the "how" and the "what", a connection which factually

exists despite many of Buber's assertions. I cannot make the matter simpler than it really is, but I shall try to explain what I mean, despite the need to be concise. Buber means a presence which is not objectlike. It has not the reality of the *thing*, that is, the thing comprehended in its contents; it is not comprehended in itself. Buber expresses this by saying that presence is in the "between". It is the relationship, and in the encounter it exists in my turning to and addressing the "Thou". It is not an "It" or a thing about which I can speak.

"—What, then, does one experience of the You? —Nothing at all. For one does not experience it. —What, then, does one know of the You? —Only everything. For one no longer knows particulars".[6] If we seize upon these sentences, upon the strict and immediate meaning of the words, then the Thou is truly content-less, in the sense of the contents of noesis. Between the Thou and the objectivity of the person or thing which I am addressing as Thou, a hiatus opens which negates all mutuality or togetherness. Then the reality of the "Thou"—more precisely: the reality of the "between thee and me"— would be a pure "How", or, as Theunissen calls it, a pure act.[7]

But that is not the way it is. The reality of the Thou is after all the reality of a person whom I address. It is the reality of my addressing *you*, who as a person apprehended as an object remain in the background of my address, and as such are bound up in the address by some connection which cannot be defined. When Buber speaks of a tree which I contemplate and "as I contemplate the tree I am drawn into a relation",[8] then it is clear that the qualities of tree-ness of the tree I am considering do not disappear in my relationship with the tree. The hiatus between relationship and object exists—and yet it does not exist (and I cannot say here that it is "mediated", for there is no synthesis here, in the Hegelian sense). The "how" occurs together with the "what", even though I cannot determine the character of this togetherness.

From here it is possible to understand that Buber's own descriptions are not clear as to the aim of their meaning, but have within them a factual fluctuation which does indeed produce insecurity. It is a wavering as to the essence of the reality to which Buber is pointing. It exists even after we have discarded the criterion of noetic security. We are dealing here with a truly "insurmountable insecurity". Furthermore: it seems to me that the reality which we attain if we follow Buber's pointing exceeds in its factual existence Buber's intentions and descriptions. That is the fluctuations of this reality exceed the lability implicit in Buber's descriptions. This perception does not stem from the inadequacy of our understanding, but from the inadequacy of Buber's descriptions, of his ways of pointing. It seems to me that the tendency toward schematization misled Buber into making sharp distinctions and rigid demarcations which do not truly exist in reality. In any event, we cannot securely conceptualize the "reality". We have no choice but to accept this insecurity—to accept a reality which is labile, not identical within itself, even if we attain it through the consciousness appropriate to it. To put it concretely: "the presence of the Thou" encompasses different modes of reality, ranging from our being caught up in contemplation in all its plasticity, its *Gestalt*, to that mystic Nothingness of the unity of Being, as depicted in the white, empty, content-less circle which the Zen master Kaku-an drew to show the penultimate achievement in the oxherd's search for truth.[9]

I spoke of stages of insecurity. This expression must be used with a conscious reservation. If we try to distinguish between the insecurity of the first stage, the point of departure, when the reality of the relationship being pointed to is still hidden, and a later stage of insecurity, when we attain the relationship as a fact of our experience, it turns out that this division is more or less arbitrary, especially since the reality of the relationship in its fluctuation is swallowed up, again and again, in the mists of the point of departure. The result of this situation is an insecurity of being, which brings in its wake a special kind of need. Whether we want to make sure of the way to attain a basic reality, or whether we want to secure a specific event which we have attained and which seems to us identical with the reality described, in any case one need prove that that reality which is being pointed to really exists. The proof cannot be a geometric one. But we need, apparently, some indication that we can rely on it—that is, some indication attained in life-experiences which exist *beyond doubt*. But these are, of course, experiences of our reality which exist *before* that dubious event of the "I-Thou". In other words: they exist in the domain of our certainty. In this domain we seek the indication which would permit us to conclude at least the existence of a place where the sought-for-event would be possible. If we find such an indication, we can follow the pointing of dialogism with greater security.

Here we may note that a similar need arises with regard to the religions; this fact in itself reveals that dialogism belongs to the domain of religion. We never attain what is alluded to by the word

"God". We are not certain of God or of any revelation of God. Some of us will say "certainly" God exists. But most of us will say, with some embarrassment, that we feel, perhaps, the possibility of His existence; or more cautiously, that a being of the kind hinted at in the word "God" is conceivable. This is not a sign of the corruption of the times; this insecurity is of the essence of our existence, of the essence of the human situation. Therefore no rational arguments can prevent us from seeking proofs of God—a search which is only an expression for the search for God himself.

Perhaps the best way to find a sort of proof for the duality of being for man, which dialogism asserts, and which includes the event of the "fundamental reality", is to comprehend the ways language is articulated; or to be precise in the duality of our linguistic relation to being, as distinguished by language itself. What Buber calls relationship is demonstrated in the second person of language, in the *speaking to*. On the other hand, our relation to Being as to a thing, something— the I-It—finds its linguistic form in *speaking-about*. If we reflect on these ways of thinking, it becomes clear that there is no *speaking-about*, there is no statement with specific content, without *speaking-to*. That is: the statement of content exists only in the address to someone, it is intended to him and includes him; even if the one "present" is merely a nameless space of a presence which replaces a real listener, as happens, for example, when I write a diary. This structure requires that the *speaking-to* be a concrete event which leaves its traces on the entire process of speech and also on me, the speaker. The speaking-about is always influenced and wrought upon by the presence of the "to". But especially this makes it clear that the speech with addresses, creates a presence which is not an object and which I cannot turn into an object. I cannot know it, if "know" means to attain through any concepts or images.

Every speaking-about is a speaking of "It": I speak of something, I relate to an object. And conversely, we can say, every conscious process directed to an object can be converted to a linguistic expression, or at least an expression by signs, e.g. mathematical signs, to a speaking-about. But this speaking-about occurs within a presence, that of a "to", about which one does not and cannot speak: in no way can I conclude the "to" in the objective statements of speaking-about. Reluctantly, the "to" remains beyond all discourse "about". I can say something about you, but this saying is not identical with the fact that I am saying this *to you*. That "to you" cannot become part of the speaking, for the speaking moves within the address to you like a fish moving in a stream of water; the fish cannot become the stream itself. Hence we conclude that the concrete presence in which we speak to someone is itself not an object of speech and cannot be known. Thus we have indeed succeeded in attaining a sort of proof that fundamental presence in the relationship truly exists, as Buber claims. In the reality of speech, in men's turning to one another in speech, a sign and a foundation are given, from which we can attain the "relationship" of lived reality.

In the last paragraphs I have been quoting my own words, with slight variations.[10] I am returning to this line of thought here in order to ask myself to what extent this proof is valid. Indeed, today I have doubts of its validity. Language serves different functions: philosophical discussions of the phenomenon of language which have been conducted in this century have thoroughly elucidated this multiplicity of functions. But it would be a mistake to ignore the fact in any case language serves to make known objective situations, as they are mediated and presented. Language points to things and situations, and one may say that by means of it the lived concreteness is transformed to an object, part of the object that is our world. That is the basic function of language, to give information on things and to maintain for all of us a shared and secured world of objective certainty. Language maintains this world, describes it and helps us to orient ourselves within it. It carries out this task with the help of a linguistic reservoir on which it can draw. The words, word-combinations, and inflections which comprise the linguistic reservoir have fixed, objective meanings assigned to them. This is the essential objectivity of language, which even Buber acknowledges when he says that even the event of relationship acquires, with its linguistic formation, "an objectively comprehensible form."[11]

What happens when I "speak to a person"? I address him, I stand in communication with him. In this communication, which is truly an unity of being, I use the word-signs of the linguistic reservoir, which have an informative meaning that is binding upon all speakers. I address to you objective statements, whether these relate to situations in the world which we share and which surrounds us, or to you or to me alone. I cannot speak to you at all without some statement of this kind; however, this situation contains a contradiction which we have here to understand. The statements represent or realize a reality which is, in itself, fixed; it is "thus and not otherwise" for everyone, it is independent, that is—separate from the present existence of the speakers themselves. But this means that these statements are fundamentally separate from the process of speaking itself, from the unity of being which exists in this moment when we, speaking, address each other. The statements realize a dimension of being other than that of speech itself, although they integrate that very dimension into the dimension of speech in its momentary existence. But this very integration demonstrates the contradiction. The statements are alien to the event of the speaking-to, and this alienation actively exists in the fact that "I am speaking to you".

The result is a clear opposition between the relationship and the objectification—an opposition which does not exist with such rigor outside the phenomenon of language. When I contemplate a tree, my contemplation incorporates objective perceptions (for instance, that this tree stands before me in all its strength, interwoven with light and heavy with shadow, etc.) These perceptions are realizations of consciousness of that unity of being which exists now, at this moment, when this tree is present and I am contemplating it. Relationship and contemplation, with their knowledge, are not as dichotomous as in the act of speaking, with its communicative turning to the other and its statements. Language with its rules further exacerbates this dichotomy, which exists in every act of speech, to a schema of distinctions, such as that between the second person and the third person (Thou as opposed to He-She-It) or between the indicative and the vocative. In other words, relationship and knowledge, are in ontic reality—to use Buber's phrase—an "indissoluble antinomy".[12] But in the embodiment of language, they are separated if only to be reintegrated, despite the separation, by the existential unity of the act of speaking; to this integration we do not direct adequate reflective attention. How did we arrive at our proof? We relied on that very distinction between relationship and statement, as brought out in speaking and as emphasized more strongly by grammatical forms; from this we proved relationship, which truly exists and is even "conscious", yet which cannot be spoken about or known as something. Thus we have been caught in a vicious circle, a *petitio principii*. Clearly, if the statement of content exists in qualitative and concrete distinction from the event of the address, so that the address exists as it were in its purity, beyond any possible statement, then we have assumed what we wanted to prove, namely that relationship establishes an ontic dimension different from the dimension of objective knowledge.

I do not mean to say that relationship, in the meaning which Buber gives it, does not exist. Indeed, the phenomenon of language reveals the existence of this relationship: the address truly does constitute a special event which cannot be assigned to the dimension of objective statement, or to the dimension of objectification at all. From here, too, a door opens to a reality which cannot be "attained," since it is essentially non-specific. When I say non-specific I do not mean concealing of positivity or lack of positivity, that is, negation; I mean a positivity of a special kind (I am using these formulations deliberately with reference to the difference of opinion between me and Michael Theunissen). But as we have already said, after new considerations, we must somewhat correct these thoughts. The correction is limited to the determination that language, in its own way, emphasizes the uniqueness of relationship, singles it out with an extra distinction. It is natural for language to make distinctions, as concepts differ from each other and as the things attained by means of concepts differ from each other. But it is at least possible that what is distinguished here is *not* distinguished in the manner of a concept—that relationship is "nonspecific" and yet not "not" specific.[13] If so, the "proof" which we thought we had found is no longer secure.

Still we may assume (the assumption is confirmed in many ways) that there is indeed a relationship which is not an object-like being, and yet does not "negate" object-like being in the way opposing concepts negate each other; that is, one cannot say of it that it "does not" belong to the domain of concepts and existent things. If we connect this with a preceding reflection, we can say: there is a reality "without content," which yet cannot be disconnected from the "what" of the contents of consciousness.[14] With this we have formulated a principle with far-reaching consequences. We are still in touch with the conceptual world of dialogism, but if we intend, in Buber's words, to "attain as experience"[15] the reality of relationship, we must also be prepared for certain deviations from the schema of dialogism. Probably, for example, contemplation as such will bring us to a numinous presence, without a reversal in our basic attitude, in the "basic word." It is also probable that contemplation does not occur at all without the existence of such a presence. It is also probable that we can arrive at the unity of being by means of concepts or imaginative images—and that unity of being will be of the wholeness of relationship, even though the concepts and the images which bring it forth are not the direct crystalizations of the relationship.[16] The point is that the absolutely nonspecific can be reflected in specific contents or can be brought forth by them, for it does not "negate" specificity. These reflections are not mere hairsplitting; they touch on the focal points of our existence. They concern, for instance, the essence of religious faith. They make it clear, in opposition to Buber, that faith can and must be, by its very nature, "acknowledgment of a specific truth."[17] They also determine the nature and capability of religious or theological language, which is fundamentally a form of religious symbolism. The symbol, too, is specific and points to specific contents, even while representing the absolutely non-specific. It is no coincidence that Buber neglected to discuss the concept of the symbol. These reflections also have a bearing on the phenomenon of love. It is noteworthy that Buber never reflected on the fact that love is directed toward *one* in particular, and that love knows its specificity in contemplating this one and in desiring this one, sensually, especially this one.

However, I do not want to break out of Buber's conceptual world, but to remain within the domain of the problems he raises. Hence I must resume the discussion with Michael Theunissen. We have seen that Buber makes a clear and schematic distinction between the reality of relationship and the It; Theunissen carries that distinction to its ultimate conclusion. If we hinted to a conception which would overcome Buber's schematic distinctions; Theunissen supplies us with an opposite conception. The confrontation between our two positions will determine the direction in which dialogism is going—its entelechy.

I shall try to sum up, with extreme brevity, Theunissen's basic thesis as it concerns us here.[18] Theunissen bases his argument on the negative attributes which characterize the "Thou" in Buber. Buber tells us that with the Thou we do not receive "a 'content' ", it is not a "what".[19] Theunissen refers particularly to the sentences: "Whoever says *You* does not have something; he has nothing" and "What, then, does one experience of the *You*?—Nothing at all. For one does not experience it."[20] By this, says Theunissen, Buber interprets the Thou as a "nothing".[21] But behind that nothing, Being is hidden: therefore Buber can continue: "What, then, does one know of the *You*?—Only everything". The "everything" points, according to Theunissen, to the totality of being.[22] Nevertheless, the "nothing" predominates in the theory of the Thou.[23] Why? Because Buber, according to Theunissen's argument, wants to make clear that the Thou is not an existent thing: "The Thou is nothing because it is no existent thing."[24] Hence Theunissen concludes that the relationship to the Thou is conceived as an existence beyond all existing things. What does "all existing things" mean? The world is the "totality of existing things"; therefore relationship is beyond the world: "the relationship to the Thou is the overcoming of the world as universe of all existing things".[25] Hence we must understand that the "momentariness" of the Thou means that the Thou does not exist in time, since ontically it does not exist at all—therefore it has no existence whatsoever.[26]

Thus Theunissen carries the dichotomy between "Thou" and "It" to its extreme conclusion. The "Thou", he says, is "freed" from the world,[27] and *a fortiori* from any particular It. In exactly the same way, the basic word I-Thou, that is, relationship, is freed from the factual I, which turns toward existent things, speaks to them, and strives to "attain" the experience of reality. In determining this, Theunissen assumes that one cannot understand relationship as deed. In other words, it is a "pure act", in which one is at once acting and acted upon, so that action and passion constitute an absolute unity. Relationship, then, is not "composed" of the actions of those who encounter each other, nor is it the result of their actions. Quite the opposite is true: the I and the Thou of the basic word I-Thou are the result of the "between", that is, the relationship. The encounter preexists the reality of those who encounter each other; they are born from the "between", from the pure act of the encounter.[28]

The consequences of this line of thinking are weighty. They are especially evident in connection with Buber's theology. This connection is decisive, for according to Buber dialogism directs itself to the duality of man's relating to God, that duality which is implicit in the relation of the creation to the Creator.[29] Even in the seemingly limited relationship of "life with nature", "we gaze toward the train of the eternal You".[30] On the authority of such sayings, Theunissen arrives at his formulation that the "Thou" with which we address the one who encounters us is, in its pure and perfect state, God.[31] If we apply those conceptual distinctions at which Theunissen arrives to the level of theological discussion, the conclusion is—I am still using Theunissen's careful formulations—that the particular Thou "breaks through the world, because it is beyond the world." As that which is beyond the world, it already participates in the mystery of He who is capable of encompassing me and the whole world, "because He Himself is not of it".[32] From this perspective it is clear that the birth of the I and the Thou from the Between means an extreme theology of grace, which denies man any independent power of doing in general and of therapeutic and sacramental doing in particular. It seems evident that behind Theunissen's philosophic decisions there are determined theological opinions.

There is no doubt that Theunissen's analysis, with its conclusions and implications, is completely opposed to Buber's intentions. When I say "intentions", I do not mean some inarticulate tendencies which would have to be inferred from the texts. On the contrary, I mean explicit intentions, which could be demonstrated by many quotations. In my book, *Die Aporie des Du,* I put considerable effort into amassing such evidence. But Theunissen will rightly reply that the intentions of a philosopher are sometimes inconsistent with the essential implications of the manifestation of his thought. This manifestation is dual in its intentions, and therefore the "entelechy" of his teachings—as I called it earlier—can even turn its back on the declared intentions of its author. When we read the text with this way of seeing, we read it, as Theunissen puts it, "against its flow". Such a reading cannot be refuted from the declared intentions of the author alone, but only from the logic of the basic assumptions of the manifestations of the thoughts. The intentions of the author must be defended from the substantiality of his foundations. I attempted to do this in *Die Aporie des Du.*[33] Here I shall summarize, again with extreme brevity, my reply to Theunissen, not in order to repeat myself, but in order to test that reply once more, as befits this occasion.

Buber distances the "Thou" from noetic knowledge: he insists on the dichotomy between the reality of our being-in-relation and the existent thing which is within our knowledge. If we call the objectively existing thing "something", then the reality of relationship is not something. In other words: "we do not know anything". This sentence merely repeats the claim of the dichotomy between relationship and noetic knowledge: Thus "knowing" here is merely an expression for knowledge. What is being said to us here is: When I am in relationship, the reality which occurs and surrounds me is not a reality which I know by way of noetic and objective knowledge.

Theunissen thinks he can express this by saying that relationship is "nothing", that is, it does not exist at all. Hence, in his opinion, we must conclude that the relationship is freed from reality in its totality and overcomes the world. This way of thinking is both incredible and seducing. Seemingly, it merely follows Buber's thought, and illuminates it, and yet it breaks through his conceptual world and becomes alien to it. What is happening here? Are there in truth potential tendencies in Buber's thought which bring forth this contradiction? And if not: wherein lies the error of Theunissen's interpretation, which seems so consistent and so close to the original? Where is the hidden twist by which this interpretation deviates from the original and shoots off on an alien track?

I think we can put our finger on the exact spot where the logic of Theunissen's thinking becomes estranged from the essence of dialogism—precisely by being absolutely "logical". This is Theunissen's argument: since the relationship is no longer an existent thing, it is freed from the existent thing and exists transcendent of it. But the "existent thing" exists only by being experienced through objective knowledge. At this state of his analysis Theunissen himself emphasizes that the noetic act which takes place in the I-It is the existing thing itself: One must abandon the transcendental distinction between the thing in itself and the act of knowledge directed towards it. The real reason for this identity between the object and knowledge of the object is the character of the realization of the I-It.[34] In a formulation similar to Theunissen's, we may say that the noetic act of knowledge is *the admission of the existent thing to existence*.[35]

It follows that when we say the relationship is nothing, we must apply this "nothing" to the existent thing, but also to noetic knowledge, which is the admission-to-existence of the existing thing. When Buber says that we do not know anything of the Thou, he means that we must abandon not only things, but also noetic knowledge. But then we cannot attain the "nothing" through noetic knowledge. The "nothing" of the I-Thou is not a modus of negation of noetic knowledge and therefore it is not a modus of negation of the thing in itself. The opposition between relationship and existent thing excludes the admission-to-existence of the existent thing from the event of relationship, but—and this is the point—it does not exclude the existent thing in the way that one existent thing, by existing, excludes another. That is, the relationship does not negate the existent thing in the way one existent thing negates another. Therefore this "nothing" does not transcend the existent thing, nor does it help us to transcend universe of things as a whole, nor do we, with its help, "overcome the world". On the contrary, we must assume that the relationship and the presence which occurs in it even though it be opposed to the existent thing, *is identical with that existent thing*, even though we cannot grasp the nature of this being identical, that is, we cannot analyze it by our concepts nor elucidate its meaning in a logical discussion. In the statement "one knows nothing of the You", Theunissen sees a kind of hole punched in the universe of things, through which we can get beyond it. But according to their spirit these words mean nothing more than that a presence has opened up which is indeed not the admission-to-existence of the existent thing—there is indeed a gap between it and objectivity—but nevertheless this presence is identical with objective reality, though we cannot define this identicalness.[36]

Once more I emphasize: presence is not the presence of a thing. And yet in that presence, this or that is present, for instance "this tree". I am speaking, specifically, of the presence of the "world-concreteness", from which the existence of existing things does not disappear. On the contrary, everything which I experience in noetic knowledge becomes real in the presence of the relationship. When it is in relationship to me, what is known is in its complete reality. I encounter it with all my being and am affected by its being. The paradox is illuminated, almost too brightly, by the theological conclusions of dialogism, precisely because here the internal contradiction is carried to its extreme. For instance, in the sentence "The real communion of man with God not only has its place in the world, but also its object".[37] The fervency of Buber's relationship to the world, his affirmation of the world, do not contradict the reasoning of dialogism, but are founded on its assumptions.

Even now, my reply to Theunissen seems to me to be consistent and appropriate to the essence of the question. I would go so far as to say that it is the kind of argument which cannot be appealed against. Yet I must admit that upon renewed examination a breach nevertheless appears, which might open the way for a valid reply. According to Buber the Thou is "not" an existent thing. Theunissen concludes from this that the "Thou" frees itself from the existent thing and transcends it. To this I reply that the "not" of the Thou is not a "not" in the logical sense which belongs to the domain of existent things; in other words, it is not the "not of the It". Since it is not the "not" of the It, it does not negate the existent thing as one existent thing negates another. Hence it is possible that the Thou is identical with the being of the existent thing. (We must be careful not to give this negation of the negation a meaning in accordance with conceptual exactness, that is, we must be careful not to determine the affirmation in this negation of negation.) But now when I say that the "not" of the Thou is not the "not" of the It—and therefore does not negate as that "not" negates—am I not, in this reply, again using the "not" of the It? I am objecting to negation as exclusion, but am I not thus negating and excluding the negation of exclusion? Am I not driving out Satan by Beelzebub? I am objecting to the elucidation of the Thou, when the elucidation is aided by conceptual reflection which is not appropriate to the Thou. But this response reflects in a logical manner against logical reflection.

One thing is clear from these thoughts: I cannot "prove" the identicalness of which we are speaking. From the theological point of view, what follows is that I cannot prove Buber's affirmation of the world against the alienation from the world toward which Theunissen is moving, in a manner reminiscent of the theology of the Fourth Gospel. Where, then, do we go from here? It seems to me that there are only two possible ways. The more radical way, which is paradoxically the more logical, is to totally abandon rational thought as a way of living our existence and of leading to attainment of reality. We shall then stand in the situation of the person attentive to the meaning of the Zen Buddhist koan, which opens only upon a reality that cannot be attained by any concepts whatever. The second way experiments with the assumption of identicalness of which we spoke earlier: we rely, without reflection, on the event of presence, and only from here do we try to crystallize our concepts in accordance with this event. Thus, in fact, every philosophical work begins—with a reliance on a specific vision of reality before the thinking and the beginning of conceptual work; the philosopher as it were leaps into his reality, and only from there does he develop a conceptuality appropriate to it; he cannot learn about this reality by deductive means, for it is given before all reflection to the personality of the philosopher and to the historical moment in which he is working. If we do something similar here, if we leap into the midst of Buber's experience of the world and arrive from here at the concept of "identicalness", then we reach the conclusion that presence is essentially irrational and yet does not negate the *ratio*, just as it does not absolutely negate the specific concreteness known to our knowledge, but belongs to it in a way that cannot be understood by our concepts. We arrive at a certain logic which can claim to bring reality close, but which cannot claim to attain it with its concepts. Thus we return, by a circle of thought, to the beginning of this road. For the conclusion justifies the way of thinking with which we set out to challenge Theunissen's thought. This thinking was indeed reflective when it challenged the pretention of reflection to master the reality of relationship, but we have the right to demonstrate through reflection that the reality refuses to submit to the reflective distinctions of reason.

The authority thus granted to the *ratio* should not be underestimated. At an earlier stage we voiced a suspicion against the distinctions implicit in language, from which, as it seems, Buber develops the schema of "basic words". We conjectured that the concept and the objective image have the power to lead us to the unity of being, to reality.[38] Now we can confirm this conjecture and understand it more clearly. In fact, even Buber acknowledges the concept's power to lead us to reality, only it seems that this does not happen in the manner Buber supposed. That is, we cannot accept his claim that the unattainable is as it were "translated" into the language of It, or that language "opens a window" through which we must "look outside". The connection between verbal language and reality is more direct: there is truly a kind of identicalness between them. And yet, it is clear that this identicalness occurs within a hiatus and cannot be attained by means of concepts.[39]

On the other hand, we must also avoid overestimating the authority of the *ratio*. It is reflected in the words of the Zen master: "Words are only vessels and props to carry the Way, the Truth . . . Truth, the Way, is fundamentally wordless. But the truth is proclaimed by the word. Whoever sees the truth forgets the words".[40] Indeed, the distinctions of words carry us only to the threshold of truth; they do not reach truth itself. For this reason Buber's effort to attain reality by the dualism of the "basic words" is futile. It becomes clear that we cannot maintain this duality. It breaks down because in the final analysis one cannot make a clear distinction between Thou and It. The branching-off of Thou from It is not to be grasped in clear concepts.

This does not remove the justification for dialogical thinking. This thinking did indeed succeed in pointing out, in the midst of daily life with all its reification, a reality which is not that of things and concepts. But as we said: in the midst of life and not in the "beyond". Not in ecstasy, not in introversion nor in turning away from existing things. On the contrary, it is here and now that that reality opens up, as Alice enters the mirror and finds herself in Wonderland, but the mirror remains. Only, one cannot distinguish this inconceivable reality through concepts, and one cannot limit it; and therefore one cannot grasp the substance of its occurrence, nor its essence. The reality which dialogism points to breaks through the schema of dialogism. The justification of dialogism contains its futility. But let us not ignore the converse of this sentence, which is also valid. The very futility of dialogical thinking flows out of that reality which breaks through every schema, and at which we arrived by the demonstrative power of dialogical thinking. Indeed, when we are persuaded of the futility of Buber's distinctions, we abandon his words. Only in this way can the truth to which he pointed remain with us.

Discussion After Jochanan Bloch's Lecture

H. GOLLWITZER

I was surprised, Jochanan, that you would begin a paper with a sentence which you then prove to be incorrect. Thought about dialogue does not reflect upon a human reality about which it is impossible to think or speak. The mode of objectifying cognition is not the only mode of cognition there is. Our language does not speak only of existing things which we can grasp noetically in the sense of objectifying cognition. You speak here of the unity of the act of speech, which is simultaneously a statement of content and an address. But you seem to me to be placing undue stress on the informational purpose of language. In your view, the main purpose of language is to transmit information about things. This is debatable. When we speak we convey much more than information about things. We convey information about feelings. Every "Ow" at the dentist's informs the dentist about the pain I am feeling.

You yourself say that language has many different functions. In posing your question you distinguish between an objectifying rationalization, which you seem to identify with Buber's I-It relationship, and an I-Thou relationship which cannot be grasped conceptually. Then, like a magician, you create a Gordian knot, a terrible difficulty, which at the end you can easily disentangle because you know the trick: language is not merely a mathematical language of information, rather it also expresses the totality of our relationships with things, our present, in which the object confronts us.

Buber had inherited from previous philosophers an epistemology which constantly practices the schema which Bloch attributes to it. This traditional epistemology recognizes only one part of this schema, that is, the I-It relationship. But Buber in *I and Thou* developed a new approach. He found that there are two ways of relating to the world of things—the I-It relationship, which characterizes both conceptual thinking and the treatment of things as objects of use, and the I-Thou relationship. The latter had been mostly ignored by traditional epistemology, which always starts from the solitary I. Buber wants to show that man's primary relationship to the world is the relationship between man and man, and that so-called primitive man, as is shown in myth, relates to nature and things as to something fraternal, not objectified, not instrumentalized. This is the fundamental relationship. After that comes the relationship to things as

61

objects of use, and this most secondary, abstract, and inhuman relationship is the I-It, which today has grown to such huge dimensions that it threatens to smother us all.

J. BLOCH

You have certainly not made things easy for me. But I think there are more misunderstandings here than real differences of opinion. The first sentence of my paper is perfectly correct. The stress here is on the word "about", "about which it is essentially impossible to think or to speak"; we are speaking about dialogical thought. There is a reality here about which it is impossible to speak or think. You are objecting to this because what is at issue here is the problem of theological language. Now the problem of theological language cannot be solved by my denying that theology speaks of something of which it is impossible to speak. The difficulty is that our language—I have never denied it—nevertheless does have ways of making it possible for us to approach this reality which cannot be spoken about. I never said that language has only informative content; on the other hand it is necessary to state the simple truth that one of the principle aims of language is informative; language is objective. And nevertheless it does touch upon things about which one cannot speak. The possibility of theological speech does exist. And I would emphasize this more, and see it more simply, than Buber did. There is no logical solution to the riddle: language speaks of that about which it cannot speak. Language can legitimately speak about that of which there is no legitimate speech.

And here is the one point at which I permit myself to deviate from Buber. He tried to solve the riddle by way of a relatively pure dualism—"I-Thou" and "I-It". But this schematization breaks down. You can see how hard Buber tried to make it work from the fact that at a later period he tried to explain this dualism as a dualism of reality— but in this he failed. Buber says more than I-Thou is the true reality on which everything else is based. I cannot live only in I-Thou, I have to live in I-It too. This is not a deficiency; the I-It realizes worlds and, if you like, realizes God, just as much as the I-Thou. That is why it is difficult to understand the dualism. Buber tried to understand it as a way of realization, and I would argue that the dualism is not to be understood—it exists, and I have to accept it. And by the way, only if I think that the It also has legitimate being can I establish, and justify, theological language.

B. CASPER

My question is: are you not removing the sting from Buber's thought by assimilating him to a transcendental-philosophical viewpoint? To put it concretely: Can the alternative, the "either-or" of I-Thou and I-It, or as Buber's text has it, the statement that the I of the I-Thou is *other* than the I of the I-It—can this be assimilated to the difference between Being (Sein) and What-is (Seiendes), a difference which the great philosophical tradition has always perceived? Or does Buber's alternative of I-Thou and I-It not signify, after all, something else, something other than the classical distinction? Something which could perhaps be called the existential or existentialist factor in Buber's thought. Theunissen's interpretation calls this a "theology of grace", but there is one point of support for such a theology of grace in Buber's text, where he says, "The Thou encounters me by grace".

J. BLOCH

It seems to me that there is a basic misunderstanding between us, and that is the main thing I want to deal with now. I want to take the distinction between "Thou" and "It" as radically as possible. It is strange that Theunissen has not noticed this, nor, I think, have you. I have no intention of assimilating Buber to a transcendental-philosophical viewpoint. I am afraid that what is in people's minds here is the business about the so-called transcendental-philosophical model which Buber supposedly started out from and had to destroy. I consider that a philosophical legend; there is no transcendental-philosophical model anywhere in *I and Thou*. But to the main point: When I understand the "Thou" quite radically as having nothing to do with the "It", then the "Thou" also breaks through the noetic way of perception and it also breaks through the antinomies of our logic. But this means that I cannot separate the "Thou" from the "It" in such a nice, clean, logical manner as you still can in your distinctions, when you say the "Thou" is no existing thing, therefore it is beyond the world, it transcends the world. I'd like to know where it arrives at then—at God? As if I could make a nice, clean, logical distinction between God and the world and say, like Theunissen, that God transcends the world or doesn't belong to it.

If I carry this idea to its radical conclusion, then I must say that the "Thou" cannot be grasped by logical distinctions, and that therefore the negation of the "It" which is associated with the "Thou" can coexist in a congruence with this "It", although I cannot call this, in purely logical fashion, a negation of the negation, that is, something positive. What remains is that the negation which accompanies the "Thou" breaks through the logical distinction, but that this negation is no longer a negation of the "It", and therefore is not opposed to the "It" in the way "It" is opposed to "It", and that therefore a degree of congruence is possible, and does indeed occur factually, when I stand before a tree and am drawn into a relationship with this tree, as Buber's language suggests. This congruence coincides with Buber's basic theological experience of a relationship between man and God, which affirms the world both through and in spite of the difference between God and world.

Thus I do not want to assimilate Buber to transcendental philosophy, I take the distinction extremely radically, but precisely for this reason I cannot and must not come to Theunissen's conclusions, I have to take Buber as he is in his book. Theunissen changes the function of what is written here when he says that the "I" emerges from the Between. This is to lose the pathos of the deed which exists in Buber, the pathos of Creation, the pathos of the partnership of man in the fate of the world, which is a divine fate. What is hard to see is how Buber can retain this pathos even while separating the Thou from the empirical I. Even though I understand that this separation has to be radically carried through the boundaries of the It, for then the negation of the "It" is also broken through, and then I can return to the genuine Buber.

L. WACHINGER

The evocative rhetoric of *I and Thou* misleads the reader into a feeling of having understood which does not stand up to close examination. My objection is that the center of Buber's thought lies outside the objectifying, noetic domain of critical philosophy since Descartes. Our task in dealing with Buber's work is to thematize the practical components in a philosophically appropriate manner: to pay attention not only to its concepts and logic, but also to the dynamics of intersubjective relations which accompany his logic, or are mixed in with it—the delicate or direct play of the struggle for power over and influence on the Other, the pressure toward a desired change and the resistence of the other to that pressure, in short, that game which is played wherever two or more people confront each other. Buber's interest in problems of psychotherapy shows his sensitivity to the dynamic aspect of language, and only from this aspect can he be adequately understood.

J. BLOCH

I would like to say one more thing: the supposed simplicity and beauty, especially simplicity, of Buber's conceptual and linguistic execution disappears the moment I try to translate him into Hebrew. You cannot imagine what a tangled-up, mysterious book *I and Thou* is in the available Hebrew translation. I know this because I have to read it in Hebrew with my students. Here, as with Nietzsche, a certain gracefulness of language can be misleading.

Notes

JOCHANAN BLOCH

1. See Franz Rosenzweig's letter to Buber on 22.9.1922 in Martin Buber, *Briefwechsel aus sieben Jahrzehnten*, Hrsg. Grete Schaeder, Heidelberg 1973, Bd. II, p. 137.
2. Alan W. Watts, *The Wisdom of Insecurity*, Vintage, New York, 1968, p. 24.
3. Jochanan Bloch, *Die Aporie des Du, Probleme der Dialogik Martin Bubers*, Heidelberg, 1977, p. 176, 223f. (Aporie).
4. Martin Buber, "Replies to My Critics", *The Philosophy of Martin Buber*, ed. Paul Arthur Schilpp and Maurice Friedman, London, Cambridge University Press, 1967, p. 693.
5. See, among other things, Martin Buber, "Dialogue", in *Between Man and Man*, translated by Ronald Gregor Smith, The Fontana Library, London and Glasgow, pp. 29-30; compare Aporie, pp. 20, 24ff.
6. Martin Buber, *I and Thou*, trans. Walter Kaufmann, Charles Scribner's Sons, New York, 1970, p. 61.
7. See Michael Theunissen, *Der Andere, Studien zur Sozialontologie der Gegenwart*, Berlin, 1965, p. 314ff (TDA); also Theunissen, "Bubers negative Ontologie des Zwischen", *Philosophisches Handbuch*, 2. Halbband, München 1964, p. 326. (TOZ)
8. *I and Thou*, p. 58.
9. D. T. Suzuki, *Manual of Zen Buddhism*, New York 1960, Plate IX.
10. Aporie, p. 216ff.
11. *Between Man and Man*, p. 20. (In German: "in einer sachlich erfassbaren Form".)
12. *I and Thou*. (In German: "unauflösbare Antinomik".)
13. What is meant here is not "dialectic mediation". See Aporie, pp. 66f., 106, 218f.
14. See above, p. 383-384.
15. See above, p. 382.
16. That is, they did not take shape amid the "fulgurations of the Thou-relationship" (*Philosophy of Martin Buber*, p. 692).
17. Martin Buber, *Two Types of Faith*, trs. Norman P. Goldhawk, Harper Torchbooks, New York, 1961, p. 8.
18. Theunissen sums up the main points of his view in TOZ. This essay was published before TDA, but written after it.
19. *I and Thou*, p. 158; *Between Man and Man*, p. 30.
20. *I and Thou*, pp. 55, 61.
21. TOZ, p. 325.
22. TDA, p. 30.
23. TDA, p. 307.
24. TDA, p. 325.
25. TDA, p. 325; cf. TOZ, p. 326.
26. TOZ, p. 326.
27. TDA, p. 311.

28. TDA, p. 269.

29. See *I and Thou*, pp. 150-151; cf. Aporie, p. 70ff.

30. *I and Thou*, p. 57.

31. TDA, p. 341.

32. TDA, p. 346; cf. Aporie, p. 86.

33. Aporie, pp. 235-240, 280-286, 288-295.

34. According to the exact nature of the concepts, if we speak of "realization" we cannot speak of "noetic knowledge" or the "act of noetic knowledge" in the meaning attached by transcendental philosophy to these concepts. The above paragraph must be read with this reservation.

35. TOZ, p. 328; TDA, p. 302.

36. The reader's attention is called to the similarity of certain of Martin Heidegger's thoughts after his "turning". The similarity is seen in such sentences as "Das Nichts ist die Ermöglichung der Offenbarkeit des Seienden als eines solchen für das menschliche Dasein" (The 'nothing' is the making-possible of the revelation of being as such for human existence). Martin Heidegger, *Was ist Metaphysik?*, 10. Auflage, Frankfurt-M, 1969, p. 35. Further examples may be found in note 37 to this essay in *Eshel Beer-Sheva*, vol. 2.

37. Martin Buber, *The Origin and Meaning of Hasidism*, ed. and trans. by Maurice Friedman, Horizon, New York, 1970, p. 94. (In the quotation "object"—the accurate translation of the German "Gegenstand"—has been substituted for "subject".-Translator.)

38. See above, p. 389.

39. Thus it is doubtful whether the expression "leap words" (Abstossworte) is still suitable to our meaning. It seems that we must here understand the function of the words of language on the model of the function of the "sign".

40. Bi-Yän-Lu, Verdeutscht und Erläutert von Wilhelm Gundert, München, 1960, Bd. I, S. 240.

The Finite Thou and the Eternal Thou in the Work of Buber

YEHOSHUA AMIR

1

In setting out to clarify the relationship between the "eternal Thou" and the finite Thou, as Buber portrays it specifically in *I and Thou*, I am asking about the place of the religious element in the totality of Buber's thought. It is certainly not my task here to fortify Buber's conception of the "eternal Thou" against attacks from without. Such an attempt would be contrary to Buber's intention. For Buber felt that his task was to point to reality. With an interlocutor who, following Buber's pointing finger, does not plainly see the reality being indicated, Buber has no further means of conversation. Any attempt at discursive "proof" would lag hopelessly behind the immediacy of presence which alone is possible here, and thus miss its mark.

We are concerned, therefore, with the question whether the connection which Buber sets up between the finite Thou in its different formations, and the "eternal Thou", is internally consistent. Such a criticism from within is found in Michael Theunissen's book *Der Andere. Studien zur Sozialontologie der Gegenwart*, which appeared in 1965, preceded by a brief essay "Bubers Negative Ontologie des Zwischen", in the *Philosophisches Jahrbuch* of the Görresgesellschaft for 1964. Theunissen speaks consistently of a "quasi-theological imagery" in which Buber's philosophy of the 'Thou' breaks forth. He argues that Buber pursues the solution to his real concern, which is seen as "social-ontological," through a daring step from the sphere of the interhuman to the sphere of statements of faith—a step not justified by the assumptions of Buber's own thought. Whoever is determined to maintain the inner coherency of Buber's world cannot avoid coming to terms with Theunissen's profound internal criticism of Buber. Such a coming to terms can be found in Jochanan Bloch's profound study *Die Aporie des Du* (Heidelberg, 1977). But I still believe there is need of a closer examination of Theunissen's interpretation and criticism. And the vulnerable point

at which this criticism is directed is precisely the relationship between the worldly "Thou" and the "eternal Thou." To this point we
must now turn.

2

"Extended, the lines of relationship intersect in the eternal You."[1]
This sentence, with which Buber opens the third part of *I and Thou*,
requires a particularly careful interpretation, for the relationships of
which he speaks here are the three worldly I-Thou relationships
developed in the first part, while the eternal Thou forms the theme of
the third part. This sentence which formulates the reciprocal relationship of these two basic concepts answers for the conceptual unity
of the entire work. And the intention of my exposition is to give as
accurate an interpretation as possible to this sentence.

The reader who up till now has followed Buber's discourse point by
point, or (to put it in Buber's terms) who has until now responded to
Buber's message, may find this sentence surprising, for it introduces
a new theme for which what precedes has not prepared him—aside
from a single hint whose significance could have remained concealed.[2] Theunissen rightly observes that up till now the reader could
not have expected the lines drawn from I to Thou to be capable of
extention.[3] The reader is therefore confronted with the expansion of a
circle which to him seems closed, and he asks himself to what extent
this expansion is meaningful or justified.

But if we look at this connection with Buber's own eyes, it takes on
an entirely different aspect. What impelled him to work on his book
were not I-Thou encounters with nature, with other humans, or with
spiritual beings, which he might study to see whether they were
capable of a final apotheosis through a Divine Thou; rather he was
driven by a desire to understand religion. The preliminary work for *I
and Thou* was a series of lectures "Religion als Gegenwart (Religion as
Presence)", which was recently edited with comprehensive commentaries by Rivka Horwitz (Verlag Lambert Schneider). Buber himself
called *I and Thou*, as it lay already finished before him, "a volume of
prolegomena to my work on religion,"[4] a work originally expected to
comprise five volumes.[5] Rivka Horwitz considers it possible that
Buber began the writing of *I and Thou* with the third part.[6] But even
if one does not accept this possibility—and Buber's own testimony
seems to me to contradict it[7]—one must still say that the whole book
is designed to lead up to the third part. It is not, then, that a social

ontology is being elevated, belatedly to theological or quasi-theological heights, but rather that an experience of religious encounter gives rise to a dialogical anthropology. This course of events is most palpable in the second, historical-sociological part. According to Rivka Horwitz's statements,[8] the lectures "Religion als Gegenwart" contain no parallels to the section; thus only in the final stage of work it must have been added onto the religious foundations.

This order of composition of the book must prejudice us in advance against an interpretation which tries to understand it as proceeding from a basically sociological-ontological question and to free that question from theological excrescences or encroachments. As a counter-position to Buber such an offensive is, methodologically, entirely justified; but where it is presented as an interpretation of the author's own teaching whose course has been altered by deceptive influences, it can only meet with displeasure. It is of course conceivable that an originally religious impetus led Buber to social-ontological discoveries, which in turn, over a period of time, caused the impulse that had given rise to them to atrophy, so that at last nothing remained of it but a hollow ideological declaration. The spiritual history of the last two centuries could easily furnish us with parallels for such a process. However, we may note that Buber, who had an extremely delicate sense of the inner transformations he had undergone a few years before, was at least not aware, in the time of "inspired labor" marked by the year 1922, of any such profound change as this conjecture would force us to assume. It would therefore require, strong proof to make credible such a factual invalidation of the immediate encounter with God in *I and Thou*.

Buber's own intent in *I and Thou* was to follow the emanations of the One, Divine reality in the real, earthly lives of men. Rivka Horwitz has related Buber's later statements concerning preparatory work for *I and Thou* to his address "Cheruth," from the year 1918.[9] I would like to go one step further and include in the discussion the address "The Holy Way,"[10] given slightly earlier in the same year. In this address Buber calls God "the sun of mankind"[11] and elaborates: "Just as the sun's substance has its being among the stars yet beams its light into the earthly realm, so it is granted to human creatures to behold in their midst the radiation of the ineffable's glory." Thus he set himself the program of seeking the rays of the Divinity "in the midst" of humanity. These rays, he said then, shine "in the Between, in the seemingly empty space."[12] How these rays make this space of the "Between," which Simmel had earlier called "empty,"[13] into the true place of realization, is from now on Buber's problem, of which his social-ontological dimension is an outgrowth. In this sense *I and Thou* may be regarded as the execution of the program he had sketched out earlier.

Now it is certainly possible to argue that with the shift to a worldly perspective the origin of those rays in a "substance . . . among the stars" which he had proclaimed at that time, had become superfluous and could be only declaratively maintained. A criticism in this direction, if justified, strikes not some incidental point, which might if necessary be conceded, but the essential intent of the book. If the tie which the earthly Thou in its threefold manifestation has to the eternal Thou turns out to be an umbilical cord which must be cut if the child is to live its own life, then Buber's book misses its mark. Its only significance is in testifying to an illusion of its author with regard to the religious encounter as the redeeming act that can restore reality to human life threatened by alienation. An illusion—because its basic assumptions are insufficient to provide a basis for such an encounter.

Before we admit such a self-deception on the part of a thinker concerning the inner possibilities of his own thought, we have the obligation and also the right to exhaust all possibilities in order to extract from Buber's thought an internally consistent meaning. We may assume that he is conscious of the powerful inner tensions, the centrifugal forces, to which his spreading motives of thought are subject, and that he will not easily lose sight of one of its basic components.

3

With this intention we return to the sentence on which we shall concentrate our interpretive efforts: "Extended, the lines of relationship intersect in the eternal You." Here Buber daringly reduces the connection of the finite and the eternal Thou to a geometric formula.

The difference between I and Thou is defined by Buber by, among other things, the fact that one can *discuss* the It, but can only *address* the Thou. But now Buber has taken upon himself to write a book *about* I and Thou. That about which one writes becomes one's object of discussion. By thematizing the Thou, Buber necessarily makes it into an object. Only at this price is he able to communicate to us what he has known. As to why he regarded it as his lifetask to communicate to us what revealed itself to him concerning the twofoldness of relationships, he has said, in his answer to his critics,[14] what was possible for him to say. But having assumed the task, he had to pay its price. He had to clothe the Thou in the language of the It.

The language which discusses the Thou remains inadequate whether the Thou is approached through feeling or through thought. A language arousing emotions, such as Buber was accustomed to employ in his predialogic past, does not lift the individual out of the immanence of the I and into the space of the encounter, any more than does the language of thought. The manner in which Buber, once thrown back on the language of the It, strives for the strictest, most objective form of that language, is certainly part of the means by which Buber—as he often confessed—impresses language into his service. If one must think about what by its very nature does not have its place in thought, at least the thought should not remain vague; its possibilities should be fully exploited. Thus Buber arrives at his geometric parable. It is, to be sure, no wonder that we soon become aware that the language of geometry, applied to that which is in principle outside the realm of thought, quickly entangles us in a geometric absurdity. But precisely by testing itself on what is by nature real and not conceptual, it helps us to mark the boundaries of the thinkable and thus to make expressible what is inexpressible in itself.

Such is the case with the sentence on the extended lines of relationships which intersect in the eternal Thou, conceived as the point in infinity at which all parallels intersect. That a line A-B may be extended infinitely and that at a point in infinity it will intersect with all its parallels is mathematically quite unobjectionable. But a mathematician would certainly find it surprising that the point C in infinity is singled out so that the final part of the book is devoted to it. For now C too appears as one of the points to which the line is drawn. But this makes the line A-B-C into a geometric monstrosity: a straight line with three determining points. Such an over-determined line has no place in a healthy geometric logic, which would attempt a rational cure of the mathematical absurdity. Since point A, that is, the I which enters into relationships, is immovably fixed as the point of departure, there remain only two possibilities of clearing up this grotesque situation:

1. Since all lines, whatever their path, finally intersect in the one point C, the intermediate point B, which neither adds nor detracts, may be eliminated as an intermediary and ignored.

2. Line A-B is self-sufficient. It may be extended ad libitum, but with

regard to the definition of the line such an extension adds nothing essentially new. Therefore any attempt to ascribe a particular valence along this line to point C is doomed to failure.

The first way characterizes the dialogical thought of various religious thinkers close to Buber,[15] but as far as I know it has never been applied as a critical interpretation. We need elucidate this possibility briefly. But we shall treat the second way at greater length, since this is the line along which Theunissen has proposed the critical demolition of Buber's thought of the eternal Thou. From the autarky of the finite Thou, which may be inferred from the first part of Buber's book, Theunissen erects a bulwark by which all encroaching claims are rebuffed at the threshold. Thus he flatly denies the claims for the eternal Thou which are made in the third part.

Incidentally, Theunissen's critical strategy may well create a false impression of his own standpoint. A critic who systematically forbids Buber to "break out" into theological escapades can easily be understood as a representative of a laicist humanism which insists on a purely intramundane settling of basic social-ontological questions and must therefore bar any thinker's retreat to a transcendental *asylum ignorantiae*. But this is by no means Theunissen's position. On the contrary, he is close to dialectic theology, and what he finds objectionable is not the opening up of the religious perspective as such, but—in his opinion—the inadequate methods which Buber employs for this purpose. The establishing of a wordly Thou, whose extended lines are said to reach the Divine Thou, seems to him to obliterate an inexorable opposition between God and world, which leaves room only for a vertical word of command spoken by God into the world, but not for the merging of action and passion with which man enters into the encounter. Since Buber does not start from the assumption of this radical antagonism, Theunissen sees in Buber's conception of the Thou an insufficiently covered loan from a realm to which he has no legitimate access. By warning him back into his own limits he tries to drive him back to a purely secular position.

When criticism is impelled to play off Buber against Buber, we shall have to ask, in a final section, whether the unspoken assumption of this criticism does justice to Buber's intention. Is Buber obliged to comply with his critic's demand that he choose between an interpretation of the I-Thou line as A-B or as A-C? Or does the line A-B-C, despite its geometric absurdity, give legitimate expression to Buber's teaching in *I and Thou*?

4

Man as Buber sees him enters life with an "inborn Thou," that is, with an urge built into his nature to seek his Thou. Thus he describes the first groping movements of the infant in this search: "soft projections of the hands reach, aimlessly to all appearances, into the empty air toward the indefinite . . . precisely these glances will eventually, after many trials, come to rest upon a red wall-paper arabesque and not leave it until the soul of red has opened up to them. Precisely this motion will gain its sensuous form and definiteness in contact with a shaggy toy bear and eventually apprehend lovingly and unforgettably a complete body."[16] The child's mind wanders about in this manner searching for something, without knowing what it is. This formulation is naturally imprecise, for the Thou which is sought with an obscure urge is not a "something." But it is nevertheless the goal of a search, and thus the difference between It and Thou cannot be that there is no "intentionality" toward the Thou. True, it is not that "world-projecting" intentionality which transcendental philosophy knows. For by the presumptions of transcendental philosophy we would expect that the factual Thou, when it appeared, would not come as a surprise to the I, since its image is already engraved in the inborn Thou. But this "world-projecting" ability is precisely what the dialogical I necessarily lacks. The urge toward the Thou which from earliest childhood throbs in man and allows him to seek a response does not have any capability of fulfilling its own demands. That such a Thou as the I has always carried within itself as an activating dream arises to meet him in bodily form, remains for the I the greatest of all possible surprises.

However, what happens with the forms in which a person encounters the Thou may be similar to what happens with the Platonic Eros. According to the description in the *Symposion*, Eros awakens at the sight of the body of a beautiful boy. It deepens into a love for the soul of this boy in its beauty, to the love of all beautiful boy-souls, and so on through various intermediary stages to the loving contemplation of the idea of beauty in its perfect and imperishable radiance. Only in this blissful contemplation does Eros come to rest. At this moment man sees the earlier moments when Eros was aroused in him as unripe and he abolishes them. Consistently, in the writings of the elderly Plato boy-love is repudiated, albeit it gave the first stimulus to the awakening of Eros, and to the ascent of the soul from its earthly existence to that supra-celestial contemplation of ideas. Once the height has been reached, the ladder is no longer needed and is pushed away without misgivings.

One could imagine the quest of the innate Thou as something analogous to this proceeding. In the passage from Buber quoted above there was mention of a red spot on the wallpaper and a shaggy toy bear, which compose the Thou for the infant at a certain stage; and as soon as the child has outgrown that stage, they no longer mean anything to him. And so it may well happen that domains in which the Thou has once flowered will later be neglected because the person has meanwhile come closer to his true Thou. And where he stands before the final, the eternal Thou, everything provisory which has once been Thou to a person will die away.

Here it is instructive to read the criticism which Florens Christian Rang voiced concerning *I and Thou*.[17] Buber, he says, should have spoken of the Thou only in a language which would be "usable in immediate prayer," for here our word approaches the circle "where it addresses itself to God." In particular he criticizes Buber's term "Beziehung" (relationship), which seems to him out of place, because it is not "a praying word." And he asks himself how Buber comes to such a pale word, whereupon he answers: "Because you start from I-Thou (and I-It) as if this existed on the human level, still without God." And later: "In truth, there is no I-Thou, only Thou (spoken to God), out of which the I merely echoes." Only to God, then, can one truly say Thou, and only in a language in which we can address God should this Thou find its expression. An earthly Thou is not sufficient to justify the use of the holy word, Thou.

This criticism of Buber does indeed come close to the position we have indicated. Such close criticism, which presumes to be only a nuance away from Buber, perhaps even expects Buber to agree with it; still it is not Buber's own position. Later we shall consider for what reasons Buber would admit that "still without God" there can be no human I and Thou. But he still cannot renounce the human I-Thou as his point of departure. Why?

In the passage where Buber speaks of the three "spheres" "in which the world of relation arises,"[18] we have not yet heard anything about an inborn Thou. It comes into play only when the question is raised how man reaches these spheres. For the spheres are not nature, other humans, and spiritual beings, but, as Buber very precisely formulates, life with these three. And we would certainly not succeed in entering life with one of those three that wait outside, without this inner urge, this "inborn Thou" with which we are initially provided. Not that the inborn Thou would be in any way capable of producing the spheres of I-Thou out of itself. The actions of the infant which we cited above are surely to be understood in the sense that in the child, who has not yet encountered a true Thou, the "inborn Thou" which has already started on its quest creates for itself a temporary substitute-Thou; as proof the Thou is scarcely acquired before it is immediately forgotten. It is otherwise with the three spheres of encounter with the external world which is not fabricated by us. Here the I finds itself before a personal call. He can stand up to this call or he can evade it. For the inborn Thou this is the astonishing moment when something is opened up to it which it could never have secreted out of itself, namely that there is a reality in which the Thou of its dreams is embodied. That is what Buber means by the dual character of the encounter as active and passive: an urge that emerges from the person and meets a presence.

To be sure, this dual nature of the encounter is nullified if we allow ourselves to be instructed by Theunissen that the Thou is in truth "nothing."[19] Buber, however, is not accessible to such instruction. Concerning the Thou he knows nothing except what he learns in the encounter. He is not in a position to make any statements, whether positive or negative, about what the Thou is in itself, aside from the fact that it encounters us. "We try to lift more than we can if we speak of it (the Thou) as something beyond the encounter,"[20] and this obviously applies even when we hazard the statement that it is "nothing." Hence we are astonished when Theunissen takes it upon himself to prove his thesis that the Thou is "nothing" out of Buber's words. I hope that no one will blame me for relating to these exegetic efforts with a substantial negative prejudice. I shall recur to this attempt at proof later.

If we are satisfied with what is given directly in the encounter, then the three realms of the worldly Thou have an advantage over the one-sided gropings of the "inborn" Thou: here the urge toward the Thou is met by realities which respond. Hence Buber can say that the inborn Thou actualizes itself in each of these relationships. Why he adds that it does not perfect itself in any of them,[21] we shall soon consider. This much has become clear: the encounters in the three spheres of the earthly Thou are real encounters. Whatever the encounter with the eternal Thou may add later on—it would no longer be an encounter if it set about to efface the factuality of these encounters. It must be in alliance with these encounters—however

we may attempt to understand this alliance. Hence Buber's passionate debate with Kierkegaard in "The Question to the Single One."
The choice with which Kierkegaard sees himself confronted—
whether to involve himself "essentially" with God *or* with humans—
is for Buber a "sublime misunderstanding" of God. It is an utterly
vacuous idea that God would require us to choose between Him and
His Creation.[22]

5

Thus on the extended line A-B, which leads at infinity to a point C,
I cannot eliminate the point B and content myself with the sufficiently
determined straight line A-C, without completely missing Buber's
intention. The finite Thou must remain immovably in its place if
Buber's basic concern is to be understood. There remains the other,
previously mentioned theoretical possibility of freeing the dialogical
construction from its overdetermination. We can construe Buber's
dialogical thought as a social ontology whose legitimate subject is the
relation of the I to its finite Thou. By arbitrarily extending line A-B
beyond itself to a point in infinity where it must intersect with all its
parallels, I still do not acquire the right to load this imaginary, purely
constructed point with the full weight of a content borrowed from
religious tradition. Such an assertion assumes that Buber, in addition
to his experience of faith, had an I-Thou philosophy which would be
separated objectively, even though not biographically, from that
experience. This separation, which Buber could not perform for
personal reasons which certainly must be respected, Theunissen is
now ready to perform in his stead.

For this purpose the teaching of the I-Thou relationship must be
developed in such a manner that it remains autarkic, one must dim
the religious perspective which it opens. Its point of departure is
transcendental philosophy, which in its general outlines parallels
Buber's teaching of I-It. This is the part from which Buber's *I and
Thou* pushes off toward a new continent asserted or discovered by
dialogical philosophy. Hence, one may ask which new aspects does it
bring to the already existing stores of philosophy. From this argument it is clear that the cross-examination to which Theunissen
subjects the new beginning is being conducted with the old categories, or, in Buberian language, with the concepts of the It-world.

But in this order of investigation the Aristotelian opposition be-

tween the "first for us" and the "first in itself" has not been taken into
account. Theunissen has shown extensively that the source of dialogical thought, as far as the history of problems is concerned, is
transcendental philosophy.[23] But the innovation of dialogical thought
was not intended as an addition to the teaching of I-It, as a problematic kind of exception within the It-world, but as a new foundation
vis-à-vis which the It-world was to be secondary. Whoever critically
contemplates the Thou-world on the conditions of the It-world
cancels out that step. The philosophical opponent is at liberty to do
this, but then he can no longer pose as an interpreter of the text from
within.

The twilight area which results from the blurring of boundaries
between these two roles seems to me to be responsible for the way
Theunissen interprets his argument that the Thou is "nothing." The
argument is almost self-evident to the critic determined to classify
the Thou-world among the aspects of the It-world. Whatever is not a
thing among things can hardly be anything other than nothing.[24] Not
having absorbed in his analysis the fact that for Buber the Thou-world
is not a variation of the It-world, but the primary foundation from
which the It-world is derived by alienation, he evidently expects a
similar judgment from Buber. But as already stated, it would be a
blatant inconsistency if Buber were willing to subject the Thou to a
"what is . . . ?" question. Theunissen[25] finds the support he so
confidently expects in Buber's explanation: "Whoever says You does
not have something, he has nothing. But he stands in relation."[26] Only
he who has been expecting with certainty the definition of an essence
will find it in this sentence. Rather, what is being emphatically stated
is: the Thou, in contrast to the It, is not something one *has*. We would
not need Gabriel Marcel's book which, parallel to Buber, places the
opposition between the Thou-world and the It-world under the signs
of the verbs *être* and *avoir*, to make this interpretation secure. Buber
had long since dismissed the question of the ontological status of that
to which I stand in relationship. But Theunissen continues undeviat-
ingly. Having acquired the sentence that the Thou is nothing, he
applies it to weigh all Buber's other writings concerning the Thou. At
one point he is even so careless as to apply his sentence, which he
merely "derived" from Buber's statement, retroactively to the same
statement, obtaining the result:[27] "Because the Thou *is* nothing,
whoever says Thou also *has* nothing" (italics in the original). Here,
then, Theunissen knows an ontological reason for what Buber merely
experiences. He is in a position to draw from the behavior of the Thou

in the encounter a stringent conclusion about its being. And here, too, he does not seem to sense how far he has moved from Buber, who said: "When we walk on our way and encounter a man who comes toward us, walking his way, we know our way only and not his; for his comes to life in the encounter . . . But we try to lift more than we can if we speak of it as something beyond the encounter."[28] There can be little doubt that Buber would have seen in Theunissen's venturing to abstract a definition of the partner from the experience a flagrant case of such lifting more than we can.

From this fortified position, Theunissen[29] approaches a Buberian statement which poses for him, given his exegetical assumptions, peculiar problems. Buber's words are: "What, then, does one experience of the You?—Nothing at all. For one does not experience it.— What, then does one know of the You?—Only everything. For one no longer knows particulars."[30] I can no more find in these sentences the claim that the Thou is everything than the claim that the Thou is nothing. But for Theunissen, Buber here is making an "about face": "the Nothing transforms itself into Being and thereby 'nothing' becomes 'everything.' " Without going into the question of the legitimacy of the presumed "about face," we may simply note that with its help the "everything" is absorbed as a dubious variant of the "nothing." Moreover, there is no consideration of the fact that in Buber's scale of values an "everything" which is "known" must have more weight than a "nothing" which is "experienced." The "nothing" as essence of the Thou is already so firmly established for Theunissen that small inconsistencies can no longer call the general picture into question.

But the decisive superiority which the "nothing" has over the "everything" as a characteristic of the Thou in Theunissen's interpretation of Buber, has a deeper root. The question of the essence of the Thou in Buber's dialogical thought to which Theunissen— erroneously, in my opinion—attributes central importance, acquires its full trenchancy when one comes to speak of the eternal Thou. For according to Buber every worldly Thou must by natural necessity sink back again, into the status of the It. Therefore it is also It, and as such is assured of its natural subsistence as an It among Its. True, when it leaps into the "Thou" state and becomes present to us, nothing new—according to Theunissen—is added to its existence, since the Thou is supposed to be "nothing"; but the existence of the world of things stands on another basis. But the eternal Thou, according to Buber, does not have this security of the It to fall back on; the eternal Thou is "the You that in accordance with its nature cannot become an It."[31] All the audacity of Theunissen's interpretation is characterized by the fact that this distinction of the eternal Thou, which exempts it from becoming an It, and hence from the dread of alienation is seen by him as a *deficiency* of the eternal Thou. Since it is only Thou and nothing else besides, and since Thou in itself is "nothing," point C in infinity, at which the parallels intersect, is thereby exposed as an imaginary point. All Buber's asseverations, which come from a root not relevant here, cannot restore to the eternal Thou the infinite fullness of being which sober analysis has taken from it.

Theunissen attempts by glancing at Buber's own teaching about God to confirm that for Buber the philosopher, however little he admits it to himself, God is, in a more radical sense than any other Thou, Nothing. He analyzes Buber's statements on the eternal Thou one by one and shows that they have a basically negative character, that is, they express what God is *not*. With this it seems to him that Buber indirectly admits his failure to establish a theology of his own, and hence Theunissen feels justified in using the word theology, in relation to Buber, only in quotation marks.

I spoke at the outset of the necessity in which Buber finds himself of speaking of the Thou in an It-language. Where the eternal Thou is to be discussed, the pertinent It-language is of course theology. Now all theological literature, when it hazards statements concerning the Divinity, has at its disposal two alternative methods, the *via elationis* and the *via negationis*. Precisely with his negative attributes of the Divinity, Buber joins a long and distinguished line of theologians of all denominations, of whom Maimonides, in Judaism, is the most famous. It is impossible to elaborate here what is expressed time after time in descriptions of theological efforts toward forming a concept of God: that it is precisely the negative attributes of God that generally convey a lofty content of faith that cannot find an ideational symbol in any more direct form.

But in Theunissen's view the negative formulation seals the judgment that the eternal Thou, not being anchored in an It, is a mere boundary concept, to whose "nothingness" the philosopher can in no wise give substance. All the aforementioned assumptions of Theunissen's criticism finally gather themselves for the decisive blow which is to strike at the center of Buber's teaching on the eternal Thou: "There is no relation to God."[32] In the reasoning with which Theunissen accompanies this decisive thesis, Buber is as it were stood on his head: "There is actually no relationship *to* God, because God is not an objective point of reference." Buber characterizes as "objective" the It in contrast to the Thou; therefore there can be no relation to God, because He is Thou and not It. Here is no longer any possibility of an understanding with Buber, for whom "relation" constitutes the superiority of the Thou over the It. And so Theunissen must forbear to cite Buber himself as the authority for his destructive conclusion. He cannot avoid acknowledging that Buber does indeed speak of such a relation. But the fact that Buber asserts the relation with the eternal Thou is nothing in comparison to the fact that precisely this relation was the real motive force of his life's work: "the Baal Shem's converse with God" was what did not let him escape from the fascination of Hasidism; exposing the immediate relationship to the eternal Thou is the real enterprise of his Bible translation and Bible interpretation; it compels him to struggle against the religious establishment; from it flows his ethic of "responsibility," which also determined his position with respect to nationalism and his position in inner-Jewish politics; and from it, finally, stems his philosophical effort to find an worldly counterpart to the man-God relationship in life with the earthly Thou. This thesis, to which Theunissen regretfully misses Buber's resigned acquiescence, is nothing more nor less than a negation of Buber's existence, including his philosophy.

Nevertheless Theunissen cannot resist trying to find some support for his thesis in Buber's writings, an attempt which is of methodological interest. When Buber begins his presentation of earthly encounters with the sentence "Three are the spheres in which the world of relation arises"[33] and then specifies life with nature, with men and with spiritual beings, he leaves no room for a third kind of encounter, which is to be the highest and the perfect one, namely the encounter with God. Therefore, Theunissen infers,[34] what is later wrongly designated as relation to the eternal Thou can mean nothing other than the leading to its completion of the presentness of the already acquired Thou, so that it no longer has "bounds"[35] and all It is included in this presentness. When Buber says,[36] "In every You we address the eternal You," Theunissen understands the eternal Thou as something which is "in" this separate Thou and develops in it. Theunissen's argument may most briefly be expressed in our formula: If the line A-B designates the I-Thou relationship in its various developments, then there can be no other point C on the same line which makes a further original contribution to the I-Thou. The possibilities are already exhausted. However conclusive this chain of reasoning is, we have already seen that Buber cannot be closed in by it: not only his philosophy, but also his whole spiritual existence forms a passionate protest against it.

6

Thus neither of the two simplifications of the three-pointed line suffices to contain the meaning of Buber's teaching and existence. "The innate You is actualized each time (in every finite relationship) without ever being perfected."[37] If only the eternal Thou is in the field of vision, the relationships are deprived of their realization; if only the separate Thou, they are deprived of their perfection. Each of the two relations, therefore, must continue to stand in its full meaning.

Such would be no extraordinary demand. The view that man lives simultaneously in two circles, or that his duties may be arrayed in two basic categories, those toward God and those toward his fellowman, is accepted in many religions and philosophies. But such an interpretation would err toward the decisive element in Buber's teaching. Mathematically speaking, the three points A, B, and C lie on one and the same straight line. The same way that leads to the "world" leads to God. "Looking away from the world is no help toward God; staring at the world is no help either."[38] And if the world is to be a world in which the Thou has its place, then we may add in Buber's sense: staring fixedly at the world is no help toward the world either. The two aspects must be fully dependent upon each other. And yet each one of them must remain in its original independence. That is the Buberian paradox of the three-point line. Where he speaks of the earthly I-Thou relationship, as it occurs in the three spheres of encounter, he closes with a hint which leads further:[39] "In every sphere, through everything that becomes present to us, we gaze toward the train of the eternal You; in each we perceive a breath of it; in every You we address the eternal You, in every sphere according to its manner." Here the "separate" Thou is present, the eternal, however, is only intuited. We do not stand before its countenance, we merely gaze toward its train. This is one of the passages which could lead us to think that Buber knows a real relationship only to the earthly Thou, whereas God is only an idea, intuited on the farthest horizon.

But we have also to cite the parallel passage from the third part of *I and Thou*:

The demanding silence of forms, the loving speech of human beings, the eloquent muteness of creatures—all of these are gateways into the presence of the word.

But when the perfect encounter is to occur, the gates are unified into the one gate of actual life, and you no longer know through which one you have entered.[40]

Here the eternal Thou is no longer intuited at an immeasurable distance; man has covered the distance and has entered in at the gate. The word, the eternal Thou, God is present. But the event of encounter has lost its presentness. You know that the earthly encounters have led you up to this gate, but everything that encounters you has now become One.

Thus, as in the presence of the earthly event the eternal Thou is only intuited on the horizon, so on the one hand, when man enters into the gate of the Divine Presence, the exact contours of what lay before the gate become blurred. In other words there can be no earthly event of encounter in which, however vaguely, the eternal Thou does not appear on the horizon, and there can be no entrance into the gate of the real life in the presence of the Divine Word at which man has not arrived through the earthly encounter. The impossibility of severing this connection is Buber's deep concern.

From this comes Buber's much-discussed reservation against the formation of a separate sacral realm. In such a formation he always senses the danger of isolating the relation to the eternal Thou from the "world." The world of earthly relationship as the true sphere in which God is served is in danger when an institutionalized sphere of worship, which is to be represented as "service to God," is cordoned off. His resistance against sacral actions as such is not as general as it seems. To be sure, at this time he is unable to ascribe legitimacy to any act of Divine worship. But for his attitude as a whole what he says on one occasion about the meaning of a sacral architecture seems to me symptomatic: "This simple essential turning 'thither' has today, in my observation, become something rare and lone. A liturgical or a sacramental occurrence with its techtonic place—ark, altar—can represent and thus make a home for that There; when it displaces it, it obstructs it."[41] Hence for the sake of the immediacy of the turning to God Buber rejects the established ritual; it would be a complete misunderstanding to conclude that Buber's God can only be intuited and thought about, but not addressed.

But the real language with which man addresses God is his action in the world, namely the redemption of the world from its alienation, from the decline of the Thou to an It. The separation between "state" and "church," between "spiritual" and "worldly" concerns, the "mentality of compromise" with which a purified faith makes itself at home in an unredeemed world, seemed to him the hereditary evil of European civilization.[42] The field in which believing man's relation to God must prove itself is human society.

Thus the people of Israel were for Buber a community standing before God. A covenant concluded between God and this community, which does not constitute itself as a "church," but remains a "people" in the whole breadth of its reality, cannot lead to a separation between a "sacred" and a "profane" domain. This community must regain its natural basis, its own land, because only activity in a naturally developing society can give Judaism a test by which to prove itself. We are not sent into the world to teach it that there is one God, but "to show it how God lives in us" (the statement comes from Buber's earlier, mystical phase; in the dialogical phase he would probably have said "among us" rather than "in us"). Thus the building of a true human community became the content of his Zionism. Concerning the manner of realization of this ideal his views diverged very far from those of the political leadership, but such differences could not lead to a separation from the Zionist undertaking. The formula of "critical identification," in which he summarized his relation to the state of Israel, was for him an inner necessity, for Israel as the meeting-point of the relationship with God and the relationship with man was and remained for him the key to his battle against the alienation of life and of the world. In this lies his lasting value as an interpreter of Judaism.

But that is another story.

Discussion Following Yehoshua Amir's Lecture

B. CASPER

You have given us a truly outstanding description of the interlocking of the encounter with the Other and the encounter with God. But your report did not quite do justice to Theunissen. His central question is: how can I as a philosopher grasp the Other as Other?

Y. AMIR

I am glad that Prof. Theunissen, who was unfortunately prevented from coming here, has found such an able representative. I must admit that I did not have the intention—nor the expertise—to confront Theunissen's central concern. For the theme of our conference I found his book relevant only insofar as it deals with Buber's theology, or "pseudo-theology," as Theunissen calls it in accordance with his views. The Other as the other human being, who is central to Theunissen's book, is not the question from which Buber starts. In my opinion it is only because of the relationship with God, which Buber discovered when he turned to dialogical thought, that dialogue enters into his new vision of human community. Theunissen's critical strategy in dislodging Buber from the encounter with God strikes at the heart of his thought. To reduce Buber to the social ontologist is to be left with something which is essentially not Buber. These questions with which I have been dealing are only tangential to Theunissen's main concern.

Notes

YEHOSHUA AMIR

1. Martin Buber, *I and Thou*, A new translation with a Prologue "I and You" and Notes by Walter Kaufmann, Charles Scribner's Sons, New York, 1970, p. 123 (Kaufmann translates du as "You" and not the generally accepted Thou).
2. Ibid., p. 6.
3. Michael Theunissen, *Der Andere: Studien zur Sozialontologie der Gegenwart*, de Gruyter, Berlin, 1965, p. 342.
4. Buber, Briefwechsel aus sieben Jahrzehnten, II: 1918-1938, ed. by Grete Schaeder, Lambert Schneider, Heidelberg, 1963, p. 99.
5. Rivka Horwitz, *Buber's Way to I and Thou*; an historical analysis and the first publication of Martin Buber's lectures "Religion als Gegenwart", Lambert Schneider, Heidelberg, 1978.
6. Ibid.
7. See "Zur Geschichte des Dialogischen Prinzips", Werke I, Kösel-Verlag, Munich, and Verlag Lambert Schneider, Heidelberg, 1962, p. 298: "when I wrote the third and last part". These words are most naturally understood as also referring to the temporal conclusion of a work.
8. Horwitz, op. cit., p. 7.
9. Ibid., p. 6, cf. especially note 37; "Herut: On Youth and Religion", *On Judaism*, ed. by Nahum Glatzer, Schocken, New York, 1967, pp. 149-174.
10. In *On Judaism*, pp. 108-148. According to Hans Kohn (*Martin Buber: Sein Werk und Seine Zeit*, J. Melzer Verlag, Köln, 1961, p. 171) this address was given in May, 1918.
11. *On Judaism*, p. 109.
12. Ibid., p. 110.
13. Ibid.
14. Buber, "Replies to My Critics", in *The Philosophy of Martin Buber*, ed. by Paul Arthur Schilpp and Maurice Friedman, Cambridge University Press, London, 1967, p. 689.
15. E.g. Fr. Ebner and Florens Christian Rang.
16. *I and Thou*, p. 26.
17. Buber, *Briefwechsel* II, p. 133.
18. *I and Thou*, p. 6.
19. *Der Andere*, pp. 301-307.
20. *I and Thou*, p. 76.
21. Ibid., p. 75.
22. Buber, "The Question to the Single One", *Between Man and Man*, trans. by Ronald Gregor Smith, Becon Press, Boston, 1955, p. 54.
23. *Der Andere*, pp. 252ff.
24. Ibid., p. 302.
25. Ibid., p. 301.
26. *I and Thou*, p. 4.
27. *Der Andere*, p. 314.

28. *I and Thou*, p. 76.
29. *Der Andere*, p. 306.
30. *I and Thou*, p. 10.
31. Ibid., p. 75.
32. *Der Andere*, p. 334.
33. *I and Thou*, p. 6.
34. *Der Andere*, pp. 333ff.
35. *I and Thou*, p. 4.
36. Ibid., p. 6.
37. Ibid., p. 76.
38. Ibid., p. 79.
39. Ibid., p. 6.
40. Ibid., p. 102.
41. Martin Buber, *A Believing Humanism*, Simon and Schuster, New York, 1967, p. 123.
42. Buber, "Der Staat und die Menschheit," *Der Jude und sein Judentum*, J. Melzer, Köln, 1963, p. 302.

A Critical Review of Martin Buber's *Epistemology of* I-Thou

STEVEN T. KATZ

Introduction

Given the occasion which called forth the essays contained in this volume I hope it will not be considered out of place if I begin this paper with the following personal comment. I did not, unfortunately, like most of the participants in this symposium, have the "zechuth" (merit) of knowing Buber—yet I too value his memory. I have learned more than can be said from his work, even when, as is often the case, I am in fundamental disagreement with it. But more than his books, the *man* has been important to me. I trust it will not be misunderstood if I say that it now seems clear to me that Buber was greater than his philosophy. Perhaps this is, in fact, the signal tribute to be paid to the author of *I and Thou* who always was impatient with philosophical abstractions, who always criticized classical philosophers for their unconcern for the quality of life as compared to their concern with theories or ideas.

Some Exegetical Preliminaries

This occasion calls for a large assessment of Buber's philosophical work, rather than a narrow focusing in on more particular philosophical topics. Nothing is more essential in drawing this wider picture than an appreciation of the structural elements—drawn in broad strokes—of Buber's epistemology. To begin, a brief review of certain foundational factors is required.

I. Buber's Kantianism

A close reading of Buber's work, especially if formed by a reasonable acquaintance with Kantian and post-Kantian German Idealism, will reveal a significant dependence of Buber on the Kantian tradition. Not only did the great master of Königsburg save him from madness at the age of 15, but he remained *the* philosopher, *the* philosophical influence on Buber's mature thought as spelled out in *I and Thou* and other post World War I works. This abiding influence is still very clearly seen even in such late works as "Distance and Relation". We need *not* (nor does space allow) review the specific details of this dependence, let it suffice to note that Buber's system is structurally and fundamentally built on the back of Kantianism.[1] Buber assumes for his own work that Kant is, in some fundamental way, right. We see this more clearly in his dichotomous account of reality described through the realms of *I-Thou/I-It* which parallels Kant's noumenal/phenomenal distinction in striking ways. We can begin to explicate this dependency by first noting the structural items: (a) Like Kant, Buber sees the world as essentially "two-fold"; (b) Kant's understanding of "noumenal" reality is the *basis*, though, of course, not the sum total, of Buber's understanding of the *I-Thou* reality; (c) Kant's understanding of "phenomenal" reality is the basis, indeed here much more nearly the entire basis, of Buber's understanding of *I-It* reality. These three structural items can be fleshed out through a consideration of the following:

1. For both Kant and Buber "what we know" is determined by "how we know", i.e. the "knower" is central to all epistemic activity even to the point of determining that which is known as well as the conditions under which it is known. In Kant's system the categorical conditions of mind determine the "phenomenal" nature of things, whereas in Buber's account the knower, the *I*, determines through his activity whether he enters into and 'encounters' reality in all its manifoldness as *Thou or It*, i.e., as *I-Thou* or *I-It*. One must always remember that it is not any 'fixed' nature of the 'other' that determines its character for us but rather our relation to it, i.e. we can have either *I-Thou* or *I-It* relations with the same "thing". Likewise Kant's "noumena" is not something different from "phenomena" rather it is the same reality "known" differently, i.e. without the structure imposed by the categories of mind.

2. The general specifications provided by Kant of what constitutes phenomenal knowledge is nearly exactly duplicated by Buber in his description of the *It*. Both the "phenomenal", and after it, the "*It*" reality are defined by the presence of the following conditions: (a) determined by and subjected to the co-ordinates of spacial location and temporal succession; (b) determined by and subjected to the laws of causality; (c) available, because of its orderliness, to us as *objective* knowledge. Indeed it is only "phenomenal" reality that we can claim

to *know* in the objective sense; (d) as a consequence of (a), (b), (c) it can be described in language; (e) as a consequence of (a), (b), (c), (d) it is subject to the rules of logic.

3. Kant's understanding of the "noumena" is the basis for Buber's *Thou*. I note only the basis for here Buber's relation to Kant stands at the end of a century of post-Kantian thought which had already well begun the alteration and widening of the concept of *noumena* which it had inherited. Nevertheless the basic structure is the same. Note should be taken that both "noumena" and *Thou* are not subject to (a) to (e) as set out in 2 above describing "phenomena" and *It* respectively. (For a more detailed description of *Thou* see pp. 5-7 below.) As a general observation on this whole structure it is clear to see that Kant gave Buber, as he had given to the whole 19th Century, the doctrine both of fixed limits to "knowledge" i.e., phenomenal reality, as well as the grounds for holding that the sum of the real extended beyond the phenomenal. In this sense his remark in the "Introduction" of *The Critique of Pure Reason* is to be taken with the utmost seriousness: "I have destroyed reason in order to make room for faith."

Moreover, though Kant essentially limited even our contact with the noumenal to morality he did postulate the general nature of the noumenal which Buber among many others followed. That is, the *noumenal* is a realm of freedom, i.e., it operates independently of the limiting conditions which govern the phenomenal, which one relates to by means of an "intuitive" apprehension. Kant's technical term for this sort of apprehension was "practical reason" as compared to the "pure reason" which provides one objective knowledge gained in the phenomenal realm. Likewise, Buber's epistemology is built around the asserted "intuitive" apprehension possible of others as *Thou*. The term "intuitive" is used advisedly with regard to Buber's position and is based on the recognition of his demands that awareness of an 'Other' as *Thou* is *not* subject to any of the ordinary epistemic conditions which operate in the domain of objective knowledge, i.e., it *necessarily excludes* all the limiting conditions noted in 2a to e outlined above. As a consequence, Buber following Kant, argues that the "knowledge" gained in such epistemic situations is not only different from that gained in *It/phenomenal* matrixes but that it is also subject to altogether different rules of meaning and criteria of verification, if one indeed can legitimately speak of verification in these altered circumstances at all.

This brief sketch of the basic skeletal parallelism and dependence will have to suffice in support of my contention of Buber's indebtedness to Kant's position. Moreover, Buber's philosophical anthropology, as well as his ontology and epistemology, has its roots here. Of course, all these themes become deepened, in some cases even transmogrofied, after Kierkegaard and Nietzsche, but their basic explanatory force remains Kantian.

We have taken the time to examine Buber's relationship to Kantianism not in order to enquire into questions of historical primacy, i.e., who said what first; or to belittle Buber's own contribution. Rather it is done to highlight a fact that seems almost always underplayed if not ignored altogether by Buber's scholars, namely, the ultimate success of Buber's epistemology, as of his philosophy as a whole, depends on the correctness of some form of Kantian Idealism. We shall return to consider the implications of this element in Part II of this paper.

II.   I-Thou/I-It[2]

As the basic epistemological skeleton of Buber's dialogical philosophy is constructed around his famous *I-Thou/I-It* dichotomy it is important to briefly spell out, in a shorthand summary, my understanding of its essential characteristics, for it is on the basis of this understanding that I shall later predicate certain reservations. I begin by noting the general rule that for Buber *I-Thou* are 'personal' relations and *I-It* are 'impersonal' relations, but one must remember that according to Buber's basic metaphysical *I-It/I-Thou* schema one can have 'personal' (i.e. *I-Thou*) relations with non-persons, e.g., objects of nature, and 'impersonal' (i.e. *I-It*) relations with persons.

The Term *I-It* in Buber's thought is the counterpart of what is referred to in a more philosophical language as the subject-object relation. In such a relation the self, the subject, treats all objects of experience, including other men, and all possible content of human knowledge as things which can be ordered and itemized but which, though adding to the information and experience of the knower, in no way touch the deeper level of his personal existence and the meaning of his own life. *I-It* relation is primarily a utilitarian relation. The *I* observes, calculates, uses, manipulates the *It* (even if another person) for his advantage without concern or regard for that which is the object of consideration or manipulation. The prominent feature of such a relation is the detachment which governs the intercourse between the active knowing consciousness and the object to which this consciousness is directed. This is not to suggest that in such relation the knower and known are unrelated as this would contradict Buber's relational premise that everything is in some relation, rather it is to suggest that in such relationships the parties do not 'affect' each other. "The object may be 'present', but we are not in the 'presence' of the object."

The most general characteristics of *I-It* relations, strongly reflecting that profound indebtedness of Kantian metaphysics already sketched, are to repeat: (1) they operate under and reflect the law of causality—causality has an unlimited reign in the world of *It*—and (2) they are located in and regulated by space and time: The world of *It* is set in the context of space and time. (3) As a consequence of (1) and (2) Buber argues the important proposition that all objective knowledge is by definition *I-It* because such knowledge is inextricably linked to and requires the causal and spatio-temporal nexus. In addition to these metaphysical categories, objective knowledge requires sytactical and semantical correctness, logical coherence, rules of criteria, falsifiability, verification and evidence. All these objectivity concepts are, according to Buber, opposite to the dialogical immediacy of *I-Thou*. Moreover, Buber argues, all knowledge gained through *I-It* relation is necessarily indirect and mediate.

I-Thou

To understand what Buber means by an *I-Thou* relation it is helpful to begin by simply inverting the description of *I-It*. Thus when *I-It* is a "subject-object" relation, *I-Thou* is not; When *I-It* is determined by its subjugation to indexical procedures, to categorization, to refined and precise measurement, *I-Thou* is not. If in *I-It* the knowing self is unaffected in an essential way by the relation, in *I-Thou* the opposite is true. Whereas causality and the spatio-temporal order reign supreme in the world of I-It, in I-Thou other conditions are operative. Just as *I-It* knowledge is mediate and indirect, *I-Thou* is immediate and direct. Significantly, in so far as *I-It* is neutral on matters of moral concern, *I-Thou* is not.

We gain a great deal of information from this not very rigorous inversion. However, what one learns from such an oblique method is limited: positive statement of Buber's doctrine is required. But here a serious difficulty arises because Buber claims that language does not make a true 'fit' with *I-Thou*—*I-Thou* can only be pointed to, it cannot be described. (This claim is itself of major critical importance and we shall return to it.) Description itself is a characteristic of *I-It* and is out of place in *I-Thou*. Despite Buber's insistence on this point, I shall make some statements about *I-Thou* for two reasons. First, and in anticipation of my critical view on the issue of the relation of *I-Thou* to language, because I maintain that Buber's position here needs to be rethought, and second, because despite this cautionary proviso, Buber actually does provide his readers with a considerable amount of descriptive information on all aspects of *I-Thou*, notwithstanding his assertions to the contrary.

Buber fills out the skeleton of *I-Thou* relation as follows: (1a) In *I-Thou* relation, both partners retain their own subjectivity in the encounter and (1b) in the meeting one is aware of the other as a subject. The *I* of the primary word *I-Thou* makes its appearance as a person and becomes conscious of itself as subjectivity.[3]

(2) Learning that the "other" is a subject means learning that the "other" is essentially a free being like the knowing self: an echo of Kant's noumenal self. Man is unique in creation in that he alone possesses possibility and potentiality. This awareness brings with it the recognition that the constitutive properties of the *Thou* cannot be measured, quantified or translated into propositions.

(3) The freedom of *I-Thou* entails the total autonomy of both dialogical partners. To act in accordance with external rules is heteronomy, and this violates the premised freedom of the 'other' as *Thou* and the self as *I*.

(4) As *I-Thou* encounter is an intersubjective relation between equals, at least in terms of their relation to each other for the duration of the encounter, this relation is characterized by its mutuality. This is an especially important feature of *I-Thou* meeting. The symmetry of the relation is a basic premise of the whole dialogical life.

(5) What emerges from *I-Thou* relation, and only from *I-Thou* relation, is not objective knowledge but rather an ontological certainty about the foundations of one's life and a surety about the unbreakable umbilical cord which runs from man's spiritual navel to the centre of Being itself. This presentness, Buber tells us, 'does not help to sustain you in life, it only helps you to glimpse eternity'.[4]

III.   Revelation

Separate note must be taken of a, if not *the*, central component of Buber's dialogical outlook—his account of revelation and the role it plays in his thought for two reasons. First, in Buber's epistemology the kind of knowing which is labeled "I-Thou" is synonymous in character with what passes under another name as 'revelation'. The *I-eternal-Thou* relation is structurally parallel to human *I-Thou* dialogue, indeed is modeled in this epistemology on it. Secondly, Buber's is an epistemology wedded to a theistic metaphysics, i.e., Buber is aware in advance which objects of reality he wants to be available in his ontology as provided through epistemology and so constructs his epistemology accordingly.[5]

I will give a somewhat detailed outline of the constitutive elements of dialogical "revelation" because of the importance of the subject—and because despite its significance, little solid exegetical, not to say critical, work has been done on it. We can summarize the essential features of Buber's account, either stated or implied, in the following six propositions.

(1) God does not reveal propositions.

(2) Revelation is NOT about God, but about God acting on man.

(3) Because of (1) and (2), revelation, when translated into human life, must take on human meaning.

(4) Despite (3), and Buber would agree it is paradoxical, we still have in that which issues from revelation an authentic pointer to the original dialogical situation.

(5) The goal and the result of revelation is the improvement of man's own understanding of himself. Anthropological, rather than cosmological or metaphysical, insights result from revelation.

(6) Due to its anthropological character, revelation must have the following characteristics:

  (a) It can never be perfect; all human truth is always partial, limited and liable to error.

  (b) It can never be tested by any criteria, except the knowledge that one acts with the personal certainty that what one does has been revealed.

  (c) It can never be definitive: a 'once and for all' truth.

  (d) Man himself decides what calls to him as revelation, and only those things which he feels are addressed to him have obligatory force.

  (e) Responsibility to act in accordance with revelation

means one thing only: to act 'authentically', i.e., with "Kavanah" (inward concentration and full commitment).

(f)   Revelation must always remain personal, spoken to and acted upon only by the one addressed in dialogue.

(g)   It can never be the basis of universal prescriptions.[6]

(h)   As the content of revelation cannot be universalized, one can never know the meaning of revelation for a specific act in advance of the event.

(i)   There is always the possibility of new revelation whatever 'revelation' may be.[7]

Review of each of the items outlined is presently impossible, and for our limited purposes, unnecessary. We need only call attention to the most important and the most striking feature of this review, namely, Buber's insistence that man is incapable of understanding himself in isolation from God and that man's universe finds its direction and its grounds only there. Revelation informs us, and this is its essential epistemic—as well as metaphysical—purpose, that God alone justifies human existence by guaranteeing its essential integrity; without God, and without knowledge of God, man's life threatens to be engulfed by nihilism. The revelation of 'Presence', while unhelpful to those seeking the security of a finished way, provides, for Buber, a more profound existential (and ontological) certainty. Though revelation forces man to return to the world and to "realize creation" such revelation at one and the same time discloses the transcendent capacity, the ontic depth, of the immanent, which we now know not to be immanent alone.

Criticism

With these exegetical remarks we hope we have set the groundwork for the critical review of the outstanding features of Buber's epistemology to which we now turn.

I. Buber's Kantianism: A Criticism[8]

"Kantianism" is certainly the most suggestive and highly influential of all modern philosophical systems, yet, more and more it seems clear to me that for all its suggestiveness and explanatory force ultimately Kantianism is unacceptable, and hence any essentially post-Kantian system which takes over the fundamental epistemological and metaphysical skeleton of Kant's Critical Philosophy, as, for example, does Buber's, is also flawed. To state the most essential objections as simply as possible: (a) Kantianism is unable to protect itself against subjectivism of the sort evident in Buber's dialogical view, as well as in all the other existentialist heirs of Kant, and despite claims to the contrary, most existentialists are his heirs if only at one remove through Kierkegaard's position. Modern conceptual relativism is the logical outcome of the Kantian "Copernican" revolution. Given the conditions of knowledge and the role of the "knower" in Kant's speculations it is impossible for the final results of a Kantian-like position to avoid being construed as knowing only the "appearances" of "appearances", or, again as being unable to provide any conditions for determining the objective character of one's knowledge. This 'subjectivity' is clearly evident in Buber's epistemology, all his attempts to defend himself against such subjectivity, as well as his claims of success in this direction, notwithstanding. (b) The various transcendental metaphysics, among which I count the basic form of Buber's *I-Thou* outlook, modeled after that metaphysical schema sketched in the *Critique of Pure Reason* seem to me confused and finally incapable of justifying any coherent metaphysical schema and *ipso facto* Buber's metaphysical schema. Indeed, "transcendental deductions", in the Kantian sense, which it must be appreciated are constitutive and essential for the Kantian program, seem mistaken. The consequence of this is both to undermine the metaphysics of the critical philosophy and any subsequent philosophy which builds upon it, e.g. Buber's dialogical metaphysics. Though Buber does *not* provide anything like the elaborate architectonic arguments of the *lst Critique* it is evident that he assumes their essential validity. This implicit assumption, *in fact*, provides the *a priori* theoretical constellation of the dialogical structure. As a specific example, one might even argue that it is a paradigm, of what is being envisioned here consider Buber's employment of the inherited Kantian formulation of the nature and employment of space-time. Kant's dicta about the source of space-time being grounded in the 'self', the employment of space-time as the regulators of phenomenal reality and the inapplicability of the categories of space-time to the noumenal are all accepted by Buber and reappear in his own formulation of the nature of the realms of *I-Thou/I-It*. To briefly repeat for the sake of clarity my earlier exegesis of this particular structural dependency: *I-It* parallels the 'phenomenal', i.e., is subject to the category of space-time (& causality); *I-Thou* parallels the 'noumenal' and is not subject to the categories of space-time (or causality). The dependence and parallelism, however, has unacceptable consequences for a truly existential dialogical philosophy for many compelling reasons, only one of which can be discussed here. Buber's employment of these notions creates philosophical confusions because it stretches beyond any legitimate employment, the very character of the space-time-causality continuum and its absence as postulated in Kant's system. It must be remembered that Kant was careful to demand that while we postulate the noumenal, we do not have any further detailed information of its character. It is true Kant himself traversed his own limitations on talking about the noumenal in some of his formulations regarding morality, but he was sensitive to the problematic element in his very postulation of a noumenal reality, and certainly of saying anything about it. Buber, however, and here he is as much an heir of the 19th century neo-Kantians as of Kant himself, despite his constant attempt to eschew characterizations of *I-Thou* still said more than was permissible to say, ending up in unintelligible formulations. Consider, for example, with regard to our present consideration of the employment of the categories of space-time in the dialogical structure, the following difficulty: To say that *I-Thou* relation is a way of meeting that takes place *in* the space-time frame seems, given other conditions are met, to possess intelligibility while to say that space-time is only a capacity of selves, and then only of selves insofar as they relate to others in the form of *I-It*, makes all claims for *I-Thou* meeting difficult to maintain for it is hard to know what we mean by "I", "Thou" and "meeting" in such circumstances. What the non-spatio-temporal "meeting" of a non-spatio-temporal "I" and non-spatio-temporal "Thou" could be is unimaginable, even unintelligible. (c) Buberians, like their master, concentrate their attention on the explication and meaning of the *I-Thou* dimension. They tend to assume that the realm of *It* has been adequately anatomized by Kant and his Kant-like successors, leaving the real vacuum with regard to the explication of the *I-Thou* encounter and its corollaries. This, however, is a consequential error. Kant's description of the phenomenal was built on a now outmoded model of Newtonian physics and Euclidean geometry. After Einstein, Planck and Heisenberg this model is dead. Hans Reichenbach,[9] among others, has I believe, demonstrably shown the difficulties of being a Kantian after the theory of relativity. The significance for Buber of this fact is that he *cannot* describe, and then tend to ignore, the realm of *It* in the inherited Kantian fashion with any philosophical security. Then again, the realm of *It* and our encounters in the *I-It* relation are far richer, more pliable, more variegated, than the dialogical philosophy allows. Franz Rosenzweig already saw and communicated this to Buber on his first reading of the still unpublished manuscript of *Ich und Du*. To this objection Buber replied that indeed Rosenzweig was correct, but that *Ich und Du* was only the first volume in a larger work and this failure would subsequently be remedied, with the *It* receiving its proper due. These later volumes were never forthcoming; Buber never gave the *It* and the *I-It* relation their proper explication. The resultant distortion is significant not only because it fails to adequately represent the dimension of *It*, but also because it thus distorts the character of the dimension of the *Thou*, for *It* and *Thou* are two halves of one whole. What each 'reality' is, especially where its limits are and what its mode of interaction with its "other half" is, has a *definitive* effect on what the other is, especially what its parameters are, and how it interacts with its other half. It appears to me that we will require a more adequate, more contemporary, more technically sophisticated account of *I-It* if we are to get a proper equation regarding the relation and complementarity of *It* and *Thou*. And this account we must have for reality is of an integrated character.

In place of Kantianism a more sober philosophical realism seems to be required to account for our world, and our place in it. Only some form of philosophical "realism", accepted as a working hypothesis, seems able to account for all we have come to know about nature, and how we have come to know it. I think that, in his way, even Kant saw this point when he insisted that his position is one of empirical realism wedded to transcendental idealism. Unfortunately, the transcendental idealism undermines the empirical realism for it finally reduces both to "appearances" only. In summation of this point, the same may be said of Buber's epistemology of dialogue which, as a species or mutant, of idealism, is also unable to serve as the model for a contemporarily informed, philosophically rigorous theory of knowledge.

II. I-Thou/I-It: A Criticism

(1) The "I" of Relation

The I of man is twofold.
For the I of the primary word *I-Thou* is a different
I from that of the primary word *I-It*.

So Buber tells us in the opening paragraph of *I and Thou*. The relational quality of the *I* is here primary, its self-isolated character denied. But can this account, for all its real epistemic and metaphysical suggestiveness, be held or do we not need a different account of the *I*, even the *I* of *I-Thou* relation? Several theses need consideration.

(A) The concern to make central the relation defining character of the *I* does not adequately handle the reality which we usually know by the term "self-consciousness". I would argue that there is a form of "self-consciousness" which is neither to be classed as *I-It* nor as *I-Thou*, and that any such classification would be arbitrary or doctrinaire.

(B) The dialogical dictum looses sight of the fact that there *must* be, and this is a logical-ontological *must*, a necessary unifying center of consciousness which is *not* touched by talk of *I's*, *Thou's* and *It's* as this talk is presently performed. Here two clarificatory remarks are called for. The first is descriptive: Buber, again relying on Kant, does actually employ a doctrine of *self* which is close to the master's "transcendental unity of apperception", for example, in *Distance and Relation* he writes: "It is only man who replaces this unsteady conglomeration (sense data), ... by a unity which can be imagined or thought by him as existing for itself." (cf. here Kant's *Critique* B 130ff., A 117 and throughout.) And again, Buber's entire view of man as free and transcendental echoes Kant's noumenal "self" who is an autonomous moral being not subject to the constraints of the phenomenal environment, as Kant says: "But though I cannot know, I can yet 'think' freedom" (*Critique* B. XXVIII). Secondly, an evaluative remark: Buber needs to explicate the nature and implications of this self-consciousness, the character of this act of self-awareness which he notes "replaces this unsteady conglomeration . . . by a unity", though a philosophical description of the mechanics of this extraordinary yet necessary behaviour in a manner consistent

with his other dialogical requirements, especially in that its employment seems to violate the essential relational thesis which we quoted
above. Buber himself seems to have become increasingly aware of
this philosophical requirement after World War II and his most
sustained, yet still fragmentary and unsatisfactory efforts in this
direction, are to be found in his essay, which we have already
referred to, "Distance and Relation". Though incomplete Buber's
work in this direction is significant for it reflects Buber's continual re-
thinking of his position and its implications, and also indicates that he
became aware, as I would argue, that the employment of a doctrine
something like Kant's unity of self-consciousness, though shorn of its
full-blown transcendental Kantian superstructure, is a *necessity of
thought* in general; it is, perhaps, *the* basic necessity of human self-
consciousness. Thus, Buber came to recognize that he *must* employ it
even at the risk of self-contradiction, though trying, without too
much success, to accommodate it within his pre-existent dialogical
thinking.

(C) Given (A) and (B) we require a detailed investigation of the
nature of this "self" which provides, or put more strongly, which
makes possible, the conditions of all knowing, that is, the ordering of
all series of happenings into an assimilable form of reality which can
be coherently understood as a world, be it the world of *It's* or of
Thou's, of which *It's* and *Thou's* are part and are known as part.

As an element of this enquiry, we need to remember, as noted,
that there *must* be a self which sustains itself through time, which is
marked out especially by a common memory, if not by a common
body. Not only must there be an enduring order to external space-
time for it to be knowable, there must also be an enduring order to
what we might call internal self space-time for this order to be known
as knowledge. In other words, here we must entertain the question of
the conditions and criteria of the use of the term "I" in its empirical
and trans-empirical contexts.

Buber clearly did not enter into this sort of an inquiry in any
fundamental way. For whatever reason, he felt it incompatible with
his main dialogical objectives to enter this discussion. Yet, this
neglect is not a plus. For all philosophizing, including dialogical
philosophizing, has at some point to offer a thorough justification of
its anthropology. It has to argue—not just assert—a view on such
issues as: the mind-body problem; the correctness or otherwise of
philosophical behaviorism; the dilemma of "personal" ascriptions
without reference to a body; the relation of 1st person ascriptions,

their nature and conditions of predication, as compared to 3rd person ascriptions, and the like. In other words, we need a defensible theory of personal identity. Buber's account of the "I" which alternates according to its relational modality is *not* such a theory. It neither accounts for the enduring character of the "self" who enters into the chain of relational encounters as the subject, nor the nature of the identity of the "self" which is moulded by each encounter in succession so that throughout the sequence one can say either "it is all happening to me" or "it is all happening to 'X' ". It is the case that Buber relies generally on Kant's model, but this is not justifiable, even if Kant's model itself were adequate, which it is not. This is so because the thoroughly dialogical model which must be provided for the relational "I" of *I and Thou* is *not* that provided, and providable, for the isolated "I" of classical idealism. Indeed, this is one of the major attractions of *I-Thou*, but to sustain its attractiveness it must be able to supply a new dialogical theory of the self for which there is philosophical support. I take this to be one of the major items which Buber has left on the agenda of his heirs to accomplish.

(2) *I-It/I-Thou*

Though, as we have noted, there are difficulties with Buber's view of what is involved in knowing something in an *I-It* manner I will, due to lack of space, pass over them. More interesting will be to interrogate Buber's version of the epistemological characteristics of *I-Thou* knowing.

As Buber's account relies on his analysis of the sort of dialogical knowing found paradigmatically exemplified in interpersonal relations it is best to begin with these. The first question must be whether in knowing other persons as *Thou's* we are ever, or could ever be, completely free from objectivity concepts as Buber argues, or whether in contra-distinction to Buber, these delimiting and identifying concepts are necessary and integral to the knowing of others as *Thou* such as the absence of these concepts would preclude *all* knowledge of the other, including knowledge of the other as *Thou*. The most direct answer to this epistemological question is that in all inter-personal relations, no matter how intimate, we cannot do without objectivity concepts if the reality, and our knowledge of that reality, of the other with whom we are in relation is to be maintained. That is, we must take full cognizance of the substantial and particular nature of the *Other* in order to relate to him as a *Thou*. The concept of 'Thou-ness' is a conceptual abstraction however it is employed and to whomever it is applied.

Here it is instructive to consider the logic of pronouns, something which is always as philosophically difficult as it is necessary, especially in light of the essential pronominal character of Buber's epistemology. To do this, consider these two examples: (a) Buber and I say: "Beersheva is warm in January". Here we are both making the same assertion, i.e., ascribing the same predicate to the same object. But, (b) if Buber and I say: "I like Beersheva"—we are saying two different things though we are uttering the same words, because of the logic of "I"; namely, every "I" context is different because every "I" is different. Of course the same is generally true of the other 2nd and 3rd person pronouns, i.e., *Thou* or *You* can have many references. But here a proviso is required noting that the logic of *Thou* and *He* is *not* exactly the same as that of *I*, for several *I*'s can refer to a *You* (or *Thou*) and mean the same thing, i.e., Buber and I can both say "You" and be referring, for example, to Kierkegaard.

I believe that Buber caught this important fact: he chose to work with pronouns because he thought their inherent ambiguity would protect his concern for real people rather than philosophical abstractions, and this concern for "existing individuals" and their situation was itself seen as a reflection of what he took to be fundamental ontological realities. Thus his employment of a pronominal schema is integrally tied to his most fundamental anthropological cum ontological commitments. Recognizing these factors it is interesting to note that despite Buber's essentially correct intuition here he failed to appreciate its full weight and thus the results of his employment of this insight run counter to his intention.

To speak of *I*'s and *Thou*'s etc., as Buber does, fails to recognize the implications of the necessary ambiguity of pronouns; an ambiguity only clarified by providing more concrete contextual information about the *I*'s and *Thou*'s in question. Unfortunately, however, Buber's epistemology precludes the possibility of providing the needed concrete referential information because of the overly strict rules governing the employment of pronouns in Buber's epistemology. As a consequence, the primacy of pronouns produces, in spite of the existentialist intent, an abstract essentialist and reductionist quality, i.e., to use Kierkegaard's phrase, abstracting and reducing "existing individuals", to ghostlike *I*'s and *Thou*'s, which is the opposite effect of that desired. It even begins to appear that every time that one writes *I*, in accord with Buber's dialogical notation one means the same thing, some general class-indicator, rather than a particular existing being. This occurs because Buber's phenomenology does not allow reference back to the speaker of the *I*, or the addressee of the *You* or *Thou*, for such reference would require the abandonment of the strictly schizophrenic reading of the relation of *It* and *Thou*, i.e., to individuate the speaker of every "I" utterance means conditions of identity and identifying criteria which have been defined in advance by the dialogical philosophy as being only illegitimately applicable to *Thou's*. Note should also be taken that his individuation of the referent of pronouns would begin to involve us more directly not only in personal categories but also in ontological ones, for the items we count as filling out the notions of *I* etc. will be part of some ontological schema. That is to say, to describe the nature of being an *I* will involve a more determinate and concrete procedure relative to the detailed investigation and description of what sort of understanding one has of reality and its constitutive elements. Thus, for example, one will have to consider questions regarding such items as the relation of being an *I* to bodily and material conditions or alternatively, the possibility of disembodied existence, or again the conditions of being an *I* relative to the larger spatio-temporal manifold and the identifying conditions of all other individuals in one's ontology. Still further, one needs to enquire into issues such as the nature of memory in the criteria of establishing the identity of an *I*, the roles of names and naming, the difference between self-consciousness and our consciousness of others as well as the relation that obtains between physical and non-physical behaviour and identity. One can therefore begin to see that the quantification, i.e., the fleshing out, of the employed dialogical pronouns will begin to introduce, as well as to considerably deepen, some of the truly interesting aspects of the present dialogical philosophical situation.

These remarks about the relation of objectivity categories to dialogical language coupled with the character of pronominal speech suggest, as a consequence, that as a minimal condition for employing dialogical language meaningfully some identifying skeleton of the notion of *Thou* must be given and this will require understanding the indissoluble tie between *what* the other is and *who* the other is. This is necessary to avoid transposing the notion of *Thou* into a form which violates any acceptable standard of intelligibility. This means that when I know another as *Thou*, say in the case of husband and wife, I know my wife as *Thou* only in and through her being 'objectively' and determinately who and what she is. Of course there is more than her behavior and the related objectivity concepts in her being a *Thou* for me, but her behavior and aptitudes, and the corollary conditioning concepts, e.g., her bodily form, her spatio-temporal locus, her memory, her intelligence, her education, as well as all the manifest and introspective characteristics that constitute what can, for a short-hand, be called her personality and character, must also be present and not as incidentals or marginalia. Thus, for example, my relation is affected by my memory of past shared (as well as private) events, by my knowledge that we are building a life together and all the public and private realities this entails, and even by the simple yet easily overlooked facts that I know that she is a woman, she is my wife, she is the mother of my children. I do not just have a spontaneous *Thou* relation to her in some space-time vacuum. The meeting with my wife as *Thou* for me, i.e., my knowing her existentially as a true dialogical partner, is grounded firmly in space and in time and is the product of events and conditions in the general spatio-temporal continuum which Buber would separate off and relegate exclusively to *I-It*. Moreover, in any *I-Thou* relation with my wife the relation is affected by the assumption, which we would call in the everyday commonsense world "knowledge", that this Other who now stands over against me is the same One who stood there yesterday and will do so tomorrow. And this easy, unquestioned assumption (questioned only by philosophers!) rests on metaphysical, ontological, philosophi-cal, psychological, physical and social criteria which are integral to the other being a *Thou* for me; without them there is no other and there is no *Thou*. Likewise in the case of "knowing", i.e., relating to God, the *eternal Thou*, parallel assumptions about continuity and the like (all the metaphysical theses tied up in using the term 'God' or *eternal Thou*) and all that such assumptions imply is surely involved.

Moreover, with reference to the *eternal Thou* it should be noted that the oft used term 'Presence', i.e., that what is "revealed" in the dialogical moment is God's Presence and nothing more, only starts the epistemological discussion, it does not end it. The meaning of the 'Presence' of the *eternal Thou* is dependent on the meaning of *eternal Thou*, which in turn is an intelligible notion (i.e., a notion that is given its intelligibility) only within a larger linguistic cum metaphysi-cal framework. For example, the *eternal Thou* is meaningless to a Buddhist for his ontology has no place for such a personal God—nor even for permanent selves, *I's* and *Thou's*. Again, it is not enough to assert that revelation understood as 'Presence' means "event" and not content and thus that all talk of logic and criteria is out of place, for an 'event' is also something that has to be made sense of and it too clearly is grounded in the necessary conditions of our experiential life. Likewise, any valid account of what it is to be a person will involve bodily criteria and objectivity concepts and any valid account of the *eternal Thou* will involve similarly identifying predicates which are appropriate to His ontological status. These considerations force themselves upon even a dialogical outlook for they are of the essence of such unavoidable philosophical issues as the problem of identification and re-identification; continuity and discontinuity; permanence and impermanence; the attribution and use of 1st person ascriptions and other person ascriptions; the ability to specify with whom one is having a relation, etc. In other words, they are integral to any discussion of "selves" or persons, even be they dialogical "selves" or persons, i.e., *I's*, *Thou's* and *It's*. They certainly are consequential for a theological vocabulary which talks of God as *eternal Thou*.

Here the context must also be reconsidered. Buber's signal contribution is his insistence on the "social" inter-human nature of man's reality: "There is no I taken by itself." The direct consequence of this emphasis was the theory of dialogical relation with its demand that pre-eminence be given to relation over substance, a demand which has had the effect of radically altering the entire form and focus on the epistemological dimension. The insight contained in this Buberian re-orientation of the direction of thought is considerable, possessing the seeds of powerful illumination in many areas of philosophical concern. Yet one is uneasy with the account as it stands for Buber's fundamental intuition(s) about dialogical relation, the ontology of "the between", to use his technical designation of the correlative metaphisical issue, is under-developed. Though there are many pressing considerations with regard to it, I mention in line with our present concerns only one of them. Despite his intentions, can Buber maintain his existential claim that dialogue is true meeting with an Other when he insists that this encounter is a-spacial, a-temporal, wholly non-sensual, and non-experiential in all the ordinary senses? Can there be any residue of substantial meaning left in the notions of 'meeting', 'encounter', 'Other' and 'Thou' when all experiential and empirical content is denied them? Can there be any ontology of "the between" in such a situation? Likewise, can Buber's original intuition that we must understand our basic and most important relations to nature, other men and God in *personal* terms be maintained when the terms 'Person', 'personal', 'personality' are divorced from all behavioral or material predicates. Thus, to say: 'I encounter a Thou' when none of the ordinary limiting-conditions and experiential concepts apply is to over stretch the limits of language for we do not have a clear sense as to what is being asserted with regard to the terms 'encounter' and 'Thou'.

What seems to be the case is that Buber's use of 'encounter', 'meeting', 'Thou', etc. is at best metaphorical and analogical, dependent on the non-metaphorical use of these concepts in ordinary discourse, and that Buber's usages retain a descriptive appearance because of the covert retention of attachments which have been overtly rejected in his dialogical presuppositions. However, even this route may be closed to the philosophy of dialogue, for one has to consider whether we can properly understand an encounter to which no predicates apply even as a metaphor or analogue of ordinary encounters, or whether Buber has gone so far with his negative stipulations that even the notion of a metaphor or analogue is saying more than it is permissible to say. In any case, this metaphorical "justification" seems closed to Buber who explicitly tells us that: '*Thou* is no metaphor'.

This sort of difficulty is seen to be particularly acute in ascribing *Thou* predicates to God, i.e., as the *eternal Thou*, as all such predicates which are ascribed to things in this world are tied to experiential conditions obtaining as a minimum yet constitutive feature of such ascription. Yet in God's case, none of the ordinary experiential conditions obtain. In fact, God is defined, so it seems, by the very absence of these conditions. A necessary regressive logic seems to be operative in which every predicate is required to point beyond itself. In what sense then is God a 'person', even the *Absolute Person,* and in what sense is it legitimate to predicate 'personality' of the Divine? This is a crucial question and in Buber's work the way the problem presents itself is only a new way of putting a classical problem about God-language. To say that ascribing certain personal predicates to God is 'more appropriate' than ascribing impersonal notions like 'creator' is no answer in itself for this preference, this "appropriateness," has itself to be justified. Why is God more correctly spoken of as *Thou* or *eternal Thou* to be precise rather than as *Creator?* In what way is God a 'Person'? In what way the *eternal Thou?* What are the criteria of 'appropriateness'?

These critical considerations bring to the surface a related hermeneutical concern: the need for a more rigorous, more substantive, personalist, dialogical metaphysics. And this for two reasons. First, to disentangle the difficulties inherent in the *I-Thou* philosophy. Secondly, to support, or rather to deepen, the structural foundation of the positive accomplishments of the *I-Thou* position. Buber, like many if not most of his existentialist colleagues, has erred in thinking that a considered disregard, one might even say disrespect, for metaphysics is a satisfactory substitute for it. This is not the case; and dealing with such issues as man, nature and God it is doubly not the case. Firstly, a statement critical of metaphysics is at least partly a metaphysical statement. Again, every philosophically interesting proposition in, for example, *I and Thou* or *Between Man and Man*, is wedded, if only implicitly, to an entire spider's web of metaphysical assumptions from which it is spawned, toward which it appeals for intelligibility and support, and whose structural contour or dynamic principle(s) it is trying to explicate or point to. Not to appreciate this, not to see the profound philosophical implications of this, is not to be philosophically self-reflective. It is a dis-service to the valuable insights of the philosophy of dialogue to leave it as a philosophy without a metaphysics.

(3) Revelation

We need now to briefly review the epistemological implications of Buber's account of revelation. Its importance and complexity have to illuminate the world we live in and the phenomenological character of the human situation.

Our line of criticism will center on item 6 of our outline given in the first half of this paper, that is, items 6a-6i, of our description of Buber's account. We begin with a consideration of the position which emerges from the cluster of views in 6c to 6g. This means beginning with the familiar question: "What does the concept of 'revelation' mean?" On the negative side we know, from the combination of items (1), (2), (6a), (6b), (6g), that it does *not* mean a set of perfect, eternal and universal propositions. Further, it does not mean information about God in Himself, or about God's will. Switching to the positive, we must go more slowly. We know it is supposed to entail God's "Presence"; that it means human form and human meaning, and that it guarantees that life is authentic and salvage from the absurdity of sheer radical contingency. But we must ask, do we know what it really means to talk in this way?

Let us ignore this question for still another moment, and consider instead the implications for dialogical existence of items 6c through 6h.

> The key to truth is the next deed, and this key opens the door if one does what one has to do in such a way that the meaning of the action here finds its fulfillment.[10]

When the 'presence' is translated into human life, no specific program of prescribed actions is necessarily entailed by the "revelatory" event. Here, instead, we have the result of the coalescence of four major trends in Buber's thought: (1) his pansacramentalism; (2) his antinomianism; (3) his adaptation of the thesis that 'truth is subjectivity' in the light of his understanding the Hasidic *Kavanah* and the influence of Kierkegaard and his heirs; and (4) his Kantian insistence on the ultimacy of human autonomy where we have an open-ended, i.e., non-deterministic, non-heteronomous, non-coercive, human situation, which is not subject to any prescribed norms, in which *any* action can be translation of revelation if man chooses it so.

The nature of that which is revealed is here that which out of the manifold of our experience man chooses to treat as revealed. The criteria of 'revealed' is no longer related to something spoken by God in propositions, rather it has been turned around, and the source of its content transported from the Divine to the human will. Autonomous activity is now holy activity because human autonomy is vouchsafed by God's act of self-limitation in the revealing of 'Presence' alone. It is not that God, as *eternal Thou*, is a *Deus Absconditus*, for He meets us in dialogue and reveals His Presence, becoming in this dialogical intercourse a *Deus Revelatus*. But the *eternal Thou*, in the very act of being a *Deus Revelatus*, respects the *Thou-ness* of His human partner, and turns him back upon himself with the assurance that no Divine coercion will interfere with man's freedom which is exercised in the face of the Divine Reality. Ontological truth and anthropological truth merge here in the existential situation of the existing individual.

What are the implications of Buber's position, which attempts to harmonize the reality of God as *Deus Revelatus* and also to protect human autonomy? Does it really do these two things without injury to either? Though there are many difficulties with this view both with regard to its significance for the human situation as well as for its implications in respect of the *eternal Thou* space limits us to two critical considerations.

(1) What is the relation between those human acts which Buber claims are free but guaranteed by the act of meeting with the *eternal Thou,* and the *eternal Thou*. Another way of putting the question is: "In what sense are man's free actions guaranteed by the *eternal Thou*?" If revelation is to maintain any meaning whatsoever, there must be a *necessary* tie between the act of revelation and that which flows from it—in Buber's case, free human actions. Yet at this point in Buber's reasoning a paradox arises for, if human action is causally determined by revelation, then of course it is heteronomous and dialogically illegitimate. On the other hand, if human action is severed from any revelational ground, then revelation seems purely a formal and not a material notion. Therefore, what relation does exist between revelation and human action? Even if we take with the utmost seriousness Buber's idea of revelation as 'Presence', this notion seems unable to provide the necessary clarification of the above dilemma, for, if knowledge of God's 'Presence' *causes* man to choose to do 'X' rather than 'Y', the situation is still a heteronomous one. Although the ground is now God's Being rather than His Will, the human agent has acted out of respect for an external consideration, i.e., God's Being. If, however, a sense of God's 'presence' in no way determines the choice of a human agent, then we can say that this sense of 'Presence' is without existential import, as it makes no material difference to human action. The entire area of what the significance of the revelation of 'Presence' is for human action is ambiguous.

(2) Our second consideration concerns the extremely problematic Buberian idea of a "moment God". In *Between Man and Man*, Buber asks the question "Who Speaks?", to which he gives the following suggestive answer:

> It would not avail us to give for reply the word "God", if we do not give it out of that decisive hour of personal existence when we had to forget everything we imagined we knew of God, when we dared to keep nothing handed down or learned of self-contrived, no shred of knowledge, and were plunged into the night.

> When we rise out of it into the new life and there begin to receive the signs, what can we know of that which—of him who gives them to us? Only what we experience from time to time from the signs themselves. If we name the speaker of this speech "God", then it is always the "God" of a moment, a moment God . . .

In such a way, out of the givers of the signs, the speakers of the words in lived life, out of the moment Gods there arises for us with a single identity the Lord of the voice, the One (pp. 14f.).

Given that this "moment God" leaves nothing behind but an awareness of His "Presence", if we can even claim this, we need to ask: "What are the considerations for identification and reidentification of this 'Presence' as God?" i.e., how do we know that the "Presence" revealed is the *eternal Thou*, The "Lord of the Voice, the One"? And again how do we know that the *eternal Thou* revealed in Situation *A* is the same *eternal Thou* as revealed in situation *B*, and so on? Moreover, and perhaps more pressing is the question: "How does Buber get to the notion of *eternal Thou* from a series of encounters with "moment Gods"? In other words, how do "moment Gods" become God?

The present format forbids an elaborate review of these central questions and requires instead a direct reply: despite the centrality of the *eternal Thou* for his epistemology Buber is unable to handle such difficulties regarding the identification and reidentification of the *eternal Thou*, indeed his *a priori* claims as to the structure of the *I-Thou* relation makes it impossible for him to give any convincing answer to the question as to how the "moment Gods" become "God". Buber himself in the passage quoted above, suggested that the only grounds for this identification is that which we experienced when "plunged into the night". (p.15) That is, this connection between the "moment Gods" and "God" is established only by dint of a mystical experience. While this at first seems a justification it is not. For Buber cannot just *posit* this fact, he needs to establish it. And this is more difficult than it first appears because *even* granting the reality of mystical experience, it is not at all obvious how such experience can give us the sort of knowledge required to identify the "moment Gods" with "God" given Buber's embargo on "content" in such a mystical experience and his overall understanding of what such an experience entails.[11] Moreover, there is a deep internal problematic to be attended to between what Buber writes of the encounter with "moment Gods" and his claim that these are united by some unifying mystical experience, i.e., he needs to show us the link between the 'One' and the 'many'; that is he needs to explain, or at least suggest, how the eternal is manifest in the momentary. Consequently, Buber's "defence" itself needs defending, yet keeping in mind the entire structural matrix of his thought it is hard to imagine how this could be accomplished.[12]

The critical significance of this inherent inability to provide more orderly and substantive rules for the description of elements and relations necessary for Buber's entire dialogical philosophy, as well as rules for identification and re-identification and the like, can be clearly seen when we consider, for example, and as a paradigm of the problematic element of Buber's whole hermeneutic, as essential contention of the entire dialogical enterprise, Buber's claim that: "The *eternal Thou* can never become an *It*". The ramifications within the dialogical structure of this claim for the *eternal Thou* are many. For the readers of this volume, I trust I need not spell them out in detail. Instead I would only call to attention the fact that this statement is a universal proposition of the sort it would seem the dialogical system can *not* offer—and even probably, if not certainly, requires that we explicitly rule out. Consider, how could we know as a result of a dialogical relation or of a mystical relation, with a "moment God" that this "moment God" could *never*, note the universality, become an *It*? Given the conditions set out for *I-Thou* relation with a "moment God" one is justified solely, if at all, in speaking of the fact that, *for the moment,* he is not an *It*. Here we again run into the need—and the absence—of metaphysical delibera-tions which are essential. Here again we recognize that our language, even or perhaps especially, our dialogical language is not ontologi-cally neutral. Its ontology may only be implied for the most part, but the need for its necessary clarification is no less pressing for that.

A corollary of these difficulties with the Buberian concept of a "moment God" is that it rules out references, for example, to "God as Creator", or more familiarly, to the "God of Israel". For the claims necessarily entailed by the proposition "God the Creator", which Buber does not like to talk of, or "God of Israel", which in fact is one of Buber's main concerns, transcend those permitted by the dialogi-cal account of revelation. The nub of the difficulty is that saying that 'moment God' A encounters at time T is either the same or different from 'moment God' $A1$ at time $T1$ while seeming a simple exercise in identification, similar to identifying the Talmudic tract in the study, or the dog's biscuits in the kitchen is, in fact, far more difficult, because what criteria of re-identification is Buber able to employ? Anything to do with time and space is ruled out and all psychological states are subject to the now familiar embargo on content. Thus, what is Buber going to use to decide that $A1$ at $T1$ is the same as A at T, and what criteria is he going to employ to check whether he has decided correctly or not? It would seem that to decide correctly whether A at T is the same as $A1$ at $T1$, A would have to have some constancy and internal coherence that could make it available to the faculty of human judgment. But it is precisely this quality which the very name "moment God" is intended to deny.

Translating the significance of this technical idiom into its more pragmatic implications means arguing that the dialogical model makes it difficult to construct an epistemology which is capable of dealing adequately with history, a philosophy of history, or a God of History. Again, it runs counter to a coherent epistemological analysis of social inter-action, which is public and endures through time and space, and social history past and present. These are just two of the more critical wider entailments, which run parallel to the above mentioned problematic, of Buber's account of dialogical revelation.

One of the pressing needs for the ongoing discussion is another look at revelation.

Conclusion

To use a geographical idiom, we can say that we have stretched over much of the Buberian epistemological landscape. It is certainly a rich environment, suggestive in its contours and the directions in which it points for further philosophical rumination. It is not, however, a landscape free of weeds, boulders or pitfalls. It is terrain well worth cultivating but the hand(s) of some skillful gardner(s) is pressingly needed if the weeds are not to choke the roses.

Discussion Following Steven Katz's Lecture

M. WYSCHOGROD

I listened to the paper with great interest—it was an excellent, well thought-out paper. At the same time, I really cannot escape the feeling that to a large extent it is irrelevant. All the paper really proves is that, analyzed from the "I-It" point of view, the "I-Thou" makes no sense, and I think that is obvious, and Buber would certainly admit it. It struck me that the whole rhetoric of your paper is inappropriate. You have points—one, two, three, four, five, six, a, b, c, d, and sub-points—1, 2, 3, 4, and so forth. That kind of structure is clearly "I-It". Compare that with the tone and rhetoric of *I and Thou* which has a dimension of mystery in it. I can't imagine *I and Thou* being numbered—1, 2, 3, and sub-point—a, b, c, and so on.

I am sure you all know the story of the engineer who wrote a very long and learned paper about how the bumble bee cannot possibly fly by the laws of aerodynamics; but the bumble bee *does fly*, and it hasn't read the laws of aerodynamics. Therefore the trick is not to ground the bumble bee, but to adjust the laws of aerodynamics to take account of the fact that the bumble bee flies.

The "I-Thou" flies, and the job of the philosopher is not to show that the "I-Thou" doesn't fly, but to show how we must readjust our ontology, our logic, our categories of thought, to deal with this, or at least cope with it. So I think it comes down to the fact that one speaks out of one's own life-experience. And if one experiences the "I-Thou" in prayer, in human encounter, then one is bound to this mystery, even if sometimes we cannot explain it by previously known laws.

S. KATZ

Prof. Wyschogrod makes an important point and the criticism he makes is a sharp one. I think that the criticism, however, is unfair, for the following reasons: First of all, as I tried to point out, and the reason I went so carefully a,b,c,1,2,3, is that most people who talk about Buber are not careful enough; in fact they are not careful at all for the most part. I think that clarity and rigour are never out of place in philosophical discussions. Secondly, what I hope at least to have shown by drawing out the details of Buber's position for example, with regard to his theory of revelation, was that despite what Buber says about not saying things about revelation, about being "beyond" language, he says, in fact, a great deal about it. So you have to read him very closely in two senses—not only do you have to pay attention to what he says but, like all philosophers involved in what one might call the technical aspect of philosophy, one has to try and see what is always implied below the surface of any philosophical argument. Buber's style cloaked a whole metaphysical theory, a whole theory of the world which is conceptual and part of the modern Western tradition; it is built on certain views that Buber inherited from Kantianism among other influences.

What I was trying to say in addition is that your view, that the "I-Thou" flies by itself, is false. The intention of the paper was to show that, in fact, Buber's position just doesn't fly as such. It is tied to the world in such a way that if one takes a close look at it, even if it may fly in the future, say if you redesign it, because it catches something inherently true, something about the human condition you call mystery, yet it is not a reality that it is totally divorced, totally independent, totally free of everything else. Moreover, I would say that the way Buber describes it and points to it is much more structured than it appears, on first glance, to be the case. Let me give you a simple analogy. Buber claimed at times that he did not tell you things but rather he merely pointed to a reality. In effect, he was saying: "I am not a philosopher, I merely point to things". But even consider the analogy of pointing. To point in normal conceptual terms and in normal space-time means having a direction. If I point over in that way, say east or west, it is because I can locate east or west on a map.

Now, what is it that Buber points to? Moreover, how does Michael Wyschogrod know that when he says the term "I-Thou", he means what Buber meant by it, if nobody can say anything about it? How does he know that his "I-Thou" is what Buber meant by "I-Thou"? It would seem that a true Buberian response at this point would be silence. And those of you who are sitting there silent and smiling may either be agreeing with me or you may be true Buberians because you realize that if you start the conversation with me then you have to play it by certain linguistic, philosophical and logical rules. When Buber criticizes Heidegger, Sartre, and Husserl, which he does for example in his lectures—in "Between Man and Man", or when he criticizes Jung, and so on, he has standards, and he applies them; when he criticizes Hegel he has standards and he applies them. And it is not fair for him to say "I can criticize everybody but nobody can criticize me". Once you enter the game, then the rules of the game apply.

Notes

STEVEN KATZ

1. The complex nature of Buber's use of and relationship to the Kantian tradition cannot be dealt with adequately in this paper. Moreover, I recognize that many readers, if not most, may be surprised in varying degrees by the importance which I attribute to this relationship. In support of my position here I can only note that this relationship has been studied, analyzed and worked out by me in considerable detail, including full explication and analysis of the essential themes and with full supporting documentation from the primary Kantian and Buberian sources, as part of my larger study of Buber's philosophical position which will appear as the second volume of my comprehensive study of Buber's work. (The first volume dealing with Buber's hasidic writing and tentatively entitled *Hasidim and Martin Buber: A Critical Analysis* is soon to go to press.) It is also my intention to make this comparative study of Kant and Buber available in a somewhat shortened form in a journal article in the not too distant future so that readers can judge the merits of the case for themselves without having to wait for the publication of my completed volume.

It should also be noted that I am aware that my remarks on this theme may be somewhat cryptic to readers who are not fully familiar with Kant's systematic discussion. Indeed, the editors of this volume have quite correctly privately communicated to me their concern that: "The connection between Buber's philosophy and Kantian Idealism should be clarified and spelled out for the average scholarly reader. . . You presume an exact knowledge and pre-understanding (of the relation of Kant and Buber) which such a reader does not possess." In response to this request some brief additional exegesis of the relationship has been included in this final version of the paper which was not included in the oral presentation given at the *Centenary Conference* at Beer Sheva. Although I am cognizant that the additional exegesis is still brief and may well still leave the "average scholarly reader" no better off, I have chosen to retain these remarks in the final version of this paper because they do raise fundamental issues for those technically equipped scholars working in the field, issues which I consider too important to delete altogether.

2. A more detailed exegesis of Buber's views is given in my "Dialogue and Revelation in the Thought of Martin Buber" in *Religious Studies* (March, 1978).

3. M. Buber, *I and Thou*, R. G. Smith (Tsl.), Edinburgh: T. and T. Clark, 1937, p. 62.

4. *I and Thou*, p. 33. See also pp. 32f. for Buber's entire discussion on this theme.

5. Buber does not even attempt to prove God's existence. Indeed, he explicitly rejects the very idea of such proof and repudiates all such attempts. See, for example, *I and Thou* pt. I; and the various essays in *Eclipse of God*, New York: Harper, 1952, p. 12f (hereafter *Eclipse*); *Between Man and Man*, Beacon Press, Boston, 1955(hereafter *BMM*), p. 12f; among other sources. Rather, Buber's position rests on his unshakable belief in God's existence and flows from this presupposition. There is nothing inductive about Buber's procedure here, nor was there any chance that he would arrive at the end of his philosophical interrogations and conclude there was no God.

6. This is a *very* sensitive point in Buber's work fraught as it is with moral,

philosophical and theological implications of tremendous import. First, to substantiate the exegesis I have given, I quote Buber's own description as given in *I and Thou*
of what does and does not occur as a consequence of revelation.

> it (Revelation) does not wish to be sealed within me, but it wishes to be born by me into
> the world. But just as the meaning itself does not permit itself to be transmitted and made
> into knowledge generally current and admissible, so confirmation of it cannot be transmit-
> ted as a valid Ought; it is not specified on any tablet, to be raised above all men's heads.
> The meaning that has been received can be proved true by each man only in the singleness
> of his being and the singleness of his life. As no prescription can lead us to the meeting, so
> none leads from it. As only acceptance of the Presence is necessary for the approach to the
> meeting, so in a new sense it is so when we emerge from it. As we reach the meeting with
> the simple *Thou* on our lips, so with the *Thou* on our lips we leave it and return to the
> world.

For a second essential source of Buber's views see his discussion of the issues of
Revelation, Law, Torah, and Mitzvot in his letters to Franz Rosenzweig reprinted in
On Jewish Education (ed.) N. Glatzer. For the debate generated by Buber's view
see: A. A. Cohen, in *Judaism* Vol. I #3 (July 1952); M. Fox in *The Martin Buber Vol.*
in *The Library of Living Philosophers* (1965); M. Diamond, *Martin Buber, Jewish
Existentialist* (1960); M. Friedman's defence of Buber in *Judaism* Vol. III, #1
(Winter, 1954).

7. Items 1-5 are distilled primarily from Buber's remarks in *Eclipse*, pp. 135ff; *I
and Thou,* pp. 109-120; *BMM,* pp. 67-70. Item 6 and items 6a to 6i are also derived
from these sources but, in addition, the list of items 6a-6i is based on the following
sources:

(6a) *Israel and the World,* Schocken Books, New York, 1963 (hereafter *Israel*), p.
    87f.; *Hasidism & Modern Man,* trans. M. Friedman, New York, Horizon Press,
    1958 (hereafter HMM), p. 227ff., 232; *The Prophetic Faith* p. 164.

(6b) *Israel,* p. 114, p. 87 f.; *HMM* p. 227 ff., 232.

(6c) *HMM,* p. 229 ff.

(6d) *BMM,* p. 16; *Eclipse* pp. 95, 129.

(6e) *Eclipse* p. 125 f.; *The Knowledge of Man* p. 85 f.

(6f) *On Jewish Learning* p. 115; *BMM* pp. 12, 14; *Eclipse* p. 129.

(6g) *On Jewish Learning* p. 115; *Good and Evil* p. 43; *BMM* pp. 114, 182; *Eclipse*
    p. 129; *Moses* p. 188.

(6h) *HMM* p. 135; *Israel* pp. 163.

(6i) All of the above.

8. Again, I realize my remarks on Kantianism in this critical discussion may be
obscure to readers unfamiliar with the fine details of Kantianism. I refer such readers
to note 1 and my "self-defence" given there.

9. Hans Reichenbach, *Kant and the Theory of Relativity*.

10. "Hasidism in the History of Religion," *Origin & Meaning of Hasidism,* trans.
M. Friedman, Horizon Press, New York, 1960, pp. 228f.

11. Buber's appeal to "mystical experience" raises many interesting, if difficult
philosophical issues. Internal to Buber's own thinking is what the appeal means
given his own criticism of certain forms of appeal to mystical experience. See, for
example, Buber's discussion in part II of *I and Thou*. For a relatively sympathetic
exegesis of Buber's position, in particular with regard to this appeal to mystical
experience, see Jochanan Bloch's discussion of "Die Symbolfrage" in his *Die Aporie*

des Du (Heidelberg, 1976). Space prevents my discussing here all the philosophical issues relevant to this issue. Instead, I refer readers to my paper "The Logic and Language of Mystery" in *Christ, Faith and History* (ed.) S. Sykes and J. Clayton, (Cambridge University Press, Cambridge, England, 1972); and to my paper "Language, Epistemology and Mysticism" in my *Mysticism and Philosophical Analysis* (Oxford University Press, New York, 1978), pp. 22-74. Note should also be taken of the further sources given in note 78 of this second essay.

12. Buber's attempts to clarify his meaning here by drawing an analogy which he recognizes is weak, between the mystical experience which establishes the unity of God and the unity of the poet known to us through his many poems. He writes: "I will now use a *gauche* comparison, since I know no right one.

When we really understand a poem, all we know of the poet is what we learn of him in the poem—no biographical wisdom is of value for the pure understanding of what is to be understood: the *I* which approaches us is the subject of this single poem. But when we read other poems by the poet in the same true way their subjects combine in all their multiplicity, completing and confirming one another to form the one polyphony of the persons's existence" (*Between Man and Man*, p. 15). This comparison, however, is not only weak, what in the original Buber characterized as a "linkischer Vergleich", but in fact helps make one of the essential points of my approach to the problems under consideration, namely, that, in contradistinction to Buber's claim, *embodied* existence seems essential to the knowing of an Other when this Other is a person. That is to say, we know the *I* of the poet because the poet is embodied, has a memory, and is locatable in space-time, etc. as well. It is easy to overlook, or forget, these "trivial" facts about the poet when we seek some "higher" poetic truth, but they cannot really be forgotten if we are to arrive at a fully coherent, defensible account of the unity of the being of the poet. Now in the case of God, by analogy, we of course do not require *embodied* existence or material predication, but we do require some intelligible form of linguistic usage, some reasonable form of non-material predication, if the term "God", and related terms such as *eternal Thou* and the like, are to find significance employment in our—*and Buber's!*—dialogical vocabulary.

Ferdinand Ebner as a Source of Martin Buber's Dialogic Thought in I and Thou

RIVKA HORWITZ

I and Thou is Martin Buber's most important book; with it the period of dialogical thought in his life begins. Because of its religious and social importance, the book has been translated into many languages and has received various interpretations. Even today, fifty years after its publication, tens of thousands of copies are printed every year, and many young people read the book and are influenced by it.

The book's great contribution is its concentration on living man and his relationship to his fellow-man. Buber's thinking in *I and Thou* is based on the sincere relationship of man to his fellow-man, which can express itself in speech or in a glance, in love and connection. The solitary man, who is the basis of philosophical analysis, is relegated to a secondary position. This other relation which Buber discusses—the "I-It" relation—is rational and impersonal; sometimes it is even calculated and utilitarian. The "I-Thou" and "I-It" relations are both possible between man and man and between man and nature, but with God—in Buber's view—only the "I-Thou" relationship is possible; God is the "eternal Thou" of man, and God is also present in every encounter of the relationship between man and man.

The book has been discussed from many different points of view. But until now no scholar has taken it upon himself to examine Buber's philosophical sources, which can illumine the plain meaning of the text and the problems with which the author struggled on the way. This is particularly important with respect to existentialist philosophy, in which a close link exists between thought and life. The present essay is one result of such an examination—that is precise examination of ideas, philology and historical influence—an examination whose basic conclusions have already been included in my book *Martin Buber's Way to I and Thou*,[1] which also includes the first and only publication of Buber's important lecture series, *Religion as Presence*, which are the early stage of *I and Thou*. This essay is concerned with a subject which I did not develop completely in my book, for it was not absolutely clear to me at that time, but developed only after the completion of the book: namely the influence of the important Catholic thinker Ferdinand Ebner and his book *The Word and the Spiritual Realities* (1921)[2] on the formation of the thought of *I and Thou* (1922). The fact that this obscure, forgotten thinker had a decisive influence on a famous philosopher like Buber has not been recognized until now. Only Ebner himself committed this possibility to writing, in words which were not printed at the time and which found no echo when they did appear. In the following pages we shall try to show that Ebner was justified in his conjecture, and we shall attempt to establish what Buber received from Ebner and in what respects he differed from Ebner and went his own independent way.

Ferdinand Ebner (1882-1931) was a sickly man, a teacher in a public school in a small village in Austria; he died young. Buber did not know him personally, nor is there any evidence that the two ever corresponded. But Buber pointed out that Ebner's book, *Das Wort und die Geistigen Realitäten* (The Word and the Spiritual Realities) was in his hands for some time before he wrote *I and Thou;* however, scholars and critics have not paid attention to this fact. Emil Brunner, for instance, in his essay, "Judaism and Christianity in Buber", speaks of *I and Thou* and of *The Word and the Spiritual Realities* as of two exceptional discoveries which occurred simultaneously, without one thinker's knowing of the other.[3] It is, he says, a rare phenomenon in spiritual history, when two thinkers, independently of each other, come to an identical conclusion. But Brunner's words do not fit Buber's own testimony. In his afterword to *Das Dialogische Prinzip,* "Zur Geschichte des dialogischen Prinzips" (On the History of the Dialogical Principle), he writes: "While I was writing the third and last part, I ended my abstaining from the reading of books and began with Ebner's fragments."[4] And in a note to these words he adds: "At first I saw some parts of his work which are published in (the Austrian quarterly) *Der Brenner,* and at this time I ordered the book." This is clear testimony that we are not dealing with the phenomenon of two thinkers independent of each other; rather, Buber read Ebner in several stages at the time he was writing his work. He read Ebner's work for the first time in the above mentioned quarterly. Ebner's editor, who was also the editor of the quarterly, saw that because of financial difficulties the appearance of Ebner's book would be postponed for a year or two, hence he published selected passages from the book in *Der Brenner* in 1920. The passages published were fragments 1, 2, 3, 16, and 18, that is, five of the eighteen "fragments" of which the book is composed reached Buber's hands as early as 1920. These five chapters already contain the essence of Ebner's philosophy, for the book is written in aphoristic form, with many flashes and innumerable repetitions, but the main ideas are clear and are repeated in various ways. A gifted thinker like Martin Buber would be capable of recognizing the basic ideas of the book from reading the third of it which he had seen in the journal. In any case there is no doubt that the reading of those sections deeply impressed Buber, and he ordered the book when it appeared in 1921.

In my opinion, Buber received the concept of divinity as developed in *I and Thou* from Ebner. On every page of the book, Ebner recognizes God as the "true Thou" who cannot be God in the third person; but this is one of the decisive innovations of *I and Thou*, that God can never be grasped in the third person, but only in presence. The similarity exists not only in the substance of the concept, but also in the whole structure and development of the idea. To be sure, the concept of God as "Thou" can be found in some of Buber's writings even in the years before his encounter with Ebner's work—in the years when he was moving away from his mystical approach—but these were quite isolated instances, with no continuity among them. "Thou" as the basic and fixed name of God is found in Buber's writings only after his encounter with the writings of Ebner. We come upon this concept for the first time in *Religion as Presence*— Buber's lectures at the beginning of 1922, in which God is regularly called "the absolute Thou." The similarity is greater between Ebner's work and *Religion as Presence* because Buber was apparently reading Ebner at the time when he was giving these lectures. Here Buber expressed himself more freely and less cautiously, and for this reason it is easier to recognize, in these lectures, Ebner's influence upon him; a few months later, when composing the lectures into a book, he took out the concepts closest to Ebner's, so that they are less evident in *I and Thou*. A philological analysis of the omitted sections shows that Buber was indeed influenced by Ebner.

From the point of view of ideas one may assume that Buber was noticeably moving away from the mystical approach to which he was attached before 1918, and was seeking a new direction in which to develop his thought on presence, and what he found in Ebner's writings impressed him deeply. He wrote as follows: "This book showed me, more than any other . . . how men coming from various traditions seek the same hidden treasure."[5] This testimony of Buber's on his absorption in the writings of Ebner has not received the attention it deserves, perhaps because it stands in contradiction to other testimony which is also found in his writings: there[6] Buber claims that *I and Thou* was not influenced by Hermann Cohen, Franz Rosenzweig, or Ferdinand Ebner. Because of this statement, much quoted by Buber's scholars, the possibility of a connection between Ebner and Buber has not yet been investigated. It seems that Buber's scholars have related to this statement more literally than its author; they did not perceive that Buber himself explicitly stated that he had read Ebner, and his statement deserves attention. The placement of Buber beside Ebner opens up possibilities of understanding his message, and our intention here is to concentrate on uncovering the roots of dialogical thought, which is of such great importance of the twentieth century, and of which Buber was one of the central figures.

Another early piece of information on Ebner and Buber comes from Franz Rosenzweig. It seems that on December 4, 1921, when Rosenzweig was visiting Buber, both of them already knew Ebner's book, and it was mentioned in their conversation. At the time Buber was engaged in the early stages of writing *I and Thou*. This testimony from Franz Rosenzweig, a thinker of stature and the author of the *Star of Redemption* (1921), is very important. He too knew Ebner's book at that early time, when it had just appeared. Rosenzweig's cousin was the thinker Hans Ehrenberg; both of them belonged to the group of young people who, in the years before the first World War, were seeking a theological solution to the philosophical problems of the generation. This group was anti-idealist: they rejected the optimistic and abstract approach of Hegel, and emphasized the Bible and the here and now and man's status as dust and ashes before God. Eventually this way of thinking was defined as existentialist. Hans Ehrenberg discovered Ferdinand Ebner by chance and was greatly surprised that in his solitude in Austria this man had written a book so close to his own world-view and that of his companions. Ehrenberg even wrote a critical essay on Ebner's book, and it was he who connected Rosenzweig and Ebner. He obtained Ebner's book for Rosenzweig, and in winter 1921-22 Ebner received the *Star of Redemption*. This was no small surprise to the Catholic writer in Austria who suddenly had a glimpse of Jewish dialogical thought. In the archive of *Der Brenner*, in Innsbruck, Austria, there is a letter written by Hans Ehrenberg on 25.10.1921 to the editor of the quarterly, Ludiwig von Ficker, in which he says: "I am happy and surprised . . . basically, this is precisely our opinion (note the plural—R.H.). This is definitely a case of parallelism in the history of ideas".[7] And indeed it was so, for Rosenzweig and Ebner had published similar books without one knowing of the other.

As mentioned, Rosenzweig visited Buber in Heppenheim in December 1921, in order to learn about Hasidism. He describes this visit as follows: "He [Buber] taught in a rather clumsy manner, because he wanted to explain to me very laboriously, in connection with one text, both the importance and the reality of the word, something which was not entirely unfamiliar to me."[8] The mention of the words "importance" and "reality of the word" (Realität des Wortes) is an unmistakable allusion to the fact that both of them were closely acquainted with Ebner and were using his terms, since in 1921 the dialogic terms had not yet crystallized. On March 5, 1922, in the seventh lecture of the series Religion as Presence, Buber described an experience from the autumn of 1921, which one may call "an answer in the train."[9] The story is woven around two motifs. The first in his lack of certainty as to his belief in the existence of God, the second—that the God in whom one can believe is always Thou, never the third person—he took from Ebner. Buber relates that, some years previously, he had made the acquaintance of a clergyman by the name of William Hechler. The latter visited him in his home in Berlin in 1914, and when Buber accompanied his guest to the train station, Hechler asked him: "Do you believe in God?" This direct question shook Buber, and he could not find an answer. Buber had once written: "To believe in God is a risk." He felt that he had failed. But in the fall of 1921, while traveling in a train to a meeting with friends, he finally "heard" the answer: it stood before him without his thinking about it at first. He heard the following words: "If belief in God means the possibility of thinking about him in the third person, then I am not sure that I believe in God, or at least, I do not know if it is permissible for me to say that I believe in God."

Buber questioned faith and received a sudden clarification or illumination: the living God can be attained only in the second person, for this is the God who is always present, whom one addresses, and whom it is possible to encounter. The power and vitality of the book I and Thou, which was about to be published, is based on the new name of God which he discovered at that moment.[10]

According to his testimony the train trip occurred in the fall of 1921, that is, after Buber had read Ebner's work in Der Brenner, and before the lecture series Religion as Presence, which did not begin until January 15, 1922. What is common to Buber and Ebner is the idea that God can only be called Thou, and that it is impossible to speak about God in the third person. In contrast to his early writing, Buber in Religion as Presence always calls God Thou, or "the absolute

Thou", and never talks about him in the third person. This proves that he knew Ebner's view.

The fact that Buber learned the basic name of God from a Catholic theologian, who takes his authority, on every page of his book, from the New Testament, is nothing exceptional in the history of ideas. The Christian character of Ebner's thought is certainly in utter contradiction to Buber's Jewish faith, which completely rejected the Christian approach; nevertheless, he had no reason to reject a religious approach which seemed convincing to him. In all generations, thinkers of one religion have learned philosophic truths from other religions: Maimonides, for instance, learned from al-Fārābí, and Thomas of Aquinas learned from Maimonides. Or, to mention an example from recent times, Rosenzweig learned the basics of dialogical thinking from the Protestant thinker Rosenstock-Huessy. Dialogical thinking in itself is not Jewish or Christian; it is anti-idealist. Buber, found in Ebner's words truths which seemed acceptable to him, even though he rejected the Christian motif.

The theory of "I and Thou" expounded in Ebner's book is connected with the New Testament Gospel of John, and especially with the well-known beginning: "In the beginning was the Word, and the Word was with God . . . all things were made through him . . . in him was life; and the life was the light of men. And the light shineth in the darkness; and the darkness apprehended it not." Ebner interprets the "Thou" as the spiritual being of man. It is the God of the human I; there is no "I" without a "Thou", nor a "Thou" without an "I". The point of departure is anthropocentric. According to his view there is no God without man. "In the beginning was the Word" means, according to his theory, that God created language and the word, which are the link between God and man; God has no share in the world. Therefore Ebner's Christianity has a Gnostic tinge, and he sees the world as something dark; the light shines only on the soul of man. For Ebner this is Christianity, and it is the true and only religion; there is only one true way, and that is faith in God as "Thou", as presence and as presently existing, and this idea is also connected for him with Jesus. In Ebner's opinion, Soren Kierkegaard had already attained this truth, but has not yet discovered the importance of language, and this was his, Ebner's, task. Ebner (like Buber after him) conceives of God both pantheistically and personally; for both of them, God is the Infinite and also the personal God; as the Infinite he fills the present and the soul of man, but as the personal God he is incarnate, according to Ebner, in Jesus, who became man in order to show humanity the right way and the right faith.[11]

Ebner was greatly influenced by the great German philosopher Hamann and also by Karl Kraus, who saw God as the creator of language. The light which was given to man in Genesis is language, speech. Only man and God can speak with each other; the connection between them is language. Nature, in contrast, is mute. Ebner states that there are basic sentences: "Du bist, ich bin" (Thou art, I am) (which can be translated into Hebrew only as "attah" (thou) or "hinkhah", "ani" (I) or "hineni", because Hebrew does not use the present tense of the verb "to be" in such sentences.) These words are absolutely different from third-person language, the language of the idealists, the language of objective description and rationalism.[12] The story of creation, which speaks of God in the third person, is without theological importance in Ebner's view, for in creation it is impossible that God should be facing man; therefore he writes: " 'God created man' means in truth nothing other than that he spoke to him."[13] In another passage he notes that "concerning God's relation to the world we know nothing, really nothing whatever."[14] Ebner sets the Gospel of John in the place of the Creation story of Genesis. His basic interest is oriented toward man; his relation to vegetable and animal life is negative, for they have no recognition of the "I", and they cannot speak.[15] They are not and cannot be "I" or "Thou", they are always "It". Nature, according to Ebner, is dark, for the word cannot illumine it, and it cannot attain the "I-Thou". The heavens and the earth may pass away, but the word "love" will abide forever.[16]

In Ebner's writings man stands between God and the world. The more man is interested in science, or in information about the world, the more he estranges himself from God and from the true task that was entrusted to him. A man who immerses himself in knowledge arrives, according to Ebner, at "Ich-Einsamkeit", "the isolation of the 'I' ". At first the soul was anchored in the "Thou", but the separation occurred, the "I" left the "Thou", this was the fall, the original sin. Man, expelled from the Garden of Eden, "knows" everything, but his obligation is to return to his origin, to the connection with God, to the "I-Thou". This is the myth which is implied in Ebner's words, and which returns with variations in *I and Thou*.

It is also very important to prove philologically the connection between *The Word and the Spiritual Realities* and *Religion as Presence*. One example of the philological connection is the rare use of words found both in the writings of Ebner and in *Religion as Presence*, namely the characterization of the third-person God as "anthropomorphism". Of course, anthropomorphism generally means the attribution of human qualities or forms to God. Ebner hated this usage: to him the God of the theologians, the creator and ruler who is called "He" represents a materialized God; this is an anthropomorphism, as opposed to "Thou", which designates the true God. I submit that this is an exceedingly unconventional use of the concept "anthropomorphism", and that the recurrence of this deviant usage in Buber's lectures *Religion as Presence* is evidence of Ebner's influence. In these lectures, which Buber gave in order to crystallize his ideas before writing *I and Thou,* Buber speaks a number of times against the appellation of God in the third person (a point mentioned only once in *I and Thou*). Thus he writes that to speak of God as "He" is to use a metaphor, which is not the case with the name "Thou".[17] In the seventh lecture of *Religion as Presence* he writes: "The religions speak of God in the third person, usually as 'He'. One seldom realizes the extent to which this pronoun already means an anthropomorphism, or rather a transference of God to the world . . . of It, that is, to a creation which has run away from God. In other words: in history God is only a thing."[18] Compare this with the following paragraph from Ebner's book:

> The spiritually idle question of how God created the world from nothing, sustains it, and rules it, aims at God in the "third person", that is, God outside his personal relationship to us and ours to him, where he is and remains incomprehensible to us for all eternity. "God in the third person" was created by the imagination of man, it is a fruit of the spirit which draws sustenance from earthly fare and worldly experience. This is creation in the image of man, with anthropomorphism in it, whether it takes shape as concrete, visible image of God, as an idol, or as a non-sensual abstraction of metaphysics.[19]

Ebner and Buber both affirm that "I-Thou" relations are the full truth; both hold that one should not think or speak of God in the third person; both scorn the theologians who speak of God as "He", who discuss the attributes which may or may not be assigned to Him, and who argue over questions of Providence and of His essence and characteristics as Creator. But most surprising is that Buber also says that God as He is an anthropomorphism. For in truth "He" is not an anthropomorphism; there is no more materialization in the name "He" than in the name "Thou" or "I".

Another similarity between *The Word and the Spiritual Realities* and *Religion as Presence* is the negative and, if one may say so, gnostic approach to the world. In the fifth lecture Buber develops the idea that the world of "It" is absolutely different from the world of

"Thou", and thus he creates a dichotomy similar to Ebner's. However, this dichotomy is not characteristic of Buber; on the contrary, it is opposed to his basic approach. In general Buber's world has a positive being, and thus the negative relationship in this case is striking and exceptional. Here we are dealing with the following problem: the I-Thou relationship is a relationship in the amount of revelation, and after that moment the relationship disappears. Then the two between whom the relationship occurred stand opposite one another and return to everyday life, to the world of "It". Buber calls the fact that it is impossible to escape the "I-It" the tragedy of human existence. What, then, is the importance of all "I-Thou" relationships—Buber asks—if they have no continuity and are characterized merely as isolated moments not connected with one another? How shall we assure ourselves of continuity, if "I-Thou" relationships are only "like lightnings in the heavens of life?" In the world of "It", the world of orientation (or of realization, as Buber put it in *Daniel* (1931) and in *Religion as Presence*), there is coordination of time and space, but in the more exalted world of the "Thou", the moments are isolated and each moment stands alone, and thus there is danger that the world of the "It" will swallow up everything. The world of the "Thou" needs an anchoring that can only be found in an absolute "Thou" which can never be "he" or "it"; it needs to be anchored in a present, a presence, which can never be past, in "I am that I am". (Exodus 3, 14.) The momentary, human "Thou" is thus directly connected with God, with the "absolute Thou." Buber warns us not to cleave to the world of "It". He speaks of the world of "It" as of a "fall" or a "betrayal", or a "moving away from a task which is placed upon us". The world of "It" is almost connected here with the motif of evil, of the satanic, and in these lectures it rises to an intensity for which there is no parallel in the rest of his writings, *I and Thou* in particular. This concept is not characteristic of Buber; it is closer to the pessimistic, almost Gnostic approach.[20]

Buber's attack on the world of "It" places him in a dilemma with regard to the relation of God to the world. The moments of the human "Thou" are transitory and need the eternal Thou in order to assure their continuity, hence there can be no relation between the eternal Thou and the world of "It". The world of "It", which is the entire empirical world extending in the dimensions of time and space—can that world not be connected in a relationship with God? There is no such question for Ebner; It is perfectly clear to him that only the soul is connected with God. But for Buber the problem is not so easily solved. Are not time and space connected with God in some way? Is there only at moments a connection with God? Is there, according to the structure of Buber's thought, no possible connection between the eternal "Thou" and the world of "It", which is in space and time? Is there contact between God and the world?

In a paragraph from the fifth lecture, whose content we summarized above,[21] Buber, using Ebner's terminology, calls the world the "world of the fall"—an allusion to original sin which is hardly characteristic of Buber's basic thought, and does not appear in *I and Thou*. Some years after *I and Thou*, in an essay written in 1936, Buber criticizes Kierkegaard, who thought that it is impossible for a person who loves God as "Thou" to have any other love-relationship. He writes: " 'In order to come to love', says Kierkegaard about his renunciation of Regine Olsen, 'I have to remove the object' (of love). This is sublimely to misunderstand God. Creation is not a hurdle on the road to God, it is the road itself. We are created along with one another and directed to a life with one another. Creatures are placed in my way so that I, their fellow-creature, by means of them and with them find the way to God. A God reached by their exclusion would not be the God of all lives in whom all life is fulfilled."[22] Buber goes on to compare the one to the God of the philosophers and the other to the God of Abraham, Isaac and Jacob.

Buber's essay was written under the influence of Rosenzweig, who had urged him[23] to believe in God as creator of the world, whom Buber did not recognize at the time he wrote *I and Thou*. In 1936 Buber recognizes the creator of the world, and he attacks Kierkegaard because he does not want to say publically that he is essentially attacking Ebner and expressing an opinion absolutely different from that which he expressed in 1922 in *I and Thou*. Perhaps this is the reason why in an essay as strong and clear as "The Question to the Single One" Buber mounts such a crushing attack on Kierkegaard, who required him to choose between God and creation—and is this not an attack on *I and Thou*?[24]

In the years of the Second World War, when Buber was already living in Israel, he tried once again to clarify this point in an important essay, "What Is Man?". Here Buber declares that "The God of Kierkegaard can only be either a demiurge outgrown by and suffering from his creation, or a saviour who is a stranger to creation . . . Both are Gnostic figures."[25] Buber held that Kierkegaard was wrong in seeing in Creation an obstacle to the religious ideal of the solitary man who loves God.

As we mentioned, Buber learned from Rosenzweig to see creation as a way to God. In the *Star of Redemption* Rosenzweig bases his thought on "I-Thou" and "I-It". But "I-It", according to Rosenzweig, can be spoken only by the Holy One, blessed be He, to whom the world belongs, who created the world by his wisdom. Rosenzweig protested with great vigor against Buber's thinking, which he argued was based on the "I-It" of man. In the sentence "I see the tree", according to Rosenzweig, the "I" of idealistic thought reveals itself, for the object is connected with the intelligence of man alone and thus the necessary link with God is removed.[26] In Rosenzweig's interpretation, the world is not anchored intellectually in man, but in God, as written in Psalms: "He spoke and the world came to be". The world is the world of the Holy One, blessed be He, and it is good, even very good. Like Ebner, Buber in 1922 thinks that the way of "I-It" does not lead to God. In their opinion, man does not approach God, but goes away from him, by learning the world and feeling it. They differ from Maimonides and other rationalistic thinkers, who hold that the knowledge of creation leads to the creator. According to Ebner it is the other way around: to the extent that man is occupied with the creation, he is occupied with the "I-It" and is distancing himself from his true task. Like Ebner, Buber does not establish a contact between God and the world. Nevertheless, for Buber the world is not negative and not evil; on the contrary, he tries on several levels to develop a positive relationship to the world, in the relationship between man and man, in the relationship between man and nature, and in the relationship between man and the work of art. In all these things he is different from Ebner and close to his own writings of earlier years. In his conception of society, of the "We", the company of believers, Buber also tries to realize his positive and affirmative relation to the world. In his lectures on Judaism before the first World War, Buber spoke of the Essenes, of the Hasidim, of the early Christians as ideal societies; in his later writings he spoke of the period of Judges or the time of the prophet Samuel as of societies that lived together by the realization of a common ideal of life, and he also saw the kibbutz of our generation in that light. In the days of Samuel Israel had no king, God was their king; this idea of religious, ideal society, a congregation of believers, is also found in *I and Thou*, where the relations of human beings to the true "Thou" are compared to radii which go from all points of "I" to the center and thus form a circle:[27] in this deeply-rooted social ideal Buber differs from Ebner.

Thus one may say that Buber rejected Ebner's pessimistic approach and developed a teaching that saw the world in a positive light. On the other hand, Buber is close to Ebner in his concept of the genesis of humanity, the Utopia of the beginning. In *I and Thou* he writes: "In the beginning is the relation"[28]—that is, even before there was human development there was relationship and love. This may be compared with Ebner's approach, which holds that in the beginning there was the word, in the beginning was a relationship of love between God and man. Both Ebner and Buber deal with the spiritual genesis, whether this is represented by Buber's images of the primitive man and of the infant relating directly to his environment, or by Ebner's Christian myth of the Garden of Eden and Jesus. For Ebner it is easier to express this idea by the use of the Christian myth of the "fall", which marks the descent after the ideal era; but Buber too, despite all the reworking which he did on this topic, thinks that life today is different from the primal Utopian beginning, in which there was no "It". Thus both long for that good life, for the moment of grace, in which the harmony of "I-Thou" is restored as it was then.

But the similarity between Buber's and Ebner's theories also brings out the differences between them. Buber rejects not only Ebner's Christological aspects, but also his concept of the relation of man to the world. On a verse from the New Testament which says "he that loveth not his brother whom he hath seen, how can he love God whom he hath not seen?"[29] Ebner notes that the man who cannot find his "Thou" in his fellow-human cannot find it in God either.[30] With this he thought he had explained the commandment of love for one's neighbor which appears in the Bible: the relationship between man and man must be a spiritual relationship, while the idea is never capable of being a connection between "I" and "Thou". Finally, Ebner concludes that the relationship between man and man is rooted in God. In his essay "The History of the Dialogic Principle" (1954) Buber criticizes Ebner's approach to the world and argues that Ebner closes himself off from the world more than Kierkegaard, that for him the "Thou" cannot be found in man: "There is one Thou, and only one, and that, of course, is God."[31] To be sure, Ebner, like Kierkegaard, states that man must love not only God but also man; but where he speaks of the exclusivity of being, every other "Thou" disappears, for him too, from before God. Buber concludes from this that while Ebner and Kierkegaard demand love for man, they are in truth misanthropic.

To sum up: Ebner's structure is extreme in the negation of the relationship between God and nature. Buber's attitude is less extreme, although in the theory of "I and Thou" there is no place for contact between God and nature. In *I and Thou* he develops the relationship between man and nature, a matter which frequently raises questions for the book's readers. The objection arises that the "I-Thou" relationship between man and tree is not the same as the relationship between man and man.[32] In the light of our discussion it appears that if Buber had renounced the dialogue between man and tree, he would have completely renounced the relationship between man and nature. Then his theory would have been still more similar to Ebner's, in which only dialogue between man and man or between man and God is suggested, while nature remains entirely in the world of the It. Such would have brought him closer to a gnostic approach.

This is not the place to inquire in detail how the metaphysical structure of *I and Thou* was amended by Buber in the essay which he wrote in the years immediately following, and what change occurs in the centrality of man who is connected with God on the one hand and with the world on the other. As a result of sharp debates with Rosenzweig, Buber limited this idealistic aspect. What is important in our work is to show that in the first stage of dialogue Buber recognized God as one who confronts us and also recognized man and nature as presence with which relationship is possible. Thus his approach, unlike that of Ebner's, does not tend toward Neoplatonism, in which, in the end, only God exists. He is the light that illumines the All and the soul of man; the soul can absorb this light and respond to God.

Nevertheless one may assume that Buber learned the most important point of his teaching—the "I-Thou" relationship with God—from Ebner, even though he did not accept his conclusions because of the deep need of his doctrine to give metaphysical status to the relationship between man and man and especially to the relationship between man and the world. Therefore Buber rejected the Neoplatonic ideas which shine forth from the theory of the Catholic Ebner. When he gave his lectures *Religion as Presence*, Buber accepted many opinions of Ebner's which were basically opposed to his own; he took from him, at the outset, more than he could hold onto afterward. These things he removed when he wrote *I and Thou*; but part of what he received from Ebner remained with him all his life.

Ebner died in 1931. In the following year when Buber suggested to his student to do research on *I and Thou* he wrote: "You would do best to start from the category of 'I and Thou', which you could fruitfully compare with Ebner . . ."[33] The writings of Ferdinand

Ebner appeared in 1963-65; Buber died in 1965. It is improbable that Buber, then advanced in years, knew the *Schriften,* which among other things contained two previously unpublished statements concerning him. One is a paragraph from an incomplete essay in which Ebner expressed his astonishment at the similarity between his work and Buber's. He also knew of the connections between Buber and the editors of *Der Brenner.* Ebner relates that by chance he went one evening to hear a lecture on Buber and his book *I and Thou* and was quite astonished at how much he and Buber had in common. He thought that Buber had indeed read him and understood him better than most of his contemporaries. Later on he wrote: "Buber seems to have been acquainted with *Der Brenner* . . . Perhaps he had also read the *Fragments,* and because of them added the dates of writing at the end of his book, which otherwise would have been quite superfluous. It is really striking and in this case wonderful how close the thoughts of my book are to Buber's book, though the latter appears more lyrical and mystical."[34]

Discussion Following Rivka Horwitz's Lecture

H. STEIMER

Although many have regarded Ebner as the Roman Catholic equivalent to Buber, it is well at the outset to define their similarities as well as their marked differences. Ebner's diaries are rich in insights which parallel Buber's insight in *I and Thou*. For example, the word is the bond between I and Thou. The true I in man is his innermost ear which admits the word. Spirit is present everywhere when something happens between an I and a Thou. Every relationship involving two people with one another which signifies a relation of I to Thou partakes in the eternal. The warranty for the spiritual immortality of man lies in the relation of his I to the Thou.

Rivka Horwitz's paper shows that we have ample evidence from Buber's own statements about the background to the dialogical writings of his own familiarity with references to Thou language, which goes back to Friedrich Heinrich Jacobi in 1775, and later to Feuerbach in 1843. In a curious way Ebner's writings reflect a blending of the salient aspects of both Buber's and Kierkegaard's insights into authentic spirituality. Ebner shared their respective difficulties with religion in its various institutional guises. Like them he rejected any absolute distinctions between the realms of sacred and profane. For each the personal and concrete relationship between I and Thou was the sole means of access to spiritual existence.

I agree with Rivka Horwitz in her dismissal of Hermann Cohen's influence on Buber's development of the life of dialogue. I also agree with her that Rosenzweig and Ebner probably influenced Buber more than he realized when he indicated in 1954 that they did not influence him decisively. This may be but a matter of semantics, however, depending upon Buber's use of the word "decisively". But I am also aware that even at my age I may say things about actions that occurred five years ago, ten years ago, and somebody may point out to me that I am totally in error, that I have twisted the facts, in order to enhance my own credibility or my present view of what was appropriate in my opinion at this time rather than then.

S. KATZ

Isn't it true that in his early publications of 1906-1907 Buber also uses the word "Thou" to refer to God? Wasn't that before Ebner's influence?

R. HORWITZ

It is true that Buber mentioned in "Rabbi Nachman" or in one of his early writings God as Thou; but my research deals not whether he mentioned it once or twice, but when God as a Thou became a creative force for his writings. I believe that this occurred in "Religion als Gegenwart." There Buber says: "God is a Thou and you cannot call Him by other names." But we may ask, to what extent is "Religion als Gegenwart" a departure in a new area? I showed Ernst Simon "Religion als Gegenwart" when I discovered it, and I was very excited about it. I gave him the fourth lecture, which has the first parallels to *I and Thou*—the first three don't have. He took it with him on a trip to the United States and he said he'd read it en route. Upon his return, he said that it sounded much as his early philosophy. He uses orientation and realization freely, not in an inhabitated way as in *I and Thou*, where orientation does not appear and realization very rarely. So it is, I would say, as in between stage. Perhaps he thought it was already a new stage, but now that we have *I and Thou* to compare it with, it is an in-between stage.

Also I would like to add in relation to Walter Kaufmann's paper that the manuscript of *I and Thou* is still not what we have in the printed version, because Buber corrected his writings as he was going on—he was writing and rewriting. In his correspondence with Rosenzweig things appear that are not in the book, and in the galley proofs there were things which later he took out. His writing was a creative process.

Notes

RIVKA HORWITZ

1. *Buber's Way to I and Thou: An Historical Analysis and the First Publication of Martin Buber's Lectures Religion as Presence"*. Heidelberg, 1978. Hereafter cited as "Buber's Way".

2. F. Ebner, *Das Wort und die Geistigen Realitäten, Schriften* vol I, Munich, 1963.

3. In *The Philosophy of Martin Buber*, ed. Paul Arthur Schilpp and Maurice Friedman, (Lasalle, Ill., 1967), p. 310.

4. The essay "On the History of the Dialogical Principle" was written in 1954. In the English translation there are omissions, and therefore the quotations are from the original German (*Das dialogische Prinzip*, Heidelberg, 1965), p. 309.

5. Ibid.

6. Ibid., p. 308. It is interesting to note that the two contradictory statements are found in the same essay.

7. I wish to thank the archive of *Der Brenner* for their kindness in furnishing me with a copy of this letter.

8. Franz Rosenzweig, *Briefe*, Berlin 1935, p. 462. (See also *Buber's Way*, p. 189.)

9. *Buber's Way*, pp. 128-130.

10. Buber published this story in *Autobiographische Fragmente* (Stuttgart, 1960) and introduced significant changes, wishing at that late period to deny that the start of the formation of *I and Thou* had been as late as autumn 1921. As explained in my book there are decisive reasons for accepting Buber's first version of the story in *Religion as Presence*, rather than the version published in 1960; see *Buber's Way*, pp. 176-177.

11. Ebner, *Schriften* I, p. 240.

12. Ibid, p. 254, also p. 187.

13. Ibid, p. 35, also pp. 239, 267, 281.

14. Ibid, p. 157.

15. Ibid, p. 173.

16. Ibid.

17. Martin Buber, *I and Thou*, translated by Walter Kaufmann (Charles Scribner's Sons, 1970), p. 161.

18. *Buber's Way*, p. 132.

19. Ebner, Schriften I, p. 281f.

20. *Buber's Way*, pp. 107-109. See also my study "Giluyim le-Toldot Ha-Sefer 'Ani ve-Attah' shel Buber" (Discoveries on the History of Composition of Buber's *I and Thou*), in *Divrei ha-Akademiah ha-Leumit le-Madaim*, vol. 5, no. 8, p. 25.

21. *Buber's Way*, p. 107.

22. "The Question to the Single One", in *Between Man and Man*, trans. Ronald Gregor Smith (Boston, 1955), p. 52.

23. *Buber's Way*, pp. 227f.

24. Rivka Horwitz, "Ha-Gnostikah ve-Torat ha-Briyah Be-Mishnat Martin Buber", in *Daat*, no. 2-3, 5738-5739, p. 239.

25. "What is Man?", in *Between Man and Man*, p. 179.

26. *Buber's way*, p. 218. See also the chapter "Creation" in *The Star of Redemption*, trans. William W. Hallo, New York, 1971.

27. *I and Thou*, p. 163.

28. Ibid, p. 69.

29. Epistle to John I, 4:20.

30. *Schriften* I, p. 36.

31. *Das dialogische Prinzip*, p. 306.

32. *I and Thou*, pp. 58-59, 172-173.

33. Letter of 23.12.1932 to Hermann Gerson. Martin Buber, *Briefwechsel aus sieben Jahrzenten*, vol. II (Heidelberg 1973), p. 455.

34. Ebner, *Schriften*, vol. II, p. 1096.

Franz Rosenzweig's Criticism of Buber's I and Thou

BERNHARD CASPER

Martin Buber's *I and Thou* and the philosophy of Franz Rosenzweig are usually named in one breath. For, from the historical point of view, the brief decade between 1920 and 1930, in which dialogical thought reached the public through Buber's epoch-making work, was marked for Buber by the unique friendship with Franz Rosenzweig. Buber felt from the beginning that this friendship was "pure utterance, such as one . . . would wish to be able to maintain with everyone".[1] But this friendship by no means prevented a battle of insights from taking place for the sake of the greater truth.

Only after Buber's death did it become known that Rosenzweig, in this dialogue defined by the search for the greater truth, had subjected even Buber's *I and Thou* to friendly but strong criticism. The criticism is directed not only at details, but at the innermost conception of Buber's work. It is contained in a letter which Rosenzweig wrote to Buber in September, 1922, after Buber had sent him the first galley-proofs of *I and Thou* with a request for comments.[2]

In the following pages this criticism will be presented and interpreted, in accordance with the concern which inspired both Buber and Rosenzweig. Our exposition, which will be in three parts, will keep close to the text of *I and Thou* and to the text of the letter. For the purposes of interpretation, however, other passages from Rosenzweig's work will also be quoted.

1. Criticism of the Constriction to I-Thou

Rosenzweig's decisive thesis, which immediately strikes the eye upon a first reading of the letter, is that Buber's understanding of reality is constricted, and this because it ultimately reduces all true, i.e. fulfilled reality, to the I-Thou.

If we look at Buber's thoughts as expressed by Buber himself, we see that Buber indeed makes the I-Thou relationship the authentic and exclusive relationship, i.e. the relationship which includes all reality. For the Thou has infinite meaning. It is Thou for me because it "fills the firmament" (59).[3] It possesses infinite dignity. It is pure emergence of being, and therefore it is also pure presentness. By being with the Thou, I am with "everything". This being-with, which is not a being with any isolated thing, but "only" with "everything" (61), constitutes the I-Thou world. And conversely, in the I-Thou world the I exists in pure, present attention. That is, it presents itself as an I which does not distort by any anticipation what encounters it, but allows everything to be *given* to it, in an act of pure receiving.

According to Michael Theunissen, Buber, although verbally he takes his starting-point from the "attitude" of the I (53), does not mean to suggest that the I continues the I-Thou world. Rather, Buber is concerned with the pure emergence of the I-Thou world from the Between.[4] By making the I-Thou emerge, at the very beginning, from the relationship itself, Buber seeks to overcome the intentional constitution of the world through the *ego cogito* or the *ego volo*. The encounter as such presents itself as that which founds everything, which changes man from the subject of an objective possession of world to "subjectivity" (112) in Buber's sense, that is, to the I of the basic word I-Thou. Thus in the encounter activity and passivity, will and grace, coincide. Rosenzweig does not question the factuality of such an encounter. What he does question is the notion that outside the reality *thus disclosed, thus occurring, and thus present* there is no other true and original reality for man. True, he concedes that with his analysis of the I-It Buber has accurately described an existing situation, namely, the constitution of the world of objects produced and ordered in perspective by the I. But the It thus constituted is for Rosenzweig nothing more than "the product of the great deception, which in Europe is less than 300 years old". (Br T 824)[5]. It is what is merely *thought*, that is, the I, constituted by the ego-cogito, of the Cartesian-Kantian understanding of being, from which Rosenzweig, in his own thinking, distinguishes the *spoken* It.

Next, Rosenzweig elucidates the speaking of this other It with a Biblical example—the words "He killeth and reviveth", from the song of Hannah (Samuel I, 2:6), which are spoken in the morning prayer. In this third-person sentence, according to Rosenzweig, that It is pronounced which on the one hand cannot be included in the I-Thou because it belongs to the "domain" of speaking-about—specifically, about something that lies in a past that is not completed; yet on the other hand, that about which one is speaking here cannot be assimilated to an object constituted by the subject in the modern sense. This It, however, reveals its sovereignty and its necessity to a thinking which understands itself as speech by the fact that—Rosenzweig argues *ad hominem*—even Buber cannot give up speaking in the third person when he wants to express in language that I-Thou world which is given out of the Between and in the Between. For the whole book *I and Thou* represents speech *about* I and Thou, that is, speech in the third person. It is speech about the fact that *it* is thus with I and Thou. Buber by no means escapes the necessity of putting the immediate relationship, which occurs in the moment, into the linguistic medium of third-person speech. The question is whether this may be regarded as a mere phenomenon of deficiency, imposed by fate—"the sublime melancholy of our lot"—or whether the linguistic necessity of speech in the third person is not rather an indication that in the It something speaks up which even the pure I-Thou relationship, in a deeper understanding, requires in order to be.

Going out once more from Buber's own thinking, we note that the Between, through which and from which the pure relationship *gives* itself, can be described linguistically only from my side. For this reason Buber seems at first to be verbally anchoring the I-Thou in the "attitude" of the I; but he then abolishes this attitude *as* attitude in order to express, *negatively,* the Between as what gives the foundation.[6] On the other hand, Buber postulates "being for the Between." "Love is . . . between I and Thou" (66). The basic word I-Thou creates a "mode of existence" (53). Not only does the Between show itself as "actual life" (60), but in the Thou even the "substance" (81) reveals itself. The *"secret ground"* is contemplated in the world-order as presence (82). If we ask whether this "being" with which the I is concerned in the I-Thou relationship is to be effected starting from the I, the answer must turn out negative. Neither the I nor the Other can constitute the encounter out of itself. That which concerns both, namely that the encounter should occur and be, is not solely in our hands. Nor can it be produced by a common will. For this, *as will,* would lag behind the substantiality, in Buber's sense, of the event of encounter, and would falsify it into something subjectively constituted. For this reason Buber attempts to base the event of encounter, with the removal of I and Thou, on the eternal Thou. This eternal Thou seems strangely ambiguous in Buber. On the one hand it is different from me and you. In everything which becomes present we "gaze toward the train of the eternal You" (57). On the other hand it appears as identical with the Between itself, as a "new form of God in the world" (166) or as a "God of the moment."[7]

If one considers only the beginning of *I and Thou* which Rosenzweig had before him when he wrote his letter, and leaves the later theological founding, of a sort, out of the picture, then it is clear that the Between as the origin of me and you cannot be constructed either by me or by you. At the same time, I am concerned with nothing other than that origin which allows us to be. But the origin is also, with respect to me and with respect to you, the Other. For this reason Rosenzweig can say in the last sentence of his letter: "For *my* and *your* sake there must be something besides me and you". And conversely: If I were concerned only with me and if you were concerned only with you, or even: If I were concerned only with you and you were concerned only with me, this "concern" itself would remain empty. It would remain, as something arising from individual selfhood (Jemeinigkeit), something purely formal. And the model of a mutual constitution of I and Thou would not change this. But I am concerned with your real existence, which is the existence of another who possesses world, who is at the same time a finite, historical Other, yet an Other to whom existence has been given unconditionally.

If there were nothing except I and Thou, then you and I would have to effect not only the being of the world but also the being of God.

2. The Temporality of the Basic Words

But now we must ask how "being", as the "enduring" through which I am and you are and we together receive existence in the basic word I-Thou, is given to us, from itself. If we pursue this question, we stumble over a curious relationship of Buber's basic words to *time*, the correction of which, it seems to me, is the innermost intent of Rosenzweig's letter.

Buber's lectures in the Freie Jüdische Lehrhaus, from which the book *I and Thou* emerged, originally bore the title "Religion as Presence". And the presence or presentness of the infinite remained the fundamental theme of *I and Thou*. This is evidence not only by the motto from Goethe's "West östlicher Divan"—"Thus I have finally obtained from you by waiting/God's presence in all elements"[8]—but above all the fact that in all three parts of *I and Thou* we can discover presence or presentness as the phenomenon to which, as to a common denominator, the partially contradictory descriptions of phenomena which Buber provides may be reduced.[9]

The encounter leads the one who encounters into a presence which in the end, one may say, alone constitutes the phenomenality of the I-Thou relationship. The Thou is that which is present per se; conversely, the I of the I-Thou relationship is what it is through living exclusively in the present. The difference between I-Thou and I-It is nothing other than the difference "between presence and object"(63). But the object belongs to the past (64).

The present, which Buber here thematizes as the temporality which alone actually constitutes I and Thou, is, of course, not the point-like present of transition, of the mere movement of time from the future to the past. Rather the present is the present of the *duration*, for which there is no future and no past, a kind of "nunc stans" which is inwardly in motion.

If there should ever be an "ontology of the Between", it would probably be most readily attained through a phenomenology of this specific temporality, through which I and Thou become for each other "what confronts (. . .), enduring and waiting" (64): the presence of the fidelity of the same thing, which through all its various fortunes yet shows itself as the same thing and thus as presence of "actual life" (60). One could also speak of a living identity which is not in my or your power to achieve, but which is granted to us in the Between, which leaves nothing real outside itself and thus need have no care for the future. For outside this presentness there is—nothing. "Ready (gewärting), not seeking" (128), the I of the I-Thou goes its way.

In contrast to this living granted union to life in the "one actuality" (167), the I-It appears as a separation, as something that has split off, come to a standstill, something petrified and cut out of life and thus dead, whose past is nevertheless a past founded on the living presentness of I and Thou. What is striking about the train of thought in I and Thou is that for Buber this present, in which alone I and Thou *are* I and Thou, is on the one hand a present that is occurring. But on the other hand it is also a present that exists a priori, as the doctrine of the inborn Thou, in particular, says. "In the relationships through which we live, the inborn You is realized in the You we encounter" (78).

Buber's thoughts, originally presented under the title "Religion as Presence", may be understood as concerned with bringing to light a presence which has always existed "in all things", which is ultimately Divine presence: the hidden Paradise, which we can enter through all things.

If so, then Buber's thought is certainly indebted to Greek thinking about "physis" and "metexis". The conjecture that he is indeed so indebted is reinforced not only by the passage in *I and Thou* which expressly employs the image of participation (cf. 56, 94, 115–117, 123, 127, 142–143, 149, 162–168)[10] and the comparison of the I-Thou world with the mother-goddess (108), but also by the inclusion of the phenomenon of *history* in the schema of pulsation between I-Thou and I-It, between actuality and latency. History accomplishes itself over and over in three stages—the entrance into real life, the becoming effective in the form, and the dying out in the "dominion of the dead form" (168). The revelations which stand at the beginning of history as it renews itself each time are therefore nothing other than the "eternal revelation". It is the "eternal touch" that is "waiting", the "eternal voice" that "sounds" (160), that are attained in the I-Thou and its presence.

If I am not mistaken, Franz Rosenzweig, from the standpoint of his own thought, was bound to protest against precisely this inclusion of everything in a presence which is eternal, though it falls apart, periodically, over and over. For Rosenzweig's thinking is much more historical than Buber's. At the beginning of Rosenzweig's thought stands the falling-apart and annihilation of that totality or "one reality" in which thought thinks to include the All.[11] Thus for Rosenzweig, unlike Buber, the present can never become the presence of the "one reality" in which basically anything can become Thou to me. And the famous sentence from Rosenzweig's "The New Thinking"—"The difference between the old and the new . . . thinking . . . lies in the fact that one needs the other person and takes time seriously—actually, these two things are identical"—does *not* mean merely that I need "the other in general", but that I need a very specific Other and therefore also a very specific time in order to speak. "But 'speaking' means speaking to some one . . . And this some one is always a quite definite some one".[12]

There can be no doubt that Buber's and Rosenzweig's thoughts are tangent to each other. Rosenzweig himself affirmed this. At the same time, however, we must see that Rosenzweig's historical thinking is much sharper and more concrete. For this reason, I and Thou and the present which breaks open between I and Thou and gives them being, mean different things to the two thinkers. For Rosenzweig this present is only the historical present, specific in each instance, between a specific I and a specific Thou. In the letter we are discussing this is expressed by the fact that Rosenzweig accepts the

Buberian I-Thou only as a sort of abstract formula, but underneath it, as sign for the concrete, historical occurrence of encounter, writes ICH and DU, once each, in capital letters. And it is also expressed by the fact that besides the concretely, historically understood basic word I-Thou and its temporality, Rosenzweig asserts the autonomy of two other basic words: HE-it and We-IT. The basic word HE-it, which expresses the reality of the Creation, belongs to a past which is not completed. This past, unlike the Buberian It-past constituted by the I, is not constituted but perceived by the I. For me it is an existing past, a past which must be taken seriously, with which I am therefore by no means finished, but which calls my attention to the fact that I, as a finite, historical I, presupposes something. The "it" which is expressed in the HE-it is "already there". The "HE killeth and reviveth" has already occurred. It is the occurrence which is immemorial, and with which I am not finished precisely for that reason.

The phenomenon of the past as past which must be taken seriously, which basically has no place in Buber's thought, is restored to its rights by Rosenzweig through the HE-it as the reality of Creation.

And similarly Rosenzweig—unlike Buber, in whose *I and Thou*, as far as I can see, the word "future" is missing altogether—recognizes a future which as such is not yet present in the concrete, historical I-Thou encounter. As there is an immemorial past which is the past of God's creatorhood, so there is—sit venia verbi—an immemorial future, the future of salvation, which cannot be anticipated in any way, i.e. not by the historical I-Thou. This future, however, is expressed in the We-IT.

What this means in Rosenzweig's thinking can only be hinted at here. Above all it means two things:

a) that not I, but only we suffice to constitute the world. The world as the existing world, in which one can make oneself understood by speaking in the third person, is always the "world we have in common". What is "valid" in each instance is by no means only what is dead, but that of which *we can speak in common*. This, however, exists historically.

b) And it exists, according to the author of the *Star of Redemption*, because we *hope* that that of which we can speak will finally become redeemed, i.e. wholly free, really valid IT.

Future as immemorial future is ultimately the future of the kingdom, of the kingship of God, for which we hope and pray.

I and Thou, in general, *participate* in this future as those who each time anew say what it is possible to say, speaking in the third person, *and* who are I and Thou, that is, those who have received the revelation and live in neighborly love. Nevertheless this future cannot be wholly *included* in the presentness of the concrete, historical I-Thou. Rather, the future is something else besides—a future which cannot be included in any present. This is signified by the autonomy of the basic word We-IT, the word of the exit, the word of liberation and redemption.

One may also say that through the clear distinction of the three basic words which Rosenzweig presents to Buber, the mortality of the I and Thou of the concrete historical event of encounter stands out more clearly; but so do the specific temporality of the present which occurs here, and the "between" situation of the event of encounter *between* creation (the immemorial presupposition) *and* redemption (the final unity for which we can only hope). The presence which occurs in the concrete, historical dialogue is itself mere timebound, expiring presence; by no means is it simply eternity in time. Rather there is something besides it.

3. God

Therefore God cannot be assimilated into a present such that there is "no longer any tension between world and God but only the one actuality" (157). Herein lies, I think, Rosenzweig's most serious objection to Buber. It is the objection expressed in the last two sentences but one of our letter: "But nevertheless: what will become of I and Thou if they have to swallow the whole world and the Creator too? Religion? I am afraid so—and I shudder at the word, as always when I hear it."

The reproach which Rosenzweig voices here in his friendly criticism of Buber is the same reproach which he leveled against the theology of national consciousness in 1914, when he accused the latter of dissolving God into the life of the nation and thus becoming an "atheistic theology".[13] In *I and Thou* the nation is replaced, it may be said with due respect for the difference in level between the two thoughts, by the Between, the enduring present, in which I and Thou exist for each other. Of course, God is not simply identical with the Between which in the isolate case occurs as that which gives being to me and you. For Buber God is not the "Moment-God" but rather the "eternal You" which is this "by its very nature" (160)—a formulation, by the way, which strikingly parallels the scholastic conception of God.[14] The eternal Thou is not subject to the alternation of actuality and latency. Therefore it is the Thou whose presence alone allows me to "say You in one word to the being of all beings." (157) Unlike the emerging and the disappearing presence of the human Thou, it is the constant presence, the enduring present, although it exists for the I only as the same, constant presence in the renewed event of encounter. The eternal Thou is the center in which, "extended, the lines of"—discontinuously occurring—"relationship intersect" (148). Into this one constant presence, as into the existing "magnum est" which waits in all the events of encounter which are subject to the alternation of actuality and latency, I enter in each event of encounter.

But the peculiarity of Buber's understanding of God consists in the fact that God can be comprehended *only thus*. In the encounter between me and the other Thou, the encounter with the pure, timelessly present Thou is always included as that which makes the finite encounter possible. "In every You we address the eternal You" (57), or "the central You that is received in the present" (95). The immediacy of the encounter is nevertheless mediated by "the mediatorship of the You of all beings" (123). The eternal center opens up in every Between as the basis of its possibility—and, many are inclined to add in accordance with Buber's line of thought, as nothing else. God is nothing but the Between of all beings, the eternal You.

In Michael Theunissen's opinion, what is problematic about Buber's understanding of God is not that he posits God as Thou, but that "he posits *Thou as God*".[15] But basically Rosenzweig's objection already takes aim at the problematic character of this relationship of mutual founding between I-Thou and eternal Thou: "What is to become of I and Thou if they have to swallow the whole world and the Creator too?" I and Thou are placed in the precarious position of the Kantian ontotheological being of all beings, which must ask itself, "But whence then am I?"[16]

But according to the *Star of Redemption*, God cannot be only the eternal Thou, given the seriousness with which the temporal constitution of thought as speech is taken. For speech in the second person, which can occur only in the immediacy of the present, is by no means the only authentic way of speaking. On the contrary, speech *about*, speech occurring in the mediatedness of the third person, is, where temporality is taken seriously, a perfectly serious and by no means deficient way of speaking. I myself immediately become, in the course of time, i.e. my history, a stranger and another, and therefore can only speak of what "happened then" in the third person.

In the terminology of the *Star of Redemption*: I can speak to God in the second person only in the moment of revelation, in the "occurred event"[17] itself and in prayer. As soon as I bear witness to the revelation, I must already speak *of* HIM. Such would only be deficient speech if it were no longer mindful of its origin in the past event. And even the choral speech of acknowledgment and praise in worship is necessarily a speaking in the third person, for God is the third person to us who are worshipping together, though he is not an It in the Buberian sense. Such speaking—in the letter Rosenzweig merely indicates this theory, which is worked out in the *Star* with reference to the grace after meals—requires the permission of those who share in the thanksgiving or profession of faith must be obtained, because what is to be acknowledged in common can be acknowledged only *as* something in common, that is, it must also be affirmed by *others*. One may, if one wishes, see in this a relinking of such speaking in the third person with the I-Thou. What is professed here, happened to me and you. But, precisely: *it happened*. Therefore we can speak about it in the third person.

But to speak of God in the third person is to recognize "God's being"—if we may use the term this once—as what cannot be entirely comprehended in the I-Thou relationship. In speaking of revelation, which Rosenzweig understands as concrete historical revelation, one makes clear that here something *happened* to me or us which "really is something", and about which one can now speak. It goes without saying, for Rosenzweig, that in the Biblical revelation this something is basically concerned with the relationship of man to man, which is set on a new path by the revelation.

The speech about God which Rosenzweig demands of Buber does not proceed from the assumption that God can be *directly* attained through the I-Thou relationship. Rather it is rooted in the *separation* of God and man and world, which as *thought* phenomena are merely phenomena. But in the event of revelation, in the concrete commandment, something is done to man through which the "deus absconditus" becomes the "tamen non ignotus": one now can speak of God on the basis of this concrete way of human co-existence, the way that opens up in the event of revelation. According to this way of thinking, God remains God, man remains man, and the world remains the world. They do not have to be gathered into a unity included in man. But they have something to do with each other, in the concrete historical event of encounter, in which HE directs His intent toward me and you. In this event God as merely eternal Thou becomes the wholly other—the God who historically claims man and who is thus the hidden, but no longer unknown God. And man changes, is converted, from a being that existed a priori to Man who is called forth by the commandments and given being as man along with man, and who in his historical existence experiences the "germination of redemption". And the world as something that is indifferently there becomes the world which is to be gathered, through love of one's neighbor, into the light of the future redemption (i.e. into the word of exit—We-it) which is to occur also *through* man.

From this view, which leads into the freedom of history and whose innermost center is the experience of Biblical revelation, Rosenzweig criticizes Buber's I and Thou, which he sees as swallowing up everything. The ultimate unity is not the unity of I and Thou but the unity of the creator, revealer, and redeemer, which cannot be assimilated by historical man. For the same reason God himself is "not everything", as Rosenzweig puts it in a letter, "rather everything is *from* him and *to* him . . . to put it in learned fashion, he stands in *relation* to everything".[18] This relationship becomes concrete, however, in the historically concrete event of revelation, through which humankind experiences God's unconditional love and concrete instruction. From this event they can speak of the hidden but now no longer unknown One and acknowledge the immemorial Creator and the Redeemer of times to come, the "Lord of the future".[19]

Now the question arises whether Rosenzweig's differentiated philosophy of revelation simply calls Buber's *I and Thou* into question. Does not Rosenzweig's criticism rather throw into relief a central concern of Buber's thought which had had to be obscured in the execution of *I and Thou*—for the reason that *I and Thou* is still rooted, more than is generally assumed and not only linguistically, in the continuity of predialogical thinking. The friendly dialogue with Rosenzweig of which this letter is merely the beginning, it seems to me, led Buber to at least partly integrate Rosenzweig's criticism into his own thinking. Such seems to be evidenced by the omission of the motto and the change in the name of God in the later editions of *I and Thou*. Further evidence, it seems to me, is the fact that in the German translation of the Bible Buber expressly approved Rosenzweig's proposal to render the name of God by ER—HE —when the text speaks *about* God.

In the first edition of *I and Thou* Buber gives Exodus 3:14 an altogether traditional rendition, which attributes metaphysical meaning to the passage: "I am that I am. That which reveals is that which reveals. Being is nothing more".[20] The lectures "Religion as Presence" had added in explanation: "The revelations . . . are basically nothing other than the eternal, all-present revelation, the revelation of Now and Here. Never and nowhere has anything happened which is not also happening now and here."[21] This passage, whose language incidentally recalls a well-known definition of myth,[22] is remarkably dichotomous. It speaks on the one hand of the "now and here". But on the other hand it reduces the revelation to "the eternal, all-present revelation". Thus it risks depriving the revelations of their unique, historical, factual character. God seems here to stand opposite man, all-present, transcending history. He does not involve himself actively with man. Only man relates to the Eternal in individually differing ways. And this alone would then constitute human history. But at the same time, man knows of that all-present history-transcending unity. If one follows this interpretation, one must see Buber in a tradition which is Platonic in the broadest sense.

But in the later editions of *I and Thou* Buber renders the name of God as follows: "I am there as whoever I am there. That which reveals is that which reveals, nothing more". (160) And in his own remarks on the German translation of the scriptures,[23] he expressly refers to Rosenzweig's essay "Der Ewige", in which Rosenzweig argues that the Biblical understanding of God does not differ from the pagan by its assertion of the unity of the Divine being. The unity of a "generally religious" and therefore eternal being is a tenet shared by every polytheism. The essential element of the Biblical faith in God is rather that "while it *presupposes* the God of Aristotle, it recognizes this God in his oneness with the very personally and immediately experienced . . . God of Abraham".[24] Therefore God can be named "in all three dimensions of the personal pronouns",[25] including the "HE" of "speaking about", in which "that one who was present with them, there with them"[26] is named.

Given his starting point, Buber had at first, in *I and Thou,* to reject the naming of God by the HE as inauthentic. (147) The HE would have to fall into the domain of the basic word I-It. In the German translation of fall into the domain of the basic word I-It. In the German translation of the Bible, however, Buber accepted Rosenzweig's arguments and rendered the name of God, wherever the text speaks *about* God, as HE, which of course no longer falls into the basic word I-It. To this extent, it seems to me, Buber's further thought was indeed affected by Rosenzweig's criticism—a criticism which, like its occasion, is great and worthy of thought, and whose message, even today, has not yet been thought through to the end.[27]

Discussion Following Bernhard Casper's Lecture

J. BLOCH

I would like to explain briefly why I do not think that your portrayal of Buber is entirely accurate.

First of all, there is the problem of negativism which keeps coming up. Theunissen and Casper see it as a deficiency phenomenon, but it is only a deficiency phenomenon of language.

Theunissen thinks that it arises from the fact that Buber's concept of I-Thou is a product of the destruction of an originally existing philosophical model—the model according to which "It", and presumably also "Thou", are a projection of a transcendental subject. As far as I can see, that idea never entered Buber's head. Transcendental philosophy was simply not relevant for him. He wanted to contrast the I-Thou with an attitude of the I which is remote from the world. Not: which projects the world. The closedness of the empirical, the grasping I, the I that has transitive verbs—this distance from the world was what had to be overcome. I can depict this overcoming only negatively because it stands aside from the transitive verbs. It is a linguistic problem.

This is connected with Theunissen's thesis that I and Thou arise from the Between, that the Between is the true origin. And that the Thou is God. Both these ideas are incorrect.

From "Daniel" on, the basic structure of Buber's thought is the concept of realization. The I, the I-Thou, the Thou-I, "realizes"; hence it is always an I that also acts. The Thou, from its own point of view, is also a realizing I. But this means that the I-Thou relationship itself cannot be God; rather God remains outside. I realize a destiny which is given by creation, which is therefore always related to God; in realization I come before God.

You quote a number of passages which are supposed to show that the totality of being is included in the I-Thou relationship. You say that love is between I and Thou. That has nothing to do with being. If you translate the sentence into Hebrew, for instance, the verb "sein" is eliminated; it is only a predicative statement, which in German inevitably falls back on the verb "to be". The word "Bestand" (mode of existence) signifies solely that what is to be realized exists and is given in advance. In the I-Thou I establish a mode of being, that is, I create what is already there. "Substance", in the passage which you quote, has nothing whatever to do with the I, but refers to the sphere of It. It is intended to show that the substance of It-thinking emerges from a memory of the Thou. "Grund" foundation in the last quotation refers to Creation and has nothing to do with "being".

In other words, if in I and Thou being is *not* included, God is *not* at hand; if, as indeed always with Buber, God is *not* included, then the difference between Buber and Rosenzweig is by no means as radical as it has been portrayed. And therefore Buber could unhesitatingly adopt the ER—the HE—in his Bible translation. For Buber the names of God are also signs of address. He can adopt ER because God remains outside. At one point in the "Dialogical Principle" he says that all the names of God remain sanctified because in them God is not merely spoken about, but also addressed. Therefore he is able to adopt the HE, because in Buber too the I always comes only from God.

B. CASPER

I will attempt to answer the question.

1) First, the subject of negativism—that one can speak of the Thou only in negative terms. In my understanding this is precisely not a deficiency phenomenon—I never said that it was—but rather the indication of a positivity which goes beyond the limits of ontology. The basic question is: can philosophy thematize the Other *as* Other? It turns out that philosophy cannot do this. Therefore there can be only a negative ontology of the BETWEEN. But this very fact tells us that we are dealing with a positivity of the most extreme kind. What is called negative ontology is therefore an indication of a philosophical task; to find a way of thinking which does justice to that which is of such paramount importance to us, and on which the survival of the world depends.

2) I used the term "deficiency-phenomenon" in connection with the quotation "melancholy of our lot" in the third part of *I and Thou*. Specifically, in the following connection: Rosenzweig calls attention to the fact that the whole book *I and Thou* is a speech in the third person. Now my question was: is this *only* the sublime melancholy of our lot, that we cannot linguistically maintain the strictness of the I-Thou experience and therefore lapse into deficient speech—or is this an indication that speech in the third person can mean something

completely different from what it is in Buber's I-It phenomenon? And this second possibility is what I wanted to affirm, along with Rosenzweig. The fact that Buber himself speaks quite easily in the third person about all the things that are close to his heart shows that he cannot do without this "It of Creation", this "it is already there", and that this is after all not speech *about* what I have observed, in the sense of speech that proceeds merely from the "ego cogito". The letter begins with Rosenzweig saying: the It which you present there, you can easily dispose of. For it is a cripple, the cripple of the last 300 years of the history of philosophy. Here Rosenzweig can only be thinking of the Cartesian-Kantian It, which the "ego cogito" produces as its construct.

3) On the problem of the worldlessness of the I in the I-It world: It is well-known that the concept "world" has widely differing meanings in *I and Thou*. When Buber says, "The world is twofold for man . . . in accordance with the two basic words he can speak", the world is understood as a relational concept for the I that realizes itself in either way. When he says, "The one who experiences does not participate in the world", then "world" has the full resonance of "world of Creation". Rosenzweig would also say: of the world that is to be redeemed. It is perfectly clear that in the event and moment of encounter I release myself into the world as the fullness which is given and is to be redeemed. I see a misunderstanding here, and not a difference between us.

4) What Rosenzweig is primarily criticizing, in my opinion, is Buber's fixation on the phenomenon of presentness. Rosenzweig thinks much more soberly and says: in your life, in your realization, there is something which is past, and which you must take seriously. And there is also something which you hope for, and which is thus not merely an unfolding of the present. Of course this present mode in which I and Thou are there for each other, does have an immanent future: the immanent future of fidelity between two people. A marriage, for instance, has an immanent future, which is already contained in the reality of fidelity. But Rosenzweig, particularly in the notes to "Yehuda Halevi", calls attention to the fact that future, of which one can speak only in the manner of the prophets, can be completely withdrawn from me. I have no way of knowing what it will be like when the day of God's judgment dawns. This is what I have called "immemorial future".

5) On the question to what extent I and Thou emerge from the Between: I think that here there is a misunderstanding between you

and Theunissen. Theunissen means this theology ontologically and not ontically. What is the difference? In the preliminary work to *I and Thou* which Rivka Horwitz has published, Buber speaks of the "hypostasis of the BETWEEN." If you take "hypostasis" in the sense of "becoming substance", you may end up with an ontic understanding of the Between, as if the Between were a kind of reality like other reality, from which one could derive I and Thou by causal analysis. After all, Buber had been debating the question of what the Between is since his preface to the series "Die Gesellschaft". When Theunissen says that I and Thou emerge from the Between, he means by this merely that the Between is the "ground of possibility" for I and Thou. I come into being through you, you come into being through me, therefore I and Thou can only be if the Between is. Consequently, the Between has an ontological, but not an ontic priority.

6) On the question of "Being": I did not say that Buber asserts the absoluteness of BEING. But I demonstrated that Buber first describes the basic words as phenomena of attitude. But then the basic words do after all establish a "mode of existence". And I naturally wonder: did Buber at that time think in Hebrew or in German? If you translate "Die Liebe ist" (love is) into Hebrew, then the word "ist" drops out. But in my opinion Buber at that time still thought in German.

Notes

BERNHARD CASPER

1. Martin Buber, *Briefwechsel aus sieben Jahrzehnten*, Band II: 1918-1938, Heidelberg 1973, 138-139.

2. The letter was first published by Grete Schaeder in Martin Buber, *Briefwechsel aus sieben Jahrzehnten*, II, 124-128. It also appears in Franz Rosenzweig, Gesammelte Schriften, 1. Abteilung: Briefe und Tagebücher, Den Haag, Martinus Nijhoff.

3. The page numbers in parenthesis refer to Martin Buber, *I and Thou*, translated by Walter Kaufmann, New York, 1970.

4. M. Theunissen, *Der Andere: Studien zur Sozialontologie der Gegenwart*, Berlin, 1965, p. 278 f.

5. The page numbers given in parenthesis with BrT refer to: Franz Rosenzweig, *Der Mensch und sein Werk*. I. Abteilung: Briefe und Tagebücher, Den Haag, Nijhoff, 1978.

6. Cf. Theunissen, loc. cit. Negation means here that the ontological constitution of the I-Thou is negated by the attitude, that is positing, of the I. The fundamental relationship—that the Thou does not exist by my grace—cannot be expressed in any other manner. This does not assert an ontic Prius of the between.

7. Martin Buber, "Dialogue", in *Between Man and Man*, translated by Ronald Gregor Smith, London, 1947, p. 14.

8. Walter Kaufmann's translation of the motto in his introduction to *I and Thou*, p. 26.

9. Cf. Buber, *I and Thou*, pp. 57, 62-63, 85, 107, 78-84, 126-131, 142-143, 157, 160, 161, 164, 167, 171.

10. In his later work Buber explicitly develops the concept of participation. Cf. "The Question to the Single One", in *Between Man and Man*, pp. 42, 47; "What is Man?" in *Between Man and Man*, pp. 193, 194; and "Elements of the Interhuman", in *The Knowledge of Man*, ed. by Maurice Friedman, New York, 1965, pp. 77-78, 80.

11. Cf. F. Rosenzweig, The Star of Redemption, trans. William W. Hallo, New York, 1971, here especially the first part (pp. 3-90).

12. Franz Rosenzweig, "The New Thinking", in *Franz Rosenzweig: His Life and Thought*, ed. Nahum Glatzer, New York, 1953, p. 200.

13. Cf. the essay "Atheistische Theologie" in: F. Rosenzweig, *Kleinere Schriften*, Berlin, 1937, 278-290.

14. Deus non habet quidditatem vel essentiam, quia essentia sua non est aliud quam esse suum. Thomas of Aquinas, *De ente et essentia*, chap. V.

15. Theunissen, op. cit., p. 340.

16. Immanuel Kant, *Critique of Pure Reason*, trans. Norman Kemp Smith, London, 1950, p. 513.

17. F. Rosenzweig, *Star of Redemption*, p. 159.

18. F. Rosenzweig, *Briefe und Tagebücher*, letter no. 408, p. 414.

19. In the "Sechzig Hymnen und Gedichte des Jehuda Halevi" (Konstanz, 1924), which is dedicated to Martin Buber, Rosenzweig distinguishes (p. 158) "consolation,

promise, even hope, which all gaze into the future, but from the present" from a "purely present future, the summons, the 'Be ready' ". The latter addresses me from the mouth of the "Lord of the future".

20. *Ich und Du*, first edition, Leipzig, 1923, p. 129.

21. From the eighth lecture in the series "Religion als Gegenwart", published in Rivka Horwitz, *Martin Buber's Way to I and Thou*, Heidelberg, 1978, p. 148.

22. Cf. Sallustios (philosophos): Περὶ θεῶν καὶ κόσμου, IV, 9: "Ταῦτα δὲ ἐγένετο μὲν οὐδέποτε, ἔστι δὲ ἀεί."

23. M. Buber, Werke, Bd. II: *Schriften zur Bibel*, Munich, 1964, p. 1128.

24. F. Rosenzweig, *Kleinere Schriften*, Berlin, 1937, p. 192.

25. Ibid., p. 188.

26. Ibid., p. 188.

27. Ibid., p. 193.

APPENDIX:
Franz Rosenzweig's letter to Buber

(Undated)

Esteemed Doctor,

This is not at all an easy task for me. You yourself distinguish quite correctly between that which I can say to you and that which I can say about the book. (. . .)

All the rest that I have to say goes deeper, belongs no more to the "corrections". I would like to take the bull by the horns immediately: with the I-It you give the I-Thou a cripple for an opponent. That this cripple rules the modern world, does not change the fact that it is a cripple. *This* It, you can easily dispose of. But it is the false It, the product of the great deception, which in Europe is less than 300 years old. Only along with *this* It is an I—not spoken, but thought. No I is spoken along with the *spoken* It. At least no human I. What I as a human being speak along with this It, when I speak it correctly, is: HE. Of course the "basic word I-It" cannot be spoken with the whole being. But then it is not a basic *word*, it is at most a basic thought— not even that: it is just a tip of a thought, a philosophical point. If, nevertheless, It is quite real, then it must be inscribed in a basic word which can likewise be spoken with one's whole being, by *him* who speaks it. From his point of view this basic word is called I-It. From ours: HE-It. If you once say "He kills and makes alive", then you have said it with your whole being.

From this constriction to I-Thou (which, by the way, you share with Ebner) all the rest, I think, follows. You, like Ebner, intoxicated by the joy of discovery, throw everything else (quite literally) to the dead. But *It* is not dead, although death belongs to it; It is created. But because you equate It with the "it" "for" the "I", which to be sure is dead, you *must* then raise everything which you do not want to let fall into this valley of death, because it is too much alive, into the domain of the basic word I-Thou, which therefore *must* be enormously expanded.

What happens to you is exactly the opposite of what happens to your fellow-discoverer Cohen (a real story of "four who entered Pardes"!): he discovered the I-Thou as the great exception to the rule and built for its sake an additional wing to his already completed edifice, trying hard to avoid disfiguring the finished one. Naturally, he did not succeed. Much too much wished to enter into this adjacent wing, which had previously found its place in the old house; thus the new wing threatened to become a house in itself, in which those who had frequented the old house felt least at home. You, on the other hand, erect from the very start a new building, you make of Creation a chaos, just good enough to provide you with building materials for the new building; whatever doesn't fit into it becomes inessential. Cohen was *alarmed* by his discovery, you are *intoxicated* by it; hence many *others* will follow you and will "cut off the plants". But in this Pardes there is also one who "entered in peace and went out in peace". To use your language: besides the I-Thou there are two equally essential basic words, basic words into whose one half the being of the other half is poured, just as much as with I-Thou. One, the HE-It, the word of the "entrance", I mentioned already. The word of the "exit"—that same exit from Pardes—is "WE-It" (with you, surely, I can be thus formulaically brief?). That is the second way of saying It "with the whole being". *I* cannot say It with my whole being, but HE can and *We* can. (N.B: in the We-It lie the answers to all those problems which philosophy attempts to answer in the pseudo-basic word I-It.) But by *Our* saying it, It becomes—IT. So that now the following series arises, in which the I-Thou must form the center, because in this Pardes there is a complete balance of powers, by the fact that I-Thou can unveil itself in every moment as *I*-Thou and it can equally unveil itself at every moment as I-THOU:

HE-It, I-Thou, We-I
I-Thou
I-*THOU*

The beginning and the end of this series, linked together, yield Schelling's great saying: "And then pantheism will be true". Our controversy, in all the details we have discussed, centers around the word It; not only the tree (which incidentally almost bewitched me just now, so splendidly does it shine on p. 13) and the work of art, but also the question of the "Law", the permission (a permission! only a permission! maranan ve-rabanan!! birshut!!!) to speak of God again in the third person and though that (and through that alone) the possibility of speaking even of the Creator—everything follows from this point. And do not even you continually, involuntarily pay your tribute to the despised word? By your speaking *about* I-Thou. And by your replacing Cohen's "Correlation" with the really no more German word "Beziehung". You could have chosen other words, words that I can speak to You and You to Me (can I say to You: "I stand in relation to you"??), more German words—if you had not needed to squeeze into the I-Thou so much (namely all authentic life) which can be spoken wholly and without compulsion only in the *It*, of course only in the genuine It of the HE-It and the We-It, not in the fictitious one of the I-It.

Dear Doctor— I am a very unselfish knight of the It, now more than ever. I am truly *interested* now, behind my curtained windows, only in I and Thou. But nevertheless: What is to become of I and Thou if they have to swallow the whole world and the Creator too? Religion?—I am afraid so—and I shudder at the word, as always when I hear it. For *my* and *your* sake there must be something besides—me and you.

Yours as ever,
F. R.

THE BIBLE

Buber and Modern Biblical Scholarship

BENYAMIN UFFENHEIMER

1. *Introduction*

The purpose of this essay is to evaluate Buber's work on the Bible, both in terms of the general spiritual aims which he had in view and which found their expression in other branches of his creativity, and in an attempt to sketch the lines which connect this work with Jewish Biblical scholarship and modern Jewish thought on the one hand, and with Protestant Biblical scholarship and Christian theology on the other. It is important to keep in mind that unlike professional Biblical scholars, who see themselves first and foremost as philologians and historians seeking the historical, objective truth attainable by man, Buber approached the Bible as a thinker of the Jewish national revival movement, seeking in the Bible his own truth and the truth of his generation. The information about the past which is stored up in the Bible interested him less than the hidden message it contains for the present and the future. Hence he did not set out to describe an inclusive historic context, but to bring out those episodes capable of illuminating the paths of our generation in its perplexity. We shall consider three aspects of his contribution: first, his linguistic-literary method; second, his antirationalist theology (here our discussion will focus on the question of the relation between myth and monotheism); and third, his historical approach to the origins and nature of monotheism. In the fourth section we shall try to assess his exegetical approach in the light of his philosophical assumptions and shall close with some critical remarks.

Indeed, the fact that Buber sought in the Bible the roots of our national revival brings him close to the creators of modern Jewish Biblical scholarship, which was a definite innovation in the spiritual world of post-Emancipation Judaism. Unlike the classical "Wissenschaft vom Judentum" which to a great extent sought to prepare the ground for assimilation, Jewish Biblical scholarship was nourished from the beginning of this century by the spiritual forces of the Jewish national revival movement, whose orientation was inward toward an ingathering of our spiritual heritage in order to turn it into an active factor in the process of our revival. Hence the three main attitudes which characterize this scholarly trend and which all found expression in the work of Buber:

1. Their inquiry into Biblical language and literature was part of their personal involvement in the process of revival of Hebrew. In their consciousness the language of the Bible became an inseparable part of the living Hebrew language which was once again an ebullient fact of life. It goes without saying that they were more acutely attuned than their Christian counterparts to the living sound of the language of the Bible; this is especially true of Buber.

2. In their reflections on the spritual world of the Bible they consciously dissociate themselves from the various Protestant theological approaches and methods which are still current in the West. They sought to evaluate the Bible as a creation of a national culture shaped by a central religious idea. On the strength of this recognition they tried to remove the world of the Bible in general from theology and from the Protestant theology which had nourished German Biblical scholarship in particular. Similarly, most of them turned away from the evolutionary explanation of the faith of Israel held by Wellhausen and his school.

3. The majority of the Jewish Biblical scholars were well acquainted with most of the branches of Jewish culture, and in their view the world of the Bible was a fundamental stratum of Jewish culture. In contradistinction to Western Christian scholarship, which valued the Bible (the "Old Testament") chiefly as a preparation for the New Testament, Jewish scholars focused on Jewish culture in all its manifestations, as the historical structure which arose on the foundation of the Bible.

To illustrate these points, let us briefly recall the work of men like S. Bernfeld, A. Kahana, Benno Jacob, M. D. Cassuto, F. Rosenzweig, Y. Kaufmann, M. Z. Segal, and N. H. Tur-Sinai, who were contemporaries of Buber. Most of them approached the Bible as Jewish thinkers seeking to understand their Judaism. A. Kahana, the senior member of this group, was an historian; in addition to the scholarly interpretation of the Bible which he initiated in conjunction with other Jewish scholars around the turn of the century, he translated the Apocrypha into Hebrew and accompanied the translations with scholarly introductions and a commentary. He also wrote on the Kabbalists and the Sabbataians, and on Hassidim. His declared intention was critical and secular, like that of Protestant scholarship; his own perspective, however, was Judaism in all its historical manifestations. Similarly, Kaufmann, from the publicatrion of his youthful work *Gola Ve-Nekhar* (Exile and Foreign Land) onward, approached the Bible as a sociologist of the Jewish people. True, his approach was thoroughly critical and secular, but he engaged in sharp and penetrating polemics against Protestant scholarship; one of the aims of his work was to expose the Christian and anti-Jewish tendentiousness as an arbitrary factor in the theories of Wellhausen and his disciples and of twentieth-century scholars. An anti-Christian polemical tendency is also clearly visible in Benno Jacob's monumental commentary on the book of Genesis and in the work of M. D. Cassuto; both of them set out to refute the source hypothesis which had been elaborated by Wellhausen and his school. They were striving to create a religious, non-Orthodox, Jewish antithesis to the methods of the Christian scholars. Cassuto, who started out as an historian, was able to incorporate into his work the early results of the study of Ugaritic literature, which he was one of the first to investigate. For Franz Rosenzweig the study of the Bible was one of the major stations in his return to his ancestral heritage; at the same time his interest became focused on medieval Hebrew poetry. The two brilliant linguists among this distinguished company were M. Z. Segal and N. H. Tur-Sinai. The first began his career with the study of the language of the Mishnah, while the second was a gifted Orientalist, thoroughly framed in ancient Eastern languages. Besides his important contribution to Biblical studies, he participated in the revival of the Hebrew language. Thus one may say that when these scholars approched the Bible they were already rooted in the Jewish heritage; in debate with Protestant scholarship they sought to restore the Jewish essence of Bible exegesis and scholarship. The Jewish perspective and the fact that they wrote Hebrew as a living language (or at least had some connection with Hebrew in its development over the centuries) are the two distinguishing marks they have in common.

Buber belongs to this group in all aspects mentioned; when he began his Biblical studies he had already established his reputation as the philosopher of dialogue; as a student of Hasidim and a thinker of the Jewish national revival movement he was attentive to the uniqueness of the Biblical dialogue between man and his creator. That is to say: Buber's dominant interest was that of a believer; more precisely, he tried to listen for the voice and the language of living faith, of the "Torah." It seems to me that this daring is what distinguishes him from all other Biblical scholars of our own and the preceding generation. Thus he says: "None of those books (the holy books of other nations) is like it (the Bible), full of a dialogue between Heaven and earth. It tells how again and again God addresses man and is addressed by him ... The basic doctrine which fills the Hebrew Bible is that our life is a dialogue between the above and the below."[1]

A. *Buber's Literary Method and Its Place in Modern Scholarship*

Buber took the first step toward unveiling this truth in his study of the language and literary structure of the Bible. In order to penetrate into the inner meaning of the Bible, he felt the need to develop a new linguistic and literary approach. He succeeded in this thanks to his deep sensitiveness towards the Hebrew language, including all its post-Biblical layers, though he did not neglect the achievements of modern Biblical scholarship and Oriental studies.

At the beginning of the 1920's, the inner dynamics of the historical-critical method established by Wellhausen had led to a crisis. Whereas Wellhausen had analyzed the Torah into four main sources, his disciples determined that these sources themselves were not monolithic; they in turn were composed of subsidiary sources. Under their critical gaze every source disintegrated into three or four subsidiary sources. The atomization of the Bible was the reductio ad absurdum of this direction in scholarship, to the point where Gressmann compared the Biblical scholar to the archaeologist whose task is to disentangle the jumbled-up layers in an excavated mound. It was Herman Gunkel who, with great vigour, took a stand against this destructive tendency. He asserted that this method of analysis into sources needed to be supplemented by the study of literary genres and the history of traditions (Gattungsforschung, Traditionsgeschichte). He argued that each source was the product of many developments within the oral tradition which preceded the written Torah. In the process of these developments different traditions were formed into a single version, and the literary dovetailing was for the most part so thorough that there is no possibility of arriving at the different elements by means of analysis of sources and dissection of verses; only in a general way is it possible to point to different strands of tradition within a

given literary text. Moreover, he sought to explain the literary forms
which have come down to us according to their growth in life-
situations, or as he put it, "der Sitz im Leben." His additional
assumption was that ancient Near Eastern literature tended more
than modern literature to crystallize into fixed, stereotyped forms,
shaped by the social functions which gave rise to them. In contrast to
this natural growth, the work of writers, scribes, and editors was
secondary. Thus Gunkel did not challenge historical-critical scholarship per se; he rather sought to confine it to its legitimate boundaries,
while transferring the center of gravity to the study of literary forms
and of the traditions which preceded the literary stage. His theory
was an outcome of the recognition that it is difficult to arrive at the
literal, pre-Biblical wording of the different traditions which have
been woven into the literary text which has come down to us. Then
came Buber, who claimed that he could go back far beyond the written word: not content with the oral tradition, he leaps over it to the
primordial moment of living speech: "Is it a book we mean? We
mean a voice; and do we believe our task is to read? We believe our
task is to listen for the spoken word. We want to reach the word in the
moment of its utterance."[2] Nonetheless, he does not oppose the
source hypothesis, unlike Cassuto and Benno Jacob, who attacked the
school of Wellhausen and sought to elucidate the Torah as a unified
creation. According to Cassuto the Torah does indeed contain different traditions, but the author wove them into the text in the interest
of objectivity; Buber, however, not only did he not attack Wellhausen, but paid his respects to him by saying: "I . . . regard as a secure
discovery the discrimination of two great fundamental types of tradi-
tion-compilation coming to expression in the differentiation of J and
E."[3] However, this is merely a polite gesture which places him under
no obligations, for in his discussion of Genesis and Exodus the impressions left by this "discovery" are no longer even faintly discernible.
His basic assumption is that the stories of the patriarchs, especially
the tales of Abraham,[4] and the stories of the exodus from Egypt, arose
from a single tradition whose substantial kernel can be unveiled by
removing late notes and glosses. One may conclude that by his broad
definition of the scope of the substantial tradition he exempts himself,
in practice, from having recourse to the theory of sources, and comes
very close to the theory held by Cassuto. The latter spoke of an epic,
poetic, oral tradition predating the written Torah, which was set
down mainly in prose. But unlike Cassuto, Buber maintains a critical
distance from the text, since his striving toward the substantial kernel
necessitates a critical distinction between the authentic foundation

and additions and glosses made by scribes and editors. Moreover, Cassuto sees the remnants of the oral tradition in brief passages of a poetic nature, inserted into the literary prose; whereas it is precisely in the prose style that Buber saw the expression of the living word which he was trying to reach by leaping over the tradition. In contrast to Cassuto, who cast only a fleeting glance beyond the oral traditions submerged in the Scriptures, Buber tried to go back to the moment of spontaneous, direct utterance.

However, when it came to translating the method into the language of exegesis, Buber involved himself in contradictions and inconsistencies. In the stories of the Torah he took the written word as it was, attempting to reach the living utterance which he believed to be imbedded in it. But in his discussions of the Samuel-Saul stories he tried to reach the substantial tradition by the removal of assumed glosses and expansions.[5] As against the widely accepted view which holds that the first book of Samuel, chapters 7–13, is compounded of a pro-monarchic and an anti-monarchic source, he proceeds from the assumption that there was a single basic tradition, to which words of admonition (e.g. 7:2; 1:5–3), anti-monarchic utterances (e.g. 7:15; 3:8), and so on, were superadded. After many excisions, which also entail textual emendations, we are left with brief, crystalline stories, from which the passages tending toward moralization or verbosity have been excised, and which describe the events without invoking the miraculous. The trouble is that, with the help of aesthetic categories which are entirely arbitrary and of the rationalist assumption that the authentic tradition contains no legendary element, Buber has altered the Scriptural text beyond recognition. This method is radically different from the one which he employs in the interpretation of Judges, which he does consider to be composed of a pro-monarchic and an anti-monarchic source. It is astonishing that precisely with respect to 1 Samuel, the one book which is almost unanimously regarded as containing a pro-monarchic and an anti-monarchic document, Buber abandons the source hypothesis. In any case, his inconsistency of method stands out when one compares his treatment of the Torah with his approach to the book of Judges, and the latter with his method of interpreting the book of Samuel.

The Techniques of Buber's Literary Method

My remarks are not intended as objections to Buber's literary-aesthetic approach, as realized in his German translation of the Bible

and as set forth in the many essays which he wrote during those years
(to these essays we may add those written by his friend Franz Rosenzweig, his inspired partner in the work of translation). In the translation he is struggling with three tasks which confront anyone who
wants to fathom the meaning of the text, namely:

a. The attempt to emphasize the rythm of living utterance, which is
reflected in the Scriptures.

b. The tracing of the associative element, which leads the attentive
listener to the meaning of the unit of living utterance.

c. The exploring of the concrete meanings and the original dynamics
of the basic words of the Bible.

The Rhythm of Speech

In his striving for the rhythm of living speech, Buber followed the
colometric method, which allots a line to each estimated unit of utterance. His assumption was that the unit of speech (kōlon) is established by the rhythm of breathing, which in turn is a result of fluctuations in the emotional state of the speaker. While the masoretic
accents of the text are an exceedingly important aid to him in his task,
he permits himself to deviate from them whenever his keen ear tells
him that the rationalistic philology of the Masoretes triumphed over
the attentive listening for the living utterance. Moreover, in his translation of Biblical poetry he ignores the *parallelismus membrorum*,
arguing that he wants to dissolve the petrified visual shell of the written sign, which is destined for the eye of the reader; his intention is to
arrive at the primordial word at the time of its utterance. He even
ventures to override the hemistichs of a stanza and to divide them
according to the length or the shortness of breath which his ear,
listening to the voice of the speaker, has perceived. An example of this
daring is the new form which he gives to Jacob's blessing of Judah
(Genesis 49):

Jehuda, du	יהודה,
dir danken deine Brüder.	אתה יודוך אחיך,
Deine Hand deinen Feinden im Nacken!	ידך בערף אויביך!
Deines Vaters Söhne neigen sich dir.	ישתחוו לך בני אביך.
Ein Löwenjunges Jehuda-	גור אריה יהודה־
vom Zerfleischen, mein Sohn, steigst du empor!	מטרף, בני, עלית!
Er kauert, er lagert,	כרע, רבץ,

wie der Leu,	כאריה
wie die Löwin,	וכלביא,
wer reizt ihn auf!	מי יקימנו!
Nicht weicht von Jehuda das Szepter,	לא יסור שבט מיהודה,
nicht zwischen seinen Füssen der Richtstab,	ומחוקק מבין רגליו,
bis dass kommt Dems—zusteht—°	עד כי יבוא שלה-*
ihm der Völker Botmässigkeit!	ולו יקהת עמים!
An die Rebe bindet sein Füllen er,	אסרי לגפן עירה
an die Purpurranke sein Eslein,	ולשרקה בני אתונו,
wäscht im Wein sein Gewand,	כבס ביין לבושו
seinen Umhang im Blut der Trauben,	ובדם ענבים סותה.
die Augen funkelnd von Wein,	חכלילי עינים מיין
die Zähne weissschimmernd von Milch.	ולבן שינים מחלב.

> (M. Buber, *Die fünf Bücher der Weisung,
> Im Anfang,* Köln-Olten 1946, Jakob Hegner Verlag,
> pp. 144–145)

Yehuda,
you
your brothers will thank.
Your hand upon the neck of your enemies!
Your father's sons will bow to you.
A lion's young, Yehuda—
from the prey, my son, you have gone up!
He squats, he crouches,
like the lion,
like the lioness,
who shall rouse him up?
The sceptre shall not retire from Yehuda,
nor the judging-staff from between his feet,
until comes he for whom° it is—
for him the sway of peoples.
To the vine he binds his ass-colt,
he washes his garment in wine,
his mantle in the blood of grapes,
his eyes sparkling from wine,
his teeth white glimmering from milk.

> (E. Fox, "In the Beginning,
> An English Rendition of the
> Book of Genesis," *Response* 14,
> Summer 1972, p. 137

(° Instead of שלה he reads = שְׁלֹה = שְׁלֹו what is belonging to him.)

Note that the exclamation "Yehuda!" takes the name Yehuda out of the hemistich; also that verse 9 is divided into six units of speech, some of them fragmentary sentences, some of them apostrophes. As for the literary prose, the passages spoken with relative calm, such as the first chapter of Genesis, are translated in long lines. When someone is speaking excitedly, or when excitement sets in while he is speaking, as in Exodus 19 or Kings II, 2, the units of speech are shortened; in extreme cases, as in excited prophetic utterance, the sentences are chopped to pieces because of the agitation of the speaker. A striking example of this is the book of Hosea, which had fallen victim to innumerable textual emendations. Buber was able to cope with many difficulties within the framework of the Masoretic text because his ear was open to living utterance, which at times is cut short; sometimes the speaker bursts into an outcry, an exclamation of joy, or a groan; and when the speaker wants to emphasize something in particular, the structure of the sentence is altered until it no longer accords with the rules of grammar. In such cases reading aloud, even disregarding the Masoretic accents, can help the sentence break out of the compulsory routine of language which was forced upon it. Legal passages, such as Leviticus 18 and 20, are translated in long lines; when the tension of admonition rises, or when apodictic commandments are set forth, the lines are shortened; similarly when sudden dramatics burst in upon the calm of legal exposition.[6]

Through his attentive listening Buber discovered new aspects of many texts, and exercised a stimulating and fructifying influence on Biblical exegesis. However, it seems to me that he went too far in deciding to ignore completely the structure of ancient Hebrew poetry. The parallelism of hemistichs came to Israel as an inheritance from Ugaritic; the rules in this area do not stifle or limit creative spontaneity, as his translation would lead one to suppose. On the contrary, they are the traditional framework within which creative spontaneity can function and attain its fullest expression. And yet here too Buber's daring resulted in some gains, especially in connection with prophetic utterance, since there poetry and prose are inseparably interwoven and intertwined. The many attempts of Western Biblical scholars to restore the "original" text, to "free" it from later additions, rest on mechanistic assumptions which have no foundation—as if the words of the prophets were obligated always to take on poetic form. In contrast, Buber's colometric method emphasizes the internal organic quality of the living utterance, which is distinguished precisely by an instability of meter and rhythm resulting from emotional fluctuations in the speaker.

The Associative Principle and the Key Word

The associative principle is the cornerstone of intra-Biblical midrash which forms an organic connection among all parts of the Bible—from the stories of the Torah and the First Prophets to the addresses of the prophets and the Psalms. Indeed, the book of Chronicles is partly based on an associative midrash. The exegeses of rabbinic midrash are based on the same principle; they are merely an organic continuation of the associative midrashic method practiced in the Biblical books themselves. Yitzhak Heinemann[7] called this method, which relies on plays on words drawn mostly from folk etymologies, "creative philology," to distinguish it from the "analytical philology" which we have inherited from classical studies and whose aim is to investigate the evolution of the meanings of words and sayings by critical examination of the history of literature and language. The contribution of Buber and Rosenzweig consisted in their being the first to appreciate the exegetical importance of the "creative philology" submerged in the Bible text, when they made the investigation of the "key word" (Leitwort, a term coined on the model of Leitmotiv) the pivot of their literary-exegetical method. Buber defines the key word as follows: "A word or linguistic root which is repeated within a text or a sequence of texts or a larger context in a highly significant manner. If one investigates these repetitions, one of the meanings of the texts is deciphered or clarified, or at least reveals itself more forcefully."[8] The key word appears in two forms; the more widely found is that of emphatic usage, when a word is repeated in a given literary context so frequently as to attract particular attention. The second is the *allusive* usage, when a key word appears only infrequently on the surface of a literary unit or series of literary units and forms highly significant connections. When the key words are spread out over literary units which are assigned by criticism to different sources, they constitute a challenge or question-mark with which that criticism must come to grips. The emphasized, stressed usage of a key word frees the narrator, by its very nature, from all sermonizing and didactic moralization and helps him avoid a loquacity which would destroy the strict tectonic structure of the literary unit in question. What is more, the key word forces the listener to concentrate and makes him participate in the evaluation of the episode under discussion. The reader does not remain a neutral observer, watching the events from the sidelines; the writer's hints compel him to take a stand on the problem to which the key word leads him.

As one of the many possible examples we shall mention the episode of Korah (Numbers 16:1–16:5), which is built up on two main key words. The first is the root יעד-y'd (appoint, designate) with its derivatives, especially the nouns מועד-mo'ed (assembly, set time) and עדה-'edah (congregation); the second is the root קרב-qrv (to draw near) and the double meaning of its hiphil form, הקריב: 1. to draw near, or to cause to come near; 2. to offer, and its noun derivative קרבן-qorban (offering). The word 'edah, which is repeated many times, means on the one hand the false congregation, which rebels against the hierachy established by God when its spokesmen argue: "For all the congregation ('edah) are holy." On the other hand, this noun designates the true congregation of God; as Moses says:

Am Morgen, dann wird Er kenntlich machen,	בקר וידע ה'
wer sein ist der wer der Heilige,	את אשר לו ואת הקדוש
dass er den sich nahen lasse:	והקריב אליו
wen er erwählt,	ואת אשר יבחר לו
den wird er sich nahen lassen.	יקריב אליו.

In the morning He will make known
who is His and who is holy
and will cause to come near to Him:
whom He has chosen
He will cause to come near to Him (Nu. 16:5).

That is, by means of a miraculous sign God will make known who is authorized to draw near (התקרב-hitkarev) to Him, to offer (הקריב-hakriv) to Him—who are the true congregation (עדה-'edah) of God, appointed (נועדה-no'ada) and chosen by Him, and who are the false congregation (עדה-'edah) who set themselves up and come together against Him (הנועדים על ה').[9]

The *allusive* use of the key word appears when the writer is compelled by the force of particular human circumstances, which he describes, to conceal his judgment and his moral-religious evaluation. In such cases he alludes to his own hesitant evaluation without concealing the opposing motive which prevents him from stating his judgment in the forthright terms. As a characteristic example we shall mention the stories of Jacob and Esau contained in Genesis 27–32: the key word in chapter 27 is the root ברך-*barekh* (to bless), which in various verb forms and in the noun ברכה-*brakhah* (blessing), is repeated tens of times in the course of the chapter. The writer's interest is in emphasizing that the battle between Jacob and Esau is joined on the issue of the blessing, that is the blessing of Heaven and Earth and the blessing of lordship (27:28–29). Undoubtedly, in the opinion of the author Jacob and not Esau is the son worthy to receive the blessing, for God confirms and reinforces this blessing in the dream at Beit El (28:13–15), which is mainly a promise of offspring and inheritance of the land. Nevertheless, the author does not conceal the fact that Jacob obtains the blessing by unrightful means. On the advice of Rivkah he tricks his blind father by disguising himself in the "goodly" (27:15) garments of Esau, and by answering his father with the words "I Esau your first born, I have done as you told me; now sit up and eat of my game that you may bless me" (19). In the course of the story the root רמה-*rmh* (to deceive) appears once in the words of Yitzhak to Esau, when the aged father realizes that he has been tricked. He answers Esau with the words: "Your brother came with deceit (מרמה-*mirma*) and took away your blessing" (27:35). He speaks not simply of the blessing, but of "your blessing," the blessing which had been designated for you! The censure of Jacob implied in this answer is obvious and explicit. And then in the next chapter, chapter 29, the root רמה-*rmh* appears again: realizing that Laban has tricked him, Jacob flings at him the reproach: "What is this you have done? Have I not served with you for Rahel? Why have you deceived me (רְמִיתָנִי-*rimitani*)" (29:25)? This recurrent use, in two successive chapters, of a rare word which recurs in the entire Pentateuch only one more time (Genesis 32:13) is intended to teach us about the internal connection between the two situations described: just as Jacob deceived his father by taking advantage of the darkness of his blindness, so Laban deceives him by taking advantage of the darkness of night. The juxtaposition of the two episodes hints that Jacob has received measure for measure in punishment for his sin. But the author conceals this negative judgment between the lines and does not express it openly, because after all Jacob is the man chosen by God to be the carrier of the blessing.[10] Indeed, at the end of Jacob's nocturnal struggle with the "man" comes the final confirmation of his election and his blessing: "You shall no longer be called Jacob but Israel, for you have wrestled with God and men and have prevailed." (Genesis 32:26, 28, 29) In any case, the carefully thought-out use of the root רמה-*rmh* and the powerful repetition of the motif of the blessing in chapter 32 of Genesis make all these chapters a single composition planned and executed by a writer who has left his fingerprints along its length and breadth.

An additional variation occurs when two widely separated and apparently unconnected episodes explain and clarify each other by means of key words; the classical example of this is the correspondence between the passage describing the Creation and the passage describing the making of the Tabernacle. The literary connection between these apparently quite unrelated passages has already been observed by our sages, who used it for their didactic midrashic purposes. Buber and Rosenzweig make an exhaustive study of the subject and drew from it the theological conclusions it invites.[11] They realized that the verbs עשה—to make, to do, ראה—to see, כלה—to finish; the noun מלאכה—work, as well as the recurring formula: ששת ימים ... (וביום השביעי) six days ... (and) on the seventh Day (Gen. 2:2,3; Ex. 23:12; 24:16; 31:17; 35:2) and the concluding sentence והנה טוב מאד—and behold it was good, or וירא אלהים כי טוב—and God saw that it was good, etc., are common to the two portions, as the following comparison will show. In this connection it should be emphasized that the stem עשה occurs about a hundred times in God's directions to Moses concerning the Tabernacle and again more than a hundred times in the passage telling of its actual making.

In order to get an impression of the literary similarity, it is worthwhile to place the parallel verses side by side.

Creation	Tabernacle
Gen. 1:7 ויעש אלהים את הרקיע (and God made the firmament)	Ex. 25:8 ועשו לי מקדש (And let them make me a sanctuary)
Gen. 1:16 ויעש אלהים את שני המאורות (and God made the two great lights)	Ex. 25:9 ועשו ארון (And they shall make an ark)
Gen. 1:25 ויעש אלהים את חית הארץ (and God made the beasts of the earth)	Ex. 25:23 ועשית שלחן (Thou shalt also make a table) Ex. 25:31 ועשית מנורת זהב (And thou shalt make a candlestick of pure gold)

Ex. 20:11 כי ששת ימים עשה ה׳ את השמים ואת הארץ . . . וינח ביום השביעי (for in six days the LORD made heaven and earth . . . and rested on the seventh day)

Ex. 24:16 וישכן כבוד ה׳ על הר סיני ויכסהו הענן ששת ימים ויקרא אל משה ביום השביעי מתוך הענן (And the glory of the LORD rested upon mount Sinai, and the cloud covered it for six days; and on the seventh day He called to Moshe out of the midst of the cloud)

Gen. 2:1–2 ויכלו השמים והארץ וכל צבאם ויכל אלהים ביום השביעי מלאכתו אשר עשה (The heavens and the earth were finished and all their array. God had finished on the seventh day his work which he had made)

Ex. 39:32 ותכל כל עבדת משכן אהל מועד (Thus was the tabernacle of the Tent of Meeting finished)

Ex. 40:33 ויכל משה את המלאכה (So Moshe finished the work)

Gen. 1:31 וירא אלהים את כל אשר עשה והנה טוב מאד (And God saw all He had made, and, behold, it was very good)

Gen. 2:3 ויברך אלהים את יום השביעי (And God blessed the seventh day)

Ex. 39:43 וירא משה את כל המלאכה והנה עשו אותה כאשר צוה ה׳ כן עשו ויברך אותם משה (Moses saw the whole work, and, behold, they had done it as God had directed him. And Moses blessed them)

These examples suffice to show that the striking stylistic parallelism between these two passages is not coincidental, and one may surmise that according to the Torah the building of the Tabernacle was the pinnacle of Creation: God created the heavens and the earth and all that is in them in seven days and rested on the seventh; similarly, Moses is called to the cloud on the seventh day in order to see and to make according to the pattern of the Tabernacle which God showed him on the mountain:

And let them make me a sanctuary
that I may dwell among them.
According to all that I show you,
the pattern of the Tabernacle
and the pattern of all its vessels,
and thus you shall make.

ועשו לי מקדש
ושכנתי בתוכם.
ככל אשר אני מראה אותך
את תבנית המשכן
ואת תבנית כל כליו
וכן תעשו.
(Ex. 25:8–9)

By making the Tabernacle Israel became partners with God in the work of Creation, and thus Israel became a dwelling-place for God upon earth. However, there is always the danger that this method may degenerate into a string of homiletic word-plays; to avoid this one needs caution and punctilious observance of philological fidelity. On the other hand, whoever wishes to comprehend the Bible's literal meaning in depth, and discover its meaning for our generation, must take this risk. Scholars and exegetes such as Benno Jacob, Cassuto and others made extensive use of the peculiar characteristics of Biblical style, and especially of the key word. In their sharp confrontations with the exponents of the sources hypothesis they frequently relied on this phenomenon as evidence of the internal unity of adjacent Scriptural portions which scholarly routine assigned to different sources. Cassuto emphasized the Oriental background of the key word phenomenon, deriving it from the principle of repetition found in ancient Semitic literatures and especially in Ugaritic. On the other hand, Buber and Rosenzweig insisted on the creative aspect of the key word, which in their view would seem to be an artistic development of the principle of repetition, anchored in the living utterance. This development of the principle of repetition has no parallel in the literatures of the ancient Near East.

In concluding this section it is worthwhile to note that the colometric method not infrequently combines with the tracing of a key word; that is, by means of key words Buber succeeds in determining the units of speech, as the following example (Leviticus 26:41ff) will show.

Buber distinguished nine units of speech in this passage, as follows:

1. או־אז יכנע לבבם הערל (only then will their uncircumcised hearts be humbled) — Wie dann ihr Herz, das vorhautige, sich unterwirft

2. ואז ירצו את עונם (and then they will make amends for their sin) — Wie sie dann nachschatzen für ihre Verfehlung.

3. וזכרתי את בריתי יעקב (Then will I remember my covenant with Jacob) — Will ich gedenken meines Jakobbunds,

4. ואף את בריתי יצחק (and also my covenant with Yitshak) — und auch meines Jizchakbundes,

5. ואף את בריתי אברהם אזכר (And also my covenant with Abraham will I remember)

und auch meines Abrahambundes will ich gedenken,

6. והארץ אזכור (and I shall remember the land).

und des Landes will ich gedenken.

7. והארץ תֶּעֱזֵב מהם (The land also shall be forsaken by them)

Verlassen muss das Land von ihnen werden,

8. ותרץ את שבתותיה בָּהְשַׁמָּה מהם (and shall enjoy her sabbaths, while she lies desolate without them)

dass es seine Feiern nachschatze, während es ihrer verstummte,°

9. והם ירצו את עונם (and they shall make amends for their iniquity)

und sie müssen für ihre Verfehlung nachschatzen,

(°This rendition of the Hebrew בָּהְשַׁמָּה is untenable.)

All the units, except the first, begin with a conversive *vav*. The first two units are bound by the opening words "'o az" and "az," respectively. Units 3–5 have in common the words "briti" (my covenant) in combination with the respective proper names. The third unit begins with the form "ve-zakharti" (and I shall remember), while the fifth ends with the future form "ezkor" (I shall remember), which is common to units 5 and 6. In contrast to the remembering of the *covenant* with which units 3–5 are concerned, the subject of units 6–7 is the *land* and God's remembering of it. In contrast to the opening "ve-af" (and also) which is common to units 4–5, units 6–7 open with והארץ (ve-haarets—and the land), which puns on ותרץ (vetirets—and will make good), with which unit 8 begins. Unit 2 corresponds almost word for word to unit 9, with which the passage ends. In keeping with the rules of Biblical rhetoric, which are similar to those of Ugaritic, the verb זכר (*zkhr*—remember) occurs in two sentences concerned with the remembering of the covenant and the land, first in the past tense with *vav* conversive (ve-*zakharti*) and then in the future tense (*ezkor*). The future form (*ezkor*) then gives rise to additional future forms which continue throughout the passage.[12]

Basic Words of the Bible

The third pivot on which Buber's literary method turns is his attempt to get at the concrete meaning and the dynamics of the basic words of the Bible by freeing them from the conceptual petrification and theological abstraction which have befallen them since the time of the Septuagint translation, as each generation of exegetes and translators has elucidated the Bible according to its own worldview and its own style of abstract thought. When one compares Buber's translation to translations made in the West, from Luther and the King James version on, one is struck by the artistic sweep of Buber's translation, by the stubborn consistency with which he restored the original concreteness and dynamism to the language of the Bible by meticulously preserving the identity of every Hebrew root, and the full breadth of its semantic field, in the language of the translation. As against the Western tendency to translate the basic words by essentially static theological concepts, he argued that the Hebrew noun expresses relation and connection, rather than a definite dogmatic content. In his effort to reach the concrete meaning of the language of the Bible he relied on etymologies similar to those found in the Scriptures themselves. Thus he attempted to understand the words mainly through the direct associations which gather around those readers and listeners to the Biblical word, whose living language is Hebrew. The task which he took upon himself was twofold: to retain the identity of each Hebrew root in the translation without blurring the extremely delicate shades of meaning associated with it. To this end he took the fullest possible advantage of the capacity of the German language to form nouns and verbs by the addition of a syllable at the beginning or the end of a root, as we shall see in the discussion that follows. When the semantic field of the German root was too narrow to contain all the meanings of the corresponding Hebrew root, he created compound words, in which the added word or root explained the particular development of the basic root. (See the discussion of *ruah*, below.) In such cases he was compelled to venture into uncharted territory, to enlarge the compass of the German language and to increase its flexibility by means of neologisms, in order to render it capable of faithfully reflecting the peculiar structure of Biblical language. Beyond all this he even attempted to create analogies in German to the similarities of sound, the puns and other stylistic devices. One may note that this constant striving to reach the original semantic foundations of the Bible has particular significance for a generation of revival like ours, which is groping toward its spiritual heritage along its own authentic path, without the intermediary of past generations.

To exemplify what we have said, we shall cite a few basic words from the area of ritual, from the religious-ritual and social ordinances, which Buber sought to establish in their Biblical meaning:

מזבח (*mizbeah*): The word *altar*, by which Western translators have rendered this, awakens clear associations of Christian sacral architecture. Buber restored this word to its original connection, as it presents itself to anyone who understands Hebrew, namely "slaughter site," *Schlachtstatt*.

כפר (*kapper*): In Western translations we witness a spiritualization of this act, which is not a purification or expiation, as the words "sühnen" and "atone" imply. Buber restored the original *concrete* meaning as it is explained in Exodus 30:12; it means to "cover," *bedecken, decken*. Hence the translations of nouns derived from this root such as כפר (*kofer*), *Deckung*; כפרת (*kaporet*), *Verdeck*; יום כפורים (*yom kippurim*), *Tag der Verdeckungen*. Thus he was indeed able to remove from these terms the theological-spiritual overtones which had become associated with them in the West. But a comparison with other Semitic languages reveals that this word has an additional concrete meaning, namely to erase, to blot out. In other words, in many cases we have to check Buber's versions with the help of semantics and modern comparative linguistics.[13]

קרבן (*qorban*): This is not a matter of devotion, of self-immolation (sacrifice, *Opfer*); rather, as the root קרב (*qrv*) tells us, it has to do with nearness, with bringing or coming near; hence, *Darnahung*. (See the foregoing discussion of the Korah episode in Numbers 16.)

עולה (*'olah*): This is not a description of the character of an offering, as suggested by Western translations such as *Ganzopfer*, "*burnt offering*"; it has nothing to do with a sacrifice offered *entirely* to God or entirely burnt, as these customary translations imply. The noun literally means ascent on high, as is explained in Leviticus 1:2, 6:2, hence: *Das Hochaufseigende*.

מנחה (*minha*): This is not an offering of food (*Speiseopfer*), but something which is "led," from the root *nhh*, to lead; therefore, *das Hingeleitete*. Perhaps in this case there is an identity between the scientific etymology and the associative etymology made by Buber.

ריח ניחוח (*reah nihoah*): Here Buber is careful to imitate the similarity of sound between these two terms, while deriving *ninoah* from *nahat* or *noah* (satisfaction, rest): *Ruch des Geruhens*, that is, scent of satisfaction.

יעד-מועד (*ya'ad-mo'ed*): Turning now to the area of ritual in a more general sense: the noun *mo'ed* is derived from the verb יעד- *ya'ad* (to appoint); the *niphal* (passive) form of this verb, הועד-*hiva'ed* (to be present, convene) is reflected in all the forms, hence:

אוהל מועד (*ohel mo'ed*)—Zelt der Begegnung (Tent of Meeting), and sometimes Zelt der Vergegenwärtigung (Tent of Presence).

אשר אועד לך שמה (asher ivva'ed lekha shama) (Ex. 30:6, 36)—wo ich mich dir gegenwärtige (where I make myself present to you).

מועדי ה' (mo'adei ha-Shem)—Begegnungsgezeiten bei IHM (times of meeting in the place of God). In this case the particular semantic coloring is expressed by the addition of Gezeit (Zeit, time, with the collective prefix ge).

אמונה (emunah): In Western culture emunah has become solely a concern of the inward soul of man. This is not the Biblical concept, which is derived from the root 'mn, "to be strong," as in ויהי ידיו אמונה (va-yehi yadav emunah)—his hands were strong (Exodus 17:12). Moreover, the word emunah does not imply a specific dogmatic content, but signifies a connection, a reliable bond; hence: Treue, Vertrauen (faithfulness, trust). The noun אמת (emet), in Buber's opinion, is also derived from this root 'mn. Again, it has no epistemological meaning in the abstract and objective sense of Wahrheit, truth, but expresses an interpersonal relationship, a bond founded on certainty, on trust, hence: Zuverlässigkeit, Haltung, Gewissheit (reliability, fulfilling, certainty).

רוח (ruah): From ancient times, translators have struggled with the choice between the spiritual meaning and the physical meaning, represented by the word-pairs Geist-Wind, spirit-wind, esprit-vent, spiritus-ventus; that is, the spirit dwelling in man and the wind blowing outside. In his translation Buber strives to preserve the identity of the word while emphasizing that it is not a static concept. Its dynamic principle is expressed by the addition of the word Braus (a rushing). Thus the physical connotation of the word is translated by the noun Windbraus, while the spiritual connotation is translated by Geistbraus, and where there is no possibility of deciding between the two, and the two meanings are bound and joined together, he simply writes Braus.

נגף (negef): Here the translations are groping in utter darkness: Plage (plague), plötzlicher Tod (sudden death), Niederlage (defeat), Seuche (plague), Anstoss (offense). But in this noun and its cognate מגפה (magefah) there is no trace of any meaning except "a striking," "a severe blow," Therefore the translation of Negef is Zustoss (a blow); of magefah, Niederstoff (a crushing blow).

The Tetragrammaton: Following the rationalist view which holds that this name is related to the verb forms hayah (he was), hoveh (he is) and yihyeh (he will be), and refers to the eternal being of God, Mendelssohn rendered this name "der Ewige," and later translators followed in his footsteps with the translation l'éternel—"the eternal." Others translated the unpronounceable Name in accordance with the word *adonoy* ("kyrios," "Lord," "der Herr"), which is customarily read in its place. Buber believes that the Name is simply an expansion of the interjection *yah*, which the believer uttered in astonishment as if to say: "It's He!" It is an exclamation arising from a feeling of immediate presence. Therefore Buber daringly translates it with a personal pronoun, varying according to the identity and situation of the speaker, and written in capital letters. When the speaker is God, it is ICH; when the speaker is a human addressing God, DU; when God is mentioned in the third person, ER. In contrast to this, the name *EL* designates a broad spectrum of vague, impersonal meanings, ranging from idolatrous and illusory images to the reality of the God of truth. It is translated as *Gottmacht* (Divine power), *Gottherr* (Lord God), *Gottheit* (Divinity), *Schutzgott* (tutelary divinity); at the same time the name *Elohim* always refers to the God of truth and is translated simply: *Gott*, without any qualifying additions. Correspondingly the word אלילים (elilim) which plays also on the negation אל-(no), is rendered: *Gottnichtse* (divine nobodies).

תורה (*Torah*): This does not mean "law" (nomos), as the Septuagint translated it; it signifies not a closed book but *instruction*, direction; therefore, *Weisung*. In conclusion we shall cite an example containing something of the three methods enumerated here, namely the colometric method, the tracing of associations, and the return to the concrete meanings of the basic words. The example is from Leviticus 25:10–13:

10. יובל היא תהיה לכם (it shall be a home-bringer to you)   Heimholer sei es euch,

ושבתם (and you shall return)   da kehrt ihr zurück

איש אל אחוזתו (every man to his possession)   jeder zu seiner Hufe,

ואיש אל משפחתו (and every man to his family)   jeder zu seiner Sippe

תשובו (you shall return)   sollt zurück ihr kehren.

11. יובל היא, שנת החמישים שנה תהיה לכם וגו׳, (This fiftieth year is to be a home-bringer for you)   Heimholer sei es, das Jahr das Fünfzigerjahr, für Euch,

כי יובל היא (for it is a home-bringer)   denn Heimholer ists,

12. קודש תהיה לכם וגו׳ (it shall be holy to you)   Verheiligung sei es Euch, . . .

13. בשנת היובל הזאת (in this home-   In diesem Heimholerjahr
bringer-year)

תשובו (you shall return)   kehrt ihr zurück,

איש אל אחזתו (every man to his jeder zu seiner Hufe.
possession)

The noun "yovel," which is commonly translated "jubilee," is
repeated here four times; it is defined by the key word "shuv" (to
return), which appears three times in conjunction with the phrases
"ish el ahuzato/mishpahto" (each man to his possession/his family).
The repetition in the phrase "shnat hahamishim shana" is also
intended to define the time of the return or the restoration. This,
then, is the year which restores each man to his family and his possession. Buber derives "yovel" from the stem *yvl*, the *hiphil* of which
means to bring; accordingly he translates יובל—*Heimholer*—that
which brings home.

Centuries before Buber, Nahmanides suggested the same etymology as against the Talmudic tradition which explains it as איל (ayl)—
ram (Rosh Hashana 26a), apparently the ram's horn or shofar which
was blown. This is a striking example of the use of folk etymology.
Indeed, the dovetailing of methods is complete: the division into
units of speech influences the use of the key word, which explains the
meaning of *yovel* by a folk etymology of the noun. Whether this is the
scientific etymology of *yovel* is doubtful; but that is of no importance
for the interpretation in this case, because the closest association of
yovel is the stem *yvl* in its *hiph'il* form: *hovil*.

The Philosophy of Language

The point of departure for Buber's hermeneutic method as we have
depicted it here is literary, although, as we have said, his aim was to
get beyond literature. It follows that his way is essentially different
from that of classical philology, which influenced the development of
modern Biblical research. The methods of classical philology are
adapted to the possible variations in the form of the word, the written
sign, in its evolution through generations of transmission by copyists
and scribes, whereas Buber's way is listening for the voice, for the
sound. It is not antiquarian research, not a study of a "dead" language, but a registering of the pulse of life, the voice of living utterance. Buber was convinced that only relatively few errors had found
their way into the text; thus it behooves us to listen seriously. The

traditional version, in his opinion, is the proper visual framework through which to penetrate to the spoken word. Only as a desperation measure and with great hesitation does he permit himself textual emendations,[14] in contrast to the excessive freedom, and sometimes arbitrariness, with which the "experts" in "Biblical" Hebrew related to the text. A hasty glance at Gunkel's commentary on the book of Psalms suffices to show that while Gunkel had taste and excellent literary intuition, he did not know Hebrew. It took a scholar like Buber, who had absorbed Hebrew and Jewish culture from his earliest youth, to show that after all there is meaning, sense and beauty in those texts which others "corrected" beyond repair. Buber owed his greatest achievements to his daring; he wanted to leap over the "Holy Writ" (Kitvei ha-Kodesh) in order to arrive at the *mikra* (the word for the Scriptures which means literally "what is read"), so that the Bible might be read and heard. Literary scholarship for him was not an end in itself; it was only a means to arrive at the time of speech, the instant of creation, when the living word issued from the mouth of the speaker.

Upon completing the translation of the Bible, at the age of 83, Buber felt the need to sum up his conclusions on the importance of the spoken word in human experience.[15] In an essay entitled "The Word that is Spoken" he balances the static elements against the dynamic elements in language. He distinguishes three modes of being of language: "present continuance," "potential possession," and "actual occurrence,"

> By present continuance is meant the totality of that which can be spoken in a particular realm of language in a particular segment of time, regarded from the point of view of the person who is able to say what is to be said . . . By potential possession is meant the totality of what has ever been uttered in a certain realm of language . . . with the decisive limitation, however, that nothing belongs to it except what can still today be lifted by a living speaker into the sphere of the living word . . . The third mode-of-being of language is that of its actual occurrence . . . the word that is spoken.[16]

The first two modes presuppose language as a possession acquired through history.

> But here nothing else is to be presupposed than man's will to communicate as a will capable of being realized.[17] This will originates in

men's turning to one another . . . The genuine author and genuine dialogue—both draw from the present continuance of language, hence not from the dammed-up basin of possession, but from the gushing and streaming waters.[18]

Following Goethe's saying in the introductory poem of his collection *Der West-Östliche Divan*:

Wie das Wort so wichtig dort war
Weil es ein gesprochen Wort war
(How weighty was the word there, because it was a spoken word)

Buber attempts to explain the mystery of the power of the spoken word, and not merely in the dialogue between heaven and earth in the days of creation, as Goethe intended in the above-quoted lines. Concerning this power, Buber says: "The importance of the spoken word, I think, is grounded in the fact that it does not want to remain with the speaker. It reaches out toward a hearer, it lays hold of him, it even makes the hearer into a speaker . . ."[19] That is: the spoken word creates a middle ground which permits dialogue between one human being and another. But in the midst of the discussion he leaves the path of hypostatization of the spoken word and, having set up a contrast between monologue and dialogue, arrives at the ontological basis of the true dialogue, that is, the dialogue whose foundation is the spoken word itself. He denies the essential validity of the monologue because "the ontological basic presupposition is missing (from monologue), the otherness . . . the moment of suprise."[20]

Furthermore, he knows that living dialogue is rooted in the multiple meanings of living language on the one hand, and in the different characters of the two speakers, on the other. There is never an identity in the conceptual understanding of two people; their differences of personal character are likely to affect even their definitions of a concept which both accept. And then the tension which is created in dialogue between two contents of a single concept may lead to misunderstanding, or even solidify and produce sharp oppositions. However, if kept within reasonable bounds this tension is a fruitful and fructifying force; it is the basis of the truthful dialogue which creates understanding, provided that the two sides are sufficiently open to each other.

Buber's studies of the Bible were a dialogue with it, an attempt to penetrate to its essence, to the primordial life of the spoken word as it reflects the unique character, the otherness, of the speaker. The Biblical exegesis of those generations or individual scholars who tried to stamp their own world-view on the Bible, was not a true dialogue. In actuality they carried on a dialogue only with themselves, while the dead letters of the Bible created in their minds the illusion that they were dialoguing with and penetrating into its world. As an example we shall mention the philosophers of the Middle Ages, who brought into the Scriptures their own abstract concepts and the theological problems which interested them, but which had no foundation in the text. The striving toward the spoken word appears from this angle of vision as an attempt to penetrate beyond the "dammed-up basin of possession" to "the gushing and streaming waters" of the moment of creation. Only the success of this attempt can fructify the present. The crystallized, already formed possession is the inheritance of the past. In pointing to the polarity between the *static*, which we inherited as an already crystallized unit, and the *dynamic*, Buber justifies his selective attitude vis-a-vis the inheritance of past generations. Indeed, the holiness of the Bible and the force of its imperative are not rooted in its canonical quality, that is, in the judgments of past generations. Its holiness or, better, its imperative, educating, shaping force is the fruit of two factors.

a. The human capacity to shake oneself free of the historical and anthropological circumstances of one's experience and arrive at a dialogue beyond the boundaries of time and space.

b. The Bible's capability of being deciphered by contemporary man; more exactly: the acoustical capability of contemporary man to draw from it the living voice of the speaker. We must make a principal distinction between this aim and Franz Rosenzweig's remarks about "the word before the word,"[21] meaning the language of humanity, on which empiric languages are based. In Rosenzweig's view every true translation is a kind of breakthrough to that supra-linguistic language without words, for the translation enlarges the borders of the target language by restoring to it what is common to it and the source language.

Buber has no share in this "Messianic" Utopianism, which gave the young Rosenzweig the force with which he sought to storm the final goal—the supra-linguistic language common to all human tongues. The direction of Buber's Biblical enterprise was the exact opposite: he did not aim to penetrate to the transcendental foundation of empirical language; rather he was concerned precisely with the concrete, living, unique, human utterance of the language of encounter. Moreover, he did not believe that through the Bible it is still possible to hear the voice of the living God; he considered the language of the Bible itself a translation, insofar, as it transmits the Divine utterance. In its primordial, immediate form this utterance is supralinguistic, as Rosenzweig emphasized in one of his letters.[22]

Yet if we are not capable of hearing the voice of God, perhaps we can still hear the voice of someone who heard the Almighty, someone who can tell us how the Almighty spoke with him, someone who was able to translate the speech of the Almighty to him into the language of human beings?

From this it is understandable that Buber did not believe that God is a law-giver who transmitted to man laws already crystallized and drawn up; he did not recognize a universal Divine law. At most there exists a personal Divine command addressed to a human being, a community, at a given hour.[23] Only what contemporary man is capable of recognizing as addressed to him—what he is able to fulfill in a significant manner—is a commandment. One may say that Buber's extreme subjectivism verges on a-nomism with its implicit danger of religious anarchism. In contrast to his extreme reserve, even closed-mindedness, toward Biblical *Halakhah*, to say nothing of Talmudic *Halakhah*, his wonderful openness to the great instruction for life enfolded, according to his view, in the literary prose, in the poetry of Psalms, and in the admonitions of the prophets, is all the more striking. His ability to listen opened new horizons for whole portions of the Bible.

B. *Myth and Monotheism*

And now to the second problem, which is theologically of major importance: What is the relation of monotheism, the faith of Israel, to myth?

The rationalists of classical Jewish thought, including, in the generation preceding Buber, the philosopher Hermann Cohen and his younger contemporary, the Biblical scholar Yehezkel Kaufmann, spared themselves the wrestling with myth by the art of definition: they defined mythology as the story of the pagan gods, their family histories and their fates. But the God of Israel is transcendent, and thus has neither family history nor fate; therefore it is not possible to speak of him in the language of myth. Myth and monotheism are mutually exclusive; for this reason Kaufmann contended that there is no contact and no transition between paganism, which is mythological by its very nature, and monotheism, which is an a-mythological quantity in human culture.

While still at the beginning of his way, Buber rebelled against this simplistic approach, in 1913, with his famous address "Myth in Judaism," he asserted the existence of monotheistic myth. This address remains a milestone both in Buber's development and in the development of Jewish thought to this very day. While the Jewish scholars of the preceding century, above all Graetz, did not look favorably on the mythological elements in Judaism, but ignored or decried them, the romanticism of the revival movement, which flourished at the beginning of this century, sought to teach us that precisely the mythical and popular element is the essence of the vitality of Judaism. The search for the popular element stands out in Dubnow's sociological approach to the historiography of the Jewish people, in Horodetsky's researches into the occult and Hasidism, in Berdichevsky's collection of Aggadah, and in Peretz's artistic depiction of the world of Hasidim. Buber belongs to this trend; the search for the popular, non-intellectual foundation of Judaism is of a piece with his recognition that the mythical elements have a decisive weight in Judaism. With his five speeches on Judaism he began to speak of the myth of the Jews, the monotheistic myth—which according to the rationalist view would be a contradiction in terms. Buber began thinking about myth in connection with an historiography which distinguishes between an official, normative Judaism and a popular, underground Judaism, which rebelled against and rejected normativism. This supposed folk current, for which he declared his full sympathy, was in his opinion the soil from which myth grew, as an expression of the vital forces working in the people. Furthermore, he gave a striking anthropological definition of myth: "We must designate as myth every tale of a corporeally real event that is perceived as a divine, an absolute event . . . Myth, then, is an eternal function of the human soul."[24] If we want to get to know myth more intimately, we must ask ourselves: what are the circumstances under which it comes into being? Buber answers that this occurs in moments of extreme tension, when experience becomes intensified. Then it is as if "the shackles of (causal) awareness fall off man: he perceives the world's process as being supercausally meaningful, as the manifestation of a central intent, which cannot, however, be grasped by the mind, but only by the wide-awake power of the senses, the ardent vibrations of one's entire being—as palpable, multifaceted reality." Though man is capable of placing this within causality, he nevertheless mythicizes it, "because the mythical approach discloses to him a deeper, fuller truth than the causal."[25]

But what is this truth? Buber came to understand it only at a relatively late stage in his thought, after he had corrected the anthropological definition which at one time caused Rosenzweig to condemn his approach as atheistic, and had integrated myth into his theory of dialogue by calling it "the expression of an authentic encounter between two realities."[26] From all this we learn two basic principles:

1. Myth is not a creation of the imagination, as Schlegel, the young Schelling, Wundt, Freud, and others thought; rather its source is in a real event preserved in the collective memory, which formed it in the organic historic process of transmission from generation to generation. At its core, the myth contains real historical reminiscences.[27]

2. Myth is not by nature informative; it neither transmits facts nor explains events according to the laws of causality. Its aim is communicative; its function is to express a truth too deep to be contained in the formulated language of science. This truth cannot be expressed in discursive language; man is incapable of expressing it save in the fullness of his concrete being. It follows that it would be hopeless to try to translate mythic truth into scientific language, as if myth were merely a special kind of verbal husk for a content which could just as well have enveloped itself in conceptual language. This was the error of Bultmann and his school, who diligently translated the language of mythical annunciation in the New Testament into rational terms, as their motto of "Mythos und Kerygma" teaches. Buber energetically opposed Bultmann's separation of content and form. In his essay on man's experience of evil he further clarifies the connection between myth and language by stating: "the experience which has taken place (not 'been gained') in factual encounters with evil in the world and in the soul is directly embodied in myth, without making the detour through conceptual or semi-conceptual determinations."[28] Thus myth is a document, a witness to an encounter between two realities; it expresses a truth which cannot be contained in definitions and abstractions, moral judgments and social norms. It is a direct and, one may say, concrete and pictorial expression of immediate, living experience. Thus one cannot speak of "mythical thinking" in contrast to other ways of thinking, as Lévy-Bruhl, Cassirer, Lévy-Strauss and others would have it.

When this experience is collective, in the domain of historical event, then the mythic expression takes the form of holy saga:

The holy saga is for this reporter the immediate and single way of articulating his "knowledge" about the events; moreover, this knowledge itself is a legendary knowledge, that is, one which represents the believed activity of God with His people, one which represents in the organic employment of a mythicizing memory. What is involved here actually is a religious *viewing* of history: the wonder is beheld by a wonder-expecting person and imagined by the wonder-gripped person in narrative language. It is not fantasy active here, but memory; but precisely that believing memory of individuals and generations of early times which, driven by the extraordinary occurrence, builds for it in a manner free of arbitrariness the extraordinary context—a poetizing memory, but one which poeticizes believingly."[29]

This sensory viewing which springs from the intuition of the one to whom the exciting event has occurred, *is* the religious viewing of history. The holy saga which is woven around the kernel of historic fact is elevated to an ultimate religious category, since it depicts the event as the result of Divine planning and intervention. It tells of this intervention in concrete fashion without any causal explanation, without any intention of necessity of presenting an objective picture of the world. This event is depicted as an encounter between the people and its God: "it is in the encounter itself that we are confronted with something compellingly anthropomorphic, something demanding reciprocity."[30] This God can be experienced and encountered, because he is a personal being. Hence anthropomorphism, which is one of the distinguishing marks of mythic expression, is a testimony to the vitality of faith. But the image and depictions are only signs and intimations pointing to the pure I-Thou relationship, which knows only the presence of that which is present.

Thus we see that the religious legitimacy of myth rests on its being a testimony, sign and intimation of the encounter which in itself is beyond all form and content. In Buber's language: mythical images are only forms through which God shines. But the moment the images are placed before the congregation of believers as established things, whether "in plastic or theological forms," they "obstruct the way to Him, and He removes Himself from them."[31] In other words: any objectivization of the force of the encounter, whether in external plastic formations or in abstract-dogmatic concepts which claim to deliver positive statements about God, destroys the legitimacy of myth.

Here the Biblical scholar is faced with a central question: does Buber distinguish between monotheistic myth and pagan myth?

Where is the boundary between them? The reader hoping for a clear pronouncement from Buber on this subject will be disappointed, for in discussing myths which depict man's experience of evil, he mentions Biblical and Iranian myths in one breath;[32] there is no doubt that in his opinion the Iranian myths are not inferior to the Biblical myths in ontological validity and religious legitimacy, since he speaks of them together. As stated in the foregoing paragraph, depictions of God—and Buber adds with explicit emphasis, "whether plastic or theological"—block the path to God. This means that from the point of view of religious legitimacy the graven image holds the same rank as a dogmatic theological system within the framework of monotheism; both kinds of "image" bar the way to God, close Him off and confine Him within fixed, unchanging external forms. The legitimate myth, on the other hand, is a sign and intimation which points to the presence of God, whose forms of revelation are innumerable. All fixed forms and all positively worded statements are invalid in the same degree, because they bar the way to the boundless Divine Thou. Moreover, the nature of his theory precludes a distinction between pagan and monotheistic myth, just as there is no distinction in his theory between monotheism and polytheism; any such distinction requires defining the content of monotheism, and therefore Buber opposes it: the essence of monotheism is simply "a living relationship with Him."[33] Its one and only identifying mark is the degree of intensity in the lives of the believers, their devotion to the leadership of God. The question of the existence of other gods does not interest the Bible; the important thing is that one is to worship God alone. The essence of His nature is expressed in the phrase "ehyeh asher ehyeh," I shall be what I shall be, which only intimates His being present without limiting or defining this presence as to manner, place, time or form.

Yet if there is no positive distinction between pagan and monotheistic myth in Buber's work, there are distinguishing marks which give pagan myth a negative connotation. I am referring to the introduction to his book *Moses*, in which he speaks of sacred legend and the historical substance it contains. There he says, among other things:

> The central figures of the Bible saga are not, as in so many hero-tales, merged in or amalgamated with personalities belonging to mere mythology—the data regarding their lives have not been interwoven with stories of the gods. Here all the glorification is dedicated solely to the God who brings about the events. The human being acting under

the God's orders is depicted in all his untransfigured humanity . . . This
withdrawing of the human being from the mythical element steeps the
tale in an atmosphere of august sobriety, a dry atmosphere, one might
almost say, which frequently permits a glimpse of the historic nucleus.

As for the mythical element which is concealed in these stories, Buber
asserts that "here, unlike the concept familiar in the science of religion, myth means nothing other than the report by ardent enthusiasts
of what has befallen them."[34] That is, the distinguishing mark of
monotheistic myth is the ontic distinction between the divine and the
human realm. Despite all the enthusiasm with which the ancient
writer relates the great deliverance which God worked for Israel by
the hand of his servant Moses, he refrains from drawing Moses into
the circle of the Divine; on the contrary, the Biblical story is careful to
emphasize all the human weaknesses of the man and to show that the
miracles which he carried out with his brother Aaron were not
evidence of superhuman powers, but of a unique grace of God resting
upon him. Even in this mythic narration, or one may say enthusiastic
vision, in which the event is depicted as a Divine event, the prophet
delegated to perform the task is sundered from the sphere of the
Divine; his humanity remains. Thus one may say that monotheistic
myth never abandons its sober way of seeing man, never blends the
Divine element with the human. Pagan myth is based on the assumption of an ontic continuum between God, universe, and man. Biblical
monotheistic myth, as it takes shape in the sacred legend, is aware of
the absolute ontic difference between God and His creation. On the
other hand, the distinguishing mark of monotheistic myth is the
enthusiastic way of seeing, in which the great historical events which
inflame the soul of man reveal themselves as Divine events. It seems
to me that this assumption is a cornerstone for every future non-
rationalistic presentation of the Biblical faith.

C. *The Origin and Character of Monotheism*

And now to the third aspect of Buber's work, the historical.
Throughout his life, Buber defended himself against his critics by saying that he was not an historian and that he did not intend to reassess
the scholarly approach to historical problems per se. All the same, it is
impossible to ignore the fact that all of his central statements in Bibli-

cal scholarship are bound up with weighty historical appraisals. His two main books in this area are *Kingship of God* and *The Prophetic Faith*. In these books he seeks to give an answer to one central question, which was not explicitly formulated: what is the origin and nature of Biblical monotheistic faith? The first step toward a comprehensive answer is shown in *Kingship of God*. Parallel to Kaufmann, and contrary to the general tendency of Protestant Biblical scholarship, he emphasized the ancient date of the sources testifying to the kingship of God in Israel. True, the Scandinavian school of the last generation also discerned the antiquity of these sources, but they reached this conclusion at the cost of a primitivization and mythologization of monotheism. They sought the source of Biblical faith in the ritual drama of the ascent of God to the throne of His kingdom; they hold that this is a ritual pattern common to the various cultures of the ancient Near East.

What was missing from this pattern in the Bible, they filled in from what is known or surmised of the Akitu ritual in Mesopotamia. Buber just ignored this school, whereas Kaufmann vehemently opposed it, because it uproots the faith of Israel from its historical foundations and glosses over the abyss of difference between it and the paganism of the ancient Near East. The Scandinavian school firmly insists that Yahvism originated in the ritual drama which depicted the cosmic myth of the war between Yhwh and the primordial sea-monsters. This drama was only the Israelite variation of a ritual pattern common in all parts of the ancient Near East.[35] As early as the 1950's, an Orientalist of the stature of Henry Frankfort took issue with this arbitrary assumption.[36] In his studies he emphasized the profound and essential differences between Egyptian culture on the one hand and Mesopotamian culture on the other, and showed the abyss which gapes between these two and the monotheistic culture of Israel. It is against this spiritual background that Buber's new assertions concerning the kingship of God are to be understood: he interpreted the many texts on God's lordship, leadership and kingship in the Torah (Exodus 15:18, 19:6; Numbers 10:30–31, 23:21, 33:5, and so on) and in the historical books (Judges 8:20–22, 9:8ff; Samuel I 8:6ff, and so on), together with the verses on the humility of Moses, as expressions of a theopolitical conception, that is a concrete social concept and not simply a matter of religious confession. The source of this conception is the event of the making of the covenant at Sinai; as stated above, this story is not an historical myth born of the writers' imagination, rather it is a mythicization of history, that is of an historical *fact* preserved and shaped by the organic, creative memory of generations. Buber believes that the stories of the covenant at Sinai do indeed point to the conclusion that the experience of Israel as a nation began with the covenant between the tribes and their God. In his view this was a "kingly covenant," that is, a covenant which imposed on Israel the rule of the Divine King in all areas of life. The making of the covenant was a theopolitical act by which God was proclaimed king and leader of Israelite society, who would lead the people in their wanderings in the desert and fight their wars as the commander of the Israelite army; such is attested by the song of Deborah, in which the men of Meroz are cursed for having failed to come "to the help of God, to the help of God among the mighty" (Judges 5:23), and in the short poem concerning the Ark of the Covenant (Numbers 10:30-31). This covenant was based on the assumption that the kingship of God is incompatible with the kingship of mortal man, and that the setting up of an earthly king is a sin comparable to the sin of idolatry. In the speech of Gideon (Judges 8:22-23), in the parable of Jotham (Judges 9:6ff) and in Samuel's opposition to the choosing of a king (Samuel I 8:6) Buber saw a forceful expression of this negative view of human kingship. The kingship of God, however, is a Utopia based in effect on anarchistic elements, since in that period the rejection of monarchy meant in practice a rejection of all human rule and authority. Buber sought to explain this conception as the religious guise of the longing for unlimited freedom characteristic of the nomad, the man of the desert, in whose image he portrayed the Patriarchs and the generation of the Exodus. The basis for this conception, according to his view, is already implicit in the stories of the Patriarchs. Like other scholars, Buber attaches historical significance to these stories, inferring from them that the God of the Patriarchs was a leader-god who went with the believers in all their wanderings, and in return demanded of them absolute devotion to His commands.[37] In fact, this faith was the heritage of the generation of the Exodus and the generation of the desert was not monotheistic in the sense of denying the existence of other gods; rather it was monolatrous, imposing on the believer the exclusive worship of YHWH. Buber seeks to differentiate between YHWH as Divine King who wanders with the followers and the Cananite Baalim, who were local nature gods. These Baalim were absorbed, when the Patriarchs came up against them, into the image of YHWH; their characteristics were interpreted as His characteristics, as an attribute among his attributes. Indeed, the image of the God of the Patriarchs, who was later to become the God of Israel, took

shape not according to abstract reasonings, but through a living relationship with Him; in the final analysis the core of this faith is the
consciousness of the immediate presence of God, the Divine King,
who wanders with man and with the people and is nevertheless
beyond them: "He is One above all, because He is the One in all."[38]
In Buber's view the rule of the Divine King, the "direct kingship of
God," is crystallized by three religious and social signs:

1. The Ark of the Covenant, which symbolizes the presence of the
Divine King in the camp, both in wartime and in peacetime (Numbers 10:30-31; Judges 20:23, 26-27; Judges 21:2; Samuel I 4:3, 4,
5ff).

2. The figure of the charismatic judge-deliverer, considered as the
temporary agent of the Divine King.

3. The apodictic laws of the Torah.[39]

In support of his anthropological theory concerning the longing of
the desert nomad for unlimited freedom, Buber adduces material on
the Kharidji sect which existed in the second and third centuries after
the founding of Islam.[40] On the basis of comparisons with material
from ancient central and western Asia he even attempts to establish a
universal sociological rule that the basic conceptions of many tribes
crystallize only when they become permanent settlers in the lands
they have conquered. True, these conceptions have their origin in the
period of nomadism, but their latent creative potentialities are fully
realized only in the period of permanent settlement. Thus, the conception of the direct rule of God was the fruit of Israel's nomadic period, when the tribes were still existing as the *Habiru* class—a name
designating, according to modern research, not an ethnic group but a
social class—mercenaries and hired laborers who wandered throughout the ancient Near East. The failure of the direct rule of God, to
which the pro-monarchic source of Judges (chapters 17-21) bears
witness, was due to its inability to cope with social disorder within
and its weakness in the face of the Philistines without. As a result of
the crisis which reached its peak in the debacle of Even Ha'ezer
(Samuel I 4), when the very existence of the people was called into
question by the Philistines' command of the hill region, the Israelite
kingdom came into being as an inescapable historic necessity. The
complete negation of the rule of mortal kings gave way to the dynastic principle; the direct rule of God became rule *by the grace* of god,
whose carrier was the leader, the king; Buber called this "the indirect
rule of God." Instead of the charismatic leader who is sent from time
to time comes the unofficial prophet who confronts the king and the

nobles in order to criticize their actions and make known
to them the will of God. In his three essays on the relationship
between Saul and Samuel[41] and in his book, *The Prophetic Faith*
Buber probes the character of kingship and the relationship of prophecy to it. He believes that from the time it was instituted the
monarchy sought to evade Divine guidance and to remove affairs of
state from the bounds of prophetic guidance. Against this background
he elucidates the rift between Saul and Samuel on the one hand and,
on the other, the ritual piety of the kings of Israel, who had an interest
in distinguishing between the area of the sacred and that of the profane. Thus David's bringing the Ark of the Covenant to Jerusalem,
and Solomon's building the Temple, appear to him as attempts to cir-
cumscribe God within the domain of the sacred and to remove the
affairs of the country from the guidance which He exerted while he
was "traveling in the tent and in the tabernacle" (II Samuel 7:6), as
the vision of Nathan puts it. Similarly, in the reign of Ahaz, king of
Judah, Isaiah confronted the king in one of the most difficult hours
when Jerusalem was under siege, and again the king evaded the
"theopolitical" decision with which the prophet confronted him.
Isaiah demanded reliance on the God of Israel alone. But Ahaz turned
away from this demand and rejected the sign which the prophet suggested to him, on the pseudo-religious plea "I will not ask, neither
will I try the Lord." (Isaiah 7:12), preferring an alliance with Assyria
as a vassal state (2 K. 16:7ff).

In this hour of disillusionment the first Messianic prophecy was
born—the prophecy of Immanuel (Isaiah 7:14–17, 8:5–10).[42] This
means that the Messianic idea is not rooted in ancient eschatologies;
it is the fruit of "political realism," of the prophet's disillusionment
with a monarchy which had not succeeded in establishing the rule of
justice and righteousness. The "Anointed" is simply the king who fulfills his obligations. His expected kingdom is real and earthly, yet it
fulfills the theopolitical demand, the ideal of the real sovereignty of
God in society.[43] At first Isaiah hoped that Hezekiah might be the
ideal king, but he was disappointed by Hezekiah's Egyptian policy.
Then he saw new visions: "the concept of kingship disappeared," the
house of David was to be cut off, from the stump of Jesse a new shoot
would spring up, namely the king who was to reign over the "remnant" which would survive the destruction. This king will fulfill his
mission (11:1–9). In the prophecies of the great anonymous writer of
the Babylonian exile, known as Deutero-Isaiah, this anti-Davidic and
anti-monarchic Messianic concept evolved into a vision refined of all

national-political dross. Deutero-Isaiah interpreted the prophecy of the child (9:5-6) in accordance with its "true meaning," applying it to Cyrus. He renounces the idea of an Israelite king; never again will a mortal sit on the throne of David. "The faithful mercies of David" (55:3) will become the inheritance of the entire people. God himself will again be king of Israel as in days of old. The Anointed will not be a king, he will not spring forth from the stock of Jesse; instead he will be a man endowed with the spirit, a prophet, a servant of God. This is the many-sided figure depicted in the cycle of "Servant Songs" (42:1-7, 49:1-9, 50:4-10, 52:13-53:12).[44] The Servant is a personality who takes many forms. The prophet is only one of his manifestations; he will play this role "in several forms and life-cycles." Moreover, he is the living symbol of Israel. The redemption of the world will be carried out by him in several steps. As a prophet he will spend his strength in vain, calling to a stubborn and rebellious people, and will even be persecuted and tormented. Redemption will take shape in the crucible of these torments undergone in the midst of the people Israel, on whom he will act despite persecution and suffering; he will establish a circle of his faithful, the "remnant of Israel," the true Israel, humiliated and tormented, Israel the Suffering Servant who redeems the world through his afflictions; this Israel will fulfill the mission for which it was chosen in days of old.[45]

This, in brief, is Buber's historical and social-political conception as it concerns the Jewish faith from its inception until the Babylonian Exile. This faith is the creation of Israelite prophecy, which was active among the people from its beginning until the time of the Second Temple.

D. *Philosophical Evaluation*

1. *Monotheism and the Theory of Dialogue*

Here it is appropriate to ask: what is the internal character of monotheism according to Buber's conception, and what is the connection between this conception and his theory of dialogue?

All the questions we have discussed so far are focused on the answer to this problem, for Buber's philosophizing and preoccupation with the Bible are merely two aspects of his attempt to reach the foundations of human existence. To clarify matters I shall briefly sketch the basics of his theory of dialogue and show how it is reflected in his elucidation of the inward nature of monotheism. According to his theory of dialogue there is only one kind of authentic relationship: that which is formed in the process of an encounter between two human beings, each in his own unique existence. This communication is the groundwork preceding the consciousness of the I as his statements on primitive consciousness and the consciousness of the child imply.[46] At first the I is only "latent" in the human being; it is intertwined with the universe through the texture of its "a priori" relation; but it solidifies and becomes real through encounters with the "Thou" which confronts him on different occasions.

Development toward objectivity and neutrality is the lot of man in his relations with the universe, which includes his fellow-man. The vitality of the personal relation is bound to give way to observation, which cuts off relationships and transforms the world into an object which can be grasped with the categories of reason. There is only one "Thou" which can never become neutralized, namely God. Through his encounters with the world, the Thou which is latent in man gradually takes shape, but it can realize itself fully only through a direct relation to the eternal Thou. Thus we see that the encounter with God is not qualitatively different from the encounter with the world. On the contrary, the encounter with the world contains the elements which lead to the absolute Thou.[47] The emphasis on the reciprocity of the encounter between man and God is intended to supplement and to correct the statements of Christian, and especially Protestant, theology. Its chief spokesman, the German scholar Rudolf Otto, based the religious experience, as is well known, on the feeling of dependency and on man's perception of himself as a creature standing before his Creator. It goes without saying that the dialogic approach implies a radical rejection of the two basic forms of mysticism, both that which denies the reality of the human I and claims to lead man to self-extinction in the ecstatic union with the Divinity, and that which denies the reality of the Divine Thou and identifies it with the meditating I of the person who strives to reach himself through deep contemplation. Buber speaks of the reciprocity of the encounter with God in these daring sentences: "That you need God more than anything, you know at all times in your heart. But don't you know also that God needs you—in the fullness of his eternity, you? How would man exist if God did not need him, and how would you exist? You need God in order to be, and God needs you—for that which is the meaning of your life."[48] Thus the encounter with God is conditional upon man's constant spiritual tension and uninterrupted listening for the voice which calls to him.

In his argument with Kierkegaard, Buber brings out a second aspect of this encounter. He emphasizes that this encounter should be the continuation of man's essential link with the world and with the community. God does not want man to come to Him through solitude, skipping over the world and relating to it as something inessential; rather man must affirm the world and its fullness. In Kierkegaard's a-cosmic doctrine, which speaks of the solitary individual reaching God through a constant detachment from the world, Buber senses the Marcionite-Gnostic distinction between a creator-God and a redeemer-God, although Kierkegaard did not draw this conclusion from his assumptions.

The personal quality and the otherness of the other being which man senses in the encounter become the basis for sympathy and moral responsibility vis-a-vis the world. It follows that Buber's dialogic theory, by its very nature, revokes the constriction of the religious experience, its reduction to the status of one of many different faculties of the soul. Moreover, there is no religious *experience* per se; there is only the religious *act* whose essence is the encounter with the absolute Thou. This encounter encompasses the entirety of human existence, which is in essential relation with the world.

Thus you will not find in Buber's writings any exposition of the nature of religious experience or prophetic experience—problems which have been discussed at great length in psychological and theological literature. He does not believe in the structural separateness of what is called religious experience. The encounter with the "eternal Thou" is merely a focal point at which the "extended lines" of all the "I-Thou" relationships intersect.[49] In other words, the encounter with the Absolute is not different from the encounter with the human Thou. This explains why Buber never wrote about religious experience in the Bible, or the experience of the prophets. The title of his book on prophecy is *Torah ha-Neviim,* translated as "The Prophetic Faith," but meaning literally "The Teaching of the Prophets"; in the final analysis Buber's approach is a kind of humanism, though it is a humanism sui generis, not based on the absolute validity of abstract rules but flowing from the sense of the reality of the "Thou" which I encounter. This encounter does not occur in piecemeal fashion. It encompasses the whole person. This means that the encounter with the other and with the "eternal Thou" is the basis for the moral ethos. Thus one does not find in Buber's studies of the

Bible the distinction between morality and religion, between ritual and ethical commandments. Contrary to Yehezkel Kaufmann, who argued that the innovation of the classical prophets was the "primacy of the ethical," Buber emphasized that the basic demand of Kingship of God according to the prophets is precisely the fulfillment of the will of the Divine King in all areas of life. That is to say, he feels that there is no possibility of distinguishing between the ritual and moral domains when discussing the history of the Biblical faith. The uniqueness of prophecy consists, in his opinion, in its confronting the individual, the people and the king with the alternative of accepting the will of God or rejecting it, of choosing the way of life or the way of death. And in this respect there is practically no difference between the ancient prophecy of the time of Moses and the classical prophecy of the time of Amos. The detachment of human will from all magical, sociological and psychological limitations, the proclamation of the absolute freedom to choose one's path and one's fate, is precisely the essence of the prophetic message, according to Buber.

Hence the central position of dialogic in the world of the Bible. Monotheism is not a system of ideas; it does not contain clear perceptions and statements about the nature of God. Still less is it a product of the intuitive consciousness of an entire people, an emanation of the *Volksgeist*.[50] It is simply "a living relationship to Him,"[51] and its vigor is measured by "the strength of devotion" of the believers. The recognition of the oneness and uniqueness of the God of Israel sprang from the absoluteness of their devotion and submission to His guidance: "by following God in his ways, they recognize in every domain that the authority is His; in all His appearances they recognize Him; He is the One above all because He is the One in all."[52] The reality of the God of Israel, in contradistinction to the leader-gods of other Semitic peoples, is discerned by the fact that he *confronts* the people and leads them toward a goal different from their own desire.[53] He is "the God who tears the people out of the chains which they have grown to love and forces on them His demand in all its sternness."[54] Indeed, just as the human "Thou" is realized in the process of encounter, so the Divine Thou is realized only through the dynamism and tension of the lives of the believers. Characteristic of this approach is Buber's historigenetical interpretation of the Tetragrammaton, already cited here in Part A. According to this view, which was influenced by Duhm and Rosenzweig,[55] the name of God is nothing other than an expansion of the elemental sound "yah," "yahu," "which apparently was common to several of the Semitic tribes. Thus they hinted, by enigma and excitement, at the Divinity which cannot be called by name."[56] The phrase "ehyeh asher ehyeh"—"I shall be what I shall be" (Exodus 3:14) does not contain an abstract rationalization of the Divine Name on the part of the later "Elohist" writer; rather it expresses the basic feeling of the believer who feels His immediate presence through a genuine relation to Him. The meaning of the phrase is: "I shall be with you to save you when and where I shall be with you; I shall appear when and where I shall appear, according to My will and to My mercy; there is no regularity in My appearances; everything will occur according to My choice and My mercy at the time it happens." By this the God of Israel is severed from the domain of magic: it is not possible to conjure Him, nor is it necessary, for He is always present.[57] From this one may gather that the Tetragrammaton is simply the third person of the "ehyeh" (I shall be) and means: the one who is, the one who is always present. This meaning is as old as the faith of Israel, but Moses was commanded to make it known to the people who had forgotten it under the pressure of servitude. In the same way Buber attempts to explain the germination of the special fruit of the faith of Israel, prophecy, which has existed from the very beginning of Israel. The prophet is the mediator who transmits to the people the word of the Divine King.[58] It is not coincidental that when Moses attained true dialogue with God and spoke with Him "face to face," he nevertheless remained concerned about the people, that they might be a truthful people, entirely subject to Divine guidance. With the founding of the monarchy, when the prophet became a man of the spirit without an official function, his protest was directed against the contraction of the domain of holiness into the area of worship, while the affairs of state and society were abandoned to the exclusive authority of the human king. Indeed, the prophet is the classical example of a man who comes to God through a feeling of responsibility for the society of which he is part.

2. The Kingdom of God and Buber's Sociological Writings

Finally, a few remarks concerning the connection between Buber's writings on the Bible and his sociological and political writings. It seems that the concept of the kingdom of God is woven organically into the sociological texture of his world, as it is outlined in his book *Paths in Utopia*.

Above all this book seeks to save the reputation and integrity of

social Utopia which had been condemned by the Marxists as the product of the wildest imagination, the fruit of delusions without any
basis in reality. Buber likewise repudiates the Freudian notion of
Utopia as a neurotic symptom, a sign of unconscious or subconscious
rebellion. As against these ideas, he depicts Utopia as something
which, though not found in reality, is a depiction of "what ought to
be." It is the longing for "the right thing." Although it is rooted in the
soul, there is nothing self-seeking about it; it is bound up with the
suprapersonal element, which comes in contact with the soul but is
not conditioned by it. Furthermore, Utopianism is not to be separated
from a critical approach to the world in which a person finds himself:
"All suffering under a social order that is senseless prepares the soul
for vision."[59]

This is the general outline of the psychological structure of "the
direct rule of God," as it emerges from Buber's writings on the Bible.
It is a vision born of suffering—the suffering of the Egyptian servitude which appeared to the tribes of Israel as the prototype of the rule
of man over man. As a counter-image to this reign of terror he
imagines "what ought to be" as the exclusive sovereignty of the
Divine King who rules by apodictic law, as Buber postulated following the studies of A. Alt.[60] (Alt distinguished between apodictic and
casuistic laws and argued that the former are from the period of
nomadism and desert life, the latter from the time when
Israel became settled on its land.)

Again: In the time of the Babylonian exile and on the eve of
destruction the soul was prepared by suffering for a new vision;
against this psychological background arose the prophecies of the
"servant of God" which depicted the suffering servant who redeems
through his suffering. The depiction of the Utopia of the Kingship of
God and the connection of it with the period of nomadism as the period of the most fruitful potentiality, are of a piece with Buber's constant striving toward the principle of spontaneous, primordial creativity. His interpretation of the "direct" rule of God is shaped by his
social Utopianism, which has about it a shade of anarchism since he is
in polar opposition to the political principle, as he explicitly states in
his essay "Between Society and the State."[61] In this essay he extols
the organic, social principle which grows from beneath, as opposed to
the political principle, which is forced on society from without and is
expressed in a centralized mechanism. Hence his negative judgment
on the Israelite monarchy, which to him symbolizes the centralist
mechanistic principle par excellence, and on the other hand his posi-

tive evaluation of the Kingship of God, which grew up from below in an organic and spontaneous manner. What is more, when he imputes to the king the intention of separating the sacred from the secular, and when he denounces the "sacred" domain in the form of a sacral religion founded on a system of static ritual commandments divorced from social vision and living religious experience, he in effect transfers to the Israelite monarchy the charge of promoting dichotomy which he had once brought against Western society, and the charge of institutionalization and stifling of creativity which in his youth he had leveled at the official Halakhic Judaism of modern times. In the present writer's view there is no basis whatever in the Scriptures themselves to these charges.

In Israel, Buber's historical conception received harsh criticism from Yehezkel Kaufmann; in the West, Albright expressed his reservations. What are the charges, and to what extent are they objectively valid? In my opinion one must agree with the criticism of Albright,[62] who objected to Buber's essential distinction between the nomadic king-gods of the Western Semites and the Baalim as local nature-gods. Just as there is no support in Eastern sources for the assumption that the image of a nomadic king-god indeed existed, so there is no basis for confining the Baal to the status of a purely local god, since the Ugaritic texts explicitly indicate the cosmic scope of Baal's sovereignty.

Kaufmann completely rejected the antimonarchic interpretation of the ancient theocracy.[63] In his opinion, the few texts which express opposition to the monarchy reflect the struggle of the transitional period at the time of the founding of the monarchy; one cannot deduce from them any opposition whatsoever to the rule of mortal kings per se. Rather, the longing for the monarchy is something deeply rooted in the Bible, as witness those verses in Genesis in which the patriarchs and matriarchs are being blessed on account of the kings destined to issue from them. Kaufmann also rejected Buber's literary analysis of the book of Judges as composed of an antimonarchic source containing the stories of the judges and a promonarchic source comprising chapters 17–21. Moreover, the anthropological basis of the antimonarchic idea also seems shaky to Kaufmann, since the psychology of the tribes of Israel upon leaving Egypt was not that of the nomad, the man of the desert; their goal was not to wander in the desert, but to settle on cultivated land. Their craving for land was their primary quality. From a sociological point of view they cannot be compared to nomads who are at home in the desert; on the contrary, their way of life was always that of semi-nomads, wanderers along the fringes of a more highly developed civilization.

As regards the stories of the patriarchs, Kaufmann aligned himself with the extreme criticism which completely denies their historical value; in his opinion there is no trace in them of reliable historical testimony concerning the prenational period—they were composed only in the time of the monarchy. The beginning of monotheistic faith dates not from the time of the patriarchs, but from the time of Moses. Furthermore, that faith is not merely a "living relationship"; it contains a certain fixed image of the God of Israel, and it insists on the denial of the existence of other gods.

There is undoubtedly much that is valid in these criticisms, and Buber's approach must be corrected accordingly.[64] Still, Buber's main conception has not been shaken, but stands firm and has even received some confirmation from recent discoveries on the ancient Near East: I am referring to the concrete image of the kingship of God and to the theopolitical interpretation of the covenant at Sinai as a king's covenant. This interpretation has received indirect support from modern Biblical scholarship, which has been marked since the mid-1950's by the debate on the extent of the shaping influence which the vassal contracts in the second and first millennia may have exerted on the form of monotheism. In my book, *Ancient Prophecy in Israel*, I have tried to argue, on the basis of Akkadian and Hittite material, that the covenant at Sinai is depicted in our sources in the image of the vassal treaties known to us from the Hittite kings of the second millennium: Israel is shown as the vassal and servant of the king and master, that is, God.[65]

The documents adduced in the above-mentioned work make it appear likely that the basis of monotheism was a social covenant between the tribes of Israel and God, their King. However, it was not a "kingly covenant" in the sense of a covenant between equals, but rather a covenant between the Divine Lord and His human vassal. It appears to me that the peculiar characteristic of monotheism, namely the exclusiveness of the worship of God and the prohibition of the worship of other gods, is merely a translation of a political clause from political contracts to the field of relations between Israel and its Divine King. Moreover, among Mesopotamian contract documents of the second millennium a further type of contract has come to light, which we may call a "contract of grant," that is, a contract in which the sovereign unilaterally takes on an obligation toward the subject without demanding anything from him in return. In this one-sided obligation, and in the language of these contracts, there appear surprising similarities with promises of God to the patriarchs, as recorded in Genesis. To this we may add the material from my essay which shows similarities with the "covenant between the pieces." (Genesis 15),[66] as well as the ancient Near Eastern parallels to descriptions of the God of the patriarchs.[67] In the face of such evidence we can no longer doubt that the book of Genesis does indeed have a real historical core, that JHWH was already known to the patriarchs, though not as a national or tribal deity but through a personal relationship with the patriarchs and their families. This relationship was expressed by His demand of the patriarchs to devote themselves to Him absolutely, as shown in the story of the binding of Isaac. Thus Buber is right when he places the beginning of monotheism in the patriarchal period.

3. Some Critical Remarks

And now to the criticism of Buber's conception of the monarchy. On this subject his anti-Establishment and anti-political prejudices distorted his vision of the historical truth in an extremely serious manner, for in fact there is not a single proof that the kings sought to sever political affairs from the domain of the sacred: neither Saul nor Ahaz, nor any other king, can be accused of this. The distinction between the sacred and the secular, which is the source of all sins according to Buber, has nothing in common with the political conceptions found in the Bible. The rift between Saul and Samuel has nothing to do with the sacred/secular dichotomy. Its cause is personal: Samuel's jealousy, his unwillingness and psychological inability to accept the founding of the monarchy, his pedantic insistence on his prerogative of performing the sacrifice before the people go to war. As for Isaiah's opposition to Ahaz (Is. 7), it is explained by the particular dilemma the king had gotten himself into at that time; one may surmise that when the prophet approached him he was already determined to dispatch the envoys with the message of submission to the king of Assyria, as is related in the parallel source in II Kings 16:7ff. Therefore he did not want to take upon himself the binding force of the "sign" proposed to him by the prophet at that point. Again, Isaiah 6 does not reflect the confrontation between the prophet and the king Uzziah who "betrays," as Buber interprets it, following the interpretation which the book of Chronicles places on Uzziah's contraction of leprosy; there is no connection between Uzziah's becoming leprous and Isaiah's sanctification. One must say that Buber's ungenerous treatment of the Israelite monarchy is not based on the sources, which view the rule of the house of David as the indubitable expression of God's loving kindness toward Israel. What is more, the bringing of the Ark to Jerusalem and the building of the Temple are portrayed, in the plain meaning of Scripture, as great moments in the history of the faith of Israel: at last the God of Israel has been given a dwelling-place on earth. This is clear from the prayer of Solomon: "I have surely built Thee a house to dwell in, a settled place for Thee to abide in forever" (I Kings 8:13). The story of the cloud that hid the priests while they were performing the sacrifice is intended to certify that, indeed, from now on the Temple will be the dwelling-place of God on earth—and on this assumption rests the religiosity of the psalmists and the prophets. There is not a single Biblical writer, psalmist or prophet who evaluates Solomon's building of the Temple as a negative act confining the God of Israel to the sacral domain, as Buber interpreted it. There is no question of "confining" God to the sacral domain; rather, the Temple is the guarantee of God's constant presence among the people.

Biblical eschatology is particularly distorted and misrepresented when Buber ascribes its origin to the prophets' disappointment with real kings. In the interests of this interpretation he takes particular trouble to read into Isaiah ch. 11 a transference of the mission from the house of David to another king! However, according to the plain sense of the text, the "rod" is from the stock of Jesse, that is, one of the descendants of David, similar to the image of the ideal king in the other prophets. The late image of the Messiah from the house of David is indubitable testimony that this faith never ceased in all the history of the Israelite belief. It is true that Deutero-Isaiah does not mention the rule of the house of David in his book, but one must reject the Protestant interpretation, accepted by Buber, that Deutero-Isaiah transferred God's loving kindness toward David to the people as a whole. On the contrary, at the time of Restoration, when the question of the monarchy again became pressing, the figure of Zerubabel ben She'altiel, the scion of the house of David, came to the fore, as can be seen in the books of Haggai and Zechariyah.[68] In the figure of the future king as depicted by the prophets one can see the outlines of the ancient popular ideal of the warrior king who imposes his dominion "from sea to sea and from the river to the ends of the earth" (Psalm 2:28); he crushes the enemy and is victorious in war, he is the king who does justice and righteousness and judges the cause of the needy and the widow (Psalm 72). In Isaiah 11 however, this image undergoes a spiritualizing transformation; but the prophet Micah, his contemporary, retains in his description the features of the warrior king who subdues the enemy. In all these depictions there is not a trace of disappointment with the house of David. The theme of disappointment is struck for the first time, with great force, in the oracle on the kings in the book of Jeremiah (22:1–23:5) and in chapter 34 of Ezekiel. Furthermore, the vision of the end of the days in Isaiah has nothing to do with any disappointment whatever; it is an expression of longing for a perfected world whose center is Zion and Jerusalem. Peace and the destruction of the weapons of war are bound up, in his vision, with the decision of the nations to consult the word of God from Zion for the settlement of conflicts.[69] If chapter 11 is considered as part of the vision, then the eschatological vision is essentially the vision of a perfected world in which there is no violence, even among wild animals (cf. also Hosea 2). These Utopian elements may be contrasted to the restorationist motif of the return of the Davidic monarchy and the extension of its dominion over the entire world in the vision of Micah. Is there even a hint of disappointment here? On the contrary, these visions are an expression of profound optimism. Consequently, one must totally reject Buber's attempt to stunt and reduce the stature of the eschatological vision, against the simple meaning of the Scriptures.

Concerning the figure of the prophet, Buber ignores the dialectic between the prophets' wish to show that the fate of Israel depends on their own free choice, and their growing realization that sentence had already been passed. With Amos the theme of the alternative still predominates when he proclaims: "Hate evil and love good and present yourselves in the gate of judgment, perhaps the Lord of Hosts will be merciful to the remnant of Joseph" (Amos 5:15; compare also verses 7–6 and chapter 4). The same is true of Hosea 14. But according to Isaiah 6:9ff., doom has already been pronounced, and nothing remains for the prophet to do but to harden the heart of the people in order to hasten the calamity.[70] With Jeremiah the situation is different; his prophecy begins with the recognition of the irrevocability of the expected world-wide doom (Jeremiah 1:10). In the vision of the boiling pot he hears that the punishment will also fall on Judah (Jeremiah 1:13–16); in chapter 18 he once more tries to explain to the people that their fate is in their own hands. But in the book of

Ezekiel the certainty of destruction finally prevails; according to him alternatives exist only for the individual, but the people have been irrevocably condemned to destruction (chapter 14).[71] The truth of the matter is that the prophets strove to confront both the people and the individual with the alternatives of good and evil, but the historical circumstances into which the people were thrown became worse and worse, until the prophets' faith that the people were still capable of freeing themselves from the grip of the fate into which they had drifted by their own fault, was shaken. Indeed, in the apocalyptic vision of the time of the Second Temple, historical and anthropological determinism was victorious; neither the individual nor the people could shape their own fates by the force of moral decision; nothing was left for them but to ask: "How long shall it be till the end of these wonders?" (Daniel 12:6) That is, when will the predetermined time of the redemption arrive.

Conclusion

Buber's constant investigation of the creative, spontaneous principle led him to pay attention to the primordial element in the language and style of the Bible, and his findings in this area are of special importance for the generation of the Jewish national revival. Because of his anti-rationalist approach, he was open to the force and authenticity of the mythic elements in Biblical monotheism. His concept of society predisposed him to see as present the ancient Utopia of the kingship of God. However, this very feeling made him incapable of forming a just and balanced historical evaluation of the ritual and political institutions of the monarchy, which were an inseparable part of Biblical monotheism. Moreover, his excessive emphasis on the "here and now" prevented him from attaining a balanced view of eschatological thought. On the other hand, by emphasizing the reciprocity of the encounter with the "eternal Thou," he created a Jewish antithesis to Protestant theology, which conceived of the relationship of man to God as a one-sided dependency based on fear.

Notes

BENYAMIN UFFENHEIMER

1. *At the Turning: Three Addresses on Judaism,* Farrar, Straus, and Young, New York, 1952, pp. 47–48.
2. *Die Schrift und ihre Verdeutschung,* Berlin, Schocken, 1934, p. 45. *Werke* II 869.
3. *Kingship of God,* 3rd ed., trans. by Richard Scheimann, Harper & Row, New York, 1956, p. 16. *Werke* II 492.
4. See Martin Buber, *On the Bible,* ed. Nahum Glatzer, Schocken Books, New York, 1968, pp. 22–43. *Werke* II 871–894, especially p. 88.
5. See *Darko Shel Mikra,* Mosad Bialik, Jerusalem, 1978, pp. 163–296. *Werke* II 725–846.
6. Such as Leviticus 23:38, 39, 40; from verse 41 on the sentence length. Again, in ch. 24:1–4, 5–7 the lines are lengthened; in verse 8 they are shortened, and in the story of the blasphemer the rhythm is constantly changing.
7. See Yitzchak Heinemann, *Darkei Ha-Agadah* (*The Ways of Agadah*), Hebrew University, Magnes Press, Jerusalem, 1970, pp. 4ff.
8. *Darko Shel Mikra,* p. 284. *Werke* II 1131.
9. *Darko Shek Mikar,* pp. 287–290. In this passage he cites other examples. Werke II 1135–1138. Cf. also F. Rosenzweig, *Be-Sod ha-Tsurah Shel Sippurei ha-Mikra* (*In the Mystery of the Form of the Bible Stories*), Naharayim, Mosad Bialik, Jerusalem, 1960, pp. 7–19. F. Rosenzweig, *Kleinere Schriften,* Schocken Verlag, Berlin, 1937, pp. 167–181.
10. Not until Hosea 12:4 and Jeremiah 9:3 is there an explicit and harsh condemnation of Jacob's act! Special attention should be paid to the words of Hosea, to whom Jacob is the symbol of Israel-Ephraim who has forfeited his life by his many sins. To the above discussion on the episode of Jacob and Esau compare Buber, *Darko Shel Mikra,* pp. 284–299; *Werke* II 1131–1149.
11. Buber, "Ben Dorenu veha-Mikra" ("The Man of Today and the Jewish Bible"), *Darko Shel Mikra,* pp. 54ff. (the English translations of this essay omit the passage in question); *Werke* II 865ff.
12. In my book *Ha-Nevuah ha-Kedumah be-Isarel* (*Ancient Prophecy in Israel*), Magnes Press, Hebrew University, Jerusalem 1973, pp. 247–264, I have tried to point out the limits of this literary path of the Biblical writers; I have also indicated their attempt to arrive at new literary forms. In our generation M. Weiss emphasizes the fruitfulness of the method in his book *Ha-Mikra ki-Demutoh* (*The Bible in its Image*), Mosad Bialik, Jerusalem. The two volumes of N. Leibowitz, *Studies in the Book of Genesis,* Jerusalem 1968, and: *New Studies in the Book of Exodus,* 2 vols., Jerusalem 1970, bear witness to its importance for Bible teaching on all levels. In recent years Christian scholars have also sought to investigate this literary characteristic of the Bible; see J. P. Fokkelman, *Narrative Art in Genesis,* Aachen, Van Gorcum, 1975.
13. For the latter see S. Loewenstamm, *Encyclopedia Miqraith,* 3 (1958) 595–600.
14. Compare F. Rosenzweig's remarks in his letter of reply to Rav Josef Karlebach, *Die Schrift und ihre Verdeutschung,* p. 343.

15. See "The Word that is Spoken," in *The Knowledge of Man: Selected Essays*, translated by Maurice Friedman and Gregor Smith, Harper & Row, New York, 1965, pp. 110–120; *Werke* I pp. 442–453.

16. Ibid., pp. 110–111; *Werke* I p. 442.

17. The meaning is that something latent in the language becomes realized in the dialogue of one human being with another and in the words of the writer.

18. Ibid., p. 113.

19. "The Word that is Spoken," in *The Knowledge of Man*, p. 112.

20. Ibid., p. 113.

21. F. Rosenzweig, *Stern der Erlösung*, Haag 1976, p. 121.

22. F. Rosenzweig, *Letters*, Berlin, 1935, p. 535: "Revelation . . . has only itself as direct content, with *vayered* (and [God] descended, Ex. 19:20) it is really already complete, *vayidaber* (Ex. 20:1) is already interpretation, to say nothing of *anokhi*."

23. See Rosenzweig's letter; Buber, *Briefwechsel* II p. 199 (No. 157).

24. *Te'udah ve-Ye'ud*, pp. 85, 86; *Der Jude und sein Judentum*, pp. 78–88.

25. Ibid., p. 86.

26. "The Man of Today and the Jewish Bible," *On the Bible*.

27. *Kampf um Israel*, Schocken Verlag, Berlin, 1933, pp. 85; *Werke* II 903.

28. Martin Buber, *Good and Evil*, Charles Scribner's Sons, New York, 1952, p. 116 *Werke* I 635.

29. *Kingship of God*, p. 63; *Werke* II 545f.

30. Martin Buber, *Eclipse of God*, Harper Torchbooks, New York, 1957, pp. 14–15; *Werke* I 512.

31. Ibid., p. 46; *Werke* I 538.

32. *Good and Evil*, pp. 118–119; *Werke* I 649.

33. *Torat Ha-Neviim* (Hebr.), Mosad Bialik, Dvir, Tel Aviv, 1952, Introduction.

34. *Moses*, Oxford and London, 1956, p. 17

35. See Hooke (ed.), *Myth, Ritual and Kingship*, Oxford, Clarendon Press, 1958. Compare the articles of the editor, of S. Smith and Windgren; in contrast see the well-weighed remarks of Raleigh in the same collection, pp. 236ff.

36. H. Frankfort, *Kingship of Gods*, Chicago, 1978, idem, *The Problem of Similarity in Ancient Near Eastern Religion*, Frazer Lecture, 1956.

37. See *The Prophetic Faith*, trans. by Carlyle Witton-Davies, Macmillan, New York, 1949, pp. 31–42.

38. "Hakdamah," *Torat Ha-Neviim*. This prologue is printed in the Hebrew edition alone, but omitted in the German original.

39. Meaning those commandments which are absolute and unqualified, such as: you shall not murder, you shall not commit adultery, you shall have no other gods before me, remember the Sabbath day to keep it holy. The term is taken from the work of A. Alt (see below, note 60).

40. See *Darko Shel Mikra*, p. 164; *Werke* II 685.

41. *The Prophetic Faith*; *Werke* II 725–874.

42. *The Prophetic Faith*, p. 139; *Werke* II 383.

43. Ibid., pp. 139–141, 150; *Werke* II 383–386; 395f.

44. Ibid., p. 219f.; *Werke* II 469.

45. Ibid., pp. 155–235; *Werke* II 400–484.

46. See *Dialogisches Leben*, Zürich, 1947, p. 30; *Werke* I 90.

47. Martin Buber, "What is Man" in *Between Man and Man*, Collins Clear-Type Press, London and Glasgow, 1947, pp. 223–224.

48. Martin Buber, *I and Thou*, trans. Walter Kaufmann, Charles Scribner's Sons, New York, 1970, p. 130.

49. This is a philosophical problem which has exercised Buber's critics and those who dispute the dialogic theory; but it does not concern us here. For a discussion of this problem see M. Theunissen, *Der Andere; Studien zur Sozialontologie der Gegenwart*, 1965; J. Bloch, *Die Aporie des Du*, 1977, pp. 80ff.; and Y. Amir, "The Finite Thou and the Eternal Thou in the Writings of Buber," this book.

50. See *Ha-Ruah ve-ha-Metsiut*, Tel Aviv, 1952, p. 61.

51. "Hakdamah," *Torat ha-Neviim*.

52. Ibid.

53. Ibid., p. 33.

54. Ibid., Introduction to the Second Edition (in Hebrew).

55. See Buber-Rosenzweig, *Die Schrift und Ihre Verdeutschung*, Berlin, 1939, pp. 184–210.

56. See "Moses," Schocken edition, 1951, p. 38.

57. See "Moses," p. 40;· also Königtum Gottes, 2nd edition, 1936, chapter 5, p. 145f.

58. *The Prophetic Faith*, p. 57.

59. *Paths in Utopia*, trans. R.F.C. Hull, Routledge & Kegan Paul, London.

60. A. Alt, *Die Ursprünge des israelitischen Rechts, Kl. Schr.* I, pp. 278–322.

61. Martin Buber, "Society and the State," in *Pointing the Way*, Edited and Translated by Maurice Friedman, Harper Torchbooks, New York, 1963, p. 161.

62. W. F. Albright, *JBL*, 57, 1938, 221.

63. Y. Kaufmann, *Mikivshonah Shel ha-Yetsirah ha-Mikrait*, Dvir Press, Tel Aviv, 1966, pp. 256–280.

64. Compare what I have written on this subject in my book, *Ha-Nevuah ha-Kedumah be-Israel (Ancient Prophecy in Israel)*, Jerusalem, 1953, pp. 121ff., and in my essay, "Yehezkel Kaufmann."

65. See *Ha-Nevuah ha-Kedumah be-Israel*, pp. 70–89.

66. See my essay, "He'arot Leparashat Brit Ben ha'Betarim," ("Notes on the Covenant Between the Pieces") in the volume *Hatsvi Israel*, Tel-Aviv University, 1976, pp. 15–22 (ed. Y. Licht and G. Brin).

67. See *Ha-Nevuah ha-Kedumah be-Israel*, pp. 65–66, and also my essay, "El Elyon Qoneh Shamayim va-Arets" ("El Elyon, Creator of Heaven and Earth"), *Shnaton le-Miqrah* 2, 1977, pp. 20–26.

68. On this problem see B. Uffenheimer, *Hazonoth Zechariah (The Visions of Zechariah)*, Jerusalem, 1961, 1968, pp. 3–10, 67ff., 102ff., 117ff.

69. On this subject see my essay, "Historiah ve-Eskhatologiah be-Sefer Mikhah" ("History and Eschatology in the Book of Micah"), *Beit Miqra*, 16, 1963, pp. 48–65. On the latter see also H. Wildberger, *Jesaja*, Kap. 1–12, BKAT, 1972, pp. 75ff.

70. See my essay, "Isaiah 6 and its Rabbinic Exegesis" (Hebr.) in *Bible and Jewish History*, in memoriam J. Liver, Tel Aviv, 1972, pp. 18–50.

71. See ibid., "Jeremiah's Fluctuating Attitudes and Approaches to History" (Hebr.) in *Baruch Kurzweil Memorial Volume*, Bar Ilan University, Ramat Gan, 1975, pp. 49–61.

SOCIAL THOUGHT

Existential Guilt and Buber's Social and Political Thought

HAIM GORDON

Introduction

The main theme of Buber's address "Guilt and Guilt Feelings"[1] is that the psychotherapist should relate to the whole being of his patient and not exclusively to the patient's mind, or to his behavior, or to his feelings. Specifically, Buber stressed that the therapist should not only treat the patient's guilt feelings but should also relate to the patient's existential guilt, when such guilt exists, and especially when the guilt is the source of the patient's guilt feelings. In conjunction with this theme Buber presents a definitive description of existential guilt and his suggestions as to how a person who has become guilty can attempt to restore the order of being which he has injured. These thoughts which are a crystallization of Buber's discussions of guilt in other writings are illuminating, and yet quite problematic.

Underlying Buber's presentation of existential guilt is his basic intuition that guilt is an ontic reality and that we must learn to cope with it as such. I accept this basic intuition which is also prominent in the writings of Kafka and Dostoyevsky, and hence I will not discuss it here. Rather, I will show that Buber pretty much ignored the relation of his intuition to the complexities of man's personal and social life; he thus weakened his presentation. I will also show that this weakness reflects serious faults in Buber's social and political thought.

Part I: The Essence and the Extent of Existential Guilt

Buber describes existential guilt broadly: "Existential guilt occurs when someone injures the order of the human world whose foundation he knows and recognizes as those of his own existence and of all human existence."[2] A person can burden himself with guilt "through acting or failing to act,"[3] thus one can incur guilt by failing to act responsibly in a given situation. I shall examine Buber's presentation

215

of existential guilt by focusing on four problematic areas. I call these areas: The relation of guilt to authenticity. Guilt resulting from a conflict of duties. Guilt and guilty behavior. The extent of existential guilt.

The Relation of Guilt to Authenticity

In his essay "What is Man?" Buber writes:

> This presence before which I am placed changes its form, its appearance, its revelation, they are different from myself, often terrifyingly different, and different from what I expected, often terrifyingly different. If I stand up to them, concern myself with them, meet them in a real way, that is with the truth of my whole life, then and only then am I "really" there: I am there if I am *there*, and where this "there" is, is always determined less by myself than by the presence of this being which changes its form and its appearance. If I am not really there I am guilty. When I answer the call of present being—"Where art Thou?"— with "Here am I", but am not really there, that is with the truth of my whole life then I am guilty. Original guilt consists in remaining with oneself.[4]

Why does a person incur existential guilt when he is not "really there?" Buber distinguishes between existential guilt and guilt which is an outcome of one's transgressing a social or divine law, i.e. crime or sin. Existential guilt is only infrequently related to a specific transgression; rather a person incurs existential guilt when he pursues a way of life which is not authentic—when he does not realize his potentials, when he only rarely responds with the truth of his whole life to the address of his fellow man, when life passes him by without his being "really there." Rabbi Zusya, one of Buber's favorite Hasidic masters, expressed his own quest for authenticity thus: "In the coming world they will not ask me 'Why were you not Moses?' They will ask me 'Why were you not Zusya?' "[5]

But is it possible for Rabbi Zusya to decide definitively what it means to be Zusya? I doubt it. Each person is, at times, confronted with conflicting ways of realizing himself authentically. Thus a person's strivings to realize his creative powers may diminish his ability to relate dialogically. For instance, during the decade that Bertrand Russell wrote *Principia Mathematica*, which initiated a revolution in mathematical logic, his relations with his wife and with other women were unauthentic and emotionally sterile. Russell describes himself during this period as being totally engrossed in working his way through a long confining tunnel of problems in logic.[6] Yet it would be quite unreasonable to ask Bertrand Russell, concerning this period of intense creativity and unauthentic relations, "Why were you not Bertrand Russell?"—he was Bertrand Russell! Another example is Charles Darwin, who while summing up his years of creative research, sadly observed:

> . . . Up to the age of thirty or beyond it, poetry of many kinds, such as the works of Milton, Gray, Byron, Wordsworth, Coleridge and Shelley gave me great pleasure and even as a schoolboy I took intense delight in Shakespeare, especially in the historical plays. I have also said that formerly pictures gave me considerable, and music very great delight. But now for many years I cannot endure to read a line of poetry, I have lately tried to read Shakespeare, and found it so intolerably dull that it nauseated me. I have also lost my taste for pictures or music. Music generally sets me thinking too energetically on what I have been at work on, instead of giving me pleasure. I retain some taste for fine scenery, but it does not cause me the exquisite delight which it formerly did . . . My mind seems to have become a kind of machine for grinding general laws out of large collections of facts, but why this should have caused the atrophy of that part of the brain on which the higher tastes depend, I cannot conceive.[7]

These examples reveal that by being "really there" creating and discovering new realms of knowledge, a person may reduce his ability to be "really there" relating to other people, or to works of art, or to scenery. There seems to be more than one way for a person to live authentically, hence not being "really there is a questionable indicator of existential guilt.

Buber's approach is also questionable because many people grow accustomed to a web of mendacities within which they have developed and which permeates their entire being. Responding truthfully to the address of such a person may bring that person unnecessary suffering because he is not capable of living with the truth or with the manner in which the truth has been expressed. King Lear could not accept Cordelia's simple manner of expressing her love for him. Moreover, Cordelia's true response was a link in the chain of events which ruined Lear—by rejecting Cordelia, Lear placed himself at the mercy of his mendacious daughters and brought suffering upon himself and his true friends, Kent and Gloucester. Henrik Ibsen has shown that many people live with a "saving lie" and that any attempt to expose such an individual to a truth which threatens that lie will inflict great suffering upon him and will frequently impel him to build a new structure of lies. Unfortunately, in his discussion of existential guilt Buber does not take into account the difficulties of coping with the lies which permeate human existence, and he does not mention the social and economic pressures which strengthen those lies. Hence, his presentation of authenticity is confined to those persons who, unlike Lear, have somehow learned to live with painful truths and who wish to respond truthfully. He is preaching to the converted!

To recapitulate, Buber's manner of linking a person's not being "really there" to the essence of existential guilt does not take into account the different paths which a person may pursue in his quest for authenticity; neither does he consider the intricate web of mendacities within which many persons develop and which hinders their ability to comprehend the truth and to relate authentically. Hence, not being "really there" is, at best, a concept which a person who is capable of a truthful self examination may use to help clarify to himself the extent of his responsibility.

Guilt Resulting from a Conflict of Duties

In his book *For the Sake of Heaven* Buber describes an encounter between the Holy Yehudi and his mother-in-law, Goldele, who came to Lublin to persuade him to marry her second daughter. (When the Yehudi's first wife was on her deathbed he had promised her to marry her younger sister.) Upon meeting her son-in-law, Goldele anounced that she had come to Lublin to remind him of his duty. The Yehudi replied: "It takes a long time before a man gets to understand what his duty is . . . it is the duties which prevent him from doing so."[8]

The Holy Yehudi's statement reflects his personal dilemma. Shortly after his marriage he deserted his family and wandered from town to town—for years he lived among strangers and taught their children while his wife suffered the distress of abandonment and his children grew up without paternal guidance. Through such wandering the Yehudi hoped to learn to serve God; he felt that he was fulfilling his predominant personal duty. But in the meantime he was neglecting his familial duties, he was injuring an order of the human world whose foundation he acknowledged. Can one conclude that the Yehudi incurred existential guilt? Buber does not seem to have given thought to such a question.

Furthermore, in "Guilt and Guilt Feelings" and in his studies on the Bible Buber repeatedly stressed that a sincere illumination of one's guilt can lead to an expiation of that guilt. But he overlooked the fact that the illumination of guilt resulting from a conflict of duties will not always help a person deal with that guilt or with those duties. Consider the parents of an autistic child with severe learning disabilities. They will soon realize that if they dedicate their lives to their child they will not be able to fulfill their personal aspirations and potentials, and if they choose to develop their own potentials they will not be able to assume full responsibility for the plight of a human being whom they brought into the world in a sad condition. They are confronted with a conflict of duties; an illumination of their guilt could, and in cases I know of did, lead to disgust with life. Another example is T. E. Lawrence who was aware that his role in the Arab freedom movement demanded insincerity and the shouldering of conflicting responsibilities, and who expressed a personal disgust with himself in that role.

One important conclusion that emerges at this point is that Buber did not deal with the diverging and conflicting ways in which man can injure an order of human existence; his presentation of existential guilt does not take into account many of the complexities of human existence.

Guilt and Guilty Behavior

Unfortunately, Buber's review of the life of a person who incurred existential guilt is anti-Buberian. He writes:

> The life course I have in mind is that of a woman—let us call her Melanie—of more intellectual than truly spiritual gifts, with a scientific education but without the capacity for independent mastery of her knowledge. Melanie possessed a remarkable talent for good comradeship which expressed itself, at least from her side, in more or less erotically tinged friendships that left unsatisfied her impetuous rather than passionate need for love. She made the acquaintance of a man who was on the point of marriage with another, strikingly ugly but remarkable woman. Melanie succeeded without difficulty in breaking up the engagement and marrying the man. Her rival tried to kill herself. Melanie soon after accused her, certainly unjustly, of feigning her attempt at suicide. After a few years Melanie herself was supplanted by another woman. Soon Melanie fell ill with a neurosis linked with disturbance of the vision. To friends who took her in at that time she

confessed her guilt without glossing over the fact that it had risen not out of passion but of a fixed will.[9]

It is presumptuous and wrong to label Melanie (or any person) as if she were a finished product—as having "more intellectual than truly spiritual gifts", as possessing an "impetuous rather than passionate need for love", as expressing her "remarkable talent for good comradeship" by developing "erotically tinged friendships." Furthermore, after having labeled Melanie Buber holds her guilty for acting in accordance with her own character. Such an approach is logically untenable. Existential guilt arises when one could have acted otherwise; yet Melanie, as described by Buber, could only have related to men impetuously. What is no less disconcerting is that such labeling is at variance with the main stream of Buber's thought, according to which a person's character can change through establishing meaningful relationships with other persons, with nature, with spiritual beings, and with God.

The excerpt concerning Melanie reveals an important characteristic of existential guilt: it is a self perpetuating process strengthened through acts of causing injury. For instance, the act of inflicting pain often serves as an outlet for a person whose life lacks fulfillment and who has abandoned the hope of leading a more truthful and meaningful existence. If one's life is dominated by boredom or by a brooding on being wronged, if a person fears his own feelings, if someone who has fallen becomes aware of his inability to emerge from his state of degradation, if a person loathes his cowardly compromises with the truth but lacks the courage to reject the lies which distort his being— in such cases a person may inflict injury on other people in order to affirm his untrue life.

It is very difficult to transcend the vicious cycle whereby existential guilt leads to, and is strengthened by acts which are a new manifestation of one's guilt. In the Vatican Museum of Contemporary Religious Art there stands a bronze sculpture of King Saul by Enrico Manfrini which depicts the state of a person who has given himself up to self-perpetuating existential guilt. Saul is falling sideways, as if into an unfathomable abyss, one hand outstretched to break his fall, the other hand covering his eyes so as not to comprehend what awaits him. His existence is governed by what seem to be external forces which rapidly hurl him down to his sad end. There is no hope for a change in direction. A similar situation was depicted by Tolstoy in the chapters that describe the last days of Anna Karenina. The examples of King Saul and Anna Karenina also reveal that the political or social reality which confronts a person can intensify the self perpetuation of existential guilt. Hence it is quite unfortunate that Buber did not give due emphasis to the power of spirit which a person must muster in order to emerge from the vicious circle of guilt, especially when he finds himself in an adament political or social situation.

The Extent of Existential Guilt

What is the extent of existential guilt? How far does a person's responsibility extend beyond the sphere of his intimate relations? As a member of the world community am I guilty for not doing anything to overthrow those regimes which blatantly ignore human rights? Are we all guilty, as Simone De Beauvoir asserts, for the inhuman treatment which most elderly people receive in Western society? Or, to be a bit more practical, am I guilty if, say, I believe the chief rabbi of Israel to be morally unqualified to serve in his post but do nothing toward seeing that he is replaced by a better person? Buber's writings overlook many of the difficulties underlying these questions.

Buber maintains that much too often a person fears to take upon himself the risk of amending a state of affairs which he knows to be morally amiss; he will analyze the situation and conclude that acting courageously is unrealistic, even quixotic, because bringing about a change is almost impossible. He will then adapt himself to what he believes to be an unavoidable evil and overlook the fact that he is thus strengthening the wicked. Such a person is guilty of not daring to challenge evil, or as Ernest Hemingway puts it, he is guilty by reason of his refusal to acknowledge that the bells toll for him personally. Hence, even in arduous or disadvantageous circumstances Buber is in favor of "daring the impossible." He explains:

> As in the life of a single person, so also in the life of the human race: what is possible in a certain hour and what is impossible cannot be adequately ascertained by any foreknowledge . . . one does not learn the measure and limit of what is attainable in a desired direction otherwise than through going in this direction. The forces of the soul allow themselves to be measured only through one's using them. In the most important moments of our existence neither planning nor surprise rules alone: in the midst of the faithful execution of a plan we are surprised by secret openings and insertions. Room must be left for such surprises, however; planning as though they were impossible renders

them impossible. One cannot strive for immediacy, but one can hold oneself free and open for it. One cannot produce genuine dialogue but one can be at its disposal. Existential mistrust cannot be replaced by trust, but it can be replaced by a reborn candour.

This attitude involves risk, the risk of giving oneself, of inner transformation.[10]

The approach suggested in this excerpt is valuable for interpersonal relationships but seems highly questionable as a guideline for social or political action. Buber acknowledges that in totalitarian states daring the impossible almost always leads to martyrdom and that he would therefore hesitate to recommend such an approach in those circumstances. But even if liberal states do boast heroes who dared the impossible, such as Mahatma Gandhi, or Martin Luther King Jr. or Theodor Herzl, they were exceptional persons and their success was due to exceptional circumstances. Quite often a person who risks giving himself to the service of truth or freedom will be exploited by ambitious politicians in the manner that Cassius exploited Brutus in Shakespeare's *Julius Caesar*; and if one refuses to be exploited one may become what Henrik Ibsen called "a public enemy," hated by the masses to whom one wishes to reveal the truth. Does a person incur existential guilt when, knowing these possible outcomes, he chooses to compromise with the truth?

Buber has not given due attention to the economic, social, and political forces that govern an individual's life. This lack of attention emerges in his discussion of the actions of Joseph K. the main character of Kafka's *The Trial*.[11] I concur with Buber's view that only by acknowledging his guilt could Joseph K. begin to change his way of life. But Buber does not give due emphasis to the Kafkian theme that a hostile bureaucracy can eradicate a person's willingness to acknowledge his guilt. He does not mention the anguish, the feelings of impotency and of futility which engulf a person who attempts to cope with his guilt in an adverse social environment. Buber pretty much ignores a main thrust of Kafka's work and of contemporary man's predicament.

Buber's writings do give some guidance as to the limits of human responsibility. He did not sanction the attitude of the rabbi of Lublin in *For The Sake Of Heaven* who believed himself to be personally responsible for the coming of the Messiah and the salvation of the world. On the other hand, Buber deplored the fact that many people join a political party in order to relieve themselves of the responsibility of reaching a decision on moral and political issues. Unfortunately,

Buber gives little guidance beyond rejecting these extremes and suggesting that, at times, a person "dare the impossible." He does not address the normal person who is caught up with economic worries or with the quest for social status. He has very little to tell us about the extent of our existential guilt.

Summary. Buber's presentation of existential guilt is much too simplistic—he ignores complexities such as guilt arising from a conflict of duties or the fact that political, social, and economic forces can mold a person's behavior and limit his ability to recognize his guilt or to cope with it. He gives us almost no indication of the extent of a person's existential guilt in his everyday life. Hence, existential guilt, as Buber presented it may appeal to a person who is capable of a truthful self examination of himself, but it seems to have almost no relevance for an ordinary person who is subject to the turmoils of economic, social, and political forces. To a great extent this failing stems from Buber's mistaken approach to social and political problems.

Interlude and a Question

Sahib sells antiques in the old market of Beer Sheva. He is tall, dark, and husky and has a warm affectionate gaze. He came from Iran to Israel with his divorced father eighteen years ago; his Moslem mother remarried in Iran and he has not heard from her since. His father opened the shop and Sahib went to school and took care of the home. They were never fully accepted by the Jewish community because according to Jewish law Sahib is not Jewish—the mother passes on the religion. But neither did the Moslems attract him, especially since he knew that his father was Jewish. The Israeli Defense Force never called him up for active duty and after his father's death the Jews labeled him an Arab, (which he definitely is not because the Iranians are not Arabs.) He is attractive but hesitates to approach girls—and which girls should he approach, Jewish or Moslem? He would perhaps like to officially convert to Judaism, but since his father died he does not know how to approach the Jewish religious institutions and request conversion. Even if he does eventually convert, he is not sure that Jewish society will accept him. Trapped between two cultures, two faiths, he is terribly lonely, and even though living alone has become a habit he is unhappy. He knows that he is not fulfilling himself and that his days are squandered over relentless bargaining in the market and his evenings wasted over domino and TV. He also knows that he has nobody to turn to for help. Who is responsible for his situation? Can one definitely indicate who is guilty?

Part II: Buber's Social and Political Thought

The theme of this paper can now be reiterated in somewhat different terms. The presentation of a concept such as existential guilt in a century such as ours, which is overburdened with guilt, requires relating that concept to the social, political, and historical processes which molded this century. If we cannot relate existential guilt, which occurs when someone injures the order of the human world, to our own responsibility towards society and history, the concept will not strike root in our understanding, or in our life. Unfortunately, Buber's social and political thought does not provide the ground for this concept to become potent. In what follows I shall discuss three weaknesses characteristic of his social and political thought which reflect upon his presentation of existential guilt. I call these weaknesses: A Lack of Inquiry and Involvement. A Depreciation of Politics. A Disregard of Contemporary History.

A Lack of Inquiry and Involvement

Buber's social and political essays are often personal responses to approaches developed by other thinkers and are not rooted in the terrain of social and political inquiry. Many essays lack information which could substantiate Buber's insights and could indicate the relevance of his thoughts for contemporary life. Furthermore, since Buber's manner of presenting his thoughts is not a result of detailed observation of what occurs in society, his writings convey the impression that political and social praxis is merely the realization of certain principles. And he seems to indicate that if one could only change the interaction between these principles, or perhaps the principles themselves, everything would work out right. Such an approach is prophetic rather than scientific. But more important in the case of Buber, it leads to an ignoring of the complexities of social and political life. An example of such an essay is "Society and the State."[12]

Buber opens the essay by pointing out that one must distinguish between the social and the political principles; but he himself presents no such distinction and instead turns to a historical survey of how various thinkers since Plato failed to distinguish between these principles. (The survey style of essay, which presents Buber's own views in a roundabout, often vague manner, is rather typical of his social and political writings, i.e. *Paths in Utopia*, "The Validity and Limitation of the Political Principle.") Only towards the end of the essay does he indicate that the social principle is the manner in which society is built up of groups, circles, unions, co-operative bodies etc., while the political principle is the subversion of these principles to the State. Buber holds that the social principle is beneficial for man's existence and that the dominance of the political principle in contemporary society is non-beneficial. Hence he offers some suggestions as to how one could, or perhaps should strengthen the social principle.

The suggestions are, at best, vague. For instance, he explains the difference between Administration and Government. Administration is "a capacity for making dispositions which is limited by the available technical facilities and recognized in theory and practice within those limits." Government is "a non-technical but 'constitutionally' limited body."[13] Next he suggests that "Efforts must be renewed again and again to alter the ratio between governmental and administrative control in favor of the latter."[14] The unclarity of Buber's suggestion speaks for itself. But what is no less disconcerting is that he does not seem to have fathomed the intricate relationship between government and administration; nor does he seem to have grasped—despite his reading of Kafka—that a bureaucratic administration can be no less an anathema to social and personal life than the power of a 'constitutional' government.

Buber also mentions that a larger measure of decentralization would strengthen the social principle and that we must encourage "the education of a generation with a truly social outlook and a truly social will."[15] His presentation of these thoughts is aphoristic and abbreviated and is not based on analysis or observation. He does not suggest how one could reach a greater measure of decentralization, or how one could educate for a social outlook based on what he calls "the spontaniety of fellowship." He confines his suggestions to principles which are so general that they are of no practical use. Consequently, his insight that the power of the state frequently damages man's social and personal life and that we must strive to counter this tendency, (an insight which was hardly novel in 1951 when Buber published the essay,) remains sadly undeveloped.

A similar lack of inquiry and involvement characterizes *Paths in Utopia*. For instance, in the final chapter Buber points out that the contemporary crisis in man's social life is questioning "nothing less than man's whole existence in the world."[16] To solve this crisis he declares himself in favor of a rebirth of the commune. But he does not suggest how one goes about realizing such a rebirth. Unlike most utopian thinkers who were willing to describe in some practical terms how their vision might be realized—for instance, the first and longest chapter in Thoreau's *Walden* is "Economy"—Buber provides no such information. He does not commit himself. His visionary phrases contain no practical suggestions.

Karl Mannheim has pointed out that among utopian thinkers there is a group which "takes refuge in the past and attempts to find there an epoch or society in which an extinct form of reality-transcendence dominated the world, and through this romantic reconstruction it seeks to spiritualize the present."[17] I believe that Buber belongs to this group and that he sought to take refuge from contemporary social exigencies by describing the vitality of the Hasidic community and Israel's encounter with God in Biblical times. I shall discuss Buber's detachment from contemporary history presently, here I would only like to point out that this constant turning to the past is rather inconsistent with his existentialist approach to the spiritualization of contemporary life. Buber continually stressed that we can only spiritualize the present by being involved in the present, by coping as whole human beings with problems that arise here and now. Unfortunately, Buber's writings on society do not suggest how to realize such an involvement.

A Depreciation of Politics

The basic theme underlying Buber's essays on politics is that we must strive to introduce the spirit of religion into politics; underlying this theme is the depreciation of political activity which is not guided by religious convictions. Consider the following excerpts from "Gandhi, Politics, and Us":

> The modern Occident rests upon the sanctioned duality of politics and religion. One need only listen to how the politician speaks the word 'ethics' and the theologian the word 'action.' Politics is unenlightened but powerful; religion . . . is the object of all shades of feelings of sacredness but it is not binding . . .
>
> One should, I believe, neither seek politics nor avoid it, one should

be neither political nor non-political on principle. Public life is a sphere of life; in its laws and forms it is, in our time, just as deformed as our civilization in general; today one calls that deformity politics as one calls the deformity of working life technique. But neither is deformed in essence; public life, like work, is redeemable.[18]

Buber does not explain what he means by the deformity of public life, neither does he attempt to show how that deformity arose. He seems to judge public life in relation to his ideal of religious life and not in its own terms. But such a manner of judging, especially when as in Buber's essay it is based on intuition and not on historical evidence, does not help a person understand the interaction of political forces which are molding his history; and I doubt that "public life can be redeemed" with a blessed ignorance of how that life is constituted.

Buber describes Gandhi's heroic attempts to introduce the religious spirit into politics and suggests that we have much to learn from his approach. Granted. But what is surprising is that Buber does not acknowledge the unique historical and political circumstances which allowed Gandhi to speak out and to engage in political activity even while held in jail. Karl Jaspers has pointed out that "It was only under the British, and only under their attempt at liberal rule which is unique in the history of empires, that Gandhi could succeed."[19] A religious political movement such as Gandhi's could not arise in a totalitarian regime. Even today in the "liberalized" Soviet Union dissidence is partially tolerated only as long as it is a personal affair— if it became a political movement it would immediately be crushed. Buber made no attempt to distinguish between democratic governments which allow movements such as Gandhi's to arise and to engage in political activity, and totalitarian regimes which would destroy such a movement at its inception. He puts all politics in one bag, labels it "deformed" and suggests that we learn from Gandhi how to redeem it.

Even if one agrees with Buber as to the sad situation of contemporary politics this does not imply that "one should be neither political nor non-political." (What should one be?—Such unclarity is unworthy of Buber.) Public life is too important a field to be left untended by persons with visionary moral and religious convictions such as Buber, especially since "the *raison d'etre* of politics is freedom and this freedom is primarily experienced in action."[20] Hence a person who deliberately detaches himself from the action which constitutes public life and, as Buber suggests, employs primarily religious or educative means in contending with political opponents is limiting his own freedom. And often, as the Jews of the holocaust sadly learned, much more than freedom is lost when one refuses to act forcefully in politics. Public life, as Buber once remarked, is a thorny field; but he often hesitated to acknowledge that in order to clear a trail through this field one must hack prickly vines and uproot brambles.

Buber's essay on Gandhi was written in 1930 and republished in 1957 together with other political essays. One would expect that following the Jews' lack of political involvement during the holocaust and its sad outcome some of Buber's views would have changed. Such did not occur. The theme that one must introduce religiousness into politics in order to "save" politics remains the central motif of all his political writings. For instance, in "The Validity and the Limitation of the Political Principle" he attacks what he terms "the political principle" which "means roughly that public regimes are the legitimate determinants of human existence."[21] As against this principle, whose manifestations he hardly describes, he suggests that in public life man learns to serve God—that is respond to the exigencies of a situation with one's entire being—and also to the political group to which one belongs. In each situation a person will be guided by his conscience to decide on the line of demarcation between the service of God and the service of one's political group. Those persons who adopt such an approach will help to rescue man "from being devoured by the political principle."[22]

As an appeal to act morally in politics such an essay may have some force. But as an approach to examining and changing contemporary life it is detached, romantic, and naive; and not only because Buber does not clarify the political principle nor describe the historical forces which brought about man's enslavement to public regimes, i.e. the rise of the mob as a political force. His basic mistake is that he does not acknowledge politics as an independent sphere of human endeavor which can develop its own moral goals and its own means of realizing such goals. Buber disliked politics and disparaged it. When he entered this realm he armored himself with religious morality so as to be able to cope with the evils which he encountered. He emerged unscathed, but also untouched by political realities.

A Disregard of Contemporary History

Nowhere is Buber's disregard of contemporary history more evident than in his writings on contemporary problems. Two examples should suffice. In his famous "A Letter to Gandhi" in 1939,[23] which was a response to Gandhi's suggestion that the Jews practice *Satyagraha* against the Nazi regime instead of emigrating to Palestine, Buber pointed out the impossibility of such a response to Nazism and questioned Gandhi's understanding of the Jew's historical situation. He also declared that, at times one must not respond passively but rather fight for justice and respond to force with force. But what perturbed Buber in this letter and in his other writings which mention Nazism was how to act in accordance with the dictates of his conscience; he did not attempt to understand how the functioning and the organization of totalitarian regimes destroy a person's conscience.

In "People and Leader" Buber attempts to describe the appropriate relationship between a people and its leader by depicting and analyzing the fictitious relationship between fascist leaders and their people. But his analysis is primarily based on speeches of Hitler and Mussolini and not on their deeds or on the processes which they utilized to acquire and consolidate their power. Such an abstract approach gives rise to the following:

> A decisive difference between fascist and bolshevist totalitarianism is that the latter arises from the tradition of a real idea and in vital relationship to it; bolshevism is established, therefore, on the belief in a truth, whereas fascism in contrast, basically acknowledges nothing 'but the firm will to retain power.' No matter how far bolshevism has removed itself, through its tendency to the accumulation of power, from the life attitude common to all genuine socialist thinking, it remains bound to an idea as its goal, and the glimpse of this goal is what ultimately holds together its masses.[24]

The essay was published in 1942 when the West already knew about the mass extermination of the kulaks, about Stalin's 1938 purges of the Bolshevik Old Guard and Red Army leaders, about the Gulag, about the Molotov-Ribbentrop pact. Despite these well published facts Buber still believed that the bolshevist brand of totalitarianism was better than Nazism because in Lenin's writings one finds "a vital relationship to a real idea." What is even more surprising is that Buber republished the essay without omitting the above citation in 1957 after Khrushchev's speech on the horrors of the Stalinist regime. One can only assume that for Buber a declared vital relationship to an idea is more important than what actually transpires after the declaration.

Although Buber was concerned with the predicaments which contemporary man faces, he did not discuss the historical processes and conditions which gave rise to these predicaments. To some extent his disregard of contemporary history can be justified by arguing that Buber described the ontic and anthropological aspects of human existence such as the I-Thou relationship or existential guilt, and these aspects are not confined to a specific period in history. Still, in coping with our predicaments it is helpful to understand why in contemporary life a person has difficulties relating to his fellow man as a Thou; or to return to the theme of this paper, we can learn much about coping with existential guilt if we understand how Adolf Eichmann could help administer the mass execution of millions of human beings and not be cognizant of his guilt. But for such knowledge one must be aware of the social, political, and economic processes[25] which influence our being; and as Hannah Arendt and others have shown these processes are unprecedented in human history.[26] Hence by disregarding contemporary history in his social and political writings Buber confined his thoughts to a realm of abstraction which is remote and often detached from our daily existence.

Summary

Buber's presentation of the concept of existential guilt has very little to tell us about human existence. Perhaps the main reason for the remoteness of this concept from our daily responsibilities and decisions is that Buber disregarded the milieu which nurtures contemporary man. Many a person, like Sahib in the Beer Sheva market, are influenced and molded by processes and forces which are beyond their understanding, and coping with these processes and forces seems beyond their ability. By ignoring these forces and processes in discussing an important concept such as guilt, Buber led his readers to a superficial and abstract comprehension of a very real problem.

One key to Buber's unfortunate presentation of existential guilt is his social and political thought which is detached from what occurs in contemporary society and politics. Buber advocated the introduction of religion into politics, the rebirth of the commune, and the need to act in accordance with the dictates of one's conscience in politics. But he did not relate these suggestions to our contemporary life—his writings are based on intuition and not on social involvement or inquiry, he disparaged politics, he disregarded contemporary history.

The weaknesses of Buber's presentation confront us with the problem of relating his important intuition concerning existential guilt to our social and personal life. Buber's contribution to this problem may have been much more significant if he had heeded the warning of Nietzsche's Zarathustra: "Stay loyal to the earth, my brothers, with your power of virtue . . . Do not let it fly away from the things of the earth and beat with its wings against eternal walls."[27]

Notes

HAIM GORDON

1. Martin Buber, "Guilt and Guilt Feelings," *The Knowledge of Man* (New York: Harper Torchbooks, 1965), pp. 121-148. The address was presented to the Washington School of Psychiatry in 1957.

2. Ibid. p. 127.

3. Ibid. p. 125.

4. Martin Buber, "What is Man?" *Between Man and Man* (London: The Fontana Library, 1947), pp. 202-203.

5. Martin Buber, *Tales of the Hasidim, Early Masters* (New York: Schocken Books, 1947), p. 251.

6. See: *The Autobiography of Bertrand Russell 1872-1914* (London: George Allen and Unwin, 1967), especially the chapters "Principia Mathematica" and "Cambridge Again."

7. *The Autobiography of Charles Darwin,* edited by Francis Darwin (New York: Dover Publications, 1958), pp. 53–54.

8. Martin Buber, *For the Sake of Heaven* (New York: Atheneum, 1969), p. 85.

9. "Guilt and Guilt Feelings," pp. 128–129.

10. Martin Buber, "Prophecy, Apocalyptic, and the Historical Hour," *Pointing The Way* (New York: Harper Torchbooks, 1957), p. 206.

11. See "Guilt and Guilt Feelings," pp. 140–145.

12. Martin Buber, "Society and the State," *Pointing the Way*, pp. 161–176.

13. Ibid., p. 174.

14. Ibid., p. 175.

15. Ibid., p. 176.

16. Martin Buber, *Paths in Utopia* (Boston: Beacon Press, 1958), p. 129.

17. Karl Mannheim, *Ideology and Utopia* (New York: A Harvest Book, Harcourt, Brace and Co.), p. 259.

18. Martin Buber, "Gandhi, Politics, and Us," *Pointing The Way*, pp. 135–136.

19. Karl Jaspers, *The Future of Mankind* (Chicago: University of Chicago Press, 1961), p. 38.

20. Hannah Arendt develops the theme of this quote in: "What is Freedom?" *Between Past and Future* (Middlesex, England: Penguin Books, 1977), p. 151.

21. Martin Buber, "The Validity and the Limitation of the Political Principle, *Pointing The Way*, p. 213.

22. Ibid., p. 219.

23. Martin Buber, "A Letter to Gandhi," *Pointing The Way*, pp. 139–147.

24. Martin Buber, "People and Leader," *Pointing The Way*, p. 150.

25. The fact that Buber ignored economics and refrained from using concepts from the realm of economics in his writings on society and politics can perhaps be explained by Karl Mannheim's remark: "The absence of certain concepts indicates very often not only the absence of certain points of view, but also the absence of a definitive drive to come to grips with certain life problems." See *Ideology and Utopia*, op. cit., p. 274.

26. See Hannah Arendt's seminal study *The Origins of Totalitarianism* (New York: Meridian Books, 1958).

27. Friedrich Nietzsche, *Thus Spoke Zarathustra*, tr. by R. J. Hollingdale (Middlesex, England: Penguin Books, 1961), p. 102.

Martin Buber's Address "Herut" and Its Influence on the Jewish Youth Movement in Germany

MENAHEM DORMAN

The concern and purpose of my lecture is not to explicate a specific religious or philosophical aspect of Martin Buber's teaching—though I must immediately qualify this negative statement by saying that there is nothing in any of the domains which comprise Buber's world that does not have some religious or philosophical meaning, anchored in his teaching. Nonetheless it is appropriate to say at the outset that with respect to the ensemble of problems raised by the renewed study of this teaching, the subject of my lecture—the address "Herut" and its influence on the Jewish youth movement in Germany—is somewhat out of the way. It is a kind of glimpse—a not overly hasty glimpse—into the area of the deeds which were done at one time by way of realization of Buber's ideas, as interpreted in good faith by young people in his time, who for some reason felt obliged to realize these ideas, or who thought and believed, many years ago, that they too were numbered with the great camp of Buber's disciples—"disciples" being understood by them in the sense of the maxim, "Not study is the chief thing, but action".

This verse from the "Tractate of the Fathers" brings me to the subject of my talk, for the name and theme of Buber's pamphlet "Herut", which was published in 1919,[1] are taken from another verse (6:2) of the same tractate: "God's writing engraved on the tablets— read not *harut* (engraved) but *herut* (freedom)". This pamphlet—of course, in the context of Buber's other writings—once gave rise to a pioneer action on the part of a very small and isolated group of Jewish youth in Germany, an action which eventually brought forth lasting fruits, whose traces are engraved in the annals of Jewish youth of German origin and on the map of the land of Israel. This is, at any rate, a hidden chapter in the spiritual-collective biography of Buber; it is doubtful whether Buber himself, though he had some very slight knowledge of the episode, ever took much interest in it or paid it much attention, and in any case I have not seen it mentioned in any essay on him, on his philosophy and its influence or on his effect among his people in the Diaspora and in the land of Israel. I would like now to briefly tell the story to which I refer, not from my own recollection, but according to an account which I found in an essay by Hermann Gradenauer (later: Amram Gadnaor), entitled "The Beginning of Kibbutz 'Herut' " and published about forty years ago in an internal publication of Giv'at Brenner:[2]

> It was in the year 1926. In the land of Israel, after two years of prosperity, a severe crisis set in. It seemed that everything was in the process of deteriorating and that the entire work of building was endangered. The (British) government had closed all Jewish immigration to the land. The "Stop Immigration" lay like a heavy ban over the whole Zionist movement. In the Diaspora a profound depression reigned, and the feeling arose that we had missed the time of takeoff, that there was no further hope of sustaining the work or of speeding it up to the tempo needed to save the people. It seemed that while we Jews were indeed capable of laying the foundations of the building, our strength was not sufficient to secure it against a crisis which endangered its very substance . . . And in Germany, it was the time of the complete breakup of the "Blau-Weiss", which left Zionism without youth and without a youth movement . . . Authoritative opinions were heard demanding the return to Europe of the pioneers from Germany . . . At that time Kibbutz "Herut" was formed from among the ranks of the "Brit ha-Olim"—which in itself shows that in official Zionist circles in Germany there was not the slightest confidence in that "Brit", and that because of the general crisis the whole enterprise of pioneer training there had just about scattered. If in 1925 there were still about a thousand people in pioneer training, as a result of the crisis there now remained only about twenty, twenty-five pioneers . . . In the general despair that enveloped us, we felt the need to establish a center of power, to found a group of people who believed in the building of the land and in a renewed aliyah which would train itself through self-activity and which would be ready, the moment immigration to the land was opened once more, to march as pioneers at the head of German-Jewish youth to the land of Israel, to enter the ranks of the workers there . . . Thus was formed kibbutz "Herut", as a human lever to overcome the paralysis of Zionism and of the pioneer movement in Germany. In the environs of the city of Hamelin in Westphalia, in the village of Lidge, on Rosh Hashana of 1926, the resolution to establish the kibbutz was taken, and it was named "Herut" after Martin Buber's pamphlet "Herut".

Thus far the chronicle, which ends on the names of Martin Buber and his pamphlet "Herut". This chronicle now calls for many recollections and detailed interpretations, but first I would like to emphasize the historical perspective from which we must contemplate, today, this event and this deed of a few pioneers in Germany.

In these days, in Israel and in the world, the hundredth anniversary of the birth of Martin Buber—1878-1978—is being noted. Buber was born into the second generation of the Emancipation and at the beginning of the disappointment in it, and in its possibility to continue to sustain the Jewish people in the Diaspora and in exile under the conditions created by the European emancipation. Moreover, he was a child of the fin de siècle through and through in his political, social, and cultural tendencies. When he was three years old there appeared in Berlin, signed anonymously by "A Russian Jew," Yehuda Leib Pinsker's pamphlet "Autoemancipation", and when he was a lad of twelve, already intellectually mature, Theodor Herzl's pamphlet "The Jewish State" appeared in Vienna. From the end of the preceding century to approximately the middle of this one, German Jewry—that is, those Jews who spoke and wrote in German, including those who lived in Central Europe, mostly in Austria and Czechoslovakia—was engaged in a mighty struggle on the question of whether to remain rooted in this diaspora or to become uprooted from it, to go out from it of their own free choice. In truth, this was a mighty struggle, the like of which no diaspora has ever known, except, perhaps, the Spanish Diaspora in the last hundred years of its existence in Spain. I do not know whether or how it is possible to estimate the degree of desire of a Jewish Diaspora community to cleave to the foreign people among whom they dwell; at any rate, among the Jewish community in Germany, or in the "German realm", as Gershom Scholem defines it, this desire pulsed with unusual force, and the contribution of Jews to German culture, above all to science and literature, was in proportion to this desire—a contribution it seems without parallel in all the diasporas and all the generations. Gershom Scholem makes some apposite and penetrating remarks on this subject in his essay "Jews and Germans".[3] As an example he cites the Jews' attitude toward the two German classical writers, Goethe and Schiller. It is impossible to draw up an account of German culture in the hundred years between the middle of the nineteenth century and the approximate middle of the twentieth century without referring to Jews and to people of Jewish descent, whatever the content of their Judaism and their relationship to their Jewish origins. In my opinion, Gershom Scholem is right in denying the legend of "German-Jewish symbiosis"; but if there was no true, total symbiosis, there was without doubt a partial symbiosis, that is a symbiosis of Jews with the German *language*, from Heine to Kafka and Martin Buber. Even Yiddish, which is one of the most wonderful creations of the Jews of the Diaspora, is at root a Germanic language.

But in proportion to the urge inward, into the German being, there was, from the other side, the outward rejection—and this in every sense, until rejection became total and under certain conditions of the twentieth century, meant annihilation. In the march of the swastika the Jewish Diaspora in Germany and in the German realm was annihilated together with millions of European Jews, and *thus*—and not otherwise—an end was put to the mighty struggle of the Jews in Germany to live in Germany, to take root in it, to remain there, to create in it, to leave its mark upon it as a legitimate part of it, whether as German Jews or as Germans "of the Mosaic persuasion". The historic mission of Zionism here was to see and to understand in advance why the Jews would inevitably get the worst of this struggle; its mission was to preserve the greater part of the Jewish substance, both physical and spiritual, and to prepare the Jews for another future—outside Germany, outside diaspora and exile. This was the mission of German Zionism generally and of Zionist youth in particular, especially in the period between the two world wars, when the horizon was growing blacker and blacker and the bad signs were definitely multiplying at a staggering rate.

As is known, the 'twenties, between the end of the first World War and the beginning of the 'thirties, was the period of flowering and maturing of the Zionist youth movement in Germany, and the "Blau-Weiss" formed the center of this youth movement until its voluntary dispersal in 1926, after an existence of about ten years. One may say that in the present context the term "youth movement" is slightly misleading. True, it was indeed a "movement", an organization (and, incidentally, a well-disciplined organization) which as an educational movement included people of all ages from childhood through youth and even beyond; true, the "Blau-Weiss" was saturated with the ideology of the specialness of youth, very much like the German "Wandervögel"; but nevertheless the emphasis in this combination of words is on "youth"—that is, the younger generation of a certain population, the rising generation in the biological and social sense, the generation of the future. When we speak of the members of "BILU", for example, we do not characterize them as a "youth movement", although most of them were as young as the veteran members of the "Blau-Weiss" at its height, and the same is true of the members of the Second Aliyah, most of whom made the revolution of their lives—and therefore the revolution of their people—at about the age of twenty. *Cum grano salis* we may say that youth is apt to produce decisive changes in the lives of peoples. At the beginning of his speech "Herut" Buber defines youth—Jugend—as follows:

> Youth is the time of total openness. With totally open senses, it absorbs the world's variegated abundance. With a totally open will it gives itself to life's boundlessness. It has not yet sworn allegiance to any one truth, for whose sake it would have to close its eyes to all other perspectives, has not yet obligated itself to abide by any one norm that would silence all other aspirations",[4]

and so forth. Youth is open, it can be open; its hearing can be ultra-sensitive in order to absorb the still, small voice of history before it speaks through thunder and storm.

The thousands of Jewish youth who were concentrated in the "Blau-Weiss" were part and parcel of German Jewry in the period under discussion. It is no exaggeration to say that here were concentrated some of the best of Jewish youth in Germany, with tremendous energy and superlative spiritual talents. There is no doubt that this Jewish youth movement saved many Jews for their Judaism and their people and extricated them from the false enchantments of complete assimilation and absorption. But in its main goal it failed utterly: it did not become the pioneer who leads the camp of German Jews in their self-liberation from diaspora and exile *while there was yet time*. It failed to realize its ideas, its ideals, *in the land of Israel*. This is not the place for a detailed analysis of the reasons for the failure. I shall content myself, then, with the following remarks on this subject: First, the Germany aliyah came late. With a few individual exceptions, German Jews did not participate either in the first aliyah or in the second aliyah—the waves of aliyah before the first World War. After this war, and after the revolutions which took place within it and in consequence of it, when the pioneers of the "Blau-Weiss" came to Israel with the third and fourth aliyah, they did not find here a human and social basis capable of absorbing them in a way that suited their character, their education, their customs, and their mentality. Second, the "Blau-Weiss" was part and parcel of German Zionism with its special spiritual and social character. In his essay on "Martin Buber and German Jewry" Ernst Simon points out the paradox that Herzl, who lived in the German realm, attracted people mainly in Eastern Europe, while Ahad ha-Am, a Russian Jew, attracted people mostly in Western Europe, in Germany.[5] One must also remember that the pioneers of the second aliyah, the disciples of Berdichevsky and Brenner, were counted among the most ardent champions of Ahad ha-Am. The "Blau-Weiss" incorporated both the good qualities of German Zionism, which had made such a great contribution to the spiritual treasures of the Zionist movement as a whole, and all the weaknesses of German Zionism, which did not comprehend and could not comprehend the depths of the catastrophic situation of the Jewish people in the twentieth century. And third, the "Blau-Weiss" was an assimilationist movement in its essence, post-assimilationist in its consciousness and Zionist in its goal—and in attaining its goal in the land of Israel it failed completely. Everyone who saw the "Blau-Weiss" from close up knows beyond doubt that this youth movement was essentially the Jewish incarnation of the German *Wandervögel*, in ideological concepts, in educational values, in its every day way of life. In contrast, how thin and shrivelled and external was the Jewish content of this movement!

Criticism of the assimilationist character of the "Blau-Weiss" had begun to grow within the movement itself a few years before it was finally forced to admit its failure and to dissolve itself. It goes without saying that the consequences of the inability of the "Blau-Weiss" groups to take root in the land were not confined to that organization alone. Among the Jews of Germany there was a deepening of the lack of confidence necessary to participate directly and in person in the building of the land; even before immigration to the land was stopped by the Mandate government, additional justifications in Zionist terminology were found for *not* turning one's back on the German diaspora. But as noted before, the breakup of the "Blau-Weiss" did not come as a surprise to *everyone*. Already in 1922 a pioneer Zionist opposition had arisen within this youth movement, and when it detached itself from the mother movement and established itself as an independent movement, a new factor, by the name of "Brit ha-Olim",[6] appeared within German Zionism. I have already mentioned this name in relaying the chronicle of how Kibbutz 'Herut' was founded in 1926. The *Hebrew* name "Brit ha-Olim" was chosen as a symbol, and one may easily suppose that those who chose this name were inspired by the writings of Martin Buber, including the well-known pamphlet "Herut". From Richard Markel's essay, "Brit ha-Olim", which was published in one of the volumes of the Leo Baeck Institute, we learn that the men who were then invited to lend their support to the new organization also included Gershom Scholem and Ernst Simon, but it is not known whether both or one of them responded to this call.[7] "Brit" does not mean simply *Bund*, "league". The Biblical, religious connotation of this word was perfectly clear. The same is true of the second word, "Olim", which means both a "going up" to the land of Israel and a heightening, a restoration, of man. In his essay "On the History of Brit ha-Olim" (Der Junge Jude, July-August 1930)[8] Hugo Rosenthal, the teacher and educator, writes as follows:

> "Brit" is a covenant with God and with man. The covenant with God finds expression in the religious commandments; the covenant with man, in socialism. Judaism aspires to a synthesis of religion and socialism. This synthesis is realized in the prophets. The Sabbath is its concrete expression. The task of the Jewish youth movement is to recreate this synthesis of pioneering, religion and socialism.

On the level of concrete activity four principles were defined: 1) the creation of close contact between Western and Eastern Jewry; 2) joining of the General Union (Histadrut) of Jewish Workers in Israel; 3) education toward the Kibbutz and 4) deepening of the study of the Hebrew language.

When we read accounts of the founding of "Brit ha-Olim" we run across the names of several cities in Germany which were not among the most distinguished centers of Jewish population in that country, at that time, such as Fulda, Wolfenbüttel, Hameln, and Emden. Some of these names are known, of course, in the history of the Jews in Germany, Hameln by the merit of Glückl of Hameln and her memoirs, written in "Iuri-Taitsch", Fulda for the small but ancient community, firm in spirit and of exemplary fidelity, which existed there until the Holocaust. Among the handful of members of Kibbutz 'Herut' and "Brit ha-Olim" the community of Emden is represented by a surprisingly high percentage, and this community too is well remembered in the history of German Jewry as a place of refuge for marranos from Portugal, who settled here and returned to their Judaism and also because of great rabbis, including Yaakov Emden and Samson Raphael Hirsch, who officiated there. I emphasize this mainly because natives of these districts, Uri Rosenblatt and Alfred van der Velde,[9] played a prominent role in shaping both "Brit ha-Olim" and Kibbutz "Herut". For the purpose of realizing the four clauses which I enumerated above as the principles of "Brit ha-Olim", and in the midst of their practical realization, Kibbutz "Herut" arose in the hardest and most desperate days of the pioneer Zionist youth movement in Germany, when it seemed, because of the breakup of the "Blau-Weiss", that the lid had been closed on the need and the possibility of finding, among German Jewry, young people who would take on themselves the duty and task of serving as its *pioneers* in the exodus from the diaspora and in participation in the building of the land. I have already related that when Kibbutz "Herut" was founded in 1926, in one of the villages in the environs of Hameln, the group read together Martin Buber's speech on youth and religion, and because they believed, rightly or wrongly, that these words expressed the desire of their hearts, they adopted the name of the address—"Herut"—as a symbol and a banner.

And now comes the question: What enchanted us in that speech and why did we believe that we were ready and commanded to walk in its light? I confess without shame that to this I have only a personal answer, but I have every reason to surmise that this personal answer of mine is also valid for other members of "Herut", to an extent varying according to the inclination of each person's heart and temperament. Buber begins here with a definition of the character and the mission of youth: he gives it the sign of *openness*. Youth, seeking a solution to its distresses, its uncertainties, is open, can be open, to different, new, non-routine answers, and being, in fact, the rising generation in the chain of generations, it is listening for the footsteps of the future. If the events of its life have wrenched him or her out of the fixed and solidified tracks; if he or she has not yet become subservient to the daily routine of pursuit of a livelihood and a career, the youth will feel the "touch of the unconditional" (Berührung des Absoluten), and then he or she must respond to that touch. Because there is something "unconditional", non-relative, in our lives. But there are illusory, deceptive responses. Here Buber mentions two kinds of illusory response: "superficial rationalism" and "superficial emotionalism", i.e. a sort of intellectual hedonism which obliges one to nothing, which contains no commandments and no deeds. Buber speaks disparagingly of three types of men who were found in abundance in German Jewry, including, of course, its youth movement: the "Erlebnissammler" (collector of experiences), the "Stimmungsprotz" (boaster about moods) and the "Gottschwätzer" (prattler about God), who talks a great deal about God and religion, but whose "exceedingly proud talk" does not place him under any obligations as to his way of life. Against these types Buber set the demand for a response from "the entire person" (der ganze Mensch), or, as in Hebrew, a man with all his 248 limbs and 365 sinews. Buber calls this readiness of man to place himself entirely at the service of his vision or his faith the way of *Ernstmachen*—of "putting beliefs into practice", of relating seriously, in word and deed, to his "unconditional", or, in good Hebrew, the "ani maamin". This, it seems to me, is how the members of "Herut" translated and interpreted Buber's pamphlet; even if they did not understand him completely, still they found in him, in good faith, an ideological basis and moral justification for a way of life which they adopted—and it was, without doubt, a hard, non-opportunistic way amid the German, Jewish, and German-Jewish environment, which proposed other ways, seemingly more correct, more promising, and more attractive to them in every sense, as individuals and as members of their people. For the sake of self-realization they seized on two things: the demand for response by the "entire person", that is, "with all thy soul and with all thy might", and to the demand of *Ernstmachen*, "putting beliefs into practice". Thus if you say "physical work", you work and support yourself by manual labor; if you say "Kibbutz", you merge into a kibbutz and carry out everything that follows from that; if you say "aliyah", then you make aliyah to the land of Israel, and the sooner the better. If you say "Hebrew", then you exchange the mother-tongue which you have spoken, lived in, and loved, for the time-honored language of the people. However, of all the commandments which the members of Kibbutz "Herut" imposed upon themselves, this one was the hardest to observe fully and constantly; although even here a great effort was made, as Moshe Shilo (then Berchmann) and Professor Dov Sadan (then Stuck), who served as teachers and educators to that pioneer group, will testify.

Written documents on the chronicles and characteristics of Kibbutz "Herut" are rare; such documents, as I said in the beginning of my talk, have the status of testimony to an almost unknown episode connected with Martin Buber's philosophy and educational influence. Yitzchak Tabenkin, in a talk given in Giv'at Brenner, the place of Kibbutz "Herut"'s realization in the land of Israel, said among other things that "as a human type the members of Kibbutz "Herut" had something in common with, or somehow resembled, those who came with the second Aliyah. This similarity of character expressed itself perhaps not so much in relation to the land of Israel as in relation to their country of origin, their former environment (. . .) Those who came with the second aliyah were rebelling against their environment, beginning in the inward depths of the soul. Each one had to rebel against his environment, to despair of it and also of his own world, in order to build another, new world (. . .) The members of "Herut" too had also experimented with the experience of personal, inward rebellion. And apparently there was also a psychological basis for this rebellion, this stand taken against the whole environment".[10] I recall a conversation with Berl Katznelson in which he, too, made such a comparison with the second Aliyah. But even as I point out the fact of the paucity of written documentation, a story by Tsvi Schatz, "Without Speech",[11] comes to mind. What remains are mainly personal letters, some of which were included in the book *Herut*, published in 1940 by Giv'at Brenner—a book which, like the names of the writers of the letters, is almost unknown.[12] Nevertheless it seems to me that even today, anyone who first read Martin Buber's address "Herut" and then turned to the bundle of letters in the book *Herut* could not help but discover some internal link between the address and the letters: the latter as it were illustrate the former and show how the words were realized in actual practice.

To the book *Herut* was added an introduction written by Dov Sadan, who worked with us, the members of Kibbutz "Herut", in 1929, and it seems to me worthwhile to quote a few paragraphs from that introduction verbatim:

> The compulsion to flee, the result of a seismographic feeling which sensed the horror about six years before it came, brought this group of young people with haste in immigrant ships. But before this flight came several other flights: it was necessary to flee from the two-faced reality that surrounded them. Two-faced, for on the one hand there was a type of people who was or wished to be joined to our nation and its land, but whose joinedness had become a way of loving at a distance, and on the other hand there was a type of people who were or wished to be detached from our nation and its future, and whose detachment expressed itself through great loves for foreign gods, from the delightful little gods of the salons to the tempestuous great gods of the masses! Both kinds of gods as it were stood there, cajoling: do not abandon a certain and great human purpose, the overthrow of Pittom and Ramses which are near, for a small and dubious national goal, the distant sacrifice to the God of the desert. I saw these young men and women facing these temptations: they, who had not trained their tongues in sharp dialectics for the preachment of values, but had prepared their hearts for the acquisition of values in the sphere of eternity, did not have an easy time of it. More than once they were torn by a feeling of contradiction, which they did not know how to put into words: the truth was in their hearts, but the arguments were not on their tongues. But they were able to carry it out in life—they lived according to their truth (. . .).
>
> Let us say: it is a miracle and yet no miracle. For miracles are beyond

explanation, but the appearance of "Herut" can in the end be explained. If one does not set out to the whole work of explanation, but contents oneself with part of it, one may hint at a few of the things that helped them. For instance, their solidarity with the poor of Israel. Certainly, most of the young people, born in Germany, had not themselves known poverty. I visited some of their houses and saw much prosperity there. But in the city outskirts and in the training groups in the villages lived the children of miserable poor families, most of whose parents had been *Ostjuden*—a kind of agency of Jewish poverty from Galicia, from Poland, from Lithuania . . . And it seems that this basic principle of mixing the different diasporas of Israel, a mixing which became complete in the life of the training period, which was full of toil and poor in pleasures—this contributes not a little to the explanation of this divinatory feeling which was not granted to others (. . .).

Once I returned from making rounds among the comrades who were scattered over the area. I related to them a few small, but symptomatic things. For instance, in Hamelin the Jewish cemetary was situated next to the non-Jewish cemetery. The non-Jewish cemetery was fenced off by a low hedge of shrubbery; the Jewish cemetery was surrounded by a high brick wall with a layer of cement on top into which many pieces of broken glass had been stuck, with their sharp edges pointing up. The reason: they were afraid the graves would be desecrated. In the small town of Lidge I had seen a Gentile mowing hay on a plot of land over which about a dozen Jewish headstones were scattered. From time to time the scythe would strike upon one of the stones. I asked the Gentile: "Hard work?" He answered, "Well, yes, that's the way the Jews are—even when they're dead they do damage." He said it calmly, as if repeating some basic axiom. While I was in the midst of telling this, one of the members interrupted me with the words: "Right now they are devising evil against the dead, but the turn of the living will come." And tapping his nostrils with his finger, he said: "The catastrophe is impending."

Far be it from me to say that these young people had supernatural intuition. But they were like those sheep that become terrified many hours before an eclipse, while the shepherds are lying down, singing their songs. It was not wisdom but a deep instinct, the absence of which in this much-learned tribe was revealed to us both as a shame and a grief. And I will say that in the path of these young people, in their terrified flight before the eclipse and from it, there was something that saves some honor for the entire tribe.

Thus far Sadan, and his worthy testimony.

After a time there was a noticeable tendency, among the members of Kibbutz "Herut", to move away from Martin Buber's teaching: the criticism against it was elaborated in various directions, but the central principle was the matter of self-realization. Here, as Gershom Scholem once observed,[13] Buber's statements turn against Buber, when one considers his remaining in Germany for the continuation of the German translation of the Bible; we also differed with Buber on questions of Zionist and settlement politics. Perhaps, from the beginning we had found in Buber's teaching what we were seeking in it, and what we were seeking in it was not always identical with what he intended to say and to give. As the members of Kibbutz "Herut" approached their goal of self-realization—in *aliyah* to the land of Israel, in the group life of the kibbutz, in the effort to master the Hebrew language—they left Buber's sphere of influence behind and became, at least among themselves, anti-Buberians, if it is permissible to say so. Within the Jewish youth movement in Germany new disciples then arose for him—I mean, of course, the "Werkleute" (workmen), who received more inspiration from Buber than the members of Kibbutz "Herut" ever had. This is evidence by the pamphlet "Vom Werden des Kreises" (The Circle Takes Shape), which appeared in Berlin in 1934,[14] and still more by the exchange of letters between Buber and Hermann (Menahem) Gerson, contained in the second volume of Buber's letters. It seems to me that Buber's influence on the Jewish youth movement in Germany, his direct and indirect participation in the formation of its image and its deeds, can be divided into three time-periods: the generation of the beginning of the 'twenties; the generation of the end of the 'twenties, including Kibbutz "Herut": and the generation of the 'thirties, which came to the pioneer movement after the Weimar republic, on the threshold of the Holocaust and in the midst of it. Words written by Gershom Scholem twenty-five years ago, in his essay "On the Figure of Martin Buber", for the occasion of his seventy-fifth birthday,[15] aim at distinguishing both Buber's influence on Kibbutz "Herut" and on its members' moving away from him when they turned the call into a realization—a *real* realization, according to their understanding and their way.

Martin Buber raised up students and disciples along the length of his long road, in the Diaspora and in the land of Israel, but especially in the Diaspora. His words, his philosophy were adapted and disseminated by them in different, even very different ways, including some that apparently were not at all in his spirit. For as with every great teacher and thinker, his teaching was like the saying "Cast your bread upon the waters and after many days you will find it".

Discussion Following Menahem Dorman's Lecture

H. GORDON

I am glad that you came to this conference to share with us some of your personal experiences about Buber's influence on you and your friends. That is what interests me in my search for ways of realizing educational philosophy in general and that of Buber in particular. I do not agree with my colleague, Yohanan Bloch, who declared here: Let us not realize Buber! Unlike him, I say: Let us try to realize his teaching. I enjoyed your lecture, and yet it seems to me that you did not touch upon the essential. It was not clear to me what, in fact, happened to those people who were influenced by Buber; was the influence only a manner of ideological satisfaction? Did anything actually occur in the souls of those young people? The haste with which the members of kibbutz "Herut" moved from an enthusiastic devoutness to Buber's teaching, to disillusion can only indicate that Buber did not really touch their souls. Buber was in fashion in Germany then, and perhaps you told yourselves: Let us be Buberians too, use the name of his famous pamphlet, adopt some of his ideas, and off to Eretz Israel . . . Is this what actually happened, and if not—what was in fact the substance of your disillusion? I raised this question to a representative of a different group of pioneers from Germany. We interviewed Menahem Gerson, but could not get a straight answer to this question—Was the source of your disappointment in your own souls, or were you disappointed with the essence of Buber's thought? The answer is not simple, and we should not be satisfied by saying that Buber himself did not fulfill what he demanded from others. There are teachers and thinkers whose task is to fructify the other, to point out ways even if they do not declare: Follow me! As far as I am concerned the principal problem is: What induced you to join the crowd of Buber's disciples, and what happened when you detached yourselves from him?

Z. WERBLOWSKY

Dorman showed us in his lecture how a central thinker in his time can be a catalyst, he can fructify, push towards a certain direction of realization; but to the extent that those people accepted his influence and realized his teaching to the best of their understanding, the inadequacy of the stimulator became more and more prominent. As long as you have not begun the process of realization his words stimulate and push to action, but the minute you proceed to realization, then, while doing so, it becomes clear how big yawns the gap between your actions and what was at the time "Causa Prima".

Y. BLOCH

I would like to correct the wrong impression made by my declaration: Let us not realize Buber! What I mean is the collective realization and not the personal or educational realization. The collective realization is doomed to fail. Like my friend Haim Gordon I still do not understand what exactly happened to you. Why did you embrace the philosophy of Martin Buber, see yourselves as his disciples, but after a short while regret it, and detach yourselves from him? Why?

M. DORMAN

I am not sure whether my answer will satisfy more than my lecture. However, what I can promise you, that when we followed Buber's teaching we did not do so because of his being in fashion among the German Jewry in the nineteen twenties. This "fashion" or these "fashions" were entirely different. The way of life adopted by the members of kibbutz "Herut" was anti-fashion. Fashion is the easy line of opposition. It seems to me that whoever chose strenuous physical work, agriculture, and Eretz Israel as *a way of life*, chose the hardest way possible for the Jewish youth of Weimar Germany. Haim Gordon asked: How come you were disappointed so soon? Well, it was not a question of time, but rather a question of the nature of the revolutionary change which occurred in our lives while leaving the city and the homes of our parents in order to go to the country, to live with a German peasant, to work hard from dawn till dark, and to persist in this work throughout the year, and to continue year after year, until the gates of Eretz Israel opened again for pioneer emigration. In addition we had to train ourselves how to live frugally and how to be satisfied with basics or even less, so that we would be fit for life in the kibbutz, and so on and so forth. Somewhere in this revolutionary change, suddenly, everything seemed different. In order to withstand the difficulties we had to measure everything according to the needs and the demands of the test into which we threw ourselves, including the teacher and his thought, which had helped us to choose that way. Such a judgment is neither liberal nor forgiving, you demand from the teacher what you believe he demanded from you. Probably we did not have a profound understanding of the thought of Martin Buber. In any case we took this matter of realization, of *Verwirlichung*, literally, like believers, who always seem "simplistic" when they translate principles of belief into deeds. Without knowing it we related to Buber as to a Hasidic Rabbi, since he was the one who taught us that the Rabbi must be the exemplary man who demands from his followers only what he himself can and will do in the sense of our sages saying: "Say little and do much". Needless to say we did not preoccupy ourselves with the dialogical philosophical thought of Martin Buber. We saw in him an ideologist of a *different* Zionism, not a petit bourgeois and a "landlordish" one. But suddenly we realized— justly or unjustly—that basically his Zionism was no different from the general Zionism in Germany, which was poor in actions, but very good at formulating phrases and expressing them aesthetically and elegantly. You ask: What disappointed you? My response is: from Zionism or from a Buberian Judaism which lacked the positive command in the sense of the sacred as well as the secular. Why did Buber disappoint us?—Because he remained in Germany, in his ivory tower in Heppenheim; because he dedicated his great talent to the culture of the German people, giving it a new translation of the Scriptures instead of the "Bible" of Martin Luther. Justly or unjustly we said to ourselves: Buber's philosophy is deceitful. This is neither Zionism nor Hasidism.

I brought two documents with me from that period, which I did not use in my lecture. I will read some excerpts now, which will perhaps clarify the reason why we turned away from Buber. In the Hechalutz World Pioneer Movement's newsletter "He'Atid" dated December 1929 a report was published, about a conversation in which Buber took part and in which the question about the justification of a decision concerning pioneering in Israel was raised.

> Martin Buber replied that he is not for demanding this (pioneering) as a duty. One should always take into account the personality. No one has the right to tell another person to go to Eretz Israel. It is only possible to consider the cultivation of inclinations that exist in a specific personality. One can also justify the youth who sees its role in existence here in the diaspora.

And then it said:

> Buber gave a very clear statement that what is most important is moral behaviour within a given framework and even if one is apprehensive about the possibility of a life of trading and negotiating a moral decision can still be made . . .

Furthermore:

> When Buber was asked about the plan of Zionism to establish a working people in Israel and about the idea of returning to agriculture and primal branches of work, he admitted that there are different scales of values but that they are no more committing than the cultivation of tendencies, and the specific personality always confronts him.

This excerpt clarifies that basically we were non-Buberians from the beginning and perhaps we were even anti-Buberians, in spite of the fact that we had adopted the name of his pamphlet—"Herut". Mistakes like these are made in the history of social movements. Moreover, Buber himself did *change*, he too underwent a metamorphosis in the first three decades of the century. We were enchanted by his lectures on the essence of Judaism—the ones he gave in the years 1909-1911, but in the late twenties and thereafter he must have given up the role of leading, instructing, commanding in the name of the vision of the revival of the people on its land.

The second document which authentically testifies to the reasons for our detachment from Buber is a letter written in 1930 by Shura Oshrowitz—a member of kibbutz "Herut", and later a member of Giv'at-Brenner, who fell in the War of Independence. Here is what he wrote to a friend who had reminded him of our debt to Martin Buber:

> I know that Buber's ideas deeply influenced our comrades in Germany. Over the last ten years, many of those who have come to training (centers) and have become pioneers, have done so due to his influence, and I wouldn't want to underestimate the contribution of Buber and his circle to German Jewry. I am aware that this circle brought youth nearer to Judaism and to Zionism during and after the war. And the socialist hue of German Zionism has its source in the influence of that circle. The unusual condition of German Jewry was also influenced by the general condition in that country at the end of the war and thereafter: revolution, social-democracy, pacifism—all these left their

marks on those youngsters . . . Even today Buber's ideas are extremely important among the 'Cameraden' and perhaps also among 'Kadima' (two Jewish youth movements in Germany, which have not defined themselves as pioneers yet). Today, under Buber's influence, people move from the 'Kameraden' (Menahem Gerson's movement) to Zionism. But among "Brit-Ha'Olim", which eight and perhaps five years ago was under the influence of this orientation, there *has been a change*. Reservation from the German revolution; from German social-democracy, and German pacifism, grew stronger and stronger among the Jewish youth, to which our "brit" belongs. Slowly their views changed, particularly those concerning the question of socialism—and in this connection to Zionism too . . . Today it is clear to them that we need to create possibilities for mass settling and not a spiritual center. Buber has become distanced.

As previously mentioned this is undoubtedly authentic evidence; however, the writer of this letter should have said at its end not that Buber had distanced himself from us but that we distanced ourselves from him; in fact, he had become incomprehensive to us, irrelevant in all areas.

Finally, I would like to thank the organizers of this conference, especially my friend Yohanan Bloch, for giving me the opportunity to add a certain line—perhaps secondary, but certainly not accidental—to the general, rich and colorful picture associated with the name of Martin Buber.

Notes

MENAHEM DORMAN

1. Martin Buber, *Cheruth, eine Rede über Jugend und Religion*, Wien u. Berlin, 1919. The English version of this speech is contained in M. Buber, *On Judaism*, New York, 1967, pp. 149-174.

2. " 'Kibbutz Herut'—Le-Hag ha-Asor" (Kibbutz Herut—For the Tenth Anniversary), Giv'at Brenner, 13 Kislev 5697.

3. Lecture given at the World Jewish Congress in Brussels, 1966. See G. Scholem, "Jews and Germans", *Jews and Judaism in Crisis*, New York, Schocken Books, 1976, pp. 71-92.

4. *On Judaism*, p. 149.

5. A. E. Simon, "Martin Buber veha-Yahadut ha-Germanit", (Martin Buber and German Jewry), in the collection of essays *Prakim mi-Morashtah shel Yahadut Germania* (Chapters from the Heritage of German Jewry), ed. by A. Tarshish and Y. Ginat, Leo Baeck Institute and Kibbutz Meuchad Publishing House, 1975, p. 25.

6. On the history of "Brit ha-Olim" see Der Junge Jude, 3. Jahrg. Juli-August 1930: "10 Jahre J.J.W.B"; also Haim Shatsker, "Tnuat-ha-Noar ha-Yehudit be-Germania ve-Yahsah im Tnuat 'Hehalutz' " (The Jewish Youth Movement in Germany and Its Relationship with the 'Hehalutz' Movement), part a, in *Asufot, Ktav-Et le-Toldot Tnuat-ha-Avodah be-Am Israel*, Arkhion ha-Avodah veha-Hevrah ha-Historit ha-Israelit, Sidrah Hadashah 4 (17), July 1973.

7. Probably there was a certain connection between this appeal to Gershom Scholem and Ernst Simon, and a few things which are mentioned in Gershom Scholem's new book, *Von Berlin nach Jerusalem*, Frankf. am Main, 1977. On pp. 192-193 he writes: "The hikers' league 'Blau-Weiss', against which I had polemicized five or six years previously, as related above (i.e. around 1917), at that time took a position, under the influence of similar developments which occurred in the Germany youth movement, which could justly be characterized today as semi-Fascist. It made a law for itself," etc. The law to which G. Scholem refers is the Law of Prun which was passed in 1922. The opposition to this "law" led to the splitting of the "Blau-Weiss" and the formation of "Brit ha-Olim". Further on, G. Scholem relates that a few weeks after these events he published a stinging denunciation of the "Blau-Weiss", and that this controversy "was the start and foundation of the friendship between me and Ernst Simon". One may note, by the way, that this autobiographical book by Gershom Scholem, besides its other merits, sheds considerable light on some of the topics discussed in the present essay.

8. This journal appeared in Berlin in the years 1927-1931 as *Monatsschrift der Chaluzverbände Europas*.

9. Uri Rosenblatt, afterwards Avigad, born in Lammsprünge near Hildesheim on 12.5.01, died in Netser-Sireni, 17.1.55. Made aliyah in 1923. For some years he was a member of Kibbutz Ein-Harod and Kibbutz Yagur, and from 1929 on he was a member of the kibbutz Giv'at Brenner. Alfred Van der Velde, born in Emdeon on 20.10.1905. Made aliyah in January 1929. Member of the kibbutz Giv'at Brenner. Died in Vienna in September, 1930, on his way to Germany. Some of his letters from the years 1926-1930 were published in *Herut* (see below, note 12).

10. "Anshei 'Herut': be-Sihat Haverim al Kibbutz 'Herut' " (The Men of 'Herut': a dialogue of comrades on Kibbutz 'Herut'), March 1941, Giv'at Brenner. "Dvarim" (Words), vol. 3, Kibbutz Meuchad and Yad Tabenkin, 1974, pp. 415-416.

11. Included in Tsvi Schatz's book *Al Gvul Dmamah* (On the Boundary of Silence), Davar, 5689.

12. *'Herut', Tsror Mikhtavim shel Havrei Kibbutz Herut* ('Herut': A Bundle of Letters from Members of Kibbutz Herut): Aliza Fass, Alfred Van-der-Velde, Lucie Fisser, Zev Auerbach. With an introduction by Dov Stuck (Dov Sadan), Giv'at Brenner, 5701.

13. In his essay "Lidmuto shel Martin Buber" (On the Figure of Martin Buber), in *Dvarim bego*, p. 461.

14. Published by Werkleute, Bund Jüdischer Jugend. A collection of essays and letters of Hermann (Menahem) Gerson from the years 1927-1933, which reflect the way of the members of the "Kamaraden-Werkleute" from the general Jewish youth movement for Zionism and pioneering in the land of Israel. In 1932 the "Deutsch-Jüdischer Wanderbund Kamaraden" split up into three separate currents: the Communist "Schwarze Fähnlein", the German-nationalist "Vortrupp", and the Zionist-socialist, pioneer "Werkleute"; later the last two joined the kibbutz of "Ha-Shomer ha-Tsair" in Israel.

15. *Dvarim bego*, pp. 455-462.

CRITIQUES OF BUBER

Martin Buber and A. D. Gordon: A Comparison

ELIEZER SCHWEID

1

The comparison which I am about to suggest between the philosophies of Martin Buber and A. D. Gordon is intended as a contribution to the clarification of the place of Buber's philosophy in contemporary Jewish thought. One may examine this question from the point of view of the modern Jewish sources of influence on which Buber was drawing. As will appear from the following, A. D. Gordon's writings are one of those sources, and one of the most important, but my basic intention in this comparison is to come to grips with another aspect of the subject. Buber's disciples and admirers often ask, and it is right that scholars should give their opinion on this question: Why did not Buber achieve among his own people, and especially in his own land, the same status of representative and teacher that he achieved among a non-Jewish intellectual elite in the West? One may say, that in the eyes of cultured non-Jews in the West Buber is the most important representative and teacher of Judaism in our time. He presents to them a conception of Judaism which seems to them credible and modern, and which conforms to their expectations. One may also say that there is a considerable circle of cultured Jews in the Western diaspora who see in Buber a very important representative and teacher. But in the land of Israel only a few see themselves as Buber's disciples, especially in his relationship to Judaism. His writings are read and discussed—but the characteristic reaction is reserved. In Israel, it seems, Buber's conception of Judaism does not seem particularly credible; there is some basic expectation to which it does not conform. This is a disturbing fact, and it has apparently, a significance beyond the sociology of culture, since the land of Israel is the testing-ground for Buber's philosophy as a philosophy intended to guide the building of an enterprise. The theme of realization is the central theme of Buber's conception of Judaism and of his entire *Weltanschauung*. In the land of Israel Buber's philosophy was confronted with the test of its

255

realization, and here the reservations against Buber are particularly prominent among those engaged in realization.

The comparison with the philosophy of A. D. Gordon is extremely important for the explanation of this peculiar situation because, while on the level of ideas the two are very close, the fate of A. D. Gordon's philosophy has been almost the opposite. He has neither name nor reputation among cultured non-Jews in the West. To cultured Jews in the Western diaspora his name may be familiar, but they know very little about the theoretical philosophy connected with it. I would not say that in the land of Israel A. D. Gordon has a great many disciples. But he is considered as one of the exemplary figures who influenced the movement of realization, and among educated people there is an attitude of great respect for his thinking. He is considered a typical representative teacher of the renewal of Jewish existence in the land of Israel. Even those who disagree with him see him as a teacher. Is it merely a result of the different personalities, and especially the difference in their way of realization? Is it only that A. D. Gordon set an extremely lofty example of personal Zionist realization which established his status, or is there something in the philosophies themselves which explains the differences in the manner of their dissemination and in their influence?

2

It is appropriate to begin with a note on the influence of the writings and personality of A. D. Gordon on Martin Buber. The fact that there was influence is beyond doubt. Buber read A. D. Gordon's writings attentively and was deeply impressed by them, and the result of this impression is immediately recognizable in everything he wrote about the renewal of Jewish existence in the land of Israel. This was a result not only of A. D. Gordon's unique status in the Israeli workers' movement, but also of the fact that A. D. Gordon's philosophy was addressed, more than any other thinking which took shape in Israel, to the spiritual expectations of young Jews who were leaning toward Zionism in the West. From this angle we may see in Gordon's influence on Buber part of a more widespread phenomenon. A. D. Gordon was able to influence a small group of outstanding men in the Western European Zionist movement, especially by means of his "Letters from the Land of Israel", which were published in Buber's *Der Jude* in 1916, and through his impressive appearance at the joint congress of "Ha Poel Ha-Tsair" and "Ts'irei Tsion" in Prague (April 1920). For these men, trained in the best of the new Western thought, A. D. Gordon was an impressive discovery, since, of all the representatives of the pioneering, workers' movement in the land of Israel, Gordon spoke not the language of political ideology, but the language of world-embracing thought. The Zionist realization in the land of Israel received through his words a universal human significance, even while he spoke to them as young Jews. Therefore it is no wonder that in the eyes of these young people A. D. Gordon became the representative and symbol of the profound, original being of the land of Israel. He brought them that "Truth from the Land of Israel" for which they longed. This, then, is the focus of the influence which Martin Buber received from A. D. Gordon: Gordon's philosophy is the juncture connecting Buber's general philosophy of life and conception of Judaism with the pioneering enterprise in the land of Israel. If he sought to see in the realization of Zionism the Jewish movement which interprets in our time, by the very example of its life, the uniqueness of Jewish existence in its full universal significance—A. D. Gordon, the man and his philosophy, served both as a source of inspiration and as a verification. Buber spoke of the process of "re-generation" of the Jew in the land of Israel, of a new private and collective life springing up from the foundations. A. D. Gordon was the convincing example that showed that this was not rhetoric or enthusiastic vision, but the coming into being of a reality.

3

But our concern in this lecture is not the full exposure of the ways in which A. D. Gordon was connected with Buber and influenced him, but the analysis of similarities and differences between their philosophies. With a certain interpretive effort one may find a similarity between Buber's teaching of "dialogue" and Gordon's teaching of "experience". For "experience" in A. D. Gordon's philosophy is the self-consciousness of man in his extended address to other humans, to nature, to the infinite creation. That is, experience means being oneself in relationship to all being and—in the absolute sense— in relationship to God. Thus it is no mere homiletic interpretation to say that in the concept of experience Gordon expressed an intuition similar to that of Buber, only the conceptual systems and the speculative sources on which they drew, were different. It seems worthwhile to mention this as background for the discussion, without expanding on it in detail. The obvious and immediate point of similarity is, as I said, the topic of realization. On this topic one may say that A. D. Gordon is the teacher and Buber the pupil.

Let me begin with a methodological note. I assume that my listeners are well versed in the various manifestations of Buber's philosophy, but not in that of A. D. Gordon. Therefore I shall explain Gordon's views in greater detail; I shall point to the parallels in Buber, hoping that my listeners' memory will supply what I shall not be able to spell out here in detail.

The basis of A. D. Gordon's teaching of "personal realization" is in the existence and work of the Second Aliyah. In this context, "personal realization" means simply that Zionism will not realize its vision unless many individuals decide, of their own free will, to make realization a way of life. Organization, propaganda, contributions and soliciting for contributions are not enough. It is necessary to immigrate to the land of Israel, to settle in the land, to live by working it, to establish a self-sufficient Jewish society. A. D. Gordon accepted this demand in its simplicity and all its stringency, but he developed it into a general philosophy of life. First of all, he repudiated the air of self-sacrifice which was associated with it. The pioneer does not appear as one who is sacrificing himself for his people. A people is not redeemed by the sacrifice of its individuals. It is redeemed by the redemption of its individuals. Self-realization must, then, be self-redemption. In epitome, it is not merely the individual's realization itself, but the individual's realization *of* himself. The building of the land of Israel is indeed bound up with much suffering, but it is the suffering of building, of creation, and whoever devotes himself to creation lives a full life in his suffering, *is* himself and expands himself. In A. D. Gordon's language, he lives a "life of expansion" as opposed to the "life of contraction" characteristic of the egoist who seeks pleasure in the sense of materialistic enjoyment. Second, A. D. Gordon emphasized the organic character of the way of self-realization. That is, the work which redeems the individual, the collective, the people and even all humanity will come exclusively "from below", from the stirring of individuals to change the direction of their lives and to relate differently to themselves and to their surroundings. Not party or union organization, and not the seizure of power, but an interpersonal creation expanding and extending itself to infinity. And third, A. D. Gordon always emphasized the present situation at the time of realization. The true direction of life is one, but its expressions are infinitely many and constantly changing, and a solution that was fine for the situation of yesterday is no longer appropriate for the situation of today. The true form of realization needs, then, to renew itself at every "here"and every "now" from the stream of individual and collective life. It is thus forbidden to canonize the standards and patterns of the past. The basic question must be asked afresh each time and decided from within present reality.

These statements may be specified and explained in several directions. I shall point to the ones that seem to me most important, especially in relation to the conception of Judaism. For Gordon as for Buber (both of them, it seems, are greatly indebted to Moses Hess on this subject) Judaism is initially not a "system of thought" or a way of life molded by a "Shulchan Arukh", but a life-direction imprinted on the physical and spiritual being of the Jewish people. This direction of life expresses itself in its creations of thought and behavior but one must not set up these creations as an exhaustive definition of Judaism. They must be seen as expressions of the same existence which renew themselves, which differ one from another and sometimes even contradict one another in many details. What, then, characterizes this life-direction? The question may be answered, of course, only by a comparison with the creations with other peoples, especially with the creations of Greece, which form, together with the Jewish-Biblical creation, the foundation of European culture. This comparison brings up the assumption which is common to Gordon and Buber: Judaism is uniquely characterized by its desire to unify life through man's deed, to overcome the contradiction between ideal and reality through living work, and to hallow all of reality. Indeed, this conception of Judaism carries the ideal of "personal realization" beyond its limited meaning in Zionism. Realization, in the sense of making the ideal a reality through the living work of individuals with their community, is the permanent essence of Judaism. Pioneer Zionism is only one of its expressions, perhaps the exhaustive expression of Judaism in the "here" and "now" of our generation.

In light of this conception of Judaism the question arises as to the attitude toward the heritage of the past. What is the status of the original literature—the Bible, the books of our sages, the thought and ethical writings of the Middle Ages—in the consciousness of the Jew in our Time? Like Buber, A. D. Gordon discovered his spiritual affinity to the Bible, especially the prophets; it is an intimate personal closeness which expresses an identification with the prophet's spiritual missionary state. A. D. Gordon saw himself as continuing the prophetic mission, even though he knew how problematic it was in his time, and it seems no exaggeration to say that Buber too had a personal relationship to the self-image of the prophet. Moreover, A. D. Gordon was spiritually close to Hasidism. His teaching reveals a close relationship to ideological trends which existed in Hasidism, even though he stood, of course, outside its organization. There is no need to speak at length about Buber's deep relation to Hasidism. However, the similarity between them is most evident in the way they interpreted their relationship to the sources of Judaism, and hence also in the way they interpreted their relationship to history. They held that the sources are not books possessing an external authority, such that one must pledge oneself to the truth stated in them or to the actions literally prescribed in them. Rather, the sources are founts of meaning which flow from an infinite fullness to which every human being, or at least every Jew, is directly related through his own selfhood. The sources help a person to understand himself, to arrive through self-understanding, at the unique interpretation which is reserved for him even in the words of the sources. A. D. Gordon said very sharply in one of his essays that the Bible was important to him not because of what is already stated in it, but because of what may yet be said through its power which has not been said. In the same context he stated that the true Bible was the one hidden in the depths of the soul of every Jew. What he learns from the written Bible which he has before him is only the echo which arises from within it, from the original Bible which is the internal landscape of the soul. What the Bible stirs a person to say from within his soul is thus his true Bible, which renews itself at all times from the depth of the present and not from the distance of the past. A. D. Gordon took a similar attitude to the rest of the sources, such as the statements of our sages, the books of thought of the Middle Ages, and Hasidism, without feeling, in general, the need to point out that he was using these sources. He felt that he had expressed directly what was hidden in the depths of his soul, and what was hidden in the depths of his soul of course bore the stamp of the sources.

An important aspect of this attitude toward the sources is the attitude toward *Halakhah* or the commandment, and here there seems to be a very considerable parallel to the philosophy of Martin Buber. A. D. Gordon took a very positive attitude toward the basic idea of a way of life governed by the commandments. For this way of life embodies the demand for realization in every detail of life. But in contradiction to the Orthodox outlook, A. D. Gordon did not accept the external authority of a "Shulchan Arukh". We shall see later that this does not mean he rejected all the commandments as they had been historically crystalised in *Halakhah*. But just as he saw in the Bible an expression of the internal personal experience, so he also saw in the commandment a spontaneous expression of Jewish self-hood, whose basic concern is thus to articulate its silent inwardness and to renew itself directly from the spontaneous illumination of the present according to its surroundings. Each time a person must examine what is the command that flows from his internal being now. This statement should be understood very broadly: what is the commandment concerning relations between him and his fellow-man; between him and the community, the people; between him and the natural environment; between him and infinite Being. In this connection it is appropriate to add that this demand for the renewal of the commandment from a response to an internal reality and to the circumstances of life is bound up for A. D. Gordon—as for Buber—with the awareness of a tragic contradiction between the command-ment of realization which constantly renews itself and the immanent tendency of human society to lean upon routine existing patterns whose source is in the past. Conservatism and routine are typical characteristics of an established community; and they create a con-stant lag between the commandments of realization in the present and the readiness of the community to respond to them. By the time the community becomes convinced of today's command, its hour has already been missed, and it has become the command of yesterday. A. D. Gordon struggled with this all his life. His hope was that in the land of Israel the pioneer movement would succeed in overcoming this conservatism. The concern inspired his statement on the proper attitude to his own teaching in a last brief essay which he wrote as a sort of a spiritual testament: "Matters of which I have written should be discussed only if there yet remains in them, and to the extent that there is still in them, a living value; that is to say not a literary nor a journalistic value, but a vital value for the life that is being regenera-ted". (*Selected Essays*, translated by Frances Burnce, New York, 1938, p. 295.)

A second matter connected with the teaching of self-realization is the concept of the character of the good society. A. D. Gordon in his writings developed a distinction between "organic society"—family, congregation, people—and "mechanical society"—class, state, party.

"Organic society" is a continuation of natural life, and it, in its constant improvement, is the good society, while "mechanical society", formed out of a desire to dominate nature, is the society of the masses alienated from their selfhood and their environment. In modern reality, mechanical society has reached the peak of its corruption and can no longer continue to exist; the only solution is the recreation of an organic society which will reconstruct the destroyed cells of family, community, and people and find for them the frameworks suitable for the future. It goes without saying that A. D. Gordon interpreted the goal of Zionism in the light of this vision. The people of Israel must return to their country, to their land, and through a life nourished by work on the land, establish a natural simple familial society, which will restore unity, selfhood and simplicity to the life of each individual. If we draw a conceptual comparison between this teaching and Buber's teaching on society, the similarity will not appear. But a factual comparison of the content reveals much that is identical. What is the difference in content between "organic society" and "mechanical society"? The difference may be summarized by three points: first, "organic society" is holistic, in the sense that it incompasses and unites all the fields of human activity, while "mechanical society" organizes activity in one field and disconnects that field from the organic unity of the life of the personality. Second, organic society is based on creative aspiration, which is self-expression directed toward the other. Or in other words, which according to A. D. Gordon express the same content: an organic society is a society based on love—not in the erotic and romantic sense, but in the ethical sense, the sense of the commandments. One who joins up out of love does not renounce himself, but *is* himself in turning to the other. In contrast, mechanical society is based on consumption; in it the other becomes a means. Finally, an organic society relates to the existing societies in its area in the mode of completion-expansion. It adds to expanding circles of shared creativity: from the family, through many families, to the community; from the community through many communities, to the people; from the people, through many peoples, to humanity and to the entire universe. This is organic affiliation. The family does not disappear in the community, the community does not disappear in the people, and the people does not disappear in humanity. The unique, the particular, continues to exist in all its uniqueness in its relationship to the expanding circles of the whole. Mechanical society, in contrast, clashes with surrounding societies because it is competing with them for domination: class against class, party against party, state against state. The self-definitions of these associations is more negative than positive, more against the other than for the self. If we compare this distinction to Buber's words on the true human community, we see that we are dealing with the same social vision, and it is not surprising that Buber had before his eyes, as source of inspiration, the images of the realization of the working settlement in the Land of Israel, upon which A. D. Gordon exercised a great forming influence.

In this connection we must emphasize one implication which has a bearing on the attitude toward the organizational apparatus, or, in the language of our day, the "establishment". A. D. Gordon's attitude toward organizations—the party, the Histadrut and others—was reserved. They characterize a mechanical society which does not rely on direct relations among people, but tries to dominate them and to dictate their behavior. The interest of the apparatus is focused on itself. The service which it offers to society is only a pretext. Essentially, it embodies the principle of domination for its own sake. For this reason A. D. Gordon manifested great sensitivity to the phenomenon of social apparatus becoming an establishment even in the pioneer society in which he was working. Whenever he discerned a tendency to canonize a certain framework as if it were good in itself, or in itself guaranteed the maintenance of proper interpersonal relations, he immediately sounded an alarm and a warning. No framework can guarantee morality, and the very fact of its rigid solidification frustrates any human relationship worthy of the name. A good society is a constant renewal of direct and simple interhuman relations. In Buber's language one may say: it exists in the constant dialogue between "I" and "Thou", from which "we" arises. It is clear that such a view implies a negative attitude to the state and, more particularly, to those institutions without which a state cannot arise and which symbolize its character of domination: the police and the army. In A. D. Gordon's opinion, nothing more clearly epitomizes the being of mechanical society than military order which suppresses the private personality and sets up a collective, compulsory mechanism. It is not surprising, then, that A. D. Gordon was opposed to the politicization of Zionism, to its going the way of statemanship accepted in the world, and to the attempts to establish a state and to form apparatuses anticipating the state. He saw in these attempts a missing of the true purpose of Zionism, which was the regeneration of the Jewish people from the foundation, the resurrection of the people from its individuals. In this sense, it seems, he was much more extreme than Buber, and would not agree to compromise in any way. In the face of the processes of formation of a political apparatus after the Balfour declaration, A. D. Gordon remained alone against the majority, in strife even with his closest friends.

One of the most important consequences of this conception concerns the question of relations between Jews and Arabs in the land of Israel. A. D. Gordon felt no doubt as to the right of the people of Israel to return to its homeland. The special link which Jewish thought from the Bible onwards has made between the people of Israel and its land was preserved in his thought, as in Buber's. Only in their land can the people return to their full original existence. But both he and Buber wished that the revival of the Jewish people should not entail the dispossession and deprivation of members of another people. According to his outlook, a positive national movement is not intended against others, but for itself, and the realization of selfhood is expressed in abundant creativity which increases blessing in the world. The blessing is not confined to those who create it; it enriches the world. From this it obviously followed that against the negative opposition of the Arabs one must set creative action by which the Arabs can also be blessed. In the final analysis, the question of which people's homeland the land of Israel will actually be, will be decided by that creative action. Whoever lives the most in the land of Israel, whoever creates the most out of it, will inherit the land without depriving others, for creation in one's homeland *is* the relationship to the homeland. Again we must emphasize that these statements could be made only on the basis of the assumption that the relationship to one's native land does not mean domination, and that the basic intention must be not a state but settlement of the uninhabited areas of the land in order to form a people living on the land, materially and spiritually. In other words, A. D. Gordon had no wish for any political status that might be given to the people Israel in their land at the cost of others, and therefore he did not view the Jewish settlement in uninhabited areas of the land of Israel either as a denial of the human rights of many individuals or as a denial of the national right of an Arab people. Of course, Martin Buber, who accompanied the Jewish-Arab dispute through its later extreme stages, understood the political problem in a much more sober way. But his basic point of departure is very close to that of A. D. Gordon.

4

Up till now we have been discussing certain ideological elements common to Gordon and Buber. The time has come to examine the differences between them on these topics. If we may "take the bull by the horns" at the outset: the differences are the result of the fact that for A. D. Gordon the idea of realization is not a mere idea, but the self-awareness of a man actually engaged in the process of realization. A. D. Gordon did not begin to write until after he had settled in the land of Israel in order to work the land. He wrote about realization from the inside, as one who was part of it. As noted, he did not write speculative works for the sake of speculation, nor did he find final satisfaction in intellectual or philosophical achievements. With all the fervor of his soul he opposed art for art's sake and thought for thought's sake. He demanded that intellectual and artistic creation should flow out of a fullness of life, i.e. work, and should direct the fullness of life, i.e. work. And what he demanded of others he himself performed. Even when he dealt with clearly philosophical subjects, such as epistemology or the doctrine of the Infinite, this was in connection with discussion on decisions concerning Zionist enterprise, in order *to guide it in practical detail*. The same cannot be said about Buber's writing. Of course, Buber tried to teach realization, and to bring others to realization, but in his writing one senses the pleasure of the artist in the perfection of verbal creation. The beautiful, stylized way of phrasing a profound idea brings with it a satisfaction which is its own end. The fact that we are confronted with thought about realization from who himself takes no active part in realization is very prominent. However, it must be admitted that this is only an impression. It is doubtful that it could be proved. Even the fact that those engaged in realization were also impressed in this way by Buber's style is no proof. But one thing can be proved for a fact: we do not find in Buber that concern which is the alpha and omega of the teaching of realization in A. D. Gordon, namely the concern that a man must do *physical work*, first of all on the land but also in other occupations such as factory and shop labor. One must "bring forth bread from the earth". Creative physical work is holy work, it is the foundation of human existence, both personal and social. It is the simple act which links the individual directly and organically to nature on the one hand and to human society on the other. As noted, the idea of work in its plain meaning and with this interpretation is absent from Buber's philosophy, nor does this philosophy contain any other suggestion that might replace it. How, then, is his teaching of realization to be realized? What real commandment issues from it to the person prepared not only to gain wisdom, but also to do, to keep and to fulfill? Those who turn to Buber's writings from realization, i.e., from the difficult transition to a life of work in the land of Israel, could not find in Buber's writings a satisfying answer for their lives. In A. D. Gordon the answer is found, with a determined simplicity demonstrated before their eyes by a reliable and consistent personal example.

The same distinction reveals itself in the tension created between the writer and the community he was addressing. A. D. Gordon, who expected a full response, a response in deeds, felt the existence of a widening gap between what he saw as a demand which for the sake of the true life could not compromise, and what he saw as possible within the realization, given the external circumstances. Statesmen, in such situations, resort to compromises. A. D. Gordon refused to compromise, for a compromise is only an illusory achievement. It gives up the main thing. Thus, one must vigorously demand the realization of what seems Utopian—realization being understood as proof by action. The proof, beyond speech, that to do the impossible is possible. Otherwise speech will truly be mere empty rhetoric. A. D. Gordon knew perfectly well that he was demanding the impossible. But he still dared to demand. On what basis? The simple, shockingly simple answer is: on the basis of the expectation of a *miracle*. A miracle in the special Gordonian sense, that is, not an occurrence that breaks out of the natural order of things, but an internal event, the breaking through of mighty forces from the unconscious depths of human nature. In other words, A. D. Gordon believed that there is in man a hidden potential, hidden even from himself. This potential cannot be known until the hour when it actually reveals itself in doing. There are critical situations in which man is confronted with certain danger to his life, and in the effort to overcome the danger he does what seems initially impossible. In that hour the circle of previous existence is broken through and a new circle is formed. Man leaps beyond himself and becomes superman. Israel's redemption and the redemption of humanity depend on such an effort, in the confrontation with the critical moment. It seems that this is the true depth of the idea of realization in A. D. Gordon: realization is a doing which expands human existence, elevates it beyond the level of existence which can no longer be (spiritually) sustained in order to bring into being a higher level of existence, both personal and social. But such a demand is possible only if it is anchored in a determined personal decision. Only the realization can prove its truth. Certainly Buber also understood how great is the tension between aspiration and ability in the process of realization. But we shall again permit ourselves the impressionistic note that he did not state this tension from direct experience. As a spectator to others' lives, he inclined toward literary idealization of their achievement, an idealization which does not reflect the difficulties and the soul-wrestlings which achievement entails. It is no wonder that the realizers did not identify with this description, whose loftiness actually made light of the value of their work, because it did not weigh the human effort invested. Moreover, A. D. Gordon wrote not only from constant anguish, but also from a pessimism which grew heavier as he grew older. True, his pessimism concealed within itself a paradox: within this very pessimism lay the only door to hope. Because only the cruel vision of the contradiction between the necessary and the possible was capable of discovering in the depths the powers required for realization. In the writings of A. D. Gordon there is no idealization of the present. From within a life of realization he did not know a moment of satisfying realization. Weaknesses were evident to him, and he exposed them mercilessly. I will not say that Martin Buber was unaware of this tension which characterizes the life of the realizer. An awareness of it is implied by the sophisticated formulation, the like of which is not to be found in A. D. Gordon, in which he describes life in the land of Israel as an "exemplary non-failure". The sophisticated formulation expresses a moment of satisfaction which one does not meet with in Gordon, even by way of dialectics. And indeed there is something ironical in the fact that what could be rightly evaluated as an "exemplary non-failure" was created from a feeling of non-success and in-capacity, of an unbridged distance between the minimum necessary and the maximum possible.

All that has been said above may be merely a matter of style, and yet it concerns the essential foundation. We may perhaps define it more factually by considering the manner in which they sought to guide the process of realization. A. D. Gordon's writing is an outstanding example of what may be termed the Halakhic manner of writing peculiar to the literature of the pioneer movement in the land of Israel. It is Halakhic writing in the sense that it responds to questions that arise out of a life of doing and answers them according to evaluative principles and according to the evaluation of current situations. We have said that A. D. Gordon accompanied the process of realization with his essays. To be sure, he demanded what seemed beyond the possible. He himself was always claiming that he was not a "practical" man in the political sense of that word: one of the first essays he wrote in Israel is called "A Non-Rational Solution". But there is a large measure of intentional irony in these expressions. The impractical seemed to him the sole practical possibility, and the non-rational solution seemed to him the only true solution to the problem. Therefore he did not let himself off in matters of vision. He pointed to the deed that need be done and said how it was to be done and demanded vigorously that there should be no compromises. That is, the impractical is also Halakhic, in the same sense of practical application in the defined reality of the present and its detailed circumstances. A. D. Gordon wrote about the founding of the party "Ha-Poel Ha-Tsair" (Young Workers), on the founding of "Ha-Mashbir ha-Merkazi" (the workers' marketing cooperative), on the founding of the moshav, on the founding of the writers' union, on the founding of the Hebrew University, on the recruiting for the Jewish Legion, on ways of educational activity in the land of Israel and in the diaspora, on policy toward the Arabs and on other burning issues, major and minor, of everyday life. Buber's writing is not Halakhic in that sense. True, he drew his inspiration from the frameworks of realization of the pioneers in the Land of Israel, but his essays do not crystalize the Halakhah which guided the setting-up of those frameworks. If A. D. Gordon, in his essays, transformed the Zionist legend into Halakhah, Martin Buber, from the reality formed by that Halakhah, extracted the *Aggadah*—the legend of the realization of the Zionist vision—and gave it a splendid many-colored garment. He did not return to it with building tools in his hands.

Halakhic writing demands a certain attitude toward the reality at hand. Having considered the consciously Utopian dimension of A. D. Gordon's writings, we must now consider the realistic dimension which marks it as Halakhic. This dimension is expressed, among other things, in his attitude toward the historical heritage as a foundation for the continuation of an enterprise, and it is important to understand this in order to comprehend the difference between Gordon and Buber even on subjects concerning which they held very similiar views. A. D. Gordon, as noted, took a critical attitude toward the canonization of the heritage of the past, but he considered the living, existing creation as the nourishing source of the new creation, and I mean this time not only the eternal idea which can be abstracted from earlier patterns of realization, but also the existing patterns, if they are flexible enough to be adapted to the new circumstances. This applies particularly to the religious tradition. Buber took a very negative attitude toward the "Shulchan Arukh"— toward the book itself and toward what that book symbolizes in the Jewish ambiance. Thus Buber identified with the "negation of the diaspora" in its most extreme version. A. D. Gordon struggled against the "negation of the diaspora" in this version. He did not view the "Shulchan Arukh" as the embodiment of compulsory authority. As a religiously observant man he was acquainted with the Jewish existence formed by the *Halakhah* from within, and he did not rebel against it as such. He did not rebel because he found in *Halakhah* a direct expression of the spontaneity of his religious experience. Therefore he described *Halakhah* as basically a living revelation of the will of the people. Only late in life, after settling in the land of Israel, did he neglect many of the positive commandments of the Torah. But not before he had found another *Halakhah* encompassing his whole way of life: the *Halakhah* of the working life. He preserved his love for *Halakhah* even then, and in truth, to the end of his days he represented himself as continuing its familial and communal core. And therefore he was deeply grieved by his young friends who abandoned the relationship to their heritage and the aspiration to form an inclusive personal-social way of life.

It seems to me that the substance of these differences between A. D. Gordon and Martin Buber hold the answer to the question which we posed at the beginning of this lecture. Buber's words had the linguistic, stylistic, and contentual qualities to make the light of prophetic and Hasidic Judaism, and similarly Zionist-pioneer Judaism, shine forth—to project it at great distances. Its legend—the *Aggadah*—burst forth from his words in all its beauty. But precisely these qualities removed his words from the hearts of those who took the yoke of realization on themselves. They could not recognize in this legend the truth of their lives, the truth which was severe, Halakhic, and realistic despite its extremism. But this truth was contained in the words of A. D. Gordon. Not that they always, or for the most part, agreed with A. D. Gordon. At every turn, his demand exceeded their ability to respond. But there was an essential difference between Buber's beautiful idealization and the extreme, pessimistic, painful demand of A. D. Gordon. Even if they did not fulfill it completely, they had to wrestle with it in actuality. Therefore the reality shaped by the pioneer worker movement in Israel bears the mark of its influence to this day.

Discussion Following Eliezer Schweid's Lecture

M. STRAUSS

What is the connection between the lack of demand for work in Buber's thought and his other views? Is it possible to view physical work as existing within the realm of the relation between the "I" and the "It", and not within the boundaries of the relation between "I" and Thou"? The relation to nature in Gordon's thought was probably different from the relation of man to nature in the teaching of Buber; hence the relation to work is problematic in light of the distinction between "I-Thou" and "I-It". Thus, it is probable that from Buber's point of view the I, when engaged in "physical" work, concentrates on its relation to nature, and is not really the same I of the "I-Thou" relation.

E. SCHWEID

This question provides an opportunity to reach a deeper understanding of the subject. The question of one's relation to work touches first of all on the problem of realization of Zionism. And this is directly connected to the writings of A. D. Gordon. He was writing at a time when the foundations for the establishment of the Zionist enterprise had to be laid. His writings constituted an attempt to set down the guidelines needed to realize Zionism, while attributing to this realization a comprehensive human, personal, and social significance.

It is simple: Without work in its primal sense—agriculture, labour, manufacture—Zionism would not have been realized. Therefore the absence of guidelines in this matter in Buber's discussions of Zionism is a lack which is difficult to settle. But the matter also has a broader context which touches on social relations between persons. One may disagree with A. D. Gordon who claims that physical work is a necessary element for man, any man, not only for the realization of a national cause, but also for his human integrity. I personally disagree with this claim and therefore I am not surprised that physical work as a value does not appear in Buber. What does surprise me? The lack of real guidance as to how to realize the demand for "I-Thou" relationships between persons. If work is not a mitzvah—what is a mitzvah? Where are "genuine" relations between human-beings realized? It

271

seems to me that Buber's writings on the relationship between "I" and "Thou" remain words based on a romantic experience, whereas when Gordon speaks of the relationship between man and man, he does not speak of an emotional disposition, based only on feelings, but of the willingness to assume responsibility for the existence of the other, his welfare and his integrity. This is the value he attributes to work; while working, man is producing the necessaries of life for the Other; therefore work is the basis of social relations. If so, work is the realization of love, and not some feeling expressed in mysterious ways, but in actions which make possible and which broaden our lives. Since Buber does not indicate that work is such an expression, we may ask what does he suggest in its stead? And for this, I think, we have no adequate answer.

N. ROTENSTREICH

My feeling is that the difference between Gordon and Buber is far-reaching, despite the relationship between them on the background of the Prague convention and all that is connected with it. I will not cite directly from "Zweischprache", but I think I am rendering the essence. It is stated there that our relationship to the world means to accept the world as it is given. That is to say: We are not to interfere with the course of the world. Who, in fact, urges us to interfere with the course of the world? The right approach for man in his relation to the world is that of caring and not of involvement. Whereas Gordon's basic assumption is different. The world itself is creative-dynamic. And man's relationship with the world is one of creativity, of involvement, of changing while hearing and listening, perhaps even emulates the rhythm of the dynamics of the world. There are, undoubtedly, two different starting-points here. The first: involving oneself with the order of the world, while avoiding bringing to this order harm, because every involvement brings harm. The latter is involvement with the order of the world, its aim being giving shape to the world, with all the problematics of such a shaping. Eliezer Schweid dealt with this problematics in the second part of his lecture, when discussing the relationship between "Agadah" and "Halakhah".

E. SCHWEID

I will respond to Nathan Rotenstreich's reservation. Generally I would accept his distinction, but it seems to me that two modifications should be added: one concerning Gordon, one concerning Buber; then the difference between them will not be so extreme. The modification concerning Gordon: He demanded from man an involvement with the universe in general, but he explicitly objected to the human desire to exploit nature egotistically, for his own profit, to his dominating nature and ignoring self-flowing. He demands involvement in order to stream the forces of nature towards the same direction; these forces stream spontaneously, and the permission for such involvement is rooted in the fact that man himself is part of nature. Therefore if he upsets the order of nature, he distorts himself; but when he is attuned to the inner dynamics of nature, he is also attuned to his own inner dynamics. We will thus find that we are not speaking of any kind of involvement but of an involvement which requires being attuned, which stems from a sense of responsibility for the flowing of the primal forces of nature. Of course, the question is how can we know what is appropriate for the forces of nature and what clashes with them? But this is another problem.

The modification concerning Buber: It is true that Buber does not express any wish for involvement with nature, but it seems to me that he does express a wish for involvement in the social realm. When Martin Buber speaks of the main wish of Judaism to unify life, unify reality, he speaks of the essential involvement, essential activity of man in his human-social realm. Here the demand is severe. In this he sees the essential uniqueness of prophetic Judaism, as distinct from Hellenism; that is to say—not a life of observation but a life of activity, involvement, realization. I accept the reservation concerning the exclusivity of physical work in Gordon but the question still remains: In what way is the involvement of man in the real life of society realized in Martin Buber?

Buber and Kierkegaard: A Philosophic Encounter

ROBERT L. PERKINS

Introduction

Buber's debt to Kierkegaard has been noted many times.[1] After analyzing one text in *I and Thou* where there is great congruence of specific detail between Buber and Kierkegaard and which to my knowledge has not been extensively dealt with, we will turn to the specific criticisms raised by Buber against Kierkegaard. Both Buber's positive and negative reactions must be mentioned or a biased and one-sided view of their relation will result.

I. Detailed Examination of a Similarity of Detail

One of the most profound similarities between Buber and Kierkegaard lies in Buber's characterization of the aesthete. These characterizations serve as criticisms of a less than fully human way of existing. For Kierkegaard the aesthete is the very paradigm of the romantic soul, but there are numerous aspects of his characterization that suggest the manipulative user and consumer of relation characterized by Buber in the Second Part of *I and Thou*.[2] Let us look at each characterization in some detail.

Buber asks "How is a being to collect itself so long as the mania of its detached I-hood chases it ceaselessly around an empty circle? How can anyone behold his freedom if caprice is his dwelling place?" Kierkegaard also "shows" precisely this detached, emptied, goalless, indeterminate ego. Buber specifically states several characteristics of the capricious man, and Kierkegaard attempts to evoke the reader's reaction to the aesthete by a rich literary presentation. Kierkegaard frequently sets forth his views via aesthetic genres rather than by means of logical analysis which are no less clear than more analytical means of expression.

Kierkegaard's characterization of the aesthete is written almost as a commentary on Buber's text.[3] The "Diapsalmata" and "The Diary of the Seducer" in the first volume of *Either/Or* show in full detail the

275

parallels between the aesthete and Buber's capricious man. I will now list ten characteristics of the capricious man mentioned by Buber and corresponding texts in *Either/Or* or lacking short texts, I will comment. This will show the congruence of Buber's and Kierkegaard's thought on a crucial point of criticism of modern society.

1. Buber states that the capricious man is without freely chosen goals. The same is true of Kierkegaard's aesthete. In the "Diapsalmata" we find the following entry where the aesthete indicates he has no choice of significant goals because of his single-minded catering to his own pleasure.

> I do not care for anything. I do not care to ride, for the exercise is too violent. I do not care to walk, walking is too strenuous. I do not care to lie down, for I should either have to remain lying, and I do not care to do that, or I should have to get up again, and I do not care to do that either. *Summa summarum*: I do not care at all.[4]

2. Caprice and doom belong to each other, for the capricious man is without internal meaning. The futility of a life built upon the pleasure principle may be stated even more starkly by Kierkegaard than by Buber.

> There are well-known insects which die in the moment of fecundation. So it is with all joy; life's supreme and richest moment of pleasure is coupled with death.[5]

3. Buber writes: "The capricious man does not believe and encounter. He does not know association. . . ." Kierkegaard's "Diary of the Seducer" is laced with military language and the seducer sees the seduction as a military campaign. There are literally dozens of references such as these. "I am ready. My arm is a grappling hook always in readiness. . . ." "I must first know her and her entire intellectual background before beginning my assault." This is certainly not the language used in ordinary healthy relationships between male and female. The point Kierkegaard is making is that the seducer does not believe in the possibility of human relationship.[6]

4. Buber also states that the capricious man is an uncompromising and busy utilitarian: "He knows only the feverish world out there and his feverish desire to use it." Kierkegaard's aesthete also attempts to use and manipulate the world.

> This momentary enjoyment is, if not in a physical yet in a spiritual sense, a rape, and a rape is only an imagined enjoyment; it is like a

stolen kiss, a thing which is rather unsatisfactory. No, when one can so arrange it that a girl's only desire is to give herself freely, when she feels that her whole happiness depends on this, when she almost begs to make this free submission, then there is first true enjoyment, but this always requires spiritual influence.[7]

To be sure, Kierkegaard is speaking less of the utilitarian than is Buber, for Kierkegaard's attack is on German romanticism. Among many other criticisms, he saw German romanticism as another male effort to subjugate and manipulate women for sexual ends without incuring responsibility. Else what is *Lucinde* about?[8]

5. Buber also claims that the capricious man, though he only desires to use, embellishes and sanctions his predatory ends by appeal to high sounding words. The corruption of language proceeds apace.   Kierkegaard's aesthete is also one who embellishes with laudatory predicates the basest of uses and manipulations. Freedom is manipulated and turned into control. Double-think reigns.

> She must owe me nothing; for she must be free; love exists only in freedom, only in freedom is there enjoyment and everlasting delight. Although I am aiming at her falling into my arms as it were by a natural necessity, yet I am striving to bring it about so that as she gravitates toward me, it will still not be like the falling of a heavy body, but as spirit seeking spirit.[9]

6. For Buber, the capricious man, though remarkably busy, is without either goals or destiny. The capricious man, however, knows no value higher than his whims and, as we have seen, he is subject to and enslaved by them. Thus, in familiar dialectic, the assertion of freedom turns into slavery to whims, things, circumstances and forces "beyond our control." Kierkegaard's aesthete also is possessed by this frozen will and incapacitated to act. In the "Diapsalmata" the aesthete confesses: "I feel as if I were a piece in a game of chess, when my opponent says of it: That piece cannot be moved."[10]

7. Having no essential goals, no vocation and nothing he deeply cares about, the capricious man lacks determination, (translated here by Kaufmann as "will"). In an effort to make up for this vacuum at the heart of his being, he becomes capricious and arbitrary in his hedonism. A passage in the "Diapsalmata" illustrates this vividly.

> The essence of pleasure does not lie in the thing enjoyed but in the accompanying consciousness. If I had a humble spirit in my service, who, when I asked for a glass of water, brought me the world's costliest

wines blended in a chalice, I should dismiss him, in order to teach him
that pleasure consists not in what I enjoy, but in having my own way.[11]

8. Just as the capricious man lacks a present, he also lacks a future.
The best that the future can offer him is futility. Lacking a concrete,
self-determined I, refusing to make goals, he is condemned never to
have a future different from his present. Kierkegaard likewise de-
spaired of bourgeois, romantic hedonism, for it produced an emptiness and impotence in the present which promises only to become
more desperate in the future. The aesthete writes: "Life has become
a bitter cup to me, and yet I must drink it like medicine, slowly, drop
by drop." Having made the decision for hedonism and whim, he must
now, he realizes, take the bitter consequences.[12]

9. Buber declares the capricious man is ever pushy, interfering,
neither comprehending nor respecting the natural flow of time or the
human predicament. Judge William, Kierkegaard's pseudonym for
concrete ethical existence and author of *The Aesthetic Validity of
Marriage* criticizes the seducer for interfering and disrupting the
lives of others by playing God.[13]

10. For Buber the capricious man is tangled in a web of unreality.
Kierkegaard also writes of the web of self-created unreality which
engulfs the aesthete.

> My life is absolutely meaningless. When I consider the different
> periods into which it falls, it seems like the word *Schnur* in the
> dictionary, which means in the first place a string, in the second, a
> daughter-in-law. The only thing lacking is that the word *Schnur* should
> mean in the third place a camel, in the fourth, a dust-brush.[14]

The above long section may be an example of referential overkill.
Still, it was very necessary, for we have too long dwelt in the land of
generalities where virtually any observation seems at home. The
above concentrated piling up texts has demonstrated that not only in
generality but also in fine detail Buber and Kierkegaard had profound
areas of agreement. In fact when Buber is thinking his own thought,
he and Kierkegaard frequently are thinking the same thought.

II. Buber's Criticisms of Kierkegaard

Having shown this, we must turn now to the unhappy part of the
paper where the criticisms which Buber made against Kierkegaard
will be examined. First, however, several questions must be raised.

Has Buber used Kierkegaardian language in the meaning Kierkegaard gave the terms? Has Buber respected the limitations Kierkegaard put upon ascribing remarks of his pseudonyms to himself? Has Buber respected the stages on life's way as a hermunentical principle or has he turned Kierkegaard's descriptive and interpretative apparatus into a doctrine? Has Buber paid attention to the literary expression of Kierkegaard's thought? Has he simply ignored the stages of life? Has Buber respected the polemical and historical context of Kierkegaard's thought, i.e., has he taken seriously the polemical aspect of Kierkegaard's thought or has the polemical aspect of Buber's own thought sometimes led him astray in his reading of Kierkegaard?

With these questions in mind, let us analyze in detail a passage from *I and Thou* which is usually thought of as a criticism of Kierkegaard. Following this analysis each major criticism of Kierkegaard will be examined text by text.

A. *A Passage in* I and Thou

The very first sentence in the passage on the 'religious' man suggests the confusions of language and interpretation which has been hinted at in the questions.[15] It has been suggested that this text is a criticism of Kierkegaard but if it is, Buber's understanding of Kierkegaard is suspect.[16] To be sure some language appears to be Kierkegaardian. The two expressions which appear to be Kierkegaardian are "religious man" and "ethical man." These are not precisely Kierkegaardian, but he did speak of a "religious stage" and an "ethical stage." What he said of them is at best ambiguously related to what Buber writes here.

Although I would have been stunned by the uses of language, if it had not been suggested this was a comment upon Kierkegaard, it would not have occurred to me for three obvious reasons and for several subtle ones. The first obvious reason is that Buber was willing to use proper names; he refers to Nietzsche in the text. If he had Kierkegaard in mind, he would not have used the eliptical and unclear "People speak. . . ." He would surely have used an exact rather than an inexact designation. Or is that too much to expect? He has been known to have mentioned Kierkegaard by name. The second obvious reason is that what Buber criticizes here is at best a parody of Kierkegaard. Still, is it not possible that the position criticized at least makes a distinction between the ethical and the religious that is very necessary in the face of numerous efforts in the modern period to reduce the religious to the ethical? Third, Buber surely recognized that accepting one's "place in the Plan" is utterly unKierkegaardian. My judgment is that persons who think this passage is a criticism of Kierkegaard have been taken in by Buber's ironic and misleading use of some slogan words that appear to be Kierkegaardian. If, however, on the basis of remembrance of conversation or of correspondence with Buber someone insists that a criticism of Kierkegaard is here intended then, it is charitable to think that Buber has shifted his focus in the passage from Kierkegaard in the first part to someone else who finds it religiously significant to talk about "the Plan," whatever that is. Compression of thought and unannounced shifts are characteristics of Buber's writing, but here, if there is such, it has not led to much clarity. That leads to the subtle and philosophic reasons.

The first philosophic reason this passage is not a criticism of Kierkegaard's actual view of the religious stage is that he as much as Buber repudiated any view of the religious that dispensed with relationship with the world.

In the *Postscript,* Kierkegaard sets forth in almost exhausting detail his concept of subjectivity. In the very midst of the discussion of "Becoming Subjective" he uses two examples in tandem which indicate the deep involvement of community in the task of becoming subjective: "For example, What does it mean that I am to thank God for the good he bestows upon me?" "For example, What does it mean to get married?" These examples, one of which is essentially communal while the other is religious, and all the more communal, indicate that for Kierkegaard as much as for Buber, the religious and the social interpenetrate each other. Note also that Buber uses the example of prayer later in the passage before us. Buber also refers to the separation of duty and inclination, but that opposition is reminiscent of Kant not Kierkegaard's view of ethics.[17]

However, in the latter part of this section beginning, "When a man steps before the countenance. . . ." one is again in Kierkegaard's mode of thought. But this passage seems to be at the very heart of Buber's intent also. Kierkegaard argues in his own *Works of Love* essentially the same position Buber here elucidates and recommends.

There seems to me to be no criticism of Kierkegaard in this passage of *I and Thou,* but rather an appropriation of some of his terminology to affirm in Buber's own argument the same issues Kierkegaard also treated and settled in about the same way. There is irony and an unannounced shift of emphasis.

Referring back to the questions raised at the beginning of this section, we must conclude that Buber has not used concisely Kierkegaardian expressions in a Kierkegaardian fashion. This is certainly any creative writer's prerogative. What is unfortunate is for scholars to only half-see the differences and none of the similarities and to experience none of the irony. What we have actually found is another congruence of detail. This congruence is not apparent and has to be excavated. One readily understands why some have missed the point of the section.

B. Buber's Positive Statement and Its Contradiction

In the essay, "What is Man" Buber expresses in the first part of the essay a very precise and complete way the central affirmations of Kierkegaard's existential philosophy.[18]

The text is no doubt well known, and it is perhaps the best illustration of Buber's profound understanding of the thought of Kierkegaard, which like his own, was an attempt to describe man in his "wholeness," as one existentially strives to express the "actuality of the living man" with "strength and actuality" "before God." In no other text has Buber caught the mood and the meaning of Kierkegaard more clearly.

In spite of the above positive evaluation of Kierkegaard, Buber completely reverses himself in the remainder of this essay. Later on he writes, "The relation to the individual man is a doubtful thing to Kierkegaard because in his view an essential relation to God is obstructed by an essential relation to human companions."[19] One can only wonder if Buber's prior insistence on "wholeness" and the unity of "the most secret solitude" and "public action" earlier in the essay and which is ascribed to Kierkegaard is consistent with the view here expressed. To the present writer, Buber is inconsistent. Buber cannot consistently write the above sentence and this one which also positively evaluates Kierkegaard; "Belief is a relation of life to what is believed, a relation of life which includes all life, or it is unreal."[20] Both cannot be true. Buber, however, continues his criticism, for he emphasizes, "The essential relation to God, which Kierkegaard means, presupposes, as we saw, a renunciation of every essential relation to anything else, to the world, to community, to the individual man." It is this sentence, or several others very like it which suggests the passages quoted from *I and Thou* were a critique of Kierkegaard.

The interpretation of Kierkegaard in this essay which started out with such an affirmative statement ends by contradicting what was so well said. One can only wonder why. To be sure, the logical consistency of Buber's views of Kierkegaard is now impossible to maintain. However, I do not think the inconsistency on this one aspect of his thought vitiates the whole of the dialogical philosophy. Still, it is a flaw, and one wonders how it arose in Buber's thought. To determine how it arose, one must turn to "The Question of the Single One."

C. "The Question of the Single One"

This essay is central to the problem which we now face; the logical inconsistency of Buber's views of Kierkegaard. Here Buber goes into detail and explains how he came to make the judgment that Kierkegaard's existentialism involved an I-Thou relation to God and to no other being. That it is based upon a misunderstanding of Kierkegaard is less often noted. Jacob L. Halevi's dissertation and articles are the major effort I have noted among Buber's students to rectify Buber's misinterpretation.[21]

Buber's account in this essay is founded upon two of Kierkegaard's essays published posthumously (1859) by his brother.[22]

It is necessary that we carefully exegete not only what Buber said about these essays, but also what Kierkegaard himself said in them.

There is one sentence, from Two Notes About 'The Individual' quoted twice by Buber; once here and once in "What is Man?" It is: "Everyone should be chary about having to do with 'the others,' and should essentially speak only with God and with himself."[23] After some very close exegesis, Buber concludes, "then Kierkegaard's meaning is evident that the Single One has to do essentially (is not 'chary') only with God."[24] That is, of course, very different from what Kierkegaard said, for he considered dialogue and self-reflection to be Socratically and Christianly possible. To so ignore the Socratic in Kierkegaard is to miss the very heart of his philosophy.[25]

The very next page tells us what Buber has on his mind. Buber is offended because "God wants us to come to him by means of the Reginas he has created and not by the renunciation of them."[26] Thus there are actually two strings on Buber's fiddle: a quotation and a broken engagement. Let us examine each in turn. First, the text.

When one looks at the text, one is struck by the force with which Buber argues his charges. Kierkegaard's view of faith may be monological at worst or dialogical with only God at best. There appears to be a rejection of 'the others.' Then one takes a second look, and sees the single quotes around 'the others.' Could that be significant? Rabbi Halevi examines the expression and claims that Buber, not noticing the single quotes misconstrues Kierkegaard's whole meaning. Halevi's evidence is utterly convincing, for Kierkegaard marked the expression because he gave special meaning to it. Most of the time when he uses 'other' or 'the other' there is no special meaning to it and it appears without the single quotes. Therefore, when the single quotes are used, something out of the ordinary must be meant. Halevi refers to three passages where the linguistic distinction of the single quotes is used to ·demonstrate that Kierkegaard did make a distinction which Buber ignored or missed.[27]

In the first instance, in the Introduction to *The Point of View* Kierkegaard specifies 'the others' as those who have inflicted some unnecessary and deliberate suffering upon him.[28]

In the second text, 'the others' designates the middle and upper classes who Kierkegaard thought would support his critique of the *Corsair*, a smutty little yellow sheet. He here criticized 'the others' for shirking any action against the lies and caricatures of the *Corsair* but which more largely was an offense against good morals and against good taste.[29]

The third reference to 'the others' is the one previously quoted. From these three instances it is noticeable that 'the others' is not the totality of mankind except oneself. 'The others' refers to those who from cowardice, fear of losing their dignity, and whose dignity, position or calling placed them above criticizing the *Corsair* or defending the one man in Copenhagen who had the courage to defend 'the others' from the *Corsair*. 'The others' in this book refers to persons lacking moral discernment regarding the abuses of the press and the moral courage to defend a man's reputation against slander, caricature, ridicule and lies. The point that Buber missed is that 'the other' is all those so lacking in moral courage and discernment. This is a far cry from what Buber accuses Kierkegaard of asserting.

Buber's critique of Kierkegaard based as it is upon a careless reading of a single sentence must be discounted. It is a blemish in the fabric of Buber's writings, and nothing more should be made of it. However, the interest of truth demands that it be recognized for what it is, and his students, exponents, expositors and supporters should be willing to call a blemish a blemish. Still, there is another basis to Buber's charge that Kierkegaard's view of the God-relation excluded other humans. Let us turn to that.

Buber charges, "The central event of Kierkegaard's life and the core of the crystallization of his thought was the renunciation of Regina Olsen as representing woman and the world."[30] Buber refers to Jesus' uniting of the love of God and man which cannot be separated and then he proceeds to criticize Kierkegaard for rejecting the teaching of Jesus. Kierkegaard's religion, according to Buber, is only one-directional—towards God. Buber emphasizes one passage "In order to come to love, I had to remove the object."[31] He apparently understands by this passage that Kierkegaard thought that he could attain to the love of God only by rejecting Regina, for he bursts into the denunciation which opens this paragraph.

However, as Halevi argues, this is sublimely to misunderstand Kierkegaard. Halevi weaves together an argument selected from various of Kierkegaard's pseudonomous works which reflect the break with Regina. He shows that Kierkegaard's meaning in the last quotation was to the effect that "out of love for Regina, he had to remove or repell her."[32]

Kierkegaard came to think that marrying Regina would crush her, that life with him would be too difficult for her. Therefore out of a desire for her happiness, he had to reject, hurt and humiliate her.[33] He wrote in his journals, "It is hard indeed to have made somebody unhappy and hard that to have made her unhappy is almost the only way to make her happy."[34] This is indeed a far cry from Buber's interpretation, for Kierkegaard meant in the statement Buber criticizes that the only way he could fully and without compromise love Regina was by causing her to reject him.

Buber thinks that Kierkegaard's views of the God-relationship compel him to reject marriage. Luckily Kierkegaard himself in his *Journals* has already replied to such a criticism: "I do not maintain and have never maintained that I did not marry because it was supposed to be contrary to Christianity, as though my being unmarried were a form of Christian perfection . . . my greatest pleasure would have been to have married the girl to whom I was engaged." However, Kierkegaard felt himself ill equipped for marriage psychologically, "The very simplest requirements for being a man, those are the very ones which have been denied me, whereas the exceptional ones, in another sense, have been granted me. . . I have not dis-

dained marriage out of vanity, far from it, I am its warmest defender."[35]

Admittedly, Kierkegaard was a very complex person, but one
whose self-knowledge comes very near to matching the complexity.
With acute self-knowledge he has perceived himself psychologically
unfit for marriage to the girl he loves. He could marry her for his own
pleasure and use, but that would be to make an object or instrument
out of her. Faced with his unfitness and the demand of the love of
one's neighbor, he can love her and give her the possibility and hope
of life which she deserves only by rejecting her. Far from rejecting
marriage because of any view of monastic perfection, he rejected
marriage because he would not deceive her into marriage in the false
hope of happiness. We do not need to psychoanalyze Kierkegaard
here to determine whether his self-analysis is correct. What we do
note is that one has no right to deceive a person, and he thought that
offering her the hope of happiness with him would be deception.
Further, we note a divine command of love the neighbor, even Buber
insists on it. Kierkegaard thinks that loving Regina must take the
form of rejecting marriage because of his psychological unfitness. He
may have over emphasized his unfitness for marriage, but given that
he has acted responsibly. This view of things, based on his own
words, has to be given preference to Buber's interpretation.

There is still another reference Buber quotes to prove that Kierkegaard's "acosmic relation to God" requires that he not marry. "Put the
other way around, one could say . . . in defiance of the nineteenth
century, I cannot marry."[36] As Buber interprets this assertion, it is
another indication of Kierkegaard's opposition to marriage because
the highest form of religiosity forbids marriage. Against that we have
already quoted a long, explicit denial from Kierkegaard's *Journals*:
The question Buber does not answer, even ask, "Given Kierkegaard's
putative religious rejection of marriage, why did he limit his defiance
to the nineteenth century? Why did he not declare in defiance of
every marriage under heaven that he would not marry?" Perhaps that
is just the pertinent question.

In this same context Buber refers to monasticism, an institution
Kierkegaard commended against all the Protestant cant of three
hundred years. Finally, Kierkegaard rejects monasticism because of
the incarnation: Christ was in the flesh; likewise the Christian man
should be in the midst of the world.

Since Buber has so stressed the relation to Regina, it is just
possible that the interpretation of this relation given above will

answer the question Buber should have asked. Bourgeois marriage was expounded by Hegel in his *Philosophy of Right* as a duty. "Our objectively appointed end and so our ethical duty is to enter the married state."[37] Buber, I assume, entirely agrees with this, but as shown above, Kierkegaard cannot, in his own mind at least, both marry her and love her as the neighbor-love commandment commands. In an age, like the nineteenth century when marriage is held to be a duty, Kierkegaard's dilemma cannot be understood.

One would have thought better of Buber, for if anyone were ever qualified to understand Kierkegaard's dilemma, it would have been cartographer of the I-Thou and I-It relations. In short, Kierkegaard refused to treat Regina as an It. That Buber did not perceive this indicates that he really did not ever think very deeply about Kierkegaard's ethical and religious dilemma in his relation to Regina. Unfortunately, Buber took a careless and false reading of an expression, ignored its other uses, appealed to the sorrow of Regina but failed to account for Kierkegaard's self-perception, his honoring of the moral law to treat persons as ends in themselves and the divine law of neighbor-love. Such an incomprehending reading has done great injustice to Kierkegaard. In short, Buber's interpretation of Kierkegaard in "The Question of the Single One" is false.

However, there is still one other issue raised in this essay which must be examined: the single one. Buber understands the category of the single undialectically as if the single one were only a single person. For Kierkegaard the single one is not only a special person, but he may also be *everyone*. Kierkegaard has preceeded Buber and answered this misconception of his thought that sees the single one as an atomic individual but does not see the single one as possibly everyone. Since Buber has created a whole misleading interpretation of Kierkegaard by not seeing this dialectical point, I must quote a crucial passage at length:

> In every one of the pseudonomous works this theme of 'the individual' comes into evidence in one way or another; but there the individual is predominately the pre-eminent individual in the aesthetic sense, the distinguished person, etc. In every one of my edifying works the theme of 'the individual' comes to evidence, and as officially; but there the individual is what every man is or can be. The starting point of the pseudonyms is the difference between man and man with respect to intellect, culture, etc.; the starting point of the edifying works is the edifying thought of the universal human. But this double meaning is

precisely the dialectic of 'the single individual.' 'The single individual' can mean the one and only, and 'the single individual' can mean every man.[38]

Not knowing or ignoring this dialectical complexity of 'the single one' Buber has bred a generation of misconception.

One last point needs to be emphasized before we leave our consideration of *The Question and the Single One*. Something must be said of Kierkegaard's views of marriage. In a quotation previously elucidated, Kierkegaard claimed to be "its warmest defender." In view of Buber's criticism the claim seems ironic at best and false at worst. Yet the claim is patently true.

Kierkegaard wrote a large volume, *Either/Or, Volume Two,* and a long essay in *Stages on Life's Way* explaining his views of marriage.[39] Besides this, he wrote Volume One of *Either/Or* to condemn and criticize the false views of love and marriage held by the German romantics. In fact, Kierkegaard took up Hegel's argument against romanticism and carried it further. From his dissertation onward Kierkegaard had criticized the romantic view of love and marriage as expressed in Schlegel's *Lucinde*. According to Kierkegaard, the *Lucinde* reduced all morality to play acting, sham and facade. The romantics had challenged the whole European moral tradition, but not by counterargument. The attack had come in the presentation of an alternate life style. The romantics claimed it was only irony, but Kierkegaard countered that the romantic ironizing of marriage had the highest doctrinaire character. For Kierkegaard, as for Hegel, the romantic irony was supercilious, clever, irresponsible, effete and nihilistic. This is because the romantic ironist is the sole judge of what is to be binding and serious. There are no universal principles of judgment; mere whim and caprice determine the principles of romantic morality. Whim and caprice raised to the level of moral principles spelled the end of rational reflection on morality as well as the end of the permanence of human relation in institutions such as marriage. Against this Kierkegaard, like Hegel, was firmly set. Thus, Kierkegaard when he claims to have been the "warmest defender" of marriage is on strong grounds.

For *Either/Or* Kierkegaard invented a pseudonym, Judge William, whom he also used as the author of the essay in *Stages on Life's Way*. In these long essays on marriage we find an uncommon phenomenon in western philosophy: We see a philosopher using marriage as his sole paradigm through which he presents a complete ethical philosophy. Buber's criticisms of Kierkegaard's view of marriage is based upon a misunderstanding of his motives in forcing Regina's hand in breaking the engagement. His criticism entirely fails to mention these works by the pseudonym Judge William which run to nearly four-hundred large pages in the English translation! This causes one to wonder about the thoroughness of Buber's research and the fairness of his remarks. Perhaps, to be kinder it is enough to say that Buber has ignored or missed Kierkegaard's polemical situation and has been carried away by his own.[40]

At this point, one can only wonder why so dialectically acute a thinker as Buber could have missed Kierkegaard's views of the individual and marriage so completely. We have suggested, directly and indirectly, several answers. First, he plainly and simply did not notice the single quotes in a sentence he took as crucial. Second, he did not explore in Kierkegaard's writings the whole meaning of the term he took to be crucial. Third, given that Kierkegaard may have misconceived and underestimated his capacity to make Regina happy, Buber has completely ignored the ethical responsibility of Kierkegaard in his effort to save Regina and himself from a bad marriage. Finally, Buber has not presented an iota of Kierkegaard's positive social philosophy which is formed in *Either/Or, Volume Two, Stages on Life's Way, The Present Age, Works of Love* and finally in the collection of his last polemical works which we conveniently call, *Attack on Christendom*.

Such an extended criticism of Buber is difficult to make, given how much I owe him. I am sure it is also difficult to hear (read) given how much we all owe him. Still, the question of the single one is with us as we ponder the individual's relation to society. Buber's essay still says much to us on this matter; it says very near nothing to us about the major vehicle of his discussion, Kierkegaard.

D. On the Suspension of the Ethical

When one turns to this essay from *The Eclipse of God* puzzlement rises like a tide. From a strong beginning which attempts to characterize the thrust of Kierkegaard's *Fear and Trembling,* Buber seems to switch from an analysis of Kierkegaard to a polemic against some specific evils which he never names but which he characterizes as "apes of the Absolute."[41]

First, let us access Buber's views of *Fear and Trembling* written by a pseudonym Johannes de Silentio. Buber titles his essay and centers his critique upon a partial but misleading expression derived from Problem One which is about half-way through the thin volume. The title to Problem One is "Is there such a thing as a Teleological Suspension of the Ethical?" Buber, however, leaves out the crucial adjective "teleological." He gives no reasons for this, but the omission is crucial.[42] Buber is distracted by the situation with Regina and the internal psychological struggle of Kierkegaard. He does not keep to the philosophic issues raised and further he proceeds to raise and leave unanswered questions which Kierkegaard fully perceived and answered.

Buber rightly perceives the divine-human encounter so emphasized by Kierkegaard. Encounter for Kierkegaard is the fundamental thread of the book, that man is addressed by God and trusts that whatever is in the address is the good. The command of God to sacrifice Isaac is for Kierkegaard the mark of what it is to be God's elect. To be sure, the address is terrible, a trial, absurd, etc., but still it is God who speaks and who preempts all other relations and obligations. He is the Lord. Kierkegaard has a deep appreciation for the divine mystery and even Buber recognizes at least ambiguity in Scripture even if not in God.

Here perhaps is where Kierkegaard and Buber part company. Buber suggested in the title only one part of the problematic which Kierkegaard discusses. In the text Buber once refers to the 'teleological' suspension of the ethical but in the title and the discussion he ignores the adjective. Kierkegaard as strongly as Buber argues there is no teleological suspension of the ethical except in *one-and-only-one* sense. That *one-and-only-one* sense is that God is Lord even of the ethical. There is no naming or saying of his purpose. There is only the blunt, unrevealing and unintelligible faith of Abraham that God had commanded him to sacrifice Isaac. For what ethical purpose? None that we can ascertain. For what hereditary or dynastic purpose? None that we can ascertain. For what political, social or economic purpose? None that we can ascertain. There is no telos at all except the one-and-one-only God's purpose of which we are ignorant. But if there is one, even single justifiable exception to the moral law, then the moral law is less than universal. It is relativized as Buber well appreciated.

However, Buber and Kierkegaard faced different polemical situations and Buber's use of Kierkegaard's phrase to address his own polemical situation has resulted in a confused and confusing essay.

Kierkegaard's polemical situation was conditional largely by Kant and Hegel. In other words, Kierkegaard's situation was largely a dispute over the limits, if any, of the ethical as characterized, to be sure, in very different fashions, by these two idealists. As Kierkegaard perceived matters, if Kant's and Hegel's view of the ethical as universal were true, and their views of the relation of ethics and religion were true, then religion has ended (anfgehoben) in either Kant's or Hegel's philosophy or jointly, though in different ways, in both. If religion is to survive as other than the handmaid or propaedeutic of philosophy, the claim of these two philosophies to universality must be rebutted. Kierkegaard attacks Kant's universalizable categorical imperative and Hegel's concrete ethical life with the instance of Abraham. Only one contrary instance is needed to overturn the universal, and if Abraham is not such an instance, religion should close up shop and enroll in Philosophy 1.[43]

Buber's polemical situation was quite different, for his opponents were saying "in order that." It is just this "in order that" that justified murder, blackmail, the concentration camps and all other horrors of those and our own times. However, it is precisely this "in order that" that separates these latter day "apes," as Buber calls them in one place or "well-conditioned young souls" as he calls them in another, from Abraham. This distinction between Abraham and the ordinary perpetrator of violence was emphasized several times by Kierkegaard, but especially in the whole last section of *Fear and Trembling* entitled "Was Abraham ethically defensible in keeping silent about his purpose before Sarah, before Eleazar, before Isaac"? is directed to precisely this point. If Abraham had uttered an "in order that" he would have been as justifiably condemned by the ethical as are the "apes" and the "well-conditioned young souls" to whom Buber refers. Kierkegaard was not at all confused about the pseudojustifications for murder and other violence. But it is precisely because Abraham did not attempt justification, that he is silent, that we know some other category must be applied to him. Kierkegaard argues that the only category applicable to Abraham is the religious. There is absolutely no possible way we can move from Kierkegaard's justification of Abraham to a general rationale for violence. The problem with Buber's essay, however, is that he never makes quite clear the connection he is attempting to make between Kierkegaard's book and plain ordinary violence.

There is, however, one plain instance when Buber is incorrect. Buber writes, "He (Kierkegaard) does not take into consideration the fact that the problematics of the decision of faith is preceeded by the problematics of the hearing itself. Who is it whose voice one hears." The fact is that Kierkegaard was well aware of "the problematics of the hearing itself." As Buber emphasizes, "Moloch imitates the voice of God." Reinforcing his point Buber emphasizes that God requires what Micah reports: do justly, love mercy and walk humbly with God. In all and any talk of suspending the ethical, indeed for Kierkegaard as much as for Buber the question is: "Are you really addressed by the Absolute or by one of his apes?"

Kierkegaard is aware of this question and set forth several tests. First, as stated above, Kierkegaard argues that if in talk of the suspension of the ethical, there is any "in order that" then we are dealing with neither the ethical nor the religious but with the uses of violence. Second, Kierkegaard suggests, the users of violence experience no dread.

> The ethical expression for what Abraham did is, that he would murder Isaac, the religious expression is that he would sacrifice Isaac but precisely in this contradiction consists the dread which can well make a man sleepless and yet Abraham is not what he is without this dread.

The point is if "the problematics of the hearing" sees violence as a tool to be used "in order that" we are discussing the issue of violence and not the issues raised by Abraham. Since Abraham has no "in order that" to which he can appeal the rupture between the inclinations of a father and the necessity of obedience to God fills him with dread.

Another issue raised by Kierkegaard, is that Abraham loved Isaac. That Abraham is not psychotic in his love we have the authority of Scripture, and Kierkegaard does not for a moment doubt this love. If there is talk about the "suspension of the ethical" "in order that" without Abraham's love of Isaac, then again we are back at the level of violence pure and simple. To push this point home, if Abraham's sacrifice is not costly, it is worth nothing at all. If it is not costly, Abraham has not heard God, but one of his apes. If Abraham has ulterior purposes to be served by his act, he has not heard God, but some mere mundane agitator at best or Moloch at worst.

There is at least one other test which Kierkegaard mentioned to separate Abraham from ordinary murderers. The ordinary murderers expect with their "in order that" to permanently dispose of what they think of as sufficiently evil to destroy once and for all. Ordinary murder and violence intend to put an end once and for all to some no longer tolerable situation. Abraham is very different. He has no "in order that," as noted. Moreover he expects God to fulfill his promise that all the nations of the earth will be blessed through this son whom God has now commanded to be sacrificed. Abraham has a problem of logical coherence which the ordinarily violent do not have. Unless we wish to admit Abraham to the rank of the murderers by intent we will have to allow God to command more than Micah 6^8 indicates and to which Buber appeals. But it is precisely this text with its appeal to justice, mercy and humility that makes the sacrifice of Isaac the problem of logical and ethical coherence it is. With this appeal to Micah 6^8 it appears that Buber is repudiating not only Kierkegaard's interpretation of Abraham but also Abraham himself! But Abraham has not heard of Micah; he has heard only the command of God. This command creates a logical and ethical incoherence lacking to those who have an 'in order that.'

Neither Abraham nor Kierkegaard's treatment of Abraham has opened the floodgates of violence so repugnant to Buber and the rest of us. Kierkegaard's *Fear and Trembling* does not license the apes of the Absolute. Kierkegaard was well aware of the "problematics of the hearing itself" and he has offered numerous indications to show it. This brief analysis dehorns what I take to be Buber's main complaint.

But, there is more. He quotes, "That which the Single One is to understand by Isaac can be decided only by and for himself." This quotation is hardly revealing of the point Buber attempts to make of it, for he continues ". . . it is left to the Single One to determine what that sacrifice is." The critical point is that the Single One having no direct declaration from God of what is intended by Isaac, must from his own life situation determine what is meant by Isaac. The quotation is taken out of the context. If one observes the context, which Buber did not, one discovers that Kierkegaard is disputing not about the presence or absence or an exact identification from God but is disputing whether Abraham or any subsequent knight of faith can make himself intelligible to anyone else. Abraham also apparently felt acutely the difficulty of explanation for he answered at best eliptically both his servants and Isaac. The question of intelligible explanation is the issue Kierkegaard raised.

Kierkegaard's knight of faith, Abraham, is not locked up in the darkness of his own subjectivity. Abraham has the clear command of God, a command he can neither comprehend nor of which he can speak. A modern knight of faith would have the same clear word or what does "faith" mean here? The remainder of us of little or no faith have only the other tests outlined above ("in order that", dread, love, promise, etc.). But more hopeful, those of us of little or no faith will not have the command.

Buber's quotation is also completely out of the context and so is completely misconstrued. Kierkegaard is contrasting the knight of faith and the tragic hero. In *Fear and Trembling* Kierkegaard discusses three "tragic heroes," Agamemnon, Brutus and Jephtha. This is what he says of them, the last sentence being the Lowrie translation of the sentence Buber quoted.

> The tragic hero also concentrated in one factor the ethical which he teleologically surpassed, but in this respect he had the support of the universal. The knight of faith has only himself alone, and this constitutes the dreadfulness of the situation.

What Kierkegaard is attempting in this passage (and book) is to set the limits of the ethical and the religious. Kierkegaard characterized the ethical as the universal (as did Kant and Hegel in the generation just before him). The tragic hero, though in a terrible position, as the three illustrations show, can be contained within the ethical. The knight of faith cannot. The point Kierkegaard is making is that the universal supports, explains and justifies the tragic hero. The knight of faith is without such support, explanation and justification. He is literally alone, or what is an Abraham, a Jeremiah alone in the pit, etc.? Buber, who quotes only the last sentence, and that not correctly, misses the contrast of the two sentences and causes also his readers to miss Kierkegaard's point.

That leads us to Kierkegaard's polemical purpose in *Fear and Trembling*. Kierkegaard wrote against the Enlightenment subsumption of the religious into the ethical. He rejected in equal degree Kant's, Hegel's and Lessing's rejection of the autonomy of religion and the various ways they reduced religion to a necessity postulated to resolve the dilemma of idealist formalist ethics (Kant), reduced religion to a social phenomenon and subordinated to the state (Hegel in the *Philosophy of Right*) or simply the preference for natural and ethical religion to any revealed religion (Lessing). As Kierkegaard perceived the matter, if any of these interpretations of the relation of ethics and/or society were true, then religion's autonomy was in this respect lost. *Fear and Trembling* was written to argue there was at least one case in which religion was autonomous with respect to, was superior to and of higher value than the ethical. That one case is the sacrifice of Abraham.

In *Fear and Trembling* Kierkegaard has not denied the ethical import of religion or that positive religions infer an ethical stance. He takes up the positive relations of ethics and religion in numerous works (all mentioned above). In this book he has a limited polemical purpose, and the considered opinion is that he accomplished it.

Buber has not presented this polemical purpose in the essay before us, and one can only wonder if he understood it. As a result he has misconstrued the book and contributed to it and its author being even more widely misunderstood. But why? One suspects Buber's own polemical purposes overrode any and all other considerations. As we note the date and history of the essay we can identify that polemical purpose and its worth. Still the reflections on Kierkegaard in the essay are inaccurate and misleading, and, as a result, a great misfortune for his reputation.

But Buber was aware of the issue which is here raised against him. To this passage we must now turn.

E. Hasidism and Modern Man

First, there are two points which must be considered here: Buber's discussion of the problem of autonomy and the unity of theory and practice (or community). In the last section of *Hasidism and Modern Man* Buber takes up the theme of the isolation of the religious from the ethical which we treated in the section devoted to "The Question of the Single One."[44] We will not repeat ourselves here, for his major point is not to criticize Kierkegaard but to argue that the ethical and the religious are not necessarily heteronomous to each other. His problematic here, however, is not addressed to those who have actually held that the ethical and religious are autonomous as Kant did. Thus he does not address the modern stream of secular and autonomous ethics so characteristic of modern philosophy (Kant, Mill, Pepper, Dewey) or the emotivists (Ayer, Stephenson) or anyone else who has seriously discussed the relation of ethics and religion in the modern period. Neither does he discuss those like Kant, Lessing, Hegel and Goethe who dismissed the very idea of revelation so dear to Buber and claimed by him to be resident in a community in the present essay. One can only wonder about the breadth of Buber's perception of the nature of modern ethics and its relation to religion since his sole critique is leveled against Kierkegaard. Let us examine this relation of community and theory.

The revelation referred to above as dear to Buber and resident in a community is the revelation of the law and the prophets and the community is, of course, Israel. He argues that the Hasidim rightly perceived the nature of the ethical, and into that we need not go. We can only rejoice that Hasidism created so rich a communal life in the light of God.

Unfortunately, it was not always so in Israel. There have been occasions in the more distant past when the individual spoke of God's grievance against Israel. I refer to Amos, Hosea and Jeremiah et al. At least at one time Israel had not as a community attained to the heights of the unity of theory and practice achieved by the Hasidim. It is in this kind of context that one can make sense of Kierkegaard's placement of the religious and the ethical with reference to the community.

Just as surely as Buber, Kierkegaard sees that ideally religion and ethics would be continuous as among the Hasidim, at least as reported by Buber. However, Kierkegaard does not know of such a community and in his own beloved Denmark the religious institution was a tool of political manipulation and social control. Kierkegaard's situation provoked a response more like that of the prophets than like the Hasidim. Such a unity of theory (or theology) and practice (community) as Buber claims existed among the Hasidism is rare. If one wishes to understand Kierkegaard's views of the relation of the ethical (or the religious) and the community the suffering antagonism of the prophets to Israel is a better analogy than the Hasidim.

There is at least one authentically Jewish account of the relation of theology and community other than Hasidism. Kierkegaard should not be criticized if his historical era was more like that faced by the prophets than that faced by the Hasidim. Rather he should be credited for serving his time, in some small degree, as the prophets served theirs. Amos is right against Amaziah and the religio-political-economic orders of respectable brutality. Kierkegaard is right against an ecclesiastical establishment manipulated by the state as an instrument of social oppression. The individual is on occasion right against his community, Buber not withstanding. The Hasidim in their communities are happy, but not the sole paradigm of the relation of the individual and the community.

So we must unhappily conclude that in this essay, Buber was misled by his enthusiasm for the Hasidim, by his misapprehensions of Kierkegaard and by his lack of consideration of Kierkegaard's polemical situation.

Conclusion

The conclusion can be as brief as the exposition is long. As pointed out in the first part there are many analyses and descriptions which appear in both Kierkegaard and Buber. In these, their thought moves along common paths. When, however, Buber stops to comment on Kierkegaard, his remarks are about what is especially important to Buber, but are not so illuminating as comments on the intent and content of the thought of Kierkegaard.

Discussion Following Robert L. Perkins' Lecture

S. KATZ

I agree with some of your reading of the texts, but I think you've also done Buber a disservice—you misunderstood the essay "The Question to the Single One" and its most serious problem. The reason the essay was written had almost nothing to do with Kierkegaard. The essay was written in 1936, if I am correct, and this was a time when German Jewry was under tremendous pressure. Buber himself was suspect and his life was in danger, as a leader of German Jewry. He was using his writings as a political vehicle, a moral political vehicle, not as a means of academic scholarship. The essay was an appeal to German Christianity, not an academic essay for scholarly debate, but an appeal to German Christianity to arouse the conscience of Christians, who thought that their ethical responsibility could be avoided. Therefore, I think that, if you are going to do justice to Buber, you have to mention 1935-1936 Germany, and I think that change of context will make the whole difference of how Buber is to be treated.

Furthermore, you read Kierkegaard's journals as if they are descriptions of fact rather than his rationalizations after the event. I think Buber read the journals as an inauthentic, rationalization of what Kierkegaard had done and regretted; and that he had then to explain for his own self-image, for his own psychic happiness, how this had come about. So that it is not just the case that Buber has imputed to Kierkegaard something that wasn't the case, but it was that Buber read Kierkegaard's actions differently than you do. You read them as an act of authenticity based on the journals. Buber reads them as an act of inauthenticity based on the journals.

R. PERKINS

In the first four or five paragraphs of the paper, I tried to account for your first point. Furthermore, we cannot say now: Well, this is not a scholarly matter, because people have gone around and quoted Buber about Kierkegaard for years, to the effect that a personal relationship to God precludes personal relationships to others. Buber left the impression that his is the true picture of Kierkegaard. Thousands of people have read these essays over the years, and we meet Buber's interpretation every day. Buber's characterization of Kierkegaard just isn't true. The problem with the journals is that Kierkegaard does rationalize in them, and he gives his reasons why the engagement with Regina was broken, because he is utterly obsessed by his incapacity to make a woman happy.

M. WYSCHOGROD

I must say that I cannot accept one or two of your central points. The case which you built is based on quotation marks around "the other" in which Kierkegaard says that human being should have a relationship with God and not with "the other". Bob Perkins tells us that this doesn't mean all others, it means only some others, these wicked men in Copenhagen. Therefore it is not true that Kierkegaard denies the possibility of a genuine relationship with others who are not these bad others. Furthermore he explains the break with Regina not on the grounds that as a religious person he cannot marry because of his absolute relationship with God, but rather simply as a psychological matter that might even have been worked out by a marriage counsellor, if not by a psychotherapist. I can't accept that reading at all. The fact that a human being who stands in an absolute relationship with God cannot have an absolute relationship with another human being is, after all, not only based on the Regina episode; it is also based on his exegesis of Abraham's sacrifice of Isaac. Abraham had an absolute relationship with God; God orders him to sacrifice Isaac. Once that command is given, he must do so, and that destroys the absolute relationship with Isaac. Furthermore, the whole Christian view of marriage must be understood. Bob Perkins' approach to marriage is a very Jewish one, but it is not really the Christian one. In Christianity, and I go back to Paul, it is better to marry than to burn, but it is certainly better not to marry and not to burn. This is deeply rooted in Christian anthropology. There is the tradition of monasticism, there is the tradition of celibacy, all of which are Christian concepts, and all of which are totally non-Jewish. In Judaism not to marry is a sin. Of course, Protestants marry, but I don't know of any Protestant author who says not to marry is a sin. Now, why does celibacy become possible in Christianity and not in Judaism? Karl Barth makes this point. I think it is not a matter of how you evaluate sex. Judaism waits for the Messiah. Once that birth for which we have been waiting has occurred, as the Christians think it has, all further birth is no longer essential, and therefore celibacy becomes a possibility. But Jews must continue human relationships because our Messiah hasn't come yet.

R. PERKINS

The position Prof. Wyschogrod takes, is kind of a back-handed confirmation. Your assertion that it is a sin not to marry really puzzles me, because that is not Kierkegaard's problem. Kierkegaard's problem was ethical. Did he have the right to lead this girl into marriage? After all, it was one of the most scintillating, entertaining, delightful courtships there ever was, but he was play-acting it. Did he have the right to reveal to her the melancholy? For him, this is a question of truth. Doesn't the girl have the right to know what she is getting into? And he decides, yes, she has the right to know what she is getting into; he decides for the truth, and for an ethical responsibility which he bears to her. He didn't break this marriage because of any view about celibacy. There are dozens of passages where he recommends marriage.

Y. GELLMAN

It seems to me that Kierkegaard's own personal views are secondary to the views that are expressed in his literature. Now, the work "Fear and Trembling" very clearly says that one should be prepared to deny the other completely for the sake of God. Isn't Kierkegaard defining the breaking of his engagement in those terms in "Fear and Trembling"? And when Buber says that the voice of immorality cannot be the voice of God, rather it must be a false voice, isn't this the same issue?

R. PERKINS

"Fear and Trembling" is a very important book. The problem, though, that Kierkegaard is facing in "Fear and Trembling" isn't the problem of Regina. In as far as she enters that book at all, he is confessing to her that he did not have faith. Abraham had faith, and he got Isaac back. And he writes this little book saying: "I would like to pick this up again and try it again, now with faith, a faith I've found".

Concerning Michael Wyschogrod's point, it doesn't seem to me that Abraham is violating his absolute relationship to his son when he follows God's command. What he is doing is horrible, terrible, and inexplicable. But it seems to me that he still respects and loves his son as a son. For God says: "Take this son Isaac whom thou lovest". God's demand to sacrifice Isaac brings up the question of God. It seems to me that in many traditions, and possibly in Judaism too, there is a platonic prejudice that God is good, and that this good conforms to our taste. Whereas the thing that is so appalling and so marvellous in the Old Testament, is the idea of God as a fascinating notion. He is not only good, he can also command Abraham to this deed, and that is a fascinating God. He is not very neat and sweet— He is awful.

Notes

ROBERT L. PERKINS

This research was made possible in part by a research grant from the University Research Committee, University of South Alabama.

1. Maurice Friedman, *Martin Buber, The Life of Dialogue,* 3rd. edition. Chicago: University of Chicago Press, 1976. p. 35.
2. Martin Buber, *I and Thou,* tr. by Walter Kaufmann. New York: Charles Scribner's Sons, 1970. All references to the capricious man are to this section, pp. 107-110. Since the section is quite compact, I will not refer to the page for each reference.
3. Søren Kierkegaard, *Either/Or,* two volumes. Translated by Walter Lowrie. Princeton University Press, 1949. Volume One shows some of the varieties of the aesthetic life while Volume Two shows a paradigm of the ethical life.
4. *Ibid.,* p. 15.
5. *Loc. cit.*
6. Bradley R. Dewey, "The Erotic-Demonic in Kierkegaard's Diary of the Seducer," *Scandinavica,* 10: 1-24.
7. Kierkegaard, op. cit., p. 283.
8. Peter Firchow, translator and editor. *Friedrich Schlegel's Lucinde and the Fragments.* Minneapolis: University of Minnesota Press, 1971. Of course, Kierkegaard's and Hegel's judgment was not shared by all. Firchow's interpretative essay in this edition offers an alternate interpretation.
9. Kierkegaard, op. cit., p. 299.
10. *Ibid.,* p. 17.
11. *Ibid.,* p. 25.
12. *Ibid.,* p. 20.
13. *Ibid.,* Vol. 2, p. 11.
14. *Ibid.,* Vol. 1, p. 29. I have referred in this text to typical quotations. On every point others could have been elicited.
15. Buber, *op. cit.,* pp. 155-157. Again, since Buber's discussion is quite compact we will not make further references to this section here.
16. Friedman, *op. cit.,* p. 35. The subsequent reference to Kierkegaard is Søren Kierkegaard, *Concluding Unscientific Postscript,* tr. by David F. Swenson and Walter Lowrie, Princeton: Princeton University Press, 1941.
17. The coalescence of duty and inclination is one of the major themes of Judge William in the essay, "Equilibrium Between the Aesthetical and the Ethical in the Composition of Personality." *Either/Or,* Vol. Two. The opposition of duty and inclination in Kant is well-known. See the *Foundations of the Metaphysic of Morals,* Part I, many editions.
18. Martin Buber, "What is Man?" in *Between Man and Man,* tr. by Maurice Friedman. New York: The MacMillan Company, pp. 161-163.
19. *Ibid.,* p. 178.
20. *Ibid.,* p. 162.
21. Jacob L. Halevi, "Kierkegaard's Teleological Suspension of the Ethical—Is It Jewish?" *Judaism* 8: 291-301. "Kierkegaard and the Midrash" *Judaism* 4: 13-28. A

Critique of Martin Buber's Interpretation of Søren Kierkegaard, a Dissertation Presented to Hebrew Union College—Jewish Institute of Religion, 1959. 102 pp. plus notes and bibliography. For the first time in my life I stand in that peculiar relation that scholars sometimes fall into: I discovered Rabbi Halevi's work after I had already broken the problem of the unnoticed single quotation marks referred to below. I am willing that he claim as much credit as he desires for this section of the paper. I am consciously aware that his excellent presentation, felicitous expression and well-developed argument saved me more rewriting than research. I wish I had discovered his work earlier and so saved more effort. It is exhaustive in detail and has a long valuable section on Kierkegaard's own anthropological views which deserves the gratitude of every Kierkegaard student. Since however, I had almost completely accomplished this research before discovering his work, I will make further specific references to it only twice.

22. Søren Kierkegaard, *The Point of View, etc.*, including "The Point of View for my Work as an Author," "Two Notes about the Individual" and "On my Work as an Author," tr. by Walter Lowrie. London: Oxford University Press, 1939. Besides this one should peep into the article on 'Individual' in *Søren Kierkegaard's Journals and Papers*, Vol. 2, ed. and tr. by Howard V. and Edna H. Hong. Bloomington: Indiana University Press, 1970. pp. 389-448. This reading makes Buber's misapprehensions seem even more odd. However, since most of this was not available to him in German translation at that time, I have not mentioned it in the main body of the text.

23. *Ibid.*, 113.

24. Martin Buber, "The Question of the Single One," included in *Between Man and Man*. See note 18 above, p. 51 and 171 for the twice repeated quotation.

25. On the Socratic in Kierkegaard's thought one should as a minimum see Søren Kierkegaard, *Philosophical Fragments*, tr. and introduction by David Swenson, new introduction and commentary by Niels Thulstrup with tr. revised and commentary tr. by Howard V. Hong. Princeton: Princeton University Press, 1962. Also more briefly: Robert L. Perkins, *Søren Kierkegaard*. London and Richmond: Lutterworth and John Knox Press, 1969.

26. *Ibid.*, p. 52.

27. Halevi, dissertation, pp. 18-59.

28. Kierkegaard, *Point of View*, p. 8.

29. *Ibid.*, p. 57.

30. *Ibid.*, p. 40.

31. *Ibid.*, p. 52.

32. Halevi, dissertation, p. 53.

33. Søren Kierkegaard, *Stages on Life's Way*, tr. by Walter Lowrie. Princeton: Princeton University Press, 1945. p. 212.

34. Alexander Dru, ed. and tr., *The Journals of Søren Kierkegaard*. London: Oxford University Press, 1938. No. 392.

35. *Ibid.*, No. 970.

36. Buber, *Question*, p. 53.

37. G. W. F. Hegel, *Philosophy of Right*, tr. by T. M. Knox. Oxford: Oxford University Press, 1958. §162.

38. Kierkegaard, *Point of View*, p. 126. The quotation is from "That Individual."

39. Søren Kierkegaard, *Stages on Life's Way*, tr. by Walter Lowrie. Princeton: Princeton University Press, 1945. The essay on marriage by Judge William is "Various Observations about Marriage in Reply to Objectives."

40. For an even more extended critique of Kierkegaard's criticism of both Hegel and the romantics see Robert L. Perkins, "The Family Hegel and Kierkegaard's Judge William," *Hegel-Jahrbuch*. 1967, pp. 89-100.

41. Martin Buber, *Eclipse of God*, tr. by Maurice Friedman, Eugene Kamenka, Norbert Guterman and I. M. Lark. New York: Harper Torchbook, 1957. pp. 115-120. "On the Suspension of The Ethical" was translated by Maurice Friedman.

42. Søren Kierkegaard, *Fear and Trembling*, tr. by Walter Lowrie. Princeton University Press, 1941. p. 79.

43. See the essays by Robert L. Perkins on Kant and Merold Westphal on Hegel in *Kierkegaard's Fear and Trembling: Critical Appraisals*, University of Alabama Press, forthcoming. These two essays are cumulatively very near exhaustive regarding Kierkegaard's polemical situation. That Buber did not attempt to evaluate Kierkegaard in his own time is a mark of unhistorical scholasticism that is incomprehensible in view of Buber's acute sense of time.

44. Martin Buber, *Hasidism and Modern Man*, ed. and tr. by Maurice Friedman. New York: Harper Torchbooks, 1966. pp. 225-256.

Martin Buber, Gabriel Marcel, and Philosophy

EMANUEL LEVINAS

I and Thou, which appeared in 1923, revealed the existence in Germany of a whole current of ideas which, whether as presentiments or as echoes, converged more or less with Buber's line of thinking. Texts of a kindred inspiration appeared shortly before and shortly after the publication of his book. They were signed by Ferdinand Ebner, by Hans and Rudolf Ehrenberg, by Eugen Rosenstock-Huessy, by Eberhard Griesbach, and a few others. However, these authors belonged to the same cultural sphere. The encounter between the work of Martin Buber and that of Gabriel Marcel is stronger and more significant proof of a spiritual reality independent of the accidents of discourses. At the time Gabriel Marcel composed his *Metaphysical Journal*, he did not, in fact, know Martin Buber. Moreover, he was drawing on an intellectual tradition which at that time was far removed from the German university atmosphere. In comparing, in their general characteristics, the speculative formulations of these two remarkable spirits, so generously gifted in so many different fields, we shall be asking ourselves above all to what extent the thought which broke through in their works, in sharp contrast to the style of traditional philosophy, responds to the vocation of philosophy, in what respect it renews that vocation and, more particularly, what this new response, in which the source and model of understanding is sought in interhuman relations, means for the traditional privilege of ontology.

The affinity between Gabriel Marcel and Martin Buber was recently the subject of a brilliant and profound study which appeared in Hebrew in a collection devoted to "Jewish Thought in Confrontation with Universal Culture". Its author, our friend Professor Moshe Schwartz of the University of Bar-Ilan in Israel, known especially for his work on Schelling and Rosenzweig, who was scheduled to speak of the Congress at Beer-Sheva on religious language in Buber, passed away a few weeks before the opening of the Congress. In rereading his essay it occurred to me that, for everything which concerns the historical confrontation between Buber and Marcel, I could borrow the essentials from him. May this be considered as a tribute to the memory of a friend who was a penetrating and sensitive thinker. Shall I succeed—according to the rabbinic interpretation of Song of Songs 7:10—in "causing the lips of those that are asleep to speak"?

I

Between Gabriel Marcel and Martin Buber there is a remarkable commonality in essential views: the I-Thou relation described in its originality with respect to what Buber calls the I-It—the originality of sociality with respect to the subject-object structure, with the latter not even necessary as a foundation for the former; the Thou par excellence, invoked as God, whom Buber calls the Eternal Thou and who, according to Marcel, cannot meaningfully be named in the third person; the invocation or address to an eternal Thou as God indicating the dimension which alone makes possible the encounter with a human Thou (even if the human might allow himself to be treated as an object); and thus the founding of all truly interpersonal relations in an original religion. Such, at first approach, are the essentials of a discovery common to the Jewish and the Christian philosopher. It consists in the affirmation that human spirituality—or religiosity—lies in man being close to man, neither lost in the crowd nor abandoned in solitude.[1] This implies both the religious import of inter-human relations and, inversely, the original possibility and the fulfillment of the relation to God—to the Invisible, the Non-given—in man's approach to the human Other addressed as Thou; an approach with addresses, an I-Thou relationship, a relationship basically *other* than the perception of the other in his nature or his essence, which would lead to truths or opinions expressed in the guise of judgments, as in the experience of objects in general.

The object is not to the subject as the subject is to the object; but in the encounter between the I and the Thou in which the address is articulated, the relationship is reciprocity itself: the *I* says "thou" to a Thou inasmuch as this Thou is an I capable of saying "thou" to him in reply. Thus there is an initial equality of status between the one who addresses and the one who is addressed. But status here is only a manner of speaking. Strictly speaking, it would be appropriate to the subject and object, terms which posit themselves, or are posited, for themselves; the I-Thou relationship stands in such sharp contrast to the subject-object relation precisely because, as Buber describes it, it takes shape in some sense before its terms, as a "between" (Zwis-chen). And Marcel very early discovered, in his *Journal Metaphysi-que* (p. 207), the necessity for a strong conception of this "Between": "the eminent value of *autarkia*, of the sufficiency of oneself" is deprecated in the assertion that "only a relation from being to being can be called spiritual". And in the study which Marcel devoted to Buber in the collective work of 1963,[2] he seems to confirm his agreement on this point: "in all these situations the encounter does not take place in each of the participants, or in a neutral unity encompassing them, but *between* them in the most exact sense, in a dimension accessible to them alone". The two philosophers agree in questioning the spiritual primacy of intellectual objectivism, which asserts itself in science, taken as a model of all intelligibility, but also in Western philosophy, of which that science is a product. Buber and Marcel contest the claim of the intellectual act of knowing to the title of spiritual act par excellence—a challenge which is common, in a sense, to them and to existentialist philosophy. Buber and Marcel join the latter in seeking an ecstatic plenitude of existence as a whole and of a presence which can only be limited and deformed in the objectivity of things-to-be-known. This search permits these philoso-phers to elevate to the rank of categories—of "existentials", as they have been called since Heidegger—certain concrete terms of anthro-pological resonance which until then had appeared only in psychol-ogy. But for the philosophers of coexistence, the "ekstasis" around which the human plenitude gathers is not the thematizing intention-ality of experience, but the address to the other, the relationship from person to person, which is summarized by the pronoun "thou". The ultimate significance of that relationship would be not truth, but *sociality*, which is not reducible to knowledge and truth.

We may now note that, even while breaking, in the description of what Buber calls the Encounter or the Relationship, with an ontology of object and substance, both Buber and Marcel characterize the I-Thou relationship in terms of *being*. "Between" is a *mode of being*—co-presence, co-esse. According to the letter of the texts, being, presence, remain the ultimate support of meaning. It would be important, however, to see whether the two philosophers turn toward ontological language for the same motive, whether, in Buber, the break with ontology is not more radically proclaimed, whether the persistence of ontology in his writings is not more startling than in Marcel, who, so remarkably liberated from all schools and all scholas-ticism, and so deliberately hostile to the objectivist interpretation of being, nonetheless remains deeply rooted, despite all the reversals introduced by the concept of the Thou, in ontology. He would thus rejoin the lofty Western tradition for which the supreme characterization of the Divine amounts to identifying it with Being, and for which every relationship with being is, in the final analysis, reducible to an experience (that is, to a knowledge) and remains a modality of that being. Whereas the philosophy which affirms the originality of the I-Thou relationship teaches that *sociality* is irreducible to the *experience of sociality,* that, as an extreme rectitude, it does not curve back on itself as the be-ing (esse) of the being (etre) which always gives itself, that is, is destined for the "understanding of being", or, in other words, authorizes idealism again and again. Such a leap whose direction is signified in an absolutely straight thought does not touch on being; reflection, afterwards, can find only an ambiguous trace of it.

II

Already in his stance with regard to the medieval dispute on the universals, Buber preferred nominalism. He refused the tendency which would recognize the absolute only in the universal and, in consequence, would imply the privilege of knowledge. This, even Spinozan monism, was in his view merely a flight from lived experience. Contemplation, the visual, optic life, means recourse to ideal notions. Knowledge of the object, impossible without idealization, is merely the freezing of an existential state. It puts an end to the personal plenitude achieved in the encounter, in relationship, in the covenant between single ones, which rests solely on the pure co-existence of the I with the absolute Thou, on the *with* which is pure transcendence!

To ask oneself how such a covenant between the singularity of the I and the absolute Thou is possible is to assume something that according to Buber's message, has been left behind: the concern for a unitary principle beneath the essential duality of Relationship. Buber's fundamental thesis, indeed, sounds like: in the beginning was Relationship. The concrete mode in which this Relationship realizes itself is language which thus verges on divinity. Dialogue here is not a metaphor. In his analyses Buber insists on the inherent movement of the word, which cannot remain with the speaker, which takes hold of the listener, or is received by him, and transforms him into an answerer (even if he remains silent). The word is the "between" *par excellence*. Dialogue functions not as a *synthesis* of the relationship, but as its very unfolding. Beyond the immediate essence of the encounter which accomplishes itself in the *between* of the word, one cannot grasp anything which is not already a retreat from language, a going farther away from the presence, from the living relationship. Relationship through language is conceived as a transcendence irreducible to immanence. And the "ontology"—since there is ontology here, after all—which takes shape in this way draws all its significance from this irreducible transcendence.

Marcel, in the studies which he devotes to him,[3] recognizes Buber's views, even while stating that he himself has not gone as far on the common path "in elucidating this structural aspect of the fundamental human situation."[4] Still, his reservations, which seem to bear on details, point to a different philosophical attitude. "To be sure", he writes, "the fundamental intuition of Buber remains to my mind absolutely correct. But the whole question is to know how it can be translated into discourse without being denatured. It is this transposition which raises the most serious difficulties."[5] Upon language weighs, for Marcel, the Bergsonian mistrust: language is inadequate to the truth of the inner life, whereas the I-Thou is lived as the very immediacy of co-presence, therefore above the level of words, of dialogue. In fact, its structure is approached by Marcel through the notion of "human incarnation" and "ontological mystery".

Incarnation, according to Marcel, is "the central 'given' of metaphysics". It is "the situation of a being which appears to itself as related to a body". In opposition to the "cogito", "this 'given' is opaque to itself."[6] Opaque: the incarnate I is not, in its self-consciousness, for itself merely; it exists in such a way as to have something impenetrable in itself. Not a foreign body! Its being-to-itself is from the first a *being exposed to others*, and, in this sense, it is obscure to itself. "The shadow is at the center."[7] The impenetrable "something" in it is not the adjunction of an extended substance to a thinking substance, but a way of being of the spirit itself by which it is, before all thematization of the universe, *for* the universe and thus united to the universe. It is a way of belonging to oneself precisely by belonging to the other-than-self—which identifies it. An ontological modality of the verb "to be" which is mediation itself—and here we find one of Marcel's most beautiful speculative constructions: "Of this body, I neither say that it is I nor that it is not I, nor that it is for me (object)"[8]; and yet it is impossible to distinguish between the *I* and the body: "I cannot validly say: 'I and my body'."[9] No Cartesian separation between me and my body, nor a synthesis, but from the beginning an unobjectifiable, lived participation. The body is essentially a mediator, but irreducible to any formal or dialectic mediation; it is the absolute or original mediation of being: "my body, in that sense, is myself; for I cannot distinguish myself from it unless I am willing to reduce it to an object, i.e., unless I cease to treat it as absolute mediator."[10] Hence "we are related to Being."[11] And, inversely, everything that exists refers us to our body: "When I affirm that something exists, I always mean that I consider this something as connected with my body, as able to be put in contact with it, however indirectly."[12] And in the same sense: "It is permissible to ask whether the union of the soul and body is, in essence, really different from the union between the soul and other existing things. In other words, does not a certain experience of the self, as tied up with the universe, underlie all affirmation of existence?"[13] Thus Marcel can say that "A blindfold knowledge of Being in general is implied in all particular knowledge."[14]

In incarnation a universal structure of being manifests itself: its coherence is certainly not assured by a few ideal links, but it is not assured by dialogue either. "All spiritual life is essentially a dialogue" (*Journal Metaphysique*, p. 137)—but dialogue is not the final arbiter of communication. Being knits itself in unity across human communication. The "one *with* the other" of being is thus oriented to the incarnation of the I, is located on an "essential orbit", as in a magnetic field. The interhuman encounter is only one modality of that ontological coherence, mediated by incarnation, in which the *I* is *for* the other. Thus we find beyond the Buberian Relationship, but at the heart of the co-presence, the participation on which every relationship is founded. It is not a dialogue. It is an intersubjective nexus deeper than language, which, according to Marcel, is uprooted from the original communication. As principle of alienation, language petrifies living communication: it is precisely in speaking that we pass most easily from the "Thou" to "He" and to "It" and objectify the other.[15]

Whereas for Buber to say "Thou" is an absolute relationship, having behind it no founding principle, Marcel is opposed to understanding language as the *element* of the encounter; he is opposed even to the term "Relationship", to which he prefers "encounter" or "tension" (spannung).[16] He decries the conceptual character which attaches itself to the terms in relation and to their objectivity which this word suggests.[17] Going deeper, beyond incarnation, he advocates substituting for Relationship the more fundamental structure of the ontological mystery. "It seems to me", he writes, "that to say: 'in the beginning was the relation' is to speak imprecisely. At the beginning is rather a certain presentiment of unity which continually dissolves, giving way to an All formed by reciprocally linked notions." Marcel certainly is not opposing Buber's Relationship, nor supposing behind it some reality conceived on the model of objects or idealities or some closed system. He is concerned with a concrete life which overflows and leads man to the heart of his being, which is where the link— original love—is knitted, in the heart of his being, which is not entirely his. "We do not belong entirely to ourselves." is one of the consequences of the Marcelian analysis of the ontological mystery: the subject does not belong entirely to itself. The divine being which we are not, the absolute Thou which we encounter as transcendent, is also the being which carries us and loves us. Marcel reproaches Buber specially for designating as *Gegenwärtigkeit* the situation of the I-Thou encounter. It is certainly not the reference to presence as a modality of being, the implicit recourse to ontology, which he finds reprehensible, but the idea of the *gegen,* the "against", which evokes the "gegen" of *Gegen*-ständigkeit[18] and suggests the possibility of a pure exteriority, while what is invoked as transcendant according to Marcel already establishes both the invocation and the invocant. The mystery of being is the way in which our being which "goes toward God" already belongs to God, and it is the way in which the being of God holds the "I" of man. The "I" of man is no longer the central, nor the initial, nor the final point, of the All.

This mystery is recognized, for example, in the question "What is being?" A first reflection reveals that the questioner himself is already within what he is calling into question; the problem turns out to be meta-problematic. Nothing is pure problem, nothing is entirely proposed: in thinking of Being, I participate, by that thinking, in that of which I am thinking. In the final analysis the interrogation is not *in* me, but in Being itself; and the I is thus revealed, in a second reflection or contemplation, as not belonging totally to itself, but as plunged in the "ontological mystery" which envelops its functioning as a subject. The encounter with the absolute Thou is thus enveloped by the mystery of being: "The *heart* of my existence is what is at the center of what we might also call my vital interests; it is that by which I live, and which, moreover, is usually not an object of clear aware-

ness for me. The community between *Thou* and *me*, or the co-
belonging, is the more real, the more essential, *the closer it is to this
heart.*"[19]

Contrary to Buber, the encounter with one's fellow-man, of the
human Thou, presupposes a "co-belonging to the same history", or to
the same destiny, and not the unconditionality of the approach.
According to Marcel, we do not encounter all those whose paths cross
ours.[20] The I-Thou does not occur just anywhere. For example, it is
the fear for our existence in a train which unexpectedly stops in open
country which draws us, the travelers, who were previously merely
side by side with one another, close to each other, and tears us out of
our banal and egocentric perspectives; it is not, as in Buber, the mere
fact of the appearance of the Other which is the encounter.

For Gabriel Marcel the ontological mystery acquires, in *contemplation*, a luminosity of its own—the luminosity of faith, which is not
an incomprehensible and unreflected act, but the height of intelligibility. Throughout the discovery of the I-Thou, Marcel remains
faithful to the spirituality of the knowing: the spirit oriented toward
God is also the event of the *ens manifestum sui*, Being's self-
revelation. To say God as Thou does not emphasize transcendence,
but is a modality of the revelation and of the truth of the Absolute. As
the common source of thought and of being, the mystery which is
love signifies the immanence of I to God and of God to I. It is, as
Schwartz summarizes, what Schelling would call transcendence
made immanence. Buber eliminates the gnoseologic foundation of
the encounter. The unconditioned event of the encounter surpasses
thought and being. It is a pure dialogue, a pure *covenant* which no
common pneumatic *presence* envelops. I am destined for the Other
not because of our *preexisting* proximity or that of our substantial
union, but because the Thou is absolutely other.

III

The work of Marcel and Buber, which, regardless of the differences
between them, has become the classic expression of what is called
dialogic philosophy, is not merely a discovery of a "curious" relationship, the Thou-relationship, as an intellectual novelty, existing side
by side with objectification. For the history of ideas, that approach to
God as to an eternal Thou or an absolutely Other would testify, in any
case, to the end of a certain metaphysic of the object, in which God,

in particular, is deduced as the unconditioned, starting from the object by a movement of founding or conditioning. "Dialogic philosophy" questions the exclusive *intelligibility* of the *founding*, as well as the questioning of objectification and even thematisation as the sole sources of understanding. But how does dialogue respond to the essential vocation of philosophy?

What was that vocation? It was understood traditionally as an appeal to live in such a way as not to submit passively to the social, cultural, political and religious decisions and imperatives, not to be duped by ideologies—which is probably the negative definition of thought itself and of reason in their ancient opposition to opinion; and, in the final analysis, it is to be able to say *I*, to think while saying *I*, to be able to say in all sincerity: *cogito*. What assured that power in our Western world was objective knowledge, consummated in communicable evidence, attaining the unshakeable, substantial being, affirming itself on the firmness of the earth—a knowledge attaining that very substantiality and firmness, in the presence, in the identity of being as such, miraculously equal to the knowledge that sought it, miraculously *made to measure* for that knowledge. Knowledge and being—a correlation of the highest utility! The rigorous development of that knowledge led, indeed, to the full consciousness of self. To think being is to think to its measure and to coincide with oneself. And the way in which the power to say *I* was understood in that adequate knowledge which was equal to itself in being equal to being, so that nothing could remain outside it to weigh upon it, was called freedom. But on this royal road the philosophers found themselves fogbound.

Let us not insist on the fact that the mastery of the being adequate to thought revealed itself as technical mastery of being as world and that, freed by scientific reason, men saw that they had become the toy of technical necessities which dictated their law to reason. It is that the presence of being to reason—the reason of pure speculation—was also called into question. The history of thought reveals a growing uncertainty as to the exact extent of the domain of thought won from opinion and ideology, as to the presence of being itself and not of its simulacrum in the forms which enfold it and in which appearance is suspected of being delusory; as to the foundation and the significance of the sciences themselves, which, despite their soaring flight, are ignorant from what place in being and under what conditions their so confident voice resounds. The history of philosophy is an ever-renewed struggle with the imprudence of the spontaneous exercise of reason, which is incapable of assuring its own security, of preserving itself from paralogisms and from resurgence, in always unexpected forms, of naivete in the very heart of reflection. Even criticism, whose face and figures of speech reason has adopted, is still misled by a traditional logic accepted as invariable, and stands in need of a phenomenology—whether a Hegelian one which would surmount the separations of logical understanding by means of a reason in motion, or—more humbly, but more radically—a Husserlian phenomenology which, this side of logic, would seek in a *living present*, and its proto impressions and their syntheses and passive explanations, that full lucidity which could already be clouded by the first constituted structures of objectivity, blocking the horizon of the critical gaze.

The privilege of presence is called into question by an entire current of contemporary French philosophy, a current which has been characterized as "a merciless critical search." A criticism proceeding from a reflection on all the conditionings and all the "mediations" of supposedly immediate experience—political, social, epistemological, psychoanalytical, linguistic, poetic: what is being contested is no longer the "other worlds", it would seem that there is a transcendental illusion in what is immediately given, in the world which stretches out, unhidden, before us. A criticism which one may, of course, be tempted to reproach for not turning against its own possibility; but one cannot take advantage of this reproach in order not to take the criticism seriously. It is not a matter of adopting it as one adopts a fashion from some great Western capital; but not to see in it the testimony of a crisis which harrows us on the royal road of philosophy that identifies meaning and intelligibility with the intellectual act of knowing, would be more frivolous still.

The dialogic philosophy of Buber and Marcel, despite all that separates them, attests, indirectly, that crisis which, undoubtedly, had already begun between the two World Wars, but which is not a malaise produced by circumstances. We have asked: does their contestation of the philosophical privilege of the *relationship* to the *Other* understood as a *being* thematised and assimilable to knowledge by virtue of the ideal generalities, their doctrine of the *relationship to the Other* assuring the otherness of the Other and thus his transcendence, as that of a Thou addressed in God and in the other man encountered in the wake of that address—does that thought respond to the vocation of philosophy?

Of course, the two philosophers still have recourse to ontological language to describe the encounter with the Thou—and we shall return to this recourse. But the question remains: does the doctrine, in its novelty, assure the power to say *I* without finding it on the liberty of a consciousness equal to being?

IV

Let us return to the relation of transcendence, conceived by Buber as ultimate and irreducible in the I-Thou and not to be enveloped by any deeper unity. The very comparison between Buber and Marcel has made it possible to emphasize this. Language—dialogue—is the proper element of this transcendence. Is that element adequate to its immediacy? Even if Marcel feels obliged to derive the I-Thou from a previous, deeper bond which is not dialogic—from the structure of incarnation and ontological mystery—is not his criticism of language as the element of Relationship independent of his fundamental position? Is not language also *a* language, words and a system of words in which no signification is immediate, in which everything depends on a conjunction of signs? To Marcel's criticism of language, nourished by Bergsonian reminiscences, may be added all that contemporary thought, especially French thought today, has taught concerning the persistence of linguistic symbolism in what is most immediately lived, and the resulting mystification of metaphor and of verbal idealization. Can language as "what is said" procure respect for the immediacy of the I-Thou relation?

But above all, as *what-is-said,* language speaks *of* something and expresses the relation of the speaker to the object of which he speaks, telling what is the case with it. To the extent that it is agreed that one speaks in order to say something and not in order to speak, dialogue itself appears as a modality of the I-It. The relationship with another person—is it not, then, a circling around truth and objectivity, rather than the I-Thou? A notable example of this would be the conception of inter-subjectivity in the Fifth Cartesian Meditation of Husserl.

But what is the case with language as "saying"? Is it absorbed, indistinguishably, in what-is-said? Can it not be examined in its purity? It says this or that, but at the same time it says *Thou*. The word *Thou* is *something that is said,* but it is not simply, like this or that, something which it is possible to say; it is the what-is-said of Saying as such. The Saying says Thou—often without saying it—by its very nature as the direct discourse which it is or to which, in the final analysis, it belongs. This address in which—even without crossing the lips—the word *Thou* says itself and *appeals* to the other: does it still have the structure of an experience and the precautions of an aim? In this vocative, it does not suffice to recognize, as a grammarian, an incomparable *case* among the other *cases* of the declension. In it an appeal resounds, an event which does without mediation, even the mediation of a fore-knowledge or an ontological pro-ject. It is nothing but the irruption, without ceremony or preparation, of Thou-saying, which is also all the risk of disinterest, all grace—and all gratuitousness—but also all the ethic of sociability, of covenant, of association with the unknown, which, we think, is pure allegiance and responsibility. The immediacy of the I-Thou of which Buber speaks is surely, not negative, in a thought cut off from all recourse to the conceptual system of the world and of history; it is rather in the very urgency of my responsibility, which precedes all knowledge.

Here we are certainly taking a few steps to one side of Buber—not to "understand him better than he understood himself", but to rejoin him and to recognize him as a pioneer. Is not this irreducibility of the association with the Other to any previous knowledge what he is teaching us by declaring the independency of the I-Thou, not convertible to I-It? That the Thou par excellence signifies the Thou of God and the Thou in God, means also that to *say Thou* is not an *aim*, but precisely an allegiance to the Invisible, to the Invisible strongly conceived not only as what cannot be grasped by the senses, but as that which is by its very nature unknowable, not thematisable, and of which one can say precisely nothing. The saying of Thou to the invisible merely opens up for itself a dimension of meaning in which, contrary to all other dimensions of thought, there occurs no recognition of an *essence* depicted in what-is-said. Neither representation, nor knowledge, nor ontology; but a dimension in which the other addressed from the start as Thou places himself.[21]

It is a dimension of meaning in which man encounters his fellow, an ethical dimension which thus specifies or determines the religious character, the excellence or the elevation of the relationship of the eternal Thou. The relationship with the Other is possible only in the wake—even if unknown, unavowed—of the original religion; and, inversely, in describing a circle about which there is nothing vicious, Buber, starting from the relationship with the human Thou, succeeds in capturing the relationship even with the eternal Thou, the latter being, in the final analysis, the foundation of the former. And this even if the Relationship, captured in the relationship to the other, is extended to orders which no longer have anything of the ethical: The world, the spiritual entities! To be sure, the I-Thou relationship, the reciprocity of dialogue, which sustains all human conversation, is described in Buber as a pure and in some sense formal face-to-face confrontation, but then appears immediately as qualified: responsibility of the one for the other, as if the "face-to-face" were from the start, and always, an ethical concreteness. The responses which constitute the dialogue mean—it is no mere play on words—responsibility. And even Marcel insists on the relatedness of these words in Buber and sees the response as a condition of responsibility.[22] Intersubjectivity thus appears in Buber's work as a reciprocal responsibility, as in the ancient Talmudic formula: "All Israel are responsible for one another."[23] Buber's entire *oeuvre* is a renewal of ethics which does not start from a mythical validity of certain values as Platonic ideas, nor from a previous thematisation, knowledge and theory of being leading up to self-knowledge of which ethics would be a consequence or appendix, nor from the universal law of Reason. Ethics begins in the face of the exteriority of the other, in the face of the other—that face which enlists my responsibility by its human expression, which, precisely, cannot be held objectively at a distance without changing and becoming fixed. An ethic of heteronomy which is not a servitude, but the service of God through the responsibility for my neighbor, in which I am irreplaceable. We are probably beyond freedom and unfreedom. The radical distinction between the I-It of knowledge and the I-Thou of dialogue and the *total* independence of the latter with regard to the former—this thesis, common to Buber and Marcel, signals the new ethic and the new intellectual order.

But this new ethic is also a new way of understanding the possibility of an I, and therefore it responds to the vocation of philosophy. This time, it is not a question of that freedom which would be assured by the knowledge of the totality of being; but of ethical responsibility which also means that no one can substitute himself for me when it is I who am responsible: I cannot hide myself from my fellow-man, I am *I* through this uniqueness, I am I as if I had been chosen.

This is an ethical interpretation of transcendence, but it is certainly not always preserved from falling back into a vision in which the I-Thou—the ethical—is interpreted once again as a certain—privileged—mode of presence, that is, as a modality of being. We have continually pointed out, in the present study, Buber's recourse to ontological terms to describe the relation to the Thou, and his admitted search for an ontology, starting from the I-Thou, as if being (or the being of what-is) were the alpha and omega of meaning. Now, it would be reasonable to wonder whether the I-Thou relationship, in its transcendence, encounters being primordially, whether it does not name it in an act of reflection which is merely secondary, whether that act of reflection is always legitimate, whether the Thou as God in his invisibility does not have a significance of sociality which eclipses the clarity of the givens and their being. Does not the ethical relationship signify precisely the non-significance of being, even if the theologians, in reflecting, insist on refinding its meaning in the trace of sociality and interpret sociality as an experience? And to use once more, in articulating it, the word which expresses that non-significance—Relationship—is Relationship not *the* disinterestedness in being, an uprooting, outside of being—the straightness of a leap that does not return upon itself? A disinterestedness which does not mean indifference, but allegiance to the Other.

It is not simply a question of vocabulary. The interpretation of the I-Thou relationship as presence, as co-existence, or as the superlative which the meaning of the word being (être) would acquire in the proposition: "all real (wirklich) life is encounter", of which the inverse must also be true—do these things, in the final analysis, attest the impossibility of thinking outside being or beyond being? Does this impossibility recall us to the necessity of carrying our thoughts to their final conclusion and rediscovering Being there? Could reflection claim to seize in disinterestedness itself a modality of being? In that case dialogic philosophy would be merely a specification of ontology and of the "thought of being"; consequently, all theology, all ethics, all theophany and all religion would turn out once again to be the "thought of being", in the Heideggerian sense, or transcendental idealism.

Such is, indeed, the destiny of the philosophy which has been transmitted to us. The final pages of Husserl's *Krisis*, especially, show it in its modern avatar and in its noble grandeur. Here is psychology, conceived as science, carried to its final conclusion, revealing itself progressively—without any special methodological procedure performing the "phenomenological reduction"—as transcendental philosophy. Every being is reduced here to those noems of constitutive intention of which that being's experience is made, and these are apodictically analysed by phenomenological reflection; thus every being is confirmed or illuminated in its being. Every being, even the other person. The other person, to be sure, in a privileged manner: as presupposed in the "consciousness of the world", so that the "reduced" subject, on the road that leads, stage by stage, to the ultimate suspension (epoche) of transcendental consciousness, still retains his human condition before being posited as absolute subject. Husserl writes: "It is unthinkable, and not merely on the level of *fact,* that I could be a human being in a world, without being *one* among others."[24] And, a little further on; ". . . each one in his having-to-do with others has, in his consciousness of the world, at the same time the consciousness of others, different each time with each other person."[25] And he adds: ". . . in the living flux of intentionality, in which the life of an ego-subject, every other ego is intentionally implied in advance, in the mode of sympathy (Einfühlung) and of the horizon of sympathy."[26] *In the mode of sympathy,* which Husserl understands as an experience: "(every soul) has experiences of sympathy, experiential consciousness of others."[27] It is thus by a certain structure of experience that ego-consciousness is linked to other consciousnesses. Husserl, faithful to the history of our philosophy, converts the welcoming of the other into the experience of the other, that is, he grants himself the right to reduce the gratuitousness of the relationship to the other, to a *knowledge* which reflection will measure. The relationship to the other which the *human* perception of the world presupposes is thus not necessary to the transcendental subject as an absolute for which that whole relationship has yet to constitute itself: "But if I perform the reducing suspension (epoche) on myself and *my* consciousness of the world, other humans and the world itself also fall under the *epoche,* and are therefore, for me, only intentional phenomena. Thus the radical and complete reduction leads to the *absolutely unique ego* of the pure psychologist, who renders himself absolutely solitary and therefore no longer has the self-validation (Selbstgeltung) as human being and as a real entity in the world, but is the pure subject of his intentionality (which the radical reduction has rendered universal and pure) with all its intentional implications."[28] So that, in the final analysis, even the privileged relationship which the ego maintained with the other in the consciousness-of-the-world and in the psychological discourse of that consciousness—a discourse which, being scientific, is held *with* and *for* others—amounts to a monologue going from *oneself to oneself,* like thought according to Plato, a silent discourse of the soul with itself. "What I say there scientifically", writes Husserl, "I also say from myself and to myself, but also, paradoxically, to all others, as they are transcendentally implied in me and in each other."[29] An implication which is based on *Einfühlung,* which, as experience, is convertible into knowledge.

Is not Husserl thinking *to the final conclusions* in order to find, in reflecting on the relationship with the other, *Einfühlung* in the guise of experience? Can one seriously wonder whether it is necessary to think to the final conclusions, or whether it is necessary to think by reflecting? Does one not damn oneself even by asking such questions in the eyes of thinking humanity? Unless these questions consist in asking merely whether thoughts without return—pure leaps—are unthinkable? Whether the necessity of thinking to the final conclusions can be suspended *only* by the effect of non-thought and nonsense and blind passion and distraction and the fall into the everyday? Whether the relationship with the other person, the appeals of one's neighbor, the demands of *sociality*, all those returns to the other, to one's neighbors, to those close to one, to all that sociality that one expects and which awaits one upon leaving the laboratory or study, when one closes the book or puts down the pen (all those returns in which, by Husserl's confession, the thread of the world of life, the *Lebenswelt*, is tied once more, but in which the founder of transcendental phenomenology sees only a provisory level of the *epoche*)—if all these returns are not merely interruptions permitted by pure concession to the weakness of our non-angelic nature? Is not the philosophy of dialogue precisely—by reference to what, outside all ontology, *otherwise*, but just as rigorously, is valid as the *source of understanding*—the affirmation that it is impossible to enfold the encounter with the other in a theory, as if that encounter were an experience whose meaning reflection may succeed in recovering? Does not this philosophy testify that it is impossible to comprehend in any concept the significance of the human face? A reasonable significance which Reason does not know! Has not the philosophy of dialogue made us attentive to the ambiguity or the enigma of thoughts which think together the world and the other human, knowledge and sociality, being and God? Is not alternation, from now on, the lot of a modern spirit?

A talmudic fable relates the protest of the angels at the moment when the divine Torah was about to leave Heaven to be given to men. The Eternal pacifies them: the laws which the Torah contains are made for earth; they are inapplicable to the condition of angels who are not born and do not die, who neither work nor eat, neither possess nor sell. The angels submit. Did they fall silent solely because their pride had been flattered? Or did they, on the contrary, suddenly glimpse the superiority of men on earth, capable of *giving* and of being-for-one-another and thus of making possible the "human comedy", above and beyond that comprehension of being to which the pure spirits are devoted?

Notes

EMANUEL LEVINAS

1. See the collective work on Buber which appeared in German (1963) and in English (1967) and whose English version is entitled *The Philosophy of Martin Buber*, ed. by Paul Arthur Schilpp and Maurice Friedman, Cambridge University Press, London, 1967; see the article by Gabriel Marcel, p. 42. We shall refer to this work below as "the collective work of 1967"

2. Op. cit., p. 43.

3. Besides the study published in the collective work of 1963, which we have already cited, there is an essay entitled "Anthropologie philosophique de Martin Buber", which appeared in a collection published in 1968 by Editions de l'Institut de Sociologie de l'Universite Libre de Bruxelles: *Martin Buber, l'homme et le philosophe*, pp. 17-41.

4. Cf. the collective work of 1967, p. 41.

5. Ibid, p. 45.

6. Gabriel Marcel, *Being and Having*, Fontana Library, London and Glasgow, 1965, p. 16.

7. Ibid, p. 18.

8. Ibid, p. 16.

9. Ibid, p. 18.

10. Ibid, p. 18.

11. Ibid, p. 33.

12. Ibid, p. 14.

13. Ibid, p. 15.

14. Ibid, p. 33.

15. Collective work of 1967, p. 44.

16. *Martin Buber, l'homme et le philosophe*, p. 19.

17. Collective work of 1967, p. 45.

18. Ibid, pp. 45-46.

19. Ibid, p. 47.

20. Ibid, p. 46.

21. Is not Brentano's celebrated thesis that every psychic phenomenon is either a representation or founded on a representation—a thesis that never ceased to preoccupy Husserl—refuted or at least contradicted by the psychism of the I-Thou which needs no I-It for its foundation? See, on the contestation of the "autonomy" of the I-Thou, the very important book by Jochanan Bloch, *Die Aporie de Du-Probleme der Dialogik Martin Bubers*, L. Schneider, Heidelberg, 1977.

22. *Martin Buber, L'homme et le philosophe*, p. 31-32.

23. Tractate Shevuot 39a, Babylonian Talmud—a formula in which Israel must be understood as shorthand for humanity.

24. Edmund Husserl, Gesammelte Werke, vol. VI: Die Krisis der europäischen Wissenschaften und die transezendentale Phänomenologi, Martinus Nijhoff, Haag, 1962, p. 256.

25. Ibid, p. 257.

26. Ibid, p. 159.

27. Ibid, p. 158.

28. Ibid, p. 260.

29. Ibid, p. 262.

BUBER AND THE FAR EAST

Oriental Themes in Buber's Work

ROBERT WOOD

In the East and in the West today, religious and philosophical traditions seem to be in a rapid state of decay brought about by the geometrical increase in the It-World of scientific and technical mastery that emerged out of the West since the time of the Renaissance. If such an It-World seemed overpowering in 1923 when Buber's classic *I and Thou* appeared, it has moved lightyears beyond since then in its industrial-scientific component and in the social regimentation connected therewith.[1]

The religious ecumenical movement within the West and the developing dialogue between world religions today have infrastructural roots in this situation of scientific-technical development. Traditions which for centuries and even millennia viewed each other with attitudes ranging from lofty indifference through suspicion to outright hostility are now more inclined to accord to each other the respect and even reverence which their own traditions have taught, for they all have their backs to the wall before a common threat of their growing irrelevance.[2] But whatever its sociological roots, the dialogue of world religions is an important component on the contemporary scene.

Buber entered into dialogue with the East very early in his career and maintained contact with it to the end of his life, guided by his conception of the community of his birth. Buber was a Westerner, but he was a *Jewish* Westerner; and that meant for him one who stands at a peculiar confluence of Western and Eastern sources, for he saw Judaism as essentially Oriental and as the religion which brought the spirit of the Orient to the West.[3]

In this essay we will explore the presence of Oriental themes in Buber's thought. We will continually take our point of departure from the explicit citation of Oriental sources in the very center of Buber's work, in *I and Thou*. In the process, we will move on to consider some Oriental themes in *I and Thou* that have not been explicitly identified as such. We will consider, in turn, Buber's treatment of Hinduism, Buddhism, Taoism and Zen. Implicated in all this is a form of the spirit[4] which Buber termed "teaching" (*Lehre*) and which we will treat in a penultimate section. Finally, we will deal with the question how the philosophical conceptualization that has developed in the West and to which Buber contributed, stands in relation to the basic teaching of the Orient to which Buber attended.

1. Hinduism

The Hindu notion of *Brahman*, the Ultimate Reality underlying the multiplicity of appearances, manifest on one level as a personal God, but at a deeper level as the impersonal Absolute, Buber considers briefly in *I and Thou*, Part One (section #23 in the numbering sequence I have adopted in my commentary)[5] in connection with the primitive notions of *mana* and *orenda*. Buber suggests the equivalence of these notions and uses them to illustrate his claim that "in the beginning is relation". These notions are rooted in the stirring of the whole psycho-physical person by what is met in primitive experience. Movement, interpretation of inner and outer, stirring of the whole person are characteristics of what Buber calls the "motor" type of man peculiarly cultivated, among the higher cultures in the Orient.[6] The vedic *Brahamana of the Hundred Paths* Buber cites in Part Two (#38), in the midst of a discussion of the alienated I who lives exclusively in the I-It relation, and before the contrast between such an *Eigenwesen* and the authentic *Person*.[7] In the Brahamana, the gods and the demons are contrasted in terms of whether they offer sacrifices to each other or each to himself alone. Prajapati, The Lord of Creation, offers himself to those, gods indeed, who entered into relation with each other, the *persons* of the I-Thou relation, not the demonic *Eigenwesen*. Buber repeats the mythic tale without explanation, but sets it in a context where an existential reading of the myth is possible.

Both the preceding citations are significant in showing Buber's contention that the great religions know the Thou, since he will later criticize the Oriental traditions for their tendency to remain within the self.

In Part Two (#36)[8] *Karma*, the Hindu doctrine that the results of our actions remain with us as we pass from existence to existence, illustrates, in its historical transformation, the transition from a human cosmos, rooted in a relational event and developed into a house in which the spirit can live and grow, into the oppressive weight of the It-World where causality rules. *Karma* is originally, in pre-Buddhistic times, the promise of a higher existence as the result of our good deeds in this existence. The negative result of *karma* as the weight of past misdeeds is relieved by sacrifice and meditation. But by the time of the Buddha, the negative has taken over: *karma* is the oppression of the wheel of rebirth, from which the Buddha offers liberation. The early function of *karma* formed part of a meaningful *cosmos* in which one could meet the eternal Thou. But times change—that's part of the Way of God and man in history: the Thou disappears from the world and the forms which expressed it remain as empty shells and become oppressive to the spirit.

The three citations mentioned thusfar Buber brings up by way of illustration and, as it were, in passing. Of greater significance and of greater substance is his lengthy encounter with Indian mysticism in Part Three (#50), by far the longest section of the book.[9] The section is anything but clear, though Buber later refers back to it as the clearest statement of his position on mysticism.[10]

The immediately preceding section (#49) rejected the positions of Schleiermacher and Rudolf Otto on the essential relation to God as one of the feeling of dependency or creaturehood. Buber rejected them because, in effect, they collapsed the human pole of the relationship. In the supreme relation, creature-feeling and the feeling of free creativeness unite in one, a case of the *coincidentia oppositorum* essential to all wholeness (of which more later). In the section in question here (#50), Indian mysticism is considered together with Christian mysticism as maintaining the opposite error: collapsing the divine pole in favor of the human. Buber calls them both doctrines of "immersion" (*Versenkung*, which can also mean "meditation") or descent into the self. Though they seem to move in opposite directions, Buber sees them as identical at base. The Christian mystic is stripped of all I-ness, all subjectivity—which would seem rather to be an extreme version of the collapse of the "I" side of the relation. In ecstasy, standing outside himself, he is united with God, or God enters into the self. Buber chooses Eckhart for this version of Christian mysticism. According to this doctrine (and in contrast to the Indian), there is duality between Creator and creature, but it is overcome in the moment of ecstasy.[11]

Buber sees this mysticism as doubly mistaken. It is, first of all, a misreading of the Johannine Gospel, seeing Jesus as identical with, rather than in purest human relation to the Father. Secondly, it is a misreading of authentic meeting with God where the actual relation seems, but only *seems* to obliterate the poles of relation (and this would apply to the Indian doctrine itself, insofar as it is rooted in authentic meeting). Buber sometime speaks as if such meeting with God can only occur in meeting with others in the world; but elsewhere he acknowledges such encounter apart from the world.[12] However, in these cases, meeting with God does not exclude the world and community with other men, but rather involves mission to that world. Buber's basis for assessment is a combination of reference to the literature of world-wide testimony to such meeting, and also apparently to his own experience. It is, I think, important to note that the dialogue style appears here in the text (as it does in several other places, breaking the normal flow of exposition). For authentic dialogue, one must speak from where he stands while attending to the other where he stands. Buber listened to the mystical traditions and spoke to them from out of his own experience.

The actual encounter with the Indian tradition speaks from the tradition as a single whole, from the *Upanishads* to their culmination in the teaching of the Buddha. Throughout the *Upanishads* it is repeated again and again that *Atman* is *Brahman*, the Self is the All, an identity hidden by *maya*, the veil of the appearance of otherness, of multiplicity.[13] The famous "Tat tvam asi", "That art thou", said of any encounterable other, though suggesting genuine relation, actually precludes it according to Buber, for the otherness of the other is proclaimed as deception.[14] Each and every thing is, in fact, absorbed into the Self. Contrary to the Christian mysticism of Eckhart, the real duality of things is not simply surmounted in the moment of identification with God; it is reduced to the status of illusion.

In this context belongs the Upanishad's teaching of deep, dreamless sleep which annihilates the difference between the Self and the other. The *Mandukya Upanishad* relates this to the mystical syllable OM (also transliterated as AUM), where the *A* represents the waking world from which we begin, the *U* the state of sleep and dream designated as "the brilliant", and the *M* the culminating deep, dreamless sleep which is contact with "the source of all, the controller".[15] The latter is a state of no consciousness or memory, yet it is an *experience* which Buber speaks of as *resembling*, not *being* actual sleep. For Buber it is one of the phenomena at the edge of real life, at its limit, and thus confusing, difficult to interpret in any satisfying way. He admits that there may be truth here, but we have no means of knowing for sure in this life. It is, *at best*, an object of living experience, but it is not something that can be lived, i.e., integrated into the whole of one's life, which is, after all, life in the midst of the multiplicity of beings. Later Buber will be less cautious about mysticism in general: he declares it to be an experience whose "object" is the self. But because it takes place in a sphere apart from encounter and thus comparison with other creatures, the principle of individuation is lost sight of and one confuses the self with the All.[16]

In the context of his discussion of Eckhart, Buber appeals, to his own experience. He speaks of the experience where all the souls powers—sensual, emotional, volitional, intellectual and spiritual— are united: this is an indispensible precondition for producing the works of the spirit; but it is an experience whose object is the self, not God. There is also an experience arising out of the meeting with any other where the relation seems, but only seems, to swallow up the partners. This latter is apparently what he understands by the claim of Christian mysticism. But the Hindu experience seems to be neither. It is a straining after the pure, the essential, and therefore a rejection of the sensual and emotional. Ultimately it is a straining after the void, which for Buber has a demonic rather than a divine character.[17]

But what Buber regards as his most important testimony here is that God can be met in the everyday: "a streak of sunshine on a maple twig and an intimation of the eternal Thou" is "for us"—i.e. for those who share his experience—greater than all mysticism, all phenomena on the edge of life.[18] Mysticism for Buber is a gathering of the powers of the soul between encounters with other creatures and with God. It is "on the borderline of faith, where the soul draws its breath between word and word".[19]

Granted that confusion is more likely here than in other realms of experience, the curious thing is the temptation (if temptation it be) to identify the self with the "All". Why "All"? This is important for Oriental teaching—and it is critically important for philosophy as well. The aim of the teaching is to find reconciliation, unity, not just with this or that, nor simply within oneself, but with the All. Philosophy itself emerges as a kind of design on the All, seeking a vision of the whole as Eros for the One that makes the multiplicity of things into a universe. There is a structural feature of humanness here, one to which much of the contemporary world seems blind. We will have occasion to attend to this again in the last section of this paper.

Buber dealt briefly with the Hindu position in his *Daniel* where, in an apparently autobiographical section, he describes it as the beginning phase of a maturing process. It is a feeling of unity detached from appearances and thus from the rest of life. But it awakened a striving for unity in the whole of life, realized finally in *I and Thou*.[20]

2. Buddhism

Returning now to section 50 of *I and Thou*, Buber devotes several pages to a discussion of the Buddha as the culmination of the *Upanishad* tradition.[21] It is difficult to untangle the various observations and evaluations Buber makes here. However, the observations do fall into three parts: 1) the character of the teaching, 2) the nature of the goal of the teaching, and 3) the ultimately negative evaluation Buber attaches to it as the culmination of the Hindu tradition.

First, Buddha's teaching involves no theoretical account of the world. It rather shows a way, a path to walk toward salvation. A theoretical account belongs to the It-World, a world of division because it divides subject and object and because it involves a division of objects from one another. But walking the way involves indivision. The categories of thought neither can contain this nor are they relevant to the actual walking. For this reason, in an early essay (1913) "Buddha", where he claims a substantial agreement between the Buddha, Socrates and Jesus on this point, Buber warns that the Buddha must not be approached in terms of a doctrine of "Buddhism".[22] Buddha indeed does not elaborate a metaphysics; rather by means of his Four Noble Truth, he points directly to life. Men suffer because of desire and can be liberated from such desire by following the Eight-fold Path.[23] As he remarked, we are like one shot with a poisoned arrow: the immediate task is to remove it, not seek for who shot it or why.[24]

Second, as far as the goal is concerned, three things go together in Buber's account: expressed negatively, the goal is "the annulment of suffering; expressed in terms of its effects, it is "salvation from the wheel of rebirth", from the necessity of returning to the disjointed world; and expressed positively in itself, the goal is, in Buber's reading, "to confront the undivided mystery undivided". And this seems to involve at least one theoretical claim, that "there is an Unborn, Unbecome, Uncreated, Unformed,"—the undivided mystery as the goal.

Thirdly, as to the ultimate Hindu character of the Buddha's teaching, according to Buber the Buddha knows "Thou-saying" to this mystery; and in the Buddha's dealings with his disciples, he shows that he knows "Thou-saying" to his fellow men; but he does not *teach* them. The claim is indeed confusing since Buber had just spoken of confrontation with the Unborn, the undivided mystery as the goal of the way. Buddha does also teach a compassion that "includes in the heart all that becomes", a variation for Buber on the Hindu "Tat tvam asi", that takes place *in the self* and not in full encounter with what is over against the self. For the Buddha claims (another theoretical assertion that he is not supposed to make) that the world dwells in him when he passes beyond the deception of forms. Ultimately, then, the Buddha's teaching becomes a doctrine of immersion where the world is in the self, a position Buber himself had praised in his 1913 Buddha essay: Buddha, the Indian Prometheus of inwardness, stands above the gods and *is* the world.[25]

Buber thus claims, in effect, to discern the encounter with the Thou at the root of Hinduism in the primitive notion of Brahman, and at the root of Buddhism in undivided encounter with undivided mystery. Each tradition develops a way for its followers and brings the everyday world into contact with the eternal Thou through the establishment of holy times and places, holy practices and teachings, and a view of the cosmos in relation to the Holy. But their primal encounter is confused with certain experiences whose object is not the eternal Thou, but the self. For Buber genuine encounter with the eternal Thou is not so much the transmission of a *content* as it is a matter of a confirming *Presence*. This position is apparently related to the Burning Bush revelation to Moses in which Jahweh said: "I will be there in the way I will be there". The relation between content and presence is one of the basic problems of Buber's philosophy, since he is not inclined to abstract the universal from the situation—a move absolutely essential to *any*, including (by his own admission) Buber's own, philosophy.[26] The translation of encounter into a content depends upon the character of the culture and thus opens it to misrepresentation.

3. Taoism

Returning once again to our point of departure in *I and Thou*, we find that the Chinese tradition appears in an immediately identifiable way only once, in Part Two, #32, in a discussion of art as one of the "forms of the spirit", one of the ways encounter with the Absolute expresses itself in the observable world.[27] Buber recounts the tale of a

Chinese poet who played his jade flute before the people and was rejected. He then played before the gods and was heard; and from then on, the people listened to his music. For Buber, all art that is more than decoration or amusing distraction speaks of relation to that which transcends the world of changing, relative values: true art speaks of the Absolute.

But in spite of this solitary explicit mention of Chinese things in *I and Thou*, Buber's thought was actually closer to the Chinese tradition than to the Indian. Recall his early publication of *Chinesische Geister und Liebesgeschichten* in 1911,[28] and especially of *Reden und Gleichnisse des Tschuang-Tse* in 1910.[29] The latter contains an essay on "The Teaching of the Tao" (written in 1909) which was one of the few early pieces Buber allowed to be published in his collected works. For Buber it represents a stage he had to pass through, very close to the position represented in 1913 in *Daniel*. It was a stage, he said, without which he could not have reached his final position.[30] And even after he reached his mature thought, in his 1928 lecture on "China and Us", he claimed that, while we of the West could no longer fully appropriate the Confucian side of the Chinese tradition, we could still learn much from the Taoist side.[31]

There are at least six interlocked Taoist notions that became important for Buber: 1) *Tao* itself as a way, discovered and traversed by 2) *non-action*, that involves 3) the *coincidence of opposites*, and 4) the *realization* of what one already knows, terminating in 5) the *unity of one's life* as a whole, which establishes 6) the *unity of the world*.

Tao means essentially "the Way", the path on which to walk, and thus involves not so much seeing as doing. Tao is the path of oneness, holding together *Yin* and *Yang*, the basic opposites: male and female, light and darkness, active and passive. Tao is a path that can only be known if it is walked, i.e. knowing at this level is coincident with doing, for it is a knowing-*how*. Such know-how is taught, not by prescription but by example, and is learned by plunging in, muddling through and gradually forgetting ourselves and our prescriptions in their verbal, conceptual form as we live them out.[32]

The essential reality here is termed *wu-wei* or non-action. It is one of the central notions of *I and Thou*.[33]. It involves a fusion of activity and passivity, so different from what we ordinarily call activity as to be called *non*-action. As in any graceful performance, there is a coincidence of opposites: conscious and unconscious, mind and body, where "it acts in me" as much as "I act". To attempt to force one's actions from the outside, as it were, by a detached picturing of positions, remembrance of prescriptions, marshalling of multiple forces and deliberate willing of movement is to issue in an extremely ungraceful performance. "Grace" is a gift, the gift of instincts and of situations. And it is only by allying oneself with one's gift, by creating in ourselves the conditions for "letting things be", that graceful performance ensues.

Non-action likewise involves a parallel non-knowing in which, just as action fuses with passivity, so knowledge fuses with love.[34] Thus knowing and doing, activity and passivity, conscious and unconscious, knowledge and love are joined in the essential act that follows the Tao. Such action both gives expression to and aids in establishing the unity of one's life which, for the Taoist, is a matter of combining the strongest change with the purest unity.[35] Such unity, in turn, both expresses and helps establish the unity of the world itself.[36]

This theme of the establishment of the unity of the world through one's own life, is both crucial and difficult to clarify, foreign as it is to the atomism and sensism of the past few centuries of Western thought. Entities are understood as circumscribed units, in principle identical with their here-and-now present sensory form. Field-theory, ecology and sociological thinking are breaking down the atomism, but the implication of sensism we have not yet surmounted. That an individual might have cosmic relations, affecting the totality—indeed, that there might be an in-principle unobservable dimension of the presence of the Eternal in the finite and temporal as the very ground of religiousness—is foreign to the modern Western tradition, though certainly not to the more ancient roots of the tradition. For the latter, my most private acts affect the totality, not simply in terms of the direct or indirect effects of my overt acts, but in terms of what has been called "winning God's blessing for the world", the deepest theological rationale for the contemplative life.

The unity of one's life as a whole is *the* central concern of Buber's thought. Unfortunately, Buber's way of speaking lends itself to the serious misinterpretation that the best that humans can achieve is alternation between a largely drab existence in the It-World, punctuated by ecstatic episodes with a Thou. This interpretation—or rather misinterpretation—disregards Buber's notion of the latency of the Thou in the It and his distinction between *Begegnung* or momentary encounter and *Beziehung* or perduring relation open to the necessary alternation between "inspiration" and "work". It fails to attend to the overall thrust of his thought.[37]

In a letter to Max Brod in 1913,[38] Buber pointed out some of the affinities between his recently published *Daniel* and the work of Tschuang-tse, who, after Laotze himself, was the greatest of the Taoists. Buber contrasts both *Daniel* and Taoism with the ecstatic experience of his own earlier preoccupations. Ecstasy has the soul as its object; its character is passive, receptive; its time-relation episodic. His own and the Taoist positions, on the contrary, have the world as their object; the character of their central experience is active; temporal relation lasting and binding. But in *Daniel* itself, Taoism is apparently the third of the three levels, after Hinduism and Idealism, that "the faithful one" had to pass through,[39] for the Taoist dwells in the midst of life in the mode of indifference. According to Tschuang-tse, the perfected one is essentially without direction; he leans neither to the right nor to the left; for him all things are equal.[40] But in *Daniel*, one of the key notions is finding one own's direction in the midst of things.[41]

Some aspects of *Daniel* can further aid us in understanding Buber's assimilation of Taoism. That work closes with the observation that the book had been basically a reflection of life and death, the basic polarity of life itself for Taoism.[42] Reflection upon our awareness of this relation will shed light on a second basic polarity in *Daniel*, that between knowledge by way of *orientation* and by way of *realization*,[43] which, in turn, foreshadows the central polarity of Buber's mature thought: the polarity between I-It and I-Thou.

Orientation is a mode of knowing which considers a given entity in terms of its fitting into a scheme developed through past experience. This mode comes into *I and Thou* as the I-It relation characterized by pastness. Our orientational knowledge of the inevitability of our own death is merely one of the items of information within our repertoire of factual knowledge which we can repeat to ourselves at any moment and whose truth we can readily verify. But there are times when death takes hold of our life: we "see" it, or rather are apprehended by it, touched by it. And then it is as if we had really never seen it before: we *realize* it for the first time, or perhaps it would not be incorrect to say that we *believe* it for the first time. As Laotze said, everyone seeks to know what he does not yet know; but few seek to realize what they already know.[44] The "motor" type, the Oriental man, does not simply look detachedly, but is moved in the whole of his being by realized thought. Orientational knowledge, knowledge in the usual sense of the term, is only one mode of truth. Buber in effect parallels Heidegger's distinction between truth as *orthotes* or correct representation and truth as *aletheia* or original emergence into presence.[45] Orientational knowledge affords a valid *object* of knowledge but not a real *presence*. And it is presence that is the key word in understanding I-Thou. When death becomes a presence for one who seeks reality and flees illusion, life itself is opened up in its strangeness and preciousness. As Daniel says, "The script of life is so unspeakably beautiful to read because death looks over our shoulder".[46]

Once more, however, the coincidence of opposites in the mode of realization has still to be brought into the whole of our life. For the "motor" type, following the Way is not simply a matter of experience (*Erlebnis*), no matter how "lively" and moving; it is a matter of life itself, for which the coincidence of opposite feelings is only a sign.[47] The realization of one's death brings life as a whole into focus—for that moment. But life itself is many moments. Realization enters the fabric of life and is fully "realized"[48] in action.

4. Zen

Zen does not enter into *I and Thou*, at least not explicitly. However, it has clear affinities with Buber's thought by reason of its own Buddhist and Taoist background. Buber published nothing on Zen until relatively late, and in each case it was in the context of a comparison with Hasidism: in the early 1940's, in "The Place of Hasidism in the History of Religion",[48a] and in 1963, in "Noch einiges zur Darstellung des Chassidismus".[49] In the latter, Zen, Hasidism and Islamic Sufi are compared in terms of the basically oral character of the transmission of their teachings, which received written expression only later in their development. The total relation of teacher to disciple in the lived context of total psycho-physical encounter is the way to teach "the one thing necessary".

In the earlier essay Zen is presented as an originally Chinese synthesis of Buddhism and Taoism that traces its line of descent back to the Lotus "Sermon" of the Buddha. Here the Buddha's speech was his deed: he simply held out a lotus before his companions. The one thing necessary is the silent unfolding of the Buddha nature, as in the flower. From this the way leads to the Mahayana *Lankavatara Sutra* and also to Laotze, for both of which the highest things do not admit of conceptual expression: "He who knows does not say; he who says does not know".[50] The truth is to be done rather than said. For this, silence is crucial, and yet it too can be deceptive. Silent unfolding terminates in concrete, but not in conceptual expression: the Zenist paints as the Hasid dances.

Rejection of conceptual expression for Zen is of a piece with the rejection of all mediation. For example, the enlightened one is often pictured destroying Buddhist scriptures or statuary. One passage reads: "If you meet the Buddha, destroy him!" The Buddha nature can only be found by direct pointing to the soul of man, only in oneself. For this, everything exterior is, at best, symbol.

For all their similarities in certain respects, this is where Zen and Hasidism part company. They agree that unity is to be achieved in the midst of the world; this they share with Taoism. Zen even provides a new twist to Buddhism by uniting *nirvana* and *samsara*, the blowing out of desire and involvement in the ceaseless round of becoming. Unlike Taoism, Hasidism and Zen consider the dream world inferior, and to be measured by the waking world. But it is the relation to otherness in the world and the mediating role of tradition that proves to be the dividing line between Zen and Hasidism (and thus also Buber's thought). The measure for the waking world for Hasidism is not individual experience shorn of history characteristic of Zen, but the *Torah,* teaching of the tradition anchored in the decisive historical events of the Jewish people in their encounter with Yahweh, the Wholly Other who draws near. But decisive also (the "also" here is not a sign of mere external conjunction but of necessary connection) is meeting with the Other in the world, encounter with the Other as full reality, not as mere symbol. Like Kant's "Humanity", for Hasidism and for Buber, every other is an end and not a mere means, not even a means to the Ultimate. Response to the full otherness of the Other opens out to the eternal Thou.

Tradition and encounter anchor the Hasid firmly in history and in community. But like the compassionate Buddha to whom Zen owes its historical roots, the Zenist may or may not be concerned to transmit the teaching to others. The teaching itself involves no necessary reference to others. It is an option the Buddhist takes: rather than enter *nirvana*, he becomes a *boddhisatva*, a savior for others. For Buber, meeting with God, with the Ultimate, involves mission to the world. And community with others opens the Between within which God speaks, at different times and in different places, as He will, and as the way of history.

5. Lehre

At the center of all these manifestations of the spirit of the Orient which Buber considered is the phenomenon of what Buber calls

Lehre, "teaching". Teaching is the most fundamental of the *geistige Wesenheiten*, which I prefer to translate as "forms of the spirit".[51] Buber speaks of spirit in different ways: it is a relation between man and that which transcends the world; it is the Between and thus more than man; it is the word into which man enters; it is closely related to *Urdistanz*; and it is that which timelessly envelopes nature.[52] Encounter with the spirit's forms, along with encounter with things of nature and with other persons constitute the three regions of the I-Thou relation. The forms are the original inspirations, Thou's that are not empirically "there", but which speak of the unconditioned, the Absolute and eternal, and lay upon the inspired one a demand to give empirical shape to the unconditioned out of the conditioned material available in the age. Though closely linked to man, spirit is more than man, for it "breathes into", in-spires him: it appears through man in temporal conditions and yet timelessness envelops nature because its inspirations speak of the eternal and unconditioned.

There are three types of these forms of the spirit, in the three realms of what Hegel characterized as the region of Absolute Spirit: art, philosophy and religion. Buber speaks of responding to the forms *bildend, denkend, handelnd*,[53] shaping in art, thinking in philosophy and acting in religion, realized paradigmatically for the West in Goethe, Socrates, and Jesus respectively.[54] Elsewhere Buber speaks of responding to the same trinity of forms *bildhaft, gedankenhaft, traumhaft*:[55] shapingly, thinkingly, dreamingly, where *traumhaft* appears in place of the former *handelnd*, as characteristic of religious *Lehre*.

Traumhaft recalls the Hindu teaching of the dream state as on the way to the highest state of dreamless sleep; it likewise recalls Tschuang-tse's equating of waking and dreaming—perhaps indeed holding for the superiority of the latter which exhibits the Tao in us without our intervention. Buber rejects the claim of the non-waking states to be the highest. He prefers rather the Heraclitean claim that the waking is superior because it follows the common world of the *Logos*, whereas the sleeping involves retreat into a private world. The Orientals retreat into the self and lose the ability, or rather consider as inferior the ability to dwell together with others in the struggle to build a common cosmos. Solitude has the primacy, and the dream state approaches absolute primacy.[56] However, dreaming does suggest, negatively, the non-intervention of the purpose-oriented waking self; and positively, contact with the unconscious and with inspiration. It thus points to non-action as centrally characteristic of the source of religious teaching.

The form of the spirit that lies at the source of "pure effective action" results in a life that is itself teaching, the showing of the Way.[57] The empirical shape given to the inspired form is the shape of a life, and is thus far superior to the forms created outside the self in art and in philosophy, in shaping and in thinking. In an entirely secondary sense, teaching translates into words and works that lie at the base of a common cosmos, a shared world of meaning taking shape in the restructuring of time and space into holy days and holy places. Dwelling in such a cosmos leads to inspired works of the spirit in a growing number of followers: to the development of new forms of art and new developments in philosophy. It leads to the possibility of the life of the spirit becoming unified as religion, philosophy and the arts embody and evoke the same spirit. The object of teaching, the one thing necessary, being truly one, being whole, may be realized in several ways. First is the unity of the simple people *(Einfältigen)*, the incomplex, those who maintain their peace and balance in the midst of change.[58] Such simple ones live in a collective world created, in its original inspiration, by a second type: those who, out of the swirling multiplicity of their natures, have become one *(Eingewordenen)*,[59] and are thus able, as the simple are not so able, to create the works of the spirit in all three regions of the spirit. Buber speaks also of the becoming one of the soul as apparently identical with this type.[60] There is, in addition, a third type, associated with the becoming one of the spiritual life which involves the organic interplay of all the forms of the spirit in an individual and in a culture.[61] Beyond, but not above this, is the experience of the void in Hinduism, at best an anticipation of unity, but not its possession.[62] But the highest type is one who has achieved unity throughout the whole of his life in relation to the primal mystery, the eternal Thou: he is the holy man, the *arhat*, the *zaddik*, the saint who has himself become *Lehre*, who has become *Torah*, whose very existence opens up a Way for a community.

There is another type of unity, unity of thought or what we might call philosophic unity, the search for which has become characteristic of the West. Buber sets up a contrast between Eastern and Western types of ideal unities in terms of the "motor" East (which we have already met) and the "sensorial" West. Western man is primarily "sensorial", dominated especially by vision, the "objective" sense par excellence. Contrasted with touch, for example, which involves the reciprocal experience of the felt other and the feeling organism, vision, in its normal functioning, involves the disappearance of the

organic self from the field of experience and the appearance of the
detached other. Furthermore, the other appears in terms of relations
of spatial exteriority to other visible individuals as well; and it
manifests itself as relatively static. Such visually observed others are
worked into a world-picture through subordination to conceptual
eidoi that are the objects of intellectual "seeing". Individuals so
conceived are fit objects for mastery, the underlying aim that lies at
the heart of Western man's orientation. At an early phase, the object
of such a stance might be contemplative—though it is still object of
conceptual or experiential mastery. But when this mode of knowing is
conjoined to a peculiar mode of *praxis* in experimental science, it
attains to an open-ended dynamism that transposes more and more
area from the unconscious and semi-conscious and deliberate refash-
ioning by a humanity bent on conquest and the imposition of its own
order upon things.[63]

Oriental man, by contrast, is essentially "motor". Where static
images and concepts guide Western *praxis*, movements and actions
guide Oriental thought. Here Buber speaks of Laotze, the *Upanishads*, Zarathustra, and the prophets: the Chinese, Indians, Per-
sians and Jews. Indeed, the latter are the "motor type in its purest
expression". For Oriental man experience is essentially dynamic. The
movements in the "outer" world reverberate through our "inner"
world as well. As we are interconnected with others, so the others are
linked with each other, and the movements within us act upon each
other: all things interpenetrate in action; all the perceptual powers
interpenetrate in the active life of a person. Oriental man, thinking in
terms of movement, is thus more temporally than spatially oriented.
The world is not primarily a set of things to be seen and comprehended in a conceptual system, but a way to be walked, a path, the
Tao. And walking the path is also, at the same time, finding response
by "doing the truth", "the one thing necessary", realizing the One
within which the split world is healed. The recognition of a split into
opposites pervades all the Oriental cultures: a split between the
knower and the world in Hinduism, within the world itself for
Taoism, between the agent and the world in Zoroastrianism, and a
split within the agent himself in Judaism. With the recognition of
different dualities, different paths are proposed. But they all are part
of the Way of the One. Teaching of the way is the dominant
characteristic of the religious teachings in each of the cultures.[64]

Overcoming the split is more than a conceptual-theoretical
overcoming—in fact, the conceptual may constitute a fundamental

obstacle to it. Hinduism, Buddhism, Taoism, Zen and Hasidism all place conceptual expression in an inferior, if not a negative position. Overcoming the split involves not so much a view as a path, and therefore not so much a knowing-*that* or a knowing-*what* as a knowing-*how*. Such knowing is taught more by example than words.

In the Hindu-Buddhist-Zen line, such knowing is referred to variously as *moksha, nirvana, satori,* or "enlightenment", in the different nuances that term has in each tradition. Though often spoken of as a single experience, what it effects is a shift of level for the whole of one's life which then attains its unity. Buber's equivalent is "the experience of faith", prepared for by encounter with many Thou's, but realized when the many are heard as messages from a single Voice.[65] But the unity of life is not simply meeting with the Thou, not even with the eternal Thou. It is rather the coming and going from meeting with the Thou to mission into the world of It; but the process now no longer loses its relation to the Center. For Buber, "the unity of life . . . once truly won, is no longer torn by any changes".[66]

Of great significance is the fact that achieving the unity of one's life is not simply something that occurs to and in an individual person, but something which has cosmic repercussions. For Hinduism, the Self is identical with the All; for Taoism as for Zen, the unity of the world is achieved through the unity of the self; and in Hasidism, the world gains its unity through the unified man.

The latter notion appears in the last part of *I and Thou* where the I-It and I-Thou relations are said to mirror a two-fold movement in the cosmos: the movements of being and becoming.[67] Becoming is the unfolding of the potentialities of beings as they move out from their divine Source, whereas Being involves the return of these beings to that Source. Man can aid in the former through his activity in the world; but it is only through man that things are returned to their Source. In Hasidic terms, man is the cosmic mediator sent to release the holy sparks from things and to establish the carriage of God's majesty in the world.[68]

Teaching has come to the West from the East. Today it is in the process of eclipse in the West and in the East, even though it shows "the one thing necessary", without which human life, and likewise the created world itself, is torn apart, unredeemed. Teaching differs from era to era, and yet it is the same. It is the same in that it displays an ultimately ineffable Presence that heals, that makes whole. It is different because it finds different expression, different content at different times and places. When the content fits both the one who has become whole and his expression and the age to which he speaks as its message, a Way opens up for a people, a common *cosmos* that speaks of the eternal Thou. Today, however, our situation is such that, for Buber, there is no common Way.[69] But there is the place where a Way may eventually show itself: the place where the Thou is met, the flashing forth of presence when we are open to it and not closed within the well-trod paths of the It-World. Buber's task has been to ponder the traditions of teaching and to point to the place. If these flashings-forth cohere in the experience of faith for many,[70] perhaps there will arise in our midst those who can teach a Way for us who now dwell in the age of the eclipse of God.

6. *Lehre and Philosophy*

Near the conclusion to *Daniel* Buber refers to a progressive maturing of *Lehre* in him, from Hinduism through philosophic Idealism to Taoism, and on to the position maintained in that work,[71] which was itself superceded and brought to full maturity in *I and Thou*. The level of philosophic idealism was the level where he achieved the unity of life, but only in thought, or, in Kierkegaard's terms, only as a possibility of existence. Buber returned to the level of philosophical comprehension in a significant way towards the end of his life in the essays collected in *The Knowledge of Man*. In this concluding section I wish to clarify and extend Buber's reflections in terms of the relation between philosophy and religious teaching.

Buber sees philosophy, as well as religion, fragmented into many traditions and thus each in some way relative to the historical conditions out of which they arose. But just as religion is a mixture of conditionality and unconditionality, of the age and the one thing necessary, so also with philosophy.[72] This relation to the unconditioned through the conditioned is what makes dialogue between differing traditions not only possible but obligatory. However, the anchorage of each in an historical context is not a superfluity that can be abstracted from to achieve a pure, universal message. Anchorage in the concrete is where the truth is to be found.[73]

There are a number of philosophic claims involved in the above, i.e. claims to universal truth that transcends conditions. If we accept Buber's claims, then we are forced to distinguish two levels to the philosophic enterprise—both, I think, indispensible. There is first the level at which the above claims operate, the level of the conditions for the possibility of distinctively human existence as such. There is, secondly, a level concerned with the concrete unfolding of human existence. The two levels implicate each other, since the coming into light of the first level is part of the unfolding of the second and stands open itself to the development in the light of further concrete unfolding. One discovers the universal imperative of dialogue and the conditions that make it possible and necessary in the particularity and contingency of one's own concrete existence; and these conditions can be brought to greater clarity in the course of that existence.

Philosophical thought lays hold of individuals in terms of universals, principles, laws; but that is only following out in an explicit way the path laid out by language itself. This involves certain underlying structures both on the part of the knower and on the part of the known. *On the part of the knower*, this involves a reference beyond the individual to the broader context within which it fits. It involves a reference to all actual or possible instances of the kind dealt with in a given instance of knowing, a reference to a universal context, a network of universals within which the kind is understood, a world of meaning. But that itself is made possible by the human knower being, at base, reference to the whole of reality itself, to all actual or possible instances of being, a reference which Buber termed *Urdistanz*.[74] Any sensorily encountered individual is taken up into this ultimate reference: the notion of all actual or possible instances of being is contracted to all actual or possible instances of the kind in question in the empirical encounter, and the empirically given individual is displayed as an instance of its kind.

On the part of the known, since thought reveals it as what it is, it must be more than its empirical individuality; it must itself actually *be* an instance within a set of universal networks, ultimately an instance of being, a relation to the whole. Particular networks are a combination of construction and discovery, and they develop in the light of the expansion of empirical encounters. But the existence of such networks displays certain necessary structures of thought and things upon which science itself rests.

What has this to do with the Orient and with its *Lehre*? The level of being in us is the level of our unconditional reference to the whole of reality, and thus also to the wholeness both of ourselves and of any encounterable other. The level of being in things is the level of their reference to the whole. Empirical encounter and conceptual interpretation afford us aspects of the wholeness of things—appearances, revealing in part, concealing in part, pointing to the wholeness from differing positions, differing cultural angles, differing methodologies, while never encompassing that wholeness. Yet there *is* the wholeness of each thing, the wholeness of ourselves and the wholeness of reality; and we are referred to that in the depth of our being. This structural feature of our humanness points to the possibility of a mode of relation to things other than empirical and conceptual, thus a relation beyond appearances (though not without them); a possible relation of the wholeness of ourselves to the wholeness of others, and a possible opening through that relation to the wholeness of reality itself. This would explain why, in certain modes of self-experience, "I and the All are one", for the self in its depth is a reference to the All. This would explain why meeting with the Thou is an intimation of the eternal Thou, and why the cosmos itself is implicated in any experience of such wholeness. This approach allows us to explain the foundations of *Lehre* without explaining it away.

But the philosophical explication of these conditions is not the living through of the one thing necessary. Philosophy here points to the possibility of that which *Lehre* lives. And in so doing, philosophy performs a service to *Lehre* by holding open the space of that possibility at a time when so many factors converge to close it. It heads off a now popular psychologizing of Oriental teaching in which meditation is considered a mere intra-organic event of learning how to "relax", but having nothing essential to do with the ontological concern of relation to the whole of reality so central to all teaching. This psychologizing is itself expression of a doctrine that claims scientific sanction which reduces the self to its empirical inspectability, and thus, in effect, cuts off the roots of science itself. It is that, above all, which closes off the space of openness to the spirit. The experiential testimony of religious teaching is dialectically related to philosophical explication of the sort we have here indicated. The teaching points to such explication, and such explication points to the teaching. Western "enlightenment" eliminated both, and now rules the world. A return to the relation between teaching and philosophy is a requirement of the age. Buber has set us on the way to such return.

Such structural analysis likewise supplies the conditions for the possibility of dialogue that moves from such analysis, on the basis of such analysis, to encounter with the concrete richness of the multiplicity of cultures and individuals. Dialogue would then be not merely a pragmatic matter of alienated cultures and individuals bound together by reason of a common threat standing over against them all. It would be dialogue rooted in the underlying structures of the human situation itself. To such structure and such dialogue Buber has led us, a dialogue of East and West, a dialogue between two forms of the spirit, a dialogue between religious teaching and philosophy, a dialogue that is one of the urgent requirements of our age.

Discussion Following Robert Wood's Lecture

C. VERNOFF

I know that Buber was very well intentioned in seeking to open up a gateway to other traditions, but I wonder if his philosophy of dialogue is not so profoundly rooted both in Hasidic perspective and in the Kantian idealist tradition, so as to finally prejudice his method against the very end which he sought. Having arrayed the various traditions in some kind of hierarchy which relates to their capacity to reflect the Thou, how can a Buberian methodology actually enter into dialogue with Hinduism? I mean if Hinduism, from its own intracultural perspective radically denies the Thou which Buber upholds, would not Buber's methods simply amount to another form of cultural imperialism?

R. WOOD

I think we have to distinguish between two levels of dialogue: the level—fundamental for Buber—of the relation between the partners of the dialogue, and the level of the content about which the dialogue occurs. We can only assume the first level is respected by Buber. The question concerns the second. Here dialogue involves not only openness to the other's position, but also speaking from where one stands himself, and that also involves judgement of the other's position. All positions for Buber are partial and therefore require correction and supplementation. Buber's treatment of the Orientals is indeed a dialogue. In his early days he read the Hindu-Buddhist line with special sympathy and in terms of his own "mystical" experiences. But he subsequently came to a greater appreciation of the superiority of the Taoist tradition for the problem with which he himself was struggling. And in time he came to see the need for sublimating the Taoist tradition as well. However, he proceeded from his mature position to re-read the Hindu-Buddhist line and thought he discerned a meeting with the Thou at the base of these traditions as well. But even in this judgement an element of openness is discovered. Buber admits that there may be more to those traditions than what he was able to see, for they involve experiences "at the edge of life" that are difficult to interpret. But, he says that for those who share his experiences, meeting in the everyday, with a glimpse through to the eternal Thou, is more valuable than these experiences "at the edge of life".

J. BLOCH

I have only a short comment. Yesterday evening Prof. Gollwitzer insisted that the I-Thou is a reality which can be spoken about and which calls for speaking, for language. He was very much opposed to an interpretation which I gave on the first day which uses what Prof. Wood calls Oriental themes. Now, the affinity of Buber towards Oriental thinking and religious thinking, Zen, Taoism, etc., seems to have an implication upon the interpretation of the I-Thou and its linguistic probabilities. Buber thinks that Judaism belongs more to the Oriental way of Lehre than to the Western kind of theological thinking. Their affinity reflects on the way I interpret the I-Thou relationship and its relationship to language.

R. WOOD

Language enriches the momentary present by relating it simultaneously to the past of our own memories and to the community of others past, contemporary and to come, as well as to the as-yet not-fully-disclosed totality. But language itself is perpetually rooted in the present of encounter, a presence opening out to the totality, a lived presence that flashes forth in its depth from time to time in a moment of realizing what we already *know*. Buber saw both as "language": the language, ordinarily understood, of I-It, and the primordial "language" of individual address and response, the language of I-Thou.

Notes

ROBERT WOOD

1. Cf. Peter Berger, Brigette Berger and Hansfried Kellner, *The Homeless Mind, Modernization and Consciousness*, New York: Vintage, 1973.
2. Peter Berger, *The Sacred Canopy*, Garden City, New York: Anchor Books, 1969, especially chapter 6.
3. Both during the period when he began writing *I and Thou* (in 1916, in his lecture on "Der Geist des Orients und das Judentum", originally in *Reden Uber das Judentum*, 1916, reprinted in the volume of Buber's collected works on Judaism, *Der Jude und sein Judentum*, Köln: Joseph Melzer, 1963, pp. 46-65) and also several years after his mature thought had been formulated (in his 1934 lecture on "The Power of the Spirit", reprinted in translation in Martin Buber, *Israel and the World*, New York: Schocken, 1965, pp. 173-182), Buber held that Judaism could only be understood by comparing it with the "reality systems" of the Orient because it was a product of Oriental thinking.
4. Cf. *infra*, n. 51.
5. *I and Thou*, Walter Kaufmann (tsl.), N.Y.: Scribner, 1970. (Henceforth referred to as IT.) The translation is a significant improvement over the older English translation, several problems with which I have pointed out in my *Martin Buber's Ontology, An Analysis of I AND THOU*, Evanston, Illinois: Northwestern University Press, 1969. There is still one problem with Kaufmann's translation: cf. *infra*, note 50.
6. "Geist des Orients", pp. 47-50.
7. IT, pp. 110-111.
8. IT, pp. 103-105.
9. IT, pp. 134-143.
10. Letter to Will Herberg, 1/25/53 in Martin Buber, *Briefwechsel aus sieben Jahrzehnten*, Vol. 3, Grete Schaeder (ed.), Heidelberg: Lambert Schneider, 1975, p. 326.
11. This very aspect of Ekhart's mode of speaking, obliterating the distinction between God and creatures, thus suggesting pantheism rather than theism, was the reason why Ekhart was regarded as suspect by his own Church. Orthodox mystics use the language of *union* rather than *identity*.
12. Cf. John Caputo, "Fundamental Themes in Ekhart's Mysticism", *The Thomist*, vol. 42, no. 2, 1978, pp. 197-225 for a different—and textually well-grounded—interpretation of Ekhart which is closer to Buber's own understanding of meeting with God.
13. Cf. e.g. the *Isa Upanishad*, 6 & &, 16; *Chandogya Upanishad*, VIII, xi, 1-3; *Brhadaranyaka Upanishad*, III, iv, 1 and vii, 15 & 23.
14. Cf. e.g. *Chandogya Upanishad*, VI, ix-xiii.
15. *Mandukya Upanishad*, 1-12. Actually there is a fourth state described here, beyond even the dreamless sleep and wherein the "cessation of becoming" occurs.
16. "Foreword" to *Pointing the Way*. Maurice Friedman (ed. and tsl.), N.Y.: Harper and Row, 1963, pp. xv-xvi—henceforth the book will be referred to as PW. Buber returned to this assessment of the dreamless sleep in "What is Common to

All", in *The Knowledge of Man*, Maurice Friedman and Ronald Gregor Smith (tsls.), N.Y.: Harper and Row, 1965, pp. 94-96—henceforth the book will be referred to as KM.

17. *The Origin and Meaning of Hasidism*, Maurice Friedman (tsl.), N.Y.: Harper and Row, 1960, pp. 117ff.

18. IT, pp. 135-136.

19. *Ibid*, p. 239.

20. *Daniel, Dialogues on Realization*, Maurice Friedman (tsl.), N.Y.: McGraw-Hill, 1965, pp. 137-140.

21. IT, pp. 138-143.

22. "Buddha", *Neue Blätter*, Hellerau and Berlin: Erich Baron, 1913, pp. 63-64.

23. *Samyutta-nikaya, v, 420; Majjhima-nikaya*, iii, 248-252.

24. *Majjhima-nikaya*, 63.

25. "Buddha", p. 65. Cf. my *Martin Buber's Ontology* for his early mystical phase (pp. 5-15).

26. Cf. *The Eclipse of God*, New York: Harper, 1957, pp. 38-42.

27. Cf. *infra* n. 50.

28. Frankfurt am Main: Rütten and Loening, 1911.

29. Leipzig: Insel, 1914.

30. "Vorwort" to *Schriften zur Philosophie, Werke*, vol. 1, Heidelberg: Lambert Schneider, 1962, p. 8.

31. "China and Us", in PW, pp. 121-125.

32. "Die Lehre vom Tao", *Werke*, vol. 1, pp. 1021-1051—henceforth referred to as LT.

33. *I and Thou*, 46, p. 125; 59, p. 157; 14, p. 62.

34. LT, pp. 1043-1045.

35. *Ibid*, p. 1039.

36. *Ibid*, pp. 1039-1041. Cf. *Daniel*, p. 141.

37. Cf. Walter Kaufmann's "Buber's Failures and Triumph" in this volume. On the notion of "latency" cf. IT, p. 69; on *Beziehung* and *Begegnung* cf. "Replies", *Philosophy of Martin Buber*, pp. 105 and 712; on unity as the basic thrust of Buber's thought, *Martin Buber's Ontology*, especially pp. 16-18. Cf. also n. 65.

38. Letter of 6/12/13 in *Briefwechsel*, vol. 1, 1972, pp. 350-352.

39. Cf. *supra*, n. 14. There is a problem here with Buber's own later assessment of this phase. In the Forward to PW (cf. n. 16) it was in reference to the essay on Taoism, which Buber had reprinted there, that Buber spoke of his "mystical" phase, preoccupied with special ecstatic moments without relation to the much more frequent non-ecstatic moments of life as a whole. This would seem to be a lapse on Buber's part insofar as the essay itself calls attention to the perfected one who lives the Tao as combining unity and change throughout his life (cf. LT, p. 1039).

40. *Chuang-tzu*, ch. 17, 6; 17b-21b.

41. *Daniel*, pp. 49-59.

42. LT, p. 1040.

43. *Daniel*, pp. 22-31.

44. LT, p. 1037.

45. Martin Heidegger, "The Essence of Truth", in *Existence and Being*, Werner Brook (ed. and tsl.), Chicago, Ill.: Regnery, 1949, pp. 292-324.

46. *Daniel*, p. 91.

47. Cf. IT, #49; p. 130.

48. Throughout *Daniel*, Buber plays on variations of the verb *wirken*, "to do, to effect, to produce, to act", in *Wirklichkeit*, "reality", and *Verwirklichung*, "realization".

48a. *The Origin and Meaning of Hasidism*, pp. 220-239.

49. *Schriften zur Chassidismus, Werke*, vol. 3, pp. 991-998.

50. *Laotze*, ch. 56.

51. Kaufmann (p. 57) follows the older translation in rendering this as "spiritual beings". In *Martin Buber's Ontology*, p. 43, I have argued for "forms of the spirit". Kaufmann's choice leads him to ignore some nuances in meaning elsewhere, e.g. p. 126 where he conflates *Wesen* and *Wesenheit*, claiming that "in English the single word 'being' must serve for both terms". It shouldn't. This is the one expression which, I think, Kaufmann has not translated well—a rather minor flaw in an otherwise excellent translation.

52. "On the Psychologizing of the World", in *A Believing Humanism*; Maurice Friedman (tsl.), N.Y.: Simon and Schuster, 1967, p. 147; IT, #32, p. 89; "Distance and Relation", in KM, pp. 59-71; IT, #25, p. 75, CF. *Martin Buber's Ontology*, pp. 38-40.

53. IT, #9, p. 57.

54. IT, #40, pp. 115-117.

55. IT, #28, P.81.

56. "What is Common to All", in KM, pp. 89-98 and 102-105.

57. IT, #32, pp. 91ff.

58. Cf. IT, #35, p. 98 and #36, p. 103.

59. LT, p. 1026.

60. *Ibid.*

61. *Good and Evil*, R. G. Smith (tsl.), New York: Scribner, 1953, p. 129.

62. "Philosophical and Religious Worldview", *A Believing Humanism*, p. 133.

63. "Geist des Orients", pp. 47-50.

64. *Ibid*, pp. 47-54.

65. "Replies", pp. 689-690.

66. "Dialogue", *Between Man and Man*, R. G. Smith (tsl.), Boston: Beacon, 1961, p. 25.

67. IT, #54, p. 149.

68. *Hasidism and Modern Man*, p. 33 and 118.

69. *For the Sake of Heaven*, Ludwig Lewisohn (tsl.), N.Y.: Harper and Row, 1966, p. xiii.

70. Cf. "Replies", p. 693.

71. Cf. n. 20.

72. "On the Situation of Philosophy", in *Believing Humanism*, pp. 136-137.

73. Cf. "China and Us", in PW, p. 122.

74. "Distance and Relation", in KM, pp. 59-71.

Buber and Japanese Thought

YOSHIMORI HIRAISHI

I

The purpose of this paper is to clarify the significance of Buber's philosophy to the modern Japanese mind, rather than to analyse, criticize, or develop his thought in a philosophical context from the view-point of Japanese thought. My reason for this is that before we discuss this problem, it will be necessary to know something about the philosophical climate in which Buber was accepted by, and confronted with, the Japanese mind.

Someone may ask, "What relations are there between Buber and Japanese thought? Japan is a country far away from Israel; moreover Japanese thought has been influenced much by both Chinese and Indian philosophies for more than one thousand years; and they are quite different from the Jewish way of thinking; how can there be any inner connection between them?" This is a natural question, of course. But, as a matter of fact, Buber's books have been read widely among Japanese today. We have not only Japanese translations of most of his important works, but also several monographs on Buber by Japanese authors, as you can see them in the exhibition. Furthermore, Buber's key words, such as "I and Thou", "Encounter", "Dialogue", and "Sphere of Between" etc., have become quite popular and have settled in Japanese vocabulary as everyday words. We can find them often in literary works, newspapers, everyday conversations, and sometimes even in the statements of politicians and economists, to say nothing of articles by scholars and specialists. I am not sure how accurately the meaning of these words is understood by them, but this fact will show us that there is something akin, and something deep in Buber's philosophy that appeals to the ordinary Japanese mind.

Why, then, is Buber so highly esteemed in Japan? Of course, we can share with you the same reasons which would commonly be given in most Western countries. For Japan today is no longer isolated from the actual situation of the world; and she confronts many of the same problems which you have in your own countries. But these common reasons may be omitted from my discussion here today. Along with

351

them, I believe that there are some others which are peculiar to the Japanese mind alone. I think I can point out at least two reasons for this. One is that Buber himself was rather Oriental-minded. Not only had he shown great interest in and sympathy toward Taoism, Zen Buddhism, and similar perspectives from his early youth; but he tried also to find a gleam of hope in the Oriental spirit at his time of world crisis. (cf. "Der Jude u. Sein Judentum, S. 648 'In der Krisis') So it is rather natural that there should be some similarities and responsiveness between Buber and Japanese thought. And this also makes Buber more understandable to the Japanese mind, not just in outward comprehension by mere knowledge.

There is, however, another and more weighty reason for my treatment of Buber's thought here. That is, in Buber's philosophy we can find out something positive which will contribute to the betterment of Japanese thought. For, in my view, that which is most lacking in Japanese thought can be supplied from Buber's philosophy. In most cases, they will appear as dissimilarities, or opposites, in which Japanese thought must confront Buber. It is true that Buber would not always take delight in the enumeration of such dissimilarities between his thought and the other, and what he sought most would be the dialogue between them. But the acceptance of this confronting encounter will be most important for the future development of Japanese thought. So my purpose is to clarify Buber's significance toward Japanese thought through these similarities and dissimilarities. It should be important both for us and for the interpretation of Buber itself to carry out this type of comparison.

II

Before we discuss these problems, it will be helpful for us to look briefly at the process by which Buber was introduced into Japan, and how much he was understood by Japanese philosophers of the past. This will give us the philosophical background, in order that we may understand him more easily in relation to Japanese thought. This process will be divided into three different ways. The first is one in which his most celebrated work *Ich und Du* was introduced directly into Japan for the first time. But, at that time, however, it is probable that no one knew who Buber was. Perhaps he might have been taken as just one among German philosophers, because his book was written in German. But this did not mean that Buber was absolutely neglected by Japanese philosophers. The philosophical circle of Japan was, at that time, mostly under the strong influence of the philosophy of Neo-Kantians; there was also the newly rising philosophy of Husserl's Phenomenology, whose concept of "Intersubjectivity" was not yet recognized as important in connection with the problem of "the other". So even if some people read *Ich und Du*, it was natural that they could not understand its full meaning.

As far as I can determine, it was only in 1935, twelve years after the publication of *Ich und Du*, that the name of Buber appeared in Japanese literature for the first time. In a small, but famous book called "Philosophy of Religion", S. Hatano (1877-1950) refered to Buber in a foot-note as follows: ". . . The book of Martin Buber, *Ich und Du*, will be one of the pioneer works, in which the problem of 'Ich' und 'Du' has been most fundamentally discussed. I should like to express my hearty thanks for all that I learned from this book. But it is regretable for me that this Jewish scholar seems to be satisfied with a kind of romantic view of the world, whose outline is quite obscure, and cannot escape from a mere worship of man, probably being much tempted by the Greek spirit. He did not notice that in as much as he had started from the problem of 'Ich und Du', he should have gone straight on the road of Love—Morality—Person . . ." Nobody can deny how unsatisfactory Hatano's comprehension of Buber was at that time. But he well recognized the importance of the "Ich-Du" relation in overcoming the philosophy of "Idealism"; and he developed his own religious philosophy, called "Personal Realism", which is, in some sense, akin to Buber's philosophy. His philosophy of religion, unlike others in Japan, which are usually founded on a Buddhistic way of thinking, greatly influenced the formation of Jewish-Christian philosophy in Japan. Hatano's followers, as a whole, were naturally good students of Buber. The late Prof. Y. Hamada, one of the eminent among them, further developed Hatano's philosophy, and made clear its peculiar meaning against the Self-centered, mono-logical tendency of Western philosophy since the Renaissance.

The second is the way in which Buber was introduced indirectly into Japan by German Protestant theologians, such as E. Brunner and others. As a matter of fact, Hatano's philosophy of religion seems to be much affected by them. However, their influence was not limited only to the Christian world, but also extended to the general circle of philosophy. In other words, we can say that Japanese philosophers learned the importance of Buber's thought through them, and not directly from Buber himself. So when they alluded to such a phrase as "Ich und Du", Buber's name was rarely mentioned, but instead the name of Brunner, and other theologians. Here we should consider two important pieces of writing: one is an article called "I and Thou" written by K. Nishida (1870-1945); the other is a book called "Ethics as Anthropology" written by T. Watsuji (1889-1960). Both of them were among the outstanding leaders in Japanese philosophy in recent years. Nishida is well-known as the founder of what is called the "Kyoto School" of philosophy, and Watsuji was also a notable scholar in Moral Philosophy. The characteristic feature of their philosophies will also indicate the general tendency of Japanese philosophy today. Their feature may be described as an attempt to build their own philosophical systems permeated with the Oriental spirit, but using the Western methods of logical thinking. First, let us consider Nishida.

Nishida's essay "Watakushi to Nanji" ("I and Thou"), which belongs to the earlier part of his philosophical thinking, appeared in 1932. He was probably the first in the history of Japanese philosophy to use such a phrase as this, and it was three years earlier than Hatano's discussion of the problem of "I and Thou". I am not sure, however, whether or not he had already read Buber's book at that time, because no mention is made of Buber in any of his works. Instead of that, the names of German Protestant theologians, such as Gogarten, are quoted several times. He might, therefore, have received the idea of "I and Thou" from them, rather than from Buber himself. He showed much interest in and sympathy toward the "I-Thou" relation, and actually comprehended it as the most concrete reality. But one thing gives me reason to pause; it is whether or not he tried to understand the full meaning of "I and Thou" along the line of Buber's way of thinking, because, in his essay, he makes no allusion to Buber's other fundamental phrases such as "I and It", "I and the eternal Thou" etc. . . . Moreover it seems that he rather tried to interpret it from his own philosophical standpoint, which was much influenced by Zen Buddhism. Thus he thought that both "I" and "Thou" derived their existence from the Supreme Universe, which enfolds both of them within it. According to his own words, ". . . The one which determines 'I' as 'I' will also be the one which determines 'Thou' as 'Thou'. Both 'I' and 'Thou' can be said to have come from the same environment, and exist within it as the denotation of the same Universal . . ." Nishida named this Universal, which is supreme, sometimes "Nothingness", in accordance with the Buddhist tradition; or sometimes the "Topos", the idea borrowed from Greek philosophy;

or sometimes the "Topos of Nothingness". It is clear that this Supreme Universe is not originally thought of as the same as the "Personal God" in Jewish-Christian tradition; but in another passage he plainly writes as though he had such a kind of notion himself. ". . . If we think that 'I' will be absorbed into oneness with the Universe, there exists 'I' no more. It will be nothing but mere non-consciousness (this is the weak point of Pantheism). So it must be that 'I' talks with the Great Universe as a person. We must be not absorbed into oneness with the Great Universe by becoming non-consciousness, but rather by standing face to face with It at the point of the self-determination of 'Self' as a person . . ." Nishida's idea of person mentioned here is rather obscure; and I doubt if he had recognized the "Personal God" beyond His immanent power in the Universe, as well as the inter-personal relationship between God and man, as Buber himself did. I dare say probably not!

Next, I must say something about Watsuji. In the case of Watsuji, I am also not sure whether or not he had read Buber directly for himself. But in his works he refered to Brunner and Gogarten several times, although no allusion to Buber can be found. So he too might have been influenced by German Protestant theologians in connection with the problem of "I and Thou". His book, *Ethics as Anthropology*, was published in 1934, in which he tried to construct an ethical theory based upon the concrete relationship between man and man, against the ethics of Idealism, whose effort consists only in the analysis of moral consciousness, and neglects the actual situation, in which men interact with one another. It is certain that he had arrived at such an idea from Buber's thinking. It is written, ". . . A German sociologist uses such words as 'Zwischen den Menschen', or 'das Zwischenmenschliche' by binding two words 'man' and 'between', and thus he expresses a standpoint of seeing a society as based on human relations . . ." Whom he meant by this German sociologist, nobody knows. But, if I understand correctly, the word "das Zwischenmenschliche" was used by Buber himself for the first time in the preface of Sombart's work, *Das Proletariat*, which appeared as the first volume of *Die Gesellschaft*, a series of the works on social philosophy, for which Buber was working as editor from 1905 to 1912. But this concept was used at that time merely to denote "das Soziale" which did not necessarily imply the concrete human relationship between man and man, as Buber himself later recognized. (cf. *Die Schriften über das dialogische Prinzip*, S. 257 f.) If this is so, a German sociologist whom Watsuji mentioned, would be no other than Buber himself. Along with "I and Thou", the phrase "Between man and man" became a completely new item in Japanese vocabulary. And it was Watsuji who first applied it to the traditional morality of Japan which was chiefly based on the ethical principle of Confucianism, being rather feudalistic in its essence. In this sense, although he used the concept of "Between" as the basis of his ethical theory, yet in terms of its inner contents, we must say he was quite different from Buber. This becomes clear also where he discusses the relation between the individual and the whole, in which he, regardless of the relationship of "Between", insists on the concept of "Non-Self" becoming oneness with the whole, according to the Buddhist view-point. None the less, it was his contribution toward Japanese thought that he treated the problem of "Between", how it was discussed in the history of Western philosophy from the Greek age to modern times.

The third way in my sketch of the introduction of Buber's thought into Japan is that of the post-war period. Up till that time, we knew the name of Buber only as the author of *Ich und Du*, and were not much aware of his career or his other works. But now the whole picture of Buber was shown to us, and the new era of Buber studies started. We owe this entirely to many well-known overseas scholars and specialists, whose works stimulated us and helped us in understanding the true face of Buber. One of the main achievements of this period was the work of the late Dr. Z. Watanabe, a well-known scholar on Biblical studies in Japan. One of his books, *The Interpretation of the Bible*, published in 1954, showed a most correct and profound understanding of Buber's thought from a Jewish-Christian point of view, unlike that of other philosophers previously mentioned. The main point of his work was to apply Buber's principle of "Ich und Du" to the interpretation of the Bible in order to understand more profoundly the true meaning revealed in it. No need to say that his achievement was also followed by some Japanese Christian theologians of today.

Another achievement of this period was that most of Buber's important works were translated into Japanese; at the same time, as mentioned already, a few monographs on Buber were also published by Japanese authors. The third achievement of this period was the encounter between Buber's thought and some of Buddhist philosophers. We have as yet no special works which were particularly devoted to this purpose, but in some of their essays and books they express a great deal of sympathy with Buber's thought. The reason for this will be that not only are they inspired by the deep religious insight of Buber, but they feel also some inner affinities with his thought, as will be discussed later. Furthermore, this also opened the way for dialogue among religions in Japan, especially between Christianity and Buddhism. In addition to these achievements, we cannot ignore the contribution of Buber's thought to Psychotherapy and Pedagogy in Japan, just as in most Western countries.

Up to this point, then, we have examined the philosophical climate, with regard to how Buber was introduced and how he was understood by Japanese philosophers. Now we must proceed further to a consideration of the significance of Buber for the Japanese mind through the comparative understanding of both similarities and dissimilarities between them.

III

First of all, we must say that there seems to be some similarities between Buber and Japanese thought in appearance, but they are essentially different from each other in their way of thinking. I will consider some examples along the line of the main concepts of Buber's philosophy. The first one will be "Ich und Du". This is a concept which has greatly fascinated the Japanese mind. We do not discriminate between "Du" and "Sie" in our vocabularly. Nevertheless, I think, Japan is one of the nations which can understand the meaning of the "Ich-Du" relationship most innately. Though it may be a mere feeling, somewhat simple and naive, we have often such experiences as this in our everyday life. And it is not only limited to communal life in families, villages, and towns, but is also extended to a stone, a tree, a bird, an animal etc.—that is, the whole of nature. Generally speaking, until recently this is the inner attitude which Japanese have continued to have toward everything. I say until recently, because today this kind of feeling as this has been completely destroyed here as elsewhere under the heavy pressure of the "It-World". We used to encounter in Japan numerous persons who might be called "Hasidim" of Japan, whose lives were quite simple, pious, and full of compassion, as Buber understood them.

We should realize, however, that their underlying philosophy was quite different from Buber's. The Japanese attitude toward the "Ich-Du" relationship came mostly from Buddhist philosophy, whose doctrine was to transcend all discrimination and opposition, sentient and non-sentient, into oneness with all-inclusive Buddhahood. In Buddhism all particular things are nothing but the manifestation of Buddhahood. So there is nothing disagreeable and offensive in this phenomenal world. Consequently, everything is welcomed with the feeling of compassion as the symbol of Buddhahood. In the case of Buber, however, although he recognizes the immanent power of God in everything in the world, his emphasis is rather put on the mutual, inter-personal fellowship between "I" and "the other", and not dissolution of "Self" into Buddhahood, nor becoming "Non-Self", as taught by Buddhism. And, moreover, what Buber strives for, is the realization of the "Ich-Du" relation in this concrete situation of society; in other words, the positive involvement in the suffering of the world, against the pessimistic view of life in Buddhism.

Another example which shows both similarities and dissimilarities, is the concept of "Ich und das ewige Du", which is very highly valued by the "Shin-Sect", one of the most influential sects of Japanese Buddhism. There is no need to say that Buddha originally meant the "Awakened One", the Self who awakens to his original Self, namely the True Self. But in the case of the "Shin-Sect", through keenly felt afflictions of religious experience of the founder, Shinran, it was rather personified just like the "Personal God" in Jewish-Christian tradition. Here the "Shin-Sect" shares the same sentiment with that of the personal relationship between "I" and the "eternal Thou", and are helped greatly by that in understanding the Founder's teaching at a deeper level. And, moreover, "Amida", their personified Buddha, was interpreted as the "Buddha of Salvation" who gives himself for the redemption of the distressed. In this sense, the teaching of the "Shin-Sect" if often compared with the Pauline doctrine of the "Salvation by Faith", rather than with that of Buber, who insists on the mutual co-operation between God and man. But it cannot be denied that there is a strong resemblance between their interpretation of "Amida" and Buber's idea of the "eternal Thou". In spite of such a similarity, there must be some fundamental difference between them. This difference concerns the nature of the personified "Amida". Is not "Amida" a mere symbolic expression of Buddhahood? If so, "Amida" will essentially be no other than impersonal "Buddhahood", which undoubtedly differs from Buber's idea of the "eternal Thou".

As a third example, I shall use the concept of "Dialogue", which is also most important in Buber's philosophy. Generally speaking, those who appreciate this concept of "Dialogue" belong to the circle of Zen Buddhists. It is rather natural that they should think highly of "Dialogue", because, unlike the "Shin-Sect", they try to achieve their final object, the "Enlightenment of Self", through "Dialogue" between a master and a monk, which shows apparently the same inner relationship between "Ich" and "Du". As Buber had already discussed the similarities and dissimilarities between Hassidism and Zen Buddhism in detail, there is no need to take them up here anew. (cf. *Die Chassidische Botschaft*) But one thing I should like to notice here is that for Zen Buddhism "Dialogue" itself is not necessarily its final object, but rather a means to attain its object: while for Buber "Dialogue" is itself the ultimate object. And, moreover, for Zen Buddhism it is mainly limited to the master-monk relationship, whereas for Buber we must say it is obviously all-inclusive.

Finally, I have to consider Buber's idea of "person" in connection with Japanese thought. According to Buber, both "I" and "Thou" in the context of the "Ich-Du" relation are also called "persons"; so his key word "I and Thou" will be exchanged in other words for the "person to person" relation. Here comes the importance of the idea of "person" or "personhood" in Buber's thought. But, as a whole, this concept of "person" is what we lack most in Japanese thought. So it is necessary to make some comments on this subject, because the situation in which we are placed is rather different from yours. As a matter of fact, Japan was slow in establishing the idea of real "personhood" in recent times because of her traditional, feudalistic social structure on the one hand, and the metaphysical thinking of "Non-Self" on the other. Some illustrations of this fact come immediately to mind. For example, the Japanese word for "I" is "Watakushi" or "Boku". The former, i.e. "Watakushi", means "private" in contrast to "public", while the latter, i.e. "Boku", means "servant"; so both of them originally lack the notion of the awakened "Self", in the sense of Western "Individualism". But this situation has changed, and after the end of the last War, it has become most urgent to establish the real "Self" as the true basis of the coming democratic society. This cannot mean merely to go back to the Individualism, or the Collectivism of former days, but forward to "Personalism" in the sense of dialogical, "person to person" fellowship, which can only transcend both of them, as anticipated by Buber himself. (cf. *Das Problem des Menschen*, S. 159 f.) In this sense, Buber's contribution to Japanese thought will be very great. In spite of this fact, however, the two modes of thought differ essentially from each other as to the problem of the ground on which "person" is founded. Then what is the difference between them?

Generally speaking, Japanese thought has accepted the idea of "person" from Western philosophy, especially from Kant and Lipps, which comprehends it as a moral subject. But such a concept of "person" has recently been refuted, because it is rather individualistic in its essence. The real "person" must consist, not in relation to oneself, but rather in relation to the other. So far Japanese thought does not disagree with Buber, on the contrary it has learned much from his thought. The fundamental difference consists in the following point; namely, Buber sees the "Personal God" at the bottom of human "person" as its existential ground, according to Jewish tradition; whereas what Japanese thought sees behind it is "Nothingness", according to Buddhist tradition. In truth, the idea of the "Personal God" is one of the most difficult ideas for the Japanese mind to understand. Because, in the way of Buddhistic thinking, both the idea of the "Personal God" as Creator, and the created world will become meaningless. Nothing exists before the phenomena of the world, as each phenomenal appearance is inevitably nothing but what it is. So Prof. K. Nishitani, an eminent follower of Nishida, and one of the distinguished philosophers in Japan today, calls such a philosophical stand-point "Impersonal Personalism", reducing the idea of the "Personal God" into the impersonal "Nothingness", which, he thinks, is more valid for Scienticism and Nihilism of today.

Buber's answer for this will be found in his comprehension of Eckhart, which is contrary to an interpretation on him, as has often been done by some of Buddhist philosophers, in which the idea of "Gottheit", or "Nichts" was explained as if it were the same with "Nothingness" of Buddhist philosophy. Buber, however, insisted that "Gottheit" should not be a mere object of contemplation, but "Person" itself which demands and orders. In this way, he tried to unify mysticism with ethics. (cf. "Gott and Seele" in *Die Chassidische Botschaft*)

Although Japanese thought *saw* "Nothingness" at the bottom of the phenomenal world, Buber heard the voiceless voice of God who addressed him from the abyss of "Nothingness", and felt His Presence in himself and in the world as well. The difference between "seeing" and "hearing" in connection with the understanding of the ultimate reality, is what Buber made clear as elsewhere as the difference between Greek thought and Jewish thought, but this can be applied also to the difference between Japanese thought and that of Buber.

IV

This is a rough description of how Buber was accepted and confronted with Japanese thought. This attitude of Japanese thought toward Buber will also be applicable to Jewish-Christian thought as a whole. The fundamental difference between them will consist in the distinction between the idea of the "Personal God" and that of "Nothingness". This may be the most essential problem of philosophy from ancient times, and a solution can hardly be found.

Generally speaking, it has been settled in Japanese thought that, so far as God is considered to be "Being", even if it may be the highest, it must inevitably be included by "Nothingness" which transcends all the beings; nevertheless this "Nothingness" does not merely mean the negation of beings, but rather the "place" where all beings can be awakened to their true "Self"; and only through this will the actual relationship of "Ich und Du" be realized.

But we have to say that there are involved at least two fundamental problems. The one concerning the "Personal God" as "Being"; and the other the "Awakening of Self". First, is God really "Being" as understood by Japanese thought? If so, in what sense? Such an interpretation of God as "Being" chiefly depends on their misunderstanding of Western philosophy, which has sometimes confused Jewish thought with Greek. As it is often pointed out, the definition of God as "Being" came probably from the Septuaginta, in which God was named as "Being" (ho on) in Greek (Ex. 3:14), but its Greek meaning is quite different from the original Hebrew word "haya". This Hebrew word means not simply to be, but to become, to work, and to happen as well. (cf. Boman, and others). So God must be by no means interpreted as sheer "Being" in terms of Greek philosophy. This is also the point which Buber made clear in his Biblical studies. Therefore, the idea of God as "Being" must be re-examined radically from its basis. In Japan the late Prof. T. Ariga, former Professor of Christianity at Kyoto University, independently expressed nearly the same idea, and tried to establish a new concept of "Hayatologia" against "Ontologia" of Greek thinking. According to him, Hebrew-Christian God is not simply "Being", but the active, living God, who reveals Himself to man as well as to the world; only from this point can the doctrine of both divine creation and divine providence be fully understood.

So this will also lead us to the second problem. If the "Awakening to the true Self" means the realization of the impersonal "Non-Self", how can the personal relationship of "Ich und Du" come out of it? Moreover, how can such "Non-Self" be realized in oneself? Will it be by means of "Self-Enlightenment", or by means of "Encounter of Self with the 'eternal Thou', namely with the living, personal God"? Here we confront the most essential problem of either "Non-Self", or the "eternal Thou". In some sense, there seems to be correlation between them, because it is said that without becoming "Non-Self" it will be impossible for "I" to accept "Thou" and establish real relationship between "I" and "Thou". But, according to Buber, in the case of "None-Self"—whether it may be the absorption of "Self" into the Absolute, or the identification of "Self" with the Absolute—"I" is essentially deprived of the other to which it is to be related. (cf. *Ich und Du*, Dritter Teil) On the contrary, the establishment of the "Ich-Du" relationship can be realized only when "Ich" and "Du" interrelate with each other, retaining themselves as the most authentic, yet independent "persons". And this "person to person" relationship will become reality for each only by being addressed, being caught, being loved, and being lived by the "eternal Thou"; in other words, only by the "Enlightenment through the Other", not through the monological relation of "I" to oneself.

This is the problem which Japanese thought, in encounter with Buber, must grapple with. But this confrontation is not an opposition only for the sake of opposition. What Japanese thought is looking for, is the possibility of "Dialogue" between them, by which, I hope, she will realize herself more deeply, and grow stronger, especially in treating issues related to "personhood".

Discussion Following Yoshimori Hiraishi's Lecture*

W. BOETTCHER

He commented about the relationship between Nishida and Taki-zawa, a Japanese philosopher and theologian of today, that, when Takizawa was young, Nishida suggested him to go to Karl Barth for further studies, not to Heidegger, nor to Brunner, nor to Gogarten, and also that Takizawa came to Buber by a detour of Karl Barth, because his central idea of "Immanuel" showed the Buber's way of thinking in its basis, so far as it was interpreted as "eine ursprungliche Beziehung und Einheit von Gott und Mensch". Then he asked two questions, the one concerning the idea of "Topos", or "Place", which he interpreted as the "Land of Enlightenment (Satori) in terms of "Shinran", an analogical concept of the "Kingdom of God" in Jewish thought, the other about the idea of "Zwischenraum". My answer to the former is that the idea of "Topos", or "Place" in Nishida's philosophy may be interpreted in this way in a derived and deduced manner, but I am not sure whether it is the same with the idea of the "Place of Enlightenment", or not.

As to the latter, my answer is following. The Japanese word for "Zwischenraum" has two calling names, although we use the same Chinese character. In one way, it is called "Ma". "Ma" is the concept which has played an important role both in Japanese music and painting. It signifies a method of expression by means of negation, namely, in the case of music, it means "Pause", and in the case of painting, "Empty Space". Both of them, "Pause" and "Empty Space", are thought to make expression more vivid, and more effective in music and painting. And it is also the way of thinking which has appeared in every-day Japanese life, I think. The other calling is "Aida", which signifies primarily "Between", or "Person to Person Relationship". This is the concept which is particular to Buber's philosophy.

B. CASPER

His question is if there are philosophical investigations about the question of what "Buddha Amida" means, in connection with the

---

*Prof. Hiraishi edited the discussion following his lecture.

problem of confrontation between Jewish thought and Christianity on the one side, and Buddhistic thought on the other side, the concept of "Buddhahood" being equivalent to that of Greek philosophy. Next is my answer to the question. I am not sure if the idea of "Buddhahood", that is, the nature of becoming an enlightened one which every human being has primarily in himself, is the concept equivalent to that of Greek philosophy. But as a matter of fact, lots of Buddhist philosophers in Japan have been much influenced by Western philosophy, and tried to explain Buddhist thought from its standpoint. But, I wonder how can "Dialogue" be realized between Buddhism and Jewish and Christian thought. That will be our urgent future problem.

C. VERNOF

He suggested that Buber's attempt to identify Judaism with the Oriental thought could be made not only in terms of "Teaching", as Prof. Wood just explained, but also in terms of category of individuation, or the importance of the individual, which Buber understands, according to him, as the individual in terms of essence in Greek philosophy. My answer is as follows: I am not sure if the notion of the individual in terms of essence has any affinity with the notion of "Non-Ego" of the Oriental thought, or not. In some sense, perhaps, they do. But, it seems to me that what Buber primarily emphasized is the idea of the individual as the concrete existence, and this is plainly against the Oriental thought which often urges the unification, or absorption of the individual with or into the Universal. Although in the case of *Zen*, they seem to pay serious attention to the Concrete, but it is not the attention for the sake of the Concrete, but merely an expedient to attain to "Satori" (Enlightenment), if I understand correctly. This obviously differs from the standpoint of Buber.

M. FRIEDMAN

When Buber wrote his doctoral dissertation in 1904, he was much concerned with Aristotelianism, but the notion of essence in terms of Greek philosophy is primarily far from Buber. There are certain mysticisms of the particular, which are not necessarily restricted only to the Orient. In fact, there is a great deal of affinity between Hasidism and Zen, as Buber himself recognized. But he felt that *Zen* emphasized the particular for the sake of getting beyond intellectual abstractions, and realizing the Buddha-Nature within.

RELIGIOUS THOUGHT

Martin Buber's Approach to Comparative Religion

MAURICE FRIEDMAN

In his note to the English edition of his classic work *Religion in Essence and Manifestation* the distinguished phenomenologist of religion Gerardius van der Leeuw expressed regret that he had not been able to incorporate "research of the first order of importance and value" done, since the appearance of the German edition, by Martin Buber, Bronislaw Malinowski, and R. R. Marret.[1] What, we might ask, can Buber's approach contribute to the excellent groundwork that has been laid by scholars such as van der Leeuw and my own great teacher Joachim Wach to the phenomenological study of the comparative history of religion?

The "Eternal Thou"

At its simplest, we can answer: the understanding of religious symbols, myths, and manifestations as unique products of our dialogue with what Buber calls the "eternal Thou", rather than as divine expression or human projection. So far from being opposites, dialogue and the unique necessarily go together. It is only in dialogue that we can grasp that true uniqueness which is not a product of comparison but of the relation to an event, person, situation, or thing in itself and for its own sake.

The "eternal Thou" did not mean "God" for Buber. "God" meant the "eternal Thou." The "eternal Thou" was not just another, up-to-date way of reintroducing the God of the philosophers, the metaphysicians, and the theologians—the God whose existence could be proved and whose nature and attributes could be described as he is in himself apart from our relation to him. It was the reality of the "between," of the meeting itself, and there and nowhere else did Buber find the unconditioned which no fathoming of the self or soaring into metaphysical heights could reveal.

367

I-Thou as Mutual Knowing: Dialogue and the Unique

Many philosophers and theologians have misunderstood Buber to suggest that he allows no room for error in the I-Thou knowing, which would mean that Buber asserts a pure I-Thou relationship unmixed and unmixable with I-It. Focussing on the nature of what one relates to rather than the nature of the relationship, they fail to understand Buber's "absolute Person" who *is* not a person but becomes one, so to speak, in man's personal meeting with him. Knowing nothing of that bond of the absolute and the particular of which Buber speaks in *Eclipse of God,* they imagine a scale of ever-purer and ever-more-general I-Thou relationships leading to some mythical totally pure I-Thou relationship with God.[2] No one can understand the "eternal Thou" who imagines that it is some separate relationship that is only analogous to or compatible with, rather than directly given through the I-Thou relationship between man and man and that with nature and art. That the lines of I-Thou relationships "intersect in the eternal Thou is grounded in the fact that the man who says Thou ultimately means his eternal Thou."[3]

Buber rejects with equal force a reason that could be set in opposition to faith and a faith that could be set in opposition to reason, and for the same reason: both are bastions of the world of It, both are flight from life lived in the holy insecurity of the meeting with the unique present. Religion is lived *complexio oppositorum* in which every religious statement is a risk pointing to the situation in which God only shows himself in the events of human existence. The life of faith is no book of rules, wrote Buber in "Dialogue." It begins when the dictionary is put down. Some of Buber's critics have assumed that this means that he conceives of dialogue without any content. This "dialogue without content" criticism is by no means uncommon, quite the reverse—so much so, indeed, that in my Introduction to *A Believing Humanism: Gleanings* I wrote:

> Some of Buber's critics have stated that his faith is pure relationship without content—a misunderstanding which is only possible for those who have never grasped Buber's existentialism of dialogue as "grounded on the certainty that meaning of existence is open and accessible in the actual lived concrete." This is not, of course, the content of absolute objective principles, whether in the form of a theological creed or of Platonic truths . . . It is rather the wholly particular content of each moment of lived dialogue in which the reality one meets is neither subjectivized nor objectivized but *responded* to.[4]

In his "Replies to My Critics" in *The Philosophy of Martin Buber* Buber himself wrote:

> It is for me of the highest importance that the dialogue have a content. Only this content is so much the more important, the more concrete, the more concretizing it is, the more it does justice to the unique, the coming to be, the formed, and is also able to incorporate in it the most spiritual, not metaphorically but in reality, because the spirit seeks the body and lets speech help find it. This great concreteness, however, does not belong to the isolated word in the dictionary, where speech only shows us its general side, its applicability, but to the word in its living context of genuine conversation, of genuine poetry, of genuine philosophy; there first does it disclose to us the unique.[5]

Dialogue, Uniqueness, and Comparative Religion

At first glance Buber's emphasis on the uniqueness of the dialogue with the "eternal Thou" might seem incompatible with any approach at all to the comparative history of religion. A second glance affords deeper insight. "Comparative" means contrast as well as comparison. Buber uses the category of the "unique" to set limits to the tendency of comparative religionists, from Frazer to Mircea Eliade, to subsume all data under universal patterns or Jungian archetypes. Most of Buber's biblical criticism is of this nature. A third level opens itself to us if we realize that uniqueness and dialogue are corollaries, that the dialogue with the unique in every religion is the prerequisite both to understanding that phenomenon in itself and to any attempt to subsume it under ideal types and compare it with other phenomena. What we compare are not the phenomena in themselves but the phenomena as we see them. This is indeed the central message of phenomenology—that the phenomenon is the product of the relation between the seer and the seen and that we must bracket any supposed objective reality of the phenomenon apart from anyone's knowing it. If Buber is not, in fact, a Husserlian phenomenologist, it is because he is more radical than Husserl in just this respect: namely that he leaves room for a uniqueness and otherness that Husserl does not, a uniqueness that can only be known in dialogue and of which we cannot speak as it is "in itself." This and nothing else is the meaning of the "eternal Thou," which does not stand for God, or the Absolute, in some metaphysical sense but for our unique dialogue with an Absolute that cannot be known in itself.

The Divine Kingship of Israel versus the Kingly Ideology of the Swedish School

The best illustration of the way in which Buber uses the comparative history of religion in order to bring out the uniqueness of the dialogue with the eternal Thou is his study of the origins of messianism in his book *The Kingship of God*. To put forward the idea of a direct theocracy or theopolitical covenant Buber had to range through the whole ancient Oriental treatment of God as King in general and the West Semitic idea of the tribal God, or *malk*, in particular. And he had to do this in the face of the dominant Wellhausen and Mowinckel approaches that used similar comparisons to dissolve any claim to uniqueness on the part of the Hebrew Bible. Buber saw the uniqueness of the divine kingship of Israel not in the development of ideas but "in the three-dimensionality of a living fact of folk history." In the Varuna of the Vedas, in Ahura Mazda of Zoroastrianism, in the divine kingship of Egypt and still more Babylon, acknowledgement of a lord took place without there being any actual lordship over the actual community. "Only in ancient Israel, so far as I see, is there—certainly not as ruling state of mind, but as a clear, manifest tendency of mind advocated with the passion of the spiritual man—this sublime realism which wants *totally* to deal seriously with faith." This paradox of Israel appears in the pre-state period as the conception of a direct theocracy and in the early-state period as the conception of an indirect, but still genuine theocracy.[6]

Buber bases this claim to uniqueness in part on insight possessed by the general history of religion for a long time, one which "Old Testament scholarship dares not close its eyes to": that the question of origin of a specific piety cannot be derived from another historical sphere where one imagines one need not ask the question of origin.

> For centuries people have wanted to derive the religious achievement which is connected with the name of Moses from Egypt, of whose religion they knew all sorts of things; but the more they discovered about it, the more futile the undertaking proved to be. Since then derivation from the Kenites has taken its place, of whose religion they know nothing at all.[7]

Buber adduces a second principle of the history of religions in connection with the objection that "the malk-idea stands in indissoluable connection with the naturalistic myth of the ancient Orient, the kingly ideology put forward by the Swedish School, and hence is a nature-mythical schema that contradicts the fundamental essence of the religion of Israel." This principle is a dialectical one of comparison and contrast between individualities and generalities through which, again, the uniqueness of every great religion arises before a background which resembles it typologically but which nevertheless contrasts decisively. "In the concrete process of its origin it is once-for-all and individual as well as in its concrete appearance; but the incomparable in it can be scientifically grasped only from the point of view of the comparable." The religious traditions of the events themselves, as visualized in faith, alone makes this eminently historical approach possible.

The Leader of the Way versus Oriental Nature Mysticism

Buber illustrates the religious tradition of the events themselves from the relation of the God who stands to the wandering host which is his people, or 'am, in the relationship of leader of its marches, lawgiver, arbitrator and giver of decisions. This malk-idea is separated both in its origin and nature from ancient oriental nature mysticism, however many elements it assimilated from its contacts with it in the course of its history:

> If an Egyptian, Babylonian, Phoenician god is called 'king', he is called thus either as one of the princes of the gods or also as the highest lord of the state of the gods, in addition doubtless also as Kosmokrator, and then probably also as ruler of the state for which the human kind represents him as his 'son'. In Israel in the sphere of the exodus history JHWH is designated as melekh, that is, as the one who goes on ahead of the wandering people; in the mature state He is venerated, to be sure, as the proclaimed world-ruler of heaven and earth and adopts the crown prince as His 'son' and designated regent in Jerusalem, but still in eschatological promise (Micah 2:13) He strides, as formerly, along before the delivered bands as malk.[8]

In connection with the human leader too Buber points to "a religio-historical uniqueness in the strictest sense: the ever and again realized, but always intended relation of dialogical exclusiveness between the One who leads and those who are led." Here too the divine-dialogue partner of the patriarch or prophet is worshipped by Israel as its melekh, its way-determiner. Even where a more historical god, a so-called "bringer of salvation," supplants the preponderantly nature one, as in the Babylonian creation epic in which the gods proclaim Marduk as king before he enters the fight against the powers of the abyss, this is no true parallel; for the reverence is still for a lord of heaven on the part of those cultically bound to him but not also for the heavenly lord of an earthly community of his people.[9]

The Sinai Covenant versus the Cosmic King

It is to the Sinai Covenant in particular that Buber points for the unconditioned reciprocity between leader and led which he finds nowhere else in other religions and nowhere else in Biblical religion. The sacral-legal act of reciprocity is witnessed in a ceremony between God and man for which none of the parallels adduced by the comparative science of religion offers a real correspondence. In the Bible too only in the Sinai covenant "is a holy action performed which *institutes sacramentally a reciprocity between the One above and one below.*" This is not a mere matter of designations. On the contrary, the very heart of religious reality if determined by this difference; for the Cosmic King still leaves the world essentially out of his province whereas the demand of the Kingship of God in Israel is precisely to bring every aspect of life—social, political, economic, communal, family, and personal-under the rule of God.

> The unconditioned claim of the divine Kingship is recognized at the point when the people proclaims JHWH Himself as King, Him alone and directly (Exodus 15:18), and JHWH Himself enters upon the kingly reign (19:6). He is not content to be 'God' in the religious sense. He does not want to surrender to a man that which is not 'God's', the rule over the entire actuality of worldly life: this very rule He lays claim to and enters upon it; for there is nothing which is not God's. He will apportion to the one, for ever and ever chosen by Him, his tasks, but naked power without a situationally related task He does not wish to bestow. He makes known His will first of all as constitution—not constitution of cult and custom only, also of economy and society—He will proclaim it again and again to the changing generations, certainly but simply as reply to a question, institutionally through priestly mouth, above all, however, in the freedom of His surging spirit, through every one whom His spirit seizes. *The separation of religion and politics which stretches through history is here overcome in real paradox.*[10]

This dialogical exclusiveness in no way means that the God of Israel whom the prophets proclaim as the only God is only the God of Israel. God is God of the peoples, the one who has *led* every wandering people, like Israel, into a "good" land. "Did I not bring Israel out of the land of Egypt—/and the Philistines from Caphtor/and the Syrians from Kir?" (Amos 9:7) Yet even there where it is explained unmistakably that JHWH is not the God of a tribe, he is proclaimed for ever and ever God of the tribe—"You only have I known." "So strong, so central in JHWH's manifestation is the character of the God walking-on-before, the leading God, the *melekh*."[11]

"Monotheism" versus the God of Moses

Buber's concern with the comparative *and* with the unique is also central to his book *Moses*. In the Preface to *Moses* Buber holds that what is important is not the familiar category of Monotheism but "the way in which this Unity is viewed and experienced, and whether one stands to it in an exclusive relationship which shapes all other relations and thereby the whole order of life." "The universal sun-god of the imperialist 'Monotheism' of Amenhotep IV," wrote Buber in implicit rejection of Freud, "is incomparably closer to the national sun-god of the ancient Egyptian Pantheon than to the God of early Israel, which some have endeavoured to derive from him." The God of Moses is the God of the way, the leader and advance guard who acts at the level of history on the people and between the peoples.[12] Buber claims this same uniqueness for Moses, whose success in wrestling with Pharaoh proves that he is something more than a prophet. "A historical mystery always means a relation between a super-personal fate and a person, and particularly that which is atypical in a person, that by which the person does not belong to his type." Similarly, Israel's acceptance of the Decalogue as its "Constitution" Buber characterizes as "a unique event in human history"; for here only did the decisive process of crystallization of a people come about on a religious basis. "Irrespective of the importance of the typological view of phenomena in the history of the spirit, the latter, just because it is history, also contains the atypical, the unique in the most precise sense." Again in connection with the scriptural report that the Israelites made the Ark in the wilderness, Buber asserts that "it is a basic law of methodology not to permit the 'firm letter' to be broken down by any general hypothesis based on the comparative history of culture; as long as what is said in that text is historically possible."[13]

The God of Nature and the God of History

Buber's discussion of the God of nature and the God of history in *Moses* is particularly significant because of its dialectical treatment of the comparative and the unique. Already in *The Kingship of God*, in connection with the hypothesis that Moses took over the nature God of his Kenite father-in-law Jethro, Buber observed that neither Israel nor the Kenites is converted to the God of the other: "Israel observes that its folk-God also rules the earthpowers; the Kenites recognize that their mountain or mountain-fire God rescues and guides tribes. The divine image of both grows. Instead of one image which is only a god of nature and one which is only a god of history, there dawns the form of the One who is the lord of nature and the lord of history." In *Moses* Buber puts this on a still broader comparative basis. In the Biblical, which is a history religion, there is no Nature in the Greek, the Chinese, or the modern Occidental sense. "What is shown us of Nature is stamped by History. Even the work of creation has a historical tone," especially during the historical period. Later in *Moses* this is stated more subtly and dialectically: "He is the history God, which He is, only when He is not localized in Nature; and precisely because He makes use of everything potentially visible in Nature, every kind of natural existence, for His manifestation."[14] This distinction between the nature God and the God of history Buber ties in with his distinction between the Cosmic King and the *melekh* of Israel:

> The Babylonian divine thrones are nature symbols, that of Israel is a history symbol; and the tablets with the "I" of the God who has led the people out of Egypt are an inseparable part of it. Only in the period of the State, when the theo-political realism succumbed to the influence of the dynastic principle and the Kingdom of YHVH was transfigured and subtilized into a cosmic one lacking all direct binding force, did the nature symbolism prevail; since the aim then was to abstract living history from the domain of the Kingdom of God.[15]

The Concrete Event

In *The Prophetic Faith* Buber states one further, related principle for his approach to the comparative study of religion—the criterion which he describes as the *uniqueness of the fact*. This criterion must be used carefully and with scientific intuition that seeks after the *concreteness* at the basis of an evidence and thereby approaches the real fact.

> Naturally we do not by this learn the real course of an historic event, but we do learn that in a definite age in a definite circle or tribe or people an actual relationship appeared between the believer and that in which he believes, a unique relationship and according to our perception, at a definite stage too, which also has to be designated unique, a relationship which embodies itself in a concrete event, which continues to operate concretely.[16]

Ideal Types: Emuna versus Pistis, Devotio versus Gnosis

Two types of Faith, the last of Buber's series of books on Biblical faith and the origins of messianism, at first appears problematic and even contradictory in the light of Buber's repeated assertions of uniqueness. For here Buber declares that while there are very many contents of faith, there are only two basic forms of faith, a relationship of trust depending upon a contact of my entire being with the one in whom I trust and a relationship of acknowledging depending upon the acceptance by my entire being of what I acknowledge to be true. What is more, Buber finds the classic example of the former type of faith, which he calls *emuna*, in the early period of Israel and of the second, which he calls *pistis*, in the early period of Christianity. He recognizes, to be sure, that the contact in trust leads naturally to the acceptance of what proceeds from the one whom I trust and that the acceptance of the truth acknowledged by me can lead to contact with the one whom it proclaims. "But in the former instance it is the existent contact which is primary, in the latter the acceptance accomplished." He also recognizes here, as with all the typologies he uses in his thought, that in practice the types are mixed. Each of the two types of faith has extended its roots into the other camp. Buber holds, in fact, that in the teachings of Jesus himself, as we know them from the early texts of the gospels, the genuine Jewish principle is manifest, as a result of which the desire of Christians to return to the pure teaching of Jesus has often resulted in an "unconscious colloquy with genuine Judaism."[17] These qualifications, plus his statement that "every apologetic tendency is far from my purpose," were lost sight of by the many Christian theologians who accused Buber of attacking Christianity. From the other side Gershom Scholem has designated *Two Types of Faith* as Buber's "weakest book," in part, no doubt, because of the sharpening of the distinction between what Buber later called *devotio* and gnosis.

This typology of "*devotio* versus gnosis" was already implicit at the heart of Buber's Hasidic chronicle-novel *For the Sake of Heaven,* and it stands in close relationship with his contrast between the "prophetic" and the "apocalyptic." But it received its explicit formulation in Buber's dialogue with Rudolf Pannwitz, who in an essay on Buber's Hasidism accused Buber of stating the issues between Judaism and Christianity to the disadvantage of the latter. In his reply Buber disclaimed this specific intention as well as any concern in general with issues of this sort and in so doing set important limits to the proper province of *comparative* religion:

> Religions are mansions into which the spirit of man is fit in order that it might not break forth and burst open its world. Each of them has its origin in a particular revelation and its goal in the overcoming of all particularity. Each represents the universality of its mystery in myth and rite and thus reserves it for those who live in it. Therefore, to compare one religion with another, valuing and devaluing, is always an undertaking contrary to being and sense: one's own temple building which can be known from within the innermost shrine compared with the external aspect of the alien temple as it offers itself to the attentive observer. One may only compare the corresponding parts of the buildings according to structure, function and connection with one another, honestly, but never valuing: because their relationship to the ever invisible Sanctissimum is concealed.[18]

Emuna and *pistis, devotio* and gnosis Buber sees as ideal types that make it possible to approach the decisive issue *within* Judaism and *within* Christianity.

Houses of Exile

In the editorial that he wrote for the first issue of *Die Kreatur* in 1926—the journal that broke new ground by being coedited by a believing Catholic, Protestant, and Jew—Buber said almost the same thing. Borrowing a metaphor from his late friend Florens Christian Rang, Buber described each of the religions as in exile and only God as able to deliver them from this exile. Yet a greeting may come from one house of exile to the other. For the same reason Buber could not agree with his friends Franz Rosenzweig and Hugo Bergmann who spoke of the revelations to Israel and the Church as equally valid. "I stand here before a mystery that I do not know from within, but before which I shudder with awe," said Buber in 1956. "I cannot believe that here something Satanic happened; it is a divine mystery in which we cannot take part." At another time he pictured the adherents of the different religions and confessions as climbing on an iceberg that gets smaller at the top. "We are on different sides of this mountain, but is is already given us to see one another from afar."[19]

In one of the fragments on revelation that Buber preserved in his "Gleanings" he elaborated on the metaphor of exile. No religion is a piece of heaven come down to earth. Each represents the relationship of a particular human community as such to the Absolute.

> Each religion is a house of the human soul longing for God, a house with windows and without a door; I need only open a window and God's light penetrates; but if I make a hole in the wall and break out, then I have not only become houseless but a cold light surrounds me that is not the light of the living God. Each religion is an exile into which man is driven; . . . in his relationship to God he is separated from the men of other communities; and not sooner than the redemption of the world can we be liberated from the exiles and brought into the common world of God. But the religions . . . call to one another greetings from exile to exile, from house to house through the open windows.

Each religion must renounce its claim to be God's house on earth and content itself with being a house of the men who are turned toward the same purpose of God—a house with windows.[20]

The Limits and Validity of Scientific Research

Persons of different faiths can cooperate in the science of religion if they recognize that the divine revelation can never be an object of scientific research but is the reality which limits that research and thereby is its mainstay, its strength-giving origin, and its direction-giving goal. A science of religion which joins itself to a living knowledge about revelation from within this reality can provide a kind of knowledge that the general science of religion cannot provide. But it must do this only in order to be able to penetrate to the unique reality of the other religions and to do it justice. Here comparing the inner and the outer aspect of one's own religion instructs us how great an exertion of penetration and making imaginatively present is needed in order to come so close to the inner reality of another religion that we can legitimately deal with it scientifically. Here too a boundary is set. "The innermost reality of a religion, its all-holiest and all-realest, is only accessible to the consecrated." This boundary is identical with the mystery of the multiplicity of the religions.[21]

In two of his mature essays dealing with the interpretation of Hasidism, Buber attempted just such an imaginative making present of other religions in order to compare them scientifically with Hasidism. In the first, "God and the Soul," Buber makes a legitimate distinction between those theistic mysticisms which preserve the duality of I and Thou and the non-theistic ones that do not and carries this forward to a significant contrast between the mysticism of Sankara and Meister Eckhart in which the Godhead is removed from human relationship and that of the Maggid of Mezritch, in which it is precisely the Godhead which enters into relationship with us, as a father limits himself to be able to teach a child.[22] In the second, "The Place of Hasidism in the History of Religion," Buber undertakes an extended comparison and contrast between Hasidism and a non-theistic mysticism, Zen Buddhism. In reply to Gershom Scholem's criticism of his reliance on Hasidic legends written down fifty years after the formal doctrines, Buber cites Hasidism, Taoism, and Zen as three mysticisms in which the oral legends reveal the life of the mystics more faithfully than the formal teachings. In "The Place of Hasidism" too Buber juxtaposes Hasidic and Zen tales to show the importance of the present moment, the transmission of the teaching through the central relation between teacher and disciple, and the concern for the particular.

Hasidism and Zen

Buber's *contrast* between Hasidism and Zen is subtler and more problematic. The concern for the particular in Zen, according to

Buber, is essentially a way of getting away from intellectualism in order to understand the Buddha nature in oneself; whereas Hasidism is concerned with the created task of redeeming those people, animals, and things with which one has to do. Hasidism is concerned with what takes place *between* us and the things of this world, Zen with the nonconceptual nature of things as a symbol of the absolute which is superior to all concepts.[23] It is ironic that one of the attacks that Scholem and Rivka Schatz-Uffenheimer make on Buber's interpretation of Hasidism is on a closely similar point. They claim that the Hasidim were not concerned with the things for their own sakes but were interested in the particular only to nullify it, that they really were Gnostics trying to get away from the world in order to cleave to the transcendent. Buber's response to this, to which Scholem does not even allude in his reply, is that there were two streams within Hasidism—one that of the founder, the Baal Shem Tov, in which the hallowing of the everyday for its own sake is emphasized; the other, that of his great disciple the Maggid of Mezritch, in which the particular is mainly of importance as a stage of a dialectical process in which it is finally nullified in order to reach the transcendent.[24]

If we must qualify somewhat Buber's comparison and contrast from the side of Hasidism to limit it to that tendency toward the hallowing of the everyday that stems from the Baal Shem Tov, we must also qualify it from the side of Zen. We may question whether Buber has made Zen imaginatively present from within sufficiently to legitimate the contrast that he has made with Hasidism. This contrast rests on the assumption that in Zen the Buddha nature is *inside* oneself, and the texts do not bear this out. Religion is often taken to be a movement away from mundane reality to the spirit floating above it. Zen Buddhism says no such movement is possible: there is only the one spirit-sense reality. The "one" and the "ten thousand things" are identical, "nirvana is samsara." It is our minds that bifurcate existence into body and spirit, one and many. We cannot overcome our existential dilemma by fleeing from the many to the one; for this very attempt to overcome dualism leads us to still another dualism—that of the one as opposed to the many. We must instead go right to the concrete particular which at the same time is the Buddha Nature. There is no process here of abstracting from concrete reality, of uncovering the essence and shucking off this world. The very particularity of things is the only means through which we can attain enlightenment. The Buddha Nature, the particulars, and the no-particulars are all one reality.[25] This nondual duality is still not *dialogue* with the other in its otherness, as in Buber's interpretation of Hasidism, but Hasidism and Zen are closer than Buber's contrast suggested. This is not to quarrel with Buber's conclusion that Hasidism explodes the familiar view of mysticism because it is that manifestation of the history of religion in which "the line of inner illumination and the line of revelation, that of the moment beyond time and that of historical time," meet in full clarity.

The Comparative and the Unique

Martin Buber's approach to the comparative history of religion does not seek for some universal essence in metaphysics, experience, or timeless myth but guards the particularity and the uniqueness of each tradition while bringing them into meaningful connection with one another. The dialogue with the eternal Thou means in every case the wholly concrete event apprehended in the first instance in itself, enregistered in the second in the ideal types which preserve a meaningful dialectic between the general and the particular, and only on the ground of these two instances compared and contrasted with other events, phenomena, and ideal types. Only thus can the comparative history of religion remain both scientific and true to its subject. Only thus can the validity *and* the limitations of comparative scholarship be ascertained in each field and each subject within that field. *This* contribution to the methodology of comparative religion has yet to be adequately taken into account and assessed by today's historians of religion.

Discussion Following Maurice Friedman's Lecture

D. MOORE

Prof. Friedman, I would like a clarification of your statement that some people misinterpret Buber by looking on the relationship with the eternal Thou as something separate from the other I-Thou relationships of our life. I am not clear as to what exactly you mean by that. Buber refers to man's relationship with the eternal Thou as the absolute, pure unconditional relationship and says that all the other relationships of our lives lead to this one absolute or universal relationship. Then too in *Philosophical Interrogations*, you ask a similar question, namely if there could be such a thing as a direct relationship with the eternal Thou which would not be through the finite Thou's of our life. I got the impression from your speech that there is almost an identity of the eternal Thou with any finite Thou.

M. FRIEDMAN

Some people interpret Buber as looking on the relationships to the eternal Thou as separate from and purer than that to the finite Thou's. I am not denying, in Buber's name or my own, that there is a direct relationship to the eternal Thou. What Buber was saying in response to my question in *Philosophical Interrogations* was that even the lonely hermit is not cut off from the human Thou's that made him. In the Postscript to *I and Thou*, which Buber wrote in response to questions that I asked, Buber claimed that we can bring all of our relations to our fellow human beings and to the rest of nature into our relation to the eternal Thou.

You use one word which I would not accept and which I do not think I ever wrote, and that is that there is a pure relationship to the eternal Thou. In response to a statement of Malcolm Diamond's Buber said: "I am really not very interested in perfection. I am only interested in a realistic meliorism." The mix is a reality with which we live. As Buber said in his "Report on Two Talks", "We cannot cleanse and purify the name of God, but we can set it over an hour of great care".

My paper can, of course, be misinterpreted, to mean only the I-

Thou relationship with man. The I-Thou relationship can be with nature and with art, and it can also be in our lonely moments of prayer. But the American Jewish theologian Will Herberg distorted it when he made out of it a triangle with a third relationship to the eternal Thou which is interdependent with that to the finite Thou's but is not through this Thou's. I cannot agree with this because we never in fact, leave the world for somewhere else. We are in our existence. If we try to cut our I-Thou relationship down to anything less than the line that surrounds our whole concrete existence, then, as Buber said in his critique of Kierkegaard in "The Question to the Single One", we are injuring that relationship and we are not meeting the real God.

For myself, I would say that the eternal Thou is that which is eternally Thou, the reality of the present. The particular form with which I identify the meaning of my meeting with the Thou changes. But I am not talking of some universal essence of Thou. What I mean rather is that it wholly concretely becomes real again and again in the present, and that present *is* the present in which we live, the present which we have.

In those same *Philosophical Interrogations* I quoted a passage from *I and Thou* where Buber speaks of a great double movement away from the cosmos and back to the cosmos, in which the potential relations to the Thou remain actual. "Can we deduce from this," I asked, "that God has an I-Thou relationship even to what is It to us?" "I can see by words of mine that are quoted here", Buber responded to me, "that, prompted by the duties of the heart, I have said perhaps even more than I should, and I hesitate to add one single word further." In *I and Thou* Buber was, in fact, close to a metacosmic, metaphysical position, but as he went on in life he became more and more concrete.

Notes

MAURICE FRIEDMAN

1. G. G. Van der Leeuw, *Religion in Essence and Manifestation. A Study in Phenomenology*, Vol. I, trans. by J. E. Turner (New York: Harper Torchbooks, 1963), "Author's Note to the English Edition" (1937), p. vi.

2. See, for example, Ronald W. Hepburn, *Christianity and Paradox. Critical Studies in Twentieth Century Theology* (London: Watts, 1958, 1966), Chaps. 3 & 4, pp. 24-59. Malcolm Diamond, author of *Martin Buber: Jewish Existentialist* takes Hepburn's critique seriously and on the basis of it, as he wrote Buber, turned away from his earlier affinity with Buber's philosophy and published a sharply critical reappraisal in *Judaism*. For a full-scale discussion of Hepburn's critique, see Maurice Friedman, "Revelation and Reason in Buber's Philosophy of Religion," *Bucknell Review*, Winter 1971, pp. 74-76.

3. Sydney and Beatrice Rome, editors, *Philosophical Interrogations* (New York: Harper Torchbooks, 1970), "Martin Buber" section, conducted by Maurice Friedman, Chap. 7—"Evil," Buber's reply, p. 114.

4. Martin Buber, *A Believing Humanism: Gleanings*, trans. with an Introduction and Explanatory Comments by Maurice Friedman (New York: Simon Schuster, 1968), Maurice Friedman, "Martin Buber's Credo," p. 22.

5. Paul Arthur Schilpp and Maurice Friedman, editors, *The Philosophy of Martin Buber* volume of *The Library of Living Philosophers* (LaSalle, Illinois: Open Court; London: Cambridge University Press, 1967), Martin Buber, "Replies to My Critics," trans. by Maurice Friedman, p. 696 f.

6. Martin Buber, *Kingship of God*, 3rd, newly enlarged ed., trans. by Richard Scheimann (New York: Harper Torchbooks, 1973), "Preface to the First Edition," p. 18 f., "Preface to the Second Edition," p. 21 f.

7. *Ibid.*, "Preface to the Second Edition," p. 26 f.

8. *Ibid.*, "Preface to the Third Edition," pp. 47-52.

9. *Ibid.*, p. 56, Chap. 3, p. 85 f.

10. *Ibid.*, Chap. 7, pp. 121-23, Chap. 6, p. 119.

11. *Ibid.*, Chap. 5, p. 99.

12. Martin Buber, *Moses. The Revelation and the Covenant* (New York: Harper Torchbooks, 1958), "Preface," p. 7 f.

13. *Ibid.*, pp. 64, 136, 158.

14. *The Kingship of God*, "Preface to the Second Edition," p. 35 f.: *Moses.* p. 78 f., 127.

15. *Moses*, p. 158.

16. Martin Buber, *The Prophetic Faith*, trans. from the Hebrew by Carlyle Witton-Davies (New York: Harper Torchbooks, 1960), "Introduction."

17. Martin Buber, *Two Types of Faith*, trans. by Norman P. Goldhawk (New York: Harper Torchbooks, 1961), Foreword, pp. 6-12.

18. Martin Buber, *The Origin and Meaning of Hasidism*, ed. and trans. with an Introduction by Maurice Friedman (New York: Horizon Press, 1973), "Supplement: Christ, Hasidism, Gnosis," p. 242 f.

19. Schalom Ben-Chorin, *Zwiesprache mit Martin Buber. Ein Errinerungsbuch*

(Munich: List Verlag, 1966), p. 183 f.; Walter Nigg, "Die drei Stationen Martin Bubers. Eine Würdigung" in Westdeutscher Rundfunk (Köln), III Program, September 29, 1962, p. 38 f.

20. Buber, *A Believing Humanism: Gleanings*, "Fragments on Revelation," 3. "The Exclusive Attitude of the Religions," p. 115 f.

21. *Ibid.*, "On the Science of Religion," pp. 127-129.

22. Buber, *The Origin and Meaning of Hasidism*, "God and the Soul," pp. 184-199.

23. *Ibid.*, "The Place of Hasidism in the History of Religion," pp. 220-239.

24. Schilpp and Friedman, eds., *The Philosophy of Martin Buber*, Rivka Schatz-Uffenheimer, "Man's Relation to God and World in Buber's Rendering of the Hasidic Teaching," pp. 403-434; Buber, "Replies to My Critics, IX. On Hasidism," pp. 731-741; Gershom Scholem, *The Messianic Idea in Judaism* (New York: Schocken Books, 1971). "Martin Buber's Interpretation of Hasidism," trans. by Michael A. Meyer, pp. 227-250; Martin Buber, "Interpreting Hasidism," trans. by Maurice Friedman, *Commentary*, Vol. XXXVI, No. 3 (September 1963), pp. 218-225. See Martin Buber, *Werke*, III—*Schriften zum Chassidismus* (Munich and Heidelberg: Kösel and Lambert Schneider Verlag, 1963), "Noch einiges zur Darstellung des Chassidismus," pp. 991-998.

25. For my fuller interpretation of Zen as a "mysticism of the particular" see Maurice Friedman, *Touchstones of Reality: Existential Trust and the Covenant of Peace* (New York: E. P. Dutton, 1972; Dutton Books, 1974), pp. 106-117.

The Significance of Martin Buber for Protestant Theology

HELMUT GOLLWITZER

I

Since the time of Moses Mendelssohn, Martin Buber is the first Jew who, as a Jew, has affected the spiritual life of his non-Jewish environment; who has been accepted in that environment not only as a human being but as a Jew; and who has elucidated Judaism, made it accessible and noteworthy to the educated among its despisers. True, one cannot imagine non-Jewish intellectual life without Baruch Spinoza, Heinrich Heine, Karl Marx, Sigmund Freud, Hermann Cohen—to name only a few of the most distinguished names. Indeed, their Jewishness was noticed; but except where it became the target for anti-Semitic polemics, it was ignored as inessential, in order to facilitate their acceptance as partners in the intellectual process of the era. A century and a half after Mendelssohn passed before another Jew, writing as a German and with a masterly command of the German language, made his Judaism a theme for his social surrounding. He impressed upon them that they must not bypass his Judaism while interpreting his statements as a universally human contribution to humanity's struggle for truth, but must recognize precisely what was Jewish about him and take it seriously, if they were to grasp what his thinking portended for all humanity. The isolation in which these two Jews, Moses Mendelssohn and Martin Buber, stood, furnished Gershom Scholem with an argument for his provocative claim that the so-called "German-Jewish symbiosis" was in reality one-sided. It consisted in German Jews' unilateral, unreciprocated appeals to their German contemporaries for a dialogue in which they would be accepted and received as Jews and not merely as integrated contemporaries whose Jewishness was no longer recognizable.

For Martin Buber, the dialogic thinker, the assertion of his Jewishness was important not merely because of the Biblical origin of his philosophy, but as the immediate demonstration of his central thesis through his own person. Against the idealistic basis of traditional hermeneutics, which, from the Greeks to his teacher, Wilhelm

Dilthey, consisted in a fundamentally pantheistic mysticism of identity and conceived of understanding as like finding like in one's fellow-man, Buber saw the problem of understanding precisely in the otherness of the other, which is not to be abolished but welcomed in the process of understanding. This understanding which welcomes the otherness of the other occurs in the *encounter,* in which each both communicates himself to the other and opens himself unconditionally to communication from the other. The understanding of the encounter is not a process of mutual assimilation, nor yet a defiant self-assertion against the other. It is a mutual acceptance and reception of the other in the give-and-take of dialogue between I and Thou, through which each I is set in motion, carried by the very otherness of the other across its own borders, out of its own static thus-ness into a richer life, a life enriched by this other.

It was precisely as a Jew, as the other which he was for them by virtue of his Jewishness, that Martin Buber could demonstrate through his practice of dialogue with his non-Jewish and especially with his German contemporaries what he was teaching philosophically, from the source of Jewish faith, on the dialogic existence of the human being. It is one of the few small signs of consolation, in this century of bloody violence against those who are different or think differently, that this teaching of his did not fall only on deaf ears, that in the very field of Christian theology, which bears so heavy a share of responsibility for Western civilization's contempt for Jewry, a few people responded with a willingness to learn this Jew's Jewish teaching.

For this teaching no expression of gratitude, on the part of Christians, can be enough. In contrast to the polyphony of both parts of the Bible, the New Testament no less than the Hebrew scriptures, the history of the Church is marked, by the prevailing tendency toward elimination of opposition, by the drive for unanimity in the confession of faith. Unanimity was desired for the sake of the unity of the Church, which was conceived as a homophony and was established through group pressure within the Church, through hierarchic authority, and all too often by the State's means of enforcement. The counterpart of this unison within the Church (destined of course to break apart into the polyphony of the various Christian denominations, each of which, however, again insisted on internal unison) was the effort of the Christian mission to incorporate non-Christians into this ecclesiastical unison. Thus the history of the Church and of the Christian mission was anything but the history of a dialogic learning process; it was rather the history of a Christian imperialism, parallel to the monologic tradition of Western thought, to which Buber placed dialogic thought in opposition. As a Jew on whom the centuries-long experience of Christian missionary pressure had left their mark, Buber rejected the mission as he found it; he could see in it only the non-recognition of the otherness of the other. Since that time profound changes have occurred in the field of Protestant mission. It is not propaganda aimed at converting the other that now stands in the foreground—both among the different denominations (as a consequence of the ecumenical movement toward dialogue among Christians of different denominations), and with other religions. Buber's development of dialogic thought laid indispensable ground-work for these changes.

But the dialogue among spiritual alignments and forms of belief, among denominations and religions—and I would enter a plea that the difference between Christianity and Judaism be regarded as a difference of denomination, not of religion—is dialogue only in the figurative, not in the original sense. In "Dialogue" ("Zwiesprache," 1930) Buber distinguished between three kinds of dialogue: "genuine" dialogue, which is a "living mutual relationship" of real persons; "technical" dialogue, occasioned by the "need of objective understanding," and "monologue disguised as dialogue."[1] The dialogue of denominations and religions, and especially of Christians and Jews, as Hans-Joachim Schoeps' book on Jewish-Christian dialogue demonstrates,[2] has been mostly a "monologue disguised as dialogue" between "two or more men meeting in space." If, with Buber's help, it becomes a real dialogue, then it is midway between the technological exchange motivated by the "need of objective understanding" and the authentic dialogue between I and Thou. This dialogue may transcend the striving of representatives of different spiritual alignments to see each other more justly, to understand each other's motives better, to help each other progress: above and beyond these aims, it may become a genuine dialogue, in which not only agents of two complexes of ideas, but real human beings speak to each other face to face, each one seeing the Thou of the other and encountering the Thou as other.

II

After a youthful phase of mysticism had been surmounted, the dialogical principle in this primary meaning, in the relationship between two specific human beings and in the relationship between man and God, became Buber's life-theme, to which he gave ever new variations and elucidations. While Catholic theologians of the period between the two World Wars, being for the most part still under the spell of Neo-scholasticism, only marginally received the parallel initiative of Ferdinand Ebner,[3] Buber's *I and Thou* (1923) became a basic text for a broad movement in Protestant theology called "theological personalism" (a term Buber did not care for).[4] This openness of Protestant theologians to Buber's person-oriented thinking was deeply rooted in Luther's theology. Its center is the event of the Divine Word in its address to man. In this event the striking variance between man's words and God's sayings is revealed to man, and at the same time is drawn into a new life with God. Both sin and grace are conceived here in a thoroughly personal manner. Constitutive of man's existence is the situation of being face to face with the God who addresses him. The categories in which scholasticism spoke of sin and grace treat them as natural phenomena: they designate states and qualities of the human being considered per se and as solitary subject. Luther no longer spoke in the plural of sacramental powers of grace, but in the singular of the one grace of God, the *favor Dei*, the graciousness of a God kindly disposed toward men; thus for him sin, judgment and grace became definitions of situations between two different subjects—not definitions of qualities, but relational concepts which required their own personal logic, in contrast to the formal logic which holds for the definition of objects. Man is no longer righteous thanks to the possession of qualities (whether self-acquired or sacramentally conferred), but through being placed in a Thou-I relationship, in which the human I, thanks to a Thou which has bound itself to him in love, is through this grace made righteous and privileged to live in the new Divine community.

The rediscovery, in the first quarter of our century, of Luther's authentic theology coincided with Buber's beginnings as a thinker. Buber provided the categories which made it possible to carry out that same reduction of the understanding of salvation to a personal event, which may already be seen in Luther. This helped to clarify the distinction between faith and knowledge with which the nineteenth century, as a result of the rapid progress of natural science, was concerned; and the abandonment of the great idealistic tradition of the nineteenth century in particular, a step to which theology saw itself ever more strongly compelled by reason of that tradition's implications of pantheism and the mysticism of identity, could be

carried out in a more consistent manner. Rudolf Bultmann's existentialist theology, along with his hermeneutics, is also part of this
personalistic movement, whose chief exponents were Friedrich
Gogarten, Karl Heim and Emil Brunner.

One can roughly characterize the differences among these three
theologians by saying that *Gogarten* is concerned with the gaining of
an anthropology with the help of which the idealistic concept of
history might be overcome, together with its hermeneutics; *Heim* is
occupied with an epistemological turning-away from the objectivizing
relation to the world toward a comprehension of a perceptual relation
which objectivization screens out and toward the dimension of personal reality; while *Brunner*'s aim is the drafting of a Christian dogma
in which revelation and salvation are understood in a strictly personal
manner.

A political intention pervades Friedrich Gogarten's thought, which
was formed by the experience of the disintegration of the polis, of the
foundations of human community and bent on the construction of
new foundations. He believed that for this purpose a new, better
understanding of Christian faith would be decisive. Turning against
the cultural Protestantism of his liberal past, he was definitely a
cultural theologian; in this respect he resembled Paul Tillich. He
viewed individualistic thought, which he considered to be based on
the idealistic tradition, as the underlying ruination of the epoch. The
idealist tradition understands history as the "history of the I as it
comes to itself and liberates itself."[5] This I can become the central
point because it knows itself identical with the spirit, the fundamental
reality of the universe, which according to Hegel comes to consciousness of itself through human consciousness. But the great identity of
absolute spirit and the individual consciousness leads only to an
exaggerated individualism, alienated from real history and the real
problems of society. For "surely no one who studies the problem of
history can fail to see that history is not possible where there is only
one man. History is something that occurs among men. But in spite
of this they all attempt to understand history as if it were something
entirely possible in the presence of only one person, one object."[6]
Only through the I's "renunciation of its claim to be the sole authentic
reality,"[7] only with the recognition of a Thou which can in no way be
absorbed into the I—that is, only with the recognition of the absolute
Thou of God as a starting-point for the recognition of the other person
as an alien Thou could the foundation be laid for the structures of
human communal life. These structures are given by the dependency

of each person on his fellow-humans, in such stable forms as the relationship between parents and children, teachers and pupils, and in the general constant reciprocal giving and receiving and rendering of services, and finally in what concerns Gogarten especially as a prerequisite for a new ordering of society—in the authority of men over men, which originates in the Thou of God speaking authoritatively to us through His word.

These indications suffice to show, in relation to Buber's work, a shift of emphasis, reinforced by the influence which Eberhard Griesbach had on Gogarten at the time and bringing with it important consequences: for anti-idealistic, anti-mystical reasons Gogarten emphasizes the alienness of the Thou vis-a-vis the I (Buber merely asserted the *otherness* of the Thou).[8] The pathos of God's distance as the wholly Other, which was so strongly accented in early dialectical theology, had for Gogarten (unlike Buber and Karl Barth, both of whom inclined toward a democratic socialism) anti-democratic consequences. The Buberian interplay *between* I and Thou, changes, according to Gogarten, under the influence of Paul and Luther to "undialectic" (what Buber later called[9] a onesided supremacy of the Thou from which the I derives its being. On the social level this means: "Never can I and Thou be bound together in substantial equality, as the individualistic community would have it"; the binding element can only be "something removed from individuality and subjectivity, as authority is," or else "the unconditional subjection of one to the other, of the I to the Thou.")[10] That "between," always in motion, in Buber's theory of dialogue, here seems frozen. Buber's "movement" becomes dependency, superiority and subjection, the kind of authoritarian thinking about class and state which led Gogarten to points of contact with National Socialist state theory, and of whose failure he has never given an account in the years since 1945. The question of the extent to which this failure is connected, as Buber opined, with the Pauline-Lutheran doctrine of grace, will be examined later.

Gogarten's authoritarian version of the I-Thou relationship was softened by him after the war; his personalism is now in the service of a de-objectivized, existentialized understanding of Christian faith, in collaboration with Rudolf Bultmann. In this late period he does not seem to have concerned himself further with Buber. But the problem of the non-objectifiability of statements of faith was formulated in a quite independent manner, long before the hermeneutic discussion after the war and in striking parallel to the developments in theoretical physics,[11] by Karl Heim, in whose work, as Buber once wrote,[12] "the influence of 'I and Thou' on Protestant theology may best be grasped."

Heim's scholarly work was devoted to the bridging of the gulf which has opened in modern times between faith and natural science. Beginning on a deeper level than his predecessors in this effort, he not only harmonized individual elements of Judaeo-Christian tradition with the state of modern knowledge, but sought to effect a reconciliation in principle. It is already clear in the first pages of "I and Thou" that Buber's distinction between the Thou-world and the It-world means not different worlds, but different modes in which the human subject relates to the one world in which we find ourselves and to which we ourselves belong, or more precisely: different modes of speaking, different ways of hearing and addressing this world. This is precisely the distinction which Heim wants to apply in order to solve the conflict between religious and scientific ways of looking at the world. But what Buber intended more as therapy for a sick age which is "sunk in the It-world" to its own harm,[13] Heim makes into a method of epistemological and linguistic criticism which serves to eliminate apparent ideological antinomies, with apologetic intent.

In the first volume of his six-volume *magnum opus, Der evangelische Glaube und das Denken der Gegenwart* (Protestant Faith and Present-Day Thought), Heim connects the existential analysis of Heidegger's *Being and Time* with Buber's theory of dialogue: he proposes that Heidegger's existential factors of "Being-in-the-world" and "temporarity of existence" be understood as dimensions in which the human subject relates to the world. These are joined by the further dimension of the I-Thou relationship discovered by Buber. "Our task is now to put what is brought to our consciousness here (i.e. in *I and Thou*) in the impressive language of the poet, as far as possible into logical form"[14]—that is, to develop a logic of the personal.

The phenomenological analysis with which Heim supplements Buber yields the following results: 1. The I-Thou encounter is an event which happens to me, in which I am primarily passive. At first I undergo it passively, then I respond. 2. Both this undergoing and this response occur in the word. It is not the mere objective appearance of another human being that makes him a Thou for me; rather he remains in the It-world until the Word occurs between us. 3. Only in the Thou-encounter is self-knowledge constituted. In a Thou-less world I too could not be an I. 4. The dimensions stand in a hierarchy.

The phenomena of the higher dimensions cannot be grasped with the categories of the lower. Personality is either unrecognizable with the categories of the objective world, or else it appears as a paradoxical riddle. Each higher dimension contains the lower, but not vice versa.

Thus Karl Heim has answered a number of questions which have been directed at Buber—answered them phenomenologically and thus in my opinion better than Buber in his later explanations, which often end in the appeal to the necessity of experiencing these things for oneself. It is unfortunate that Heim's work has not received the attention it deserves in the discussion on Buber. Although one misses in Heim's work the intention of social significance which animates Buber's description of the personal encounter in a society which reifies everything, nevertheless Buber and Heim agree in their counter-attack on the reifying tendency and in their opposition to the omnipotence of the objective. They reject the object-oriented concept of truth in the natural sciences, which relegates statements of faith to the unreal realm of fantasy. Heim is able to make clear that this is an inadmissible elevation of categories which are valid only for a limited sphere of reality (the objective It-world) to the status of absolutes.

Beyond this, Heim's theological interest is in showing that existence in the I-Thou dimension, if isolated amid the object-world which draws everything into its undertow, is doomed to meaninglessness and despair if it does not have its foundation above, in the I-Thou relationship between man and God, which alone can give it eternal meaning. Buber concurs with Heim on this point, but he has never expressed in Heim's apologetic argumentation—"Either God or the void, either faith or despair!"—he has only testified, without making claims.[15] All this is clarification of the common ground of belief between Jews and Christians; individual questions of content, which bring with them differences between the two modes of faith, have not yet been touched upon.

Emil Brunner's reception of Buber is another matter. Brunner has several times emphatically expressed his gratitude for Buber's "simple yet ingenious discovery of the great difference between the I-Thou relationship and that of the I-It relation"; along with Karl Heim, he calls this discovery "a 'Copernican revolution' in the thinking not only of Europe but of the whole of mankind."[16] He calls his own three-volume Dogmatics an attempt "to emphasize in Christian thought the importance of this truth, which is wholly derived from the Bible," since "Hitherto this has never been done within the sphere of dogmatics."[17] This means nothing less than "a complete rebuilding of the structure of theology" from a new, Biblical understanding of faith, "which must inevitably revolutionize traditional Church Dogmatics," and which involves the "release (of theology) from the dogma of the Church."[18] And the new structure is to be based on the "fundamental distinction" between the I-Thou dimension and the I-It dimension.[19] This program is set forth in Brunner's work *Truth as Encounter* (1937, 1963)[20] and carried out in the three-volume *Dogmatics* (1946-60). All of the statements of belief (dogmas) which are treated in the traditional dogmatic writings of the Church are understood no longer as descriptions of objective, revealed truths, but as testimonies of a truth which occurs in personal encounter through God's communication of Himself to the humans He addresses. Human sin is thus not a qualitative degeneration of human nature, as theologians have often wrongly portrayed the Christian way of speaking about "original sin" (an unfortunate phrase); rather sin is man's rebellion—based on the creatural personal relationship between God and man and made possible precisely by man's personal nature—against the dependency of his existence on God, which his creation entails. This rebellion does not abolish the personal relationship, but it perverts the relationship to an autonomy which isolates man as the ground of himself, and in so doing delivers him all the more surely to the undertow of the It-world. And his fellow-man is now threatened with an instrumentalization which changes him from a Thou into an It.

All statements about Jesus Christ may be understood from this perspective as testimony to the restitution of the I-Thou relationship between God and man through a foundation-laying, and therefore unique and historically concrete new encounter of God with His human creatures. For each human creature this encounter is actualized by the annunciation of Jesus Christ as the personal Divine truth, which is addressed to him as a person and intends to turn him back to God. Once again awakened as a person, the individual is also immediately awakened to his fellow-human; he is freed—this too represents an absorption of Jewish Biblical thinking about the Chosen People of God—from his individual atomisation, to become a member of the brotherhood of the Ecclesia: the Church interpreted not as institution, but as community of persons.

These indications must suffice to show that Brunner read Buber profoundly. He could even hope, in his reconstruction of Christian dogmatics, to clear away two prejudices Buber had against Pauline Christendom and thus help Buber to transcend his own limits.

1. The opposition which Buber assumes, in *Two Types of Faith*, between Hebraic faith as personal trust and Pauline Pistis-belief as the holding of certain dogmatic statements to be true, collapses upon itself. Faith in the New Testament sense is precisely not a conviction of the truth of any dogmas, but a personal response of trust to the personal encounter with God in the person of Jesus Christ, who inspires trust and makes trust possible. "Faith as acceptance of the self-communication of God in Jesus Christ is the perfecting of Old Testament faith,"[21] not its opposite. It is a "perfecting" in the sense that God does not merely announce Himself to men, but communicates Himself to them by surrendering Himself for them in Jesus' death.

With this, as Brunner in my opinion rightly concludes, Paul—a Jew and not, as in Buber's portrayal, a Hellenist overcome by Gnosticism—does more justice to the concept of faith in the Hebrew Bible than Buber. Because in his interpretation of the Divine-human I-Thou relationship, Buber finds it difficult to give historical occurrences more than an exemplary significance; he does not allow them a foundation-laying significance, such as is after all essential to the calling of Abraham, for instance, or the covenant at Sinai. In contrast, the meaning of the event Jesus Christ for Christian faith impels us to reflect on the connection of the relation to God with specific historical events and thereby also to appreciate more justly, in their foundation-laying meaning, such acts of God in the history of Israel.[22]

2. Buber felt that Paul had abandoned the correspondence which exists in the Hebrew Bible between the freedom of God and the freedom of man. "The Pauline and the Paulinistic theology depreciated works for the sake of faith," and this "resulted in the retreating into obscurity of the Israelite mystery of man as an independent partner of God."[23] "A fundamental dualism in existence resulted: spirit and world became subject to different laws: man can accomplish nothing by himself. All he can do is surrender to the other, to redemption which has come from beyond and has assumed bodily shape in his earthly sphere.[24] To this Brunner answers: If God's personal relationship to man is, as Buber says, the foundation of human personality, then the doctrine of creation already states that God's grace is unconditional, that it precedes human decision and by doing so makes the latter possible. The same is true for the turning of man from the perversion of his existence which contradicts the new life in the Divine community: man cannot perform the turning "by himself," rather God's preceding, unconditional love calls him into

the turning, and alone restores to him the freedom to make the turning. In words very similar to Buber's, Brunner writes: "The grace of God comes first; but it is not thrown over man, but set before him. He is not overwhelmed by it, but treated as one who can and should decide freely. Grace must be accepted by man; God's love, if it is really to become man's life, must be answered by reciprocal love."[25] I would surmise that in genuine dialogue Buber's concern that man should be seen as the free partner of God, and the Pauline-Lutheran doctrine of *gratia praeveniens* could be reconciled.

Karl Barth is not as far from this answer of Brunner's as one well acquainted with both might at first suppose. He has accused Brunner of being too much attached to the philosophical concept of freedom as something like Hercules' freedom of choice at the crossroads, and this reproach is in my opinion justified.[26] But for Barth, too, it is important to fend off the notion of a magical or otherwise compulsory causality of grace.[27] His sentence "Love is free or it is not love"[28] is valid for both partners, for man as well as for God.[29] "Again, grace would not be grace if its exercise consisted only in the elimination or suppression as an autonomous subject of the one to whom it was extended."[30] Thus Barth also agrees with Buber in the rejection of the notion, tending toward pantheism, of God as the sole active force (monergism):[31] creator and creature stand face to face in real partnership. And in his understanding of faith Barth, like Buber, presses for "realization" rather than a mere lingering in feeling or thought: "Only the doer of the Word is its real hearer."[32]

Through his positive concept of freedom Barth is, I believe, in a better position to maintain all this without getting into the proximity of synergism—a proximity which Brunner and Buber have not mastered and which Buber for this reason does not avoid.[33] With Brunner it is based on the above mentioned clinging to freedom primarily as freedom of choice; with Buber it is emphasized in his concept of the turning, and he believes he must assert it as a factor which distinguishes his thought from Reformation theology.

Emil Brunner relates a conversation with Buber on sin. "He opposed sharply the New Testament, above all, the Pauline concept of sin, because he saw in this an encroachment on man's responsibility to himself and his freedom."[34] Brunner states that at that time they "parted without having reached any agreement."[35] He reproaches Buber's approach which leaves man imprisoned in his opposition to God: "He was able to close the door, but he cannot open it again."[36] He misses in Buber the understanding for the radical alienation of man from God, which is after all not alien to the Hebrew Bible, although it received its essential sharpness only with the New Testament interpretation of the redemptive meaning of Jesus' death. Whereas Buber sees no third way between assertion of the possibility of the turning to which even the sinner always has free access, and "divine monergism, in which nothing of the dialogue-character of our relation to God is left,"[37] Brunner is able to show that the Divine act in Jesus Christ is *the* call to the turning which at the same time bestows the freedom to carry it out. Thus the New Testament summons, "Be ye reconciled to God" (2 Cor. 5:20) has incorporated the meaning of the Old Testament *shuv*, insofar as in both cases the content is a plea for trust in the faithfulness of the God of the covenant.[38]

It is not clear to me, I must admit, why Buber felt that he must so stubbornly oppose this foundation of man's turning in God's "turning" of man.[39] Aside from the fact that the conditional formulation so frequent with the prophets ("If you seek me, you shall find me"—Jer. 29:13) can very well be understood as a summoning pledge of a bestowal of forgiveness which in principle has already occurred[40]—the very "personal" logic made possible by dialogic thinking does indeed show (as the exposition particularly by Karl Barth of the relation between Divine and human freedom proves) a way out of the dilemma in which Buber remains caught—and decides, willy-nilly, on synergism.

And finally a brief discussion of *Karl Barth's* relation to Buber: It is curious that these two men had no close personal contact, presumably out of a lack of mutual sympathy—and yet, objectively, were exceedingly close at least on one point, which we shall come to presently. There is only one letter of Barth to Buber and two of Buber to Barth, all three in the same connection:[41] in 1936 Buber asked whether Barth could agree to Buber's evaluation of Gogarten's *Politiche Ethik* (1932). The point in question is Buber's rejection of Gogarten's conversion of man's radical sinfulness according to a judgment passed by God, to a category of state theory.[42] Barth, who at the time was occupied with polemics against Brunner's renewal of "natural theology" and evidently sensed a similar tendency in Buber, answered somewhat curtly and—as Buber's answer shows not very helpfully, stating that the Reformation doctrine of original sin, "which also and especially comprehends the interhuman, does indeed have lasting political relevance"—though not in the meaning Gogarten gives it (the last point is not developed).

Twelve years after this correspondence, which had no sequel,

Barth published his anthropology (*Church Dogmatics* III/2, 1948). Here he defines the fellow-humanness of man as "the basic form of humanity" (45,2), very much in the sense of Buber's sentence: "The fundamental fact of human existence is man with man."[43] I know— despite Brunner's efforts—of no Christian anthropology in which the coexistence of man with man is expounded with such intensity as a fundamental and not only accidental definition of humanness as in these pages of Barth's dogmatics. And then Barth expresses surprise that "In this respect theological anthropology has to go its own way, and while pursueing its way resolutely to the end it is led to statements which are very similar to those in which humanity is described from a very different angle (e.g. by the pagan Confucius, the atheist L. Feuerbach and the Jew M. Buber)."[44] This shows, according to Barth, that "a certain knowledge of this conception was and is possible to man in general, even to the pagan, atheist and Jew," but that Christian theological anthropology has an "advantage" in the foundation of this knowledge in the "knowledge . . . of the man Jesus," and therefore in the decisiveness with which it grasps the "freedom of the heart between man and man" as the "root and crown of the concept of humanity." Barth leaves open the question of whether pagan, atheist and Jew can and want to go that far, but remarks that this does not appear to be the case.[45]

In the afterword to his *Schriften über das dialogische Prinzip* (Writings on the Dialogical Principle) Buber recognizes that Barth has taken over, "of course in the manner of genuine autonomous thought, our insights on the fundamental distinction between I and Thou and of the true being in the encounter," but "could not quite admit that such a concept of humanity could grow on other soil than the Christological," and closes with the beautiful wish: "But I wish I could show Karl Barth here, in Jerusalem, how the Hasidim dance the freedom of the heart toward one's fellow-man."[46]

The proximity in which the two thinkers find themselves will be evident to anyone, who will be surprised that Barth is surprised at it—for, by his own assumptions, he did not need to be. A few years later, with much greater freedom, he regards such coincidences between Christian and non-Christian thought less as a problem and more as a sign, which should be gratefully hailed by Christians, of the unlimited range over which the reconciliation of the world with God, sealed by Christ's resurrection, is valid.[47] But even in 1948 it should not have occurred to Barth to juxtapose so unceremoniously the pagan Confucius and the Jew Buber—after all that he himself, while determinedly combating Christian anti-Judaism, had found to say since 1932 about the continuing election of the Jewish people. For although Buber delivered his thoughts as philosopher and not as theologian, he never denied or concealed their Biblical origin; and Barth had available Buber's Biblical scholarship, which might soon have given him access to Buber (I do not know to what extent he had read them). Brunner's assurance is after all correct: "The 'I-Thou' of the divine relation to the world and to Man is certainly not a *schema*, introduced into Christian doctrine by the 'I-Thou philosophy,' but it is the true, fundamental relation between God and man."[48] For a moment Barth—in contradiction to himself—treated his Christological starting-point as narrowly exclusive, as his critics have often insinuated, thus not including Israel and the Jew Buber, despite the common Biblical basis, and despite the demand of his fundamental concept of the intimate connection of Israel and the Church. Hence, in this case Barth's Christological beginning need not have led to the expressed reservation against Buber.

III

We ought now, on the basis of this necessarily selective survey of prominent Protestant theologians' relation to Buber, to speak of Buber's significance for the Christian-Jewish dialogue which has gotten under way especially since the collapse of Hitler's Reich.
It would be appropriate to cite his own remarks about Christianity in relation to Judaism, as well as references to him in this dialogue. For reasons of space that is not possible here.[49] I therefore limit myself to a question which is called forth by a contradiction between some of Buber's remarks and his theory of dialogue. According to Buber's theory of dialogue understanding occurs between human subjects *not* on the basis of an identity of mind which can be presumed in advance, but through the encounter of two subjects whose otherness is not to be abolished. This otherness does not exclude understanding, as idealistic hermeneutics fears; rather the separation it implies is overcome through the genuine encounter, which brings about understanding and knowledge of the other, so that otherness itself becomes productive.[50]
But when Buber speaks of Christianity and Judaism, otherness becomes for him a boundary which makes full understanding impossible. For instance, the difference between the Jewish belief in Israel's election of Israel and the Church's assertion of Israel's rejection is not problematised in a polemic against the latter notion, but

recognized as the "basic difference" between the "knowledge of the Church about Israel's self-knowledge," about which there can evidently be no discussion, but at most the hope "that the Spirit alone wafts over our irresolvable differences, that though it does not bridge them, it nevertheless gives assurance of unity, assurance in the experienced moment of unity for the communality even of Christians and Jews."[51] Buber limits the possibility of understanding by distinguishing between an understanding from without and an understanding from within: "Obstinate Jew that I am," he said in 1914 to Florens Christian Rang "that we Jews know him (Jesus) from within, in the impulses and stirrings of his Jewish being, in a way that remains inaccessible to the peoples submissive to him."[52] Or: "There is a something in Israel's history of faith which is only to be understood by Israel, just as there is a something in the Christian history of faith which is only to be understood by Christianity."[53] Concerning these formulations, whose vagueness is significant, there is a good deal one might say in order to distill out a possible hermeneutic truth factor. I limit myself to the remark that Buber here—evidently without taking into account the consequences for his theory of dialogue—is setting a limit to dialogue: It can lead only to a certain point, beyond which each remains immured in his own immediate particularity. Perhaps such sayings are to be explained by the resignation into which the unheard-of difficulties of Jewish-Christian dialogue threaten to lead us. But Buber's theory of dialogue is designed not to legitimize such resignation, but to give hope against it and courage for ever new beginnings. We shall do well to resist such temptations to resignation by clinging to such experiences as happened—though seldom—even to Buber, and which that conversation with Florens Christian Rang so happily communicates: " 'In a way that remains inaccessible to you'— so I directly addressed the former clergyman. He stood up, I too stood, and we looked into the heart of each other's eyes. 'It is gone,' he said, and before everyone we gave each other the kiss of brotherhood. The discussion of the situation between Jews and Christians had been transformed into a bond between the Christian and the Jew. In this transformation dialogue was fulfilled. Opinions were gone, in a bodily way the factual occurred."[54]

IV

It is impossible, in a time like ours, to limit the report on the meaning of Martin Buber for Protestant theology to what has been said so far, which is in any case only a sketch. To do so would be to cut

Buber in half. He wanted not only to help us speak in a more
appropriate way about the living God (in this limited sense Emil
Brunner perceived and received him); he wanted to find something
healing for earthly society in a sick time, he wanted to be politically
effective, and his significance extends to the social-political challenge
under which any theology which takes its task seriously stands today.

Martin Buber was a Zionist. No portrait of Buber can be accurate if
it separates this will from his thinking, as if it were accidental for him.
His Zionist will is the practical commentary to his thinking which
presses for "realization" and "hallowing" of the earthly. Where politics and morality touch—and where do they not touch?—is the locus
of his thought and also the locus of a theology pursued in responsibility for human life and not as an erudite luxury.

In a significant essay on "The Validity and Limitation of the
Political Principle,"[55] Buber, taking his text from the pericope on the
tribute money (Matth. 22:15-22, Mark 12:13-17, Luke 20:20-26),
demonstrates the right and the limitation of the claim which our
involvement with the political makes upon each of us. Jesus' words
"Render unto Caesar the things that are Caesar's, and unto God the
things that are God's" in no way places God and Caesar on the same
level, so that one could divide life into two realms, each with its own
autonomous system of laws. Rather it means, like the Deuteronomic
commandment to love God (Deut. 6:5) that the totality of our life
belongs to God from thence we take our instructions—beginning
with the instruction to love our neighbor, and above all the neighbor
at the mercy of our power, whom God loves (Deut. 10:17-20). If the
"political principle" takes possession of us wholly, then we have fallen
under the sway of the deified Caesar, of deified power; then the
friend-enemy principle rules, then we can, "with peaceful and un-
troubled conscience, lie, slander, steal, torment, torture, murder"
the enemy. "In the factories of party doctrine, good conscience is
being dependably fashioned and refashioned." In this way "free
decision becomes unexpectedly unfree."[56]

Jesus' saying is intended to preserve us from becoming enslaved to
a political principle which has become totalitarian; thereby it would
free us to serve in the political field in a manner obedient to God: "On
the other hand, I believe that it is possible to serve God and the
group to which one belongs if one is courageously intent on serving
God in the sphere of the group as much as one can."[57]

This is precisely what Buber wanted to make true in his Zionism,
and his Zionistic activity was aimed at helping the Jewish people, who
had returned to Palestine and were again allowed to live in Eretz

Israel, to make it true, so that they might not—a danger against which he repeatedly warned—win Palestine and lose Zion. It is well known to what extent the solution of the Arab question, which, however, means the achievement of peaceful coexistence between Jews and Arabs, was for him, from the beginning, the test question of Zionism—and it is equally well known how isolated he became within Israel through his undeviating announcement of this political task.

Only when Christian theology takes the intimate connection of people and land—that is, Zionism—theologically seriously will it have found a promising basis for Christian-Jewish dialogue—even for the necessary relearning of the meaning of Israel for Christian faith. This done, the non-Jewish Christian may acquire a right, certainly not to give the Jewish people in the state of Israel, who are still in mortal danger, political advice and moral prescriptions whose real consequences the Jews and not we non-Jews would have to suffer, but: to participate, through a sharing in thought, in the deliberation within Zionism and Israel concerning the way of the State of Israel to peace with the Arabs, and to contribute to the discussion in all modesty and in the constant awareness of the great share of responsibility borne by Christians and Germans for the situation today. This second alternative is unavoidable in any case, since we as citizens of our respective countries participate, concurring or opposing, in their policies toward Israel and the Arabs.

Martin Buber took the view that a Zionism which would merely add one more Levantine state to those already existing and which would repeat all the sins of the pagan states would be of no interest either to Judaism or to humanity. The Jewishness of the new state must therefore not prove itself by the subjection of the populace to religious law *per* state law; rather it must prove itself by a persistent effort toward peaceful—and means egalitarian—coexistence with the Arabs inside Israel and with the Arabic neighbors. If there is any people that must not be a "master race" and must not drift "unexpectedly" into the position of a "master race," then it is the Jewish people; let this be a prime commandment of a Zionist politics that does not wish the word "Zion" to be misused in its name.

Buber at first failed with these postulates. They seemed to be inadequate to the real demands of the struggle for survival in Israel. And in this struggle for survival the "political principle" seems for the time being to have enforced its autonomy. Nevertheless I would like, from a deep sympathy with the problems of the State of Israel, to venture a prophetic word: Should Israel survive and obtain the peace without which it will not be able to survive in the long run, then the postulates of *Ichud,* of Buber, Judah L. Magnes and their friends will once again acquire decisive political actuality. The facts will prove them right, and it is they, not those who opposed them, who will point the way to Israel's future.

Christian theology learns from Buber and from Judaism: "spirit is nothing but that power which hallows the world," and "The world is not something to be overcome. It is created reality, but reality created to be hallowed."[58] We goyim, to whom it has been promised that we shall yet "take hold of the skirt of him that is a Jew, saying, We will go with you, for we have heard that God is with you" (Zechariah 8:23)—we goyim long to see Buber's Zionism become a real politics, so that we may learn from it a way of political action in a time when Israel's survival and in equal measure the survival of humanity are threatened, and this earth can be saved only through a new working of the spirit that hallows.

I therefore close with words written by Buber in a letter to Louis Massignon on 15.9.1953:

> Yom Kippur falls this year on September 19. If you wish, I will fast with you for Israel and for its adversaries, linking them together in my fast and in my prayer and invoking the great forgiveness of their common Father for their misdeeds—I might almost dare say: for their common misdeeds. I shall begin, as always, with myself, the only one all of whose evil I know, and then I will make the common task and the common guilt—the guilt of having failed to recognize, and still failing to recognize, the task entrusted to them. May the Merciful One hear your prayer and mine as if they were a single prayer for the unfortunate race of Adam.[59]

Afterword

The word "master race" comes from the monster's dictionary, though for its inventor it meant not the Jews, who were to be exterminated, but the eastern peoples destined to become slaves of the "nordic race." However, on being pronounced in Beer Sheva it touched wounds that had not healed; I should therefore have avoided it. But what was meant was expressed many times by Buber and is today, since the Jewish state has a large number of Arab inhabitants of Palestine under its control, a nuclear question of any settlement of the Near Eastern problem and of the future coexistence of Jews and Arabs.

Discussion Following Helmut Gollwitzer's Lecture

N. ROTENSTREICH

I shall make three points. The first is about silence. Silence, language and reflection. I think the point raised by Prof. Jochanan Bloch yesterday is a very legitimate one, not only because of the involvement in language, but because of reflection being an essential precondition of all discussion including the discussion which tries to overcome reflection. And we cannot just say that we address God or we keep silent. We are engaged in both attitudes. Because no linguistic expression is adequate, we are aware of the gap between where we stand and what we intend to express. Therefore no metaphoric descriptions like *Begegnung* or *Beziehung* can do justice to the complexity of that attitude seen from within.

My second point is related to the exegesis of St. John's very famous proposition about the word becoming flesh, and the interpretation by Prof. Gollwitzer in terms of *Verwirklichung*. There is a basic difference between *Verwirklichung* and incarnation. Incarnation is embodiment in flesh, *Verwirklichung* is the creation of a situation of interhuman relations, precisely not embodied in flesh.

My third point is about Buber's Zionism. My first encounter with Buber was with Buber as a Zionist thinker. From my early youth I engaged in polemics with Buber on his political interpretation of Zionism. Buber never understood the *Judenfrage.*, the situation of the Jews in Eastern Europe, even during the period between the two Wars. He was always concerned with the clash between living according to one's substance and being overpowered by the circumstances. This is an important analysis, but he could not combine it with an integrated view of Zionism as a full renaissance of the Jewish people, and not only of the renaissance in terms of overcoming the duality of Jewish existence between home and environment.

And when the German aliyah came to Israel, to Palestine, in the thirties, Buber said at the one meeting we had in Jerusalem, "The Halutz spirit is going away". I reported that to my teacher and Buber's disciple, Hugo Bergmann, and Bergmann said, "Who are we to be masters of history? This is how history gave shape to the events. And we have to come to grips with the situation as it is."

For years I have been critical of the status quo political line of the governments of Israel. But the problem of peace with the Arab world is how to integrate that peace with the political existence of the Jewish people—not to see that peace as a parallel line to the political existence of the people of Israel. Buber and Magnes saw peace with the Arab world as an independent constant factor and not as a part of the full gestalt. This was their historical mistake. Magnes, who was opposed to the establishment of the State of Israel, did not see the dynamic process which led to the establishment of the State of Israel. It was probably the first and the last chance in the history of the Jewish people.

It is very easy to say, as you said, Prof. Gollwitzer, "Now we shall incorporate Buber's line". But we are in a very difficult position with regard to the establishment of peace with the Arab world as the heart of the dynamic process of the Jewish revival. This is our real problem. Our problem from the Zionist point of view is to combine the two halves of Aristotle's statement that the political life of the state comes into being for life, but it exists for a good life.

M. WYSCHOGROD

I would like to address myself briefly to the concluding remarks of Prof. Gollwitzer concerning Buber's Zionism. Prof. Gollwitzer mentioned Jochanan Bloch's remark that until Christian theology understands the relationship between the people of Israel and the land of Israel it will not have understood Judaism. It was not clear to me whether he had taken this advice.

We are in the land that the word of God promised to the people of Israel. It is not possible, in my opinion, for a Christian or a Jew to discuss Israel without taking this fact into account.

One of the things I failed to detect in the words of Prof. Gollwitzer is the fear of another Holocaust here, a fear which is profound in the minds and hearts of Jews and which cannot be averted by words alone, but must be averted by reality. The image of the Jew on the cross is an image that is deeply embedded in Christian thought; it is an image that Jews no longer accept—it is a role that Jews no longer wish to play.

I also failed to detect in his lecture any words of chastisement to the enemies of Israel who time and again have attempted to destroy the Jewish people in this land. You mentioned the Arab refugees. Germany has shown us the example of resettling four million German refugees in the homeland after World War Two—resettling them with love, with affection, successfully. The analogy is particularly clear when we understand that in both cases the expelled people entered a world which linguistically, culturally and religiously was identical to the world they were accustomed to, and where the process of adjustment could have been, and in the case of Germany was, easily made.

The Jewish people is not ready for another Holocaust and with the help of God will avert that Holocaust. It has stretched out its hand in peace, but because it reads the Bible it also knows that this land, and this city where the Covenant with Abraham was first struck, is the Land of Israel. Buber stood with that and this is the real issue. If one accepts that, then in the eyes of certain persons one is an imperialist. Ultimately, a choice must be made between the mythology of the left and the faith of Israel.

W. KAUFMANN

I am in agreement with the preceding speakers that the remarks we have heard about politics contribute very little to the understanding of the problems to which this congress is devoted, or to a general understanding of Buber. People have a tendency to interpret people they like by assimilating them to their own views. Some of the speakers here have indulged in that tendency rather far. In Prof. Casper's paper Buber was discussed in a context of German metaphysics and Christian theology from which Buber always tried to dissociate himself. Prof. Gollwitzer was pursuing a similar course in his talk, long before he got into politics. What was distinctive about Buber's religiousness—whether you share it or not—was precisely that it was an attempt at a non-theological religiousness. As a matter of general method one should lean over backwards and ask oneself, when one is dealing with a person one likes, whether one is reading one's own ideas into him. It seems to me that Buber would not have felt happy with Casper's or with Gollwitzer's readings of any part of him.

J. BLOCH

I have no intention of entering on a political discussion with Gollwitzer, or of setting up one political viewpoint against another. I am concerned with something quite different. I am concerned, to put it quite simply, with the degree of justification and right which Gollwitzer has, as a representative of Christian theological thinking, to take part in the discussion of questions internal to Zionism. That is a very difficult question, and I think it should be discussed, in honesty and friendship, in a real dialogue. It is also a basic question of Jewish-Christian dialogue.

Gollwitzer is without a doubt a stronghearted man. It is certainly admirable how, without any qualms, he approaches Buber, interprets him, and simply cannot avoid coming to conclusions which correspond exactly to his own theological intentions. He interprets Buber, he interprets the linguistic phenomenon, and inevitably comes up with the justification of his own theological speaking and thinking. This reminds me of a well-known paragraph by Karl Barth which asserts that Christian theology certainly can recognize Israel's chosenness, only this chosenness flows from the Church and leads to the Church.

Gollwitzer says that according to Buber understanding occurs between two human subjects not on the basis of spiritual identity but through the encounter of two subjects precisely in their otherness which cannot be annulled. This otherness does not exclude understanding. Rather, what separates is overcome through a genuine movement which leads to understanding and knowledge of the other. What is meant by understanding is that mutuality which does not diminish the autonomy of the partner. I understand someone when I feel the basic uniqueness of another person and can grasp his acts and his utterances as proceeding from this basic uniqueness, that is, I understand how he in his otherness can arrive at certain utterances, opinions, or actions, that is, I understand the other, out of my feeling for his otherness, though it may not be possible or necessary for me to agree with him. But Gollwitzer does not want to accept the basic difference; he thinks that dialogue has to produce an understanding which will eliminate the basic difference.

Buber, the Jew, felt that there is something in Israel's history of faith which only Israel can perceive. Gollwitzer does not want to acknowledge this. But the fact is that we are special, whether we like it or not: as a people, as a community of faith that is identical with our people. Therefore we cannot ask for an understanding in commonality. We must refuse that. We do not want to be "embraced" by that understanding which the Christians practice in the hope that we will stop being what we really are. The Christian assumes that the special character of Judaism is ultimately founded and conditioned by what he himself believes, namely Jesus Christ, and therefore he, the

Christian, has direct access to Judaism—I say this not polemically, but because it is so. He always has to understand us better than we understand ourselves. And so when he engages in dialogue with us, it is in order to lead us to our own truth. And that is what is happening at every step of the way when Gollwitzer interprets Buber.

On this basis it is possible to understand the last part of Gollwitzer's lecture. He says that he takes Zionism seriously from Christian theological considerations, that is, he understands Zionism from his Christological point of view and participates in thought, as he says, in our discussions within Zionism. And he already understands them, he already knows better than most of us. He is participating in the discussion, he says, in all modesty. But, dear Gollwitzer, I must ask you: is it really modest for you, who are completely different from us, who were conscripted into the German army and went as a German soldier to the Russian front, you who were a pastor there—I know this—as a Marxist theologian from Berlin—do you have the right to tell us which Zionists know Israel's way into the future and which do not? I ask *you*, in all modesty, how do you find it possible to do that? There is a real asymmetry here. It is possible to say something, with great caution, to another people about political differences. To be quite honest, I personally would not dare to say anything, for instance, about the advantages and disadvantages of American presidential candidates. At the very most I might, after close study, say, "I like this one better because of his attitude toward the Jews". In the famous Jewish question, "Is it good for the Jews?" there is a real, genuine modesty.

But that isn't Gollwitzer's way of doing things. And I can understand even that. He comes to Israel as a true friend, he has many friends in Israel, and he decides, I like this or that opinion better. But adopting the terminology of a certain group that was close to Buber, does not allow you to say we are a "master race". That is Nazi terminology. I have to ask: are we a "master race" because we do not want a binational state? If we hold, contrary to the Brith-Shalom, contrary to Magnes, that Zionism really has to solve the problem of the Jews of the world—does that make us a "master race"? If we do not believe we can depoliticize Zionism, does that make us sinners like all the rest of the nations?

Ladies and gentlemen, I am not particularly shy, as you can see, but I would not come to a Protestant church conference and say, for instance, the Lutheran fundamentalists point the way to the future of the Church. Nor would I interfere in internal questions of German politics. I wouldn't have the nerve to say, "The SPD is terrible, vote CDU or you'll be heading for a catastrophe".

Buber wanted dialogue. In the course of the last two days we have heard very critical statements about this. But dialogue is what Buber said it was: *du-siah*—a thoroughly Jewish concept. It means that the partners in this dialogue remain in their otherness and autonomous. But from the Christian standpoint dialogue is something quite different. As Nietzsche once said, the Christians pull the Bible out from under the Jews and use it against them. And it looks to me as though here dialogue is likewise being pulled out from under us and used in a very questionable manner. This does not seem to me likely to provide the basis for genuine discussion between Christians and Jews.

M. AUERBACH

I am placed here in the odd position of having to defend Prof. Gollwitzer. I am not going to do this; rather I shall try to explain what he has said, and I shall try to be brief, although a great deal has been said against him here.

First I should like to answer Mr. Wyschogrod's objections to Gollwitzer's interpretation of Buber's Zionism. On this point I must observe first of all that Mr. Wyschogrod was speaking not against Mr. Gollwitzer, but against Buber, or rather against Buber's Zionism.

Mr. Wyschogrod, you have reminded us of the covenant between God and Israel, and you claim that Buber's Zionism did not sufficiently respect this idea, but took a political line that brought with it the danger of glossing over the historic Jewish tradition. I do not think that Buber is to be understood in that way. Buber was above all a Jew, and a Jew who stood within the tradition, the historical tradition. If I were to evaluate Buber as a Zionist, I would see him as someone who followed in the footsteps of Moses Hess, and as a contemporary of Ahad ha-Am. All three of them were well aware of both the problem of anti-Semitism and the problem of Jewish nationalism, but all three, and especially Buber, refused to consider anti-Semitism as the real underlying motivation for the rise of the Zionist movement. The Zionist movement needed something more, it needed an internal, Jewish justification. This, basically, is the essence of all of Buber's addresses on Judaism and especially on the "Jewish movement".

It should go without saying that Buber did not want a repetition of the Holocaust. Who, in God's name does? It seems to me that

Buber's aim was precisely to show a way that would make a repetition of the horrors of our generation impossible, and this in a manner that does not rely only on defiance and self-assertion. His concern was not only the restoration of the old covenant, and certainly not the restoration of Israel in the old boundaries. He was also concerned, beyond this, with coming to an understanding with other nations, including the nation that lives in Palestine. Many will find this naive and unpolitical, but it certainly was not un-Zionist. It was an attempt to integrate this people Israel, on its own land, into a humane, better society.

And now to our mutual friend Gollwitzer. My dear Mr. Bloch, I did not understand his words as an attempt to dictate to us what political line we should follow here in Israel. Moreover, I do not think we ought to dispute anyone's right to express an opinion on questions that concern another people. I would not take this as unwarranted interference. All that Gollwitzer wants is a more humane society, and in this he is really following Buber's line. The advice he is giving us, or rather the hope he is expressing, is nothing more than the hope of seeing Israel integrated in a truly humanistic manner into the family of nations. He is speaking and arguing in the way people speak and argue in the world today.

Every person is obliged to speak in the language of his surroundings; every nation is obliged to speak in the language of the community of nations. I should like to recall the mistake made by Nasser in his speeches against Israel in May, 1967. I am firmly convinced that he later regretted those words. The historians of the next ten or twenty years will decide whether he meant what he said then.

One of the basic causes of anti-Semitism is that the Jew has never been able to make himself understood as a Jew. Maybe this was because people did not allow him to make himself understood, did not want to understand him. But sooner or later this vicious circle of "Not-being-able-to-make-oneself-understood and not-wanting-to-understand" will have to be broken through. I see with great fear how this problem of not being able to make oneself understood which has plagued the isolated Jew in the Diaspora amid the non-Jewish world over the last two thousand years, is being carried over into the problem of a nation, Israel, not being able to make itself understood among other nations.

I believe that Buber had no other desire than to plead for understanding for Israel in the world, on the one hand, and on the other hand to plead for understanding for the world in Israel. I have known

Mr. Gollwitzer, not for twenty years, like Mr. Bloch, but for twelve years, and I am sure that he intended nothing more than to give expression to a very human and humanistic hope.

H. GORDON

I was happy to hear that Prof. Gollwitzer is interested in our life here in Israel and wishes to help us understand ourselves. I received the impression that he spoke in the spirit of dialogue that accords with Buber. Although for many of those sitting here, his thoughts were not pleasant to hear, I want to thank him for the courage he had to express these thoughts. As Buber remarks, one needs courage to embark upon a dialogue.

I think that many of the attacks against Gollwitzer arise from past disagreements, and I already belong to another generation and this history does not appeal to me. But Gollwitzer's thoughts and ideas do appeal to me, because I agree that in some respects the striving for power guides us here in Israel and not the wish to relate dialogically to God. In Buber's words, we serve Caesar and not the true God.

I feel sad that I must agree with Gollwitzer that the spirit of Buber's writings is missing here. I am personally attempting to teach students to relate to this spirit and to attempt to live by it, with limited success. Therefore I gladly bless any person who is ready to come to us and to help us to live in accordance with this spirit. I do not feel that Gollwitzer wishes to embrace us into Christianity and I do not feel uncomfortable with Christians who wish to criticize us in the spirit of dialogue. Thank you for coming Prof. Gollwitzer, God bless you!

H. GOLLWITZER

Perhaps after all the evening will come to a happy conclusion. But the seriousness of this evening and of the discussion, which has been going on for some years now, between Jochanan Bloch and me, is part of the subject of this conference, if we do not want to regard it as purely historical. And if it were merely that, we would not have come together here.

I should like to answer some of the critical comments and to explain to what extent I accept them or would defend myself against them.

Walter Kaufmann and Jochanan Bloch have voiced, in different words, the same accusation: what I set forth in the central portion of my lecture was an assimilated Buber, my assimilation of Buber; in Bloch's opinion, Buber is for Gollwitzer nothing but a wonderful instrument for the confirmation of his own theology. It is possible to receive this impression, if only because my own theology could not have taken shape without Buber's influence, and consequently I have indeed assimilated important elements of Buber's philosophy as I understood it. The Buberian elements which I have assimilated may help to explain theologically the problem of speech about God. The question is whether in doing so I have distorted Buber or whether I have used an authentic Buber for my own ends, which is natural and legitimate. I pointed out the meaning of language in Buber, and especially its significance for human memory and expectation and also the peculiar character of the language of witness as a language which combines the directness of confession with objective, informative language. I was able to show this in detail in Buber's writings.

My remark about the Incarnation was intended slightly provocatively. It is not to be understood in any other way. It was simply a proposal that we should think a little, together, about this question: if we read the prologue to the Gospel according to John as a Jewish and not as a Greek product (this is a matter of exegetical controversy), in the context of Jewish thought—is verse 14, "The word became flesh", so far removed from Buber's concept of realization? This is not a thesis, but a proposal for reflection.

Third: Karl Barth's remarks in vol. 2,2 of *Church Dogmatics* have concerned me unceasingly ever since I first read them. Let us assume that Christian thinkers think, like Barth—and many of them do—that all ways finally end in the Church, that Israel's way leads to the Church. This could then be taken as a peculiar characteristic of these Christians, who have to be accepted as they are, just as you Jews want to be accepted as you are. Each side would have to put up with this from the other. You know Franz Rosenzweig's story, from a village in Eastern Europe, how a Jewish boy was asked what would happen at the end of days. "Nu," he answered, "what will happen is that all people will be Jews". In that boy's Messianic faith the way of humanity leads to Israel. And in Barth it leads to the Church. But meanwhile I have come to doubt very strongly—and this too is a result of the dialogue in which I am engaged—whether it is an essential hope of Christian faith that all ways of humanity should end in the Church. I rather think that our Christian logic has been surprised by God's direction of history—by the fact that Israel has not been dissolved into the Church, as Paul still hoped. That two "chosen peoples" of God exist side by side. There is surely some good reason for this, and thus my "embrace" of you Jews is not with the intention of drawing you over to our side.

What you have said about the limits of understanding, must certainly be accepted. It is part of the learning process which we also had to go through in the ecumenical movement between Protestants and Catholics, who burnt each other throughout history just as we Christians burnt you Jews. We too had to learn—and this is the most important event among Christians in the 20th century—that we do not have to convert the others to our truth, that there is not only one truth, but that truth is many-faceted. We cannot expect the Catholic to become Protestant, and the wiser Catholics no longer expect us to return to Rome either. And this is repeated in Christian-Jewish relations. I understand the fear which we Christians have put into your hearts for centuries, and perhaps you are afraid we still have some dark purpose. But, thank God, you really do not need to have that fear today, and this new state of affairs has found expression in the remarks by Haim Gordon. We have learned to allow you to exist alongside us and with us as you are, I believe we have finally learned it, it is no longer the problem.

I must say something in my own defense, as a false impression has been created by Bloch's words. Of course, over the last 30 years I have had my own thoughts about Israeli politics, whether in criticism, agreement, understanding, or misgiving. I have expressed these thoughts again and again in my own circle, as a non-Jew and a non-Israeli deeply involved with Israel. I have often had to speak in public about Israel and have had to argue with our young anti-Zionists. And I think I do not have to reproach myself with having publicly criticized official Israeli policy. I have not even expressed my critical reflections in public. Jochanan Bloch and I have had vehement arguments, about politics as about other things, but this did not go beyond the walls of my room. Not that I think that interference is forbidden. Of course I interfere! I interfere in Chilean affairs and I interfere in Soviet affairs, of course I interfere in Israeli affairs. What sort of provincialism is that, to say I don't express my opinion about American presidential candidates? On the contrary, I expressed my opinion very strongly when it looked as if Nixon might get in, and it turned out exactly as I had feared. The question is not whether it is all right to interfere, but whether, in the situation you are in, it is all right for a person to express in public an opinion whose consequences he would not have to bear himself. And therefore what I said is not to be taken as a political prescription. And furthermore, you would have spared me the entire second part if you had prepared a program which treated Buber's Zionism with the breadth it deserves. This did not occur, and for me, with my theology, the separation between theory and practice is unbearable. It is in contradiction to Buber, and of course, it is also in contradiction to my own theological view. That's why I had to say it.

I ask you to believe what I am going to say now. I took Communion with our Christian Jews, and afterwards they were deported. And I stayed at home and did not do what the priest does in Rolf Hochhut's "The Deputy"—jump into the deportation train. I let them put the uniform on me and I was not swallowed up by the Holocaust. In my position I can only ask you, a survivor of the Holocaust, to believe that I think about this day and night, and that everything that I am doing today follows from this, and that I am profoundly aware that I am not in your situation. But nevertheless I thought that for the sake of the inseparability of theory and practice I had an obligation to speak about Buber's Zionism. And here I must say the following: in the criticisms which have been voiced I did not hear that I had portrayed Buber's Zionism in a false light. Rotenstreich points out the boundaries of Buber's Zionism; Bloch criticizes Buber. I understand this. But clearly I formulated Buber's concern correctly. I formulated it negatively, with the Nazi word "master race". That is, all nations, or very many nations, have been the "master race" at some time in their history and have oppressed other nations. This is a permanent element in the history of the European nations. If I have correctly understood Buber, and Leo Baeck, and all those from whom I have learned something about Judaism, then *this* nation must not repeat the sins of other nations, must not become a "master race".

And therefore, dear Jochanan, I have not pronounced a prophecy, but have simply spoken in the spirit of the prophets—you can, I hope, make that distinction—I have not voiced a demand, I have simply said in the spirit of the prophets that this land, the land of Palestine, has become a double homeland: it was promised to you, but you know the Jewish saying: "God promised us the land of Palestine, but he didn't give us an exact map of it". From Dan to Beersheva or from the Golan Heights to Eilat? This promised land has also become the homeland of another people through two thousand years of history. We cannot speak theologically about the significance of history for human existence while ignoring the significance of the historical fact that the Promised Land is promised to

Israel, and at the same time Arabs too have their home here. And in this situation I pointed to ideas in Buber's speeches about the Arab question at the Zionist congresses, and in the writings of Yehuda Magnes, which seem today to be of merely antiquarian interest. My "prophecy" was that the generation of Haim Gordon will read those texts once again with great interest and will find much in them that will speak to their problems and will show them the way they must go.

Notes

HELMUT GOLLWITZER

1. Martin Buber, "Dialogue", in *Between Man and Man*, trans. by Ronald Gregor Smith, Beacon Press, Boston, 1955, p. 19.

2. Hans-Joachim Schoeps, *The Jewish-Christian Argument; a history of theologies in conflict*, trans. by David E. Green, New York, Holt, Rinehart & Winston, 1963.

3. Cf. Th. Steinbüchel, *Der Umbruch des Denkens*, F. Pustet, Regensburg, 1936.

4. Cf. Gerhard Gloege, "Der theologische Personalismus as theologisches Problem," *Kerygma und Dogma* 1 (1955), pp. 23-41, reprinted in: *Heilsgeschenen und Welt*, Göttingen, Vandenhoeck & Ruprecht 1965, pp. 53-76; also H. Diem, "Dogmatik zwischen Personalismus und Ontologie," *Evangelische Theologie* 15 (1955), pp. 408-415; B. Langemeyer, *Der dialogische Personalismus in der evangelischen und katholischen Theologie der Gegenwart*, Verlag Bonifacius Druckerei, Paderborn, 1963; W. Michel, *Martin Buber. Sein Gang in die Wirklichkeit*, Rütten & Loening, Frankfurt/Main, 1926.

5. Friedrich Gogarten, *Ich glaube an den dreieinigen Gott*, E. Diederichs, Jena, 1926, p. 34.

6. Op. cit., p. 35.

7. F. Gogarten, *Von Glauben und Offenbarung*, E. Diederichs, Jena, 1923, p. 81.

8. Op. cit., pp. 76-79. Gogarten against Angelus Silesius and Meister Eckart: The world is "broken apart into I and Thou." The Thou stands opposite me "in harsh, absolute opposition." "God's Thou remains as distant, as alien from us as every other Thou—all the more distant, more alien, more unapproachable because it is the Thou of God." See, in contrast, Buber: "Of course God is 'the wholly Other'; but he is also the wholly same: the wholly present. Of course, he is the *mysterium tremendum* that appears and overwhelms; but he is also the mystery of the obvious that is closer to me than my own I." (*I and Thou*, A New Translation with a Prologue "I and You" and Notes by Walter Kaufmann, Scribner, New York, 1970, p. 127).

9. "Nachwort," *Schriften über das dialogische Prinzip*, Lambert Schneider, Heidelberg, 1954, p. 296.

10. Gogarten, *Von Glauben und Offenbarung*, p. 77.

11. Cf. E. Käsemann, "Zum Thema der Nichtobjektivierbarkeit," *Evangelische Theologie* 12 (1952/53), pp. 455-456; reprinted in: *Exegetische Versuche und Besinnungen* I, Vandenhoeck & Ruprecht, Göttingen, 1960, pp. 224-236.

12. Letter of 28.12.1936 to R. G. Smith, in M. Buber, *Briefwechsel aus sieben Jahrzenten*, II: 1918-1938, ed. by Grete Schaeder 1973, p. 628. Cf. the "Nachwort" to *Schriften über das dialogische Prinzip*, p. 296, where Buber comments that it is Heim who "has most emphatically indicated the turning which must be carried out."

13. Cf. Buber, *I and Thou*, pp. 95f., 117: "Dialogue," in *Between Man and Man*, trans. by Ronald Gregor Smith, Beacon Press, Boston, 1955, p. 36f.; *Eclipse of God: Studies in the Relation Between Religion and Philosophy*, trans. by Maurice S. Friedman, Harper Torchbooks, New York, 1957, p. 129.

14. K. Heim, *Glaube und Denken*, Furche, Berlin, 1931, p. 205, further p. 206: The insights "which dawned on Buber in a visionary manner must now be expressed logically."

15. Cf. the last sentences of the "Afterword" to *I and Thou*: "The existence of mutuality between God and man cannot be proved any more than the existence of God. Anyone who dares nevertheless to speak of it bears witness and invokes the witness of those whom he addresses—present and future witnesses." (p. 182) Similarly the last sentence of "Dialogue": "All the regulated chaos of the age waits for the break-through, and whenever a man perceives and responds, he is working to that end." (*Between Man and Man*, p. 39) Finally in "God and the Spirit of Man": "The eclipse of the light of God is no extinction; even tomorrow that which has stepped in between may give way." (*Eclipse of God*, p. 129.)

16. Heinrich Emil Brunner, "Judaism and Christianity in Buber," *The Philosophy of Martin Buber*, ed. by P. A. Schilpp and M. Friedman, Cambridge University Press, London, 1967, p. 309. Cf. Brunner's letters to Buber in: Briefwechsel II, N. 383, 424, 563; III (1975) No. 293, 552.

17. Brunner, "Preface," *Dogmatics*, trans. by Olive Wyon, The Westminster Press, Philadelphia, 1949-62, vol II, p. v.

18. Op. cit., vol III, pp. 220, 223.

19. Ibid., p. 220.

20. In his essay "Towards a Missionary Theology," in *Christian Century*, July 6, 1949, he writes that in this book he had finally attained full clarity. It was preceded by *God and Man; four essays on the nature of personality*, trans. by David Cairns, Student Christian Movement Press, London, 1936 (original German edition published 1930).

21. Brunner, *Dogmatics*, vol. III, p. 172.

22. Cf. Brunner's remarks on *Two Types of Faith* in *Dogmatics*, III, pp. 159ff, and his essay cited in note 16. See also H. U. von Balthasar, "Martin Buber and Christianity," Schilpp-Friedman, op. cit., pp. 341-359.

23. Buber, *Eclipse of God*, p. 107.

24. Buber, "The Power of the Spirit," *Israel and the World: Essays in a Time of Crisis*, Schocken, New York, 1936, p. 179.

25. Brunner, *Wahrheit als Begegnung*, 2. Aufl., 1963, p. 146 (trans. E. K.).

26. K. Barth, *Church Dogmatics*, vol. III/2, pp. 128-132. Cf. U. Hedinger, *Der Freiheitsbegriff in der Kirchlichen Dogmatik Karl Barths*, Zwingli Verlag, Zürich, 1962.

27. Cf. Barth, op. cit., vol. III/3 pp. 135f; I/2, p. 374.

28. Op. cit., vol. III/3, p. 110.

29. See especially *Church Dogmatics* IV/3, § 70,1: "The True Witness"; also "Das Geschenk der Freiheit," *Theologische Studien*, Heft 39, Zürich 1953.

30. *Church Dogmatics* III/3, p. 93.

31. Cf. Brunner, *Dogmatics* II, p. 149; Barth, *Church Dogmatics* III/3, p. 86ff.

32. *Church Dogmatics* I/2, p. 886.

33. B. Caspar speaks of "Buber's predilection for Pelagian formulations" (*Das dialogische Denken*, 1967, p. 391.)

34. Brunner, *Dogmatics* III, p. 161.

35. Brunner, "Judaism and Christianity in Buber," Schilpp-Friedman, p. 309.

36. Brunner, *Dogmatics* II, p. 106.

37. *Dogmatics* III, p. 277.

38. Cf. ibid., pp. 279ff.

39. Cf. Barth, *Church Dogmatics* IV/2, 66,4: "The Awakening to Conversation."

40. Cf. the foundation-laying essay of H. W. Wolff, "Das Thema 'Umkehr' in der alttestamentlichen Prophetie," *Zeitschrift für Theologie und Kirche* 48(51), pp. 129-

148; reprinted in *Gesammelte Studien zum Alten Testament*, C. Kaiser, Müchen, 1964, pp. 130-150.

41. Cf. Buber, Briefwechsel II, Nr. 545-548.

42. Cf. Buber, "The Question to the Single One," in: *Between Man and Man*, pp. 76-79.

43. Cf. Buber, "What Is Man?" in *Between Man and Man*, p. 203.

44. Cf. Barth, *Church Dogmatics* III/2, p. 277.

45. Ibid., p. 278.

46. Buber, "Nachwort," Schriften über das dialogische Prinzip, pp. 303ff.

47. Cf. Barth, *Church Dogmatics* IV/3, 62,2: "The Light of Life."

48. Brunner, Dogmatics II, p. 216. Of course, this sentence also shows the difference between Brunner's Buber reception and Barth's agreement with Buber. To Brunner Buber's personalism was important in the inquiry after the right way of speaking about God and faith. In this respect Barth did not need such help, he rather feared a driving-home of personalistic conclusions from a presupposed principle (cf. Diem's essay cited in note 4; hence, also, Barth's orally expressed reservations concerning my monograph *Die Existenz Gottes im Bekenntnis des Glaubens* (*The Existence of God as Confessed by Faith*, trans. by James Leitch, Westminster Press, Philadelphia, 1965.), which makes considerable use of Buber's thought). Unlike Tillich, he does not consider personality to be an inauthentic attribute of God—on the contrary; and, like Buber and Brunner, he admits the inevitability of such anthropological ways of speaking (see especially *Church Dogmatics* II/1, pp. 284-297), but he develops this not from a philosophy however rooted in the Bible, but from the totality of Divine utterance in the Bible itself. On the other hand, he is closer than Brunner is to Buber in that the latter develops the I-Thou relationship in a primarily anthropological manner, much as Barth does in the text on fellow-humanness cited above (compare with this the first pages of *I and Thou*!).

49. Cf. Grete Schaeder, "The Dialogue with Christianity," in *The Hebrew Humanism of Martin Buber*, trans. by Noah J. Jacobs, Wayne State University Press, Detroit, 1973, pp. 388-410; also H. J. Kraus, "Gespräch mit Martin Buber," *Evangelische Theologie* 12 (1952/53), pp. 59-77.

50. Cf. Buber, "Dialogue," in *Between Man and Man*, p. 8: "A time of genuine religious conversations is beginning . . . genuine dialogues, speech from certainty to certainty, but also from one open-hearted person to another open-hearted person. Only then will genuine common life appear, not that of an identical content of faith which is alleged to be found in all religions, but that of the situation, of anguish and expectation."

51. Buber, "Church, State, Nation, Jewry," in Christianity—Some Non-Christian Appraisals, ed. David W. McKain, McGraw-Hill, New York, (1964), p. 178.

52. Buber, "Dialogue," *Between Man and Man*, p. 5.

53. Buber, *Two Types of Faith*, translated by Norman Goldhawk, Harper Torchbooks, New York, 1961, p. 13.

54. Buber, "Dialogue," *Between Man and Man*, pp. 5f.

55. In Buber, *Pointing the Way—Collected Essays*, trans. from the German and ed. by Maurice Friedman, Harper, New York, 1957, pp. 208-219.

56. Ibid., p. 217.

57. Ibid.

58. Buber, "The Power of the Spirit," *Israel and the World: Essays in a Time of Crisis*, Schocken, New York, 1963, p. 180.

59. Buber, *Briefwechsel* III, p. 351.

"Jewish Religiosity" According to Buber

PINHAS HA-COHEN PELI

1

"Jewish Religiosity" is the name of the fifth speech in the series of "speeches on Judaism"[1] which Buber began in Prague at the age of 31, in 1909, and which he continued to give for decades as a "continuing address" in Vienna, Berlin, New York, London and Jerusalem.[2] But Jewish religiosity (without quotation marks), as a subject to be contended with and as a subject for creative thinking, is one of the central themes in Buber's thought. Probably, then, it is no coincidence that the speech which Buber called "Jewish Religiosity" contains certain elements of his thought, many years before the formation of the philosophy of "I and Thou" and before Buber arrived at the summaries of his studies of Hasidism, or his penetrating interpretations of the Holy Scriptures. The study of this speech will lead us, I believe, to the conclusion that in certain respects it anticipates and invites these later works.

It seems that this speech includes what in the language of literature and poetry is called "fundamental visions" of the poet, which he absorbs at a certain period of his childhood or youth: visions, or in the present case revelations, from which the poet—the thinker—can never again free himself; he returns, of his own free will or by compulsion, to wrestle with them again and again. The complicated systems of original thought and interpretation which Buber created in the decades of his creativity are impressive; but among the splendid many-storied buildings which Buber erected, those addresses on Judaism seem like temporary lodgings in which he rested from time to time, in order to speak explicitly to the broader public, or perhaps even to himself.

2

What importance should we attribute to these "addresses on Judaism" within the general framework of Buber's work? To what extent were the later ones summaries of sustained thinking in the

419

past, the early ones harbingers of future long-term work? In trying to answer this question, we need discuss the addresses from two points of view:

a. What is the real historical role which these addresses played in the influence of Buber on his generation, an influence which perhaps was not without a fruitful mutual relationship between the addresser and his hearers, between the teacher and his students?

b. What is the individual, specific weight of these addresses as expressions of Buber's thought?

As to the first question, the answer is clear. We can rely on the testimony of that generation as to the powerful influence exercised by the first addresses on Shmuel Hugo Bergmann,[3] Franz Rosenzweig,[4] the cousins Robert and Felix Weltsch,[5] Buber's biographer Hans Kohn,[6] Max Brod, Franz Kafka,[7] Gershom Scholem,[8] Akiba Ernst Simon,[9] and others. They testify that the first three addresses, then the three additional ones, and finally the eight addresses collected in the Frankfurt am Main edition of 1923 under the name *Reden über das Judentum* changed the life course of members of a whole generation of the young searching Jewish intelligentsia in Central and Western Europe.

As to the second, more essential question—a careful investigation will show, in the light of the continuation of Buber's work, that the argument[10] that people rely too much on these addresses in discussing Buber's teaching, and that do not represent his opinions, is not acceptable. On the contrary, some if not all of the addresses, and particularly the fifth, "Jewish Religiosity", indeed express what we called earlier the "fundamental visions" of all Buber's future thought.[11] The terminology changes, but the problem with which the address is concerned did not abandon Buber from the beginning of his career until the end. These two points of view, the historical and the ideational, from which we propose to examine the addresses (or "sermons" drashot, as Hugo Bergmann preferred to call them), are not separate; when we come to determine the defining characteristic of the addresses, the two join together.

3

We must remember that the "addresses" were not born detached from the problems of the time in which they were created. On the contrary, most of them were invited addresses responding to a definite, concrete, sometimes even urgent need. When Buber accepted the invitation of the Zionist students, members of Bar Cochba in Prague to lecture to them on Judaism, he knew what was required of him and why they had chosen him, in particular, to light a path for them amid the perplexity into which they had fallen on their way from the ideals and "isms" of progressive Europe to Zionism, which shifted its burden to the building of the Land of Israel, far and rejected in the remoteness of the backward East. He knew this searching youth whose soul longed for a new Jewish content, different from and other than what they found in the Jewish world which they had only just discovered. This otherness they hoped to receive from Buber, whose literary work, though still modest in quantity,[12] heralded the appearance of an European Jewish creator who was not occupied with utterances "on Judaism" or with moralistic apologetics, but with the thing itself, with authentic chapters of Judaism which were so close—Hasidism and the Hasidim were only an hour's train ride away—and yet so distant. In the form in which Buber presented Hasidism and the Hasidim there was not a trace of the repulsion aroused by those strange types dressed in black caftans who wandered in from the East. The Hasidic stories as Buber retold them spoke to the heart and elevated the spirit.[13]

In my opinion it is forbidden to us to accept the merciless indictment heard in the words of Nahum Glatzer,[14] to the effect that Buber said what he said with the deliberate intent of pleasing those young people in Prague who wanted to hear from the mouth of an authority words that would affirm Judaism even while negating it, and that Buber said the words out of self-interest, in order to become that authority for which the young generation of alienated Jews who had returned to Judaism was waiting. This is a severe indictment, and Glatzer does not have sufficient evidence on which to base this accusation. It is more correct to assume—and the continuation of Buber's struggles with these subjects over a period of decades will prove—that the words reflect Buber's real train of thought at that time; a train of thought which, in being voiced, gained a "momentum" of its own, and Buber remained its prisoner for many years, during which he tried again and again to translate it into a consistent language, theory, and world-view.

We said "his train of thought at that time", for the addresses are firmly anchored in their time and place, and Buber was reacting in them, not to expectations or to "what they wanted to hear from him", but to matters which were of crucial interest to the Jewish youth of

Central and Western Europe, to which he belonged. In their simplistic formulation, these matters had to do with the "solution to the Jewish question", which painfully and existentially concerned Jewish youth in the East and the West, in each person in accordance with his temperament and cultural background. The struggle with this question did not come into the world with Buber, or with the Zionist students in Prague and Vienna. In 1909, when Buber gave his first address on Judaism, this question already stood in the center of Jewish thought for sixty or seventy years, since Moses Hess, through all the struggling Jewish thought of the nineteenth century—a situation reflected in kaleidoscopic form in the two volumes of Nathan Rotenstreich's *Jewish Philosophy in Modern Times*[15] and in the second volume of Yehezkel Kaufmann's *Golah ve-Nekhar* (Diaspora and Foreign Land).[16] The number of attempts to find what was called a solution to the "question of Jewish existence" was equal to the numbers of thinkers and publicists who addressed the subject. And when Buber took it upon himself to address this subject, it was demanded of him both by his adherents and by himself to say something *new*, and this he indeed intended to do.

However, despite all that was new in his words, we should view them as part of the Jewish thought of his time and also as a direct reaction to that thought; a textual analysis will prove that Jewish thought, including that of Eastern Europe, was not unfamiliar to him. In the years 1906-1914 a tempestuous polemic encompassing the majority of the thinkers of the Revival, had broken out following the publication of S. Y. Hurwitz's essay "On the Question of the Existence of Judaism".[17] All eight of the addresses given between 1909-1919, relate to that polemic but to substantiate our thesis we shall confine ourselves to the fifth and central address, "Jewish Religiosity", for which all the preceding addresses, especially the first and the third, are a preparation. The "innovation" in this address is the obvious tenet seized upon by many, whether to rely on it or to attack it—namely the rebellion against halakha, which emphasizes the aridity of established religion, as against the source of living water of another hidden Judaism, subterranean. In this rebellion Buber had many predecessors, among them the trailblazers of Reform Judaism on the one hand,[18] and some of the giants of modern Hebrew literature (Yehuda Leib Gordon, Achad Ha-Am, Berdichevsky)[19] on the other hand. The "innovation" in this address is not in *negation* but rather in *affirmation,* despite the fact that Buber succeeded in polarizing and exacerbating the real or artificial rift between "Torah" and "mitsvot"—for which Franz Rosenzweig later castigated him in his letter "The Builders".[20] This affirmation contains "the whole Buber" in a nutshell. It is, if one may use a term from the lexicon of the tradition, a one-time, nuclear "revelation". And yet, if we continue in this vocabulary we shall say: And Mordechai Martin Buber approached the cloud in which God was. And in that cloud he remained. This is the problem of Buber's "Jewish religiosity".

On the one hand we stand in admiration before the daring; especially against the background of all that Jewish thinking about the "solution to the question of Judaism" that preceded him. However, on the other hand we grope along with Buber in the cloud into which he led us when, in the words of Gershom Scholem,[21] he "promised" to the rigidified Jewish world revelations of a revolutionary awakening from within. He promised the discovery of a hidden life beneath the official, rigidified forms, a revelation of riches stored up in our treasure-house, if only we knew how to cross the threshold and enter. This and much more he promised to his listeners, but he did not show a clear way. And all the attempts Buber made afterwards to dispel this cloud, to "elucidate" himself, to coin precise terms and to bring them to "realization" were unsuccessful. Some of these attempts are explicit, as in the famous Introduction to the 1923 edition of the speeches; some of them are not explicit, merely to be inferred. Nevertheless, one may say that, as they are defined here, they already herald the appearance of the eternal Thou vis-a-vis the "I" which longs and seeks Him with the deep emotion of "religiosity"; here is the cornerstone for the great structure of dialogical philosophy. However, at our present stage we do not succeed in divesting ourselves of the cloud which surrounds us when we enter together with Buber, the "dark sanctuary" of his soul, in which dwells "Jewish religiosity" as he perceived it in the days of his youth.

4

Thus, the essay "Jewish Religiosity" belongs to the thought of its generation and of the generation preceding it. The "key word" here (to use a term taken from Buber's method of Biblical exegesis) is the word *revival*, Jewish Revival. Baruch Kurzweil rightly argues[22] that the very use of the word "revival" tells us that we have before us something "dead" which has to be revived. In talk about "revival" there is a renunciation of continuous eternity, exchanging it for "a slice of wretched reality". Indeed, among the adherents of Torah and in the courts of the tsaddikim in Eastern Europe they did not speak of revival, nor seek justifications for the continued existence of Judaism, nor even new definitions of its essence, outside the traditional definition of Torah and mitsvot. However, for a large part of the people, at first in the West, and then also for the younger generation in the East, this topic became vital, a matter of burning urgency. The quest of the individual was linked to the searching of the community, and in the solution to the question of the Jews as a community they sought a solution for the distress of the individual. The words of M. L. Lilienblum, one of the great "seekers" and "reformers" of Eastern Europe, characterize this way of thinking, which appears in many different shades: "The political life which we shall live will set everything right."[23] Moses Hess, perhaps the greatest Jewish thinker of modern times, states that "national revival precedes religious revival".[24] And even Achad Ha-Am, who emphasized the revival of the hearts and the Torah of the heart, states in a reaction to Yehuda Leib Magnes (in the year 1910) that nationality comes first and that only in it is a "safe shelter not only for Jews but also for Judaism".[25] There are only a few exceptions to the general chorus of those who defined "revival" as basically national revival, among them A. D. Gordon, who spoke of a "revival of the spirit"[26]—not an academic revival, a revival of knowledge, or a political revival, "but a revival of life". Rabbi Abraham Isaac Kook speaks of a cosmic "revival of holiness".[27] Among all these Buber's voice stands out: he calls the child by its name and says that revival can only begin with the individual, and that it begins not with something general, like "life" or "holiness", but with something many preferred to soft-pedal: with religion. Buber states clearly:

> Jewish religiosity is not, as many people think, a matter of admittedly special dignity but otherwise negligible moment for the so-called "solution of the Jewish question". It is rather, now as always, the only matter of unconditional moment for Judaism—motive power of its fate, guidepost to its destiny, a force whose upsurging blaze would restore it to new life and whose total extinction would deliver it to death. Renewal of Judaism means in reality renewal of Jewish religiosity.[28]

A. D. Gordon also spoke of a revival of religion, but his emphasis was basically on the perfect life, which comprised "the *morality* of life, the *religion*[29] of life, the *poetry* of life". The medicine he prescribes is: "Labor is our cure". A. D. Gordon wanted to "save" Yom Kippur, not to "lose" it, as that would be a "national loss"; he cries out against the discarding of religion because "during all our long exile we existed by the strength of our religion".[30] With Buber, religion is not a means, but an end in itself, *the* end. Here is the innovation.

Achad Ha-Am,[31] like Hermann Cohen[32] in the West, bases Judaism entirely on morality. But Buber states, without specific reference: "The meaning of the act of decision in Judaism is falsified if it is viewed as merely an ethical act. It is a religious act, or rather, it is the religious act; for it is God's realization through man."[33] And again: "Every construct of a pure 'ethics' of Judaism misses this basic point. Wherever the unconditional deed reveals the hidden divine countenance, there is the core of Judaism".[34] From Buber's vague words there emerges, directed at Achad Ha-Am, the same devastating criticism which Yehezkel Kaufmann levels against him:

> Spiritual Zionism, established by Achad Ha-Am, relies on an erroneous distinction as to the nature of the factors at work in the history of Israel until this day, that is on a false evaluation of the workings of the *religious* factor in the history of Israel. The Jewish religion did not serve as a 'means' in the hands of the desire for national survival to ensure the existence of the nation, nor was it a storehouse of the 'tools of the Diaspora", which the desire for national survival might use to gain its end. Religion was the *primary motive* in the history of Israel, which forced the people to separate from its surroundings and to survive in its singularity.[35]

In this criticism Buber preceded Yehezkel Kaufmann by several decades, and it was an "innovation" then, as it is still today for many. In Zionist thought Buber was almost alone with this opinion. I say "almost", because at the same time words of even a greater clarity and faith concerning national revival, the renewal of religion and of original Jewish socialism, were being spoken by a contemporaneous thinker who has been almost forgotten: Shlomo Schiller, who preceded Buber by a generation in leaving Europe and ascending to the land of Israel.[36]

Buber's statement that Judaism cannot be replaced by morality, nationality, and such like, and that it is entirely based on religion, impelled him to turn to the definition of that religion. Obviously, he could not accept the Orthodox concept, not even in its Hirschian,

Germanized guise of "Torah with secular culture".[37] Nor could Buber, as a proud Zionist, a contemporary and confidant of Herzl, accept Reform religiosity, diluted as it was with much apologetics and obsequious self-effacement. On the other hand, Hasidism, as it emerges from the stories of Rabbi Nachman and the tales of the Baal Shem, enchanted the contemporary European culture. So, leaning on the antinomian element which he sees in Hasidism, Buber set out on his journey of affirming the negation, which he believes is the way of man.

The starting-point is the distinction between religion and religiosity—a distinction which he did not invent, but for which he coined new terms. The tension which exists in every religion, in every spiritual movement, between the idea and its realization, between the experiential revelation and its translation into the language of life—in Jewish terms: between "Halakhah" and "Aggadah"—this tension has been well known from time immemmorial. Buber, employing his abundant rhetorical gifts, heightened this tension to a rift that cannot be mended, a gap that cannot be bridged. "I say and mean: religiosity",[38] he emphasizes; "I do not say and I do not mean: religion". What is the difference between the two? The list of differences which Buber spells out with great fervor is long, and these words have, as Gershom Scholem testified, "broad wings whose beating sounded beautiful in our youth".[39] Here are some of the differences, according to Buber, between "religion" and "religiosity".

Religion is static—religiosity is dynamic.

Religion is cold and rigid; religiosity is fervent.

Religion is sterile; religiosity is fertile.

Religion flows out of religiosity, but continues to lead a severed existence as "unalterable law", without regard to religiosity which continually renews itself and aspires to a new form.

Religion is the organizing principle; religiosity is the creative principle.

Religion is forced by the fathers upon the children; religiosity starts anew with every young person who seeks the truth.

Religion means passivity; religiosity means activity—the elemental entering into relation with the absolute.

Religiosity has only itself as an end, but religion has other purposes, to the point that religiosity is lost on account of religion and the two become hostile to each other.

This does not exhaust the list. And Buber takes upon himself: "I shall try to extricate the unique character of Jewish religiosity from the rubble with which rabbinism and rationalism have covered it". And what does he extricate? The words of Buber in addresses on Judaism, as Gershom Scholem says,[40] "had a profoundly dual character: an awakening power, on the one hand, and a strange vagueness on the other, a vagueness which Buber never acknowledged". Indeed, when you read the words at a distance of sixty years, you feel that some lofty peak is being scaled here; but when you arrive with Buber, perspiring and weary, at the summit, you discover that there was no mountain there at all. What appeared before as a mountain shrouded in mystery has disappeared, melted away. All that remains is the cloud at the top of the mountain. The clear signpost that would show us the way to the goal which he urges us to attain. Probably, however, Gershom Scholem's verdict that beneath the words which have a "stimulating power" there is a "strange vagueness" should be mollified, for, as we have seen, they conveyed a trailblazing truth, which may also be recognized in their influence; in the lives of many people the words became a turning-point. Can such be done with beautiful and "vague" words alone?

How, then, does Buber see the "religiosity" which he so endears? Let us try to epitomize his words: a.) Religiosity means freedom. "The act that Judaism has always considered the essence and foundation of all religiosity is the act of decision as realization of divine freedom and unconditionality on earth". Here he brings in the act of *teshuva*, the turning, which is based on the freedom of choice, since "Sin means to live not in freedom, that is, decision-making, but in bondage, that is, being acted upon, conditioned. The man who 'returns' rises to freedom; he rises from conditionality into freedom; he is, as the Zohar calls it, 'alive all around, at one with the tree of life' ". And again: complete freedom without dependency is the special religious content of Judaism. The idea in itself is not original, it prevails in existentialist literature[41] and has foundations in classical Jewish thought on the subject of "turning",[42] but it is expressed here with overpowering force. b.) An aspiration toward *unity* vis-a-vis the rifts in life and in the world. In the third speech Buber broadly discussed this longing for unity, to which he joins the unifying act.[43] Inspiration and action which fill the life of a person lead to perfection. Here he criticizes Christianity, which opposes the Jewish character:

> the early Christian movement became barren for the Jew when it converted Jesus' truly Jewish proclamation that every man could become a son of God by living unconditionally into the doctrine that

nothing except belief in the only begotten son of God could win eternity for man.

In the "no" to the early Christian movement which distorted Jesus' message, one hears a "yes" to that message itself. And indeed the latter belongs, in Buber's opinion, not to "the forces of specific periods" but to the "eternal forces" which constitute the true Judaism, that is, the anti-establishment Judaism, the hidden Judaism, the revolution in the depths.

The flight from the present, ugly Judaism to the "true," beautiful Judaism is not unique to Buber. It abounds in modern Hebrew literature, which sought support in ancient myths (Berdichevsky,[44] Frischmann,[45] Schneur,[46] and others). The difference is that while we know more or less what these authors seek—a muscular Judaism, a Judaism of lusts and passions, a Judaism liberated from the complexes of exile, etc., which imply abandoning religion and religiosity together—Buber in his flight from religion wishes to reach religion; he flees from it to it. But how does one get from a rigidified, established, static religion to a fervent, living, fruitful religiosity?

Buber tries to sketch for us a map which will lead us to the true Judaism, which lies under three layers through which we must pass. The first is the "imitatio Dei", which appears already in the Talmud as an explanation of the possibility of cleaving to God.[47] The second: man's act of decision as a realization of God ("if you are my witnesses, I am God")[48]—the reality or presence of God in the world is dependent on man—an idea which was afterwards developed and broadened and serves as a basis for the religious philosophy of Avraham Heschel.[49] The third layer is taken from the domain of the Kabbala, and posits the influence of man's deed on God's destiny. By his deeds man strengthens the "household of heaven", and causes the raising of the world and the raising of the Shekhina.

Beneath these three layers is revealed "the subterranean Judaism which, secret and suppressed, remains authentic and bears witness, in contradistinction to an official, sham Judaism whose power and public representation have neither authority nor legitimacy". These are mighty words of protest against "official Judaism"; their fervor recalls expressions which have a messianic tinge, as in Sabbetaianism. With the same fervor Buber tells us that "All these concepts have in common a concept that is innate in Jewish religiosity: the concept of the absolute value of man's deed. Something infinite flows into a deed of man; something infinite flows from it." The transition from the covering layers to religiosity is sharp and swift. Suddenly, man and not God is established in the center, and his deed is an *absolute* act. Not only this: man's deed is not important in itself.

> Not the matter of a deed determines its truth but the manner in which it is carried out: in human conditionality. Whether a deed will peter out in the outer courtyard, in the realm of things, or whether it will penetrate into the Holy of Holies is determined not by its content but by the power of decision which brought it about, and by the sanctity of intent that dwells in it. Every deed, even one numbered among the most profane, is holy when it is performed in holiness, in unconditionality.

According to Buber "religiosity's counteraction to religion", has two faces. The first is the rebellion of heretics which breaks out periodically and is frequently accompanied by powerful Messianic movements which shake the world to its depth. The second is the constant and constructive activity of religious mysticism, which is expressed, he tells us, in three historical movements: the prophets, the Essenes (or the early Christians who carried the true message of Jesus), and the Hasidim. Borne aloft on the wings of this idea, Buber continues to soar on one of those winged words which have become signposts in his world: "The truth is not a What but a How". In speaking of Elijah's war against the prophets of Baal, he says that "whether worhsip-service served idols or serves God depends not on the name by which one calls one's God but on the way in which one serves Him".

In order to support his thesis, which he propounded as an attempt at "a solution to Judaism" through a revival of religiosity, Buber seemingly relies on historical experiences. He reveals to us, so to speak, a new Judaism, a subterranean Judaism existing, according to him, throughout the history of Israel. If there is not a *revival* here, there certainly is a *rejection*. A rejection of venerable portions of what kept Judaism in existence, despite—or perhaps because of—the tension between Halakah ("religion") and Haggadah ("religiosity"), as these are depicted, for example, in Bialik's essay,[50] or in the profound definitions of Rav Kook.[51] This rejection is carried out with a high and confident hand.

"Religion" and "religiosity" as Buber conceived of them, one being accepted and the other rejected, are, he tells us, archetypes of an "eternal" typology in Judaism. Here, for instance, are his words on

Moses and Aaron, in which the influence of Achad Ha-am's essay "Priest and Prophet" can be recognized.[52] In Achad Ha-am there is synthesis and reconciliation in the cooperation of these two types in order to advance society and strengthen its foundations; in Buber there is no reconciliation between the two, but a struggle.

> Here the two dominant human types who wage the struggle of Judaism's internal history are already juxtaposed to each other: the prophet and the priest. Moses is the man of demand who listens only to the voice, acknowledges only the deed. Aaron is the mediator, as accessible to the voices as to the voice, who destroys the people's discipline by his directionless and subservient formalism . . . The prophet wants truth; the priest, power. They are eternal types in the history of Judaism.

It is easy to guess toward which of these leaders Buber is directing us. Yet how do we attain the hearing of the "voice"? And how do I know what is the "how" that God wants, or that I should want, in order to reach perfection or the "great reality" to which I must aspire beyond the "what"? It seems that, according to Buber, the answer to this question—a critical question for us today—will be found in the no-man's-land between mysticism and nihilism, when we are stirred by a Messianic impulse and a heretical rebellion. From these he arrives at the sanctification of secular action. However, does such not lead us out of the domain of Jewish religiosity or any religiosity?

Already within the relatively short address on "Jewish Religiosity" and especially in the words that come after it, Buber is struggling to explain what he meant by the "great reality" which we are supposed to attain. Is it not a mirage produced by a youthful apparition and revealing itself to the poet in the fundamental visions which establish his world and of which alone he can sing, or perhaps there is here instruction in a way of life, "realization" (a word Buber loved)? Although much is said in the address on "Jewish religiosity" about the "how", at the end of the address he slightly contradicts himself and attempts to convince us that we cannot get along without the "what", which, like the "how", can find expression only in action. Thus he says at the conclusion of his essay on "religiosity":

> Religiosity is . . . man's urge to establish a living communion with the unconditioned; it is man's will to realize the unconditioned through his deed, and to establish it in his world. Genuine religiosity, therefore, has nothing in common with the fantasies of romantic hearts, or with the self-pleasure of aestheticizing souls, or with the clever mental exercises of a practiced intellectuality. Genuine religiosity is *doing*. It

wants to sculpt the unconditioned out of the matter of this world. The countenance of God reposes, invisible, in an earthen block; it must be wrought, carved out of it. To engage in this work means to be religious—nothing else. Men's life, open to our influence as is no other thing in this world, is that task apportioned to us in its most inward immediacy. Here, as nowhere else, multiplicity is given into our hands, to be transformed into unity; a vast, formless mass, to be in-formed with the Divine. The community of men is as yet only a projected opus that is waiting for us, a chaos we must put in order, a Diaspora we must gather in, a conflict to which we must bring reconciliation. But this we can accomplish only if, in the natural context of a life shared with others, every one of us, each in his own place, will perform the just, the unifying, the in-forming deed. For God does not want to be believed in, to be debated and defended by us, but simply to be realized through us.

The "how" changes back into a clear and explicit "what", whose main thrust is the reform of human society. Do not Buber's final words contradict the opening? Hugo Bergmann rightly asks:[53] if giving society a form is a moral task, how is it that the moral task turns into a religious one? "The social factor has absorbed the religious factor", is Bergmann's verdict on these conclusions. Is this the end of the dream of religious revival, the revival of "religiosity" of which the young Buber dreamed?

In the light of the teachings of Rav Kook, who tried to abolish the boundaries between the profane and the sacred, and the teachings of Hasidism on "service in the everyday reality", as understood by Buber in his writings on Hasidism, it seems to me that we must oppose Bergmann's unequivocal judgment,[54] which would exclude Buber from the domain of religiosity and confine him to the domain of secularity; let us at least give Buber the benefit of the doubt. It is possible that Buber himself, to the end of his days, was not sure of himself on this point. Characteristic of this, perhaps, is a beautiful anecdote, related by Buber in his memoirs, from the year 1914, one year after he had delivered his address on "Jewish Religiosity". It concerns his meeting with Hechler, the elderly clergyman and friend of Israel known to us from the diaries of Herzl for his help to the establisher of Zionism. The meeting between Hechler and Buber lasted for several hours.

Then I accompanied him to the railway station. In order to get there, one first had to go to the end of the small street of the 'colony' in which we lived and then on a narrow path covered with coal-dust, the so-called 'black path' along the railroad tracks. When we had reached the corner where the colony street met this path, Hechler stood still, placed his hand on my shoulder, and said: "Dear friend! We live in a great time. Tell me: Do you believe in God?" It was a while before I answered, then I reassured the old man as best I could: He need have no concern about me in this matter. Upon this I brought him to the railway station and installed him in his train . . . When I now returned home, however, and again came to that corner where the black path issued into our street, I stood still. I had to ponder to the depths of the matter. Had I said the truth? Did I "believe" in the God whom Hechler meant? What was the case with me? I stood a long time on the corner determined not to go farther until I had found the answer.[55]

Buber's memories and reflections on faith continued on, after 1914, throughout the span of his life and of his wonderful creativity; and yet it seems that even today, more than sixty years after this happened, we are still standing together with Buber at the end of the "black path", the "narrow path" covered by coal-dust, and together with him are racking our brains for the answer to Hechler's difficult question.

Notes

PINHAS HA-COHEN PELI

1. This is the title given to the first three addresses, delivered by Buber between 1909 and 1911 and published as *Drei Reden über das Judentum* in Frankfurt am Main in 1911. Three additional addresses which he gave in the years 1912-1914 were printed in the book *Vom Geist des Judentums* (The Spirit of Judaism), in Leipzig, 1916. The seventh address, *Der Heilige Weg* (The Holy Way) was given in May 1918 and printed in Frankfurt am Main in 1919. The eighth address, *Heruth: On Youth and Religion* as published under the name "Heruth" in Vienna, 1919. The collection of eight addresses with a new introduction appeared in Frankfurt am Main in 1923 as *Reden über das Judentum* and in a second edition published by the Schocken press in Berlin in 1932. After a long pause new "addresses" appeared, this time in Hebrew, first under the title "Ha-Ruah veha-Metsiut" (Spirit and Reality), Tel Aviv, 1942, and then in "Be-Mashber ha-Ruah, Shlosha neumim al ha-Yahadut", Jerusalem, 1951; they were translated as *At the Turning* (New York, Farrar, Straus and Young, 1952). Again the addresses were printed in a single volume, but not as a group, in *Te'udah ve-Ye'ud* (Mission and Destiny), Ha-Sifriah Ha-Tsionit, Jerusalem, 1953, vol. I. The latest concentrated translation into English of the eight early addresses and the four late ones is the book *On Judaism*, edited by Nahum Glatzer, Schocken, New York, 1972; it follows the last edition which was corrected by Buber himself, in the book *Der Jude und sein Judentum*, Cologne, 1963.

2. Buber himself, in his collection late work *Be-Mashber ha-Ruah, Shloshah Ma'amarim al ha-Yahadut*, asks that the three new addresses, which he gave in Jerusalem, London and New York around the time of the founding of the Israeli state, be viewed as a supplement and continuation of the seven addresses on Judaism which he delivered in 1909-1918 in Prague, Vienna, and Berlin (see the beginning of the book). Elsewhere, in the introduction to *Te'udah ve-Ye'ud* (see above), vol. I, p. 15, the speeches are called "massaot" (addresses) by the translators, and the speech with which we are dealing is called "the fifth address" (p. 17). But in Hugo Bergmann's essay in *Ha-Shiloah*, vol. 26 (1912), they are called "drashot" (sermons). In English they were translated as "addresses"; in the German original they were called "Reden". Despite the wide interval between the first address (1909) and the last (1951), it seems from Buber's words that he saw all the addresses as joined together in one concern, a sort of "serialized address".

3. See Hugo Bergmann, "Ha-Filosophiah shel Buber" (Buber's philosophy), in his book *Hogei ha-Dor* (Thinkers of Our Generation), Tel-Aviv 5695, Jerusalem 5730, p. 179. See also his essay "Shalosh Drashot al Ha-Yahadut" (Three Sermons on Judaism), *Ha-Shiloah* vol. 26 (1912), pp. 549-556, which contains the statement (p. 550): "The little book of *Three Sermons on Judaism* which were given by Martin Buber could be for us—if we ourselves wish it—the cornerstone for a new Jewish world view."

4. See Nahum Glatzer, *Franz Rosenzweig: His Life and Thought*, Schocken, New York, 1953, p. 36, the letter to his parents from 19.3.1916 on the reception of Buber's *Vom Geist des Judentums* on the Balkan front. Similarly ibid., p. 234, where he argues with Buber about the seven speeches which appeared in Frankfurt, 1923.

5. Robert Weltsch testifies to this in the introduction to *Te'udah ve-Ye'ud* (see

above, note 1), vol. I, pp. 9-13: "His first address on Judaism (was) a kind of revelation of a truth for which (Weltsch and his friends among the Jewish students in Prague) longed and aspired in their hearts . . . it brought hope into the heart of the European Jew of 1909 and set a goal before him . . . addresses which made a powerful impression and completely changed the spiritual direction of Jewish youth in central Europe".

6. See Hans Kohn, *Martin Buber: Sein Werk und seine Zeit*, Jakob Hegner, Hellerau, 1930.

7. For Buber's influence on Brod and Kafka see Glatzer, *On Judaism* (above, note 1), p. 241.

8. See Gershom Scholem, "Li-Dmuto shel Martin Buber" (On the Figure of Martin Buber), in *Dvarim Bego*, Tel Aviv, 5736, pp. 455-462: "Buber's voice, the voice that spoke from Drei Reden über das Judentum . . .was a mighty echo of the voice within us: it promised something, it cast a spell, it demanded . . . more than all the spokesmen of Zionism, he penetrated into the domain of the Jew as an individual".

9. See A. E. Simon, "Martin Buber ve-Emunat Israel" (Martin Buber and the Jewish Faith), in *Divrei Iyyun Mukdashim le-Mordekhai Martin Buber be-Milat Lo Shmonim Shanah*, Jerusalem 5738, p. 20. Also in the pamphlet "Ha-Morashah ha-Hayyah shel Mordekhai Martin Buber be-Milat Meat Shanah le-Holdato" (The Living Legacy of Martin Buber on the Hundredth Anniversary of His Birth), offprint from "Bi-Tfutsot ha-Golah", no. 83-84, Jerusalem, 1978. Compare also Simon's article on Buber, "Gosher Gsharim", in *Molad*, vol. 16, 1958; English version "The Builder of Bridges", *Judaism*, vol. 27, no. 2, spring 1978.

10. See Simon, *Divrei Iyyun* (above, note 8), p. 14.

11. See above, note 3.

12. Before 1909 Buber published only a few things, but among them were several books on Hasidism. See Margot Cohn and Rafael Buber, *Martin Buber: A Bibliography of His Writings, 1897-1978*, Magnes Press, Jerusalem, 1980.

13. On the confrontation between Hasidism as it was in the East and Hasidism as Buber depicted it in presenting it to the Gentiles, see S. Y. Agnon in "Sippur Ma'aseh, Le-Milat le-Buber Shmonim ve-Hamesh" (Anecdote, for Buber's Eighty-fifth Birthday), in *Me-Atsmi Le-Atsmi*, Schocken, Jerusalem and Tel Aviv, pp. 265-268.

14. In his afterword to *On Judaism* (see above, note 1), p. 240.

15. Nathan Rotenstreich, *Jewish Philosophy in Modern Times*, New York, 1968. Also compare his book *Tradition and Reality*, New York, 1972. ·

16. Yehezkel Kaufmann, *Golah ve-Nekhar*, Tel Aviv, 5721, 2 vols.

17. *Ha-Shiloah*, vol. 13, Nissan 5664.

18. For the attacks by spokesmen of Reform Judaism on rigid *Halakhah* see Tsvi Zahavi, "Tnu'at ha-Hitbolelut be-Israel veha-Polemos be'adah ve-negdah be-Sifrut ha-Ivrit ha-Hadasha" (The Movement of Jewish Assimilation and the Polemics for and Against It in Modern Hebrew Literature), Jerusalem, 5708, esp. pp. 86ff.

19. On the antinomian and anti-Establishment tendency in modern Hebrew literature and on the demand for a change of values and a renewal of the face of Judaism through the revelation of the "hidden", subterranean Judaism, compare Yehezkel Kaufmann, op. cit., vol. II, and also Barukh Kurzweil, *Sifrutenu ha-Hadashah—Hemshekh o Mahapekhah*, Tel Aviv, 5722.

20. Parts of Rosenzweig's letter against Buber on this subject, entitled "Die

Bauleute", in *Schriften*, pp. 107-113, were translated into English in the above-mentioned work by Glatzer, pp. 234-240; the whole of it was translated into Hebrew by Yehoshua Amir in "Naharayim, Mivhar mi-Kitvei Rosenzweig" (Naharayim, a selection from Rosenzweig's books), Mosad Bialik, Jerusalem 5721, pp. 80-93 (on p. 80 it is erroneously printed that the letter was written in 1914; this must be corrected to read 1924, since the eight addresses to which Rosenzweig refers did not appear in print until 1923).

21. G. Scholem, *Dvarim bego*, Am Oved, Tel Aviv 5736, p. 457.

22. B. Kurzweil, *Be-Maavak al Arkhei ha-Yahadut*, Tel Aviv, 5730, p. 210.

23. M. L. Lilienblum, "Ein Mearvin Sheelah bi-Sheelah", in Avraham Hertzberg, *Ha-Raion Ha-Tsioni*, Jerusalem, Keter, 1970, p. 126. (in the English version Arthur Hertzberg, *The Zionist Idea*, Harper Torch Books, New York, 1966, this sentence is translated "Within our autonomous political life everything will find its place". (p. 171).

24. Quoted from Moses Hess, "Rome and Jerusalem," in Hertzberg (English p. 134)

25. Ahad Ha-Am. "On Nationalism and Religion", in Hertzberg (English p. 261)

26. Ibid., p. 379 (English)

27. Rabbi A. I. Kook, *Orot*, Jerusalem, 5706, pp. 48-98; also the three volumes of *Orot ha-Kodesh*.

28. *On Judaism*, p. 79.

29. Hertzberg, (Hebrew) ibid., p. 289; (English p. 374.)

30. Ibid., p. 296 (English p. 384).

31. See Achad Ha-Am, *Al Parashat Derakhim*, vol. 2, p. 79. (Berlin, 1930).

32. *Dat ve-Hitbonenut Mimkorot ha-Yahadut*, Jerusalem, 5732, esp. the introductory chapters.

33. *On Judaism*, p. 83.

34. Ibid., p. 89.

35. *Golah ve-Nekhar*, vol. II, p. 355.

36. See *Kitvei Shlomo Schiller*, Jerusalem, 5687, Rabbi Binyamin's introduction pp. V-XII, and the essays "Ha-Tsionut veha-Dat", pp. 3-9, and "Mahshevah al ha-Yahadut", pp. 35-51. On Schiller and his uniqueness see Dov Shtuk (Sadan) "Goral ve-Hakhra'ah al Mishnato shel Shlomo Schiller" (The Fate and Judgment on the Teaching of Shlomo Schiller), Tel Aviv, 5703.

37. On Samson Raphael Hirsch, the father of Neo-Orthodoxy in Germany, see *Ha-Rav Shimshon Rafael Hirsh—Mishnato ve-Shitato*, (Rabbi Samson Raphael Hirsch—His Teaching and his Doctrine) edited by Yonah Emanuel, Jerusalem, 5742.

38. The quotations from Buber whose source is not given are from "Jewish Religiosity", *On Judaism*, pp. 79-94.

39. *Dvarim bego*, p. 458.

40. Ibid.

41. See Gabriel Marcel, "Existence and Human Freedom," *The Philosophy of Existentialism*, New York, 1957.

42. See Moses Maimonides, Mishneh Torah, Hilkhot Tshuvah, chapters 5 and 6; also see P. Peli, *Al ha-Teshuva*, pp. 195-258.

43. "Renewal of Judaism", *On Judaism*, pp. 34-35.

44. On Berdichevsky, his call for a change of values, and Nietzsche's influence on him and on Hebrew literature of the time, see Yehezkel Kaufmann, *Golah ve-Nekhar*, vol. II, the chapter entitled "Dor Navukh" (The Perplexed Generation).

45. B. Frischmann in the stories of *Ha-Midbar*, which are a rebellion against the establishment, on behalf of a humane, healthy and pure Judaism.

46. In the great long poem "Luhot Gnuzim" in which he tries to give us once again the lost tablets mentioned in the Bible, but rejected and not included in the "official" codex drawn up by "old, weak, cautions 'masters of assemblies' ".

47. This is the interpretation given by the Gemara (Babylonian Talmud, Sotah 14a) to the verse (Deut. 13:5) "After the Lord your God shall ye walk . . . and unto Him shall ye cleave": "It is then possible for a human being to walk after the *Shechinah*? But (the meaning is) to walk after the attributes of the Holy One, blessed be He. As he clothes the naked . . . so do thou also clothe the naked".

48. "So you are my witnesses, says the Lord, and I am God" (Isaiah 43:12) is interpreted by the Midrash Sifri (Ve-zot ha-Brakha) as follows: "When you are my witnesses I am God and you are not my witnesses I am not God".

49. See his books *God in Search of Man*, New York, 1955, and *Man is Not Alone*.

50. Haim Nachman Bialik, "Halakhah ve-Agadah", in *Divrei Sifrut*, Dvir, Tel Aviv, 5714.

51. Rabbi A. I. Kook, *Orot ha-Kodesh*, Part I, p. 25.

52. *Al Parashat Derakhim*, vol. 1, p. 179-184; vol. 3, p. 214.

53. In his essay "Buber veha-Mistikah", in *Divrei Iyyun Mukdashim le-Mordekhai Martin Buber be-Milat lo Shmonim Shanah*, Jerusalem 5718, p. 13.

54. See especially "Be-Fardes ha-Hasidut" (In the Pardes of Hasidism), Jerusalem 5707, and the introduction to *Or Ganuz* (Hidden Light), Tel Aviv, 5717.

55. Buber, "Autobiographical Fragments", in *The Philosophy of Martin Buber*, ed. by Paul Arthur Schilpp and Maurice Friedman, London, Cambridge Univ. Press, 1967, p. 24.

Buber's Concept of Faith as a Criticism of Christianity

LORENZ WACHINGER

Two Types of Faith is the title given by Buber to a book, published in 1950, about the basic difference between the Jewish and the Christian ways of belief. Like so much else from Buber's pen, it has probably been read more by Christians than by Jews—there is scarcely a theological bibliography on the concept of faith that does not include it. The eminent Protestant dogmatist, Emil Brunner, finds that *Two Types of Faith*, "without wishing to be, indeed amounts to a massive attack on Christianity".[1] Buber also remarks, in a conversation with Werner Kraft, that *Two Types of Faith* was really about the failure of Christianity, only he had expressed this more cautiously in the book, as he could not expect the Christians to accept it.[2]

Since Buber takes the Christians so seriously, Christians surely also have reason to deal seriously with his criticism. However, in its thesis—the opposition between *emunah*, the Hebraic faith allegedly still shared by Jesus himself, and *pistis*, the faith promulgated by John and Paul—this book is contestable; and in its reasoning it is questionable, as has often been observed.[3] Rather than pursue the weaknesses of *Two Types of Faith*,[4] it would be more worthwhile to inquire into the permanent meaning of presenting this critical question and its meaning for Christian theology.

I. The Locus of Dialogue

First we must ask: when we Christians speak with Buber, where are we speaking from? Where is the locus of this dialogue across borders, and how is it constituted?

Let us follow a hint from Gerhard Ebeling, who suggests that instead of two *types* of faith one should speak of two *times* of faith, that is, of two stages in the unfolding of belief which are not necessarily comparable.[5] I go one step further: must one not speak of two—or more—*histories* of faith, rather than of two *types* of faith as of fundamental types of religious relationship which always remain the same? Of course, it hurts to use the term "history of faith" (*Glaubensgeschichte*—a word coined, to the best of my knowledge, by Martin Buber) in the plural. But in order not to enter upon an ahistorical "dialogue", one must take into account that Israel's history of faith, of which Buber speaks, is not the only one. It is possible to show that he takes his starting-point primarily from a certain early period in Israel's history: from the beginning of the monarchic period, when, the people being now settled and tolerably secure in their land, the form of national life was the subject of vehement struggles: should it be a monarchically organized state, geared to power-politics, like the states of other nations, *or* a free, comradely government of the people under the royal sovereignty of God alone, who sends His impulses, new and different each time, through the dynamics of prophetic men filled with the spirit, like the Judges and Samuel, and before them Moses? In other words, a theocratic government of the people, which one could almost call anarchic?[6] The time of the literary prophets is characterized for Buber by the same struggle between the "normal" principle of state and power politics, and the "prophetic faith"—a faith that makes demands on the people in all dimensions and calls them to stand before God. In this period Israel is a clearly defined people in its own land, with strong religious and social traditions, with an unbroken will to national self-assertion. What Buber formulates as "the faith of Israel" has reference primarily to this situation: Constancy in the covenantal relationship, trust as the core of this relationship, and on God's side a corresponding faithfulness to the covenant; this is the *emunah* described in *The Prophetic Faith* and in *Two Types of Faith*.

And what of *pistis*, to which, we may say in anticipation of our argument, Buber is not entirely just?

Centuries later, after this situation of the people of Israel had been almost completely shattered, the Christian history of faith begins—the history of the "Way", as the account of the apostles likes to call it (Acts 9:2). This way has a beginning, like every way: something new appears with that unique human being, Jesus, with his otherness that so shocked his contemporaries, with his way of living and of understanding life—the "way of Jesus", as E. Haenchen calls his commentary on the gospel of Mark. This newness attains its full force in that event which we call the Resurrection of Jesus, and still more deeply in the Pentecostal pouring-out of the spirit (Acts 2). The New Testament scribes understand and narrate the "Way of Jesus" according to the Scriptures and not otherwise; the continuity of the "Way" with the long, hard way of God with his people, from Abraham and Egypt on, is of decisive importance for them. On the other hand, they understand "the Scriptures", the history of God with his people, in a new way, according to the "Way of Jesus"; here begins a new and different understanding: the history of God is *with all men*—it is no longer the history of God with Israel alone.

This corresponds to the new situation, for Israel is no longer living as a united people in its own land—still less "those who are of the Way". (Acts 9:2). Everywhere, Diaspora Jews, and along with them "those of the Way", find themselves as "new arrivals and strangers" (Letter of Diognetus) in a different environment, confronted with other, often very powerful spiritual traditions. Thus, on one branch of the "way", the theological ways began to diverge even before the New Testament was committed to writing (Matthew, John, Paul, Hebrews, etc.).[7] Paul and John articulate their way of faith by severing it cleanly from the Jewish way of salvation through fulfillment of the Law; they place faith and Law, as fundamentally different ways, in polemical opposition to each other. And from then on the *one Way of Jesus* exists only in *the ways* of the different churches. At first there are the Latin and the Greek churches; later the Reformation churches separate themselves from Catholic doctrine, while the Catholic Church rejects the Protestant way as a wrong turning. Moreover, the different forms of belief become associated, from the first century on, with specific ways of thinking and of philosophical questioning, proof, and dispute.

The history, the way of Western thought and Western theology alone, with its brilliant pages and its fateful, catastrophic ones, leads into a terrible melee of opposition, attack and defense, into ever more ramified "road-maps"; moreover, the way of science has begun to exercise an enormous fascination and has led to a basic mistrust of the way of faith.

Such is the historical fate which Christian faith must confront today; in addition there is a difficult chapter of destiny and guilt: the minority existence of Jews within the Christian states and peoples has, through the well-known social-psychological mechanisms, led to persecution and suppression, culminating in the Third Reich's program of extermination. We Christians and our churches have not succeeded in dismantling these sociopolitical mechanisms. Not only is the Christian way fully marked with Jewish blood, a trail of blood from the fourth to the twentieth, which cannot be erased; but also,

Christian theologians, with very few exceptions, have lacked the encounter with Jewish tradition of faith-thought—to their own great detriment.

In this Occidental history of thought and faith, Martin Buber occupies a specific place: it is not only that Christianity encountered him with a specific understanding, that of Protestant theology between 1900 and 1950, and that this characterizes and limits its coming to terms with him; it is also from this place in the history of faith and thought that he formulates his view of Israel's history of faith—as a criticism and corrective directed against both Jewish Orthodoxy and Christian faith-thought. From this history of the Christian way which is present to him, he rejects Pistis as conceived by Paul and John—a rejection which must not be rendered inoffensive by the techniques of critical exegesis. And it is here, finally, that Buber's personal conception of the immemorial antinomies of religious thinking and of theology must be placed.

From this same place in the history of thought and faith we must hear Buber's criticism of Christian faith, reflect on it, and examine it. The struggle with the antinomies of the concept of faith has its own interminable history, both in Christianity and in Judaism, in which are expressed the tensions of lived faith and the respective concepts of man—anthropological pre-decisions which reflect deeper historical movements. Thus it is also meaningful to inquire into the Buberian concept of faith from the standpoint of the history of the Catholic concept of faith in our century—to clarify one in the light of the other. For the year of Buber's death, 1965, was also the closing year of the second Vatican Council, whose Dogmatic Constitution on Divine Revelation is unthinkable without the influence of the dialogical and personal thinking; and Buber's beginnings as a publicist before 1910 coincide with the crisis of Modernism—that theological dispute within Catholicism which also excited the broader public, and which the Church sought to end by the invocation of its authority. The themes of this dispute are Buber's themes—one could almost call him a Jewish Modernist: above all the themes of subjective experience as against traditional faith, and the theme of Biblical faith and historical truth which can be found out by the historical-critical method—in general, the problem of "faith and knowledge".

We shall therefore first inquire into the development of Buber's concept of faith and view of Israel's history of faith, and then into Buber's critical conception of Christian faith and the understanding of faith in present-day Catholic theology.

II. The Development of Buber's Concept of Faith

The concept "faith" is so important in Buber's work that with its help the development and compactness of his thinking in his chief areas of work—writings on Hasidism, on philosophy, on the Bible, on Judaism—may be demonstrated. This is rather astonishing, for in the traditional understanding of Judaism the Law, not faith, stands as the central religious concept. The fact that in the Christian Churches faith is taken as *the* central religious act may have led Buber to feel the necessity of bringing out the element of faith more strongly in his new interpretation of Judaism.

1. At first, to be sure, in the beginning period from about 1902 to *I and Thou* (1923), Buber relegates faith, as in *Two Types of Faith* he relegated the Pauline *pistis*, to the negative side—the side of religion rigidified in dogmas and rituals, of the objective taking-cognizance of factual situations, of being tied down to a one-time historical revelation. On the positive side stand "religiosity" (Buber must have taken over the distinction between religion and religiosity from his teacher, Georg Simmel) and, above all, decision, act, realization, as characteristic of the Oriental and thus of the Jew and his relation to God. To do whatever one does with a unified, undivided soul, with the right intention, means to allow God to become real in this world; this is how the Hasidim act. More precisely, as Buber wrote at that time, it is a matter of the "religious act; for it is God's realization through man".[6] "For God does not want to be believed in, to be debated and defended by us, but simply to be realized through us".[8] Buber soon moves away from this realization of God, which in its pantheistic tendency recalls the Rilke of the *Book of Hours*.[9] But one thing he holds fast, although the concepts change: the life of man is not to be divided into a sacral domain of religion cordoned off by religious law or a fixed faith from the rest, which is abandoned as profane. In *I and Thou* faith and ritual religion still stand on the side of the It.

2. But as early as 1924 the word "faith" appears in a positive, almost religious sense in a letter from Buber to Franz Rosenzweig, stating that he cannot say "yes" to an argument of Rosenzweig's "for no other reason than that my faith forbids it. You know, my friend, that I do not use the word lightly; it is appropriate".[10]

In subsequent writings and addresses faith as contentual recognition, as "believing something", as belief in dogmas or a revelation handed down by tradition or the existence of God, continues to be rejected; rather the meaning of faith is "presenting ourselves and perceiving",[11] it is "lived life in dialogue: being addressed by word and sign, answering by doing and not-doing, by holding one's ground and being responsible in the lived everyday".[12] Later Buber will speak of decisive experiences of faith which led to the insights of *I and Thou*—to that major work which from the beginning was planned as Buber's "prolegomena" on the primal phenomenon of religion within a great theological project. He refers again and again to his subjective experience, which he calls faith-experience, insofar as it accepts "a person in all his component parts, his capacity for thought certainly included."[13] To this experience of the concentrated soul at one with itself there now corresponds the insistence on the one, experience-able world of man, which is not to be split up into Here and Beyond, Nature and the Supernatural. Faith, as Buber now calls the relation to God, which for the time being is still conceived very much in the manner of the Thou-relationship, aims no further than to the borders of possible experience in time and space; God allows himself to be experienced in the events of the world, the everyday. "In each *Thou* we address the eternal Thou", as he says in *I and Thou*. As in the Thou-relationship, in faith no content is given, nothing one can hold fast; faith is completely *situational faith*, ever new; the relation to God is radically dynamicized; any dogma would annihilate the "dia-logic force" of the situation, for "the moment is God's garment".[14] Faith is *dialogical*, it is an entering into reality, that is into the bond with things and beings and, within that bond, with God, in a real reciprocal relationship. Now as before, the moment of the deed is part of it: faith is *practical*; in action the two domains of life—mind and nature—are to be united; for that nature and mind are "the gestures of *one* hand" is a "principal item of faith".[15]

3. It is fascinating to see how this radical situational, subjective, religiously anarchic faith,[16] without continuity in space and time, almost mystical in its timelessness and lack of historicity—how this "religion of presence" is joined by the other factor: tradition, Scrip-ture as a document of great revelations in the past which made history and continue to exercise their influence; as if the radical present inevitably calls up its antithesis, History.

The beginning is the German translation of the Bible. Buber writes concerning the letter from Lambert Schneider, who invited him to make the translation: "This letter from a thoroughly Germanic Chris-tian seemed to me like a sign".[17] At that time Buber was concerned with language as such; with basic questions of theology; with the dialogue between Jews and Christians (this is discussed in his correspondence with Franz Rosenzweig) and with the Bible itself: for many years a German translation had been planned, as the common work of several men who were personally connected, among them Moritz Heimann and Ephraim Frisch; World War I intervened. In the following years Buber arrived at the decisive clarity on method, and especially on why the holy book, "despite everything, should be placed anew in the human world of the present, new, that is, renewed in its originality".[18]

To renew the Bible in its originality: this enormous, genuinely reformational task means for Buber to make audible once again, in the fixed text of Scripture, the living voice of the message, that which addresses and challenges, and the human voice answering in prayer and action. The Bible must be understood "acoustically"; in a beautiful paradox Buber speaks of the "fundamentally oral character" of Scripture, of the "spokenness of the word". Then addressing and hearing, the dialogue between God and man, dialogue in the sense of the I-Thou relationship, must be made experienceable behind the patina of agelong habit which covers it for all of us. And the *meaning* of the WORD, which after all cannot be expressed in a sentence, objectively, insofar as it concerns what is deepest, namely the relation between God and man: this meaning must be made perceptible to the senses in the spoken and heard sound-structure of the renewed text; it offers itself, made recognizable by linguistic means, "not to our discursive understanding, but to our contemplation".[19]

Thus for Buber the service to Biblical tradition does not mean subjection of the dialogical principle and dogma-less situational faith to the letter; rather there occurs a powerful transformation of the text, which is linguistically roughened up, as Gershom Scholem says, to disconcert the reader-listener. An actualization of the Biblical message takes place—Buber describes this extensively in his writings on the Bible. Actualization means first of all personalization. Buber employs his personal experience, his conscience as he would say, his personal faith, as a hermeneutical principle by which he distinguishes between what is central and what is marginal—a daring venture which would provoke opposition from any orthodoxy! He presents a subjective criterion, vis-à-vis the objectively existing word of God and the codifying tradition which interprets it—in Judaism the Talmud, in Catholicism the councils and Church Fathers. According to these subjective criteria Buber lays down the normative mean of the Scriptures: as Luther assumed as normative mean the doctrine of justification in Paul's letters in the New Testament, so Buber views the prophets, not, as customary in Judaism, the Torah. Christian Old Testament scholarship in the nineteenth century had discovered the early prophets' temporal priority over the Pentateuch; Buber also gives them the theological, contentual priority and, in true reformation spirit, criticizes later rigidifications in the light of the origin. Within the Torah he gives preference to the state of editing considered to have been influenced by the prophets, namely the Elohist. Thus the legal and cultic traditions, the wisdom texts, and especially the apocalyptic texts recede into the background. For the apocalyptic texts considerably overstep the bounds of experience and of the rationally comprehensible, since they include the end of this world's time and a coming world, are often in search of a knowledge of the unknowable, and assume that the events of the end-time will take a course predetermined by God and unalterable.

Exegetes differ over whether the apocalyptic writings are to be considered as legitimate continuation of Biblical faith or as a degeneration under the morbid influence of Hellenistic, Gnostic religiosity; whether the apocalyptic writings are "the mother of Christian theology" (E. Käsemann) or are to be rejected from the standpoint of "presentist eschatology" (R. Bultmann). Buber clearly rejects the apocalyptic writings (which has consequences for his judgment on the New Testament) and thereby assures his Biblical faith, the "faith of the prophets", of a beautiful self-completeness; he can now portray messianic faith with a brilliant rational clarity. The price he pays for this—even here, where he speaks of Israel's "history of faith"—is a peculiar ahistoricity; Buber fixes the normative mean of Biblical faith at prophetic faith, understands it as aiming at the realization of the complete kingship of God, not cultically and religiously, but in the full extension of the daily life of the people, in the social dimension. Not temples and sacrifices, but people and social justice one signs of God's presence—as the Apocalypse of John (21:22) says of the coming aeon. There is no substantial accretion in the developmental history of faith, such as the later, apocalyptic books of the Scriptures bring with their imagination of the Beyond, and certainly not a new action on the part of God, such as the New Testament confesses as having occurred with Jesus.

Thus "Israel's history of faith", as Buber sees it, certainly to his understanding of faith brings a considerable increase in continuity—from the promises to the Patriarchs through the history of God with the people of Egypt to the Exile, even to all the exiles of the Jewish people and to the expectation of Messianic fulfillment; the momentary faith of the dialogical writings thus receives a corrective. The completely contentless faith of the Thou-relationship acquires a certain contentual filling, so that Buber can speak of a "naive religious knowledge" of the earliest prophets[20] or of a "believed historical truth".[21] Moreover, the domain of the individual, the I, is decidedly transcended, since faith is now seen predominantly in the dimension of the people.

But is it possible to avoid a certain spiritualization, a certain dehistoricization of faith, when one so decidedly separates "faith" from "religion", "history of faith" from "history of religion"? Certainly the distinction between faith and religion in Protestant dialectic theology, in Barth, Gogarten, Brunner, is meant otherwise than in Buber, who wants to combat the division of life into sacral and profane, into religion and world, and understands faith in its full extension over the whole of life, up to and including political decisions. But does it not in the end amount to the same thing, whether, like dialectic theology, one understands faith as purely the work of God, or whether, like Buber, one understands it as intention in all action and as decision of a whole people? For here, too, faith is after all—despite all assertions to the contrary—conceived as God's work and moved very far into the possibilities of messianic fulfillment. As the Apocalypse of John states, quoting from the prophets: "and they shall be his peoples, and he himself shall be with them, and be their God" (21:3).

The last years have brought a noticeable move in theology away from that deprecation of religion as opposed to faith which originated with dialectic theology, especially with Dietrich Bonhoeffer, who comes closest to Buber in his thesis. (It would be appropriate to restate this problem from the perspective of Catholic Christianity, which has always been less embarrassed about understanding itself as a religion).

III. Buber's Conception of Christian Faith

What Buber presents in *Two Types of Faith* as a scholarly, exegetical study of religion is the sum and result of a critical preoccupation with Christianity of almost fifty years. In the volume *Kritik an der Kirche*,[22] he figures among the critics of the church. Let us therefore avoid, once again, the extremely difficult, and never quite comprehensive enough, exegetical specialist's question of the Pauline concept of faith as opposed to the ancient Hebraic concept; let us rather inquire into the sources and goals of Buber's criticism of Christian faith.

1. In 1913 Buber wrote to Hugo Bergmann[23] about his work on a book on Christianity, in which he wanted to treat the problem of *teshuva*, the "turning". But Jesus' public speaking also begins, according to Mark (1:15) with the call to the turning—for Buber a core-word of Judaism from the prophets of Israel to the Hasidim; he himself clings determinedly to man's power to begin and to make the turning.

But Buber sees Christian teaching, "which has distorted Jesus' meaning and basis",[24] from Paul to Augustine, from Thomas to Luther, as deviating from this through the principle of exoneration through grace alone; against man's decision stands God's sovereign election of grace, toward which man can do nothing. For faith itself, which leads to exoneration (Romans 1:17), is the act of God in man, from whom nothing else is asked, no action, no works. Thus Buber sees Christianity in its Reformed version, which he probably first came to know through Kierkegaard; the theology of Paul, of an isolated and radicalized Paul, acquires such a preponderance in it that Buber finds it easy, following the leading Protestant exegetes of the time after 1900, to remove Jesus far away from Paul; as late as 1948 he gave the title "The Palestinian Jesus" to his book which later appeared as *Two Types of Faith*. He thus set Jesus in opposition to the occidentalized, Hellenic-Gnostically alienated Jesus of Paul and John; and in 1917 he wrote to Franz Werfel: "Therefore I want to and will fight for Jesus and against Christianity".[25]

If one considers that the Council of Trent against the Reformers emphasized man's freedom of will, that is, his cooperation with grace, as well as the necessity of works, without which faith is dead, one can only regret that Buber never dealt intensively with Catholic doctrine. (There may have been other points on which Buber felt still less comfortable with the Catholic Church than with Protestant theology—in reference to Guardini in 1922 he spoke of the latter's "assured churchliness" which placed him at a distance.[26]) All the significant Christian theologians with whom Buber was closely acquainted were Protestants: Albert Schweitzer, of whom he said as late as 1963 that one must begin with his works if one wanted to understand his, Buber's, relationship to Christianity.[27] To Bultmann he wrote in 1949: "Among the theologians of our time you are the one from whom I have been able to learn by far the most, for nearly three decades now, for the understanding of the New Testament".[28] He was also personally acquainted with F. Gogarten and E. Brunner, leading exponents of dialectical theology.

2. The Reformation doctrine of justification furnishes another point for criticism of Christianity: Buber sees the split between the redeemed soul and the unredeemed world established by the belief in the fact of salvation having occurred as a unique event, which was not perceptible but could only be believed; or still worse: the splitting of humanity into one part elect by Divine predetermination, and another part rejected—Augustine's terrible phrase about the "massa damnata", which was the starting-point for Calvin's doctrine of predestination. Behind this, for Buber, stands the unacceptable division of history into a time of wrath and a time of grace, which he finds in Paul, whom he therein considers a Gnostic; with this concept, Gnosis, Buber marks the farthest distance from the Jewish type of faith. The doctrine according to which God disposes of the generations of man in an impersonal, fateful, arbitrary manner, drives man into sin and then rejects him, being himself enthroned in an unattainable distance, having given the rule of the world into other, demonic (sin, wrath) hands contradicts the dialogical view of *I and Thou*, in which all moments have an equal Divine immediacy, as well as the dialogue of the prophetic call to turning and the still human possible response of turning.

We are dealing here with the paradox of every theology—how to conceive simultaneously of human freedom and Divine effectuation of history, including the history of salvation. Paul emphasizes more the Divine workings; the Reformers and again the dialectic theologians intensify this emphasis. Buber resolves the tension perhaps too onesided toward the side of human freedom—at least when he is polemicizing against Paul. It would be appropriate to ask how he can speak of an "eclipse of God", or of "Pauline" historical epochs, such as ours, in which the contradictions of human existence fatefully consolidate,[29] if he has not after all drawn close to Paul's interpretation of history.

3. Immediacy of relationship is a basic axiom of dialogical thinking and of Buber's concept of faith. A separation between time of disaster and time of salvation must provoke Buber's contradiction, just as does the faith in a mediator who stands between God and man; but this is how he sees salvation-bringing faith according to Paul: no longer faith as a relationship of trust to God, but faith in the act of salvation through the mediator Christ. Buber is concerned that in the Chris-

tian type of faith Christ finally suppresses the Father; in a letter to
F. Gogarten in 1922 he formulates it as a "problem of the age" which
is most emphatically portrayed in Dostoevsky, "who has reached the
point where he can *really* believe only in Christ".[30] Yet Buber
understood Christology very much as an essentially religious phenomenon, even as the authentic seriousness of the Christian peoples.
Already in 1912 he himself was preoccupied with a Christological,
messianological project which he wanted to incorporate twenty years
later into his work on Messianic faith.[31] He recognized his own view of
the problem in the early Christian doctrine of Adoptianism, which
holds that Jesus was accepted as the Son of God upon his baptism in
the Jordan. He interpreted the rebirth through water and the spirit
(John 3:1-8) in this sense, devoted considerable effort in the 30's to a
book on that subject, until he finally made of it a section in *Two Types
of Faith*.[32]

What guided Buber in his understanding of the Messiah, in which
he did indeed grant Jesus a place, he liked to express with a sentence
from the apocryphal Gospel of the Hebrews, in which God addresses
Christ: "My son, in all the prophets I have awaited you, that you
might come to me and I might rest in you".[33] What is meant is that in
the Messiah humanity goes toward God, enters into the perfect,
fulfilling dialogue with Him, and thus has its part in the salvation of
the world. In the Christology of Christianity, precisely in the version
of Gogarten and other exponents of dialectical theology, who under
Kierkegaard's influence emphasize the "infinite qualitative distance"
between God and man, he finds only the direction from above to
below, the "Christology of Divine monergism", such as Yves Congar
attributed to Luther.[34]

But here, again, Buber feels that the dialogical situation between
God and man is destroyed, the spontaneity of man is not taken
seriously, and his realizing deed is excluded from the picture. A note
to the last-quoted letter to Gogarten states that the perception of the
difference between the Jewish and early Christian direction of faith
from below to above, and the late, dogmatic Christian direction from
above to below, was the germ of *Two Types of Faith*.

4. Socialistic, Zionistic and Hasidic impulses led Buber early in his
life to make a close connection between faith and one's relationship to
the community: only in community is faith in the full sense possible,
and the community of a people living in faith, and finally the coming-
together of peoples to form the people of humanity, is the goal of
humanity. Thus for him the Hebraic faith, *emunah*, is the type of faith

having to do with the history of a people; in contrast, one comes to the Christian faith, *pistis*, as an individual; the Christian type of faith has to do with individual history, its birth was a process of individualization, an exit from history, which after all is history of peoples. Nor can the Church replace the relationship with the community, for the Church is not a natural people; the existence of the Christian remains divided between Church and natural peoples. Christianity is founded on the single one, the peoples as such have remained pagan in their law. That is the dualism of the redeemed single one and the unredeemed peoples, upon which Christianity, according to Buber, has foundered.

Certainly one could object that "the individualization of the relationship to God"[35] began much earlier, could be demonstrated for instance in the Psalms, and is certainly not to be dismissed as a merely Christian problem; it is perhaps part of the destiny of our very civilization. But Buber's inquiry seems to me, precisely on this point, very much worth hearing: is the problem of the believer in relation to natural communities (family, congregation, people) if not solved in Christianity, at least clearly seen? Is the dichotomy between the single believer and the community of which Buber speaks a wound that cannot and should not be healed, because it is part of the alienness of the Christian in the world?

IV. An Answer: Christian History of Faith

Buber's criticism deserves an answer: dialogue is after all the basic model of his thinking; in 1958 Hans von Balthasar gave the name "Solitary Dialogue (Einsames Zwiesprache)" to his book on Martin Buber—the first major Catholic contribution to the understanding of his thinking. The answer has already learned from Buber's inquiry, and asks in reply.

1. A history of faith has a beginning; where faith is meant seriously, this can only be an appeal, an act of God and a hearing and obeying on the part of man. This is how the Bible, and also Paul, see the beginning of faith with Abraham; in the calling of Moses Buber already sees a new beginning of God's history with the people, together with the continuity of patriarchal faith; and a similar transition occurs when the people of Israel goes into exile. The New Testament writers experienced their faith situation in the same way, as a beginning, as a necessary answer to a revolutionary new act of

God, but in the continuity of the old faith in this same God of Abraham, Moses, and the prophets. A decision like that of Abraham when he left his tribe and his father's house was demanded—they understand this demand by quoting Scripture, that is, by interpreting Israel's history of faith.

One aspect of Buber's antithesis between *emunah* and *pistis* is the opposition of "continuity in faith" *(emunah)* versus the "leap into faith" *(pistis)*; but this describes two stages of the history of faith. The tension between a new beginning and a persistence in what has been handed down, between reformation and tradition, belongs in the inner historical dialectic of every religion; and it is surprising to find Buber so strongly on the side of continuity and tradition—that burden which, in the discussion of the renaissance of Judaism, he was rather inclined to shake off.

This, however, is probably a reminder to the Christians, who, absorbed in the beginning in Christ, are in danger of forgetting the continuity with Israel by much deprecating the so-called Old Testament in favor of their New Testament, or even, like Marcion, by cutting it out of their Bible—as late as 1900 this was proposed by Harnack. In any case the Christians cannot cite Paul as authority for this, who impressed upon the Christians of Gentile origin their true and abiding relationship to Israel: ". . . it is not thou that bearest the root, but the root thee" (Romans 11:18). It may well be that Buber with his criticism of Christian faith, with his German translation of the Scriptures, with his books on Israel's history of faith, has taught countless Christians the taste of the sap of the ancient olive-tree Israel (Romans 11:17), which nourishes both Testaments.

2. To believe in the one God, as Israel and Jesus believed, is one thing, according to Buber; to believe in Christ, the son of God and mediator, another. Perhaps it might still be possible to believe *along with* Jesus, whom the letter to the Hebrews calls "the author and perfecter of our faith" (12:2). We do not wish here to gloss over real differences in belief; but one must examine the Christological dogmas and the history of their interpretations and misunderstandings, to see if they have not exaggerated differences which are not after all so deep. Thus in a theology like the dialectical, which is very much concerned with God's initiative in the history of salvation, with the radical otherness of God, with grace which cannot be affected, Christ will appear as the eternal Son of the Father, as heavenly and alien. Thus U. von Balthasar speaks of the "Christological contraction" in Karl Barth. The ancient Church theology of the first centuries was

already struggling for the truly human being of Jesus, for instance against the misunderstanding, promulgated by Docetism, that he was simply God with an illusory human body. But it was also struggling against the other, the Arian misunderstanding—that Christ was a mediating creature, God-like, but not God. What Buber means by the Messiah, who comes from below, from man, is expressed by the dogmatic claim of Jesus' truly human nature; the other side, the truly Divine character of Jesus, says that in this fulfilling human being God Himself enters into history, suffering and acting, not represented by a mediator, but He Himself in a mediated immediacy—it cannot be expressed otherwise than paradoxically—somewhat as in the late Jewish and Hasidic imagination of the Shekhinah God appears in His world-immanent form. Hans von Balthasar hazards the bold formulation that Jesus is the dialogue between God and man in person; Schillebeeck and O. Semmelroth have voiced similar thoughts.

Buber's criticism of a supernaturalistically and monologically formulated Christology strikes the sore point of the Christian history of faith—that Christological dogma was not developed out of the dialogue with Israel, as even Paul was still attempting to do, but in the atmosphere of Greek thought. With its conceptually strict thinking, its approximation through the Greek language to the Greek style of thought, the Christology which became predominant in the Latin Church appears monologic, insofar as the relationship to the consummation of faith, to prayer, is less recognizable in it. The confusion of many Christians as to whether they should address their prayers to Christ or to the Father—that is Buber's criticism of the "ditheistic" intermediary character of Christ!—is solved in the ancient Church's practice of prayer "through Christ in the spirit to the Father"; but if the old theological rule "lex orandi, lex credendi" is valid, then this means that our way of faith leads to the one God, who becomes present to us in Christ and in the spirit. Eastern Christianity has more clearly elaborated this way, closer to the Bible, which in the West is present in prayer and liturgy, but not in theology. Here we have a piece of history of faith, encoded in the history of theology— which also has its destiny!

The historical Jesus, as a man, as one who precedes us in faith, is the discovery of many theologians after Barth and Bultmann, of many books on Jesus, and also of youth for some years now; as if Buber's criticism had reached the Christians, as if they had learned to speak of their faith in a way closer to earth. The dialectic between the workings of God and man in salvation will, of course, remain, it must remain, like the other question of whether God's imagelessness excludes every symbol of the Invisible, even the "image of God" which Jesus Christ represents for us according to Colossians 1:15. Similarly there will remain the insoluble antinomy between the alleged immediacy toward God and the practice of mediated relationships to him.

3. In *Two Types of Faith* Buber adopts a thesis of the Protestant exegete Wissmann, who in 1926 had worked out the idea of Pauline *pistis* as faith merely in the sense of holding something to be true;[36] with this, Christian faith is characterized for Buber as " 'believing that' in the fullest sense", as "acceptance of the factuality of an occurence" (Jesus' resurrection), while Hebraic faith, the dialogical vis-à-vis of human trust and Divine fidelity, the dialogical, unmediated situation between God and man, is given up. On the one hand we have faith through the mediation of a knowledge, of an assumed, rationally affirmed fact of revelation—and, against this, faith as a personal letting-oneself-be-demanded, a presenting of oneself before God.

It is certain that for centuries in the Catholic theology of faith, the noetic elements of faith were predominantly treated, most recently in the First Vatican Council, which defined faith as rational agreement with Revelation. It is equally certain that the personal factor of faith in the lived consummation of faith has not been lacking, as the rich tradition of mysticism and the history of piety shows. Was Buber simply aiming at provocation, protesting against a real danger that easily clings to every orthodoxy, every religious tradition, every theological overdifferentiation, that he overlooked the other half of Wissmann's thesis, namely: the mystically understood Christian piety in Paul, the being seized by Christ, and faith's character of obedience, which after all does contain a personal presenting of oneself? Is it because of this aim that he found in Paul only the holding-to-be-true of Jesus's resurrection and not the experience of the "power of resurrection" (Phil. 3:10)?

The protest of dialogical and personalistic thinkers since Maurice Blondel and J. H. Newman, including Buber, against the overemphasis on the elements of knowledge in the act of faith has been heard.[37] The Second Vatican Council speaks of faith as the act in which man surrenders himself freely and as a whole person to God.[38]

But here, too, the insoluble antinomy remains: how is the relationship to God to be conceived as real, and yet not completely fulfilled? Is there direct contemplation of God, whether in the depth of the soul, as with the mystics, or in a co-experience of being in every categorical recognition (of existence)? Or is there only a mediated relation to God through created things? Buber's formulation of this inevitable paradox is the concrete I-Thou relationship, in which the immediate encounter with the eternal Thou occurs.[39] With this, as we have indicated, the other paradox of the coexistence of subjective religious experience and already given revelation, which pass through both Jewish and Christian history of faith, is connected— above all the paradox of the immanence and transcendence of God, which is conceived by mystics of all religions differently than in their respective orthodoxies.

The dialogue between Catholic theology and Martin Buber is just beginning. In our gratitude to him as one of the great teachers of religious thought and the Bible we should not forget what the Bishop of Aachen, Prof. Klaus Hemmerle, has called to our attention: Buber is a kind of suture in dialogue, an inexhaustible impulse, a challenge; "—and we must not be in a hurry to make him into a cliche, a possession, a fashion; he deserves that we should question him, argue with him, listen to him". And: "Our motto should be not to stylize Buber, but to enter into what he intended for us—into dialogue".[40]

Notes

LORENZ WACHINGER

1. E. Brunner, Dogmatik III, Zürich-Stuttgart 1964, p. 187.
2. W. Kraft, *Gespräche mit Martin Buber*, Munich 1966 (conversation of 11.4.63).
3. Cf. Hugo Bergmann's letter of 30.5.49 in M . Buber, *Briefwechsel aus sieben Jahrzehnten*, vol. III, Heidelberg 1975, letter no. 160; also Gershom Scholem, "Martin Bubers Auffassung des Judentems", in his *Judaica* II, Frankfurt 1970, p. 185.
4. On this see L. Wachinger, *Der Glaubensbegriff Martin Bubers*, Munich 1970, pp. 143-204.
5. G. Ebeling, "Zwei Glaubensweisen?" in Juden—Christen—Deutsche, ed. by H. J. Schultz, Stuttgart 1961, p. 166.
6. Cf. M. Buber, *The Kingship of God*, trans. Richard Scheimann, New York and Evanston, 1956.
7. On the theme of the "Way" see G. Söhngen, *Der Weg der abendländischen Theologie: Grundgedanken zu einer Theologie des "Weges"*, Munich 1959.
8. M. Buber, "Jewish Religiosity" (1913), *On Judaism*, ed. by Nahum Glatzer, New York, 1967, p. 83.
9. F. Rosenzweig, in 1914, criticized this harshly as "atheistic theology" (*Kleinere Schriften*, Berlin, 1937, pp. 278-290). See also A. Zweig, who feels confirmed by Buber "in my kind of immanent God and atheistic religiosity—atheistic of course in relation to all rigidified religions". (M. Buber, *Briefwechsel aus sieben Jahrzehnten*, vol. I, no. 302.)
10. M. Buber, *Briefwechsel*, vol. II, letter no. 153 of 24.6.1924.
11. M. Buber, "Dialogue", in *Four Existentialist Theologians: A Reader from the Works of Jacques Maritain, Nicolas Berdyaev, Martin Buber and Paul Tillich*, ed. by Will Herberg, Garden City, New York, 1958, p. 182.
12. M. Buber, *"Philosophical and Religious World View"*, in M. Buber, *A Believing Humanism: My Testament, 1902-1965*, trans. by Maurice Friedman, Simon and Schuster, New York, 1967, p. 132-133.
13. M. Buber, "Replies to My Critics", in *The Philosophy of Martin Buber*, ed. by Paul Arthur Schilpp and Maurice Friedman, London, 1967, pp. 689-690.
14. M. Buber, *Hasidism*, Philosophical Library, New York, 1948, p. 144.
15. M. Buber, "Biblesches Zeugnis", in *Schriften zur Bibel*, Munich and Heidelberg, 1964, p. 1018f.
16. G. Scholem, "Martin Bubers Deutung des Chassidismus", *Judaica* I, pp. 197ff.
17. M. Buber, "Zu einer neuen Verdeutscung der Schrift", supplement to *Die fünf Bücher der Weisung*, verdeutscht von Martin Buber gemeinsam mit Franz Rosenzweig, Cologne, 1976, p. 38.
18. Ibid., p. 37.
19. M. Buber, "Abraham the Seer", trans. by Sophie Meyer, *Judaism* V/4, fall 1956, p. 297.
20. M. Buber, *The Kingship of God*, p. 154.
21. M. Buber, "Der Gesalbte", *Schriften zur Bibel*, p. 742.

22. Ed. by H. J. Schultz, Stuttgart, 1958.
23. Briefwechsel I, no. 223.
24. Ibid., no. 348.
25. Briefwechsel III, no. 133; the letter to Werfel, Briefwechsel I, no. 348.
26. Briefwechsel II, no. 114.
27. Grete Schaeder, "Martin Buber: Ein biographischer Abriss", Briefwechsel I, p. 88.
28. Briefwechsel II, no. 159.
29. M. Buber, Two Types of Faith, trans. Norman P. Goldhawk, New York, 1961, pp. 166-167.
30. Briefwechsel II, no. 116.
31. Letter to G. Scholem, Briefwechsel II, no. 390.
32. Two Types of Faith, pp. 116ff.
33. Letter to Gogarten, Briefwechsel II, no. 115.
34. Letter to Gogarten, Briefwechsel II, no. 116.
35. Cf. R. Bultmann, Das Urchristentum im Rahmen der antiken Religionen, Reinbek 1966 (rde 157/158), pp. 175ff.
36. E. Wissmann, Das Verhältnis von Pistis und Christusfrömmigkeit bei Paulus, Göttingen, 1926.
37. On the history of Catholic theology of faith see R. Aubert, Le probleme de l'acte de foi, Louvain 1958, 3. edition.
38. Dogmatische Konstitution über die Göttliche Offenbarung, I Kapitel, Nr. 5.
39. See J. Bloch, Die Aporie des Du: Probleme der Dialogik Martin Bubers, Heidelberg, 1977, especially chap. II, 3, "Die Widerspruchseinheit der Beziehungen".
40. K. Hemmerle, "Geleitwort", in Eckert/Goldschmidt/Wachinger, Martin Bubers Ringen um Wirklichkeit: Konfrontationen mit Juden, Christen und Sigmund Freud, Stuttgart 1977.

Buber's Evaluation of Christianity: A Jewish Perspective

MICHAEL WYSCHOGROD

There is little doubt that in the two thousand year old conversation between Judaism and Christianity, the segment that is the contribution of Martin Buber is one of the most significant. In a way, that is not saying very much. Much of that conversation has been polemical in the extreme. Perhaps the whole of the medieval segment suffers from this lack of mutual hearing. The accommodation—and there was accommodation—was a practical one. In the midst of Christendom, Israel was permitted to survive, often more than survive and some-times less. The reason for the accommodation is not self-evident. While to us it may seem a dictate of elementary decency, to medieval man the toleration of a non-Christian community in the midst of Christendom, a community that denied some of the fundamental tenets of the Christian faith, required considerable justification. Lest we are prone to forget the extent to which medieval man refused to consider religious belief and practice a private matter into which public authority had no right to inquire, we need only remind ourselves of the fate of various Christian heretical sects whose departure from recognized Christian teaching was hardly comparable to the distance between Israel and the church. While such Christian dissenters were eliminated, Israel, by and large, was permitted to exist. This can be explained only by reference to Christian theology and its doctrine of the significance of the continuing survival of Israel. But the accommodation that resulted from this theology was practical rather than one of the spirit. And so the encounter was polemical in which little more was seen than the strangeness of the other's faith.

There is, of course, a polemical element in Buber's treatment of Christianity. It is a defense of the faith of Israel against the intrusion of foreign elements, of a non-Jewish, hellenistic and even gnostic sort. But it is nevertheless an encounter of the spirit. No one can read Buber speaking about Jesus without recognizing the seriousness with which Buber takes this Galilean Jew. "From my youth onwards," he writes in one of his most widely quoted passages,

I have found in Jesus my great brother. That Christianity has regarded and does regard him as God and Saviour has always appeared to me a fact of the highest importance which, for his sake and my own, I must endeavor to understand. A small part of the results of this desire to understand is recorded here. My own fraternally open relationship to him has grown ever stronger and clearer, and to-day I see him more strongly and clearly than ever before.

I am more than ever certain that a great place belongs to him in Israel's history of faith and that this place cannot be described by any of the usual categories.[1]

Later he goes further: "All in all, the saying of Jesus about love for the enemy derives its light from the world of Judaism in which he stands and which he seems to contest; and he outshines it."[2] Jesus thus "outshines" Judaism even if something can be said for those "amongst whom he arose" who refused to set a standard that was so high as to cause men to despair. However significant the polemic here is, there is surely also a reverence that has not been characteristic of the Jewish-Christian discussion. This is, therefore, the new element in the situation.

Having located the place of Buber in the history of Jewish-Christian interaction, we can now ask what place this aspect of Buber's thought plays in the totality of his work. Can it be said that the encounter with Christianity plays a central role in the thought of Buber? Is it one of the sources of his vision, does it play a decisive role in shaping his soul? I do not think we can make such claims. *Two Types of Faith*, the central work devoted to our theme, is an application of Buber's fundamental vision, not one of its sources. If, at the risk of oversimplification, we assign *Emunah* (Jewish faith) to the realm of the I-Thou and *pistis* (Pauline faith) to that of the I-It, we can see clearly how very much we are dealing with a concrete application of what is fundamental, not the occasion for a new and unanticipated discovery. The fact that *Two Types of Faith*, written during the battle for Jerusalem in 1948, appeared as late as 1950, the same year that saw the appearance of the German edition of his *Paths in Utopia*, itself helps us understand its place in the author's work. The fundamental work of *I and Thou* and the almost equally fundamental discovery of Hasidism had to come first. Only later was it necessary to address the question under discussion today. This time-table ought not to surprise us. An evaluation of Christianity is, after all, not central to the Jewish enterprise. Jewish self-understanding, in this respect, is more autonomous than that of the Christian who can hardly define himself independently of his emergence from the spiritual world of Judaism from which, at least in some respects, he ought not to emerge at all. It can therefore be argued with some plausibility that the excision of *Two Types of Faith* from Buber's opus, while undoubtedly diminishing its total weight, would not leave a prominent lacuna.

And yet, one cannot leave the matter at that. The place we assign to Buber's writings about Christianity in his work cannot be separated from his relationship to the non-Jewish world in general. While to thousands of people throughout the world Buber has come to be seen as the arch-Jew, a term he applied to himself in accepting the Peace Prize of the German Book Trade in 1953, Buber was also, throughout his life, one of the great Jewish apostles to the gentiles, perhaps only second in stature to that most famous Jewish apostle to the gentiles, Paul of Tarsus. We need not here lend very much credence to the charge, widely repeated, that Buber has played a greater role in non-Jewish, particularly Christian, thought than within Judaism itself and that he was a prophet not very much honored in his own land of Israel. The occasion and the auspices under which we meet demonstrate the esteem in which Buber is held in Israel and among Jews throughout the world. Nevertheless, it is not possible to overlook Buber's stature in German and European literature. It must be said that not since Mendelssohn has a Jewish Jew had the impact of Buber on German literary and religious culture. Without in any way questioning the Jewish authenticity of Mendelssohn, we must however note that his Judaism, at least as he projected it toward his non—Jewish audience, was far more rationalistic and universalistic than that of Buber who brought to the attention of German gentiles and largely assimilated Jews the spiritual life of Eastern and therefore non-Westernized Jewry. We are therefore faced with a Jewish personality who is able to mediate between the inner life of Eastern European Jewry and the culture of the West that becomes the audience to which Buber addressed himself.

What was the nature of this mediation? It was not the usual one. The usual one was the language of science. The international language of Europe was the language of science. He who mastered that language gained admittance to what had previously been closed to Jews. Spinoza, Marx, Freud, Husserl are but some of the many Jews who took advantage of this opportunity. The subject matter of these was, however, not the culture of the Jewish people. But even this culture could be pressed into the scientific mold and thereby made palatable to Western man. The form it took was the methodology of historical or social "science" as applied to Jewish history. *Wissenschaft des Judentums* was the fruit of this application. Initially, the method determined the subject matter and only the more "rational" portions of the Jewish experience were found worthy of being presented in "scientific" form. But gradually even an irrational content, such as Jewish mysticism, could be absorbed into the new language and we find someone like Scholem approaching Jewish mysticism with the methods of "scientific" history and thereby gaining a hearing for what would earlier not be heard. But Buber never took this path. It is not that he ignored "scientific" scholarship. In fact, he mastered its techniques, a mastery that is reflected in various areas, including his biblical scholarship. But it did not become the platform on which he presented himself. It is more difficult to characterize that platform positively than it is to point out that, negatively speaking, he did not, as Scholem, present himself primarily as a scientific scholar. It was as a man of the spirit that Buber presented himself. His sensibilities were artistic and literary, not scientific. And because they were literary, his roots in German culture and language had to be, and were, very deep indeed. The German cultural landscape was his world and therefore Christianity, and particularly cultural Christianity, was a very large segment of his being. It is true that in spite of all this he remained the arch-Jew. But there was also a distance between Martin Buber and his Eastern European Judaism. He was not a practicing Hasid nor did he have much contact with synagogue life either in the diaspora or Israel. There was a certain alienation between Buber and existing Jewish religious life. The significance of this for his interpretation of Christianity will become apparent only after we discuss the fulcrum of that interpretation, Paul of Tarsus.

Buber's interpretation of Christianity rests on a bifurcation, that between Jesus and Paul. In a fundamental sense, Jesus, according to Buber, stands within the circle of faith that is Israel. At times, claims Buber, Jesus "outshines,"[3] "supplements"[4] and "transcends"[5] Judaism. We will soon examine the significance of this judgment more closely. But with Paul, the tie to Judaism is almost severed. Speaking of "this immediacy of the whole man," in Judaism which "is devoted towards the whole God," Buber writes: "It excludes the two great *imagines* which the Pauline world-view set over against the immediate *Emunah;* the demonocracy, to which this aeon is given over, and the mediatorship of a Christ at the threshold of that which is to come."[6]

With Paul, it is not a matter of supplementing or even transcending Judaism but of exclusion. We must therefore attempt to understand the supplement-transcend-outshine relationship to Judaism of Jesus and compare it to the relationship of exclusion that is Paul's. Since Christianity is a composite of the Jesus and Paul components, together they constitute the Christianity that is evaluated by Buber.

The best example of a "transcending" of Judaism that can be produced is, of course, the Sermon on the Mount (Mat. 5) in which Jesus contrasts what "you have learned" with "what I tell you." And of this list, the most interesting is the one which deals with loving one's enemies. The Hebrew Bible (Lev. 19:18) teaches: "Thou shalt not avenge, nor bear any grudge against the children of thy people, but thou shalt love thy neighbor as thyself: I am the Lord." Against this, Jesus formulates his teaching (Mat. 15:43-48): "You have learned that they were told, 'Love your neighbor, hate your enemy.' But what I tell you is this: Love your enemies and pray for your persecutors; only so can you be the children of your heavenly Father, who makes his sun rise on good and bad alike, and sends the rain on the honest and the dishonest. If you love only those who love you, what reward can you expect. Surely the tax-gatherers do as much as that. And if you greet only your brothers, what is there extraordinary about that? Even the heathen do as much. There must be no limit to your goodness, or your heavenly Father's goodness knows no bounds." The issue is joined here fairly clearly. How does Buber respond to this issue?

He points out that the commandment of Leviticus (19:18) does not admit of the interpretation that one ought to hate the enemy.[7] While there has been much discussion whether *re'ah* includes non-Jews, there is no reason for believing that the enemies that are to be loved in Jesus' command are non-Jewish enemies. Furthermore, Exodus 23:4-5 teaches: "If thou meet thine enemy's ox or his ass going astray, thou shalt surely bring it back to him again. If thou see the ass of him that hateth thee lying under his burden, and wouldst forbear to help him, thou shalt surely help with him." The Hebrew Bible, even if it does not explicitly command love of the enemy surely does not command hate of him and, in fact, comes rather close to commanding love of him. Nevertheless, Buber does not make much of this misinterpretation of Judaism but refers it to "a popular saying, that one was free to hate the enemy,"[8] without wondering about why Jesus substitutes a popular saying for authentic teaching. In evaluating Judaism's attitude toward the enemy, Buber quotes[9] Psalm 139:21-22:

"Do not I hate them, O Lord, that hate thee? and am not I grieved with those that rise up against thee? I hate them with perfect hatred: I count them mine enemies." It is in this spirit that *Abot de R. Natan* (16,32) can instruct: "Love all-and hate the heretics, the apostates and the informers." At this point, Buber could distinguish between one's personal enemy whose lost ox or ass Exodus commands to be retrieved and the enemies of God who ought to be hated. He could draw attention to the impossibility of loving one's enemies and, to a degree, he does so when he speaks of Jesus as "a person in the sign of the kairos [who] demands the impossible in such a way that he compels men to will the possible more strongly than before."[10] The fundamental move of Buber's, however, is rejection of the distinction between one's own enemies, who may not be hated, and the enemies of God who may be hated. This boundary line between the two kinds of enemies is a dangerous one. "In this case it is shown crudely," he writes,

> how dangerously unstable the boundary-line is. To one assured of his possession of the God of Israel it was but a short step to hold (Sifre 22) that one who hates Israel is 'as one who hates God'. Such opinions are easily transferred to the personal sphere, so that many among the people understand their own enemies as God's, instead of reckoning with the Psalmist God's enemies as their own. But we do not come to know the real danger on such lowlands as these, but rather upon the heights of faith. Not merely fanatics but precisely genuine prophets often cannot but attribute opposition to the message—God's message!—to malice and hardness of heart and their zeal for it they lose the simple love. The Gospel in which the Sermon on the Mount appears knows the same thing in Jesus' angry outbursts against the 'generation of vipers' of the Pharisees (Matt. xii. 34, xxiii, 33), the authenticity of which, it is true, has been justifiably contested.[11]

Buber thus considers hate of enemies a dangerous path along which it is easy to convert one's own enemies into those of God. And if further proof is needed that love of one's enemies is not alien to but deeply continuous with authentic Jewish teaching, Buber leaps across 1800 years to the Hasidim and quotes one of their masters "Pray for enemies that things go well with them. And if you think, that is no service of God: know that more than any other prayers, this is service of God."[12] This, together with a number of similar Hasidic sayings speaking well of enemies, convince Buber that in the teaching of Jesus we are not dealing with a break but rather with an intensification of the faith of Israel. In view of this, one might wonder why it is accurate to speak of Jesus as transcending or outshining Judaism. But that is no matter. The important point is that the teaching of Jesus, as David Flusser has more recently shown, is located within and not discontinuous with the faith of his people.

But that is not so with Paul. Here we are dealing with contentions deeply at odds with Jewish faith. The world has been handed over to gods of this age (2 Cor. 4:4) who were unaware of the redeeming function of Jesus' sacrifice, for had they known the significance of this event they would not have done as they did: "The powers that rule the world have never known it, if they had, they would not have crucified the Lord of glory." (1 Cor. 2:8). During this period, God has put into man's "flesh" and "members" a law of sin over which man has no control. "But as things are, it is no longer I who perform the action, but sin that lodges in me. For I know that nothing good lodges in me—in my unspiritual nature, I mean—for though the will to do good is there, the deed is not. The good which I want to do, I fail to do; but what I do is the wrong which is against my will; and if what I do is against my will, clearly it is no longer I who am the agent, but sin that has its lodging in me." (Rom. 7:17-20). Buber adds: "The Gnostic nature of the essential features of this conception is obvious—the derivative powers, which, ruling the world, work against the primal divine power and waylay the human soul, the enslavement of the cosmos, the problematic character of the law, the overcoming of the 'rules' and the setting-free of man. . . ."[13] Connected with this is God's hardening of the heart of Israel so that God's mercy can be shown and, in this connection, Paul (Rom. 9:17) quotes God's words to Pharaoh whose heart he has hardened and whom he tells (Ex. 8:16) that he raised him precisely for this purpose so that the power of God may be known by all. By juxtaposing with this the verse (Ex. 33:19) "I will be gracious to whom I will be gracious, and I will show mercy on whom I will show mercy," Paul, according to Buber, tells his readers that "as the mercy is God's alone, so the hardening is His alone; as the mercy is unfathomable to human understanding, so also is the hardening; as the mercy does not need to be 'caused,' so neither does the hardening."[14] Against this, Buber states unequivocally:

> In the Old Testament meaning the hardening intervenes in an extreme situation in life, an extreme perversion in the relation of an individual or a nation to God, and makes it, dreadfully enough, into an inevitable

destiny, makes the going-astray into a state of having gone-astray from which there is no returning; in Paul's usage however the process of hardening in general no longer cares about the men and the generations of men which it affects, but uses them and uses them up for higher ends. Contrary to the Old Testament Paul's God does not have regard for the people to whom He speaks out of the cloud, or rather causes His angels to speak.[15]

He concludes:

> When I contemplate this God I no longer recognize the God of Jesus, nor his world in this world of Paul's. For Jesus, who was concerned with the individual human soul and with every single human soul, Israel was not a universal entity with such and such an appointed function in the plan of the world, nor was it for him the mere totality of Jews living in his day and who stood in a certain relationship to his message: every soul which had lived from Moses to himself belong in concreto to it. In his view for everyone of them, when they had gone astray, turning was allowed, and everyone of them when they did turn back, was the lost son returned home. His God was the same Who, though He might at times also 'harden' and perhaps even at times give a statute which was 'not good', yet answered in every generation to the person interposing for Israel: 'I have pardoned according to thy words' (Num. xiv. 20). In Paul's conception of God, where the generations of souls in Israel from Moses to Jesus are concerned, this characteristic is supplanted by another, which alters everything. I do not venture to give it a name.[16]

The Gnostic element in Paul, then, comes to this, that God has placed the present age into the hands of powers through whom the heart of man has been hardened so that man cannot fulfill the Torah. Because of this, he is guilty but, even worse, he cannot turn (in the sense of Teshuva) to God to obtain forgiveness. In this situation, man is lost until God sends down his only begotten son whose crucifixion atones for man's sins. The medium through which all this is attained is the Torah which, according to Buber, is capable of fulfillment for Judaism and for Jesus but is not capable of fulfillment for Paul for whom "it was given not in order to be fulfilled but rather through its incapability of fulfillment to call forth sin—'in order that it might abound' (Rom. 5:20), that it, through the fact of the commandment, 'might become exceeding sinful' (7:13)—and so prepare the way for grace."[17] The crux of the matter, then, is the question of the possibility or impossibility of the fulfillment of the Torah. If the Torah can be fulfilled, then, even if it is not, the sin that accrues to man is not his pre-ordained fate but the result of his choice. And if he has sinned in a situation where it was not inevitable that he sin, there is a possibility that he turn to God and be reconciled with him. But if the Torah cannot be fulfilled, if it was given with the certainty that it will be violated and if it was given *that* it be violated, then the inevitability of transgression rules out the possibility of turning and then only grace can bring redemption. In Christian Gnosticism, the God of the Torah is a malevolent divinity whose snare is the Torah and who succeeds in inprisoning souls of divine origin in the world of matter until they are rescued from their predicament by an emissary of the benevolent deity. When Paul speaks of the Law as coming not from God but promulgated through angels (Gal. 3:19) he comes perilously close to the Gnostic attribution of the Torah to someone other than the God of Israel.

We are thus faced with the question of the law. Can it or can it not be fulfilled? Buber claims it to be the teaching of Judaism that it can be fulfilled. What is the Torah? Is it properly translated by the word "law?" Buber claims that it is not. "The Torah of God is understood as God's instruction in His way, and therefore not as a separate *objectivum*. It includes laws, and laws are indeed its most vigorous objectivization, but the Torah itself is essentially not law. A vestige of the actual speaking always adheres to the commanding word, the directing voice is always present or at least its sound is heard fading away. To render *Torah* by "law" is to take away from its idea this inner dynamic and vital character. Without the change of meaning in the Greek, objective sense the Pauline dualism of law and faith, life from works and life from grace, would miss its most important conceptual presupposition."[18] Elsewhere, Buber writes: "I do not believe that revelation is ever lawgiving, and in the fact that law-giving always comes out of it, I see the fact of human opposition, the fact of man."[19] And finally, in one of his most powerful passages in which he expresses his attitude toward the tradition in its legal form, he exclaims:

> O you secure and safe ones who hide yourselves behind the defence-works of the law so that you will not have to look into God's abyss! Yes, you have secure ground under your feet while we hang suspended, looking out over the endless deeps. But we would not exchange our dizzy insecurity and our poverty for your security and abundance. For to you God is one who created once and not again; but to us God is he who 'renews the work of creation every day.' To you God is one who

revealed himself once and no more; but to us he speaks out of the burning thorn-bush of the present . . . in the revelations of our innermost hearts—greater than words.[20]

We are thus faced with an interesting puzzle. Buber himself is an important Jewish critic of the law. And so is Paul. Yet, instead of discovering in Paul a kindred spirit with whom he can, at least in part, agree, Buber rejects his fellow critic of the law, Paul, as stepping outside the bounds of Judaism. How is this to be understood? Is it Buber's view that Paul identifies revelation with law and it is for this reason as we will see that he finds it impossible to fulfill the law? But if so, why does Buber characterize those who equate revelation with law as "secure and safe ones who hide yourselves behind the defence-works of the law?" The implication seems to be that objectivized law bestows security but if that is so, then why is Paul so insecure, convinced that he is guilty by the standards of the law? Or is it rather the person who has the courage to live by the maxim "First we must act, then we shall receive: from out of our own deed" and who abandons the security of the law who is bound to find himself condemned by his deeds because he can never even have a reasonable certainty that his actions please God? If we characterize the position that law can be the content of revelation and not only a human strategy to objectify what cannot be objectified as the "revelation-through-law" position and Buber's position as the "revelation-is-never-lawgiving" position, then we must ask which of these is more and which is less compatible with the Pauline judgement of the inevitability of sin.

On the one hand, those who live under the law as the revealed word of God seem more secure and therefore less guilty than others. They know what is right and wrong and even if, from time to time, they do not live up to the standards of the law, they know the power of turning and the graciousness of God who waits for the turning of the sinner. On the other hand, these same people also live under the objective and therefore rigid law which condemns them by its rigidity. Similarly, those for whom revelation is not law, there is the burden of not knowing whether they have done what is right but there is also the liberation from a rigid law so that what appears as transgression may, in fact, not be so. These questions come down to two fundamental questions: how does Paul understand the law and why does Buber find it so difficult to understand someone who feels crushed by his burden of guilt?

I do not believe that Paul shares Buber's "revelation-is-never-law-giving" point of view. For Paul, the law was of divine origin, whether revealed by God or through angels. It's effect is to make man guilty because he cannot or will not live up to its demands. But he becomes guilty because he violates a divinely given law. There is nothing in Paul that would imply that man's guilt is a result of the fact that the legal formulation is a human interpretation of revelation which is inherently not legal. Paul's problem is not lack of knowledge of exactly what God demands—this is a uniquely modern problem—but rather the unwillingness which amounts to an inability to do what one ought to do but fails to do. When Paul laments that "the good which I want to do, I fail to do; but what I do is the wrong which is against my will," (Rom. 7:19) he makes very clearly that sin is not ignorance—a position we find in Plato—but not doing what one knows to be the right. And this knowledge is derived from the Torah which specifies very clearly what is and what is not the will of God. In this respect, Paul is quite rabbinic, more so, in fact, than is Buber. Buber is right, of course that Paul is unrabbinic in his judgment concerning the impossibility of living up to the demands of the law. But even here, as we will see, the chasm is not as great as Buber seems to think it is.

If ours is a correct reading of Paul's interpretation of the law as fully within the "revelation-through-law" point of view, then we can begin to understand the absence of sympathy in Buber for Paul's critique of the law. Paul's critique stems from feeling himself condemned by the demands of the law. It is otherwise with Buber. His critique of the law is that much of it is man-made, consisting of human accretions to the living fire of revelation. Inevitably, this diminishes or totally destroys the possibility of feeling guilty for violating the law. It is true that guilt does not disappear from Buber's world. In fact, it becomes quite prominent when Buber takes up psychotherapy and its tendency to explain guilt away as the product of social and psychological conditioning. But the guilt to which Buber here returns is a guilt that grows out of a sense of having violated the human order. "Existential guilt," writes Buber, "occurs when someone injures an order of the human world whose foundation he knows and recognizes as those of his own existence and of all common human existence."[21] But this is a quite different guilt from that of which Paul is speaking. Paul's guilt grows out of having violated the divine command. It is not restricted to injuring "an order of the human world" though it, of course, includes such guilt. Guilt that is restricted to the domain "between" man and man is subject to human correction. In fact, divine forgiveness can only play a limited role in its expiation. It is the fellow human being rather than God who must be appeased. But when sin is understood primarily as a violation of the command of God, then it is divine forgiveness that must be sought and this can be obtained for Paul through belief in the redeeming sacrifice of his savior.

According to Buber, Paul believes that the Torah cannot be fulfilled whereas Judaism teaches that it can be. Buber quotes[22] Paul in Gal. 3:11, "It is evident that no one is ever justified before God in terms of law." Thus we have the Pauline contrast between faith and law. On the one hand stands Leviticus 18:5: "Ye shall therefore keep my status and my judgments: which if a man do, he shall live in them. . . ." On the other hand, also quoted by Paul, is Habakkuk 2:4, ". . . . the just shall live by his faith." Is life gained from keeping God's statutes as in Leviticus or from faith, as in Habakkuk? Paul's answer, of course, is that life is gained from faith and not from keeping God's commandments because no one fully keeps God's commandments.

It is otherwise for Judaism, claims Buber. "The Jewish position may be summarized in the sentence: fulfillment of the divine commandment is valid when it takes place in conformity with the full capacity of the person and from the whole intention of faith."[23] Several pages later, Buber adds: "According to this purpose of the Torah the decisive significance and values does not lie in the bulk of these actions in themselves but in the direction of the heart in them and through them." Here is the secret of Buber's misunderstanding of Paul. For Buber, the essence of the Torah is the direction of the human heart. If that direction is proper, then the Torah has been satisfied. While Buber does not connect this teaching with his view that revelation is never law giving, the connection is perfectly plain. Law deals with actions. If revelation as law is possible, then God commands actions. A particular direction of the human heart may also be required. But by itself it cannot be sufficient. In addition to the direction of the heart, action is required. And once that is so, it becomes—in contrast to Buber—far more difficult to say that the Torah can be fulfilled completely. But if the crux of the matter is the direction of the heart, then there is no sense about worrying whether this or that detail of the law has been fulfilled. The direction of the heart was right and therefore why worry about external details which, in any case, are probably human inventions in the first place. Buber's equanimity about the possibility of fulfilling the Torah is therefore rooted in his non-legal and therefore non-action oriented interpretation of the Torah. And it is for this reason that he has little sympathy for Paul's sense of guilt with respect to the Torah as Law. It is true that, were he so inclined and given his emphasis on the direction of the heart as that which God really requires, Buber could develop an even more intense sense of guilt since the direction of the heart is ever more difficult to evaluate than more external actions. But it does not seem to work this way. Since a wrong direction of the heart is not as visible as a wrong action, it seems easier to satisfy oneself that the direction is right than to believe that one has done what was required when that is not the case. And so guilt is diminished.

Paul's insight is that man is saved by faith and not by works of the law. Almost universally, this thesis has been taken as being sharply at odds with Judaism. But I am not convinced of this. What would the counter-thesis assert? To say that man is saved by works of the law would amount to a curious claim. Someone who held this position would, in effect, be saying to God: judge me by my actions and give me what I deserve, neither more nor less. Such a person would reject any favors from God; he would ask for no mercy but only for justice, presumably because he would feel that he does not need mercy since his actions are enough to insure a favorable outcome. The fact is that I know of no Jew who has ever taken such an arrogant point of view. In the morning liturgy, we plead: "Sovereign of all words! Not in reliance upon our righteous deeds do we lay our supplications before thee, but by reason of thine abundant mercies." The Jew approaches God with the knowledge that, were he judged by the demands of the law and in accordance with justice, he could not prevail. As a sinner, he would be lost beyond all hope. His only hope is that God will not judge him according to the law but show him mercy so that he can be saved even though he does not deserve it. But is not this the meaning of the contention that man is saved by faith rather than works of the law? Faith here means faith in the mercy of God who does not mete out to sinners what they deserve but bestows mercy rather than justice on them. For Judaism, this faith in the mercy of God does not require faith in Jesus as the messiah. For Christianity, faith in Jesus is faith in the mercifulness of God. In Judaism, at times God acts in accordance with justice and at times in accordance with mercy. But man can never know which it will be, whether he will receive his deserts or whether he will be spared by mercy. Apparently for Paul, this uncertainty is now over. With the occurrence of Jesus, man is guaranteed the mercy of God. It is as if God had decided to extend mercy almost automatically to those who invoke the name of Jesus. Is it un-Jewish to tip the scale in favor of mercy, to believe that mercy and judgment are not fully equal but that mercy somehow predominates, destined ultimately to redeem man from the deserved consequences of his action? I believe it to be the teaching of Judaism that these two *middot* (measures, characteristics) of God are not equal. In this respect, Buber rightly emphasizes two points: that "the *middot* are always united; now and then one predominates, but it never works alone, the other is never excluded from its operation."[24] And, secondly, "they are not equal to one another in power: the *middah* of grace is the stronger. It, and not rigour, is the right hand, the stronger hand (Sifre)."[25] Buber adds: "The dynamic unity of justice and grace stands opposed in this instance to the Pauline division of the justice of God in this aeon and His saving grace and the End."[26] But God's saving grace, according to Paul, is not altogether reserved for the End but is available here and now through faith in Jesus as the Christ. And if this is so, the distance between Paul and Judaism may not be as great as Buber thinks.

We must end our critique of Buber's excommunication of Paul by referring to some curious omissions. Nowhere, at least not in *Two Types of Faith*, does Buber deal with Romans 9-11, the central text in which Paul wrestles with the significance of Israel in the divine plan. In these chapters, Paul investigates with great passion the significance of Israel's rejection of the messiahship of Jesus and, at the same time, he insists (Rom. 11:2) that "God has not rejected the people which he acknowledge of old as his own." It is here (Rom. 11:18) that Paul warns the gentile church "that it is not you who sustain the root: the root sustains you" and that (Rom. 11:29) "the gracious gifts of God and his calling are irrevocable." It is not our purpose here to investigate the implications of these remarks. We can only wonder why Buber does not address himself to them. It seems to me clear that no Jewish evaluation of Paul can ignore them.

Finally, we must broach an aspect of Paul's view of the law that, in my view, is the single most suggestive reinterpretation of Paul of our time. I am referring to the observation that Paul's statements about the law are made by him to gentiles who, because their newly gained faith, are contemplating circumcision and obedience to the Mosaic Law. From Acts 15 it is clear that some Jewish Christians believed that gentiles who came to faith in Jesus had to undergo circumcision and therefore obey the law. But Paul disagreed and in Acts 15, we read of the Jerusalem Council at which this question is debated and Paul is vindicated. As a consequence, gentiles are asked only to obey the Noachide commandments (Acts 15:29) which rabbinic Judaism considered obligatory for gentiles. The very fact, however, that this matter is debated indicates beyond doubt that there was unanimous agreement that Jews, unlike gentiles, were duty bound to obey the law even after the event of Jesus as the Christ. If this is so, then Paul's discouraging views about the law may not represent his complete view. Any rabbi, when speaking to a gentile whom he is obligated to discourage from conversion to Judaism, will stress the negative consequences of the law, the record of Israel's disobedience and resulting punishment. He will speak, as does Paul, of the curse (Deut. 28:15-68) attached to disobedience of the law. But, because his purpose is to discourage conversion, he will not mention the blessing (Deut. 28:1-14) attached to obedience of the law. In short, the evaluation of the law delivered on such an occasion must be one-sided in view of its purpose. This, I think, is what is happening in the writings of Paul. As Apostle to the gentiles, he speaks to gentiles. In addition to the normal Jewish opposition to gentile conversion, Saul's opposition is greatly strengthened by his conviction that through Jesus gentiles can now enter the household of Israel as adopted sons making full conversion even more unnecessary than previously. Fired on by these views, Paul proclaims and even exaggerates the perils and difficulties of existence under the law. But this is only part of the truth, though it is the part that gentiles need to know. And if this is so, Paul probably had a quite different evaluation of the law as it applied to Jews, or the people of the covenant, who were obligated to express their faith by obedience to the law's commandments. Since total obedience is never possible, the significance of Jesus was to guarantee mercy for Israel when it sins. But the guarantee of such mercy through Jesus in no way erased the demands of the law which Jews should strive to continue to obey as before.

If the crux of the matter before Paul was law for gentiles, then the reading that Paul has received from the time of the disappearance of the Jerusalem church has been faulty because his quarrel then was not with the law but with gentiles who wished to come under its jurisdiction. While we cannot fault Buber for not having noticed this possibility, we can wish that he had done so. It might have modified his views.

Notes

MICHAEL WYSCHOGROD

1. Martin Buber, *Two Types of Faith* (New York, Harper, 1961), pp. 12-13.
2. *Ibid.*, p. 75.
3. *Loc. cit.*
4. *Ibid.*, p. 76.
5. *Ibid.*, p. 69.
6. *Ibid.*, p. 154.
7. *Ibid.*, p. 72.
8. *Ibid.*, pp. 72-73.
9. *Ibid.*, p. 74.
10. *Ibid.*, p. 75.
11. *Ibid.*, pp. 74-75.
12. *Ibid.*, p. 77.
13. *Ibid.*, p. 83.
14. *Ibid.*, p. 86.
15. *Loc. cit.*
16. *Ibid.*, pp. 89-90.
17. *Ibid.*, p. 80.
18. *Ibid.*, p. 57.
19. Quoted by Maurice S. Friedman, *Martin Buber: The Life of Dialogue* (Univ. of Chicago Press, 1960), p. 264.
20. *Ibid.*, p. 262.
21. *Ibid.*, p. 197, n. 2.
22. Martin Buber, *Two Types of Faith*, p. 48.
23. *Ibid.*, p. 56.
24. *Ibid.*, p. 153.
25. *Loc. cit.*
26. *Ibid.*, p. 154.

Summary of the Conference

NATHAN ROTENSTREICH

I

We start with a general comment on the fact that the expression "I and Thou" became very current, not only in the deliberations of the Conference explicitly devoted to Buber's thought, but also in semi-popular parlance of our generation. When Buber coined that expression, or gave it a position in his attempt to formulate a basic insight into the human condition, he wanted indeed to formulate a basic experience or intuition cognate to it. It is probably defying his intention when an expression like that becomes so easily translated and turns out to be even a slogan. This indeed is the last thing Buber contemplated since it is not congruous with his attitude and teaching. We who are interested in his teaching have to be aware of the danger, and probably one of the ways to meet that danger is to try to reconstruct some of the components of Buber's basic intuition. This, to be sure, can sound again like a paradoxical attempt, since we apply the tools of analysis to an intuitive attitude—but such a paradox or tension is unavoidable. We have, of course, to take into account that this is indeed a fact that Buber's personality and his teaching elicited that sort of resonance which as such carries with itself not only the tendency toward popularization but also the tendency to use phraseology which lacks the grounding in experience and in the various ingredients of which an experience is composed.

We already used the concept of "basic intuition"; that concept is a reformation of what Bergson said, that a philosopher is motivated by one intuition and by one only. What a philosopher is engaged in is a continuous formulation and reformulation of that intuition, and also in various attempts to transfer the intuition from one orbit to another. This would be the case, and indeed we follow here the direction outlined by Buber himself, namely that the "I and Thou" is not only a formulation and perhaps an epitomization of the inter-human context, but also the expression of the fundamental nucleus of religious experience. Thus "I and Thou" are meant to serve as pivotal points of the phenomenology of the human context as well as of the direction of transcending that context in terms of the encounter between human existence and the divine realm.

II

The Conference is concerned with the "I and Thou" in its previously indicated two contexts. Its theme was set not to include the Zionist aspect of Buber's thought and concurrently his position as a Jewish national thinker in the era of the Zionist renaissance of the Jewish people. One may question whether such a limitation is warranted in terms of the overall profile of Buber's thinking, since there are rather visible connections between Buber's philosophical conviction and the trend of his thought within the Zionist context. The fact that Buber as a Zionist thinker concerned with the fundamentals of the Jewish renaissance as well as with current issues, including the human and political aspects of the Jewish-Arab conflict—the fact that these aspects are bound to evoke controversies is no reason not to deal with Buber's ideas in this direction. Moreover, a procedure can easily be worked out to understand Buber from his immanent position, without necessarily involving him and us in polemics related to present-day issues, which preoccupy our minds and attention.

It is indeed mandatory to see the various expressions of Buber's fundamental intuition, which as such leads him not only in the direction of the Zionist ideology, but concurrently in that of his concern with the structure of social life. We have to keep this in mind when we come to our next step of characterizing this built-in presupposition of Buber's thought.

III

In our attempt to elaborate on that point by way of describing the basic intuition, we may refer in the first place to what Buber himself considered to be characteristic of his approach, namely his attempt to record the various aspects of the immediacy of human existence. He says himself that he does not construct things, but presents them as they are lived; he reports life as it is lived—and in this context he can be characterized as belonging to the trend in German philosophy of the 20th century, which was characterized, even sometimes polemically, as *Lebenphilosophie*. To be sure, *Leben* is understood here not in the naturalistic infra-structure, but in its human, that is to say, also inter-human boundaries. These in turn are not only boundaries limiting human beings, but also opening for them the horizon of their very existence. Since the emphasis is placed from the very beginning not on the naturalistic aspect but on the inter-human one, it can be understood that Buber is essentially a social thinker, who elaborates the societal manifestation of the primary inter-human dimension. Historically or retrospectively speaking, he takes advantage in this context of the well-known distinction between *Gemeinschaft* and *Gesellschaft*. He absorbed that distinction from those who presented it and mainly from Tönnies. *Gemeinschaft* was germane to Buber's own direction of thought according to which he tried to present modes of human social coexistence which are primarily imbued with a non-organized ambience. He gave preference, both descriptively and normatively, to that mode of existence. The preference he gave to it brought about as one of its consequences a skeptical—and perhaps even more than a skeptical attitude to the political organization of social life. This in turn has been echoed in Buber's interpretation of the Bible, as it was presented in our colloquium by Prof. Uffenheimer. It had also its extension in Buber's evaluation of the political aspects of Zionism and his orientation, even to belittle the extent of the significance of that aspect in his interpretation of the basic trends in contemporary Jewish life. Here the intuition, which brought about the adherence to the non-organized mode of human existence led Buber to take a polemical attitude not only against the depreciation of the immediacy, as for instance by replacing the I-Thou situation by the I-It situation. It led him also to what can be described as a polemical consequence grounded in his basic position. Hence we can trace here a line of continuity from the immediacy referred to as Gemeinschaft to the criticism of Gesellschaft in its various manifestations, including the political one which amounted in his eyes to a trend of authoritarianism.

One additional consequence can be derived from that context or atmosphere, which in turn may shed some light on the very close relationship which existed between Buber and Gustav Landauer. Out of that relationship or affinity Buber absorbed a certain anarchistic trend into his thinking, since that trend was seen by him as being akin to the immediate or even spontaneous character of human coexistence. That mode of existence qua coexistence has been viewed as imbued with its own norm, and as such stands in no need of an intervention of rigid political structures, including authorities, impositions, let alone compulsions. To reiterate this point, it has to be said that indeed there is a line of continuity from Buber's involvement in immediacy to his socio-political stand and the critical consequences which he himself derived from that stand.

IV

At this juncture it is explainable that we have to refer to Buber's adherence to socialism originating in faith, that is to say in religious faith—*Sozialismus aus dem Glauben*. Here, too, we have to observe that Buber's point of departure does not lie in a socio-economic analysis of a social class in the historical or industrial sense of that term. His point of departure lies in the immediacy of the inter-human contacts, which is obliterated and overpowered in the prevailing socio-economic conditions. Socialism as grounded in immediacy is meant to reconstruct or to redeem the underlying human situation, whereby the religious faith adds to that redemptive direction by pointing to the fact that the I-Thou relationship is not exhausted in the societal context. Human beings as partners to the dialogue or *Zwiesprache* between man and God have to be freed from the compulsary societal situation, which through its imposing and even cruel character carries them out of their fundamental context, both horizontally in the human situation, and vertically in the relationship between man and the divine realm.

Zionism in the proper sense of that term, as Buber understood it, has to be seen, at least partially, in the context which is the subject of our analysis. For Buber who, as is well known, related Zionism in his *Drei Reden über das Judentum* to the basic experiences of the Jews as individuals, pointing to the duality of their experience as being at home on the one hand in the Jewish world, and in the surrounding environment on the other. But Zionism is for him also a renaissance or activization of the particular adherence of the Jewish people and the land of Israel. The emphasis placed on that attitude led Buber probably to write his book *Between the People and its Land*, whose aim was to analyse the awareness of the land in the consciousness of the Jews over the generations. The pivotal point in that consciousness is the primary relationship of the Jewish people to the land—and this interpretation brought Buber, to mention one example, to give particular attention to the thought of the famous Maharal of Prague. For the Maharal the land occupied a position of a specially designed territory, implying that a people occupies a proper place in the world, and from that place it cannot be uprooted. This aspect is significant not only from the point of view of realizing Buber's profile as a Zionist ideologue, but also in his attempt to integrate into the spectrum of his thinking additional aspects of the immediacy of human experience, which as such in the light of the particular example before us encompasses man's attachment to a place or to a land.

V

We may move now to the second topic of our consideration, which, due to the subject matter of the Conference, was naturally at the centre of our deliberations. The matter came up—at least parenthetically—in one of the discussions, and can be described as that of the relationship between I and Thou on the one hand, and that of the in-between or *di-logue* on the other—"Ich und Du" and "Zwiesprache". One could suggest at this juncture that it might be impossible to isolate one of these two, let us describe them as prisms of inter-human relations. They are supplementary or complementary in their interaction and in the systematic attempt to posit them within the human scope. To put it negatively, neither of the two positions can be seen as enjoying a sort of primacy. This mutual reinforcement of the two can perhaps be illustrated by the following example which, to be sure, derives from a different philosophical climate from that characteristic of Buber's impetus. We take one of the formulations of Kant's categorical imperative, namely that man has to be viewed not merely as a means but at the same time as an end. In order to invest the person with the position of being an end, and not a means only, one has to be aware in the first place that we are approaching here a person and not—to put it bluntly—a stone. Such an awareness which, at least partially, precedes the imperative as such and by the same token accompanies the imperative, its exercise and application, is essential for the identification of the person as well as for the very move to the field of morality. To be sure, that awareness does not imply the novelty exemplified by the introduction of the moral perspective in the strict sense of the term, that perspective which is epitomized by the categorical imperative. The categorical imperative brings into the scope of our behaviour not only the identification of somebody as a person, but the treatment which follows that identification and is guided by it in the direction of treating the person as an end and not as a means only. At the same time the moral perspective enhances the person's position as a person and thus enhances that which is already present in the primary awareness and identification. Hence, and this we may say now, summing up the interaction between the two modes of awareness, we find a mutual reinforcement of the two perspectives. That reinforcement leads us to the phenomenological conclusion that eventually one perspective cannot be separated from the other.

Having made this insertion, we may come back to our point of departure, related to the "Ich und Du" and "Zwiesprache". It can now be said that Zwiesprache, the in-between position is possible only between two human beings, or between the I and Thou. But that position is asserted and reinforced by the awareness either of ourselves as partners or as observers. The dialogue, being the focus of the in-between situation, occurs between the I and Thou. We can say here that there is no first beginning, when we look at the order, that is to say the structure, of the human reality—the dialogue emanates from the I and Thou, and as such reinforces their partnership, but also by the same token manifests and reinforces their position as partners. A mute relationship between I and Thou would be beyond the scope of the inter-human contact; obviously silence relates to a dialogue and is not a transformation of muteness.

VI

Here we may touch upon a third point in our attempt to understand Buber's philosophical interpretation of immediacy. We may refer to some origins or sources of his thinking, not all of which easily to be identified philologically. Yet at least some of them are present in his writings, either directly or indirectly. Since we described Buber's position as that of philosophy of immediacy, and in turn some of the elements of immediacy are brought into prominence, we may point in the first place to the line of continuity which starts perhaps with Friedrich Heinrich Jacobi in the 19th century, who by the way speaks about "Ich und Du", namely that one does not recognize the "Ich" without recognizing at the same time the "Du", and vice versa. In terms of a philosophical tradition of continuity there seems to be a line from Jacobi to Buber. The existence of that line is to be seen as warranted by the fact that Wilhelm Dilthey was Buber's teacher, even when we do not say that Buber was his disciple. Let us recall that by the end of the 19th century Dilthey delivered a lecture in which he tried to establish his own version of philosophical realism, that is to say, the conception asserting the reality of the external world. In that lecture Dilthey addressed himself to belief proper that the world exists. Belief as such connoted for him the negation of the possibility to demonstrate or to prove by arguments of a philosophical character of different sorts the reality of the external world. Belief replaces demonstration and proof. It carries with itself an aspect of immediacy, and in terms of the philosophical roots it points to a concept employed by David Hume, with whose position Jacobi is concerned in a book dealing with the subject-matter.

We have to distinguish between the aspect of belief pertinent to the attitude towards the external world, and the aspect of faith in the sense of religious faith. In both attitudes one can discern from the negative point of view the acceptance of given facts or the all-embracing sphere of facticity, as is the case in terms of belief in the reality of the external world. But belief is an acceptance of given data, while faith implies also confidence, reliance, and not only mere acceptance. Yet we have to realize the line of continuity which may perhaps be drawn from the attitude of belief, which Dilthey advocated in his systematic thinking about the problem of the external world as being a mode of immediacy, and the transformation of belief into faith as a mode of immediacy characteristic of Buber. Let us not forget another component of Dilthey's system, namely that of "Verstehen", which again is a mode of immediate awareness and understanding. Speaking therefore in the context of a possible influence of Dilthey on Buber, one could suggest that Buber absorbed in his own way these two ingredients of Dilthey's thinking, namely belief as transformed into faith, as well as "Verstehen" as transformed into the dialogical situation.

Looking further into the origins of Buber's I and Thou and the interpretation of this, one may go back to the analysis of the dialectic between master and slave present in Hegel's *Phenomenology of Spirit*. Perhaps in this context one cannot refer to a text of Buber's which would warrant the suggestion about a possible absorption of Hegel's exploration by Buber. One can rather rely on personal discussions with Buber and his response to a reference to Hegel's dialectic, when he said that indeed this chapter of Hegel's phenomenology he studied under Dilthey. To be sure, one cannot disregard the basic dialectic motive in Hegel, namely that only through the dialectic process does one reach the level of an encounter between two persons. We start with the asymmetry of the relationship between master and slave. Through the discovery of the implicit dependence we notice that it becomes symmetrical since not only the slave depends upon the master, but also the master depends on the slave. That turn of the relationship in the direction of mutuality leads to the discernment of the symmetry between the two persons, and once symmetry is established, the hierarchy of master and slave disappears. Probably for Hegel the discernment of the mutuality could not be conceived as being a discernment of immediate relations between two persons, since, according to Hegel, immediacy is not immediately given, but is bound to be mediated. Buber probably could pick up as it were the result of the dialectical process and procedure, once symmetry has been reached and achieved, and focus on the mutuality understood as immediacy. As such one encounters mutuality; one experiences it without taking advantage, that is to say, without being involved in disadvantages of hypotheses, explications, explorations of genesis, etc. Here the aspect of immediacy brings about a corresponding awareness that the reality encountered is not a sum total of raw facts, but something which has a physiognomy in the literal sense of the term. As such it is to be interpreted dialogically in the first place.

VII

Summing up this part of our analysis we could suggest that among modern philosophical trends Buber represents an approach which can perhaps be described as a phenomenology of human experience from within. It is an attempt at articulating the phenomenon of the inter-human encounter without being, at least pragmatically, engaged in reflexion on that phenomenon as an outside observer, who, being outside, is bound to abstract from his own involvement. To be sure, when we apply here the term phenomenology, we are far from referring to its scholastic use, since—and this goes without saying—there can be no affinity between Buber's descriptions, and they are meant to be so pragmatically, and some of the major methods of the phenomenological school, like reduction or some of the pivotal concepts of that school, like the transcendental ego. Concurrently, the phenomenological school is formulating its reflections from the position of an observer, who eventually calls for the insight or the assurance of evidence. All these aspects cannot be found in a phenomenology of an experience aiming at the explication of the experience without detaching itself from it. Of course, any explication cannot nullify at least the conceived position of the observer. Once an observer comes to the scene, the question of distance between the experience as such and the reflexion on the experience cannot be escaped. To put it differently, attempts to articulate experience cannot be viewed as being identical precisely from the phenomenological point of view with experience as such. Most probably we touch here on some of the problems dealt with by Jochanan Bloch in his book *Die Aporie des Du*.

VIII

This attempt to understand human experience from within has its bearing on another subject, which was central in the discussion of this colloquium, that is to say, Buber's interpretation of religious experience, including his interpretation of historical religions, namely of Judaism and Christianity.

Perhaps it would not be totally improper to start off this comment with a word of skepticism or reservation related to many a philosophical attempt at explicating and articulating the major trends of historical religions by applying to them systematic philosophical concepts. These attempts, if they are valid at all, may be successful only in articulating partial aspects of historical religions—and this discrepancy is due to the nature of historical religions. The latter, unlike philosophical systems or even a presentation of a religion by a philosopher integrated into his system, are characterized by a variety of trends. Historical religions absorb these trends, they create a merger or a fusion of them, without systematizing them in order to present a major categorical structure characteristic of them. Hence consistency, which can be attributed to a philosophical system, cannot be attributed to a spectrum of motives and trends characteristic of historical religions. This skepticism applies also to attempts which we know from the phenomenology of religious experience, which differs from the systematic articulation of religious concepts. Speaking about phenomenology in this context one may refer to Schleiermacher who placed the emphasis on *die schlechthinnige Abhängingkeit* (the total dependence) or Rudolf Otto's descriptions of the various encounters of the numinous etc. What we say very briefly about these two major representatives of the phenomenological approach to religious experience applies also to Buber's interpretation, which transposes the I and Thou encounter from the human context to that relationship between man and God. A more specific aspect in Buber's interpretation related to Judaism has to be brought to prominence now.

The fact that Buber transplanted the structure of I and Thou to this interpretation of the religious experience in general and of Judaism in particular, or the other way round, that he transposed that structure from the religious context to the inter-human one, is on the one hand his well-known contribution to modern thought, but on the other hand it is a problematic contribution. The problematic aspect of that two-way shift lies in the fact that the religious context is not understood as being *sui generis*, but as having as it were an inter-human parallel. Here those who attempted to be with the experience as such without characterizing the divine realm in particular—and let us mention in this context Gabriel Marcel, the analysis of whose system was presented by Emmanuel Levinas—are perhaps on a safer ground than was Buber. The difference lies precisely in the fact that those philosophers or phenomenologists have seen the uniqueness of the religious experience, even when the term experience is used in the systems for the sake of characterizing the very religious attitude.

One could go one step further, paradoxical as it may be, namely that the characterization of religions and of Judaism, because it calls for a separation of the essence and position of God, found its interpreter in Hegel, who indeed was not a friendly interpreter of Judaism, because Hegel characterized Judaism as the religion of sublimity *(Erhabenheit)*, and thus amplified the fact that in spite of the involvement in attitudes or experience the gap between God and man is not eradicated. The employment of the categories I and Thou may carry with it a tendency to make the gap secondary, because I and Thou as a *Zwiesprache* implies a kind of intimacy and along with that a kind of symmetry between the two partners. Buber was concerned with the question since he wanted to introduce into the structure of the relationship between I and Thou in the religious realm the ingredient of distance. But we wonder whether such a synthesis between immediacy and distance is possible altogether. Immediacy is perhaps more germane to proximity between the partners than to distance between them, let alone to the ambiguous situation where both proximity and distance are supposedly present. In any case, the parallelism between the inter-human area and the area of religious experience calls for further analysis.

IX

Winding up we may try to characterize Buber's thinking as it appears in the intellectual climate of our generation. In the general atmosphere of searching for immediacy, in spite of the paradoxical conjunction of search and immediacy, Buber became popular and, as it is now said, the reception of Buber's thought is a telling example of that search. It relates of course to the affinity between immediacy and authenticity, the aspect emphasized by Walter Kaufmann's presentation. Here we find again a supposed kinship between the aspect of immediacy and the various concepts which were prominent in protest movements, that is to say, where the dichotomy was understood as one between expression and structured civilization in its various modes. Authenticity and immediacy have been felt or understood as related to spontaneity and as such the centre of the expressive

attitude has been the ego, his position and his manifestations. Therefore we could say that one of the basic components of that thrust
towards authenticity is related to the egotistic interpretation of it.

At this point we have to distinguish between Buber's conception
and the reception of it in the last generation. What is characteristic of
Buber's thought—and what puts into prominence the basic distinction between his thought and the drive towards authenticity is that
Buber never identified immediacy and authenticity with egotistic
attitudes. On the contrary, he saw authenticity and immediacy
fundamentally involved in inter-human relations. One can see his
interpretation of the phenomenon of responsibility as not fully adequate, because he stressed only the aspect of response implied in
responsibility, and not the aspect of the constant and permanent
personality which lies behind the responsibility. Yet we cannot be
oblivious of the major fact that Buber stressed the aspect of responding, that is to say, the aspect which places the person within the
framework of inter-human relations. It is because of that aspect that
the normative anti-egotistic component is inherent in Buber's presentation of immediacy. At this point the master was more adequate
than those who sometimes quoted him or attempted to present his
thought as one of the credentials for their own credibility.

Let me thank at this juncture our colleagues for organizing the
colloquium and giving us the opportunity of exchanging views on
Buber's thought and to speak freely and sometimes also critically
about it.

Participants

YEHOSHUA AMIR is Senior Lecturer Emeritus of Philosophy at Tel Aviv University. He has translated books by Buber into Hebrew; he has published essays on Buber.

JOCHANAN BLOCH was Associate Professor of Jewish Thought at Ben Gurion University of the Negev. He is author of *Die Aporie des Du, Probleme der Dialogik Martin Buber's* and also of a book on Jesus' Parables, which will soon appear. He has published essays and books on Zionism.

BERNHARD CASPER is Professor of Fundamental Theology and Religious Christian Philosophy at Freiburg University, Germany. He has published books and essays on Buber and Rosenzweig.

MENAHEM DORMAN is a writer and among the founders of the "Ha-Kibbutz Ha-Meuhad" Publishing House and among its first editors. His main books in Hebrew are: *Nicolo Machiavelli, On the Political and Military Orientation of the Secretary of Florence; Nicolo Machiavelli—A Play, a Story and Dialogue; Marcelius of Padva*.

MAURICE FRIEDMAN is Professor of Religion at San-Diego University, California. Also is editor of *The Philosophy of Martin Buber;* author of *Martin Buber—A Life of Dialogue*. He has also written books on Existential issues.

HAIM GORDON is Senior Lecturer at Ben Gurion University of the Negev. He has published essays on Buber's thought.

HELMUT GOLLWITZER is Professor Emeritus of Theology at the Free University of Berlin. Among Karl Barth's students. He has written books on Protestant theology.

RIVKA HORWITZ is Associate Professor at Ben Gurion University of the Negev. She is author of: *Buber's Way to 'I and Thou', with the First Publication of Martin Buber's Lectures "Religion als Gegenwart"* and also essays on Buber and Rosenzweig.

YOSHIMORI HIRAISHI is Professor Emeritus of Philosophy and Ethics at Doshisha University, Kyoto, Japan. He is author of: *Martin Buber, His Life and Thought* and also has translated Buber's essays on Hasidism into Japanese.

STEVEN KATZ is Professor of Religion at Dartmouth College. His books deal with analysis of mysticism and philosophy.

WALTER KAUFMANN was Professor of Philosophy at Princeton University. Among his books: *Nietzsche: Critique of Religion and Philosophy; The Faith of a Heretic*. He translated *I and Thou* into English.

485

EMANUEL LEVINAS is Professor of Philosophy at the Sorbone University, Paris. His main book is: *Theory of Intuition in the Phenomenology of Husserl*.

PINHAS HA-COHEN PELI is Associate Professor of Jewish Thought at Ben Gurion University of the Negev. He has published books and essays on contemporary Jewish thought.

ROBERT L. PERKINS is Professor of Philosophy at the University of South Alabama. He has edited and written books on Kierkegaard.

NATHAN ROTENSTREICH is Professor of Philosophy at the Hebrew University. He has published books on Jewish thought and on the history of philosophy and also on actual problems within Israel.

ELIEZER SCHWEID is Associate Professor of Jewish Thought at the Hebrew University. He has written essays and books on Hebrew literature and Jewish thought in the Middle Ages and in modern times.

BENYAMIN UFFENHEIMER is Professor of Biblical Studies at Tel Aviv University. His main books are: *The Visions of Zecharia, from Prophecy to Apocalypse* and *Ancient Prophecy in Israel*. He has written essays on Kaufmann, Buber, Cassuto.

MICHAEL WYSCHOGROD is Professor of Philosophy at Baruch College at the City University of New York. He is author of: *Kierkegaard and Heidegger: An Existential Ontology* and other books on philosophical and religious issues.

LORENZ WACHINGER is a psychotherapist in Munich. His main book deals with the concept of faith of Martin Buber. He has written essays on Buber and Freud.

ROBERT WOOD is Professor of Philosophy at Dallas University, Texas, U.S.A. He is author of: *The Future of Metaphysics* and *Martin Buber's Ontology*.

Index of Names

Indexes compiled by Niva Elkin and Haim Gordon

Index of Concepts

490